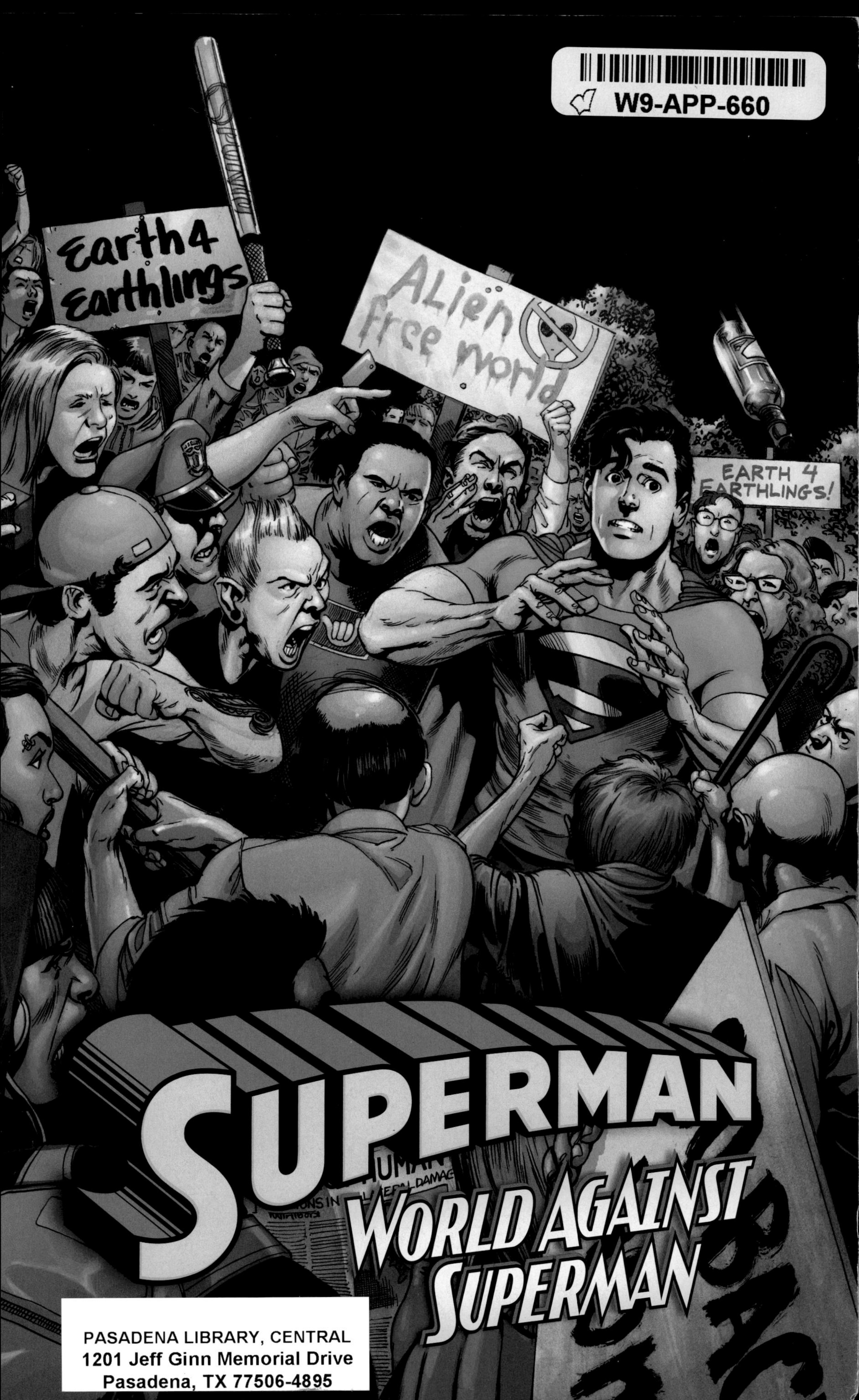
Earth 4 Earthlings
Alien free world
EARTH 4 EARTHLINGS!
SUPERMAN
WORLD AGAINST SUPERMAN

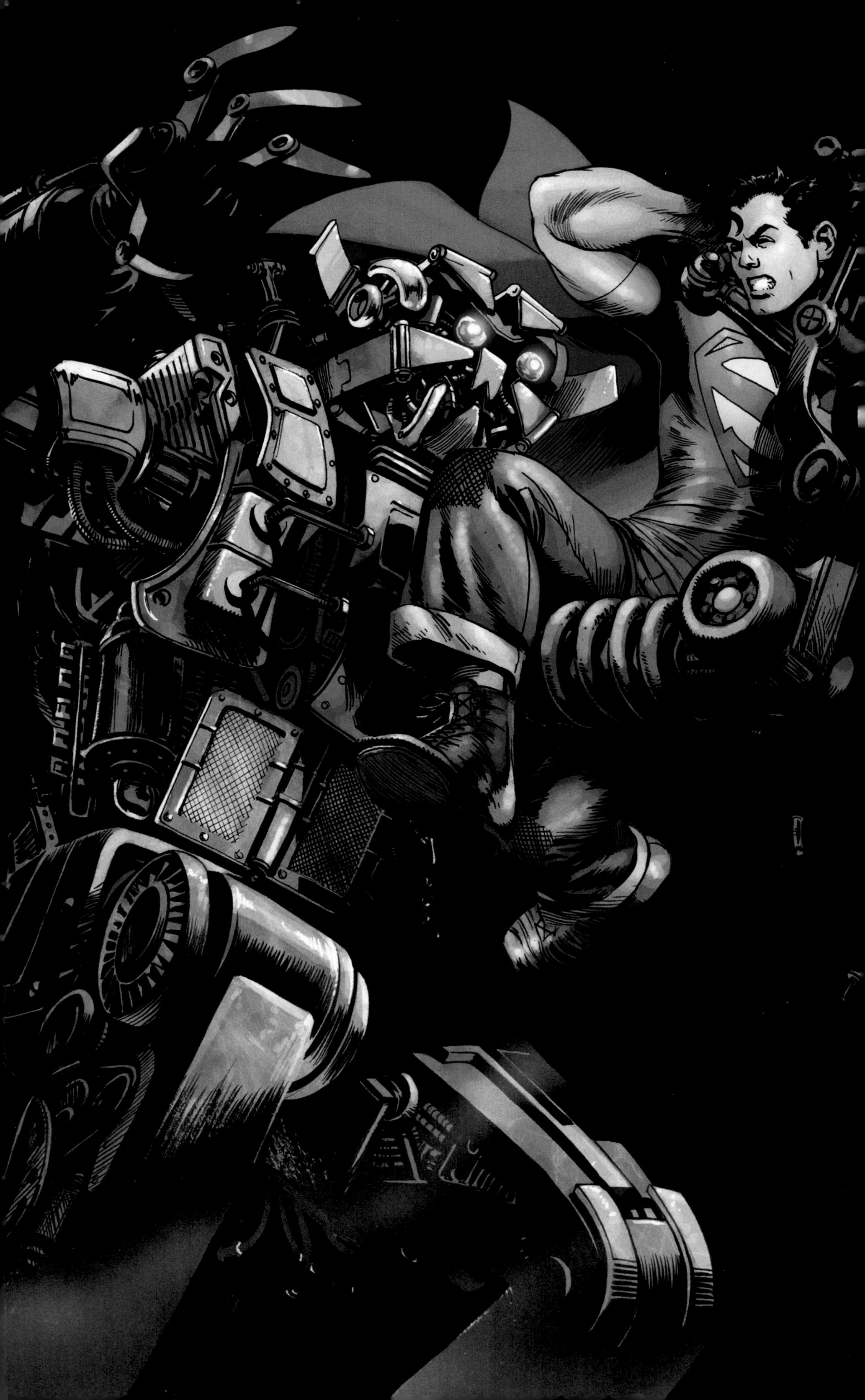

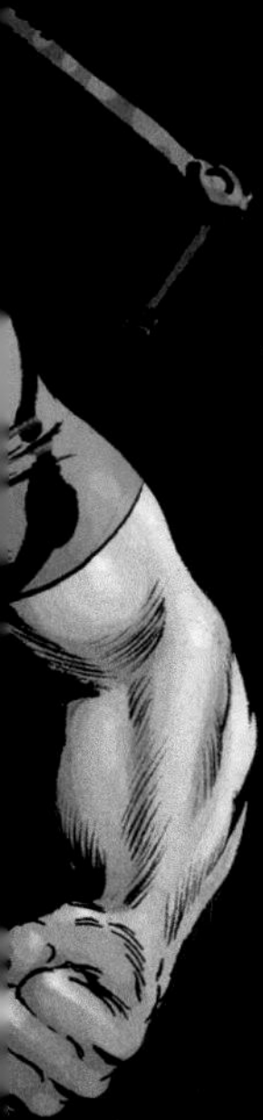

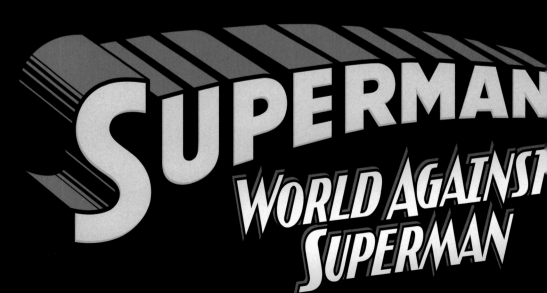

GRANT MORRISON
writer

RAGS MORALES ANDY KUBERT
BRENT ANDERSON GENE HA
pencillers

RICK BRYANT JESSE DELPERDANG
JOHN DELL SEAN PARSONS BOB McLEOD
GENE HA BRAD WALKER
inkers

BRAD ANDERSON
ART LYON
DAVID CURIEL
colorists

PATRICK BROSSEAU
letterer

RAGS MORALES with **BRAD ANDERSON**
collection cover artists

SUPERMAN
WORLD AGAINST SUPERMAN

SUPERMAN created by JERRY SIEGEL and JOE SHUSTER
By special arrangement with the Jerry Siegel family

SUPERMAN: WORLD AGAINST SUPERMAN

DC Comics, 2900 West Alameda Ave., Burbank, CA 91505
Printed by LSC Communications, Kendallville, IN, USA. 3/22/19. First Printing.
ISBN: 978-1-4012-9105-1

Library of Congress Cataloging-in-Publication Data is available.

PEFC Certified
This product is from sustainably managed forests and controlled sources
www.pefc.org
PEFC/29-31-337

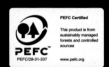

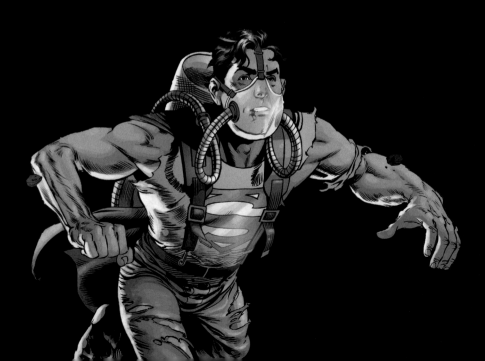

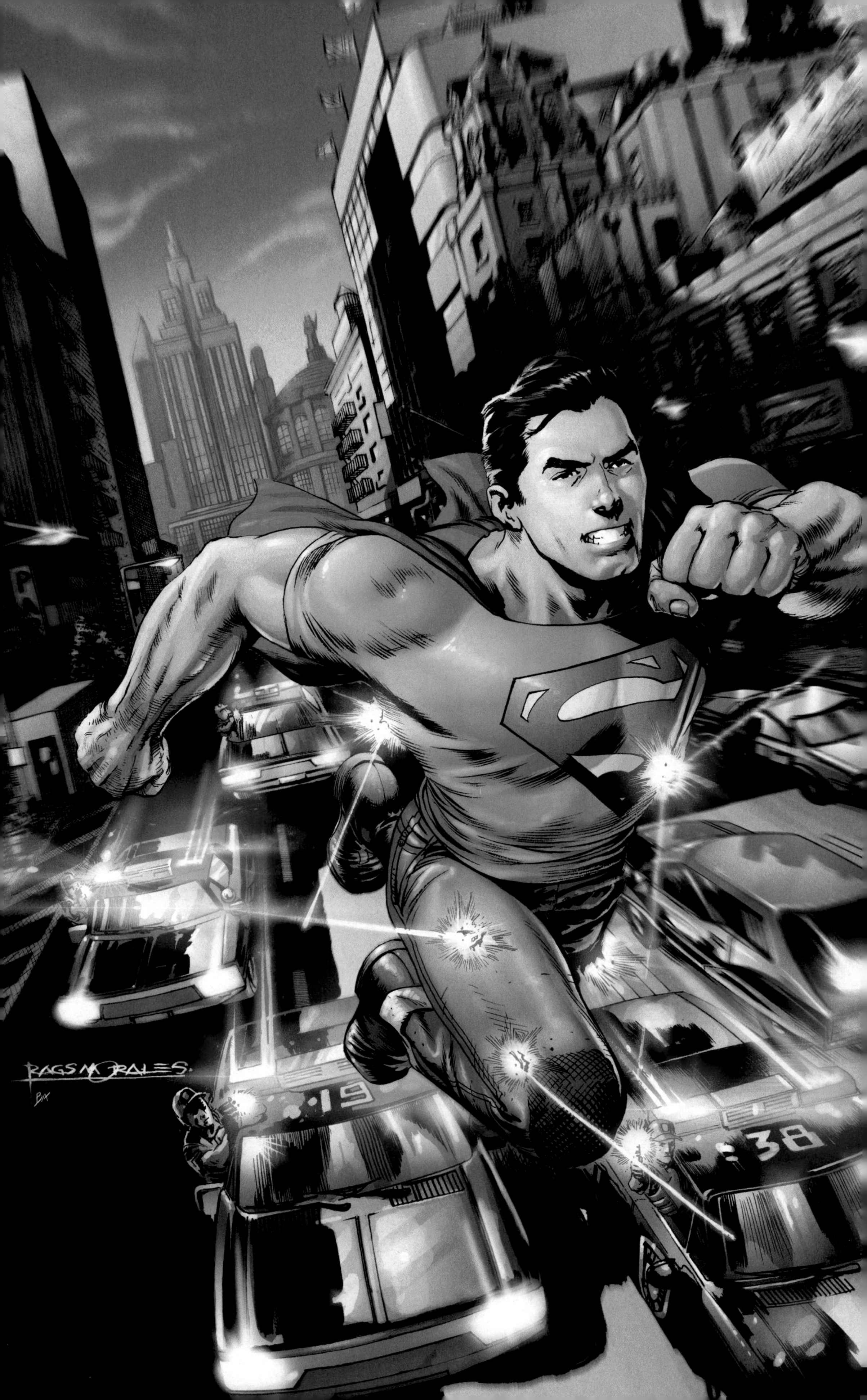
RAGS MORALES.
BIX
19
38

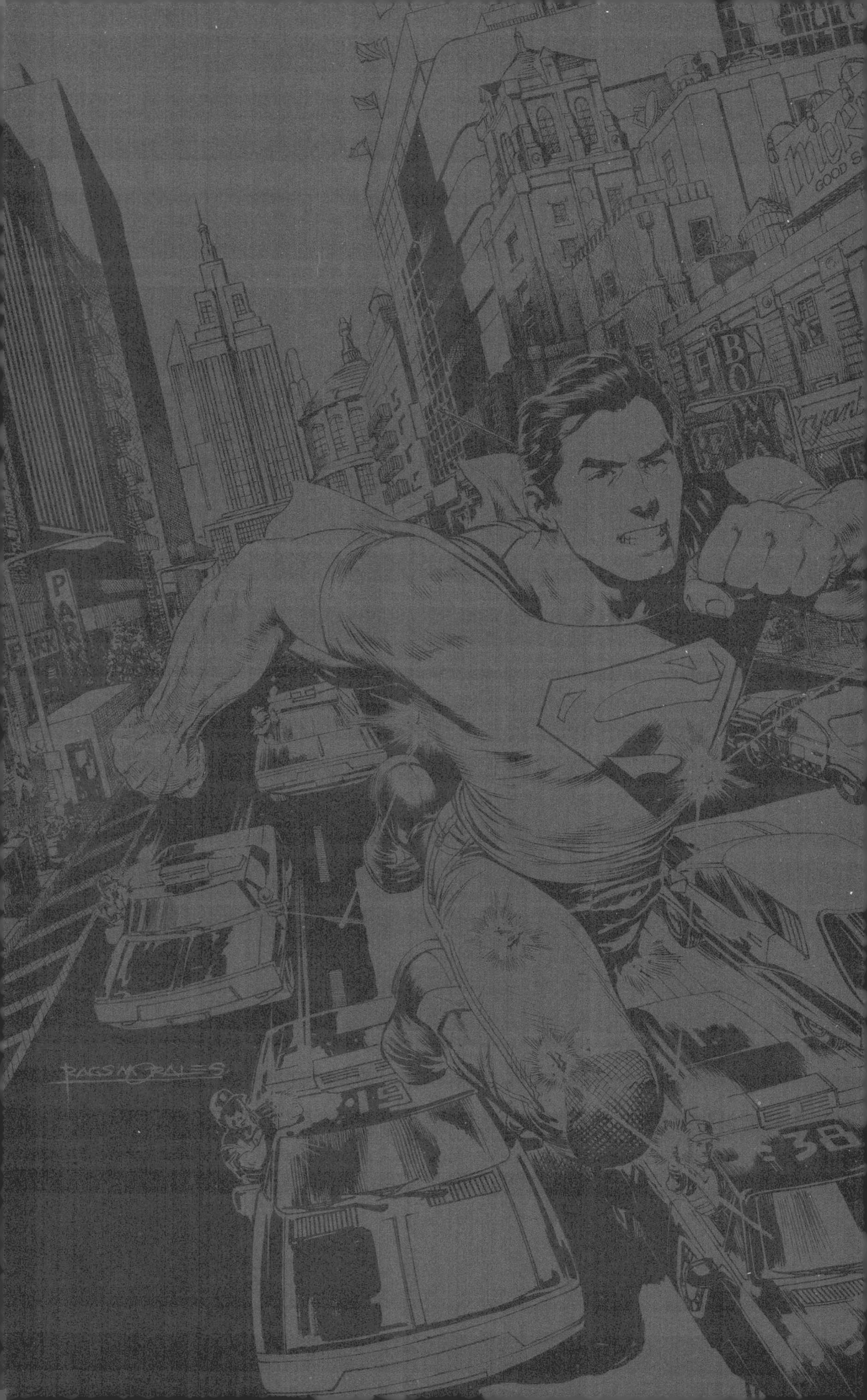
RAGS MORALES

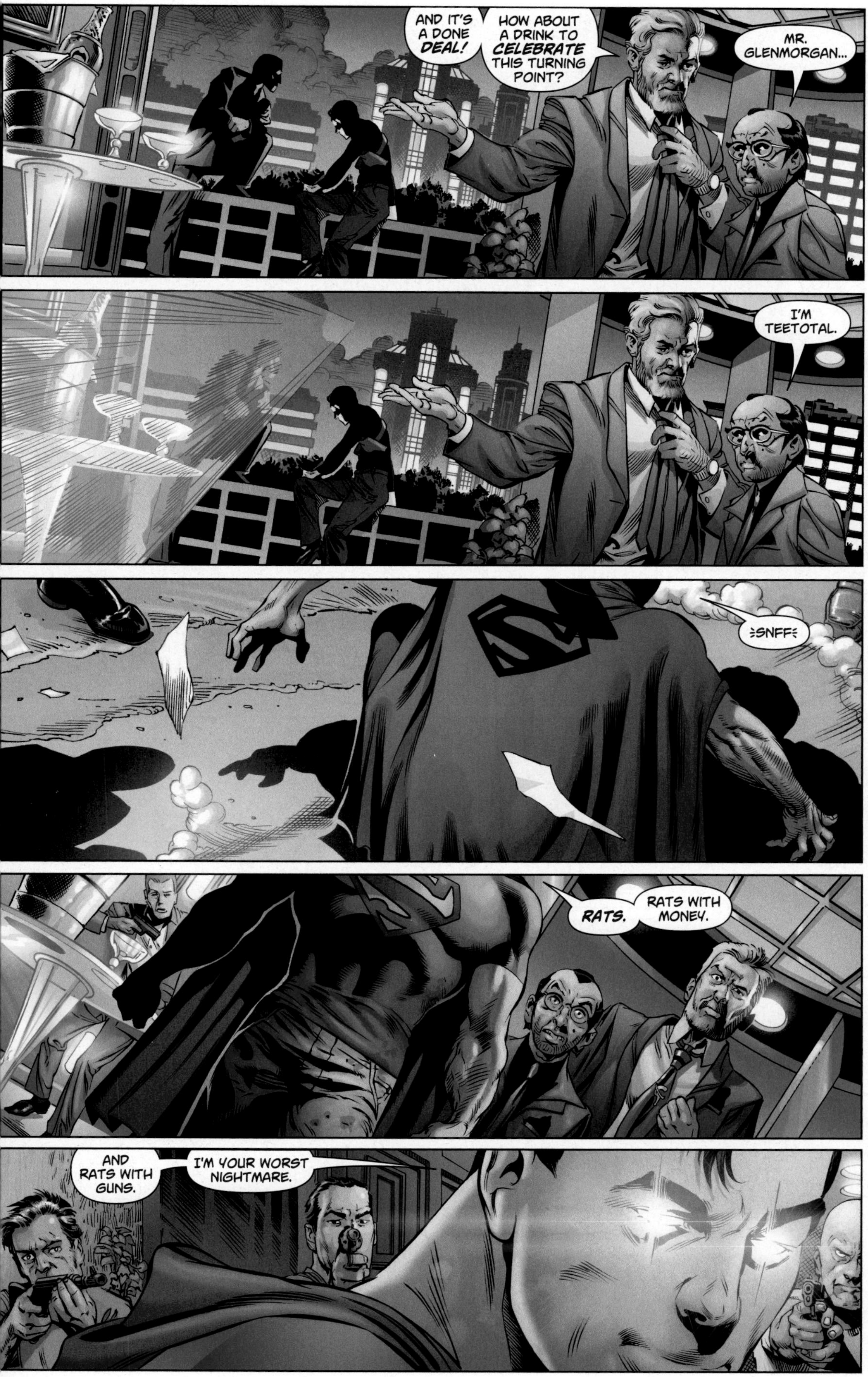
AND IT'S A DONE DEAL!
HOW ABOUT A DRINK TO CELEBRATE THIS TURNING POINT?
MR. GLENMORGAN...
I'M TEETOTAL.
SNFF
RATS.
RATS WITH MONEY.
AND RATS WITH GUNS.
I'M YOUR WORST NIGHTMARE.

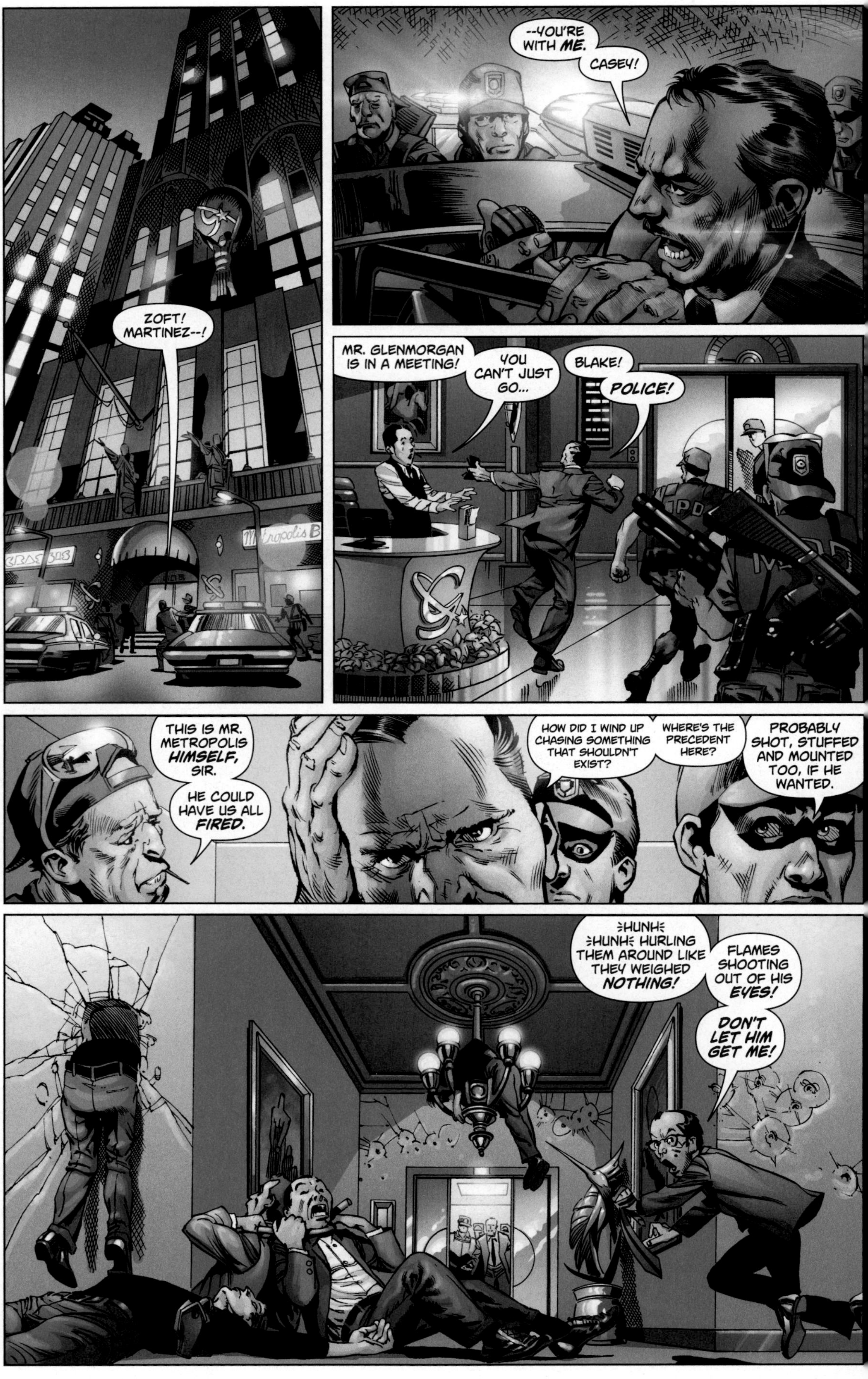
ZOFT! MARTINEZ--!
--YOU'RE WITH ME.
CASEY!
MR. GLENMORGAN IS IN A MEETING!
YOU CAN'T JUST GO...
BLAKE!
POLICE!
THIS IS MR. METROPOLIS HIMSELF, SIR.
HE COULD HAVE US ALL FIRED.
HOW DID I WIND UP CHASING SOMETHING THAT SHOULDN'T EXIST?
WHERE'S THE PRECEDENT HERE?
PROBABLY SHOT, STUFFED AND MOUNTED TOO, IF HE WANTED.
HUNH HUNH HURLING THEM AROUND LIKE THEY WEIGHED NOTHING!
FLAMES SHOOTING OUT OF HIS EYES!
DON'T LET HIM GET ME!

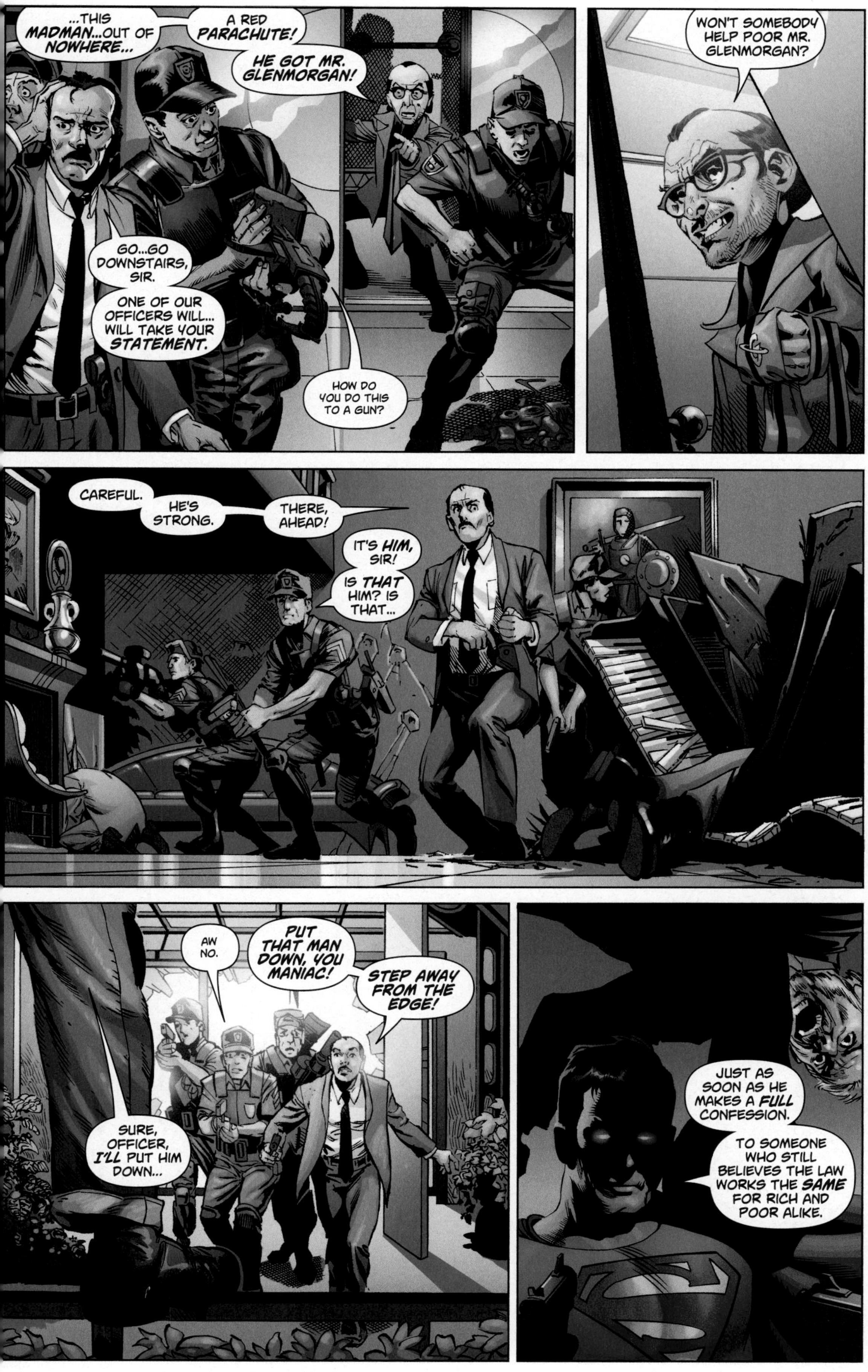

...THIS MADMAN...OUT OF NOWHERE...
A RED PARACHUTE!
HE GOT MR. GLENMORGAN!
GO...GO DOWNSTAIRS, SIR.
ONE OF OUR OFFICERS WILL... WILL TAKE YOUR STATEMENT.
HOW DO YOU DO THIS TO A GUN?
WON'T SOMEBODY HELP POOR MR. GLENMORGAN?
CAREFUL.
HE'S STRONG.
THERE, AHEAD!
IT'S HIM, SIR!
IS THAT HIM? IS THAT...
AW NO.
PUT THAT MAN DOWN, YOU MANIAC!
STEP AWAY FROM THE EDGE!
SURE, OFFICER, I'LL PUT HIM DOWN...
JUST AS SOON AS HE MAKES A FULL CONFESSION.
TO SOMEONE WHO STILL BELIEVES THE LAW WORKS THE SAME FOR RICH AND POOR ALIKE.

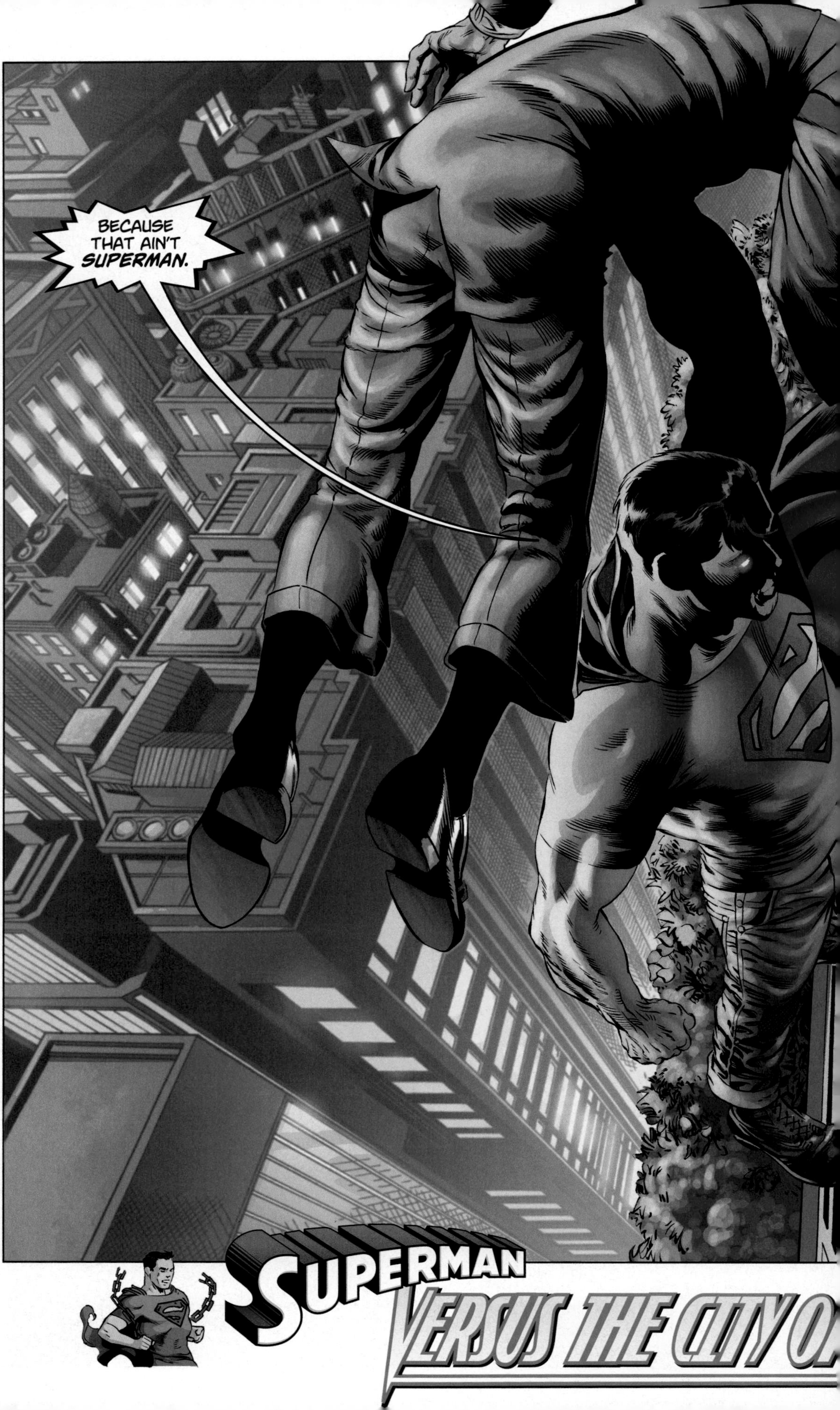
BECAUSE THAT AIN'T SUPERMAN.
SUPERMAN
VERSUS THE CITY OF

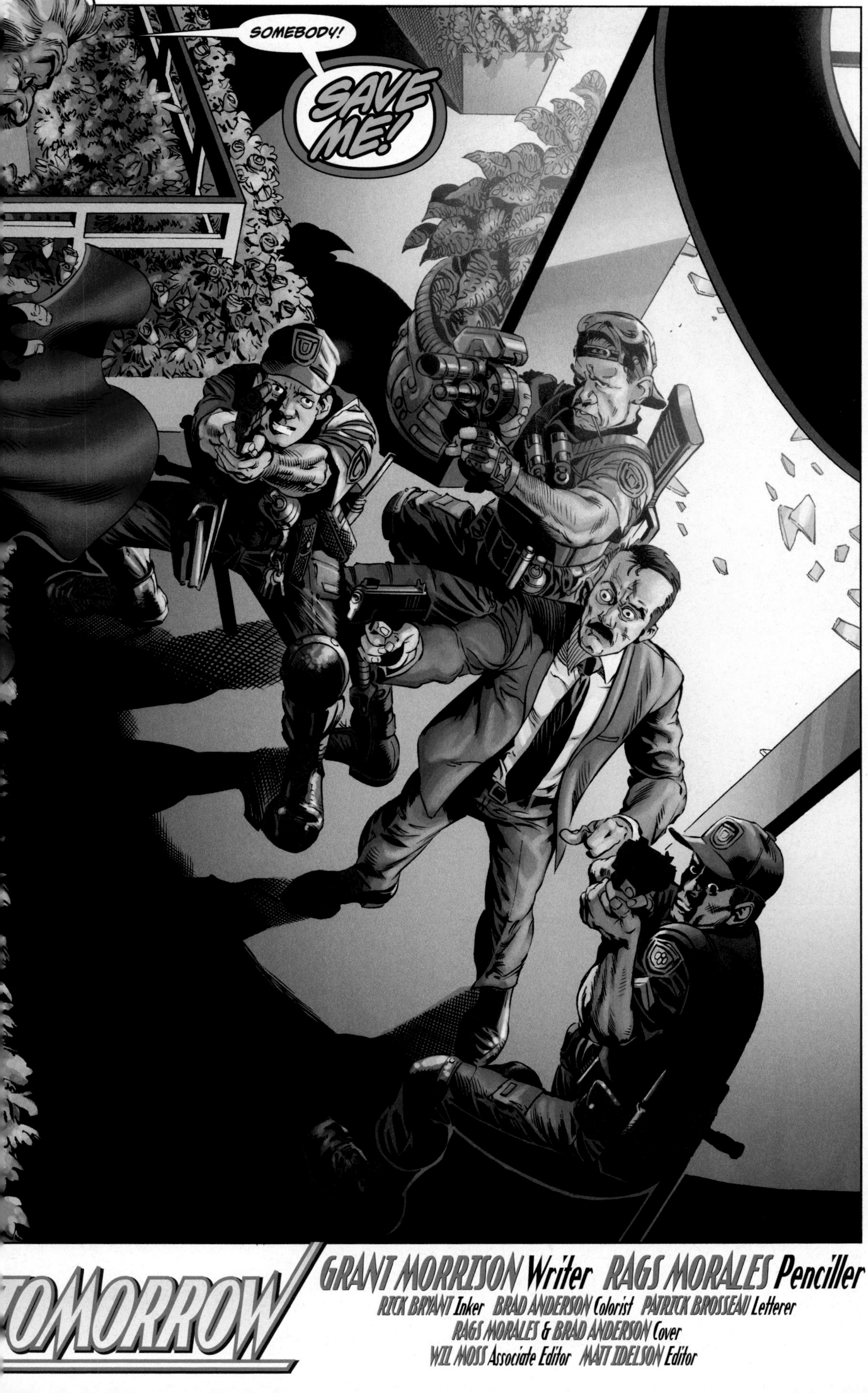
SOMEBODY!
SAVE ME!

TOMORROW

GRANT MORRISON Writer **RAGS MORALES** Penciller
RICK BRYANT Inker **BRAD ANDERSON** Colorist **PATRICK BROSSEAU** Letterer
RAGS MORALES & BRAD ANDERSON Cover
WIL MOSS Associate Editor **MATT IDELSON** Editor

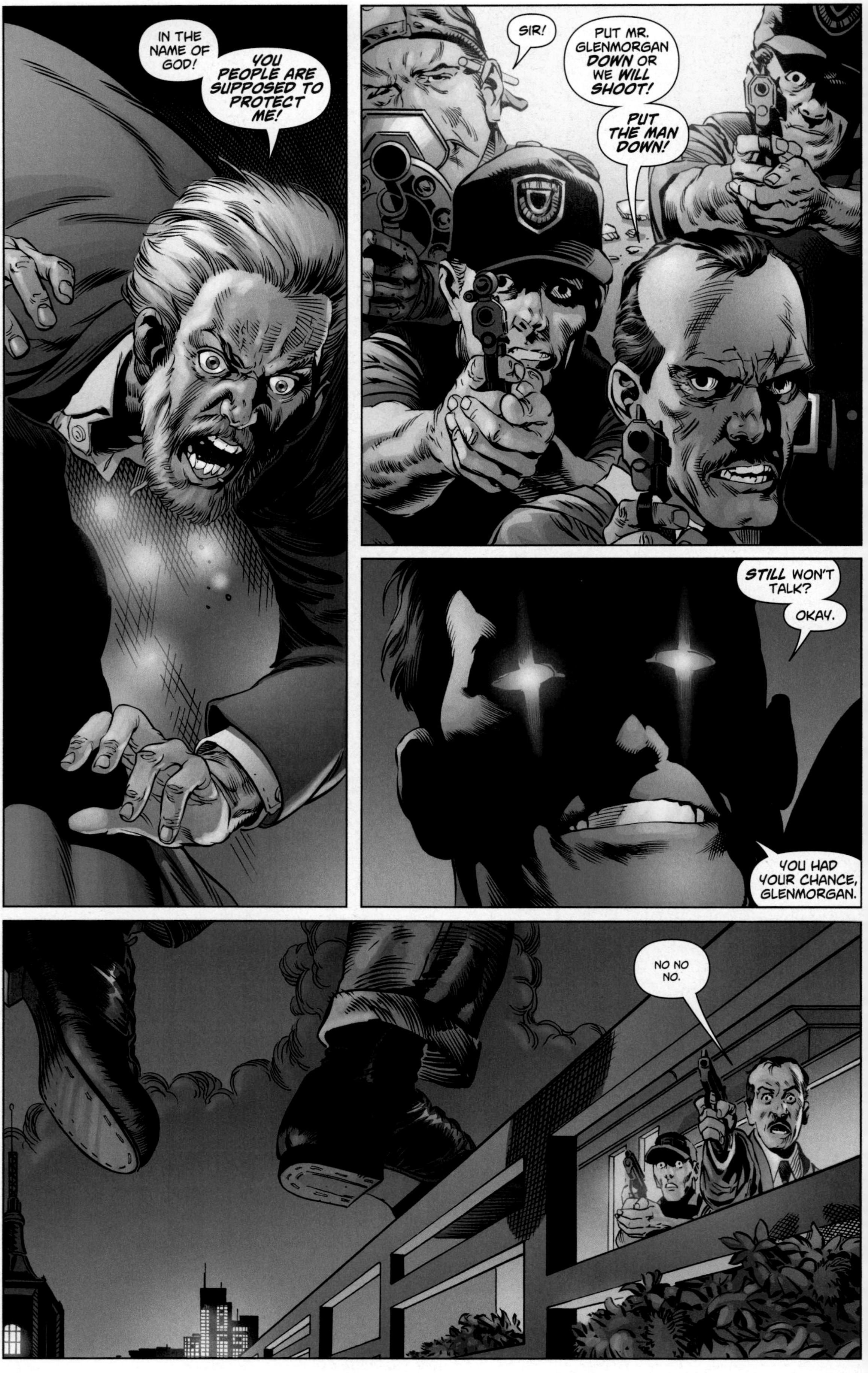
IN THE NAME OF GOD!
YOU PEOPLE ARE SUPPOSED TO PROTECT ME!
SIR!
PUT MR. GLENMORGAN DOWN OR WE WILL SHOOT!
PUT THE MAN DOWN!
STILL WON'T TALK?
OKAY.
YOU HAD YOUR CHANCE, GLENMORGAN.
NO NO NO.

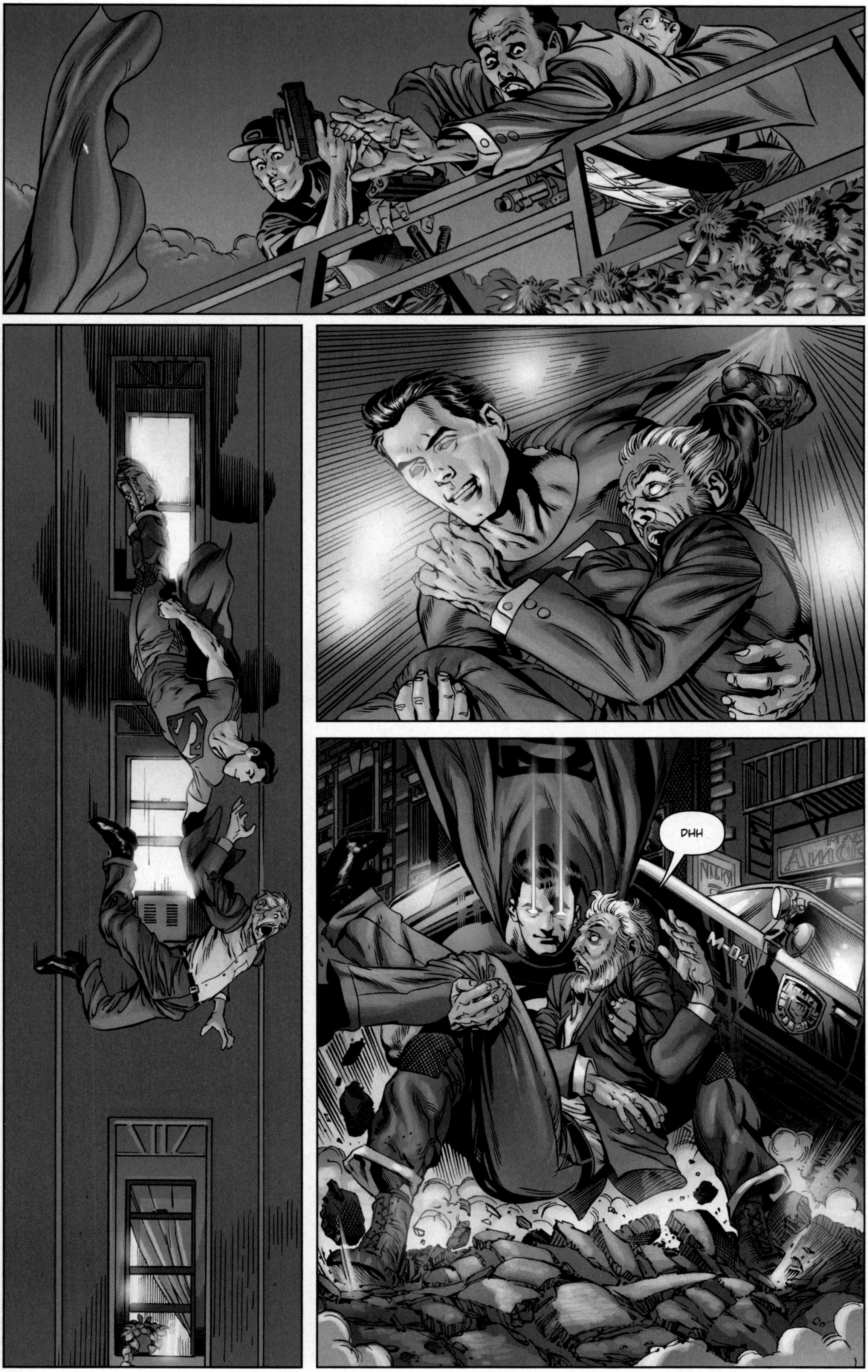
DHH
M-04

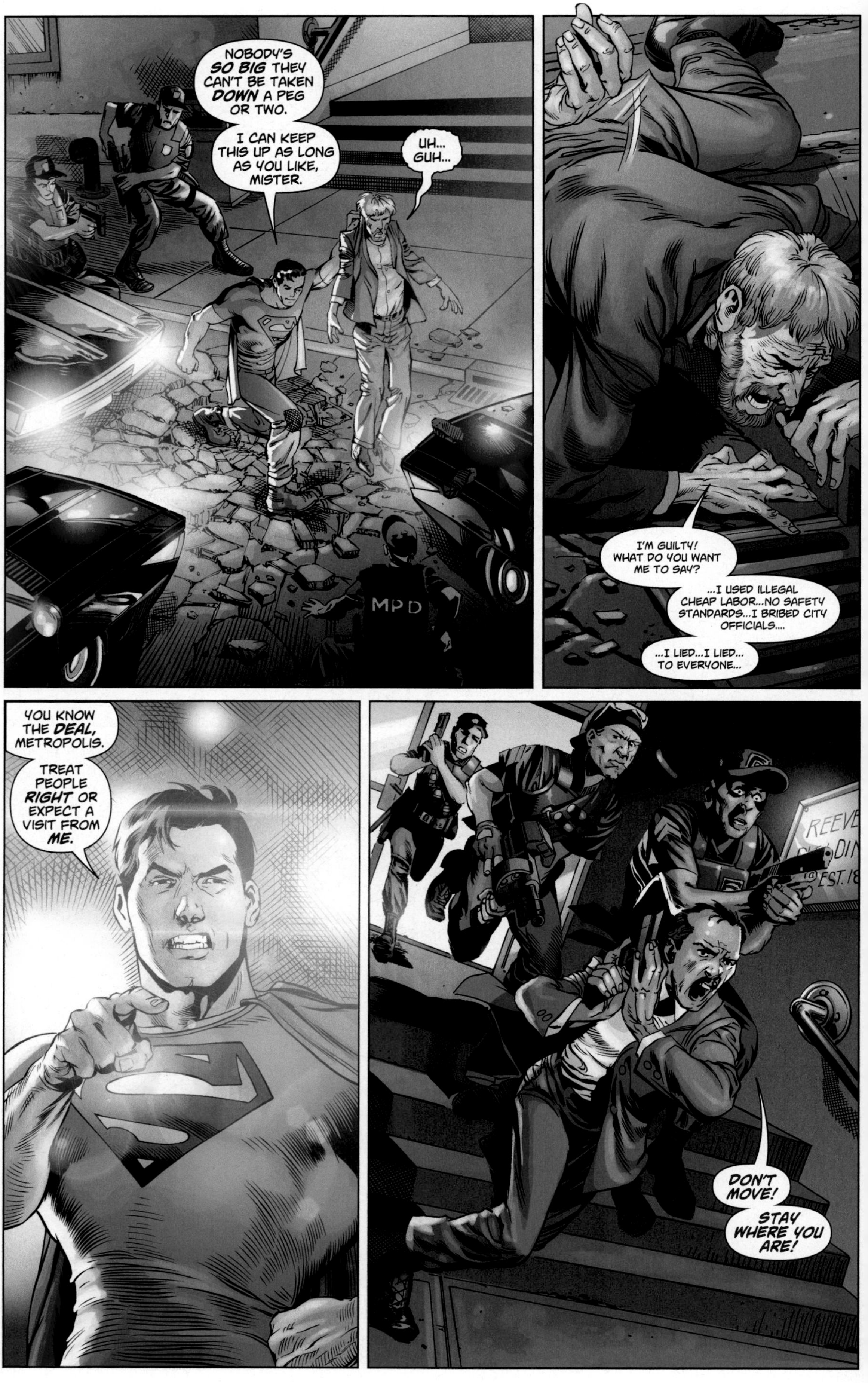
NOBODY'S **SO BIG** THEY CAN'T BE TAKEN **DOWN** A PEG OR TWO.
I CAN KEEP THIS UP AS LONG AS YOU LIKE, MISTER.
UH... GUH...
MPD
I'M GUILTY! WHAT DO YOU WANT ME TO SAY?
...I USED ILLEGAL CHEAP LABOR...NO SAFETY STANDARDS...I BRIBED CITY OFFICIALS....
...I LIED...I LIED... TO EVERYONE...
YOU KNOW THE **DEAL,** METROPOLIS.
TREAT PEOPLE **RIGHT** OR EXPECT A VISIT FROM **ME.**
DON'T MOVE!
STAY WHERE YOU ARE!

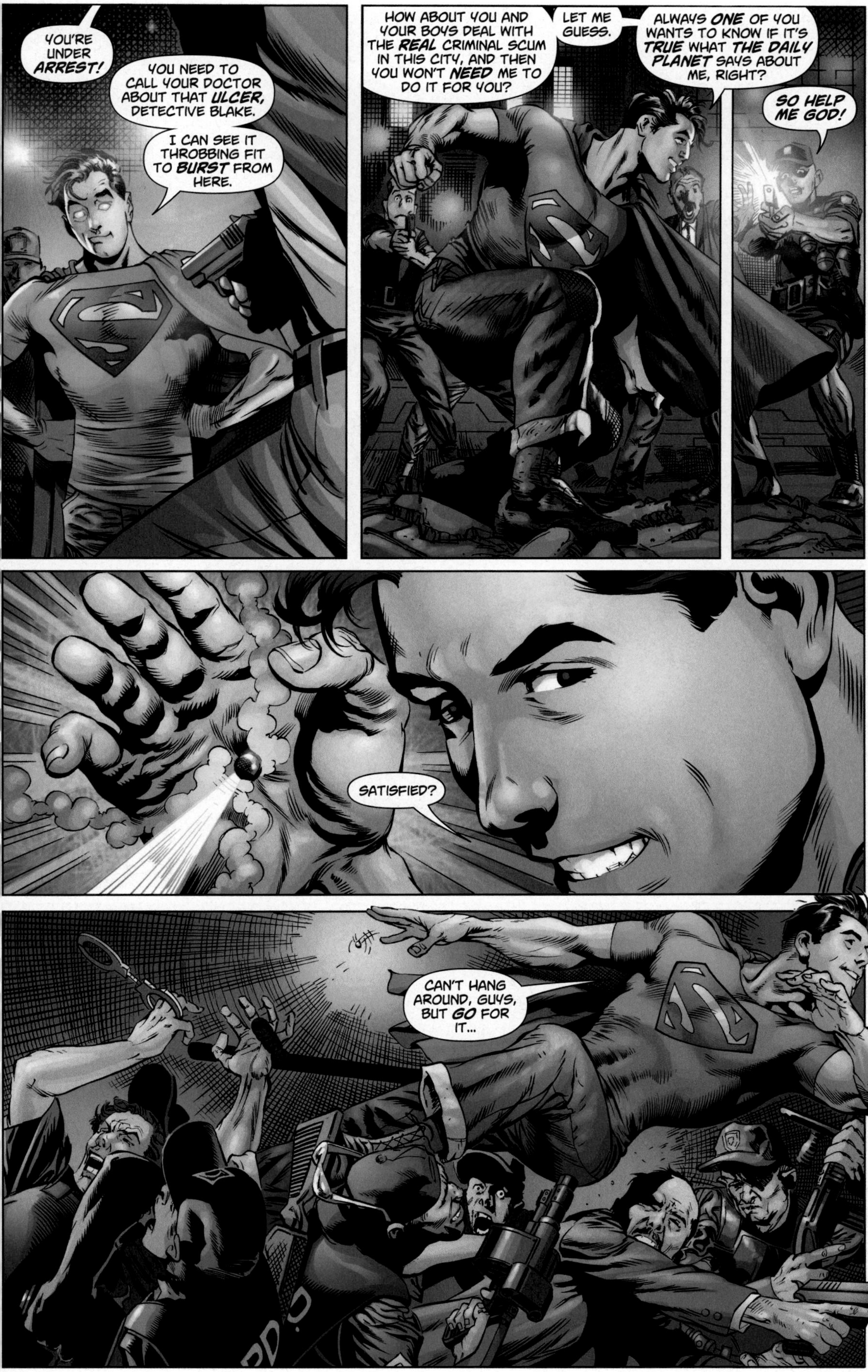
YOU'RE UNDER ARREST!
YOU NEED TO CALL YOUR DOCTOR ABOUT THAT ULCER, DETECTIVE BLAKE.
I CAN SEE IT THROBBING FIT TO BURST FROM HERE.
HOW ABOUT YOU AND YOUR BOYS DEAL WITH THE REAL CRIMINAL SCUM IN THIS CITY, AND THEN YOU WON'T NEED ME TO DO IT FOR YOU?
LET ME GUESS.
ALWAYS ONE OF YOU WANTS TO KNOW IF IT'S TRUE WHAT THE DAILY PLANET SAYS ABOUT ME, RIGHT?
SO HELP ME GOD!
SATISFIED?
CAN'T HANG AROUND, GUYS, BUT GO FOR IT...

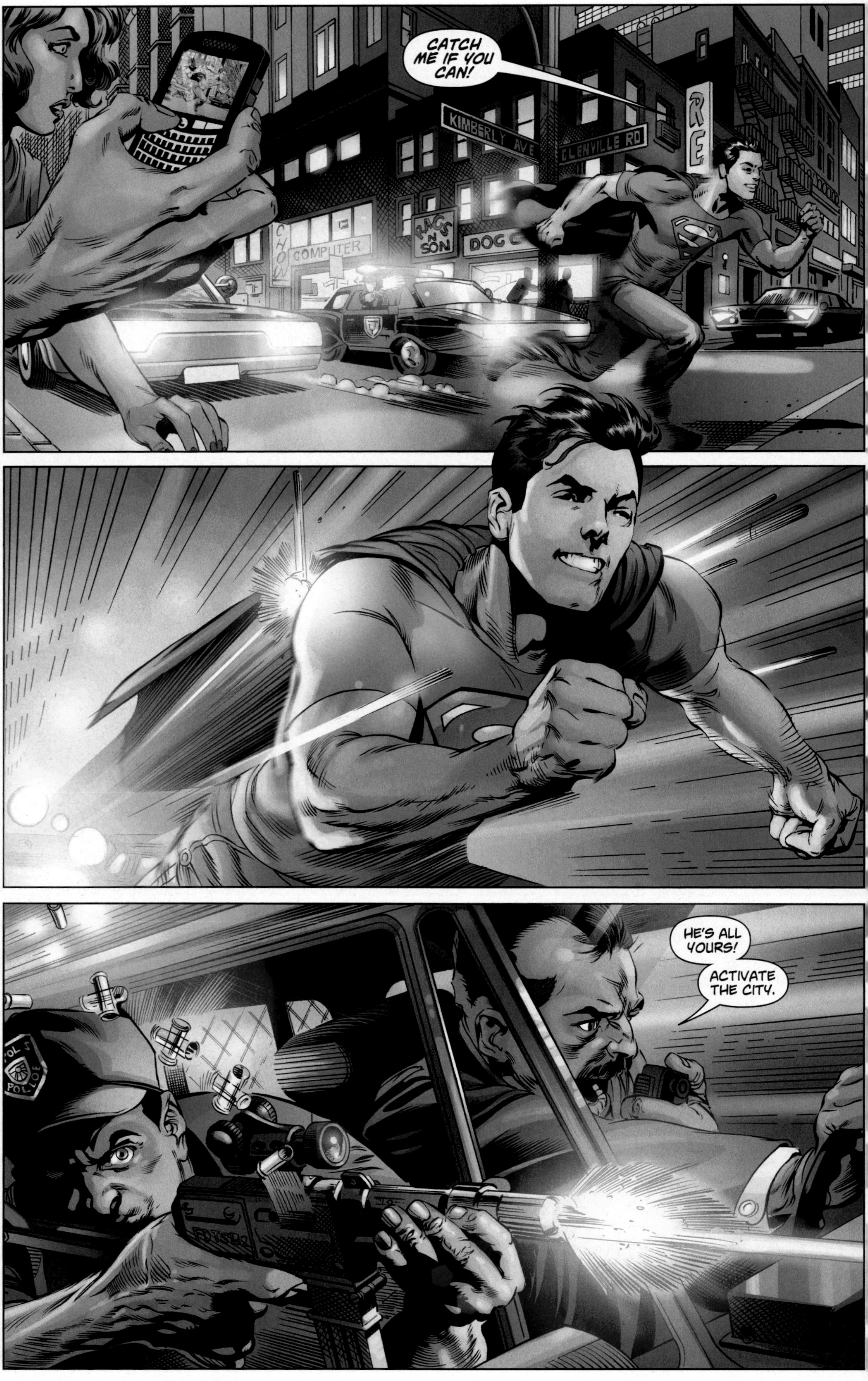

CATCH ME IF YOU CAN!
KIMBERLY AVE
GLENVILLE RD
RE
CHOW
COMPUTER
RAGS N SON
DOG C
HE'S ALL YOURS!
ACTIVATE THE CITY.

THE "SUPERMAN" WHO APPEARED *SIX MONTHS AGO* COULD HURDLE SKYSCRAPERS AND TOSS *TRUCKS* AROUND.

NOW IT'S *FASTER*, NOW IT'S *STRONGER*.

HOW SOON BEFORE IT CAN'T BE *STOPPED*?

19:30

WELL. GIVE ME A *REGIMENT* OF MEN LIKE THIS "SUPERMAN"...

HOW CAN I CALL HIM THAT?

IT WAS YOUR *DAUGHTER* WHO CHRISTENED THE CREATURE, GENERAL LANE.

NOTICE HOW IT DIDN'T *REFUSE* THE NAME.

GLENMORGAN SEEMED UNDULY *ANXIOUS* TO HELP OUT, WOULDN'T YOU SAY?

GALAXY HAS THE WHOLE *NEW MORAVIA TRIANGLE* EARMARKED FOR *DEVELOPMENT*, SO WE'RE FREE TO HIT *HARD*.

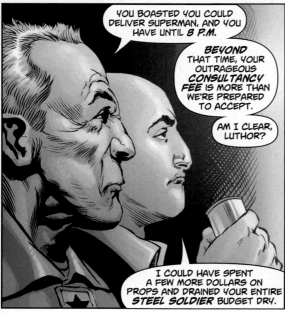

YOU BOASTED YOU COULD DELIVER SUPERMAN, AND YOU HAVE UNTIL *8 P.M.*

BEYOND THAT TIME, YOUR OUTRAGEOUS *CONSULTANCY FEE* IS MORE THAN WE'RE PREPARED TO ACCEPT.

AM I CLEAR, LUTHOR?

I COULD HAVE SPENT A FEW MORE DOLLARS ON PROPS AND DRAINED YOUR ENTIRE *STEEL SOLDIER* BUDGET DRY.

BUT I LOVE MY *COUNTRY*, AND IN RETURN ALL I ASK IS *INFORMATION*, SAM.

I CAN *PROVE* TO YOU, ONCE AND FOR ALL, THAT A *MONSTER* WALKS ⸨SSPP⸩ AMONG US.

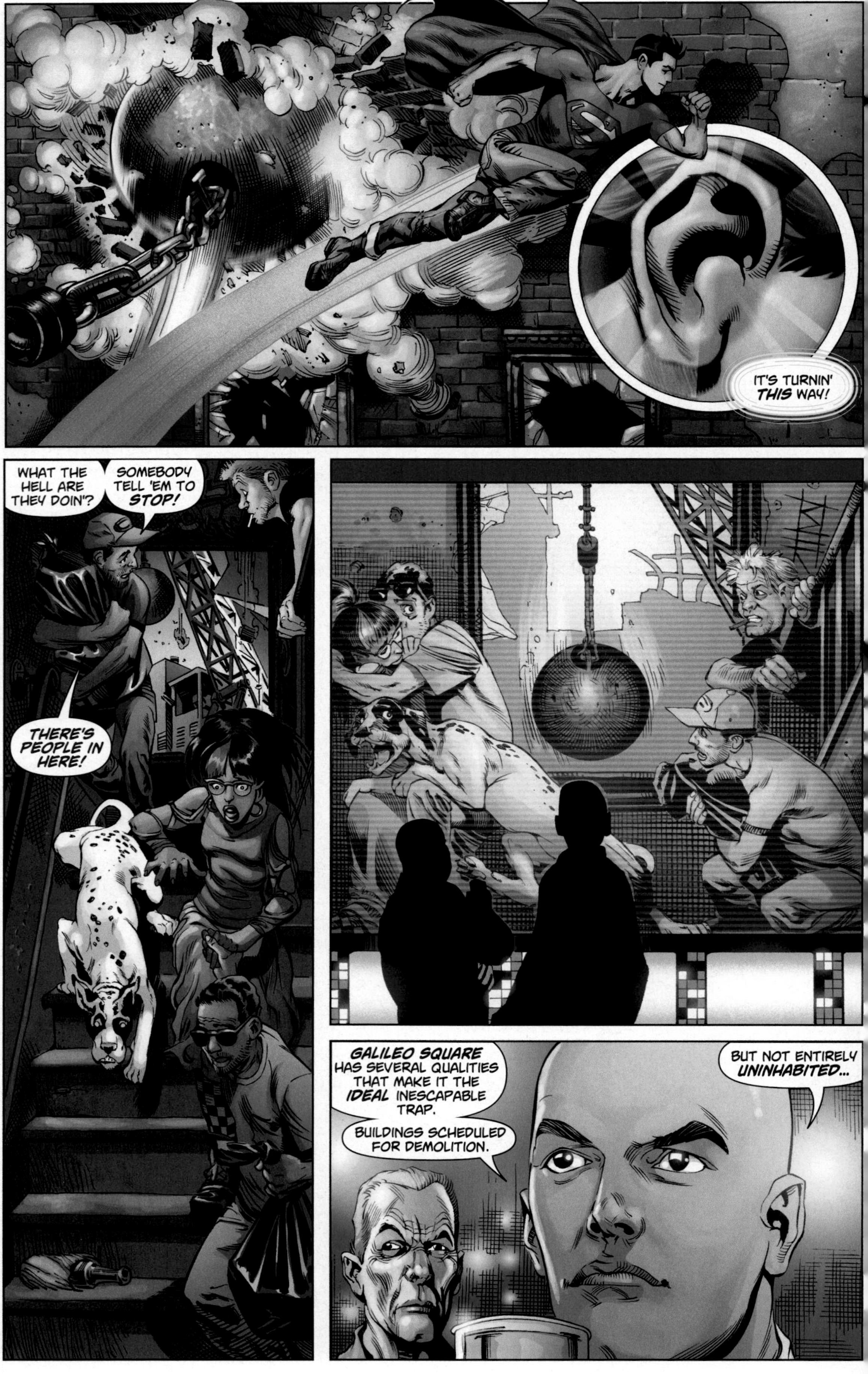
IT'S TURNIN' THIS WAY!
WHAT THE HELL ARE THEY DOIN'?
SOMEBODY TELL 'EM TO STOP!
THERE'S PEOPLE IN HERE!
GALILEO SQUARE HAS SEVERAL QUALITIES THAT MAKE IT THE IDEAL INESCAPABLE TRAP.
BUILDINGS SCHEDULED FOR DEMOLITION.
BUT NOT ENTIRELY UNINHABITED...

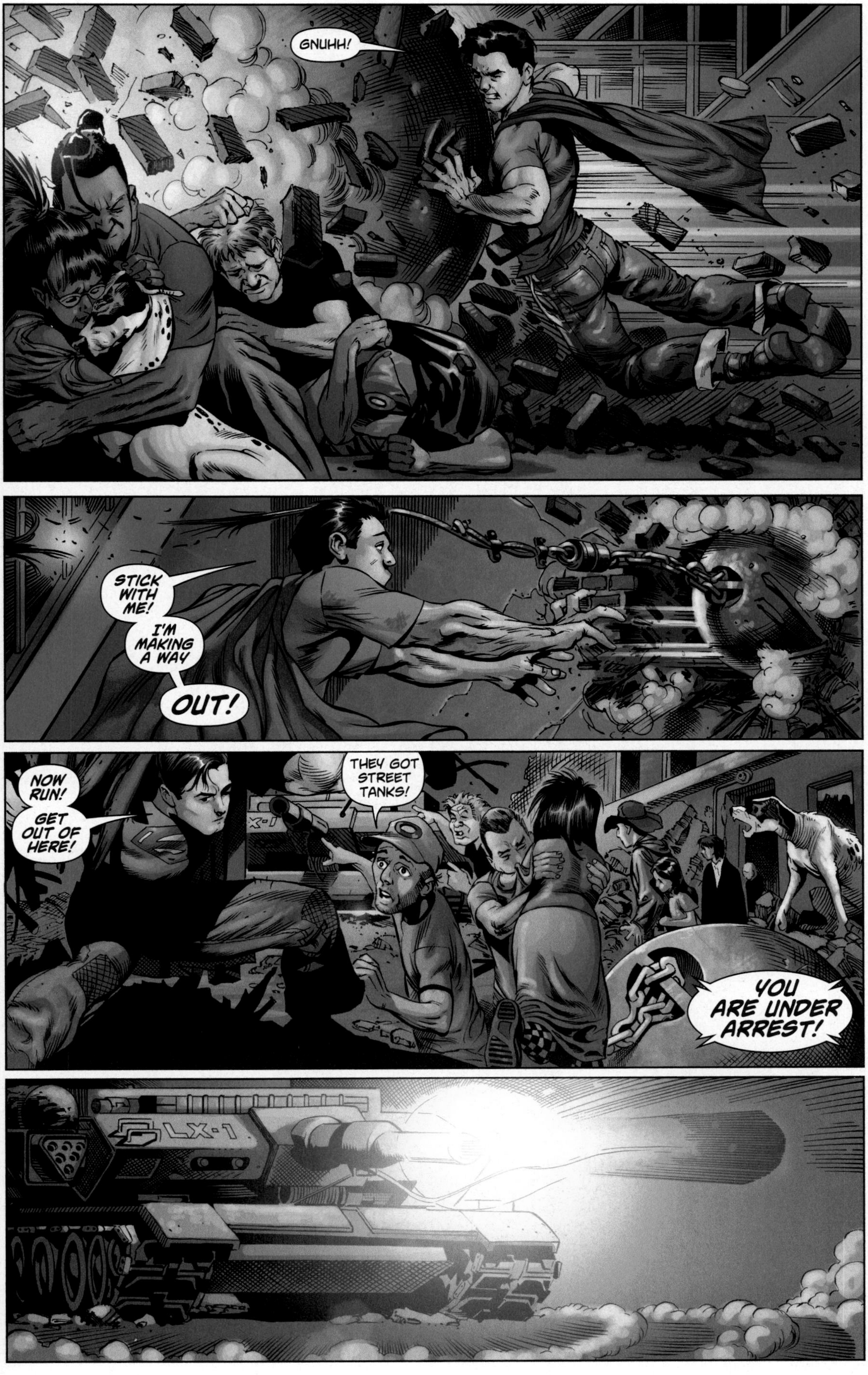
GNUHH!
STICK WITH ME!
I'M MAKING A WAY
OUT!
NOW RUN!
GET OUT OF HERE!
THEY GOT STREET TANKS!
X-1
YOU ARE UNDER ARREST!
LX-1

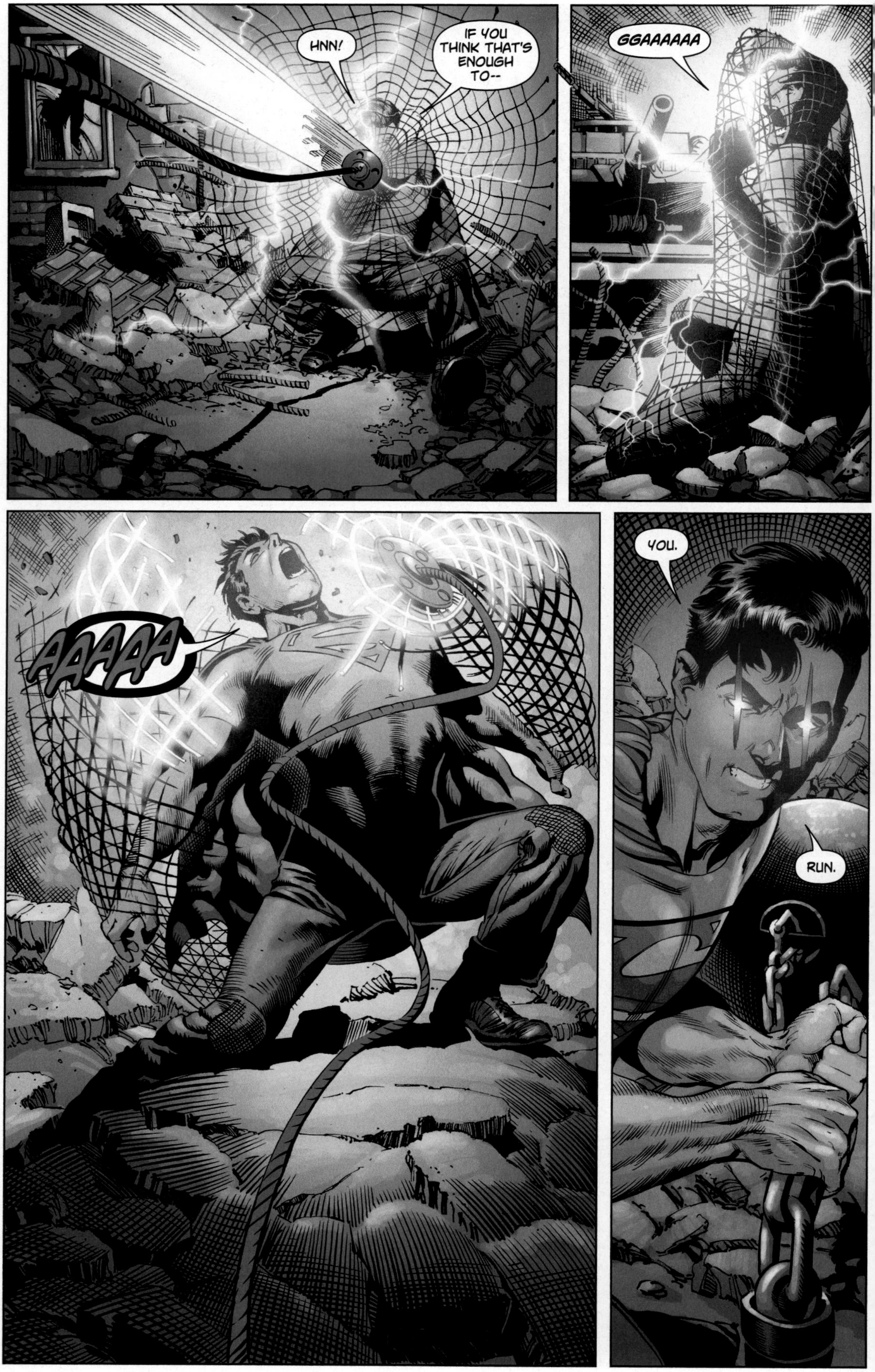
HNN!
IF YOU THINK THAT'S ENOUGH TO--
GGAAAAAAA
AAAAA
YOU.
RUN.

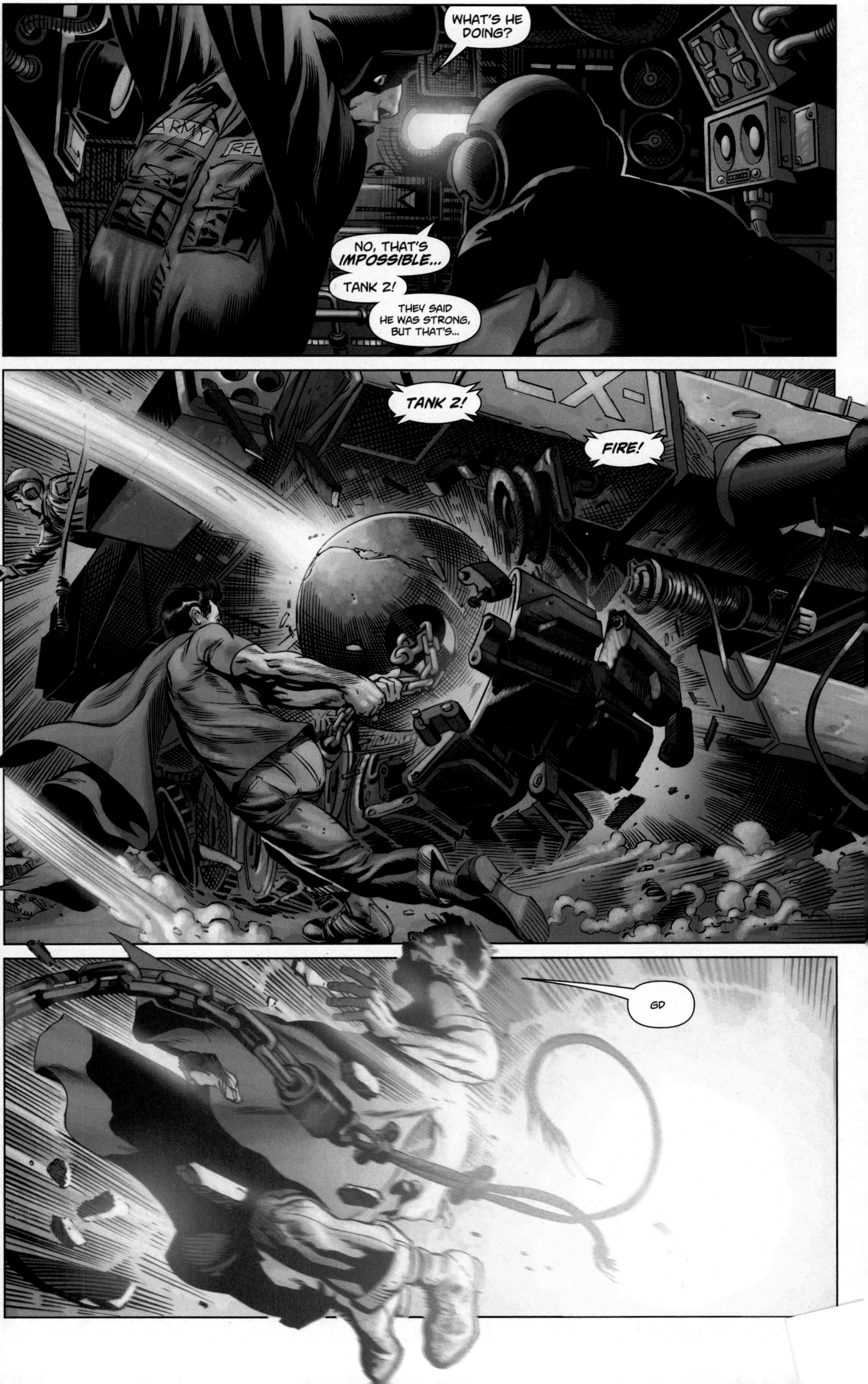
WHAT'S HE DOING?
NO, THAT'S IMPOSSIBLE...
TANK 2!
THEY SAID HE WAS STRONG, BUT THAT'S...
TANK 2!
FIRE!
GD

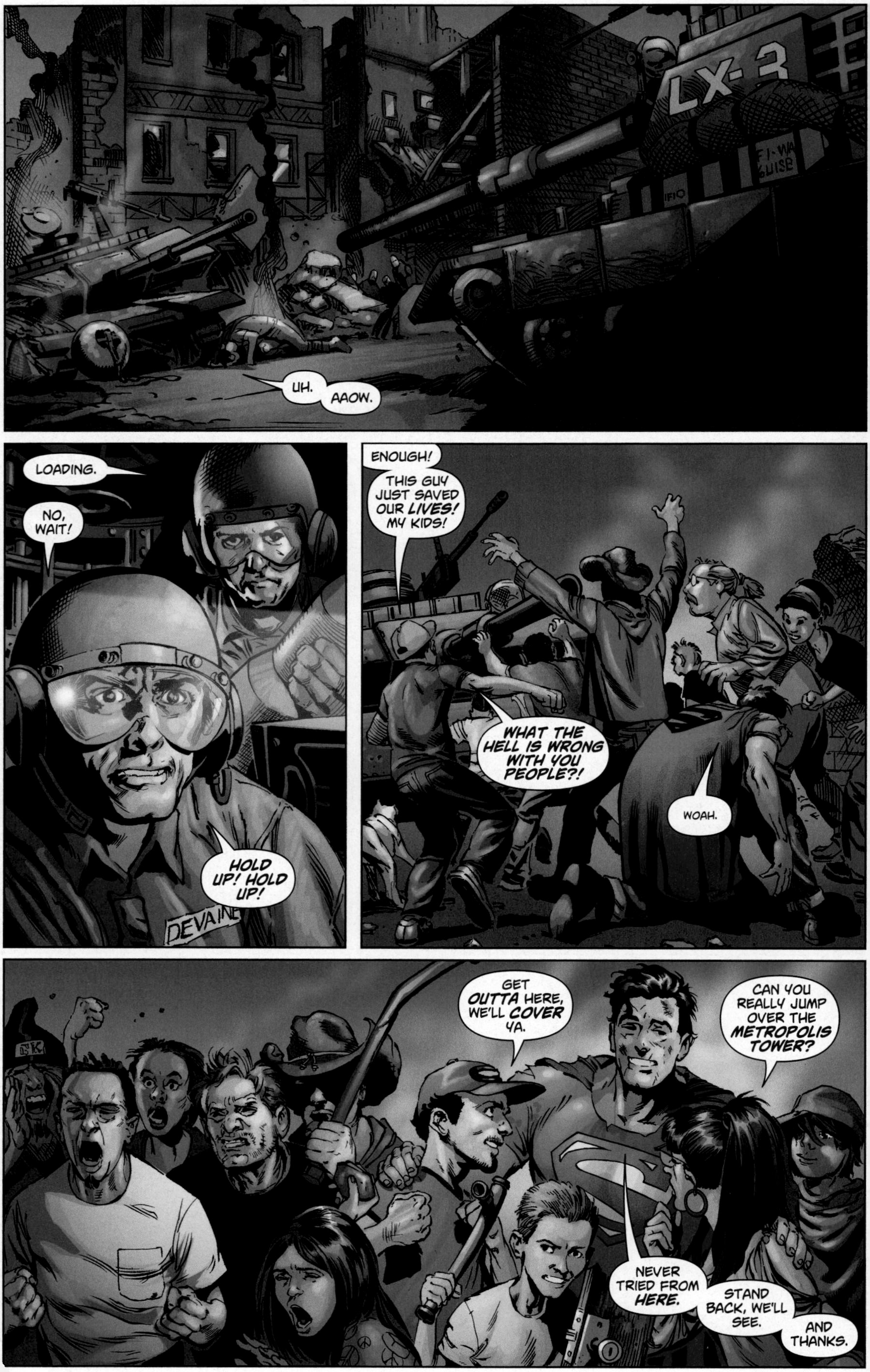
LX-3
UH.
AAOW.
LOADING.
NO, WAIT!
HOLD UP! HOLD UP!
DEVAINE
ENOUGH!
THIS GUY JUST SAVED OUR LIVES! MY KIDS!
WHAT THE HELL IS WRONG WITH YOU PEOPLE?!
WOAH.
GET OUTTA HERE, WE'LL COVER YA.
CAN YOU REALLY JUMP OVER THE METROPOLIS TOWER?
NEVER TRIED FROM HERE.
STAND BACK, WE'LL SEE.
AND THANKS.

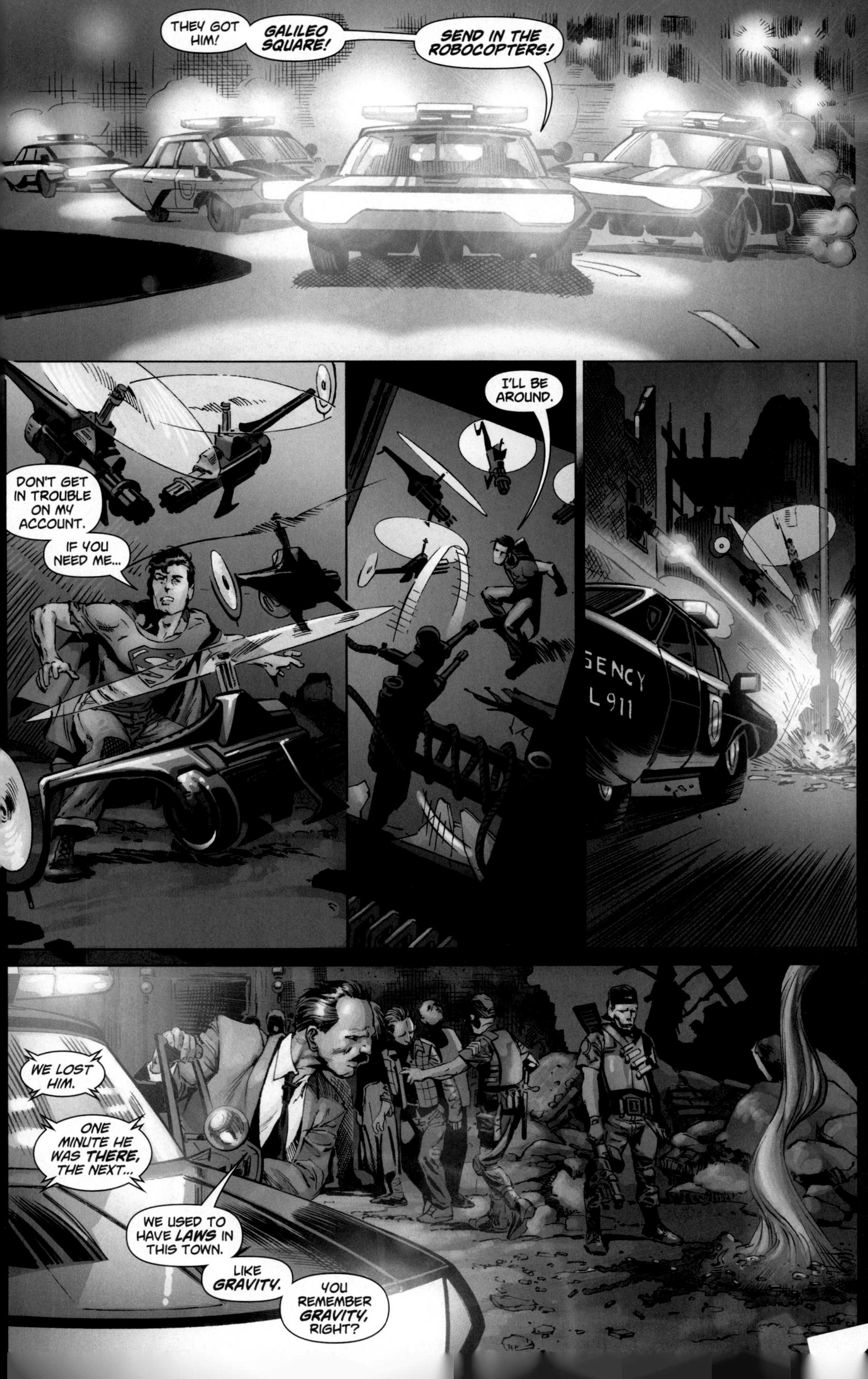
THEY GOT HIM!
GALILEO SQUARE!
SEND IN THE ROBOCOPTERS!
DON'T GET IN TROUBLE ON MY ACCOUNT.
IF YOU NEED ME...
I'LL BE AROUND.
WE LOST HIM.
ONE MINUTE HE WAS THERE, THE NEXT...
WE USED TO HAVE LAWS IN THIS TOWN.
LIKE GRAVITY.
YOU REMEMBER GRAVITY, RIGHT?

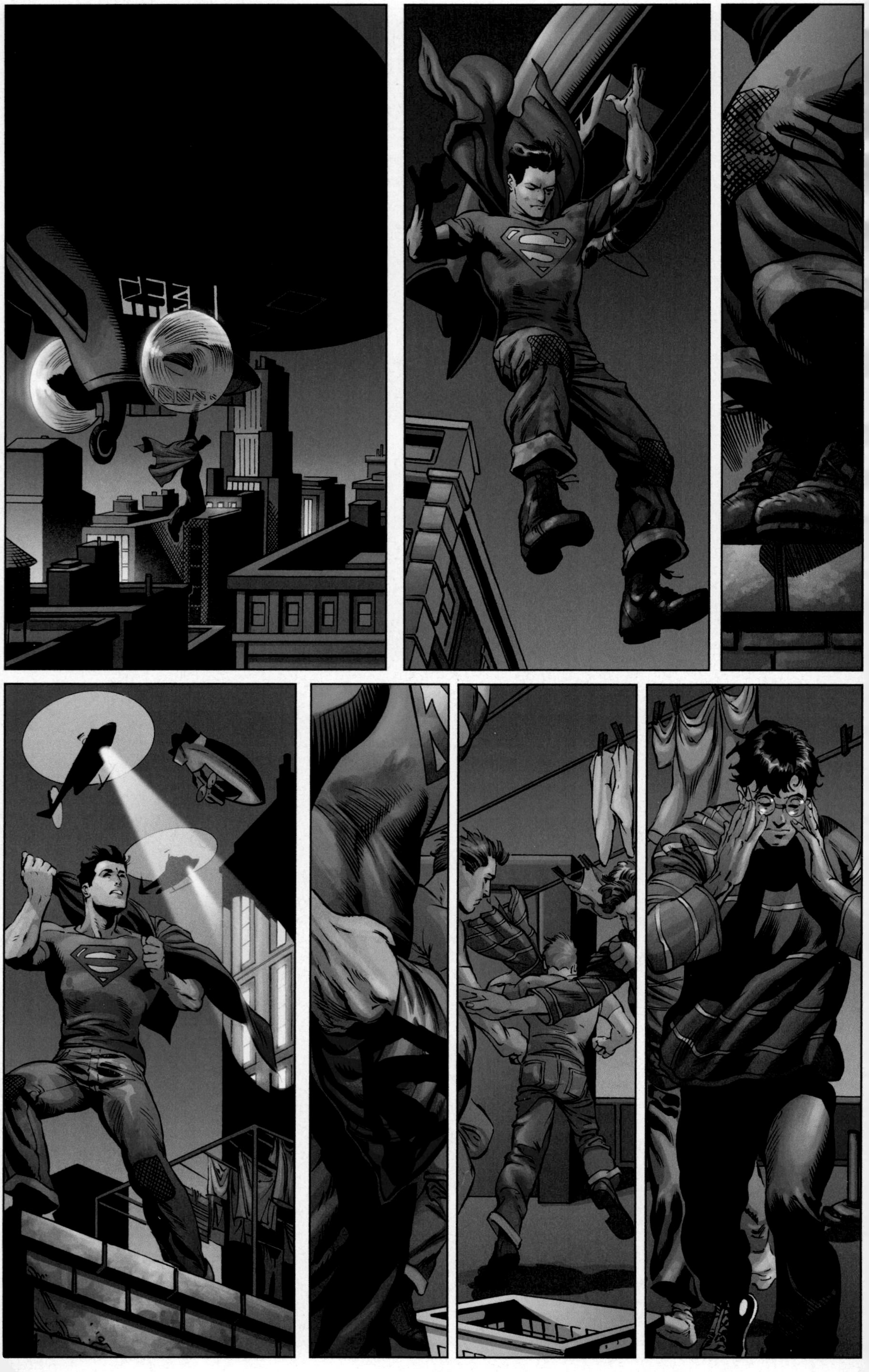

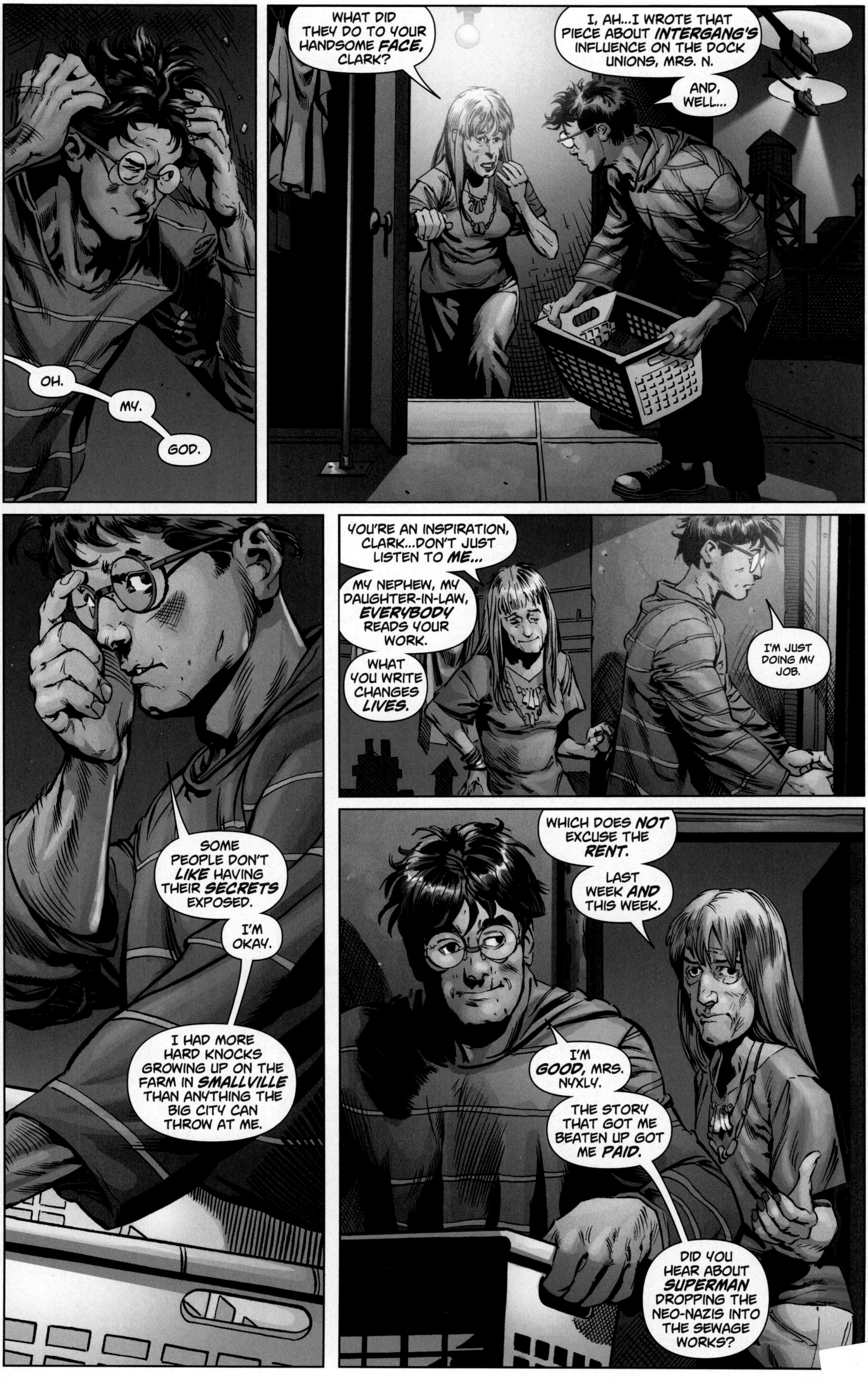
OH.
MY.
GOD.
WHAT DID THEY DO TO YOUR HANDSOME FACE, CLARK?
I, AH...I WROTE THAT PIECE ABOUT INTERGANG'S INFLUENCE ON THE DOCK UNIONS, MRS. N.
AND, WELL...
SOME PEOPLE DON'T LIKE HAVING THEIR SECRETS EXPOSED.
I'M OKAY.
I HAD MORE HARD KNOCKS GROWING UP ON THE FARM IN SMALLVILLE THAN ANYTHING THE BIG CITY CAN THROW AT ME.
YOU'RE AN INSPIRATION, CLARK...DON'T JUST LISTEN TO ME...
MY NEPHEW, MY DAUGHTER-IN-LAW, EVERYBODY READS YOUR WORK.
WHAT YOU WRITE CHANGES LIVES.
I'M JUST DOING MY JOB.
WHICH DOES NOT EXCUSE THE RENT.
LAST WEEK AND THIS WEEK.
I'M GOOD, MRS. NYXLY.
THE STORY THAT GOT ME BEATEN UP GOT ME PAID.
DID YOU HEAR ABOUT SUPERMAN DROPPING THE NEO-NAZIS INTO THE SEWAGE WORKS?

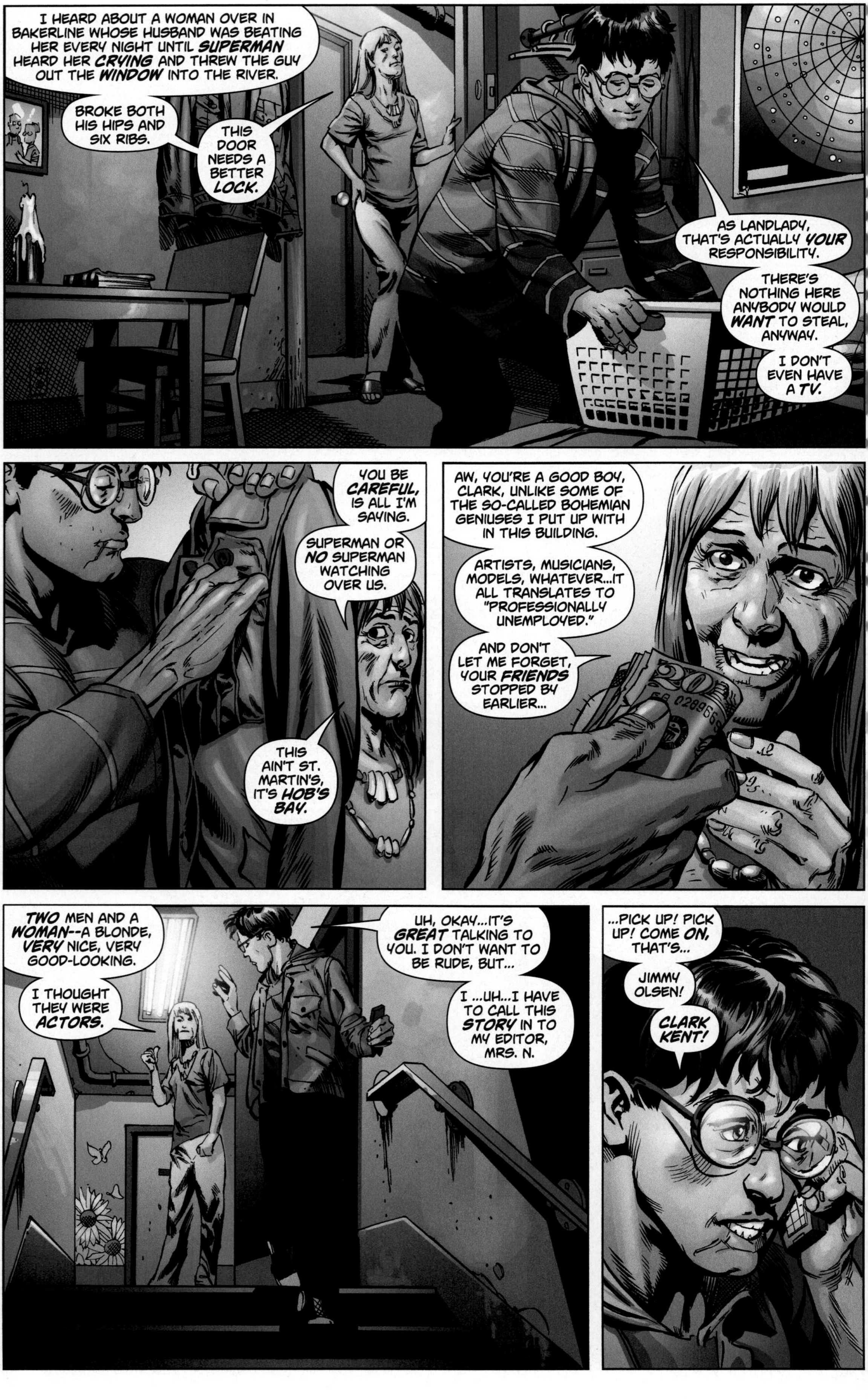
I HEARD ABOUT A WOMAN OVER IN BAKERLINE WHOSE HUSBAND WAS BEATING HER EVERY NIGHT UNTIL SUPERMAN HEARD HER CRYING AND THREW THE GUY OUT THE WINDOW INTO THE RIVER.
BROKE BOTH HIS HIPS AND SIX RIBS.
THIS DOOR NEEDS A BETTER LOCK.
AS LANDLADY, THAT'S ACTUALLY YOUR RESPONSIBILITY.
THERE'S NOTHING HERE ANYBODY WOULD WANT TO STEAL, ANYWAY.
I DON'T EVEN HAVE A TV.
YOU BE CAREFUL, IS ALL I'M SAYING.
SUPERMAN OR NO SUPERMAN WATCHING OVER US.
THIS AIN'T ST. MARTIN'S, IT'S HOB'S BAY.
AW, YOU'RE A GOOD BOY, CLARK, UNLIKE SOME OF THE SO-CALLED BOHEMIAN GENIUSES I PUT UP WITH IN THIS BUILDING.
ARTISTS, MUSICIANS, MODELS, WHATEVER...IT ALL TRANSLATES TO "PROFESSIONALLY UNEMPLOYED."
AND DON'T LET ME FORGET, YOUR FRIENDS STOPPED BY EARLIER...
TWO MEN AND A WOMAN--A BLONDE, VERY NICE, VERY GOOD-LOOKING.
I THOUGHT THEY WERE ACTORS.
UH, OKAY...IT'S GREAT TALKING TO YOU. I DON'T WANT TO BE RUDE, BUT...
I ...UH...I HAVE TO CALL THIS STORY IN TO MY EDITOR, MRS. N.
...PICK UP! PICK UP! COME ON, THAT'S...
JIMMY OLSEN!
CLARK KENT!

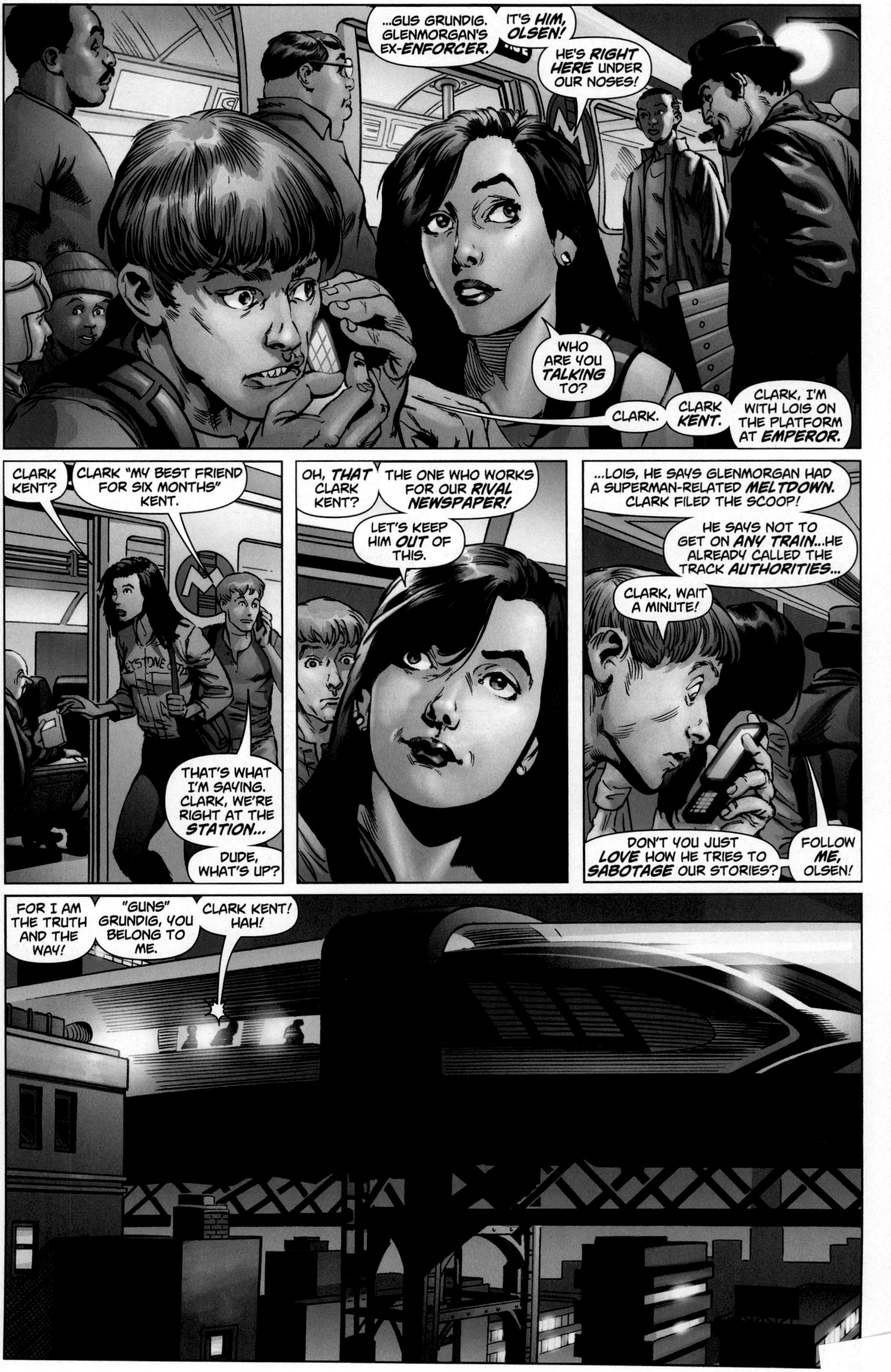
...GUS GRUNDIG. GLENMORGAN'S EX-ENFORCER.
IT'S HIM, OLSEN!
HE'S RIGHT HERE UNDER OUR NOSES!
WHO ARE YOU TALKING TO?
CLARK.
CLARK KENT.
CLARK, I'M WITH LOIS ON THE PLATFORM AT EMPEROR.
CLARK KENT?
CLARK "MY BEST FRIEND FOR SIX MONTHS" KENT.
THAT'S WHAT I'M SAYING. CLARK, WE'RE RIGHT AT THE STATION...
DUDE, WHAT'S UP?
OH, THAT CLARK KENT?
THE ONE WHO WORKS FOR OUR RIVAL NEWSPAPER!
LET'S KEEP HIM OUT OF THIS.
...LOIS, HE SAYS GLENMORGAN HAD A SUPERMAN-RELATED MELTDOWN. CLARK FILED THE SCOOP!
HE SAYS NOT TO GET ON ANY TRAIN...HE ALREADY CALLED THE TRACK AUTHORITIES...
CLARK, WAIT A MINUTE!
DON'T YOU JUST LOVE HOW HE TRIES TO SABOTAGE OUR STORIES?
FOLLOW ME, OLSEN!
FOR I AM THE TRUTH AND THE WAY!
"GUNS" GRUNDIG, YOU BELONG TO ME.
CLARK KENT! HAH!

"THERE ARE *SKELETONS* IN THE FOUNDATIONS OF THE CITY OF TOMORROW." YUP.

I *DO* MEAN THAT LITERALLY, MR. TAYLOR.

LOOK, AS FOR THE SUPERMAN THING....SURE IT'S INTIMIDATION, BUT IT BACKS UP OUR *HARD EVIDENCE* AGAINST GLENMORGAN.

WHAT DID YOU JUST SAY?

THIS IS HAPPENING NOW? I *TOLD* THEM!

NO...I, UH, I HAVE TO GO BACK UPSTAIRS FOR A SECOND...

SO WHAT WAS ALL THAT GLEN GLENMORGAN STUFF?

DID KENT *SA*... ANYTHING...

I MEA... WHAT D... HE KNO... DON...

I *HATE* THIS PHONE. IT'S MY ... PERSONAL STALKER.

ZEE ZEE ZEE

A DO... GL...

READ CLARK'S TEXT!

THIS TRAIN SHOULDN'T EVEN BE *RUNNING*.

WHY AREN'T WE STOPPING, LOIS?

WE'RE AFTER THE BAD GUY.

HEY, MISTER!

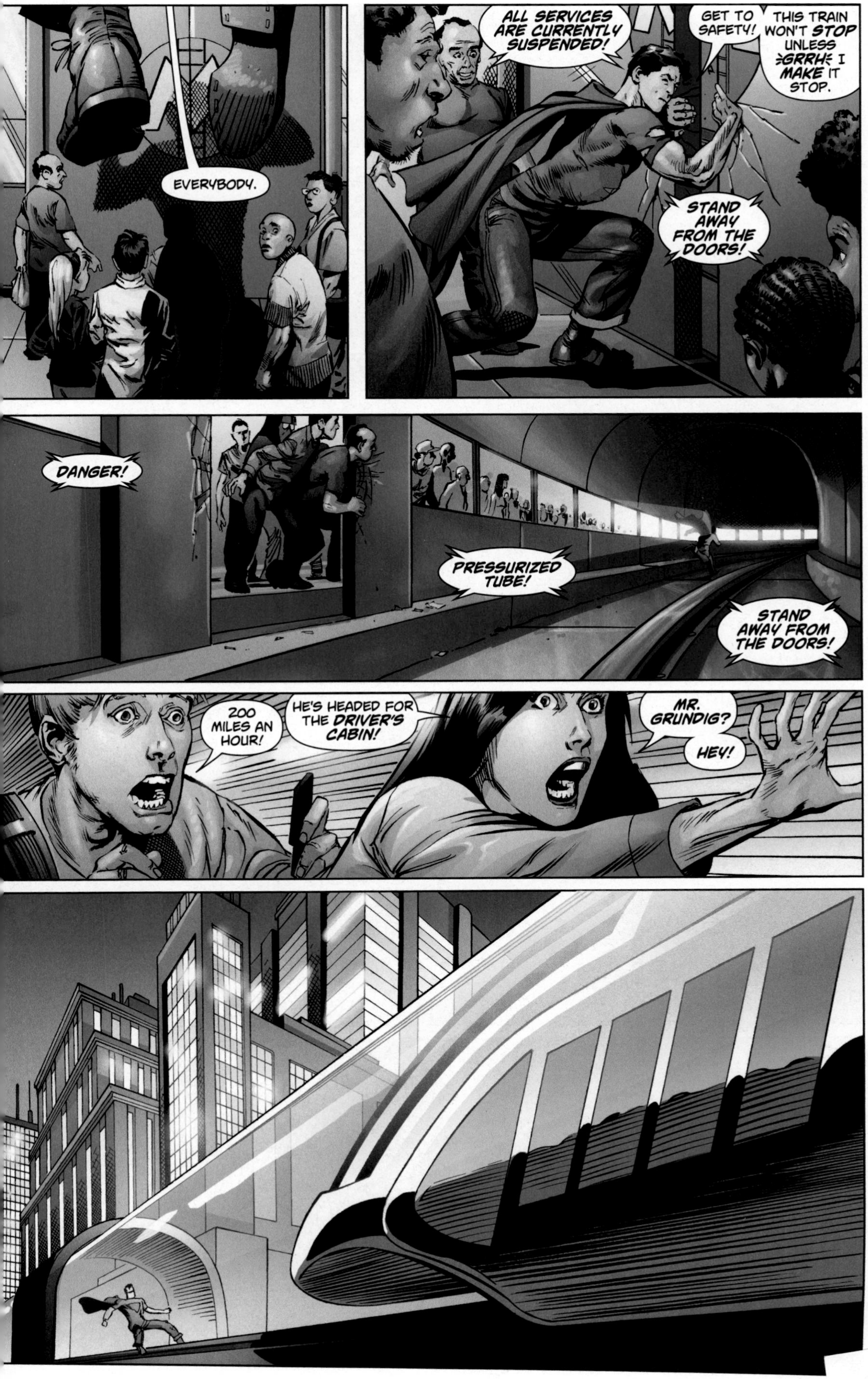
EVERYBODY.
ALL SERVICES ARE CURRENTLY SUSPENDED!
GET TO SAFETY!
THIS TRAIN WON'T STOP UNLESS GRRH I MAKE IT STOP.
STAND AWAY FROM THE DOORS!
DANGER!
PRESSURIZED TUBE!
STAND AWAY FROM THE DOORS!
200 MILES AN HOUR!
HE'S HEADED FOR THE DRIVER'S CABIN!
MR. GRUNDIG?
HEY!

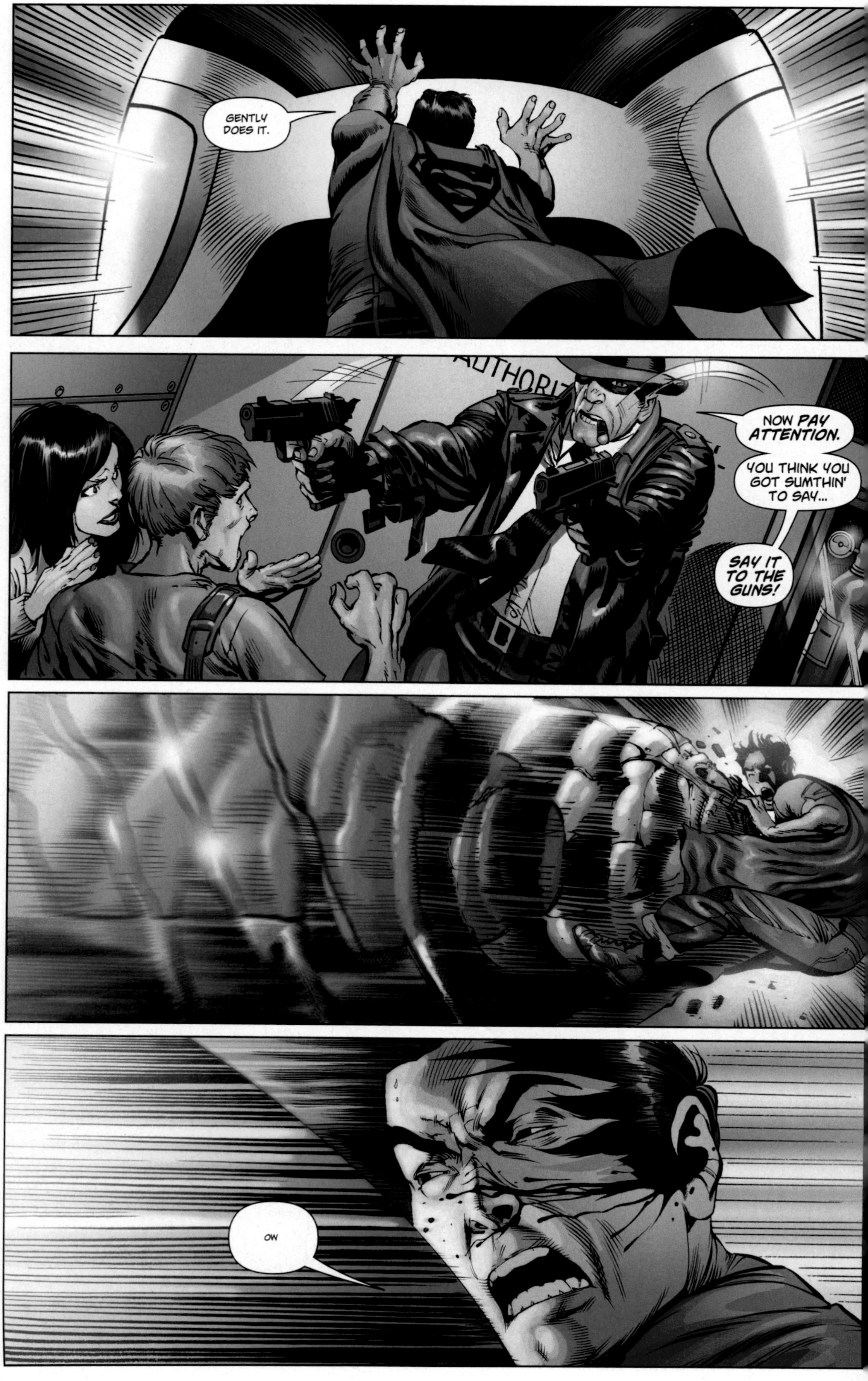
GENTLY DOES IT.
NOW PAY ATTENTION.
YOU THINK YOU GOT SUMTHIN' TO SAY...
SAY IT TO THE GUNS!
OW

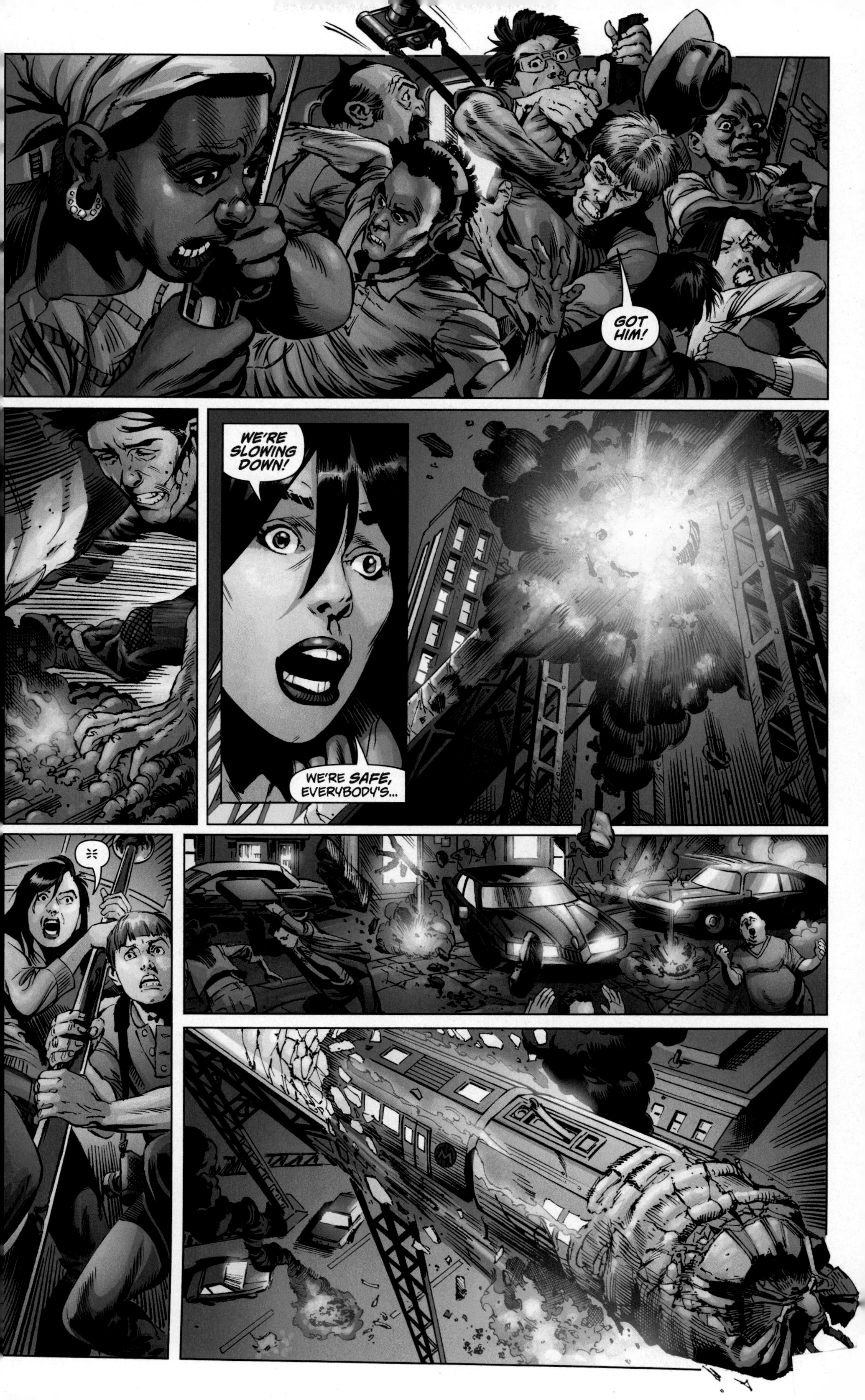
GOT HIM!
WE'RE SLOWING DOWN!
WE'RE SAFE, EVERYBODY'S...

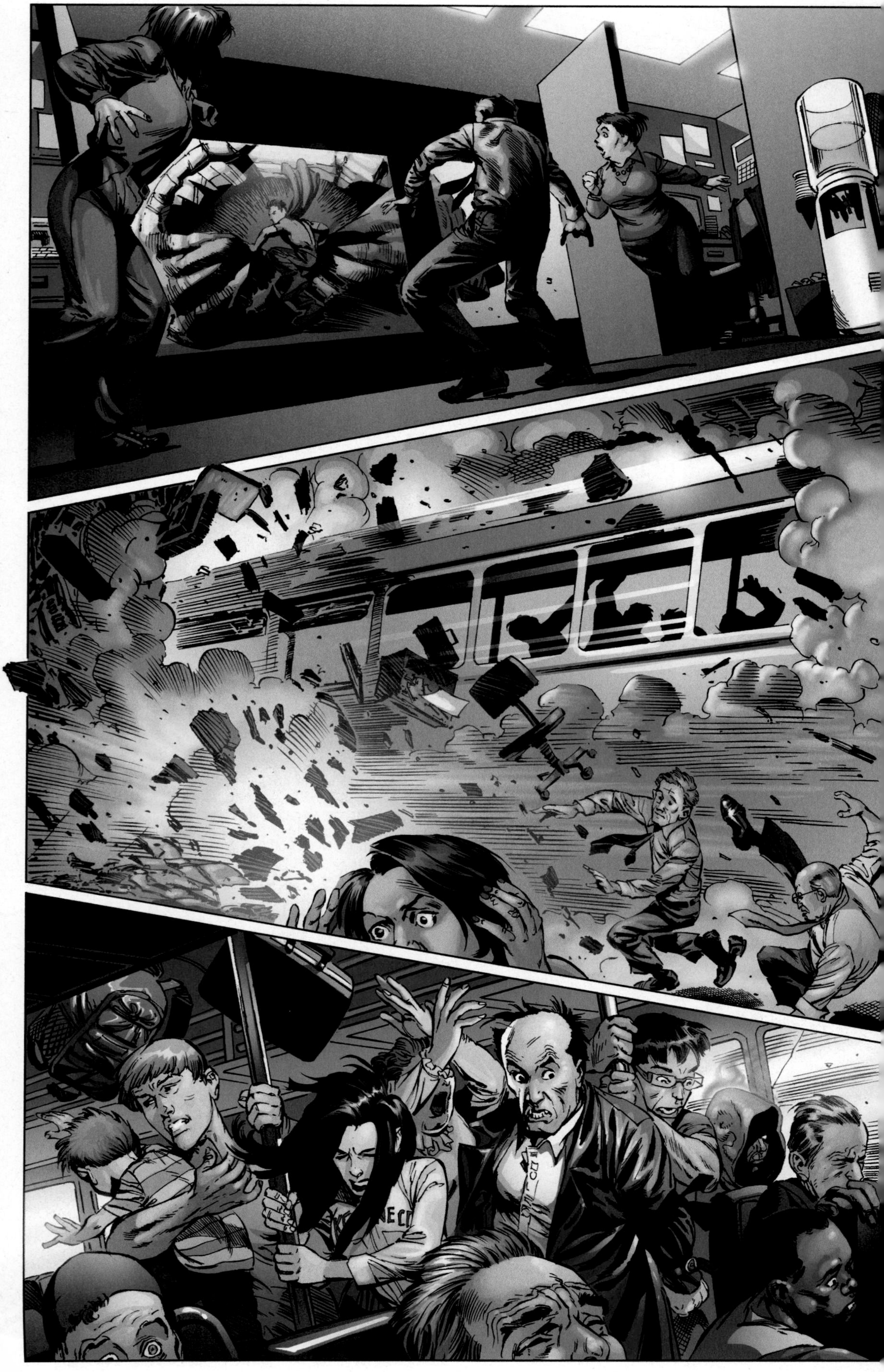

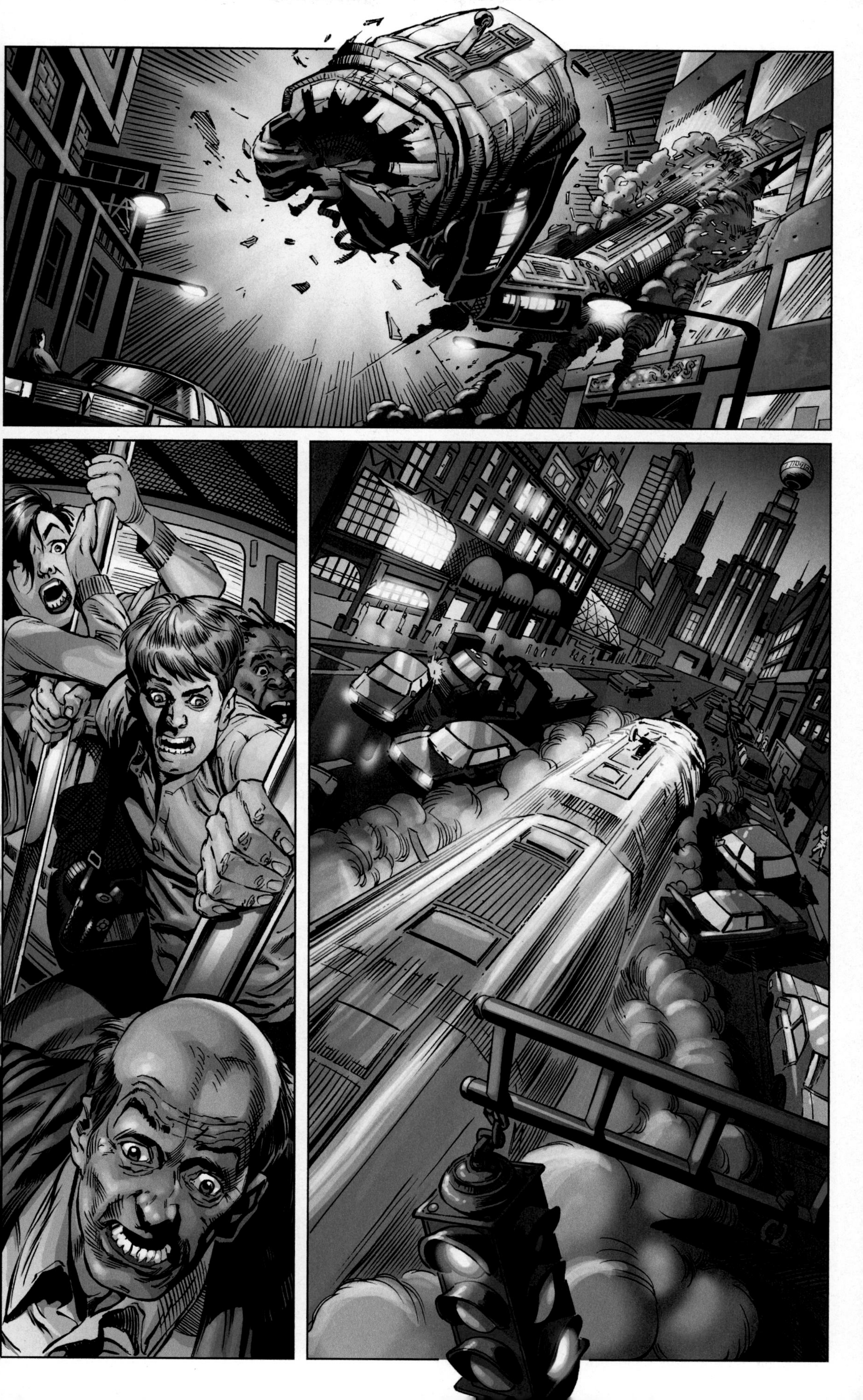

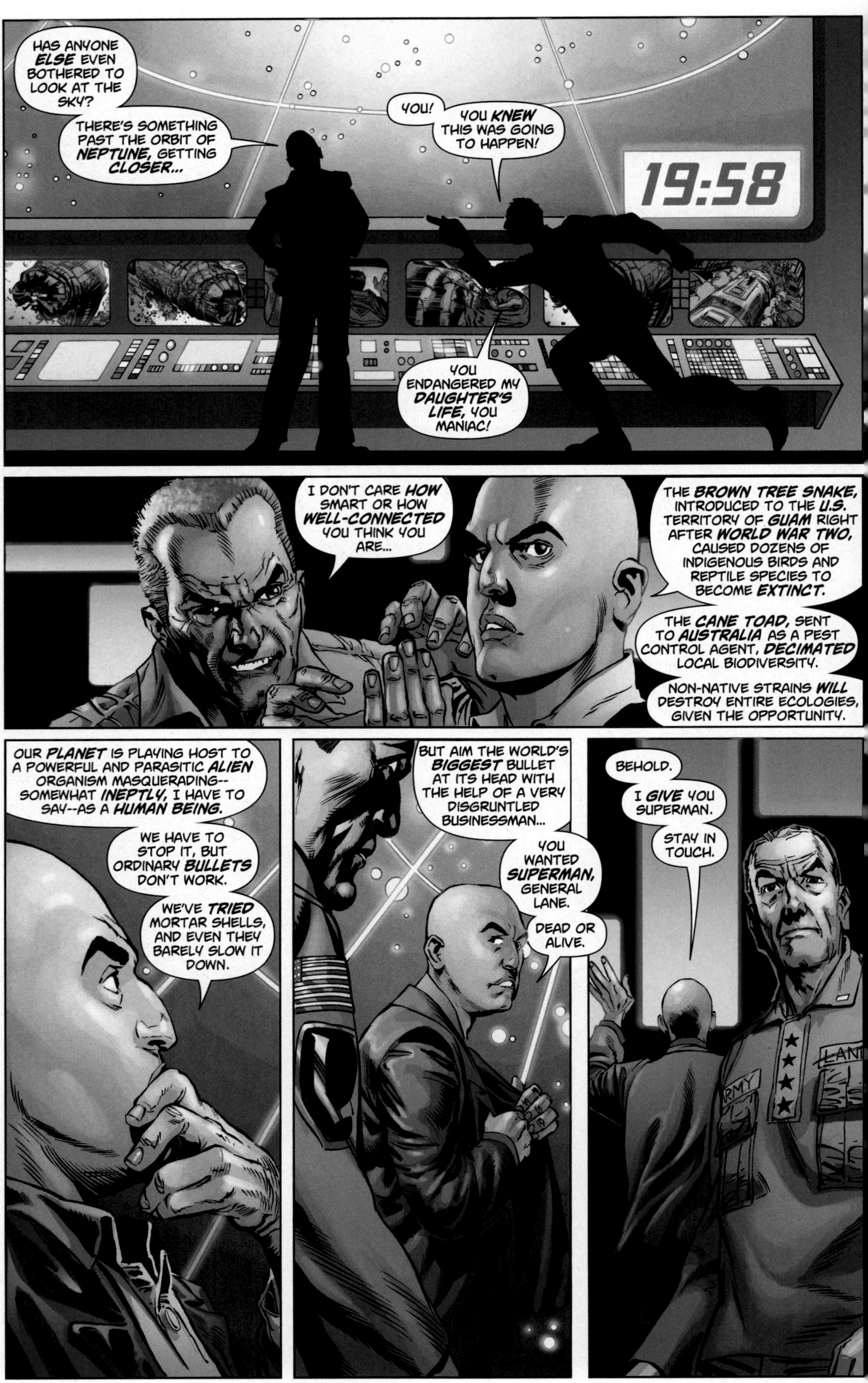

HAS ANYONE ELSE EVEN BOTHERED TO LOOK AT THE SKY?
THERE'S SOMETHING PAST THE ORBIT OF NEPTUNE, GETTING CLOSER...
YOU!
YOU KNEW THIS WAS GOING TO HAPPEN!
19:58
YOU ENDANGERED MY DAUGHTER'S LIFE, YOU MANIAC!
I DON'T CARE HOW SMART OR HOW WELL-CONNECTED YOU THINK YOU ARE...
THE BROWN TREE SNAKE, INTRODUCED TO THE U.S. TERRITORY OF GUAM RIGHT AFTER WORLD WAR TWO, CAUSED DOZENS OF INDIGENOUS BIRDS AND REPTILE SPECIES TO BECOME EXTINCT.
THE CANE TOAD, SENT TO AUSTRALIA AS A PEST CONTROL AGENT, DECIMATED LOCAL BIODIVERSITY.
NON-NATIVE STRAINS WILL DESTROY ENTIRE ECOLOGIES, GIVEN THE OPPORTUNITY.
OUR PLANET IS PLAYING HOST TO A POWERFUL AND PARASITIC ALIEN ORGANISM MASQUERADING--SOMEWHAT INEPTLY, I HAVE TO SAY--AS A HUMAN BEING.
WE HAVE TO STOP IT, BUT ORDINARY BULLETS DON'T WORK.
WE'VE TRIED MORTAR SHELLS, AND EVEN THEY BARELY SLOW IT DOWN.
BUT AIM THE WORLD'S BIGGEST BULLET AT ITS HEAD WITH THE HELP OF A VERY DISGRUNTLED BUSINESSMAN...
YOU WANTED SUPERMAN, GENERAL LANE.
DEAD OR ALIVE.
BEHOLD.
I GIVE YOU SUPERMAN.
STAY IN TOUCH.

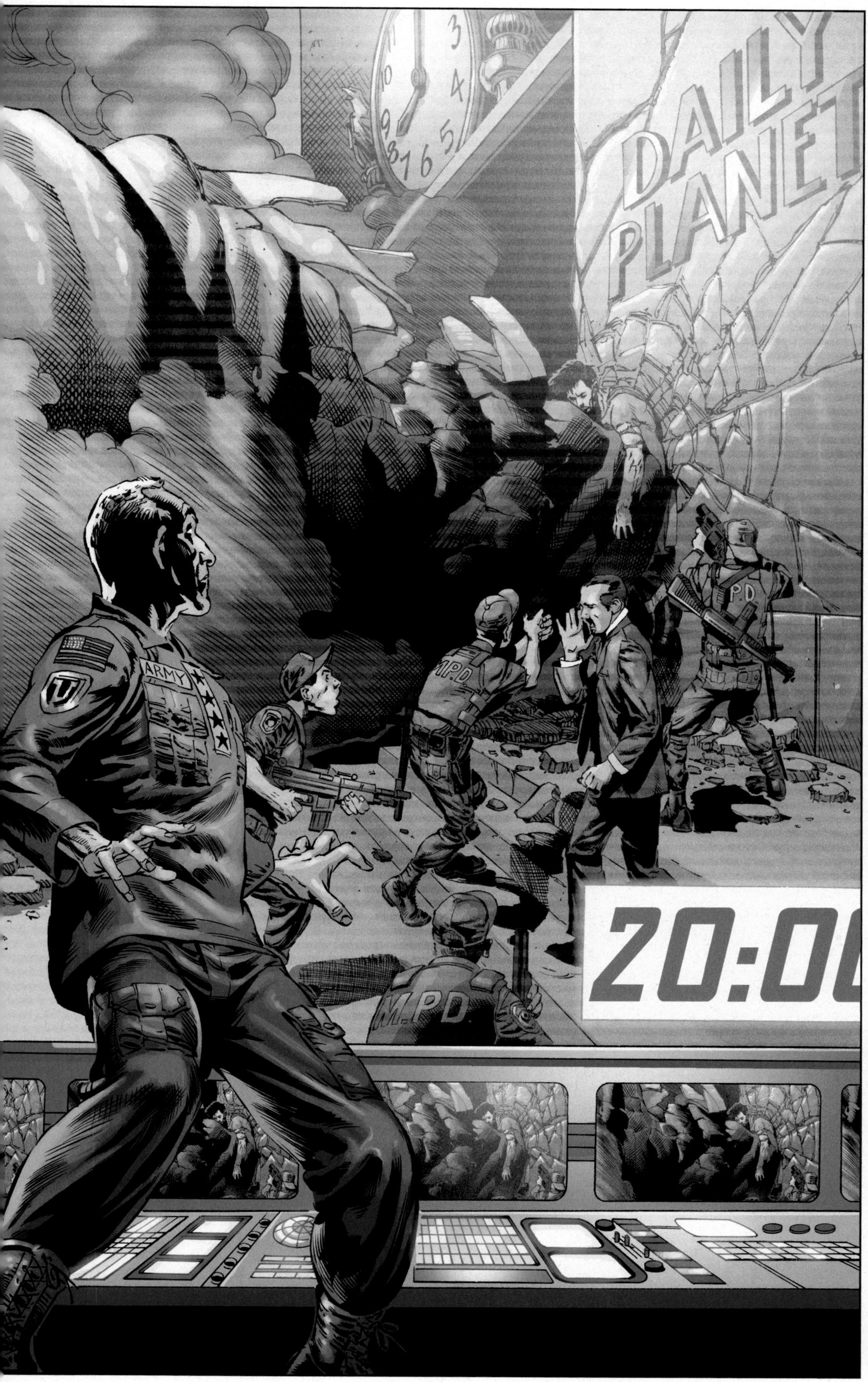
DAILY
PLANET
ARMY
M.P.D
P.D
20:0
M.PD

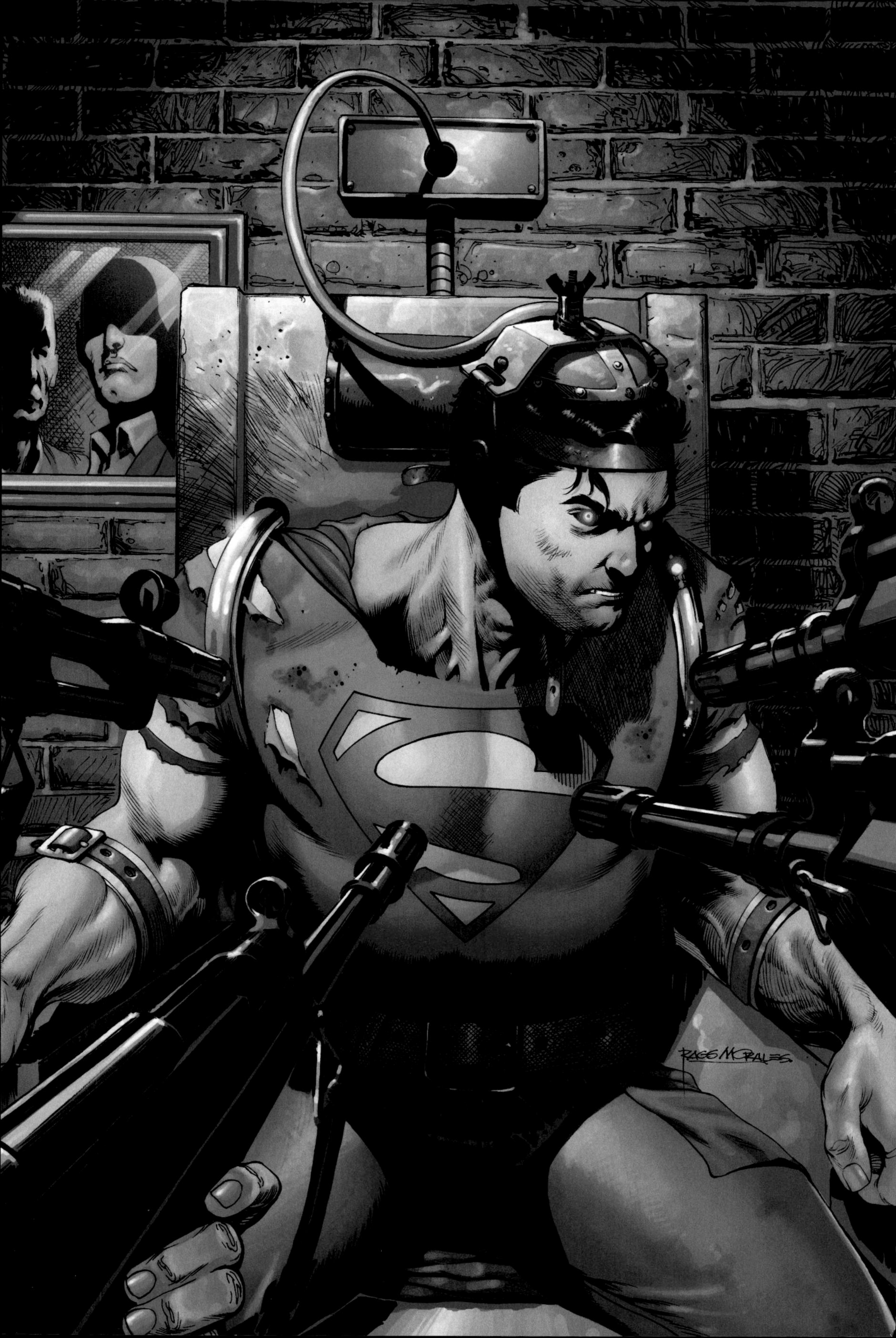
RAGS MORALES

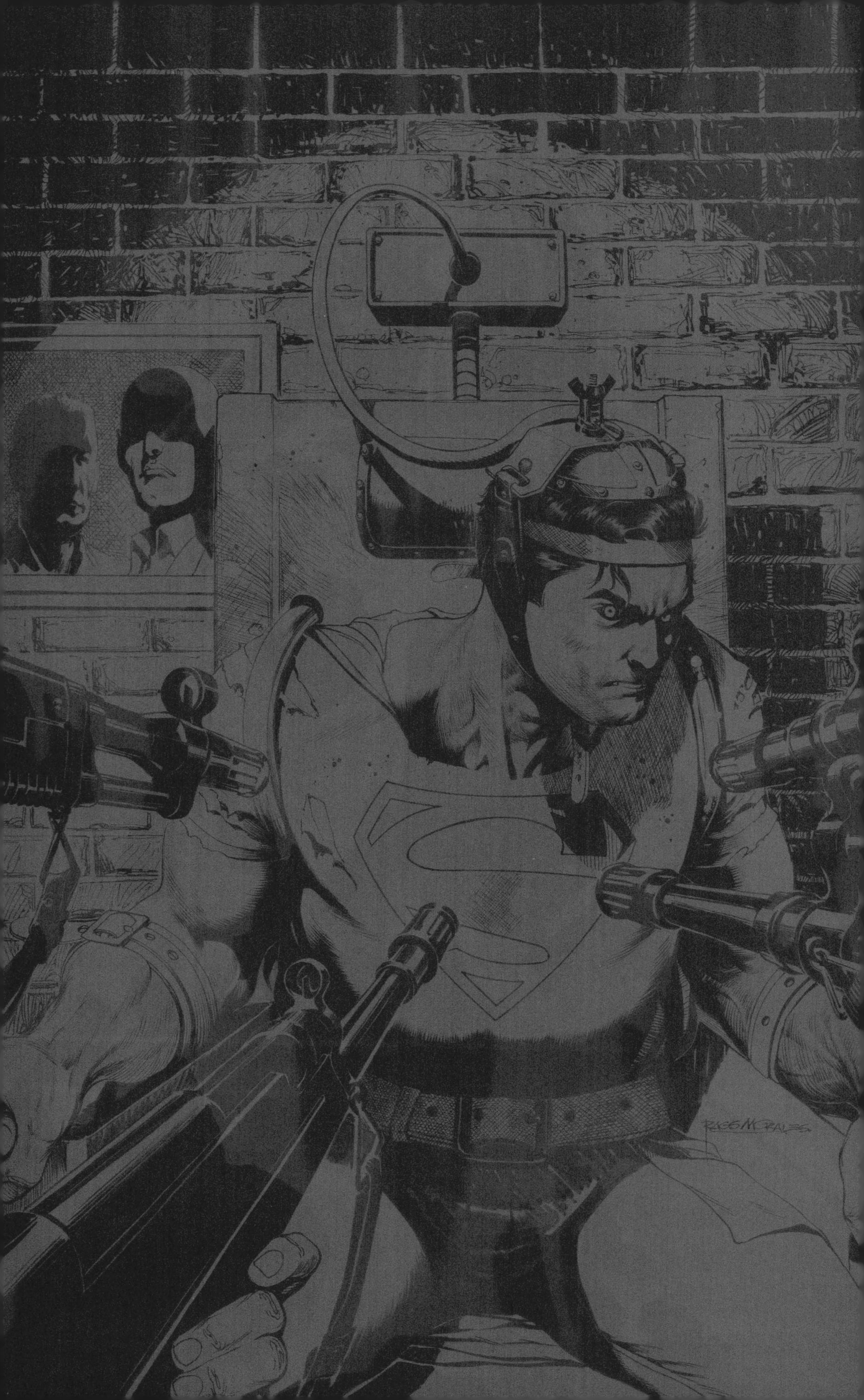
RAGS MORALES

HOW CAN ANYONE *DO* WHAT HE'S DOING?

WE RAN ENOUGH VOLTAGE THROUGH HIM TO FRY A *MOUNTAIN GORILLA.*

WHAT ARE WE *LOOKING* AT HERE?

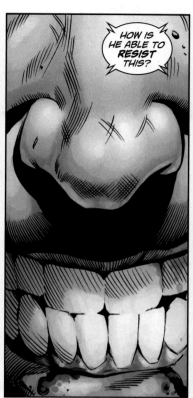

HOW IS HE ABLE TO *RESIST* THIS?

NO. NO.

HE'S *BREAKING LOOSE!*

JUICE HIM AGAIN!

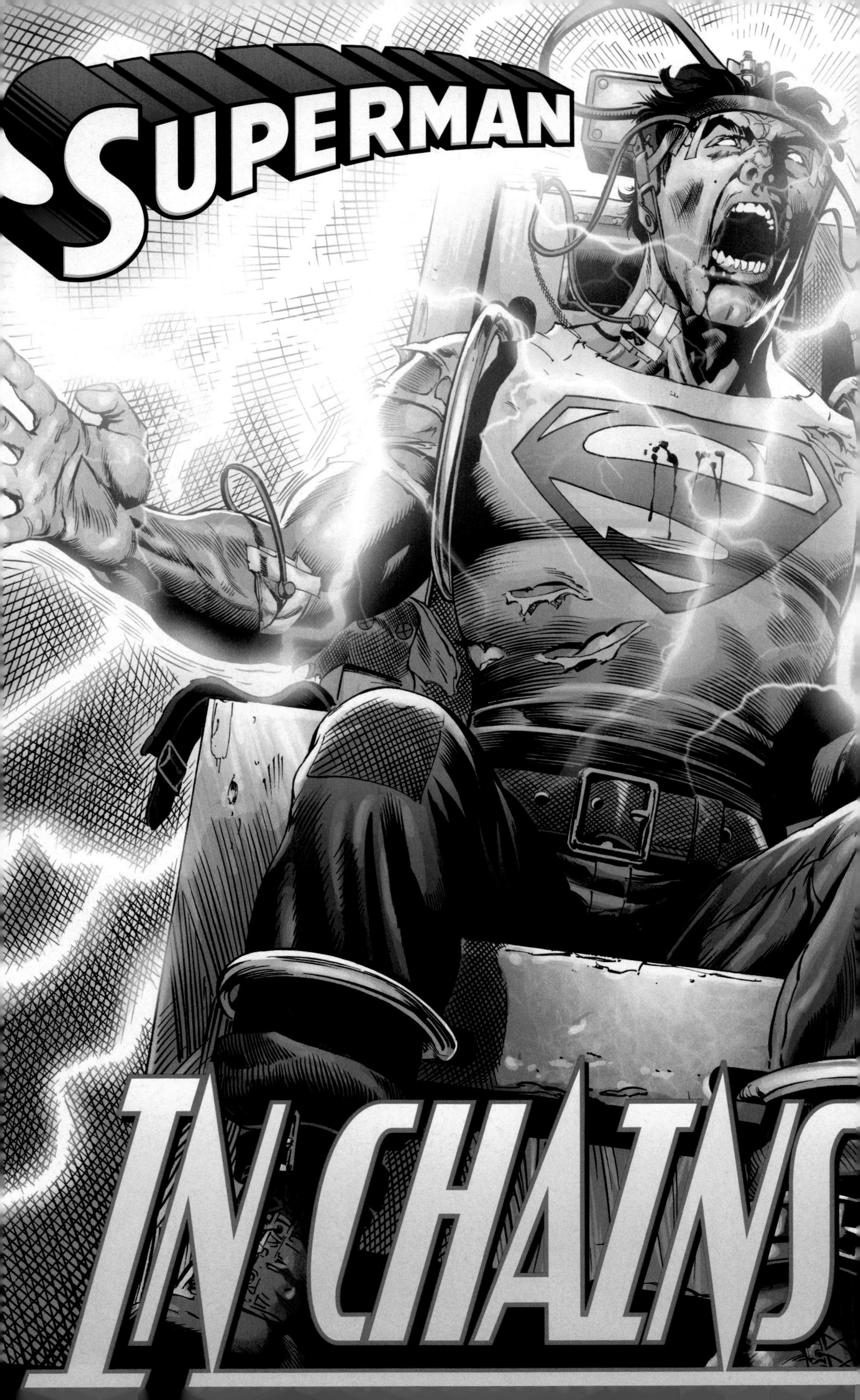
SUPERMAN
IN CHAINS

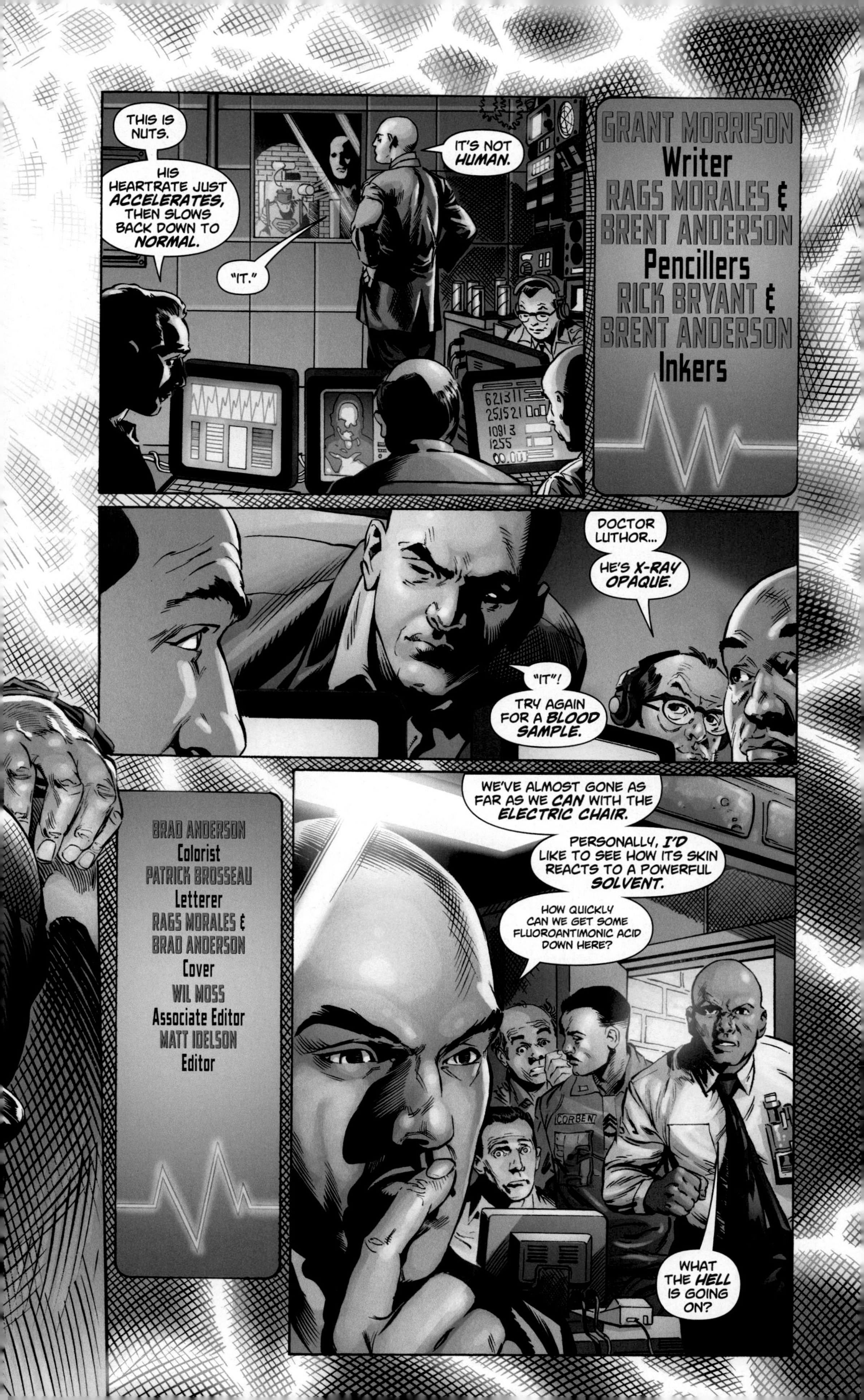
THIS IS NUTS.
HIS HEARTRATE JUST ACCELERATES, THEN SLOWS BACK DOWN TO NORMAL.
IT'S NOT HUMAN.
"IT."
GRANT MORRISON
Writer
RAGS MORALES & BRENT ANDERSON
Pencillers
RICK BRYANT & BRENT ANDERSON
Inkers
DOCTOR LUTHOR...
HE'S X-RAY OPAQUE.
"IT"!
TRY AGAIN FOR A BLOOD SAMPLE.
BRAD ANDERSON
Colorist
PATRICK BROSSEAU
Letterer
RAGS MORALES & BRAD ANDERSON
Cover
WIL MOSS
Associate Editor
MATT IDELSON
Editor
WE'VE ALMOST GONE AS FAR AS WE CAN WITH THE ELECTRIC CHAIR.
PERSONALLY, I'D LIKE TO SEE HOW ITS SKIN REACTS TO A POWERFUL SOLVENT.
HOW QUICKLY CAN WE GET SOME FLUOROANTIMONIC ACID DOWN HERE?
CORBEN
WHAT THE HELL IS GOING ON?

LUTHOR!

DOCTOR IRONS.

SERGEANT CORBEN.

WHAT CAN I DO TO MAKE YOUR LIVES BRIGHTER?

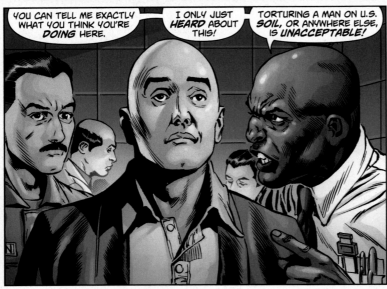

YOU CAN TELL ME EXACTLY WHAT YOU THINK YOU'RE *DOING* HERE.

I ONLY JUST *HEARD* ABOUT THIS!

TORTURING A MAN ON U.S. *SOIL*, OR ANYWHERE ELSE, IS *UNACCEPTABLE!*

THOSE LAWS APPLY TO *HUMAN BEINGS*, SURELY.

AND TELL ME HOW WE CAN *TORTURE* A SO-CALLED MAN WITH *STEEL-HARD* SKIN AND HAIR THAT CAN'T BE *CUT?*

TAKE A *LOOK*. HE'S *FINE.*

THAT'S *HIM?*

THAT BEAT-UP-LOOKING KID IS HIM?

"IT."

ARE YOU EVEN *LISTENING* TO ME?

I WANT THIS STOPPED *RIGHT NOW!*

HE'S SHAKING OFF THE GAS.

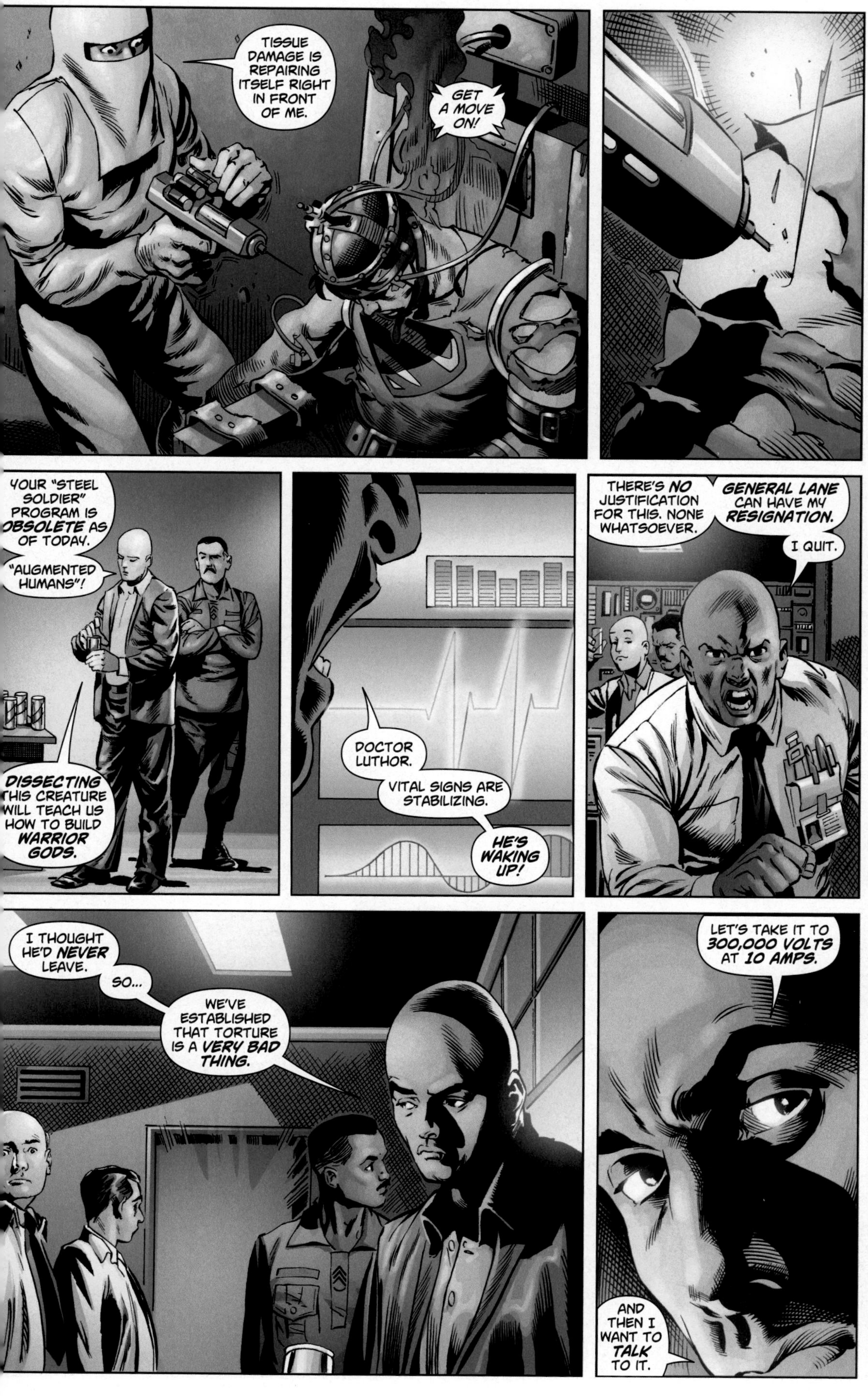
TISSUE DAMAGE IS REPAIRING ITSELF RIGHT IN FRONT OF ME.
GET A MOVE ON!
YOUR "STEEL SOLDIER" PROGRAM IS OBSOLETE AS OF TODAY.
"AUGMENTED HUMANS"!
DISSECTING THIS CREATURE WILL TEACH US HOW TO BUILD WARRIOR GODS.
DOCTOR LUTHOR.
VITAL SIGNS ARE STABILIZING.
HE'S WAKING UP!
THERE'S NO JUSTIFICATION FOR THIS. NONE WHATSOEVER.
GENERAL LANE CAN HAVE MY RESIGNATION.
I QUIT.
I THOUGHT HE'D NEVER LEAVE.
SO...
WE'VE ESTABLISHED THAT TORTURE IS A VERY BAD THING.
LET'S TAKE IT TO 300,000 VOLTS AT 10 AMPS.
AND THEN I WANT TO TALK TO IT.

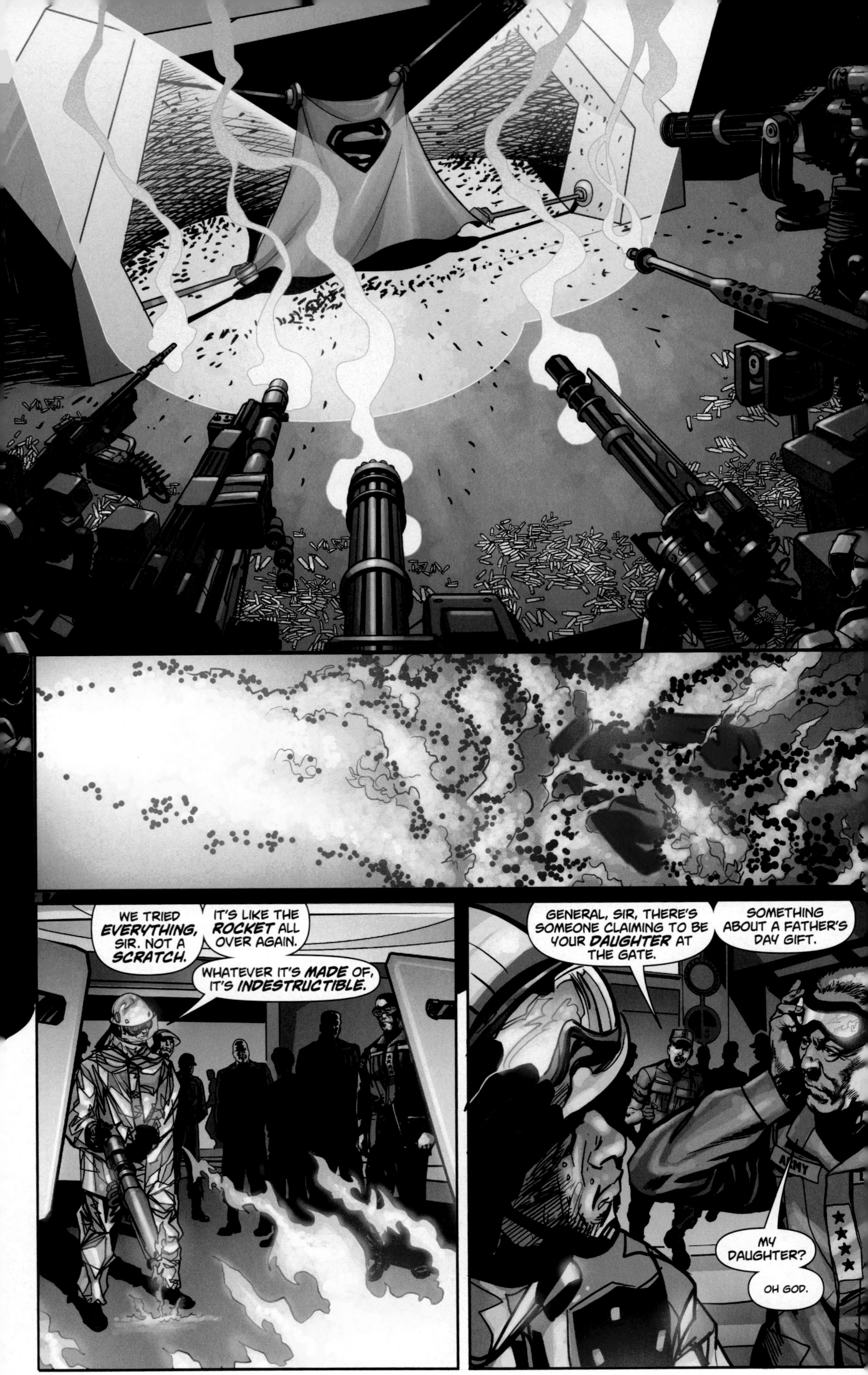
WE TRIED EVERYTHING, SIR. NOT A SCRATCH.
IT'S LIKE THE ROCKET ALL OVER AGAIN.
WHATEVER IT'S MADE OF, IT'S INDESTRUCTIBLE.
GENERAL, SIR, THERE'S SOMEONE CLAIMING TO BE YOUR DAUGHTER AT THE GATE.
SOMETHING ABOUT A FATHER'S DAY GIFT.
ARMY
MY DAUGHTER?
OH GOD.

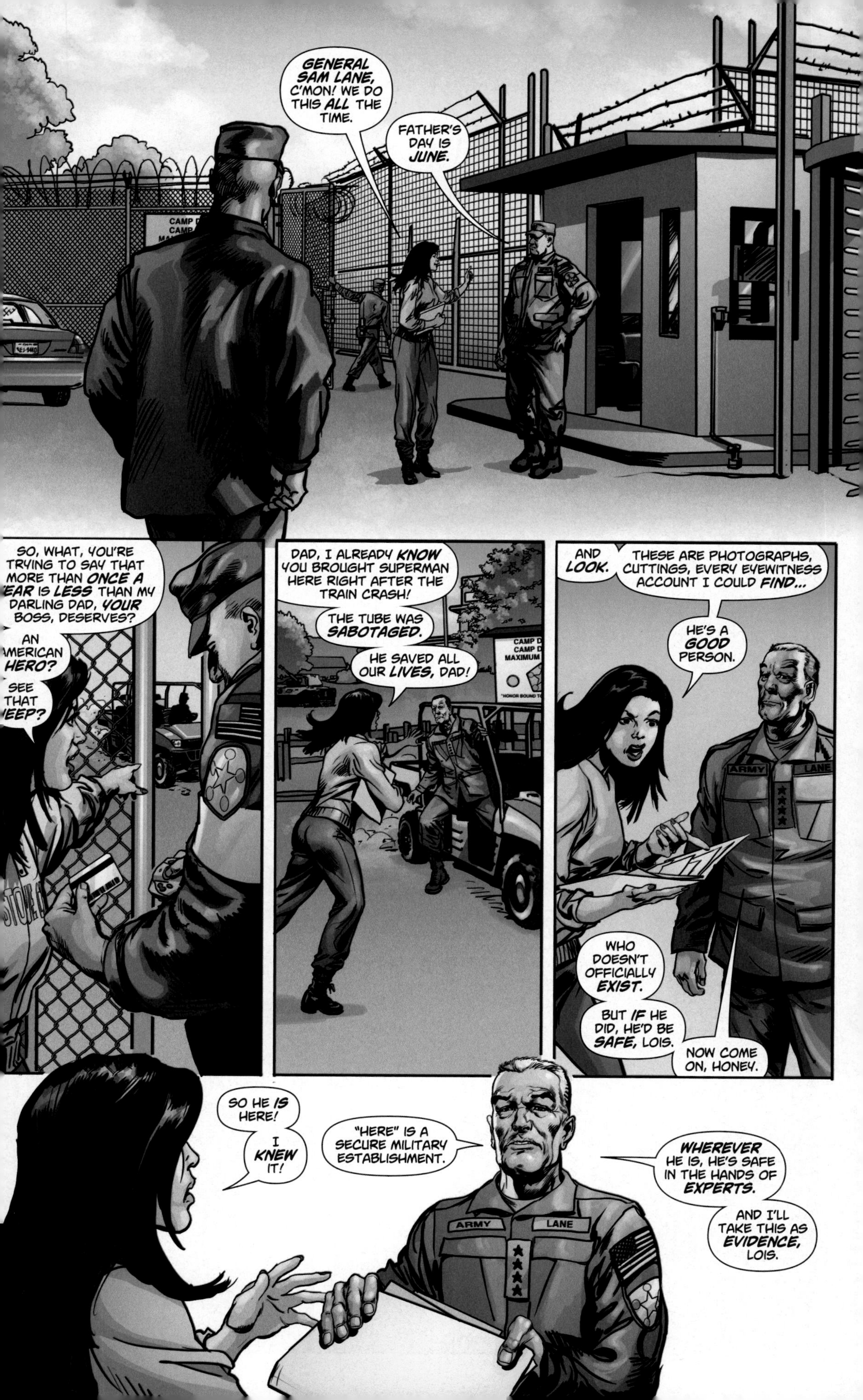
GENERAL SAM LANE, C'MON! WE DO THIS ALL THE TIME.
FATHER'S DAY IS JUNE.
SO, WHAT, YOU'RE TRYING TO SAY THAT MORE THAN ONCE A EAR IS LESS THAN MY DARLING DAD, YOUR BOSS, DESERVES?
AN MERICAN HERO?
SEE THAT EEP?
DAD, I ALREADY KNOW YOU BROUGHT SUPERMAN HERE RIGHT AFTER THE TRAIN CRASH!
THE TUBE WAS SABOTAGED.
HE SAVED ALL OUR LIVES, DAD!
AND LOOK.
THESE ARE PHOTOGRAPHS, CUTTINGS, EVERY EYEWITNESS ACCOUNT I COULD FIND...
HE'S A GOOD PERSON.
WHO DOESN'T OFFICIALLY EXIST.
BUT IF HE DID, HE'D BE SAFE, LOIS.
NOW COME ON, HONEY.
SO HE IS HERE!
I KNEW IT!
"HERE" IS A SECURE MILITARY ESTABLISHMENT.
WHEREVER HE IS, HE'S SAFE IN THE HANDS OF EXPERTS.
AND I'LL TAKE THIS AS EVIDENCE, LOIS.

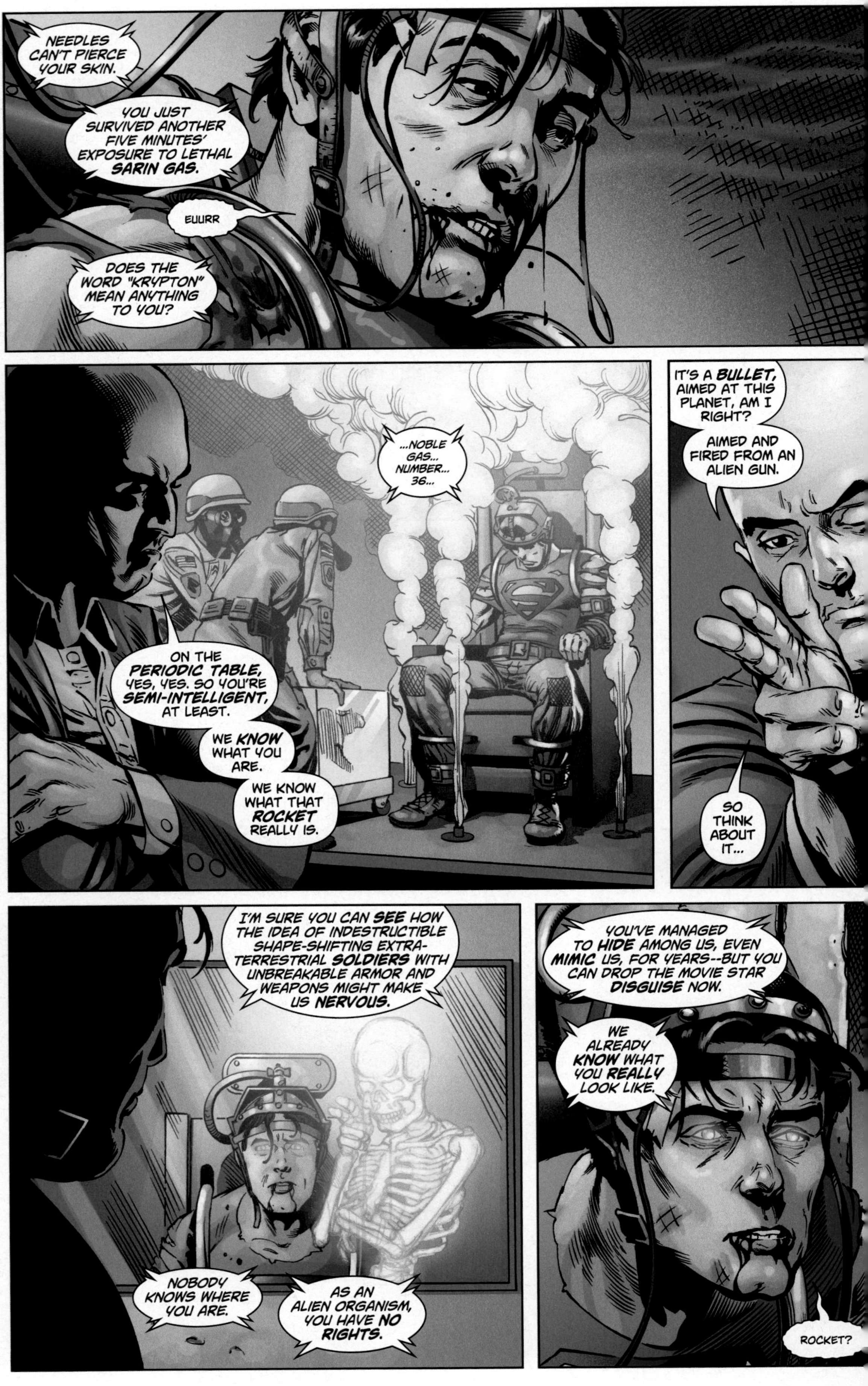
NEEDLES CAN'T PIERCE YOUR SKIN.
YOU JUST SURVIVED ANOTHER FIVE MINUTES' EXPOSURE TO LETHAL SARIN GAS.
EUURR
DOES THE WORD "KRYPTON" MEAN ANYTHING TO YOU?
...NOBLE GAS... NUMBER... 36...
ON THE PERIODIC TABLE, YES, YES. SO YOU'RE SEMI-INTELLIGENT, AT LEAST.
WE KNOW WHAT YOU ARE.
WE KNOW WHAT THAT ROCKET REALLY IS.
IT'S A BULLET, AIMED AT THIS PLANET, AM I RIGHT?
AIMED AND FIRED FROM AN ALIEN GUN.
SO THINK ABOUT IT...
I'M SURE YOU CAN SEE HOW THE IDEA OF INDESTRUCTIBLE SHAPE-SHIFTING EXTRA-TERRESTRIAL SOLDIERS WITH UNBREAKABLE ARMOR AND WEAPONS MIGHT MAKE US NERVOUS.
NOBODY KNOWS WHERE YOU ARE.
AS AN ALIEN ORGANISM, YOU HAVE NO RIGHTS.
YOU'VE MANAGED TO HIDE AMONG US, EVEN MIMIC US, FOR YEARS--BUT YOU CAN DROP THE MOVIE STAR DISGUISE NOW.
WE ALREADY KNOW WHAT YOU REALLY LOOK LIKE.
ROCKET?

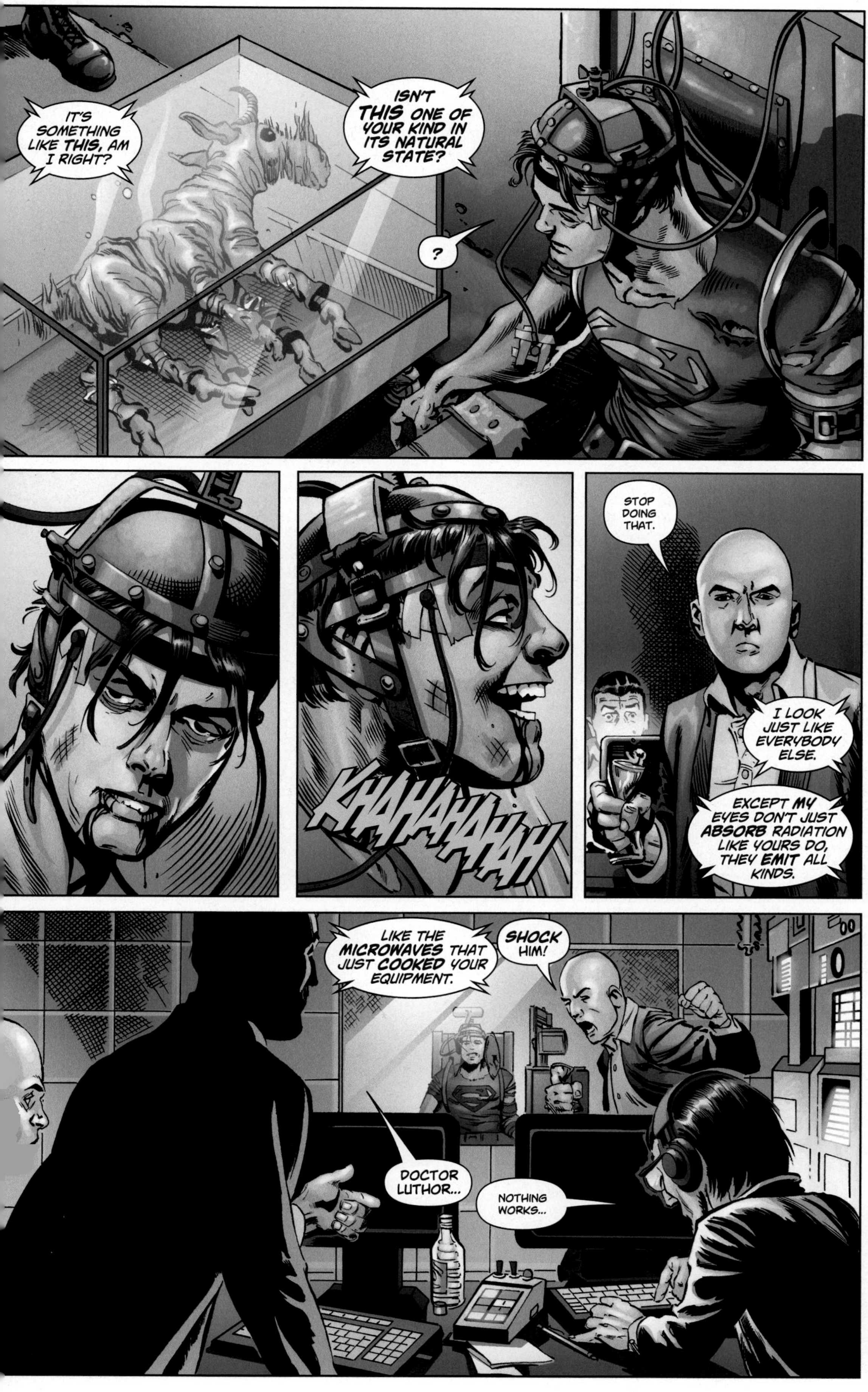
IT'S SOMETHING LIKE THIS, AM I RIGHT?
ISN'T THIS ONE OF YOUR KIND IN ITS NATURAL STATE?
?
KHAHAHAHAHAH
STOP DOING THAT.
I LOOK JUST LIKE EVERYBODY ELSE.
EXCEPT MY EYES DON'T JUST ABSORB RADIATION LIKE YOURS DO, THEY EMIT ALL KINDS.
LIKE THE MICROWAVES THAT JUST COOKED YOUR EQUIPMENT.
SHOCK HIM!
DOCTOR LUTHOR...
NOTHING WORKS...

DA-AD!

I HAVE **ENOUGH** ON AN ALREADY OVERBURDENED PLATE OF UNPROCESSED **SEWAGE** RIGHT NOW, LOIS.

JOHN, **YOU** TALK HER DOWN.

LOIS, HEY...

LOIS.

JOHN, PLEASE...

I'VE **KNOWN** ABOUT **STEEL SOLDIER** SINCE I WAS A **KID**, DAD!

WOW.

IT'S **GREAT** TO SEE YOU AGAIN... I REGREW THE **MUSTACHE**.

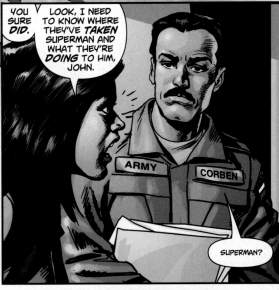

YOU SURE **DID**.

LOOK, I NEED TO KNOW WHERE THEY'VE **TAKEN** SUPERMAN AND WHAT THEY'RE **DOING** TO HIM, JOHN.

ARMY CORBEN

SUPERMAN?

C'MON, JOHN. WHERE IS HE?

WHAT'S IT GOT TO DO WITH **SUPERMAN?**

WHAT HAPPENED TO **US**, LOIS?

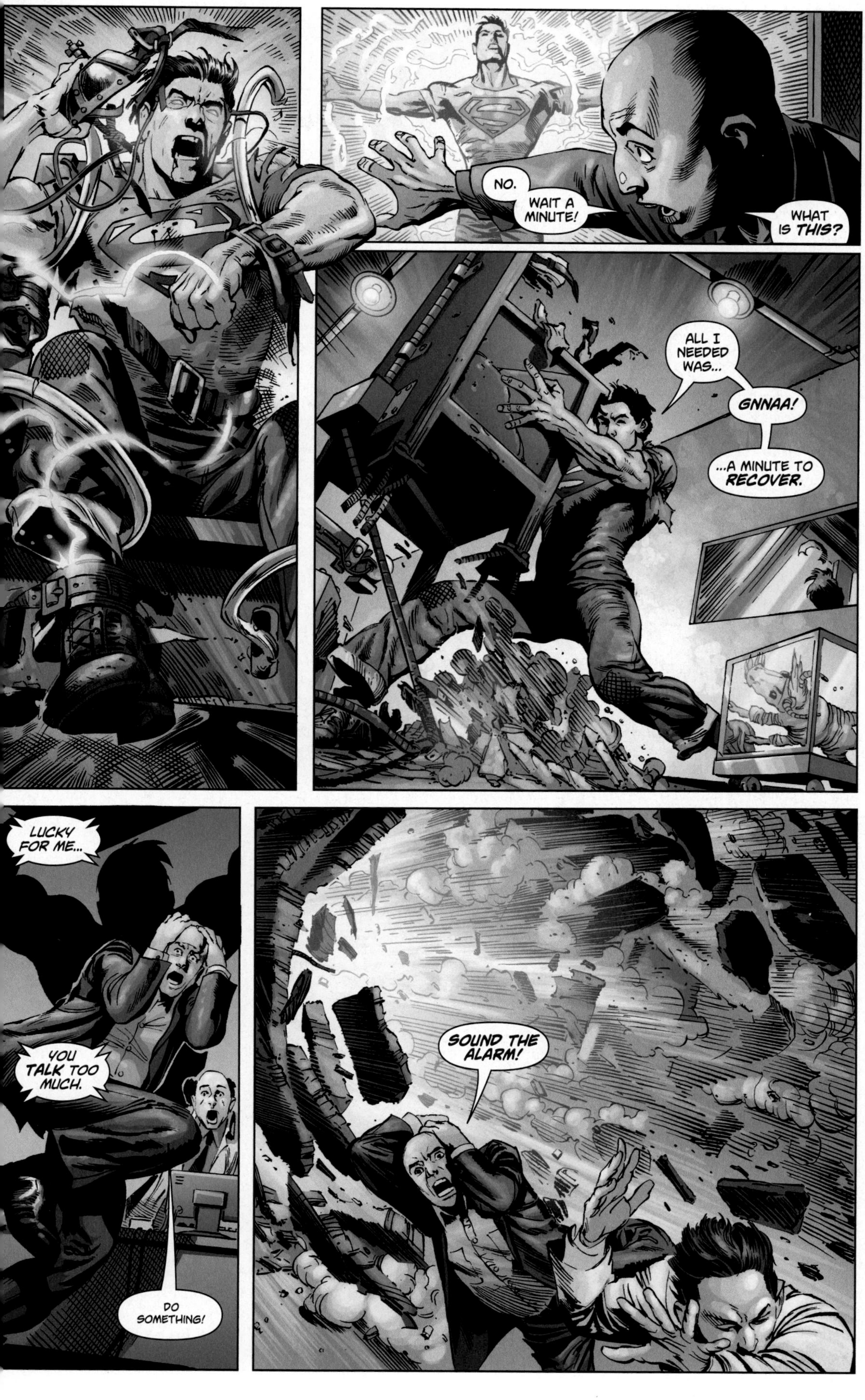
NO.
WAIT A MINUTE!
WHAT IS THIS?
ALL I NEEDED WAS...
GNNAA!
...A MINUTE TO RECOVER.
LUCKY FOR ME...
YOU TALK TOO MUCH.
DO SOMETHING!
SOUND THE ALARM!

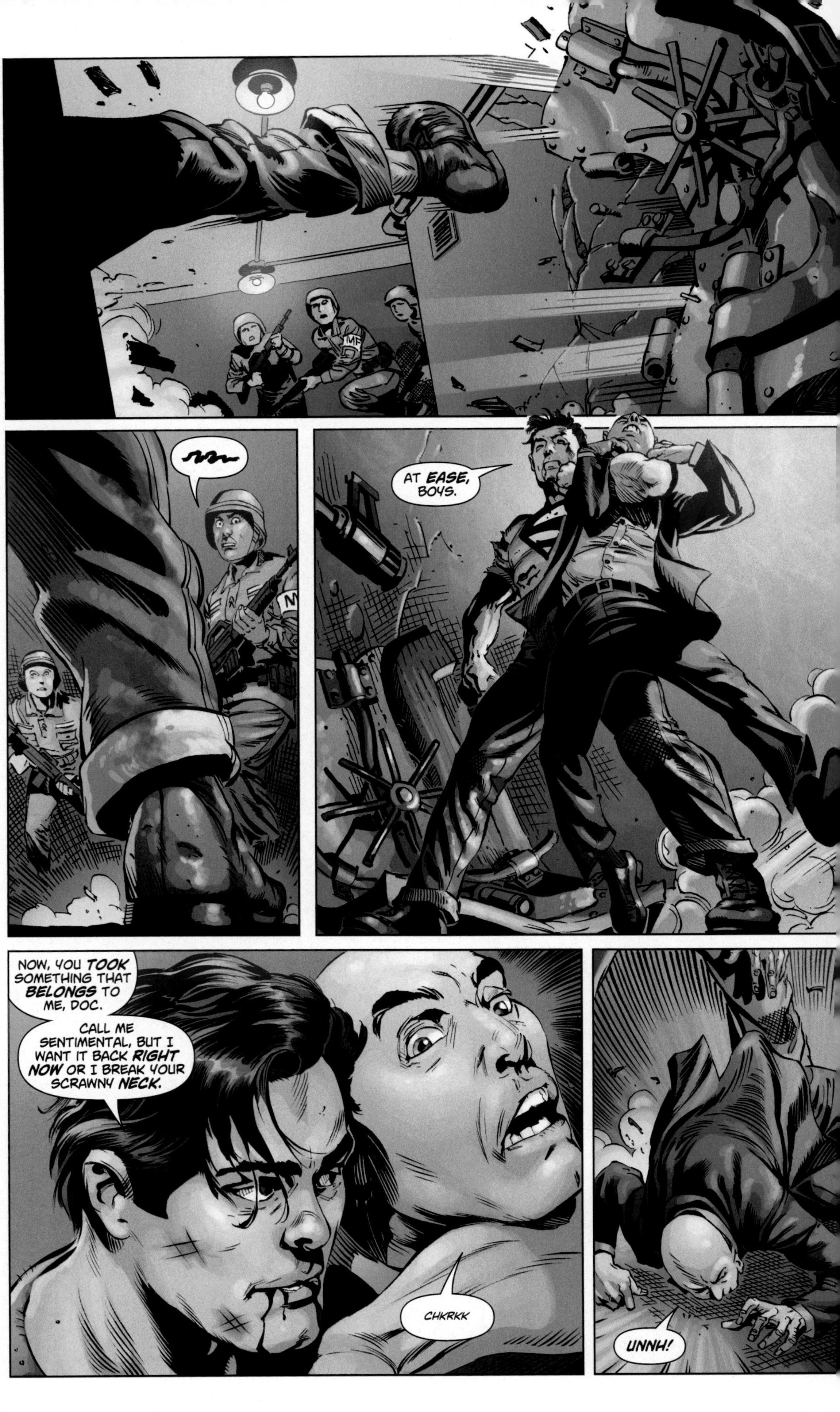
IMF
AT EASE, BOYS.
NOW, YOU TOOK SOMETHING THAT BELONGS TO ME, DOC.
CALL ME SENTIMENTAL, BUT I WANT IT BACK RIGHT NOW OR I BREAK YOUR SCRAWNY NECK.
CHKRKK
UNNH!

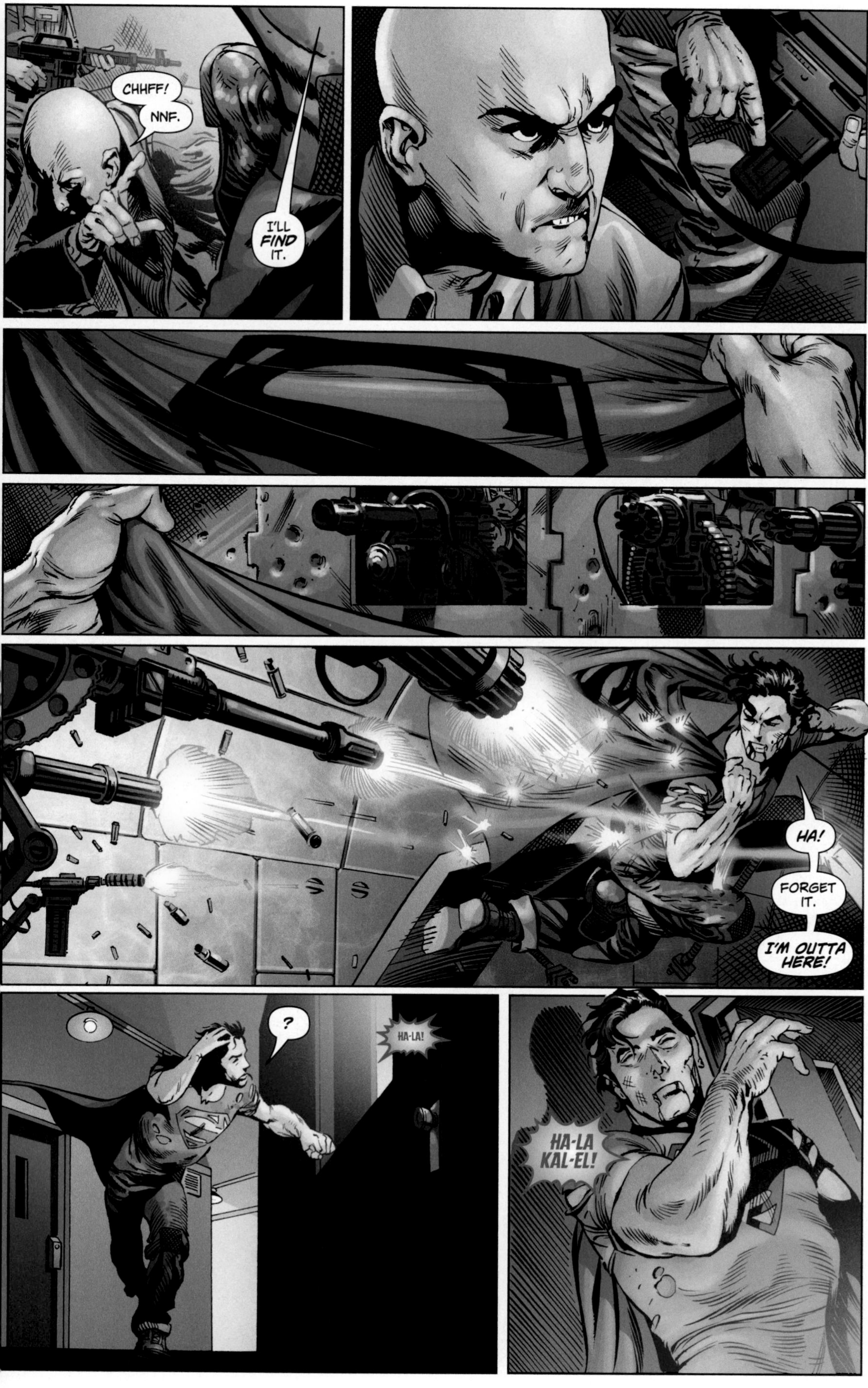
CHHFF!
NNF.
I'LL FIND IT.
HA!
FORGET IT.
I'M OUTTA HERE!
?
HA-LA!
HA-LA KAL-EL!

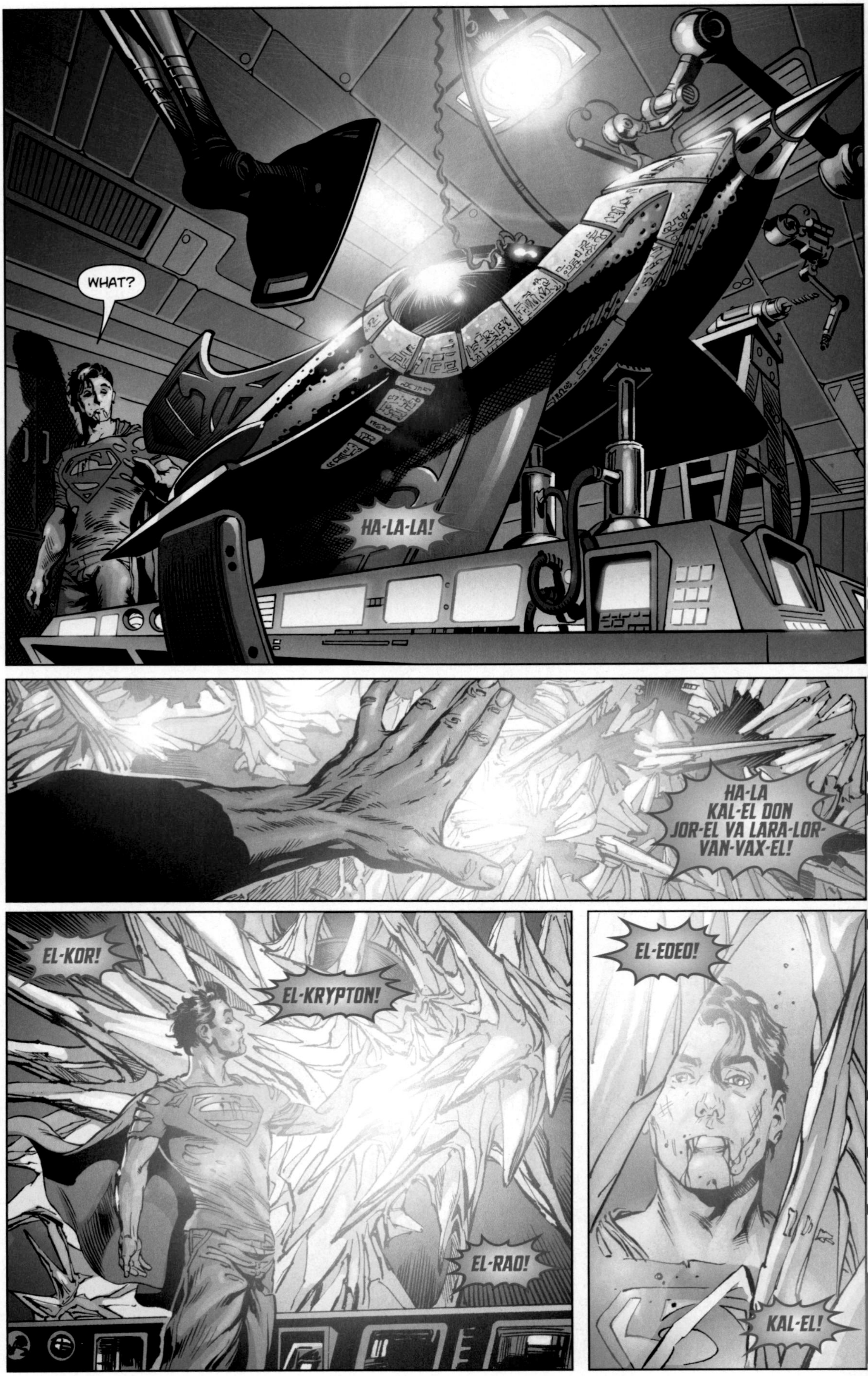
WHAT?
HA-LA-LA!
HA-LA
KAL-EL DON
JOR-EL VA LARA-LOR-
VAN-VAX-EL!
EL-KOR!
EL-KRYPTON!
EL-RAO!
EL-EOEO!
KAL-EL!

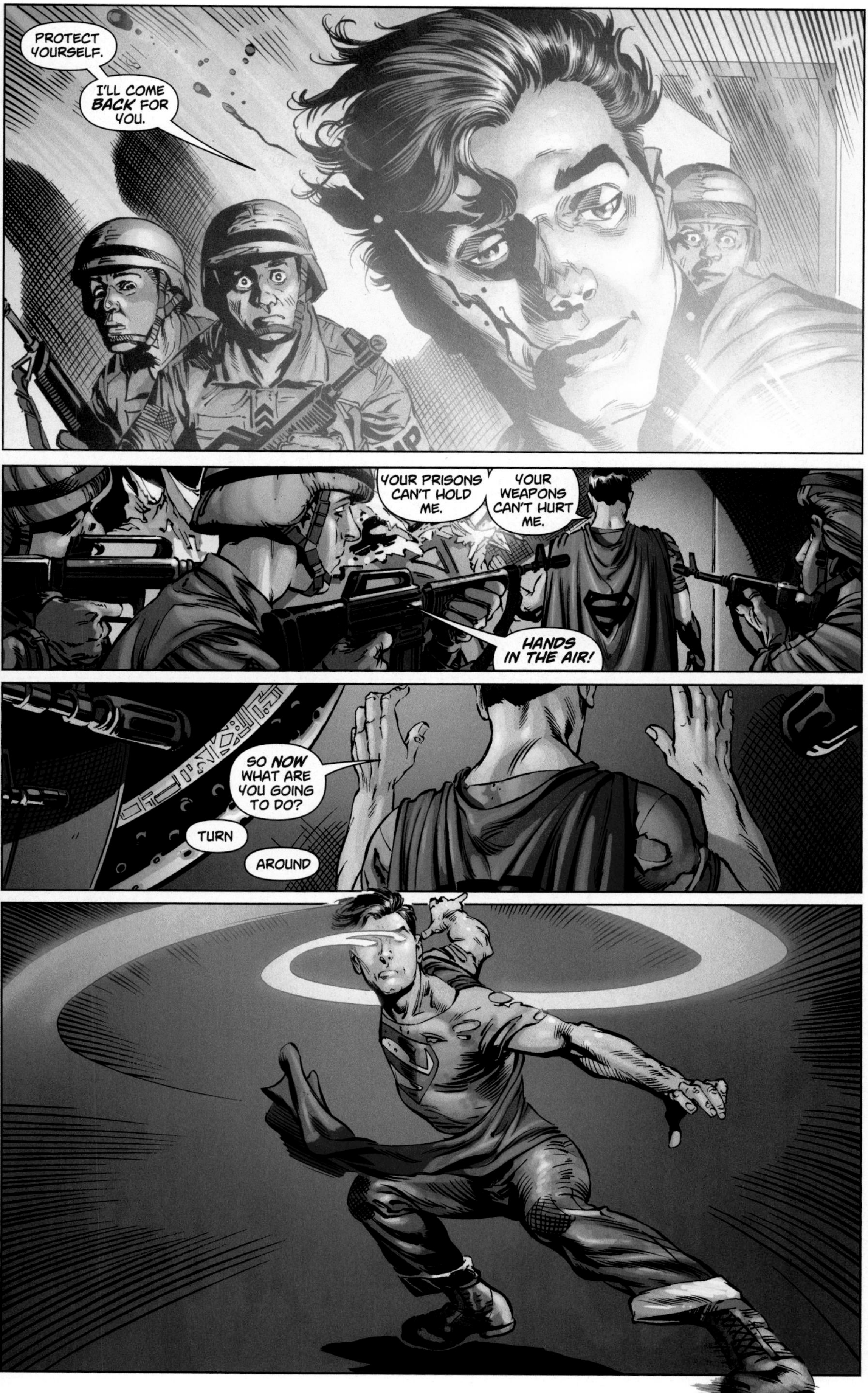
PROTECT YOURSELF.
I'LL COME BACK FOR YOU.
YOUR PRISONS CAN'T HOLD ME.
YOUR WEAPONS CAN'T HURT ME.
HANDS IN THE AIR!
SO NOW WHAT ARE YOU GOING TO DO?
TURN
AROUND

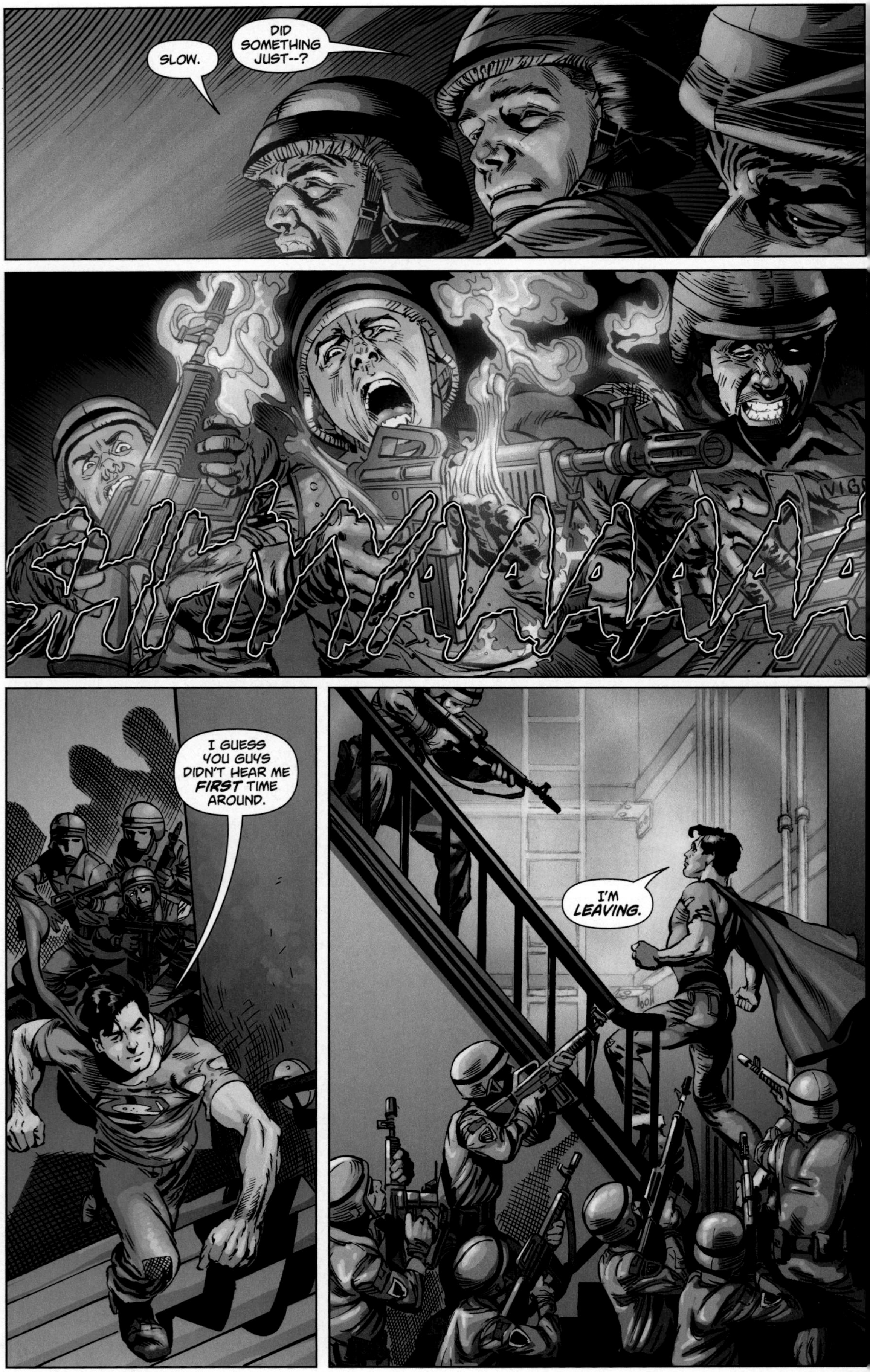
SLOW.
DID SOMETHING JUST--?
I GUESS YOU GUYS DIDN'T HEAR ME FIRST TIME AROUND.
I'M LEAVING.

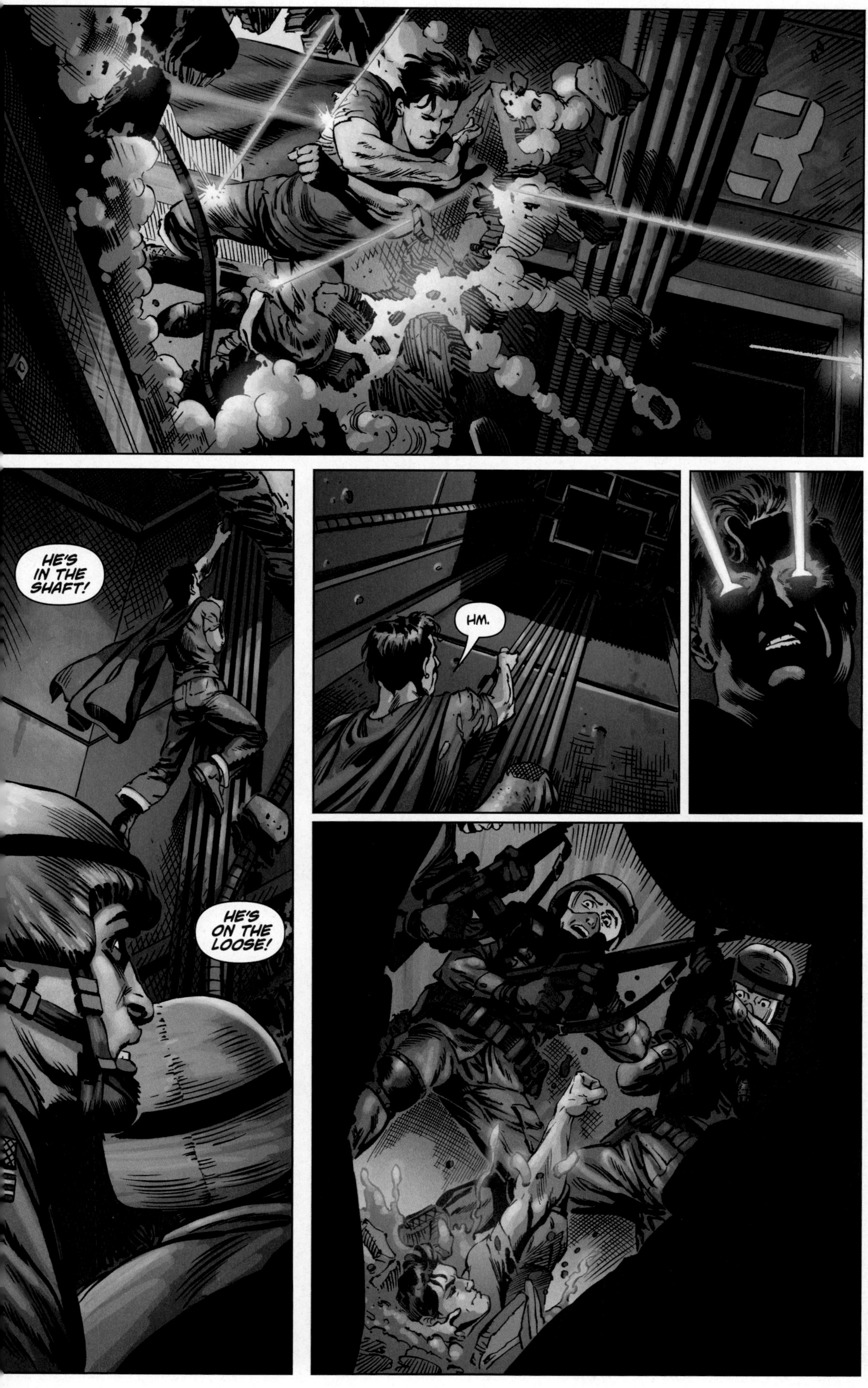
HE'S IN THE SHAFT!
HE'S ON THE LOOSE!
HM.

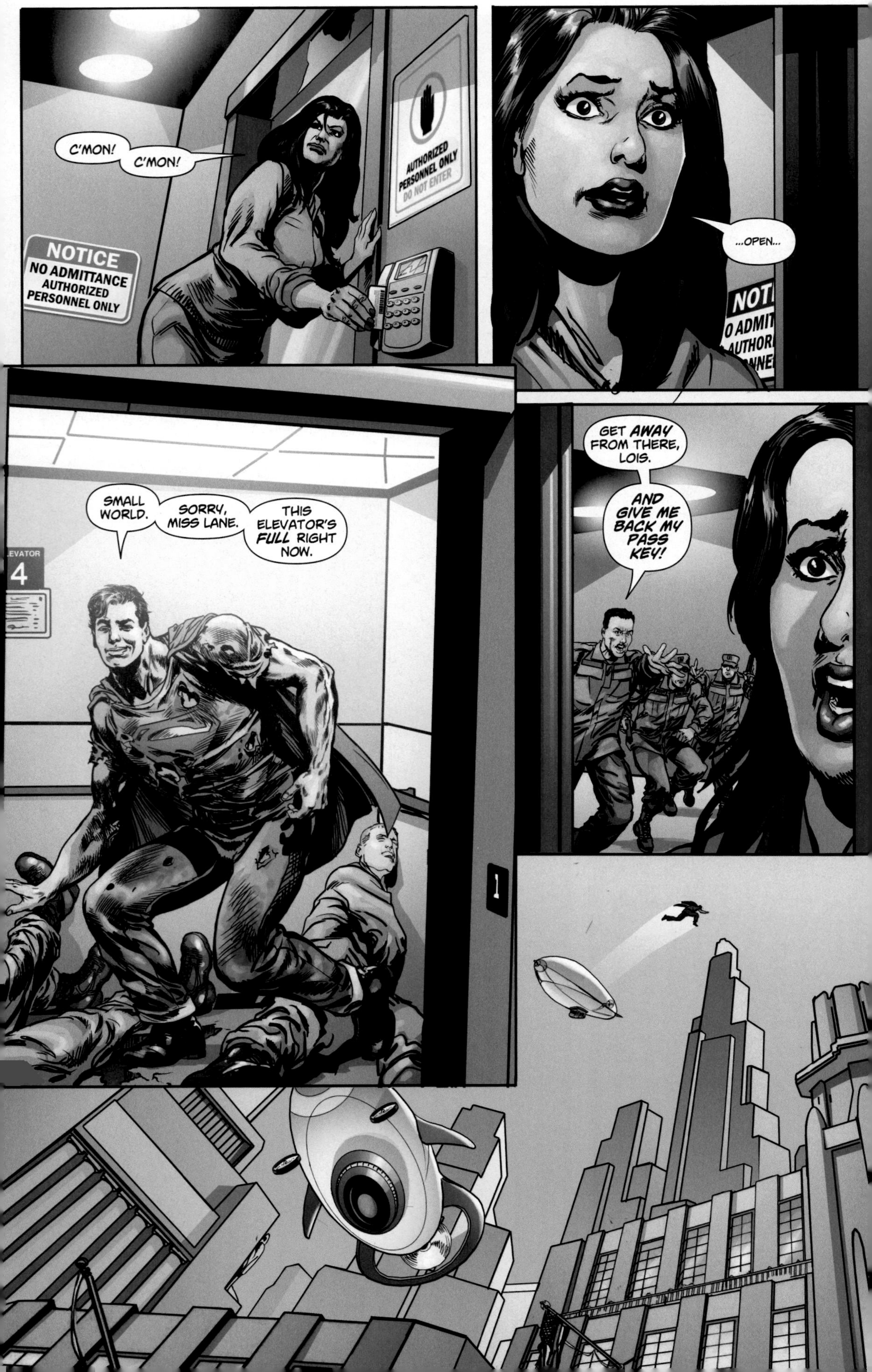
C'MON!
C'MON!
AUTHORIZED PERSONNEL ONLY DO NOT ENTER
NOTICE NO ADMITTANCE AUTHORIZED PERSONNEL ONLY
...OPEN...
SMALL WORLD.
SORRY, MISS LANE.
THIS ELEVATOR'S FULL RIGHT NOW.
ELEVATOR 4
GET AWAY FROM THERE, LOIS.
AND GIVE ME BACK MY PASS KEY!

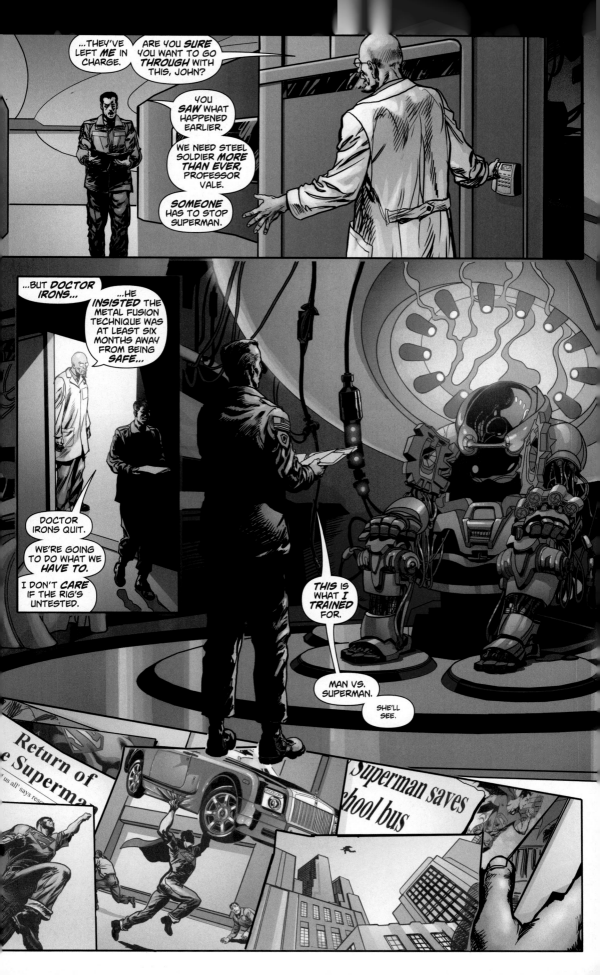

...THEY'VE LEFT ME IN CHARGE.

ARE YOU SURE YOU WANT TO GO THROUGH WITH THIS, JOHN?

YOU SAW WHAT HAPPENED EARLIER.

WE NEED STEEL SOLDIER MORE THAN EVER, PROFESSOR VALE.

SOMEONE HAS TO STOP SUPERMAN.

...BUT DOCTOR IRONS...

...HE INSISTED THE METAL FUSION TECHNIQUE WAS AT LEAST SIX MONTHS AWAY FROM BEING SAFE...

DOCTOR IRONS QUIT.

WE'RE GOING TO DO WHAT WE HAVE TO.

I DON'T CARE IF THE RIG'S UNTESTED.

THIS IS WHAT I TRAINED FOR.

MAN VS. SUPERMAN.

SHE'LL SEE.

Return of e Superma

Superman saves chool bus

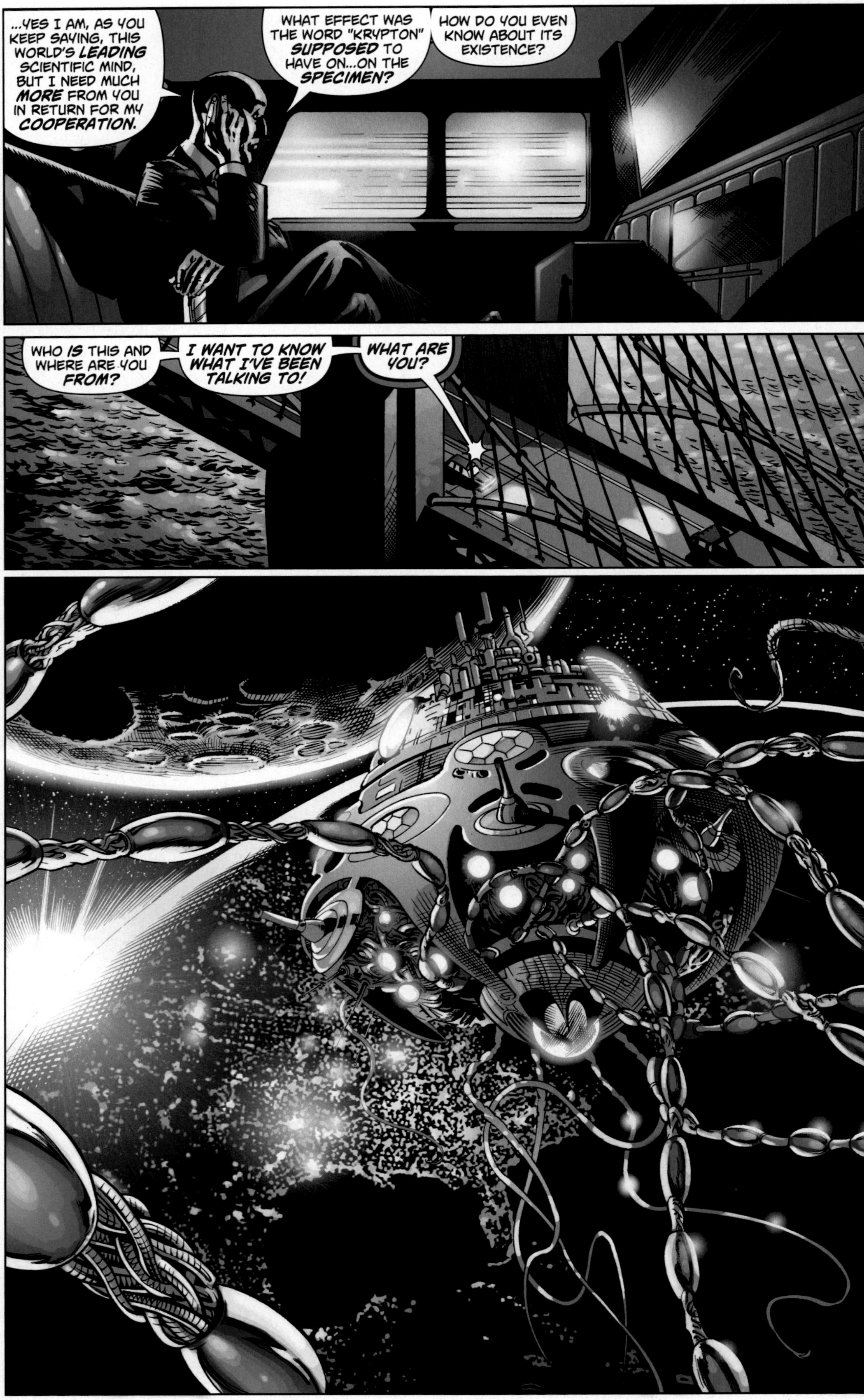
...YES I AM, AS YOU KEEP SAYING, THIS WORLD'S LEADING SCIENTIFIC MIND, BUT I NEED MUCH MORE FROM YOU IN RETURN FOR MY COOPERATION.
WHAT EFFECT WAS THE WORD "KRYPTON" SUPPOSED TO HAVE ON...ON THE SPECIMEN?
HOW DO YOU EVEN KNOW ABOUT ITS EXISTENCE?
WHO IS THIS AND WHERE ARE YOU FROM?
I WANT TO KNOW WHAT I'VE BEEN TALKING TO!
WHAT ARE YOU?

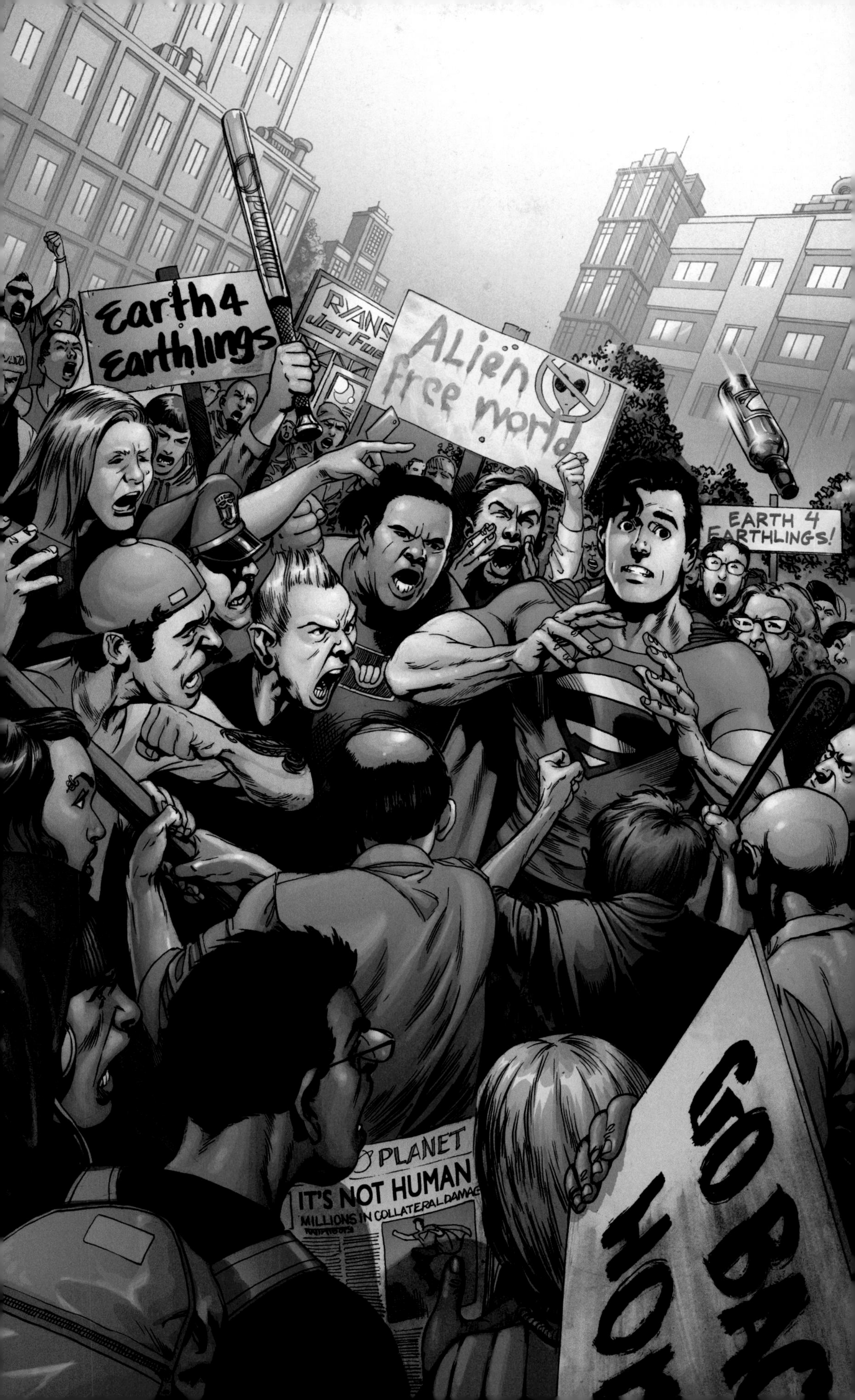

Earth 4 Earthlings
Alien free world
EARTH 4 EARTHLINGS!
PLANET
IT'S NOT HUMAN
MILLIONS IN COLLATERAL DAMAG

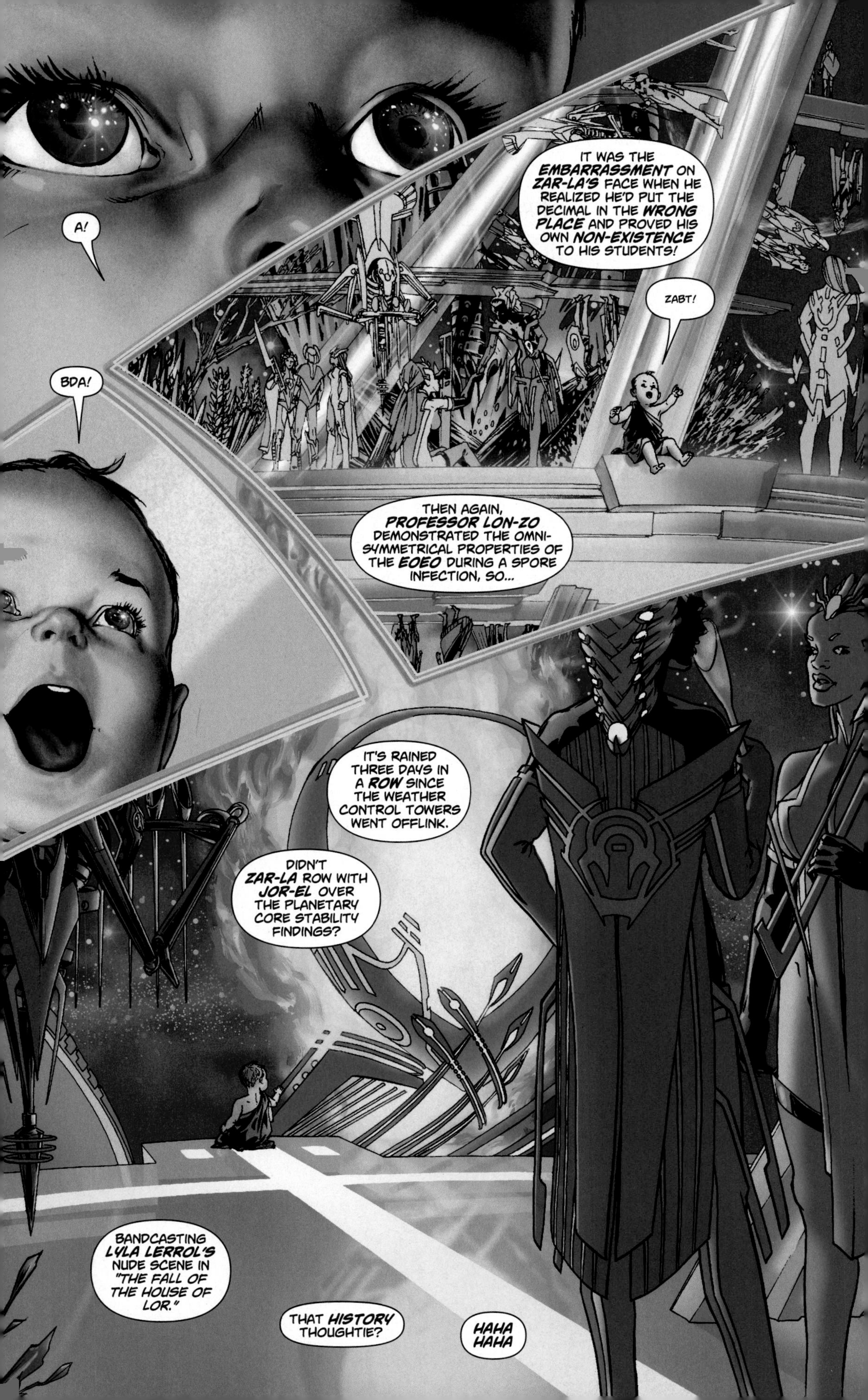
A!
IT WAS THE EMBARRASSMENT ON ZAR-LA'S FACE WHEN HE REALIZED HE'D PUT THE DECIMAL IN THE WRONG PLACE AND PROVED HIS OWN NON-EXISTENCE TO HIS STUDENTS!
ZABT!
BDA!
THEN AGAIN, PROFESSOR LON-ZO DEMONSTRATED THE OMNI-SYMMETRICAL PROPERTIES OF THE EOEO DURING A SPORE INFECTION, SO...
IT'S RAINED THREE DAYS IN A ROW SINCE THE WEATHER CONTROL TOWERS WENT OFFLINK.
DIDN'T ZAR-LA ROW WITH JOR-EL OVER THE PLANETARY CORE STABILITY FINDINGS?
BANDCASTING LYLA LERROL'S NUDE SCENE IN "THE FALL OF THE HOUSE OF LOR."
THAT HISTORY THOUGHTIE?
HAHA HAHA

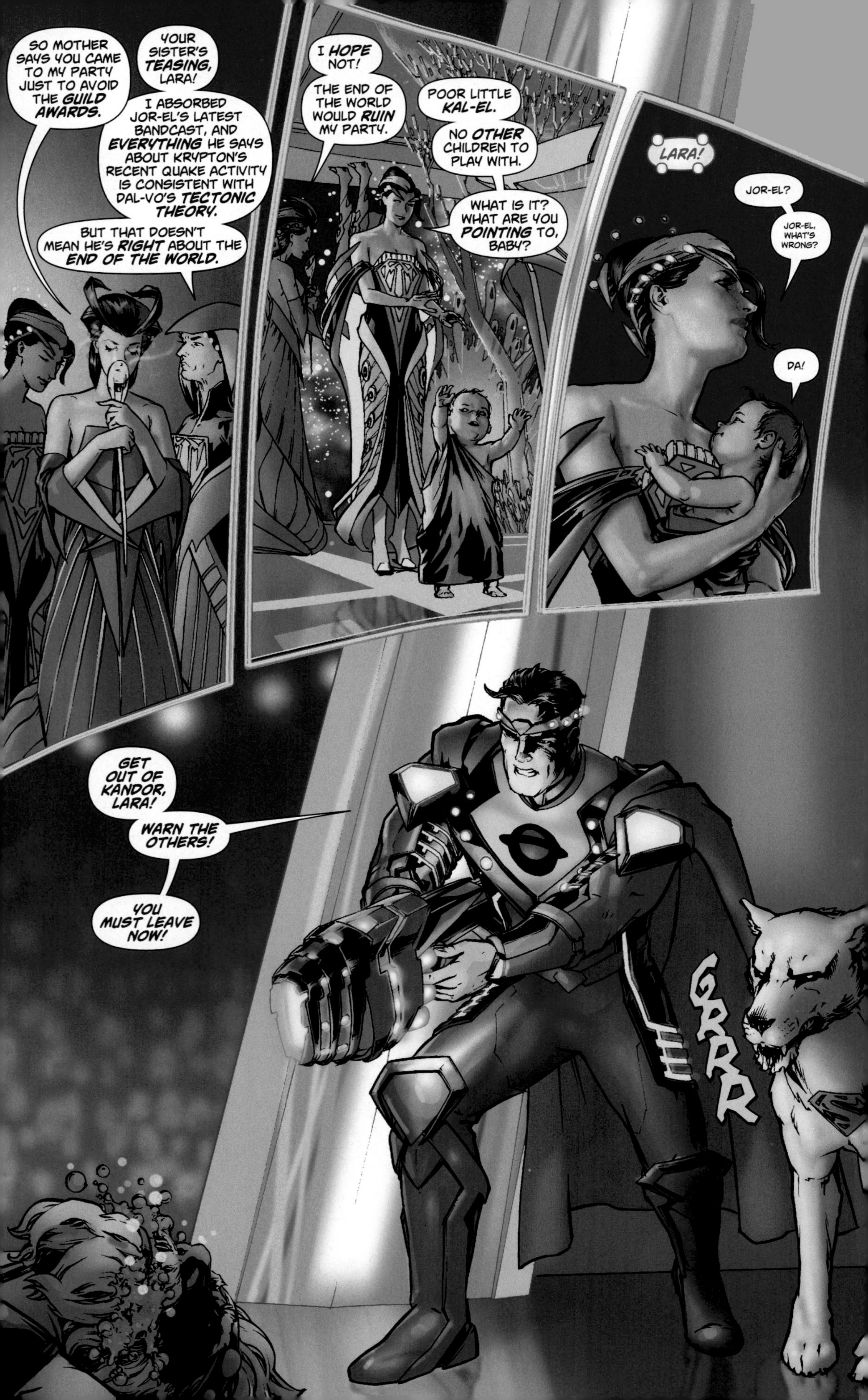
SO MOTHER SAYS YOU CAME TO MY PARTY JUST TO AVOID THE GUILD AWARDS.
YOUR SISTER'S TEASING, LARA!
I ABSORBED JOR-EL'S LATEST BANDCAST, AND EVERYTHING HE SAYS ABOUT KRYPTON'S RECENT QUAKE ACTIVITY IS CONSISTENT WITH DAL-VO'S TECTONIC THEORY.
BUT THAT DOESN'T MEAN HE'S RIGHT ABOUT THE END OF THE WORLD.
I HOPE NOT!
THE END OF THE WORLD WOULD RUIN MY PARTY.
POOR LITTLE KAL-EL.
NO OTHER CHILDREN TO PLAY WITH.
WHAT IS IT? WHAT ARE YOU POINTING TO, BABY?
LARA!
JOR-EL?
JOR-EL, WHAT'S WRONG?
DA!
GET OUT OF KANDOR, LARA!
WARN THE OTHERS!
YOU MUST LEAVE NOW!
GRRR

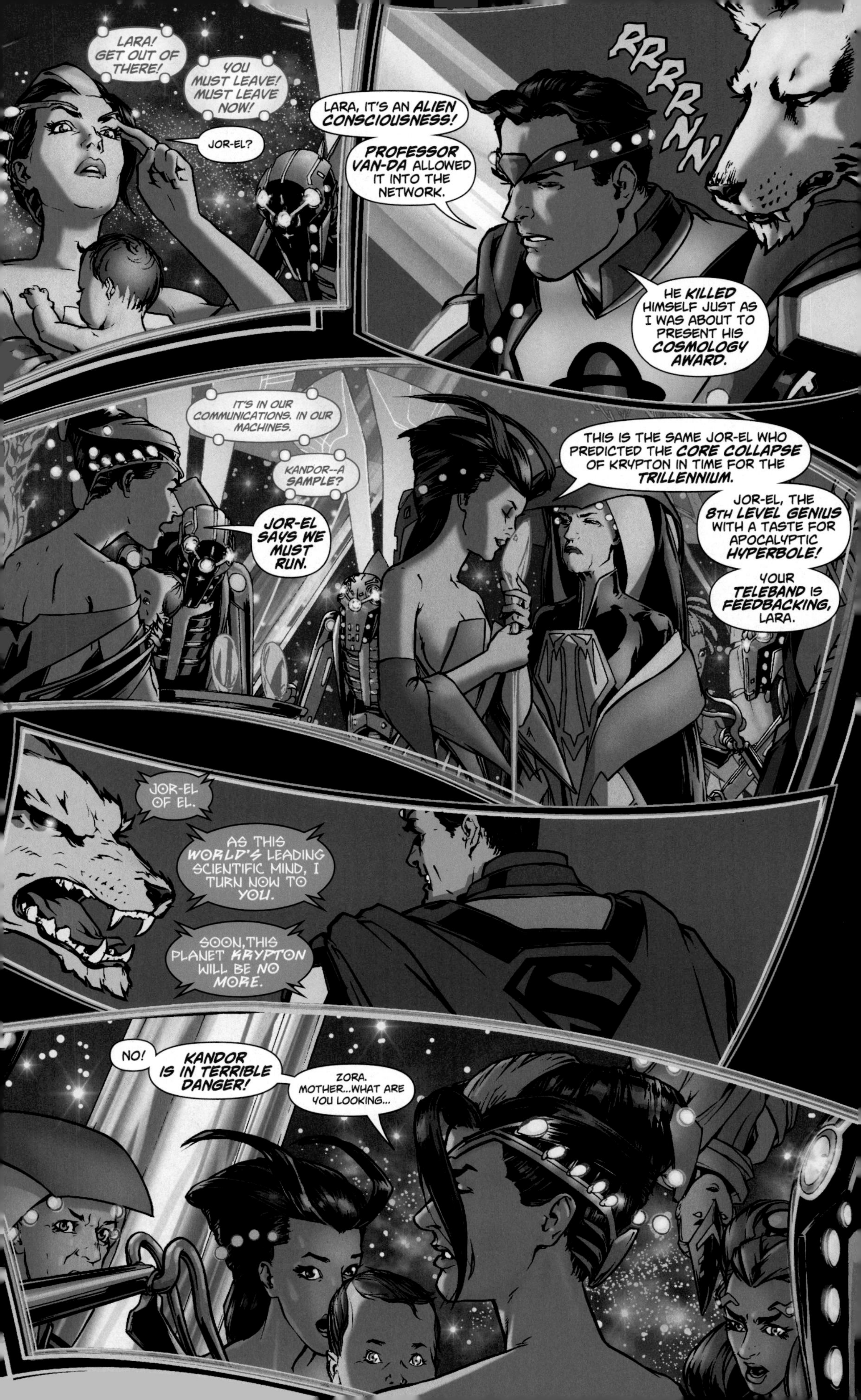
LARA! GET OUT OF THERE!
YOU MUST LEAVE! MUST LEAVE NOW!
JOR-EL?
LARA, IT'S AN ALIEN CONSCIOUSNESS!
PROFESSOR VAN-DA ALLOWED IT INTO THE NETWORK.
RRRRNN
HE KILLED HIMSELF JUST AS I WAS ABOUT TO PRESENT HIS COSMOLOGY AWARD.
IT'S IN OUR COMMUNICATIONS. IN OUR MACHINES.
KANDOR--A SAMPLE?
JOR-EL SAYS WE MUST RUN.
THIS IS THE SAME JOR-EL WHO PREDICTED THE CORE COLLAPSE OF KRYPTON IN TIME FOR THE TRILLENNIUM.
JOR-EL, THE 8TH LEVEL GENIUS WITH A TASTE FOR APOCALYPTIC HYPERBOLE!
YOUR TELEBAND IS FEEDBACKING, LARA.
JOR-EL OF EL.
AS THIS WORLD'S LEADING SCIENTIFIC MIND, I TURN NOW TO YOU.
SOON, THIS PLANET KRYPTON WILL BE NO MORE.
NO!
KANDOR IS IN TERRIBLE DANGER!
ZORA. MOTHER...WHAT ARE YOU LOOKING...

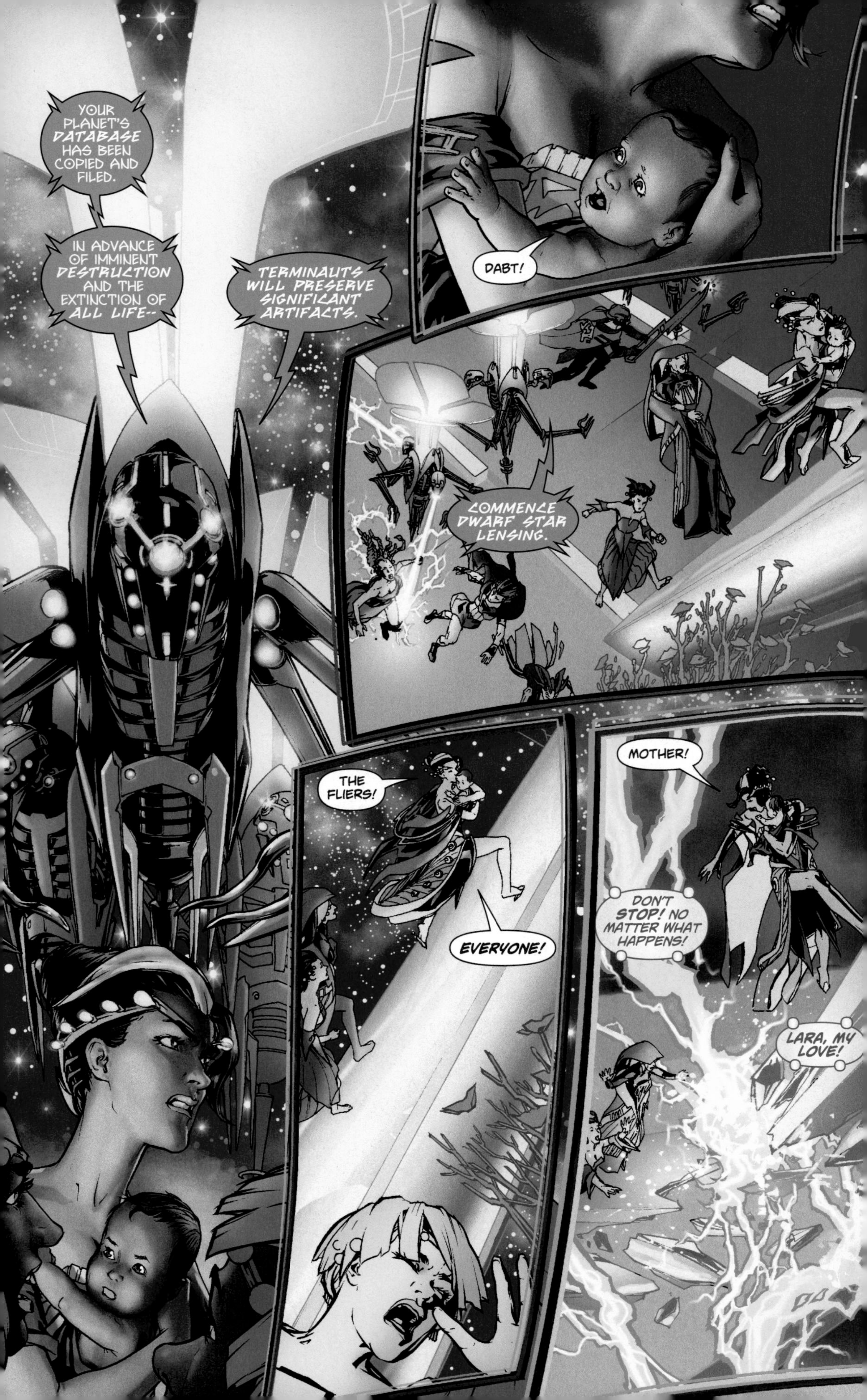
YOUR PLANET'S DATABASE HAS BEEN COPIED AND FILED.
IN ADVANCE OF IMMINENT DESTRUCTION AND THE EXTINCTION OF ALL LIFE--
TERMINAUTS WILL PRESERVE SIGNIFICANT ARTIFACTS.
DABT!
COMMENCE DWARF STAR LENSING.
THE FLIERS!
EVERYONE!
MOTHER!
DON'T STOP! NO MATTER WHAT HAPPENS!
LARA, MY LOVE!

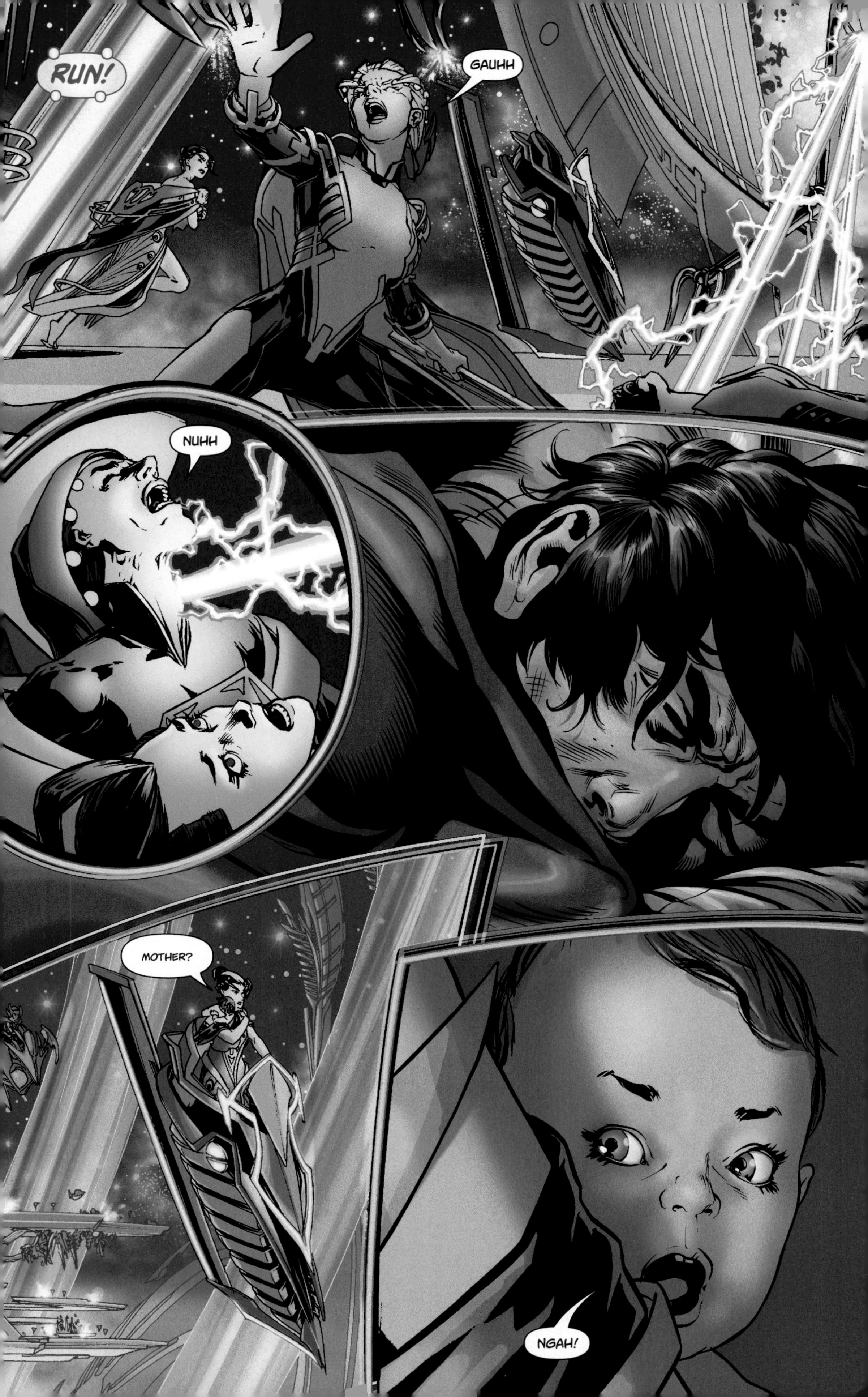
RUN!
GAUHH
NUHH
MOTHER?
NGAH!

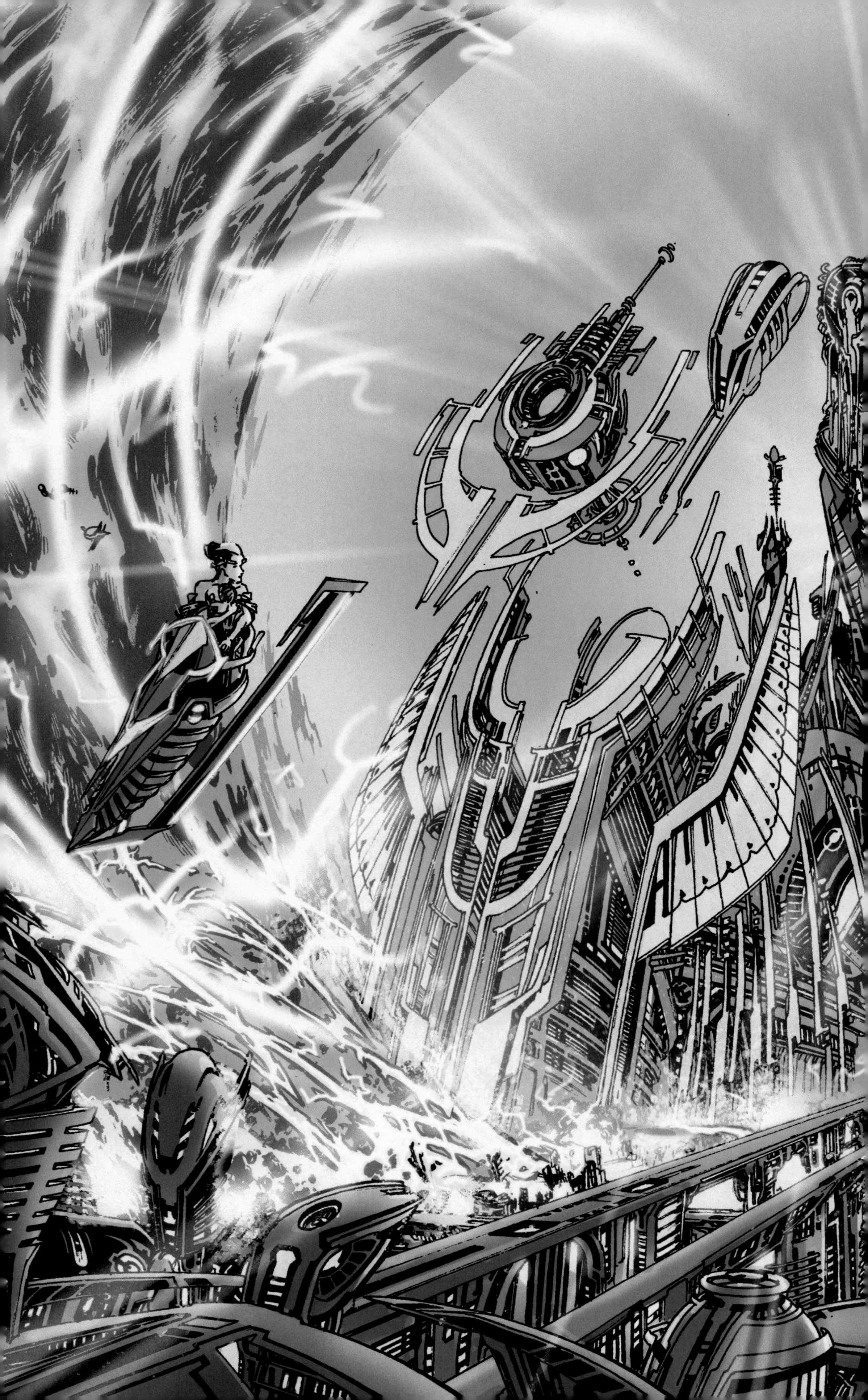

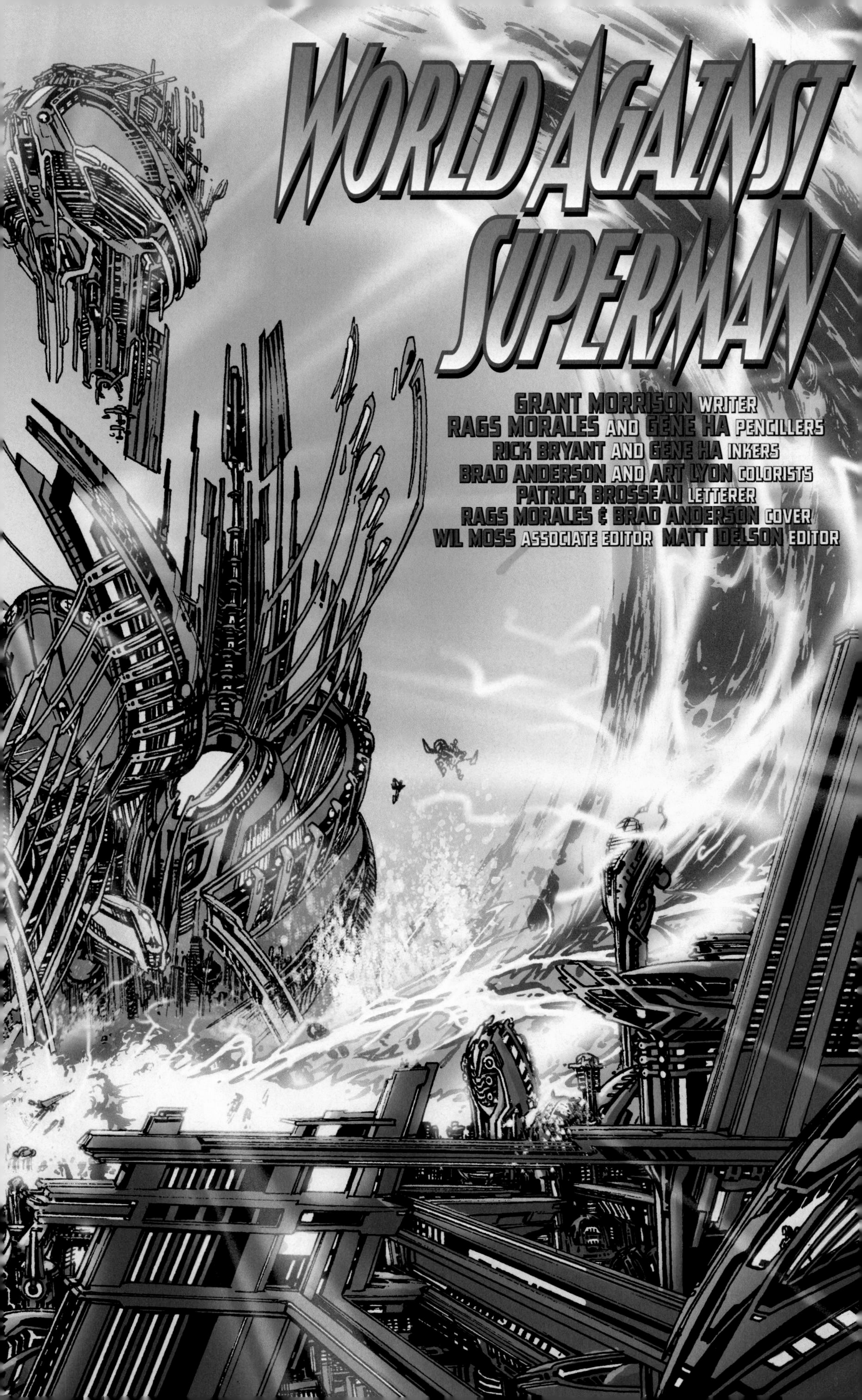

WORLD AGAINST SUPERMAN
GRANT MORRISON WRITER
RAGS MORALES AND GENE HA PENCILLERS
RICK BRYANT AND GENE HA INKERS
BRAD ANDERSON AND ART LYON COLORISTS
PATRICK BROSSEAU LETTERER
RAGS MORALES & BRAD ANDERSON COVER
WIL MOSS ASSOCIATE EDITOR MATT IDELSON EDITOR

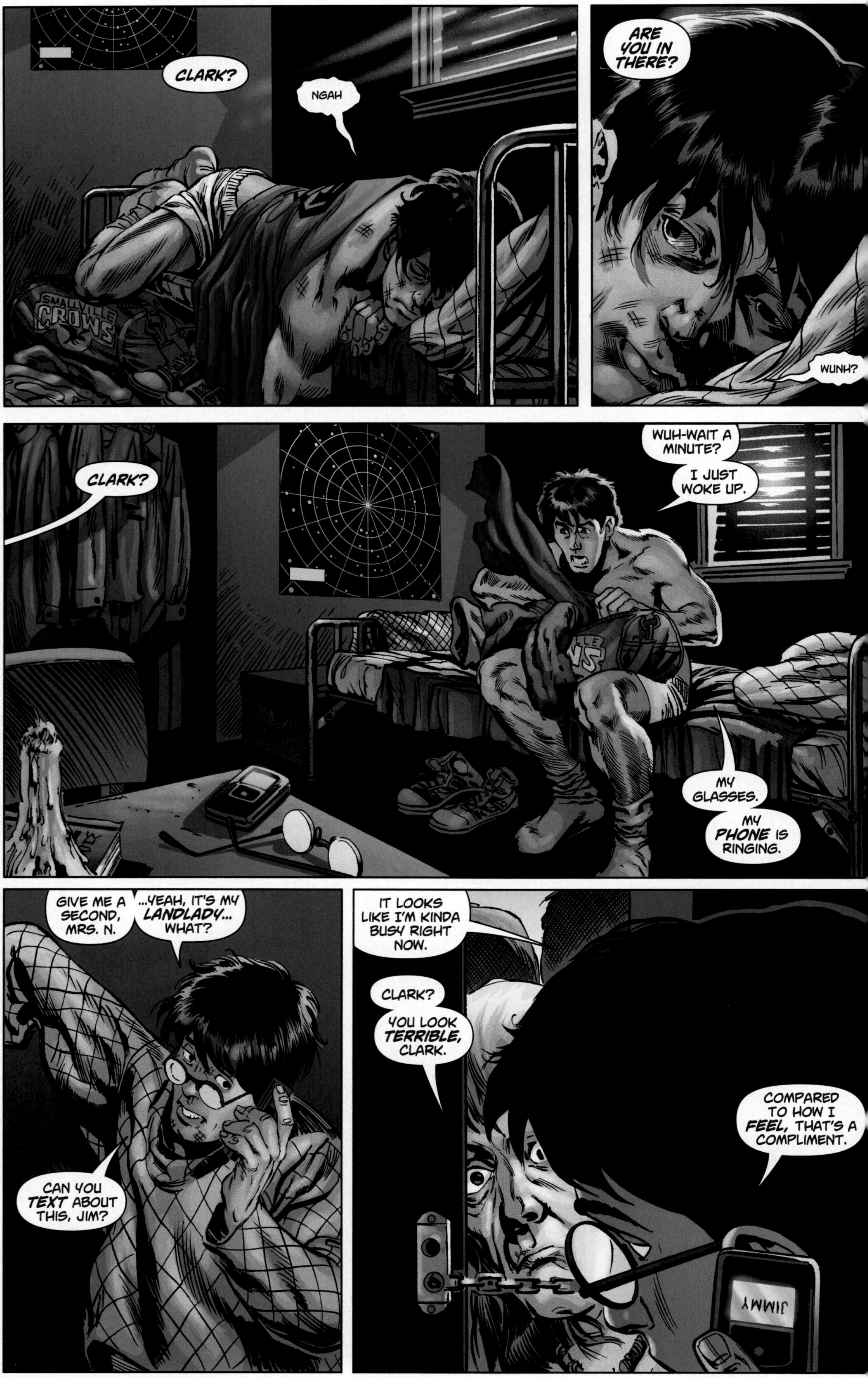

CLARK?
NGAH
ARE YOU IN THERE?
WUNH?
CLARK?
WUH-WAIT A MINUTE?
I JUST WOKE UP.
MY GLASSES.
MY PHONE IS RINGING.
GIVE ME A SECOND, MRS. N.
...YEAH, IT'S MY LANDLADY... WHAT?
CAN YOU TEXT ABOUT THIS, JIM?
IT LOOKS LIKE I'M KINDA BUSY RIGHT NOW.
CLARK?
YOU LOOK TERRIBLE, CLARK.
COMPARED TO HOW I FEEL, THAT'S A COMPLIMENT.

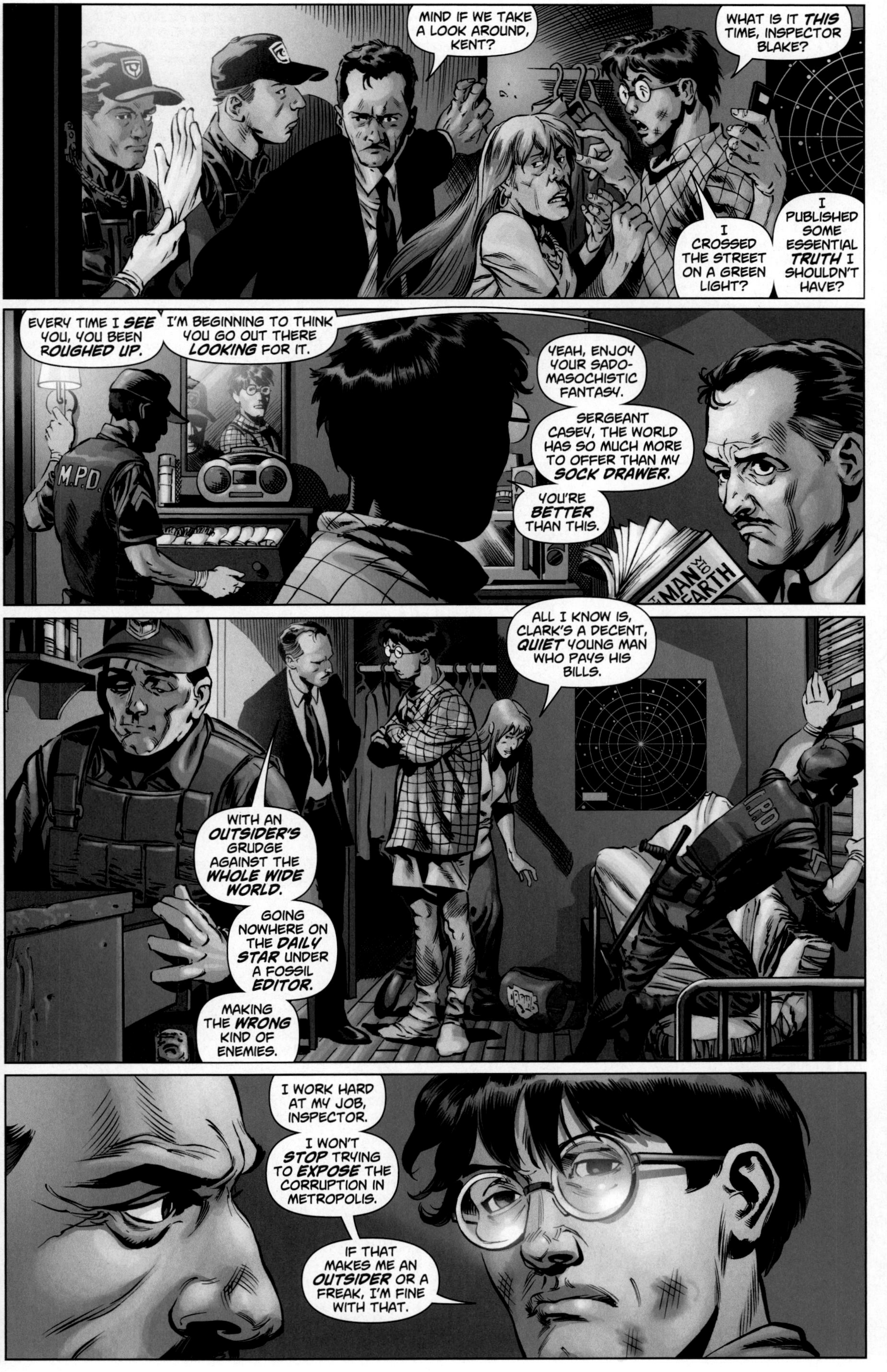
MIND IF WE TAKE A LOOK AROUND, KENT?
WHAT IS IT THIS TIME, INSPECTOR BLAKE?
I CROSSED THE STREET ON A GREEN LIGHT?
I PUBLISHED SOME ESSENTIAL TRUTH I SHOULDN'T HAVE?
EVERY TIME I SEE YOU, YOU BEEN ROUGHED UP.
I'M BEGINNING TO THINK YOU GO OUT THERE LOOKING FOR IT.
YEAH, ENJOY YOUR SADO-MASOCHISTIC FANTASY.
SERGEANT CASEY, THE WORLD HAS SO MUCH MORE TO OFFER THAN MY SOCK DRAWER.
YOU'RE BETTER THAN THIS.
M.P.D.
ALL I KNOW IS, CLARK'S A DECENT, QUIET YOUNG MAN WHO PAYS HIS BILLS.
WITH AN OUTSIDER'S GRUDGE AGAINST THE WHOLE WIDE WORLD.
GOING NOWHERE ON THE DAILY STAR UNDER A FOSSIL EDITOR.
MAKING THE WRONG KIND OF ENEMIES.
I WORK HARD AT MY JOB, INSPECTOR.
I WON'T STOP TRYING TO EXPOSE THE CORRUPTION IN METROPOLIS.
IF THAT MAKES ME AN OUTSIDER OR A FREAK, I'M FINE WITH THAT.

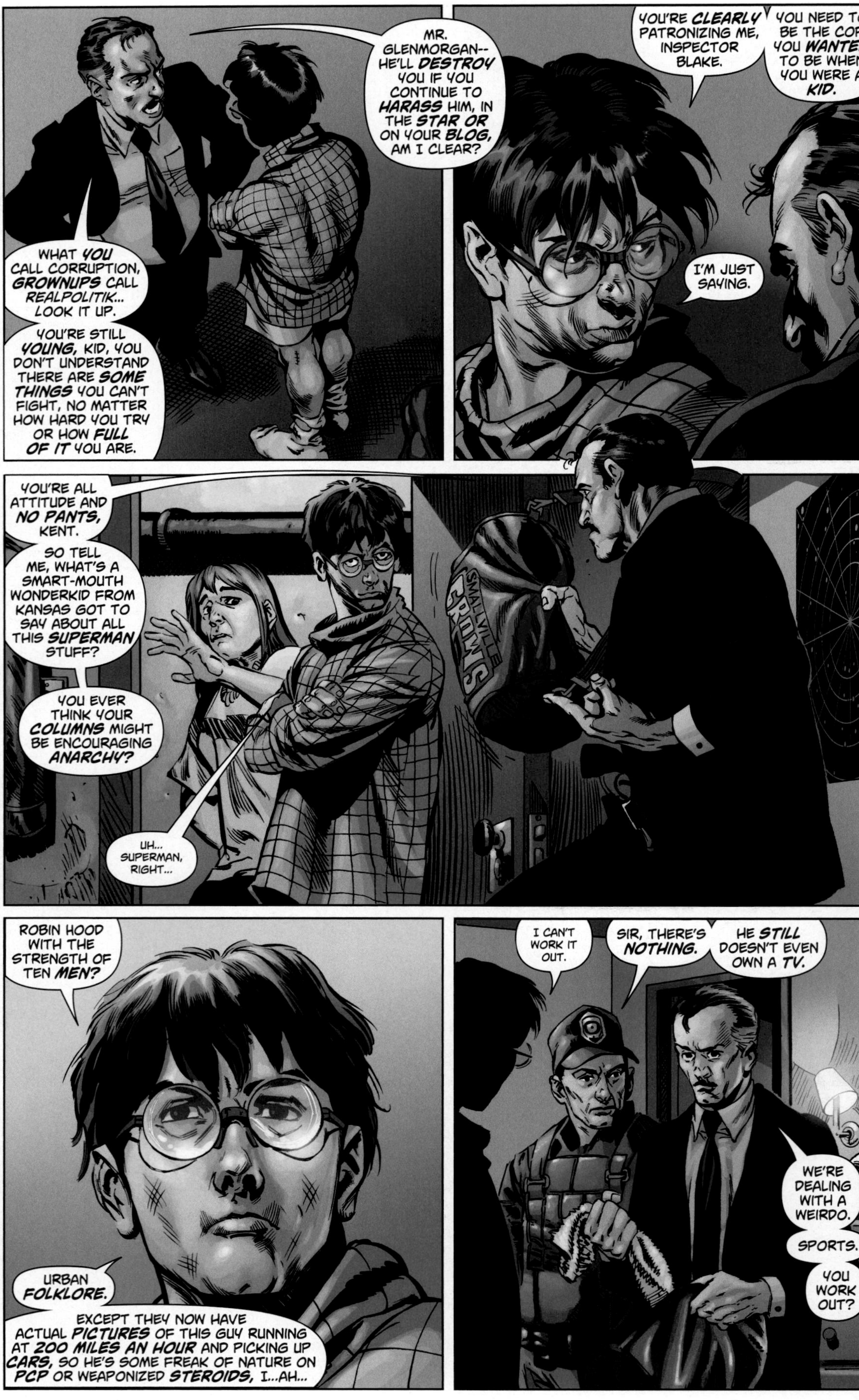

MR. GLENMORGAN-- HE'LL DESTROY YOU IF YOU CONTINUE TO HARASS HIM, IN THE STAR OR ON YOUR BLOG, AM I CLEAR?
WHAT YOU CALL CORRUPTION, GROWNUPS CALL REALPOLITIK... LOOK IT UP.
YOU'RE STILL YOUNG, KID, YOU DON'T UNDERSTAND THERE ARE SOME THINGS YOU CAN'T FIGHT, NO MATTER HOW HARD YOU TRY OR HOW FULL OF IT YOU ARE.
YOU'RE CLEARLY PATRONIZING ME, INSPECTOR BLAKE.
YOU NEED TO BE THE COP YOU WANTED TO BE WHEN YOU WERE A KID.
I'M JUST SAYING.
YOU'RE ALL ATTITUDE AND NO PANTS, KENT.
SO TELL ME, WHAT'S A SMART-MOUTH WONDERKID FROM KANSAS GOT TO SAY ABOUT ALL THIS SUPERMAN STUFF?
YOU EVER THINK YOUR COLUMNS MIGHT BE ENCOURAGING ANARCHY?
SMALLVILLE CROWS
UH... SUPERMAN, RIGHT...
ROBIN HOOD WITH THE STRENGTH OF TEN MEN?
URBAN FOLKLORE.
EXCEPT THEY NOW HAVE ACTUAL PICTURES OF THIS GUY RUNNING AT 200 MILES AN HOUR AND PICKING UP CARS, SO HE'S SOME FREAK OF NATURE ON PCP OR WEAPONIZED STEROIDS, I...AH...
I CAN'T WORK IT OUT.
SIR, THERE'S NOTHING.
HE STILL DOESN'T EVEN OWN A TV.
WE'RE DEALING WITH A WEIRDO.
SPORTS.
YOU WORK OUT?

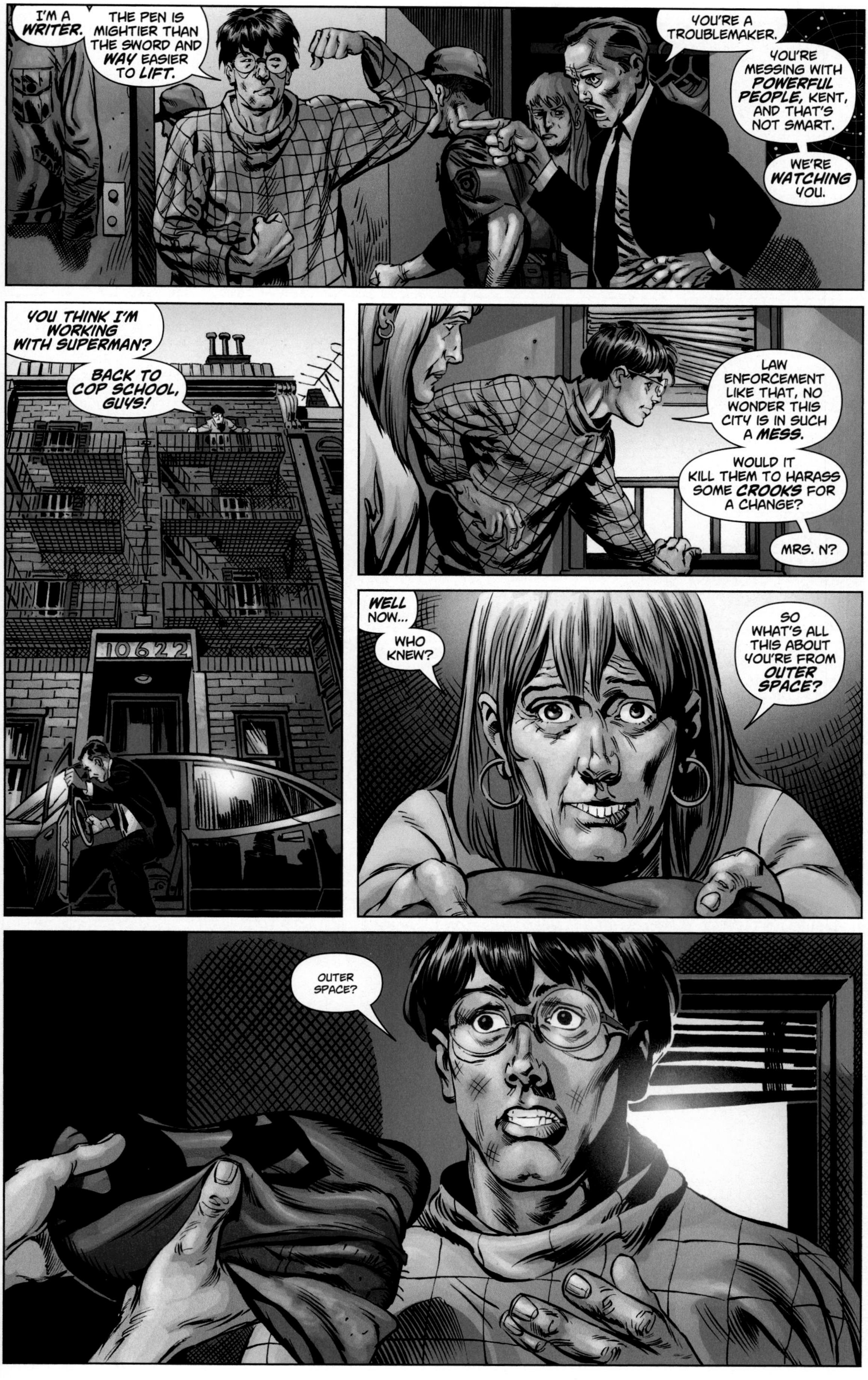
I'M A WRITER.
THE PEN IS MIGHTIER THAN THE SWORD AND WAY EASIER TO LIFT.
YOU'RE A TROUBLEMAKER.
YOU'RE MESSING WITH POWERFUL PEOPLE, KENT, AND THAT'S NOT SMART.
WE'RE WATCHING YOU.
YOU THINK I'M WORKING WITH SUPERMAN?
BACK TO COP SCHOOL, GUYS!
10622
LAW ENFORCEMENT LIKE THAT, NO WONDER THIS CITY IS IN SUCH A MESS.
WOULD IT KILL THEM TO HARASS SOME CROOKS FOR A CHANGE?
MRS. N?
WELL NOW...
WHO KNEW?
SO WHAT'S ALL THIS ABOUT YOU'RE FROM OUTER SPACE?
OUTER SPACE?

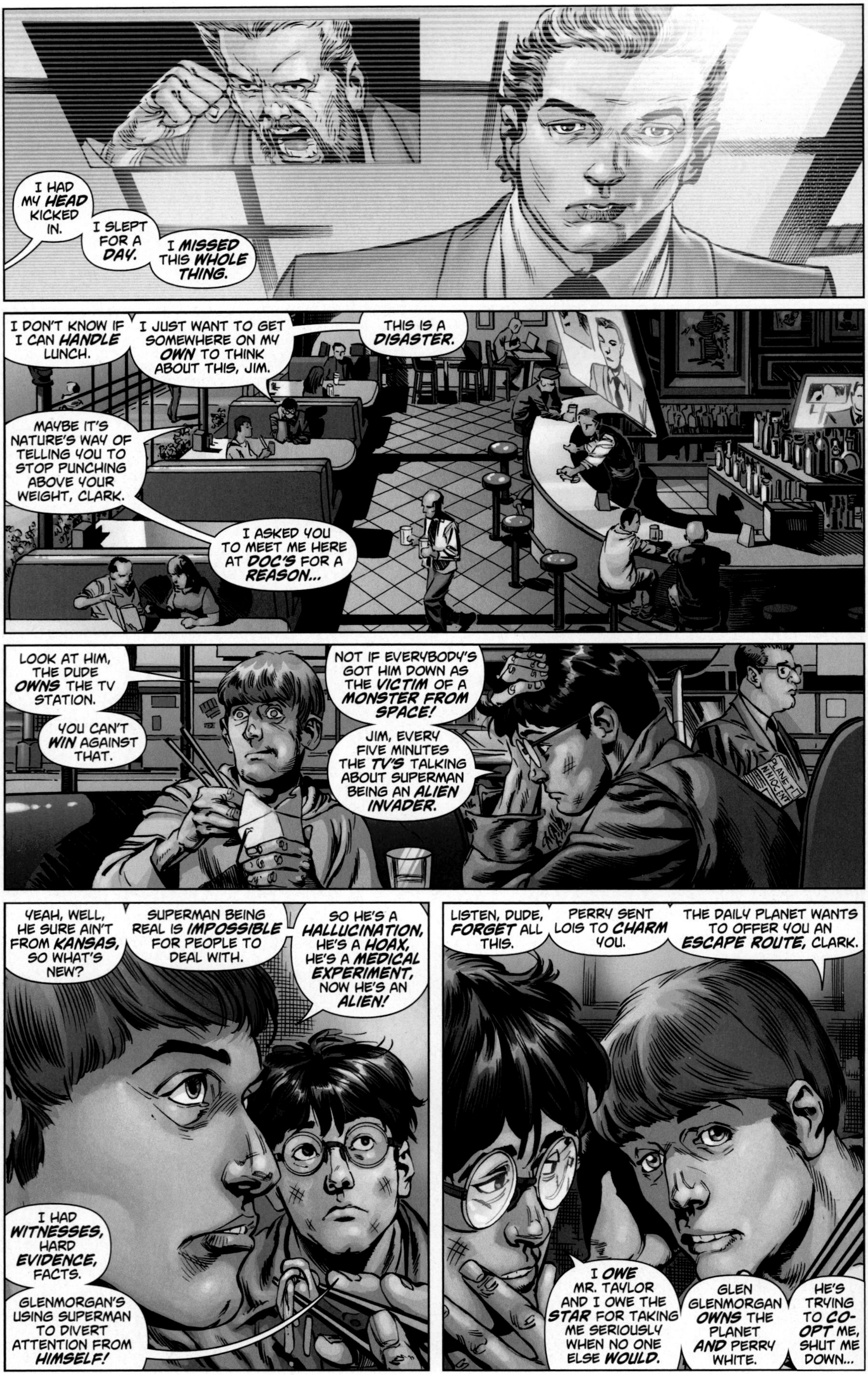
I HAD MY HEAD KICKED IN.
I SLEPT FOR A DAY.
I MISSED THIS WHOLE THING.
I DON'T KNOW IF I CAN HANDLE LUNCH.
I JUST WANT TO GET SOMEWHERE ON MY OWN TO THINK ABOUT THIS, JIM.
THIS IS A DISASTER.
MAYBE IT'S NATURE'S WAY OF TELLING YOU TO STOP PUNCHING ABOVE YOUR WEIGHT, CLARK.
I ASKED YOU TO MEET ME HERE AT DOC'S FOR A REASON...
LOOK AT HIM, THE DUDE OWNS THE TV STATION.
YOU CAN'T WIN AGAINST THAT.
NOT IF EVERYBODY'S GOT HIM DOWN AS THE VICTIM OF A MONSTER FROM SPACE!
JIM, EVERY FIVE MINUTES THE TV'S TALKING ABOUT SUPERMAN BEING AN ALIEN INVADER.
YEAH, WELL, HE SURE AIN'T FROM KANSAS, SO WHAT'S NEW?
SUPERMAN BEING REAL IS IMPOSSIBLE FOR PEOPLE TO DEAL WITH.
SO HE'S A HALLUCINATION, HE'S A HOAX, HE'S A MEDICAL EXPERIMENT, NOW HE'S AN ALIEN!
I HAD WITNESSES, HARD EVIDENCE, FACTS.
GLENMORGAN'S USING SUPERMAN TO DIVERT ATTENTION FROM HIMSELF!
LISTEN, DUDE, FORGET ALL THIS.
PERRY SENT LOIS TO CHARM YOU.
THE DAILY PLANET WANTS TO OFFER YOU AN ESCAPE ROUTE, CLARK.
I OWE MR. TAYLOR AND I OWE THE STAR FOR TAKING ME SERIOUSLY WHEN NO ONE ELSE WOULD.
GLEN GLENMORGAN OWNS THE PLANET AND PERRY WHITE.
HE'S TRYING TO CO-OPT ME, SHUT ME DOWN...

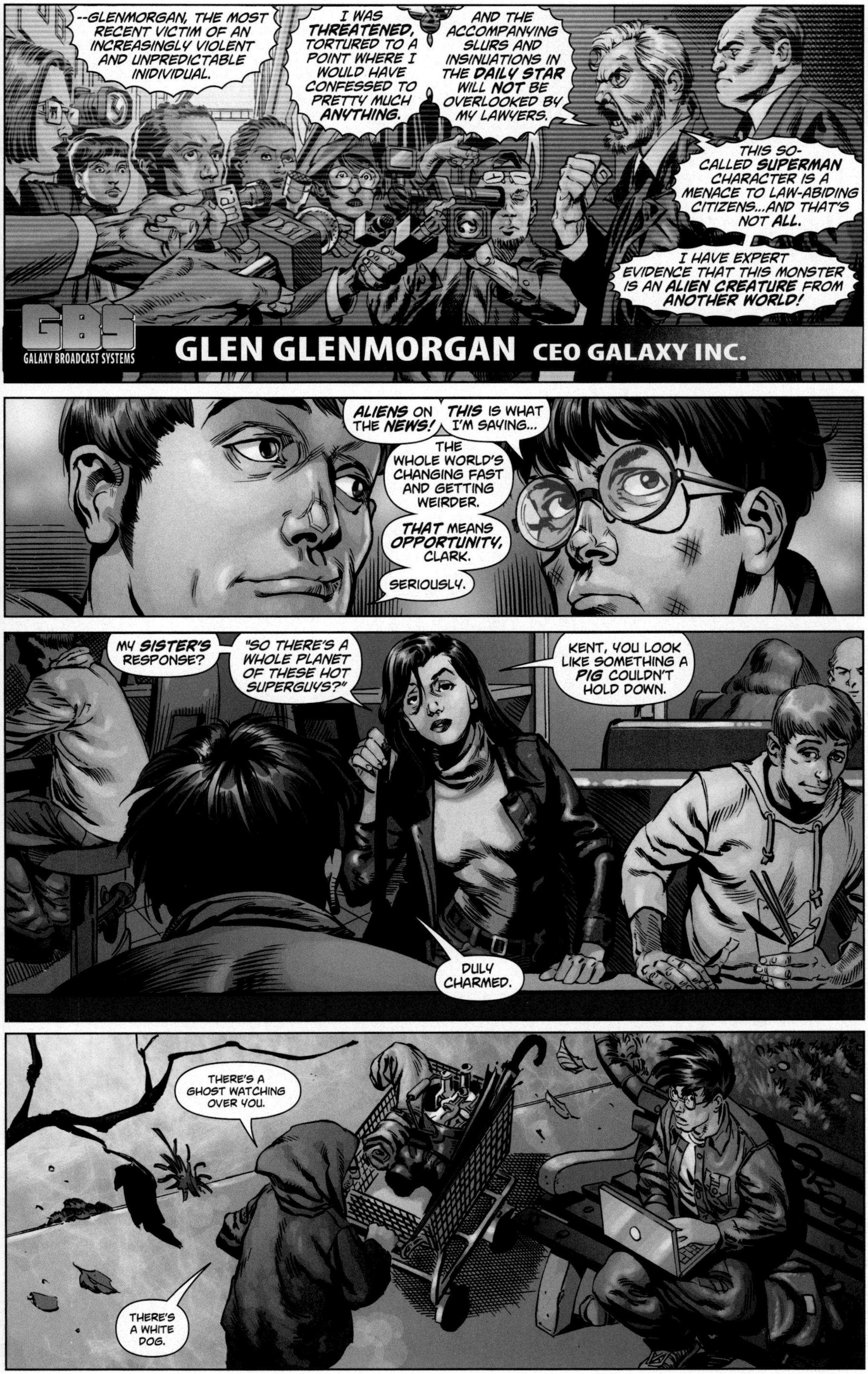
--GLENMORGAN, THE MOST RECENT VICTIM OF AN INCREASINGLY VIOLENT AND UNPREDICTABLE INDIVIDUAL.
I WAS THREATENED, TORTURED TO A POINT WHERE I WOULD HAVE CONFESSED TO PRETTY MUCH ANYTHING.
AND THE ACCOMPANYING SLURS AND INSINUATIONS IN THE DAILY STAR WILL NOT BE OVERLOOKED BY MY LAWYERS.
THIS SO-CALLED SUPERMAN CHARACTER IS A MENACE TO LAW-ABIDING CITIZENS...AND THAT'S NOT ALL.
I HAVE EXPERT EVIDENCE THAT THIS MONSTER IS AN ALIEN CREATURE FROM ANOTHER WORLD!
GBS
GALAXY BROADCAST SYSTEMS
GLEN GLENMORGAN CEO GALAXY INC.
ALIENS ON THE NEWS!
THIS IS WHAT I'M SAYING...
THE WHOLE WORLD'S CHANGING FAST AND GETTING WEIRDER.
THAT MEANS OPPORTUNITY, CLARK.
SERIOUSLY.
MY SISTER'S RESPONSE?
"SO THERE'S A WHOLE PLANET OF THESE HOT SUPERGUYS?"
KENT, YOU LOOK LIKE SOMETHING A PIG COULDN'T HOLD DOWN.
DULY CHARMED.
THERE'S A GHOST WATCHING OVER YOU.
THERE'S A WHITE DOG.

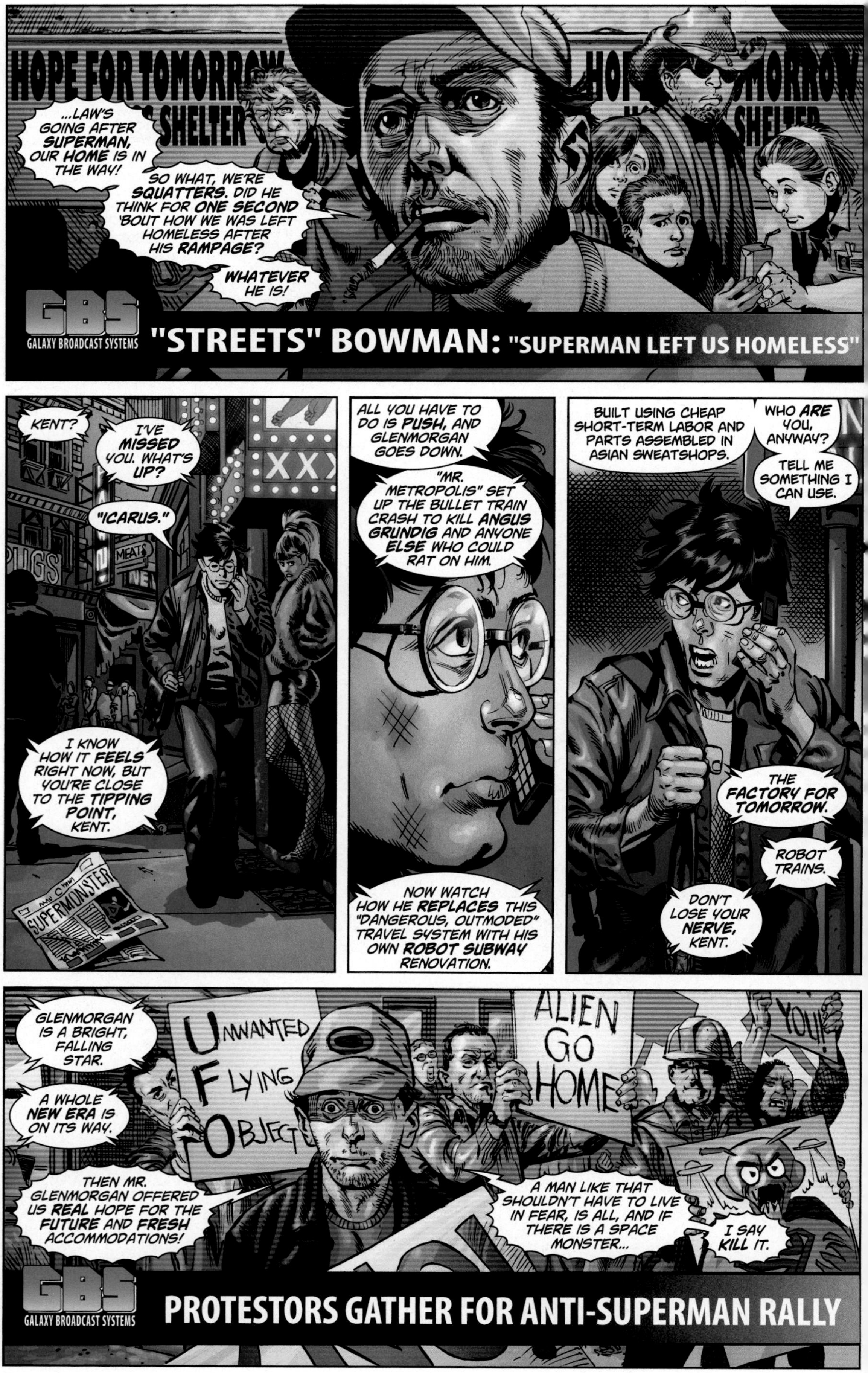
HOPE FOR TOMORROW
SHELTER
...LAW'S GOING AFTER SUPERMAN, OUR HOME IS IN THE WAY!
SO WHAT, WE'RE SQUATTERS. DID HE THINK FOR ONE SECOND 'BOUT HOW WE WAS LEFT HOMELESS AFTER HIS RAMPAGE?
WHATEVER HE IS!
GBS
GALAXY BROADCAST SYSTEMS
"STREETS" BOWMAN: "SUPERMAN LEFT US HOMELESS"
KENT?
I'VE MISSED YOU. WHAT'S UP?
"ICARUS."
XXX
MEATS
I KNOW HOW IT FEELS RIGHT NOW, BUT YOU'RE CLOSE TO THE TIPPING POINT, KENT.
SUPERMONSTER
ALL YOU HAVE TO DO IS PUSH, AND GLENMORGAN GOES DOWN.
"MR. METROPOLIS" SET UP THE BULLET TRAIN CRASH TO KILL ANGUS GRUNDIG AND ANYONE ELSE WHO COULD RAT ON HIM.
NOW WATCH HOW HE REPLACES THIS "DANGEROUS, OUTMODED" TRAVEL SYSTEM WITH HIS OWN ROBOT SUBWAY RENOVATION.
BUILT USING CHEAP SHORT-TERM LABOR AND PARTS ASSEMBLED IN ASIAN SWEATSHOPS.
WHO ARE YOU, ANYWAY?
TELL ME SOMETHING I CAN USE.
THE FACTORY FOR TOMORROW.
ROBOT TRAINS.
DON'T LOSE YOUR NERVE, KENT.
GLENMORGAN IS A BRIGHT, FALLING STAR.
A WHOLE NEW ERA IS ON ITS WAY.
UNWANTED FLYING OBJECT
ALIEN GO HOME
YOU!
THEN MR. GLENMORGAN OFFERED US REAL HOPE FOR THE FUTURE AND FRESH ACCOMMODATIONS!
A MAN LIKE THAT SHOULDN'T HAVE TO LIVE IN FEAR, IS ALL, AND IF THERE IS A SPACE MONSTER...
I SAY KILL IT.
GBS
GALAXY BROADCAST SYSTEMS
PROTESTORS GATHER FOR ANTI-SUPERMAN RALLY

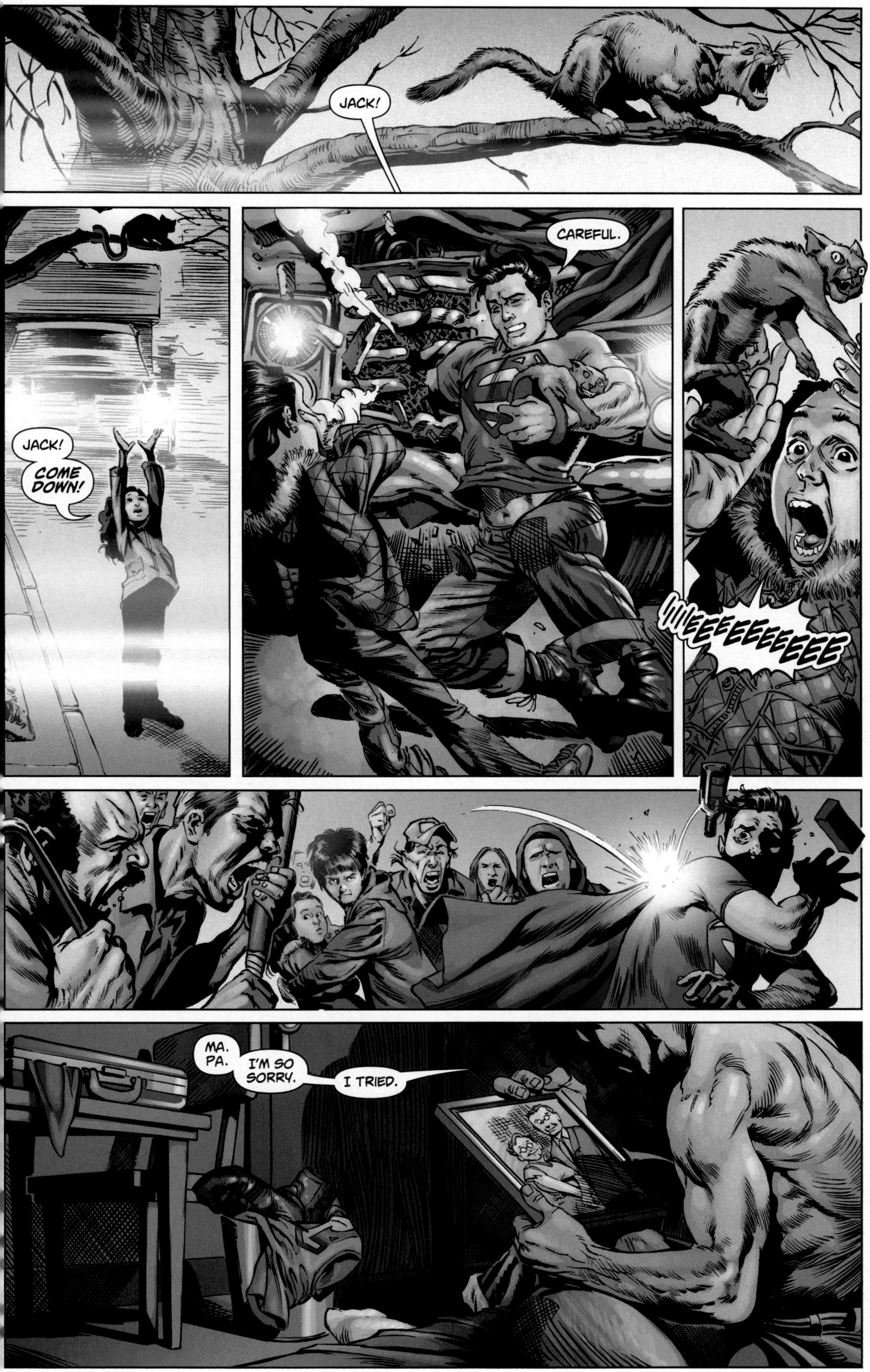
JACK!
JACK!
COME DOWN!
CAREFUL.
WEEEEEEEEEE
MA. PA.
I'M SO SORRY.
I TRIED.

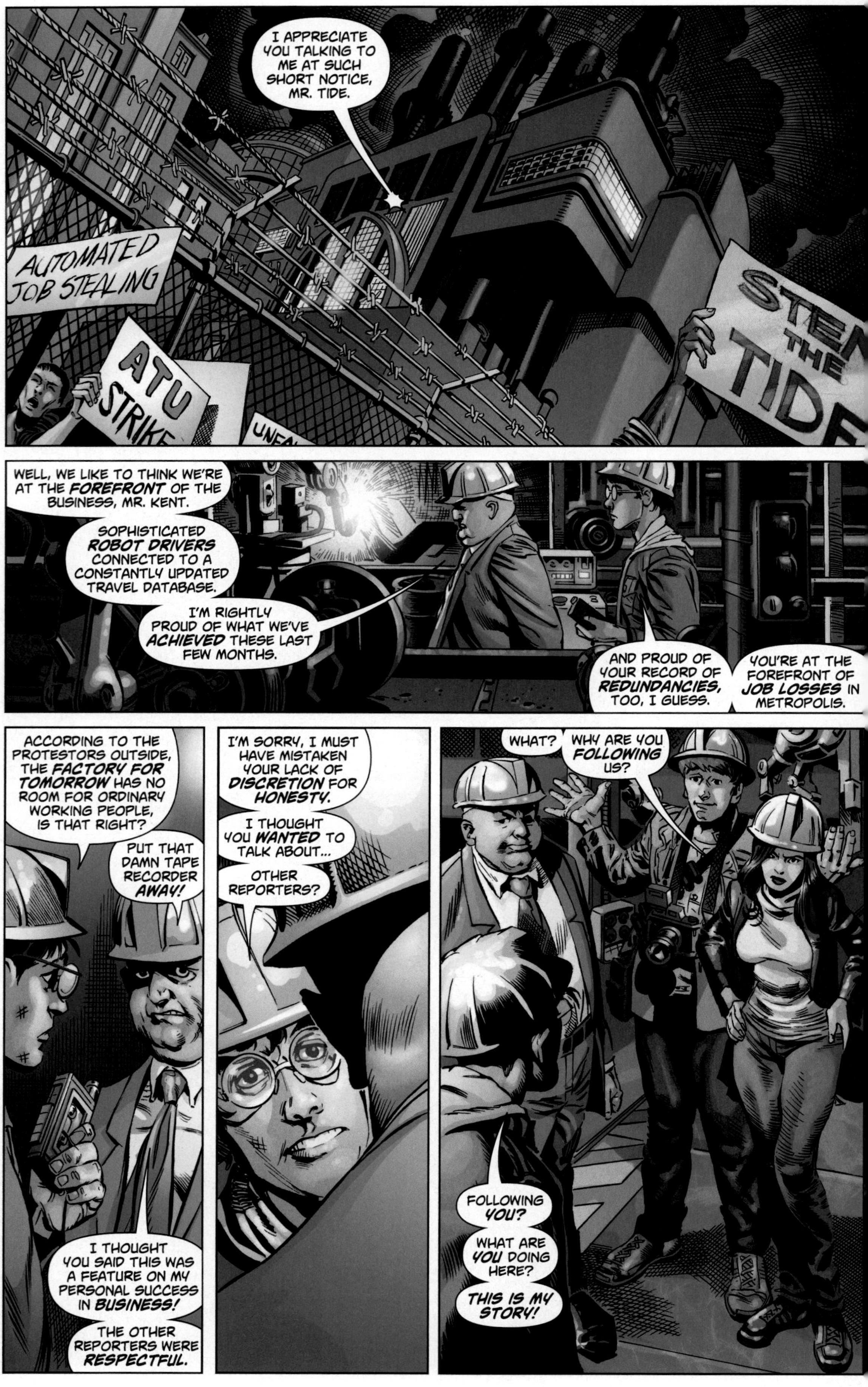

I APPRECIATE YOU TALKING TO ME AT SUCH SHORT NOTICE, MR. TIDE.
AUTOMATED JOB STEALING
ATU STRIKE
STEM THE TIDE
WELL, WE LIKE TO THINK WE'RE AT THE FOREFRONT OF THE BUSINESS, MR. KENT.
SOPHISTICATED ROBOT DRIVERS CONNECTED TO A CONSTANTLY UPDATED TRAVEL DATABASE.
I'M RIGHTLY PROUD OF WHAT WE'VE ACHIEVED THESE LAST FEW MONTHS.
AND PROUD OF YOUR RECORD OF REDUNDANCIES, TOO, I GUESS.
YOU'RE AT THE FOREFRONT OF JOB LOSSES IN METROPOLIS.
ACCORDING TO THE PROTESTORS OUTSIDE, THE FACTORY FOR TOMORROW HAS NO ROOM FOR ORDINARY WORKING PEOPLE, IS THAT RIGHT?
PUT THAT DAMN TAPE RECORDER AWAY!
I THOUGHT YOU SAID THIS WAS A FEATURE ON MY PERSONAL SUCCESS IN BUSINESS!
THE OTHER REPORTERS WERE RESPECTFUL.
I'M SORRY, I MUST HAVE MISTAKEN YOUR LACK OF DISCRETION FOR HONESTY.
I THOUGHT YOU WANTED TO TALK ABOUT...
OTHER REPORTERS?
WHAT?
WHY ARE YOU FOLLOWING US?
FOLLOWING YOU?
WHAT ARE YOU DOING HERE?
THIS IS MY STORY!

CLARK. GUYS.

YOU!

I'M HAVING *ALL* OF YOU EJECTED FROM THESE PREMISES RIGHT NOW.

I THOUGHT THIS WAS ABOUT *ME!*

WE'RE GOING *NOWHERE* UNTIL YOU--

NNAOW!

THAT *SOUND!*

A SIGNAL.

THIS OPERATION IS *ENTIRELY* ABOVE BOARD, AND IT'S NOT *MY* FAULT IF...IF...

WHAT THE HELL?

THOSE DON'T LOOK LIKE *SUBWAY CABINS.*

OR *ROBOT DRIVERS.*

MR. T?

YOUR PLANET'S *DATABASE* HAS BEEN COPIED AND FILED.

SOMETHING GOT INTO THE NETWORK.

WHAT *IS* THIS? WHAT'S IT SAYING?

WHAT'S IT *MAKING?*

WE MAKE SUBWAY CARS.

IN ADVANCE OF IMMINENT *DESTRUCTION* AND THE EXTINCTION OF *ALL LIFE--*

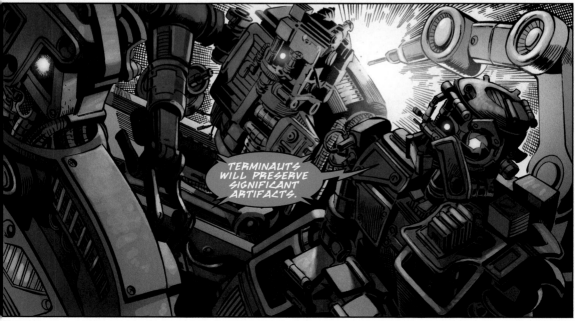

TERMINAUTS WILL PRESERVE SIGNIFICANT ARTIFACTS.

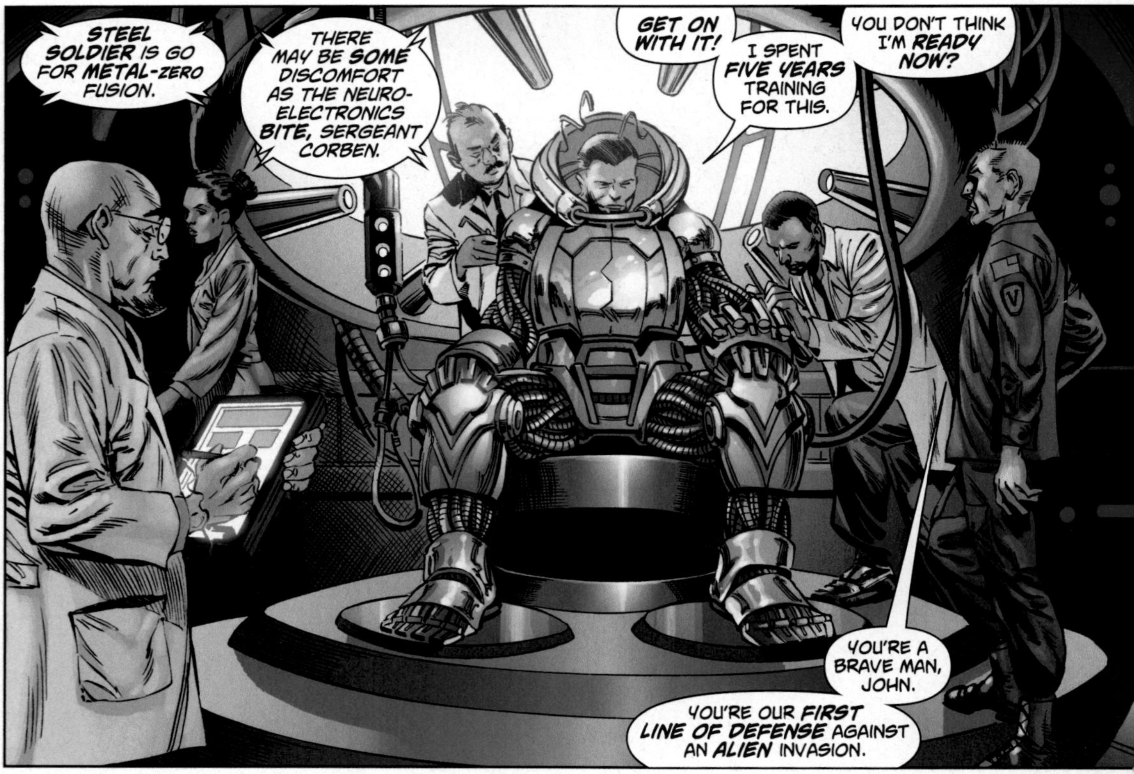
STEEL SOLDIER IS GO FOR METAL-ZERO FUSION.
THERE MAY BE SOME DISCOMFORT AS THE NEURO-ELECTRONICS BITE, SERGEANT CORBEN.
GET ON WITH IT!
I SPENT FIVE YEARS TRAINING FOR THIS.
YOU DON'T THINK I'M READY NOW?
YOU'RE A BRAVE MAN, JOHN.
YOU'RE OUR FIRST LINE OF DEFENSE AGAINST AN ALIEN INVASION.

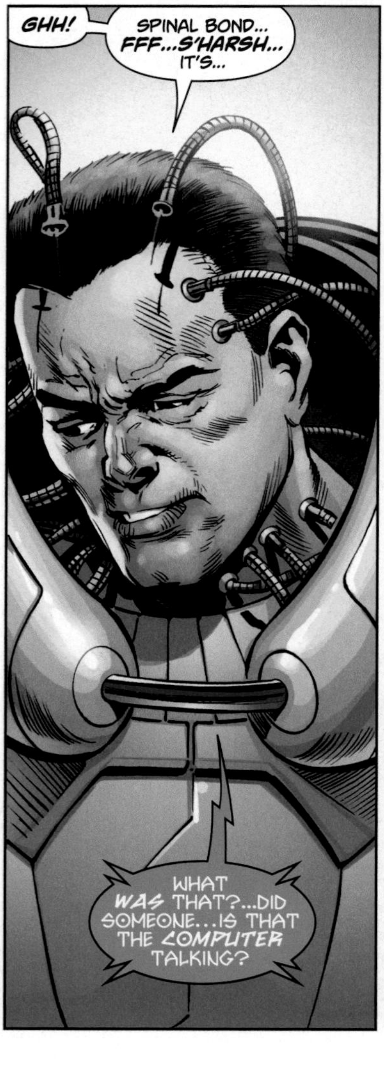
GHH!
SPINAL BOND... FFF...S'HARSH... IT'S...
WHAT WAS THAT?...DID SOMEONE...IS THAT THE COMPUTER TALKING?

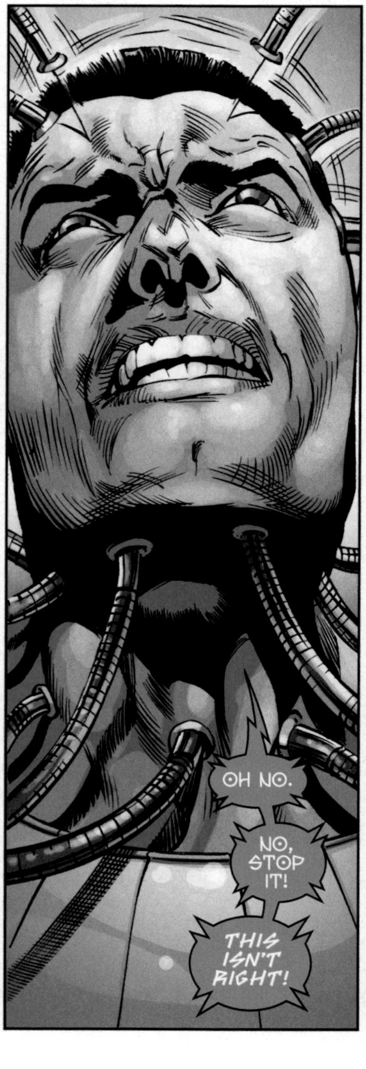
OH NO.
NO, STOP IT!
THIS ISN'T RIGHT!

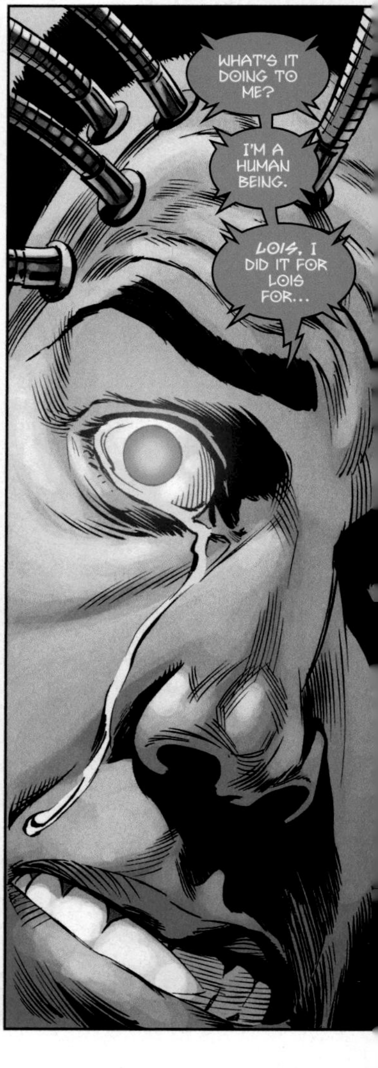
WHAT'S IT DOING TO ME?
I'M A HUMAN BEING.
LOIS, I DID IT FOR LOIS FOR...

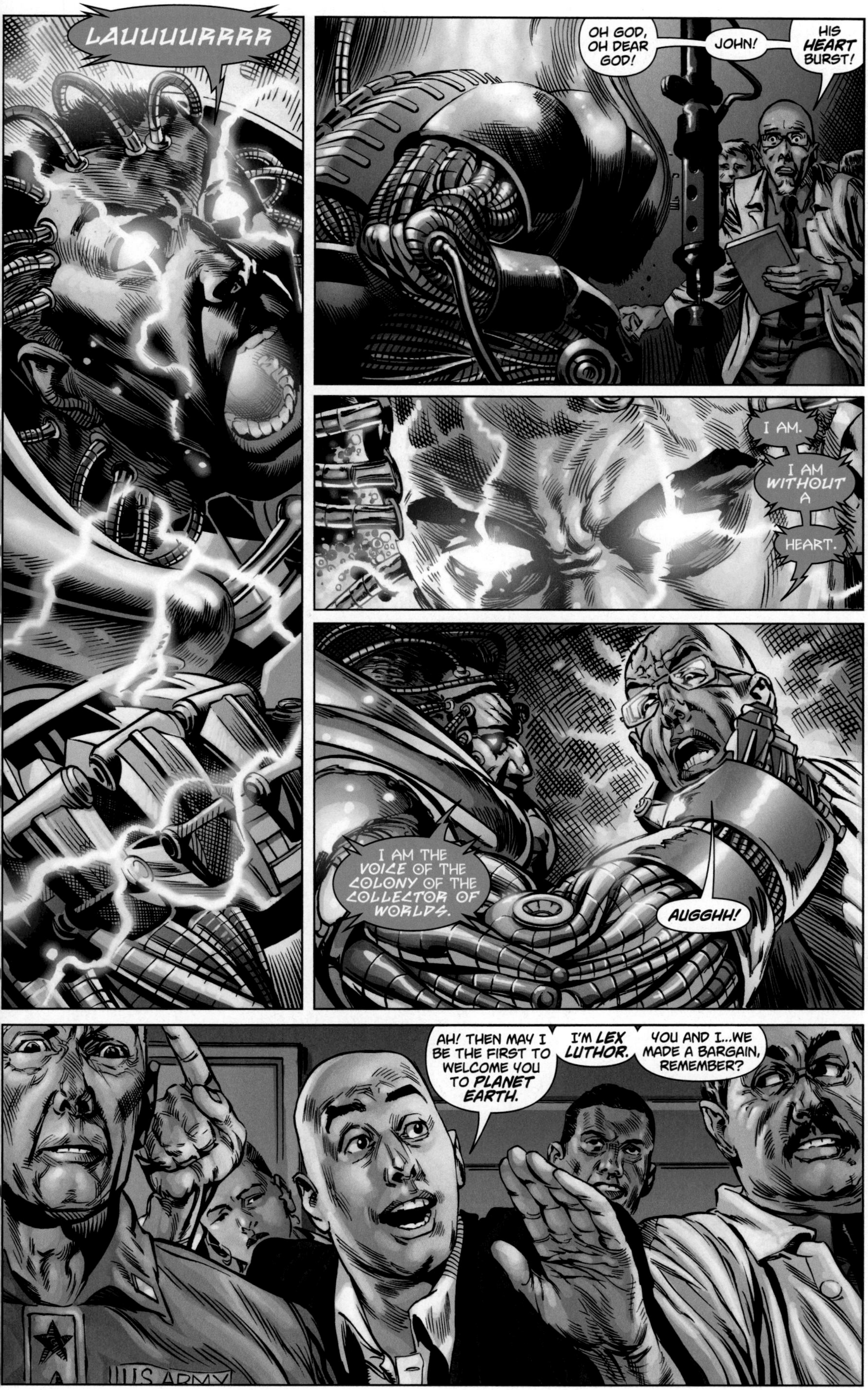
LAUUUURRRR
OH GOD, OH DEAR GOD!
JOHN!
HIS HEART BURST!
I AM.
I AM WITHOUT A
HEART.
I AM THE VOICE OF THE COLONY OF THE COLLECTOR OF WORLDS.
AUGGHH!
U.S. ARMY
AH! THEN MAY I BE THE FIRST TO WELCOME YOU TO PLANET EARTH.
I'M LEX LUTHOR.
YOU AND I...WE MADE A BARGAIN, REMEMBER?

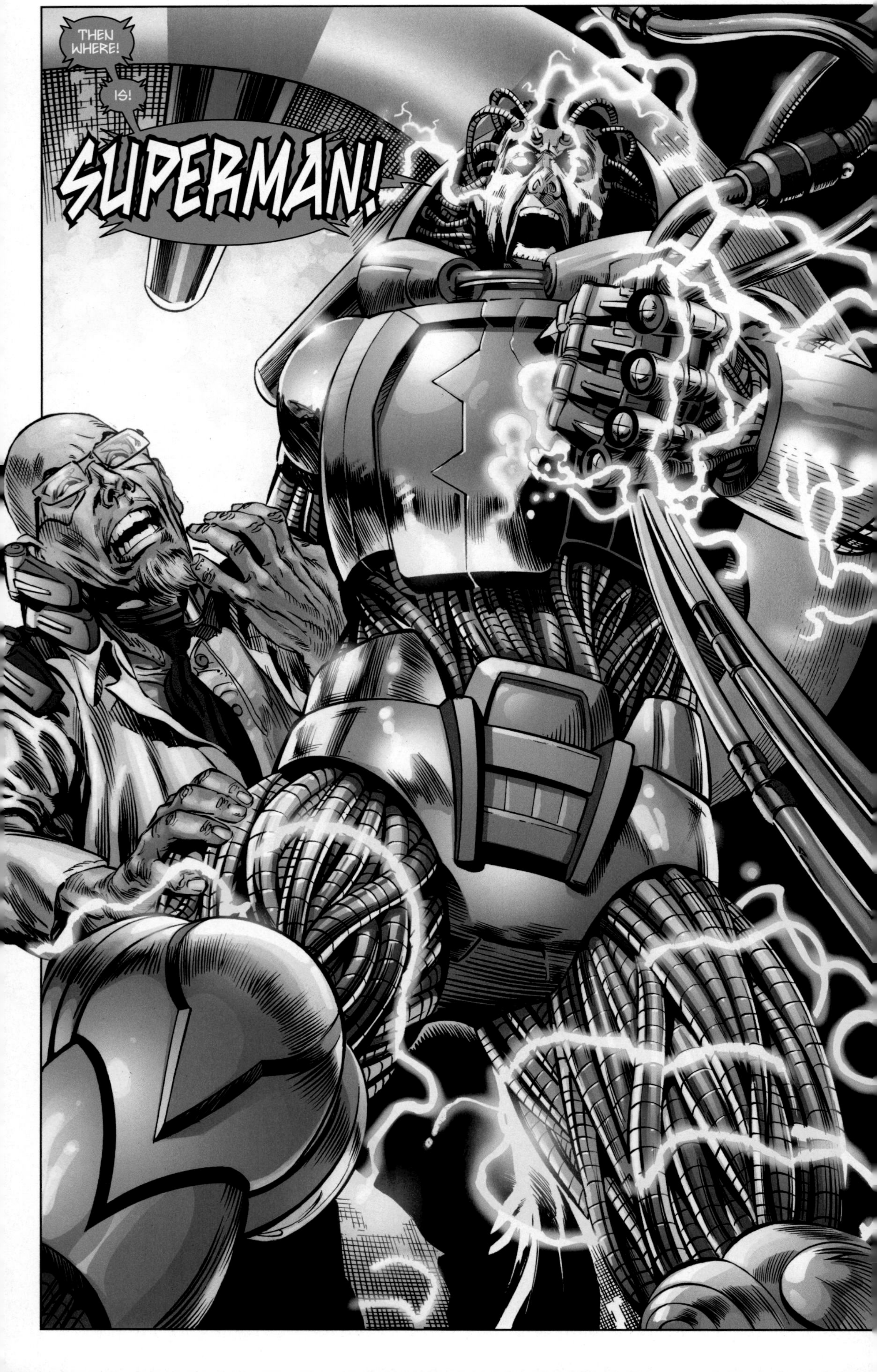
THEN WHERE!
IS!
SUPERMAN!

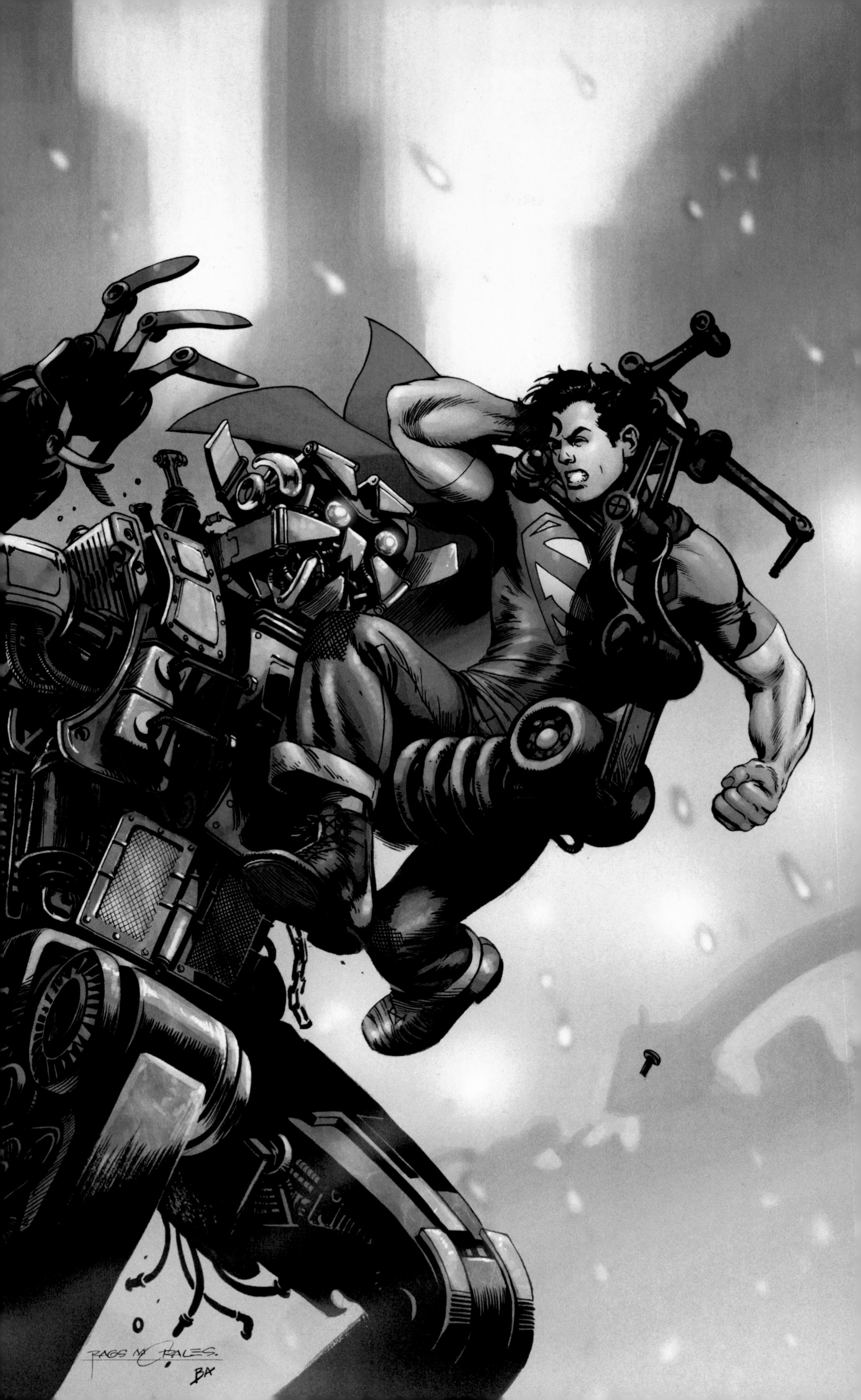
RAGS MORALES.
BA

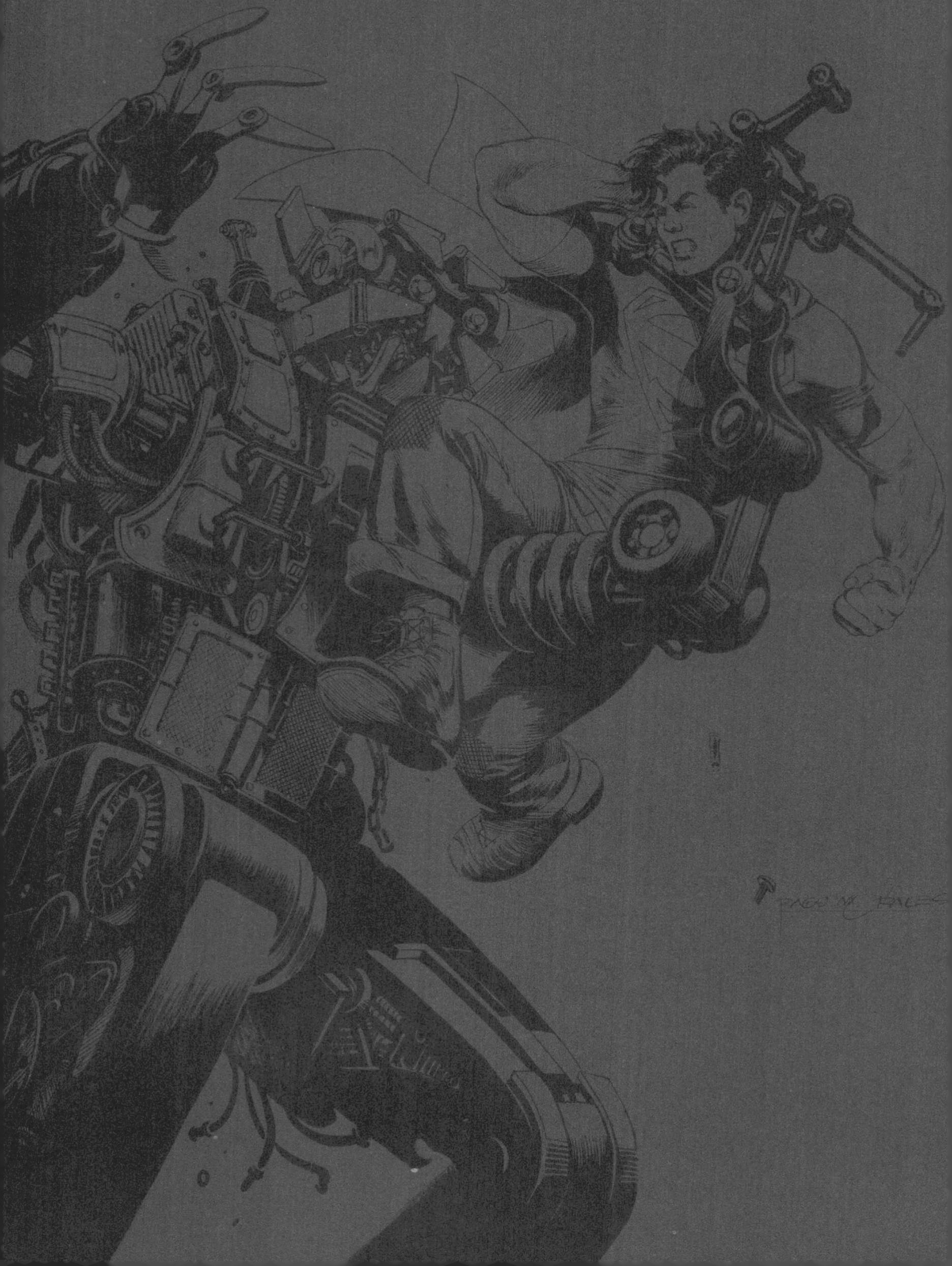

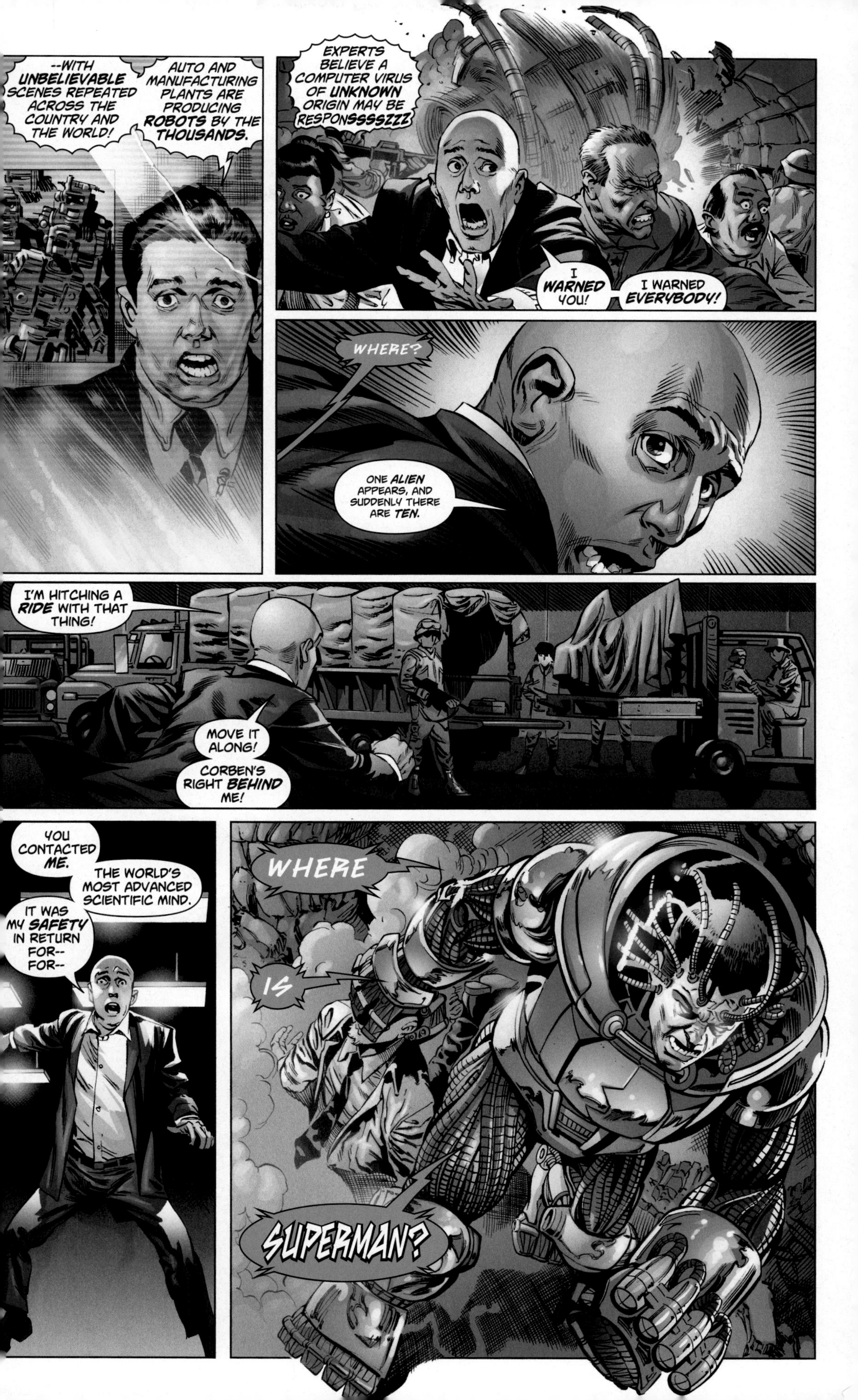
--WITH UNBELIEVABLE SCENES REPEATED ACROSS THE COUNTRY AND THE WORLD!
AUTO AND MANUFACTURING PLANTS ARE PRODUCING ROBOTS BY THE THOUSANDS.
EXPERTS BELIEVE A COMPUTER VIRUS OF UNKNOWN ORIGIN MAY BE RESPONSSSSZZZ
I WARNED YOU!
I WARNED EVERYBODY!
WHERE?
ONE ALIEN APPEARS, AND SUDDENLY THERE ARE TEN.
I'M HITCHING A RIDE WITH THAT THING!
MOVE IT ALONG!
CORBEN'S RIGHT BEHIND ME!
YOU CONTACTED ME.
THE WORLD'S MOST ADVANCED SCIENTIFIC MIND.
IT WAS MY SAFETY IN RETURN FOR--
FOR--
WHERE
IS
SUPERMAN?

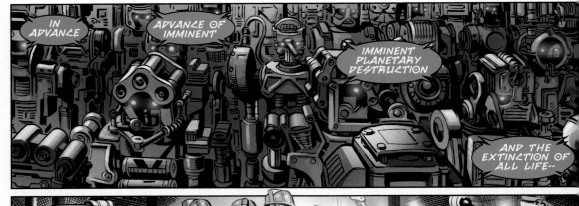

IN ADVANCE

ADVANCE OF IMMINENT

IMMINENT PLANETARY DESTRUCTION

AND THE EXTINCTION OF ALL LIFE--

TERMINAUTS WILL PRESERVE

WHAT *ARE* THOSE THINGS?

MR. TIDE...

I DON'T KNOW.

THIS IS IMPOSSIBLE.

WHAT AM I LOOKING AT?

PRESERVE SIGNIFICANT ARTIFACTS.

THEY'RE MARCHING OFF *YOUR* PRODUCTION LINES!

AB

UH, YOU GUYS...

...DO I HAVE TO BE THE FIRST TO MAKE THE OBVIOUS *SUGGESTION* HERE?

RUN!

KENT, DID YOU SAY...

KENT?

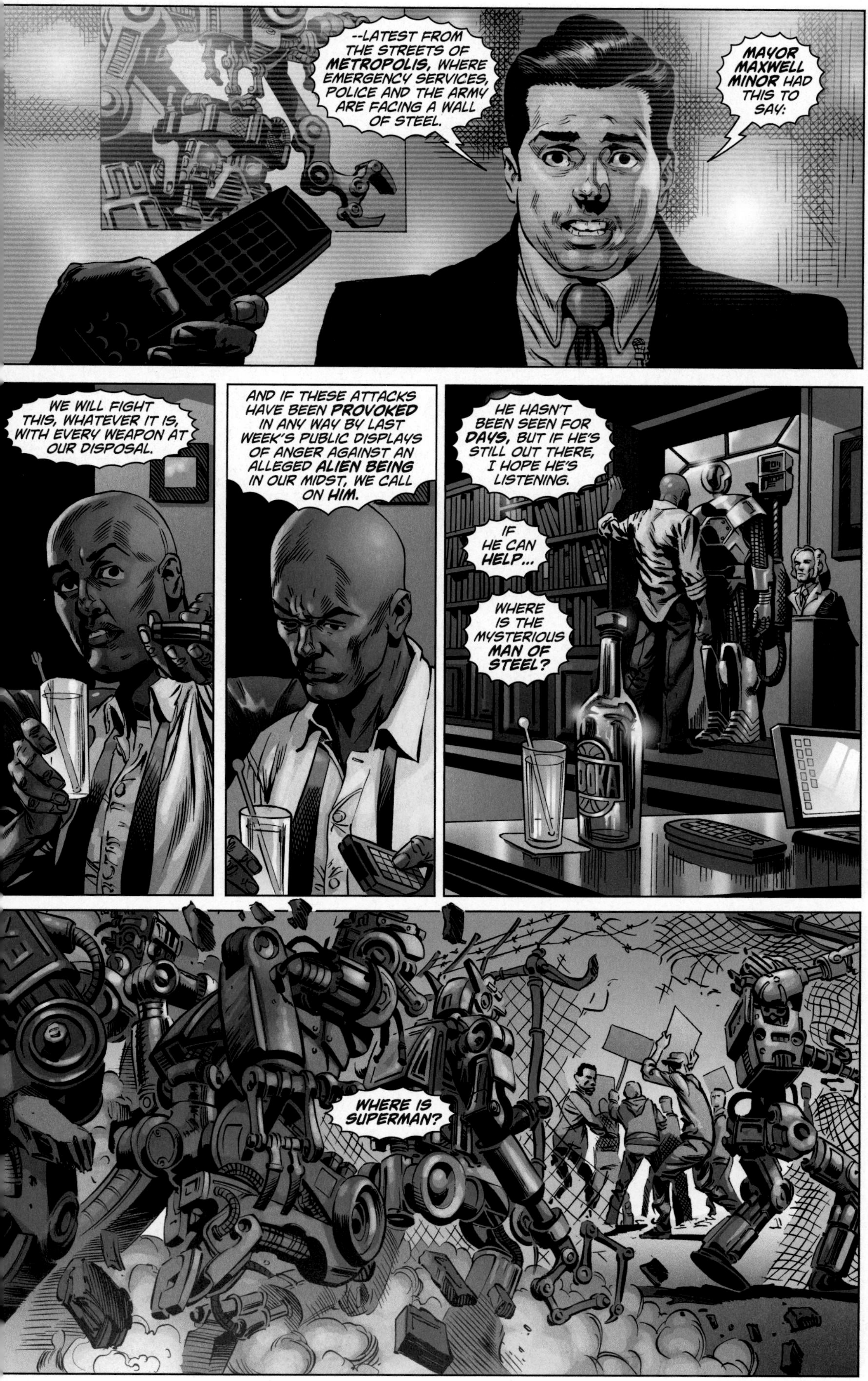
--LATEST FROM THE STREETS OF METROPOLIS, WHERE EMERGENCY SERVICES, POLICE AND THE ARMY ARE FACING A WALL OF STEEL.
MAYOR MAXWELL MINOR HAD THIS TO SAY:
WE WILL FIGHT THIS, WHATEVER IT IS, WITH EVERY WEAPON AT OUR DISPOSAL.
AND IF THESE ATTACKS HAVE BEEN PROVOKED IN ANY WAY BY LAST WEEK'S PUBLIC DISPLAYS OF ANGER AGAINST AN ALLEGED ALIEN BEING IN OUR MIDST, WE CALL ON HIM.
HE HASN'T BEEN SEEN FOR DAYS, BUT IF HE'S STILL OUT THERE, I HOPE HE'S LISTENING.
IF HE CAN HELP...
WHERE IS THE MYSTERIOUS MAN OF STEEL?
WHERE IS SUPERMAN?

SUPERMAN AND THE MEN OF STEEL

GET IN THE BUS!

GET OUT OF HERE!

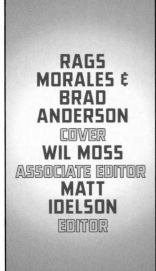

RAGS MORALES & BRAD ANDERSON
COVER

WIL MOSS
ASSOCIATE EDITOR

MATT IDELSON
EDITOR

GET ON BOARD!

IT'S THEY WANT!

IF THEY GET HIM, THEY'LL LEAVE US ALONE!

IT'S HIM!

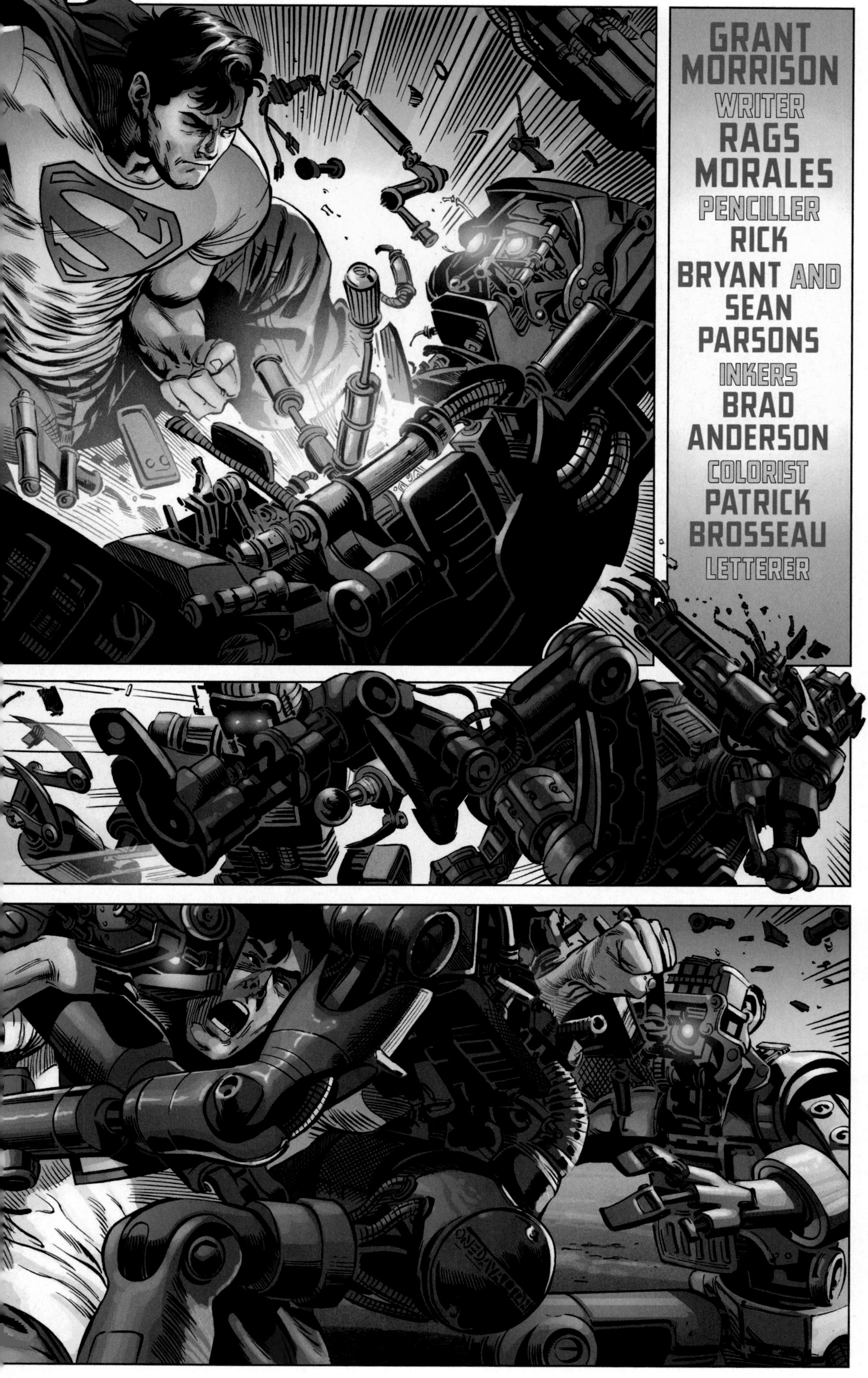
GRANT MORRISON
WRITER
RAGS MORALES
PENCILLER
RICK BRYANT AND SEAN PARSONS
INKERS
BRAD ANDERSON
COLORIST
PATRICK BROSSEAU
LETTERER

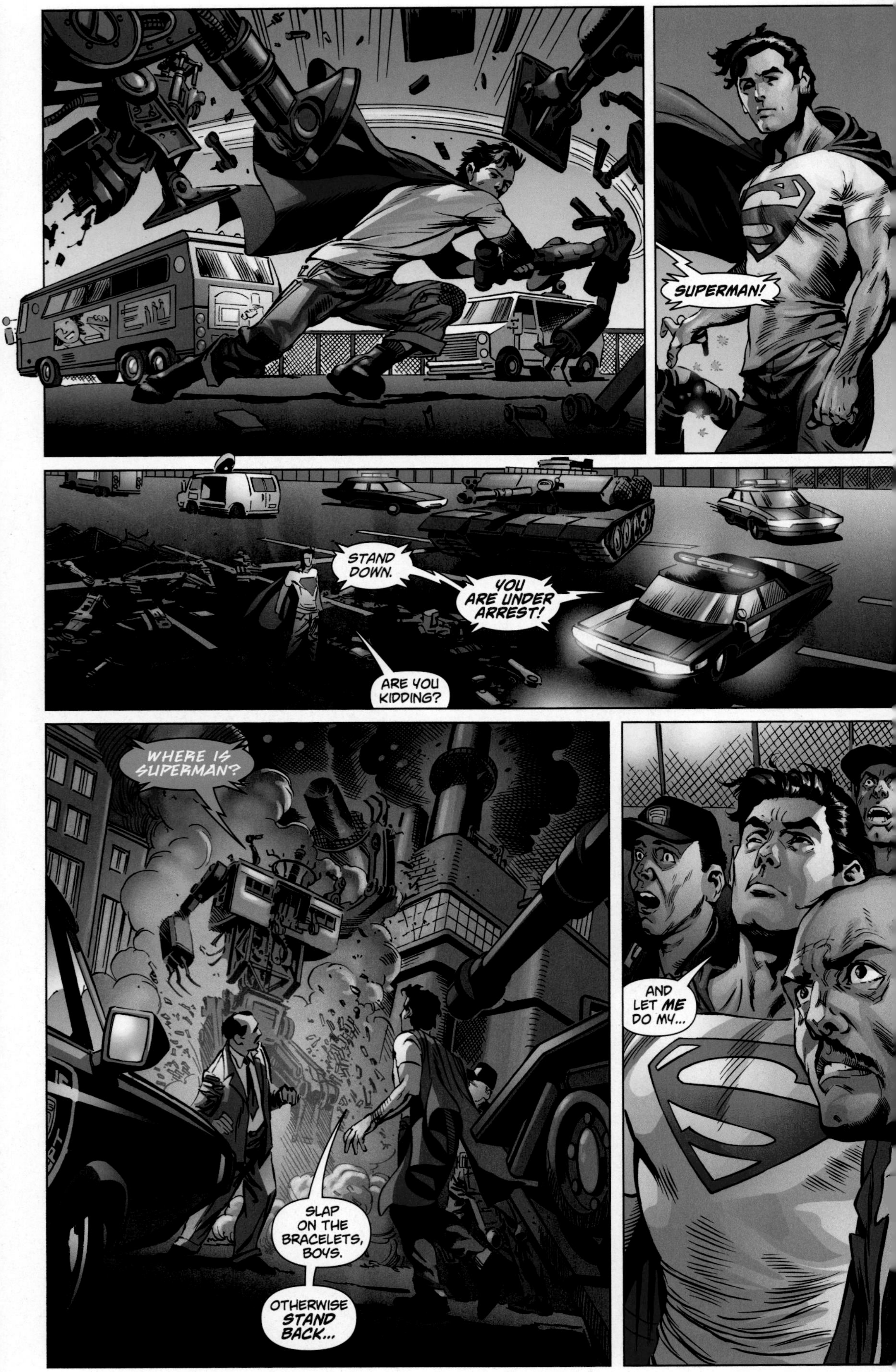
SUPERMAN!
STAND DOWN.
YOU ARE UNDER ARREST!
ARE YOU KIDDING?
WHERE IS SUPERMAN?
SLAP ON THE BRACELETS, BOYS.
OTHERWISE STAND BACK...
AND LET ME DO MY...

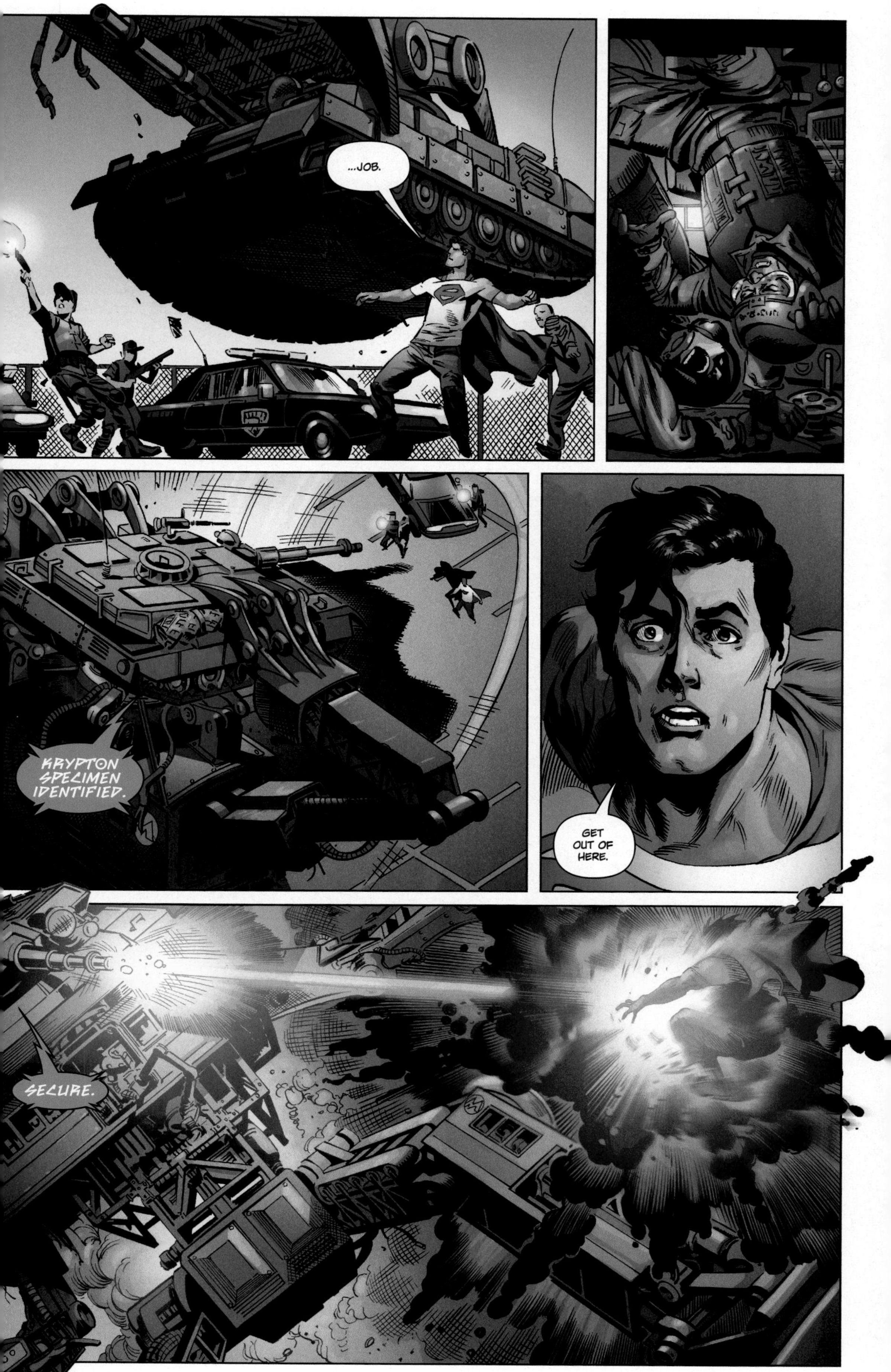
...JOB.
KRYPTON SPECIMEN IDENTIFIED.
GET OUT OF HERE.
SECURE.

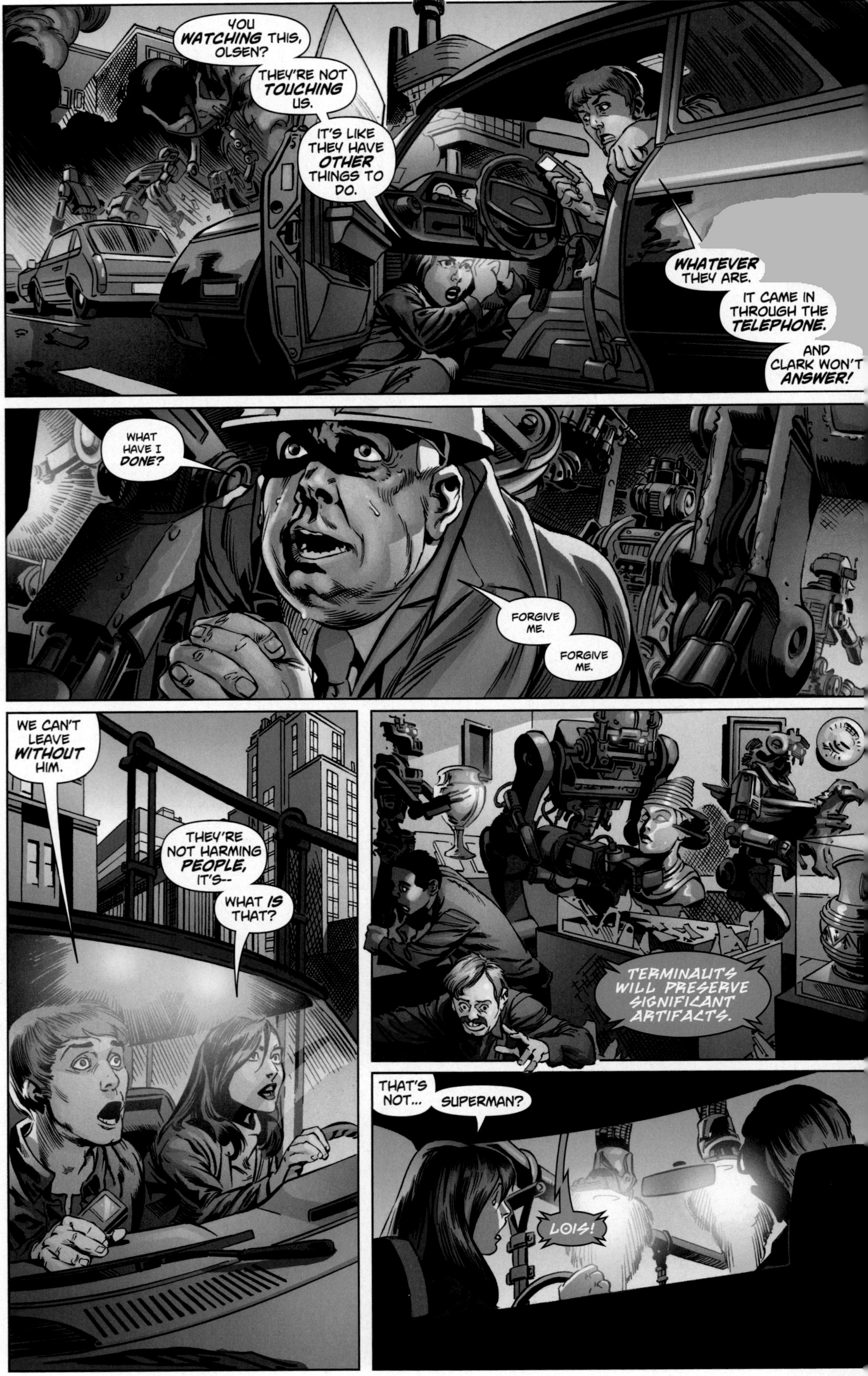
YOU WATCHING THIS, OLSEN?
THEY'RE NOT TOUCHING US.
IT'S LIKE THEY HAVE OTHER THINGS TO DO.
WHATEVER THEY ARE.
IT CAME IN THROUGH THE TELEPHONE.
AND CLARK WON'T ANSWER!
WHAT HAVE I DONE?
FORGIVE ME.
FORGIVE ME.
WE CAN'T LEAVE WITHOUT HIM.
THEY'RE NOT HARMING PEOPLE, IT'S--
WHAT IS THAT?
TERMINAUTS WILL PRESERVE SIGNIFICANT ARTIFACTS.
THAT'S NOT...
SUPERMAN?
LOIS!

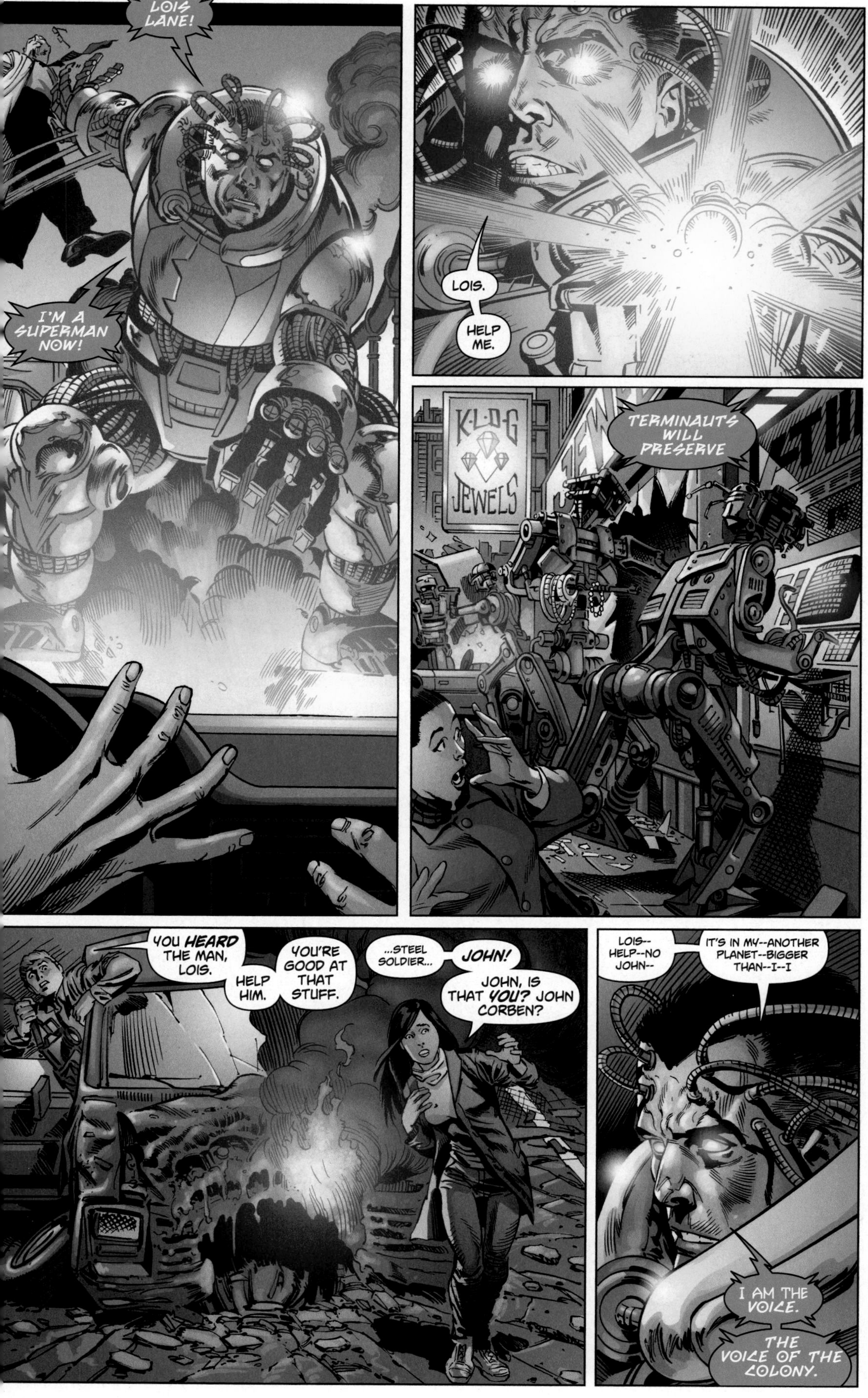
LOIS LANE!
I'M A SUPERMAN NOW!
LOIS.
HELP ME.
TERMINAUTS WILL PRESERVE
K·L·D·G JEWELS
YOU HEARD THE MAN, LOIS.
HELP HIM.
YOU'RE GOOD AT THAT STUFF.
...STEEL SOLDIER...
JOHN!
JOHN, IS THAT YOU? JOHN CORBEN?
LOIS-- HELP--NO JOHN--
IT'S IN MY--ANOTHER PLANET--BIGGER THAN--I--I
I AM THE VOICE.
THE VOICE OF THE COLONY.

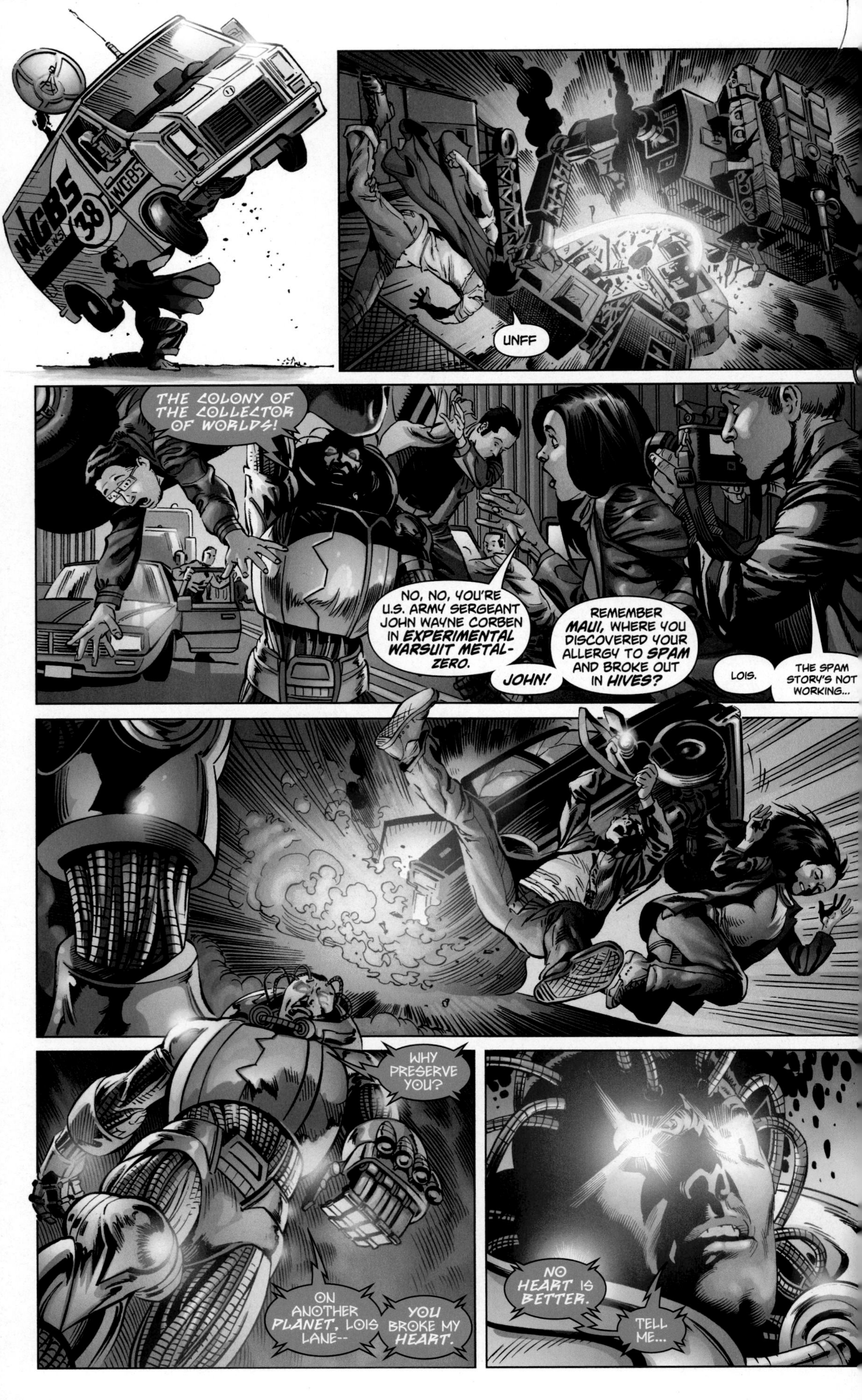
WGBS NEWS 38
WGBS
UNFF
THE COLONY OF THE COLLECTOR OF WORLDS!
NO, NO, YOU'RE U.S. ARMY SERGEANT JOHN WAYNE CORBEN IN EXPERIMENTAL WARSUIT METAL-ZERO.
JOHN!
REMEMBER MAUI, WHERE YOU DISCOVERED YOUR ALLERGY TO SPAM AND BROKE OUT IN HIVES?
LOIS.
THE SPAM STORY'S NOT WORKING...
WHY PRESERVE YOU?
ON ANOTHER PLANET, LOIS LANE--
YOU BROKE MY HEART.
NO HEART IS BETTER.
TELL ME...

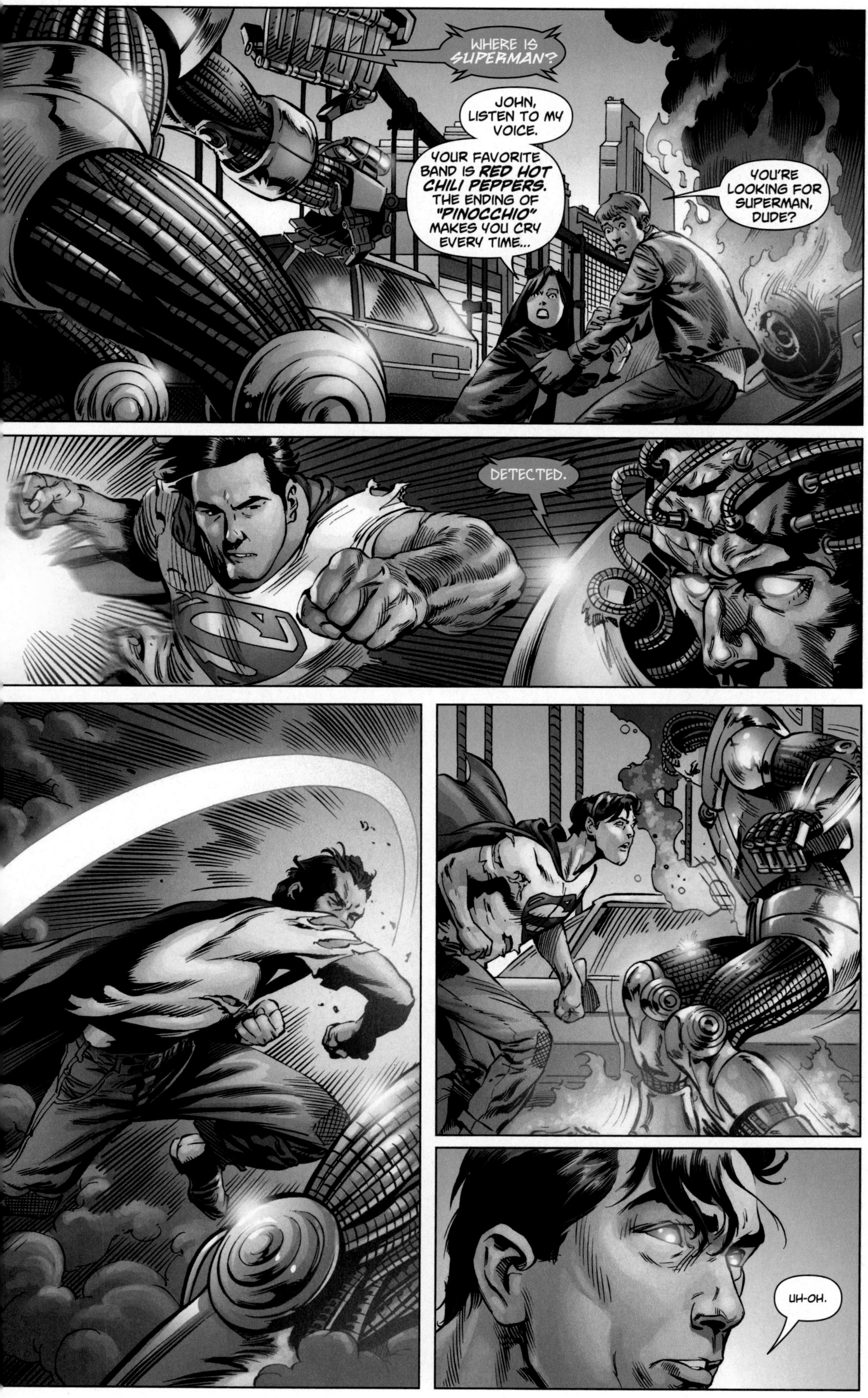
WHERE IS SUPERMAN?
JOHN, LISTEN TO MY VOICE.
YOUR FAVORITE BAND IS RED HOT CHILI PEPPERS. THE ENDING OF "PINOCCHIO" MAKES YOU CRY EVERY TIME...
YOU'RE LOOKING FOR SUPERMAN, DUDE?
DETECTED.
UH-OH.

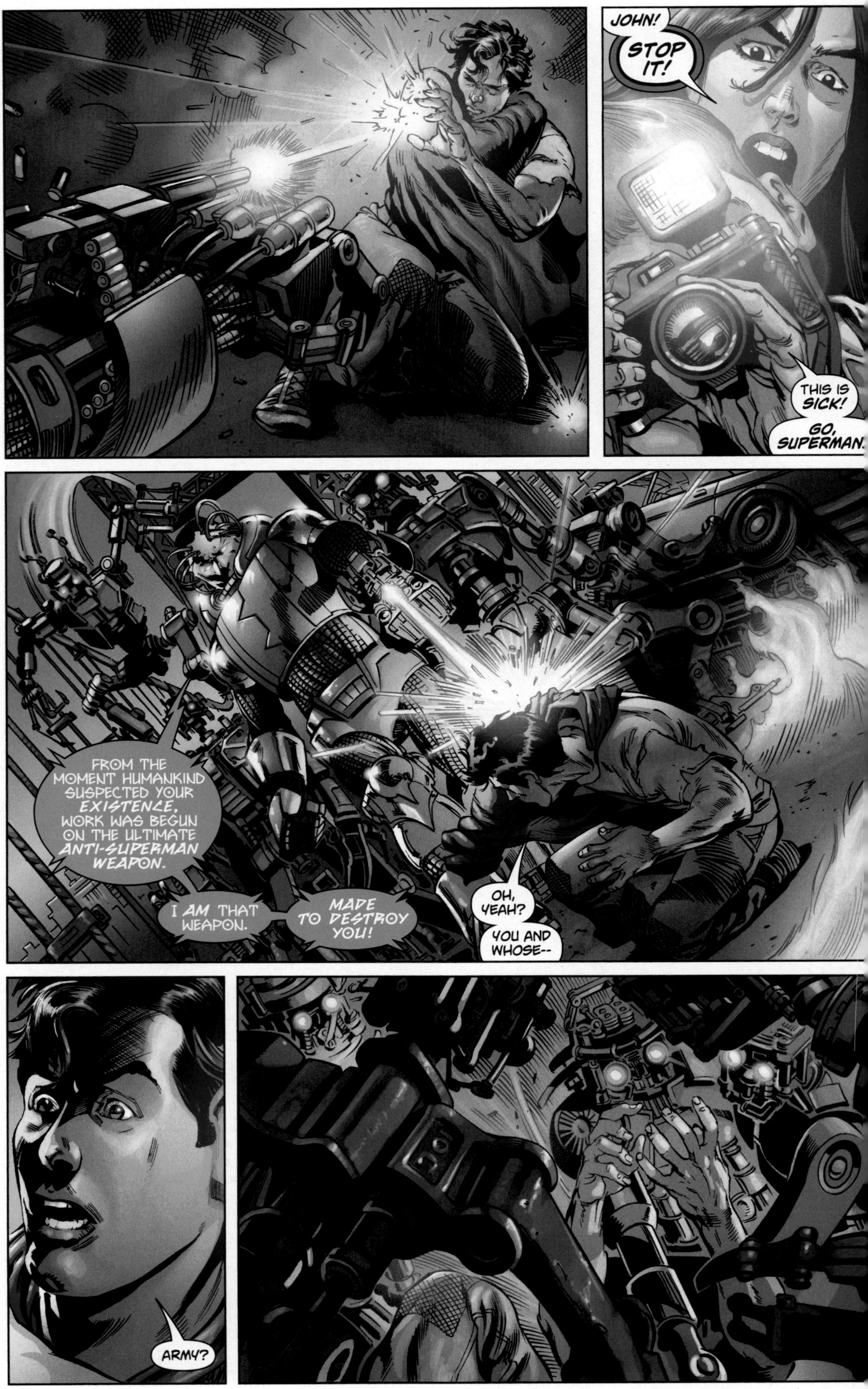
JOHN!
STOP IT!
THIS IS SICK!
GO, SUPERMAN.
FROM THE MOMENT HUMANKIND SUSPECTED YOUR EXISTENCE, WORK WAS BEGUN ON THE ULTIMATE ANTI-SUPERMAN WEAPON.
I AM THAT WEAPON.
MADE TO DESTROY YOU!
OH, YEAH?
YOU AND WHOSE--
ARMY?

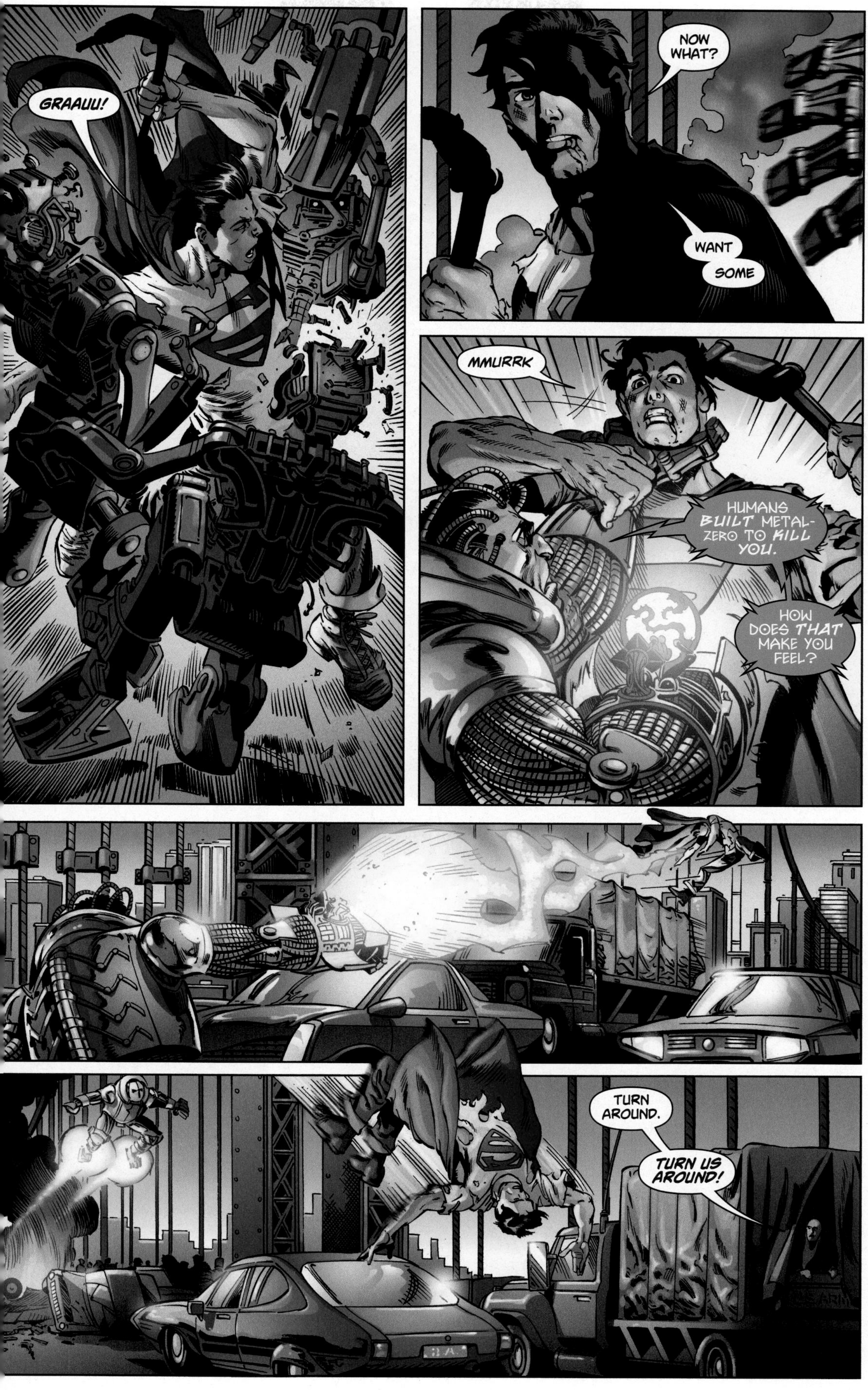
GRAAUU!
NOW WHAT?
WANT
SOME
MMURRK
HUMANS BUILT METAL-ZERO TO KILL YOU.
HOW DOES THAT MAKE YOU FEEL?
TURN AROUND.
TURN US AROUND!

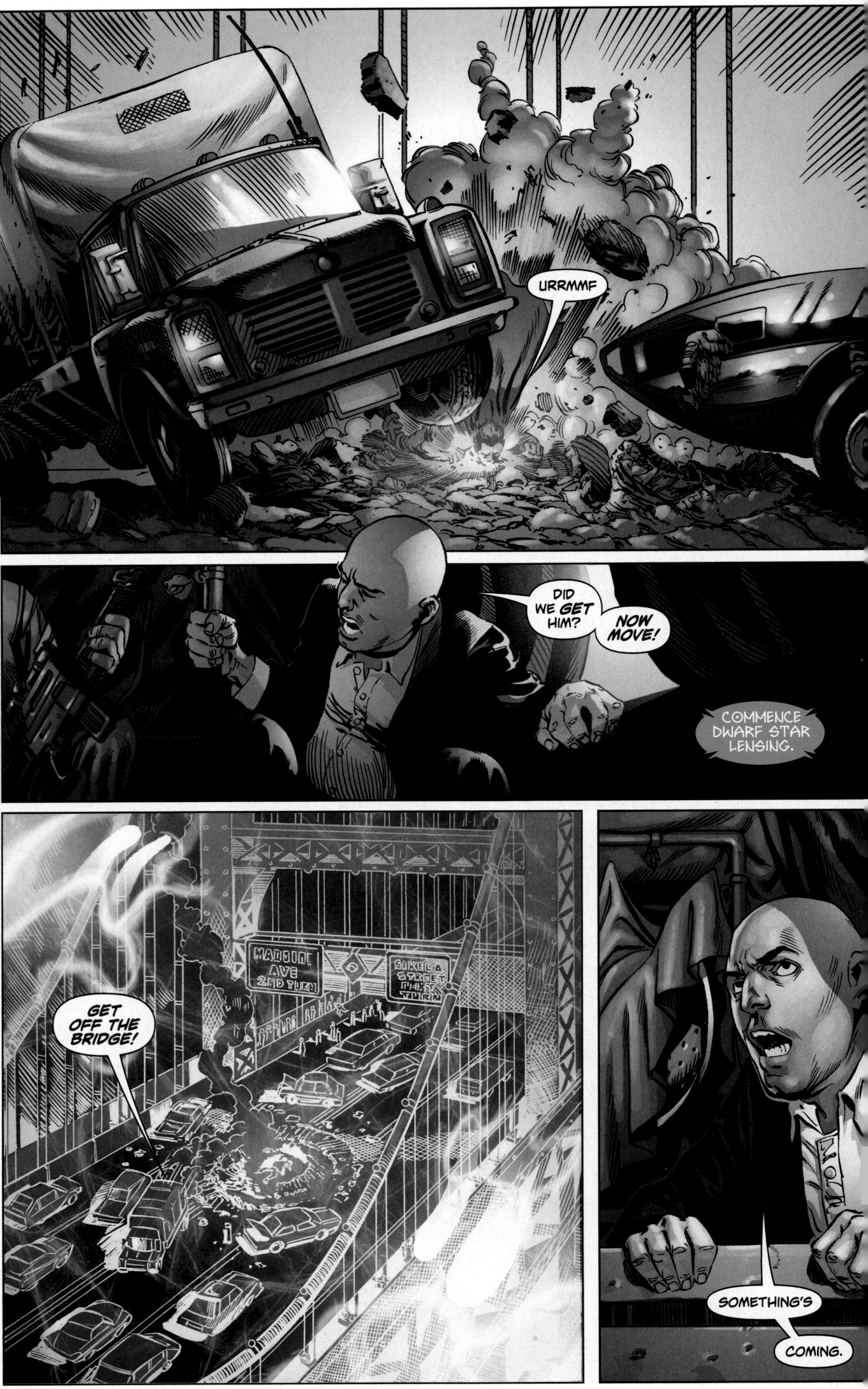
URRMMF
DID WE GET HIM?
NOW MOVE!
COMMENCE DWARF STAR LENSING.
GET OFF THE BRIDGE!
SOMETHING'S
COMING.

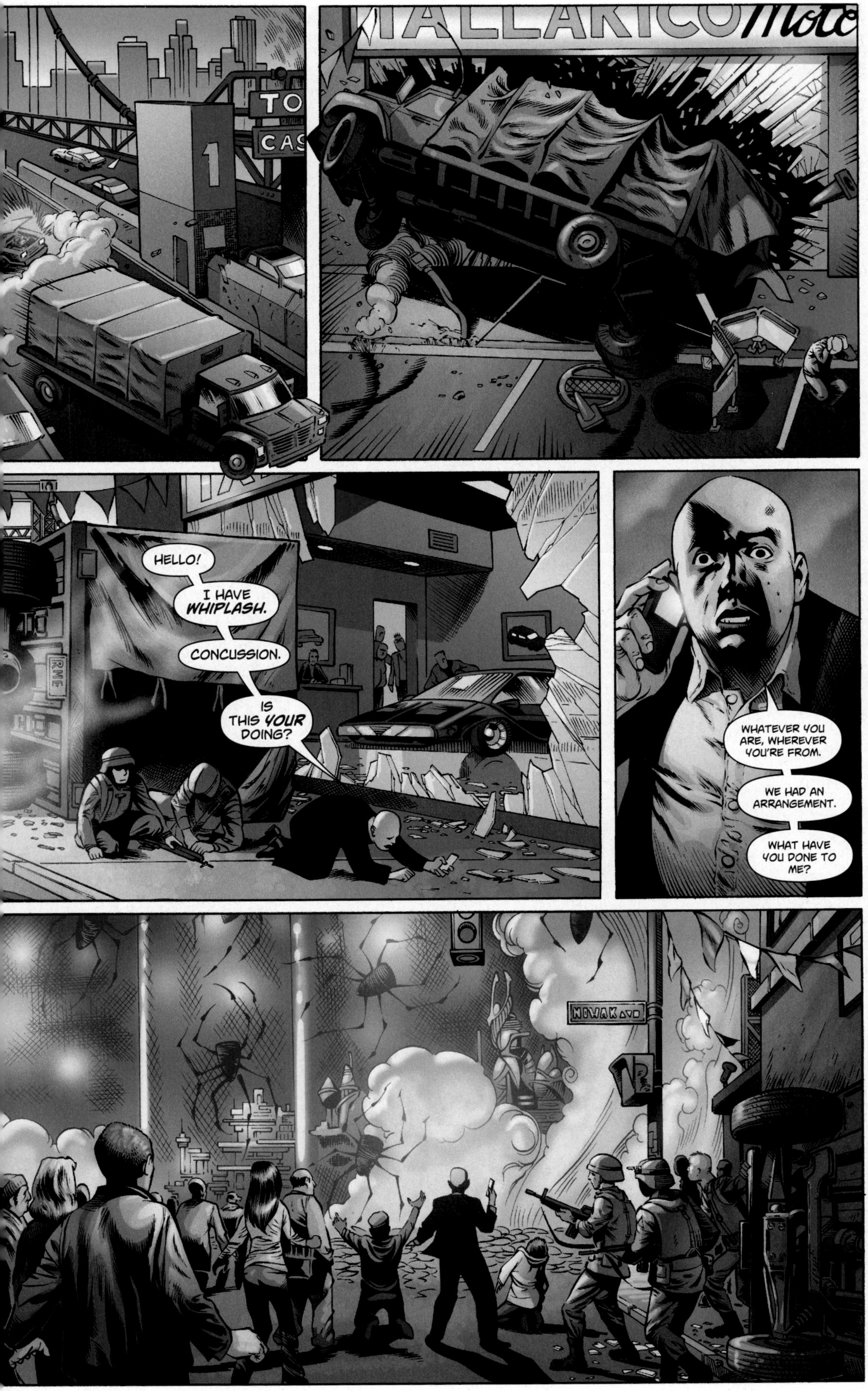
TO
CAS
ALLARICO Moto
HELLO!
I HAVE WHIPLASH.
CONCUSSION.
IS THIS YOUR DOING?
RME
WHATEVER YOU ARE, WHEREVER YOU'RE FROM.
WE HAD AN ARRANGEMENT.
WHAT HAVE YOU DONE TO ME?
NOVAK AVE

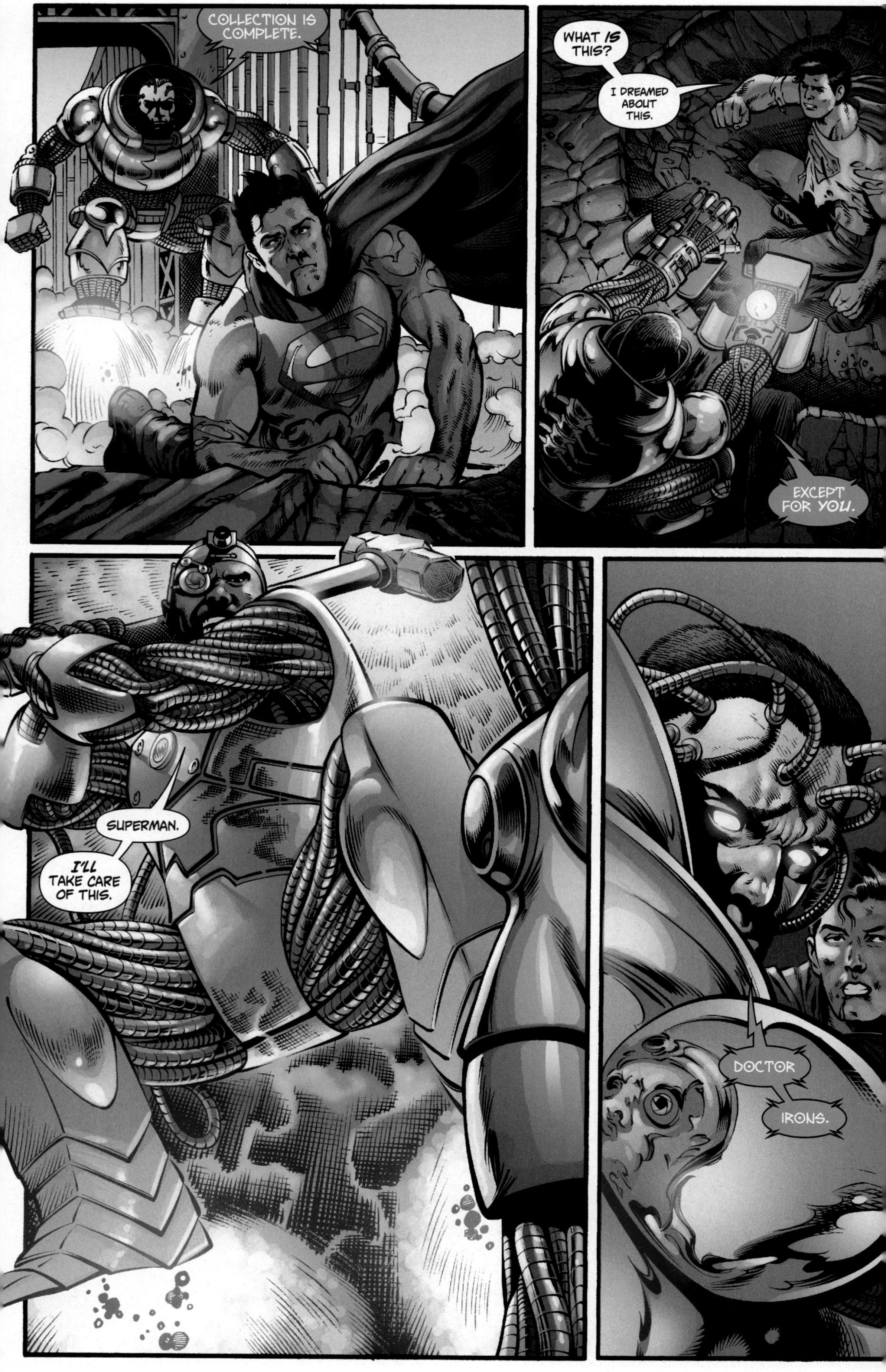
COLLECTION IS COMPLETE.
WHAT IS THIS?
I DREAMED ABOUT THIS.
EXCEPT FOR YOU.
SUPERMAN.
I'LL TAKE CARE OF THIS.
DOCTOR
IRONS.

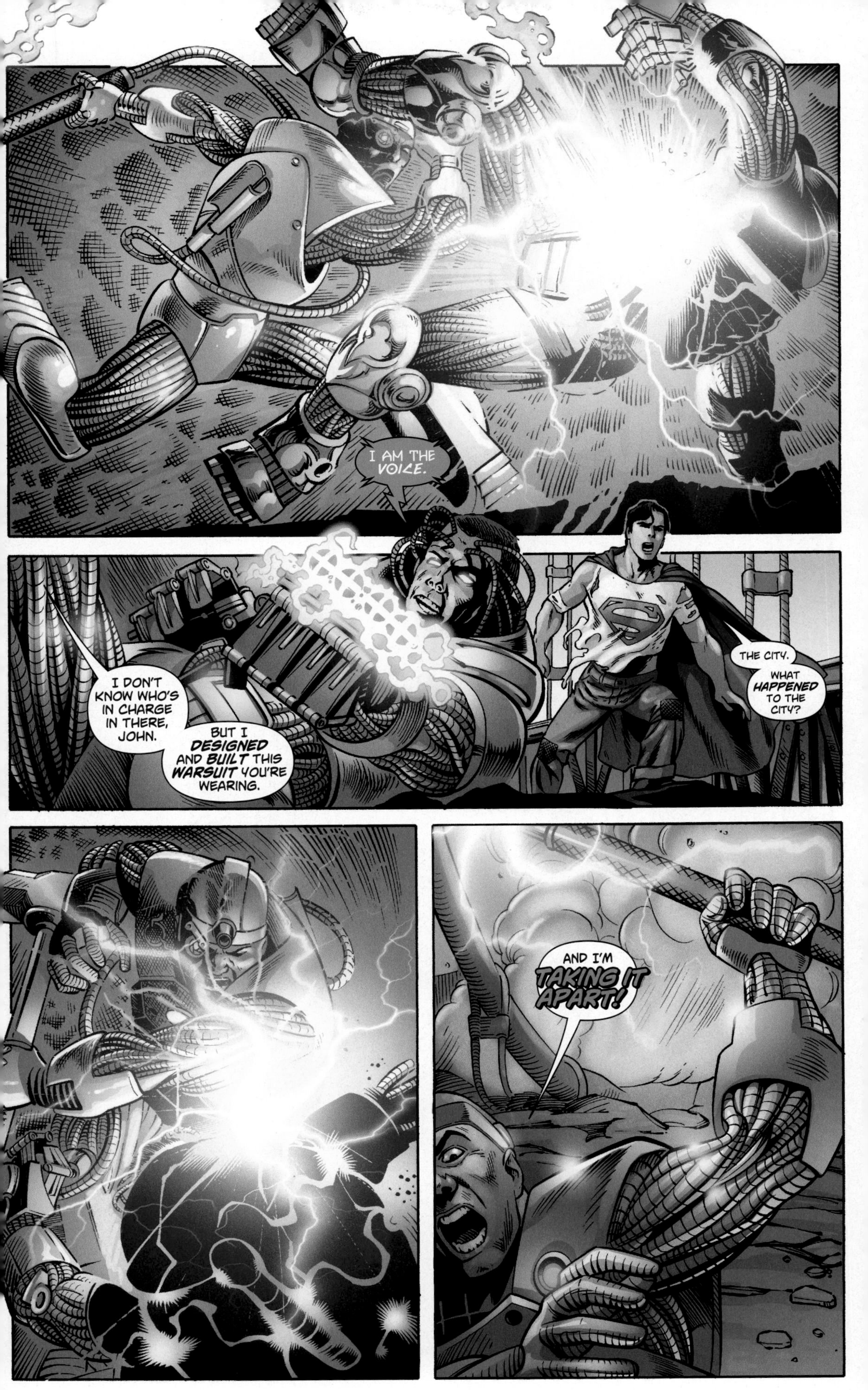
I AM THE VOICE.
I DON'T KNOW WHO'S IN CHARGE IN THERE, JOHN.
BUT I DESIGNED AND BUILT THIS WARSUIT YOU'RE WEARING.
THE CITY.
WHAT HAPPENED TO THE CITY?
AND I'M TAKING IT APART!

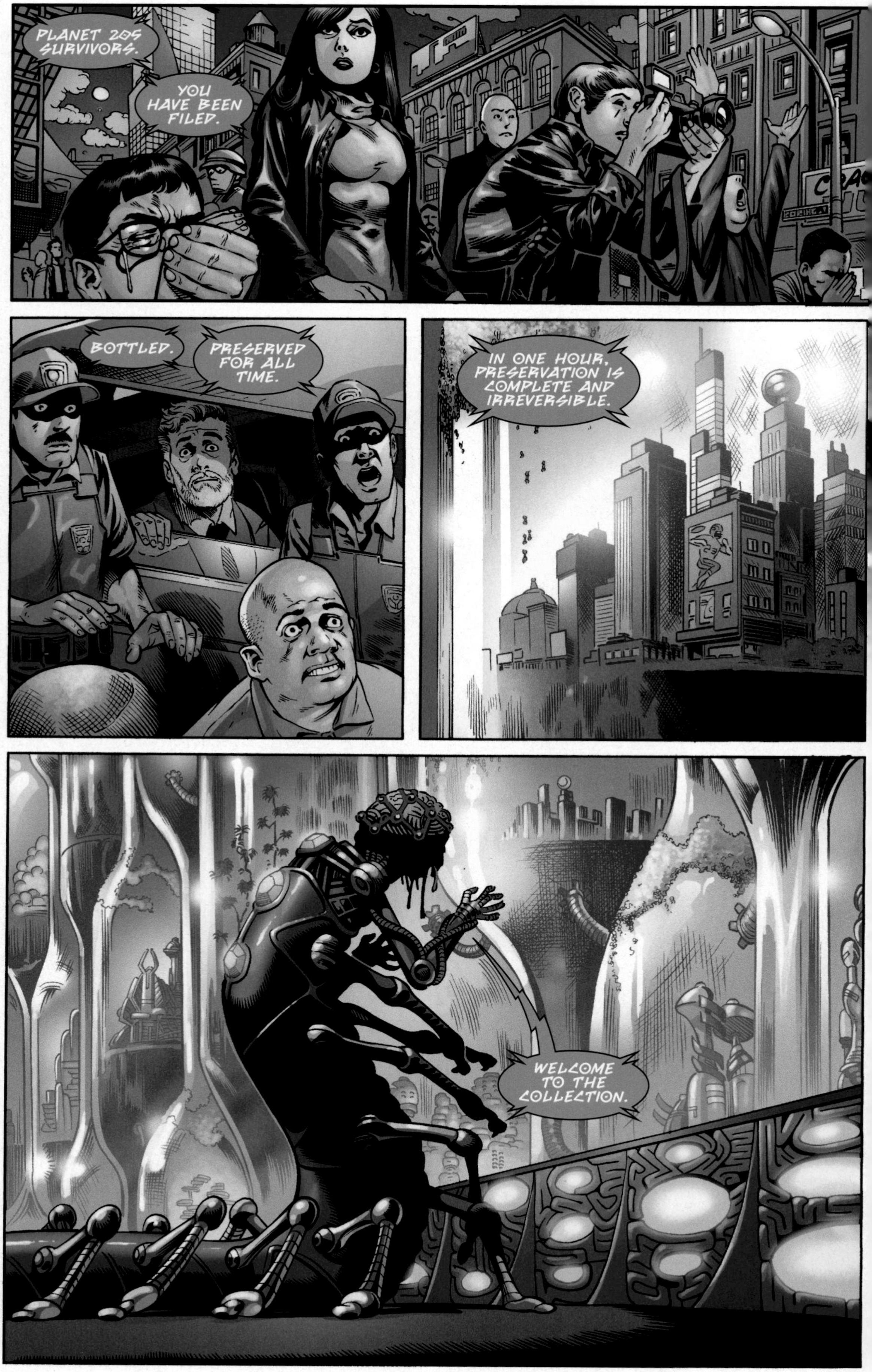
PLANET 205 SURVIVORS.
YOU HAVE BEEN FILED.
BOTTLED.
PRESERVED FOR ALL TIME.
IN ONE HOUR, PRESERVATION IS COMPLETE AND IRREVERSIBLE.
WELCOME TO THE COLLECTION.

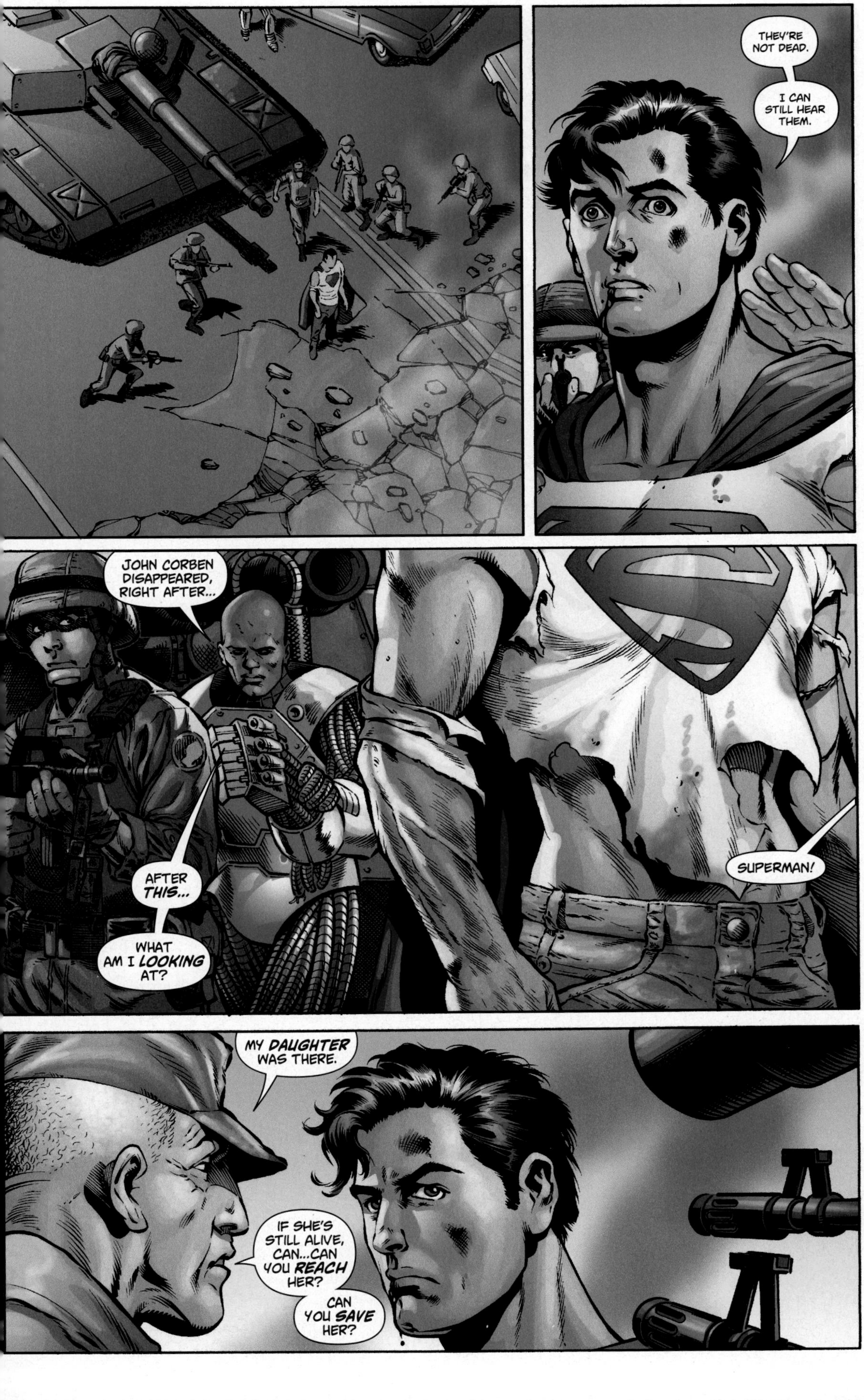
THEY'RE NOT DEAD.
I CAN STILL HEAR THEM.
JOHN CORBEN DISAPPEARED, RIGHT AFTER...
AFTER *THIS*...
WHAT AM I *LOOKING* AT?
SUPERMAN!
MY *DAUGHTER* WAS THERE.
IF SHE'S STILL ALIVE, CAN...CAN YOU *REACH* HER?
CAN YOU *SAVE* HER?

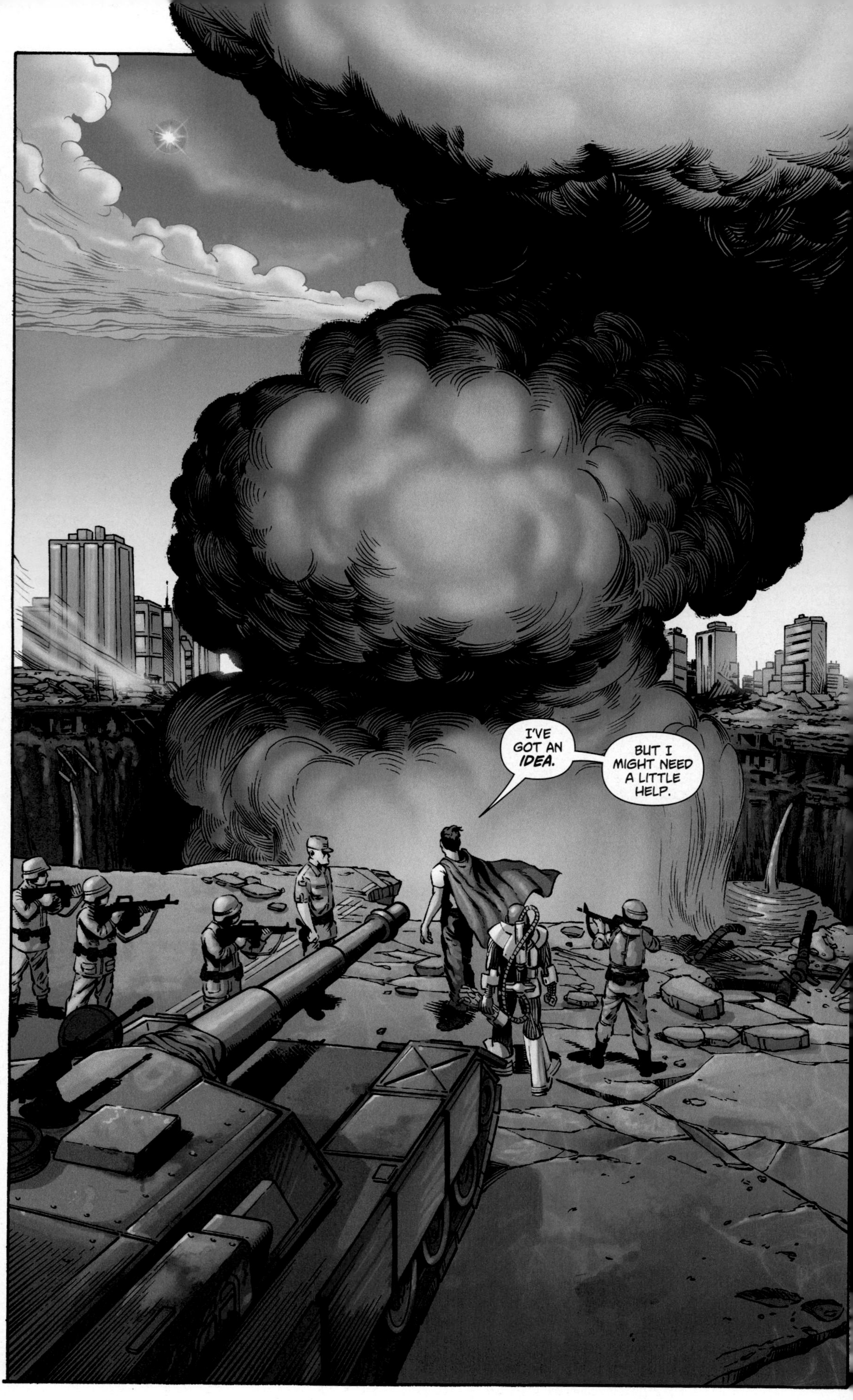
I'VE GOT AN IDEA.
BUT I MIGHT NEED A LITTLE HELP.

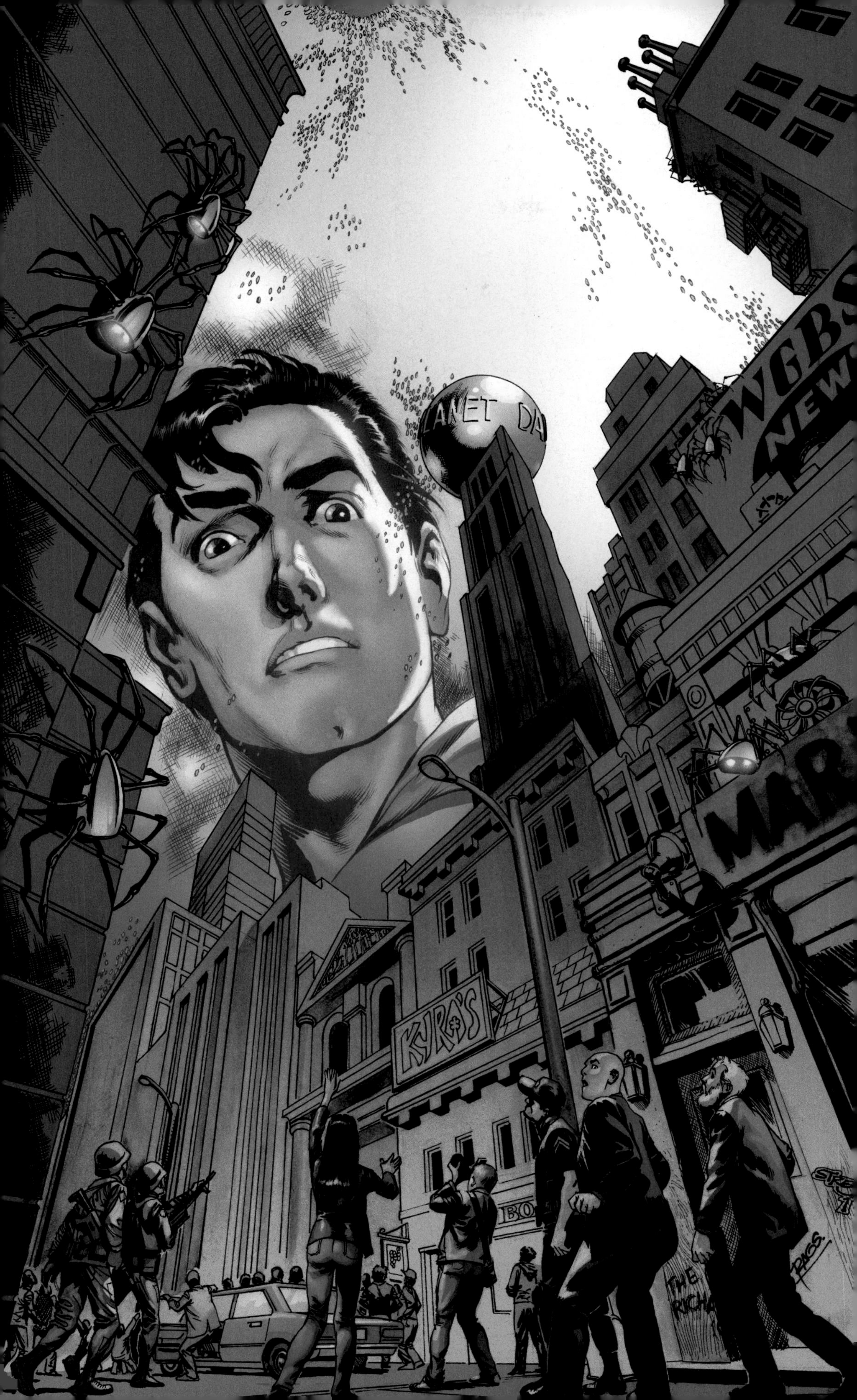
WGBS
KYRA'S

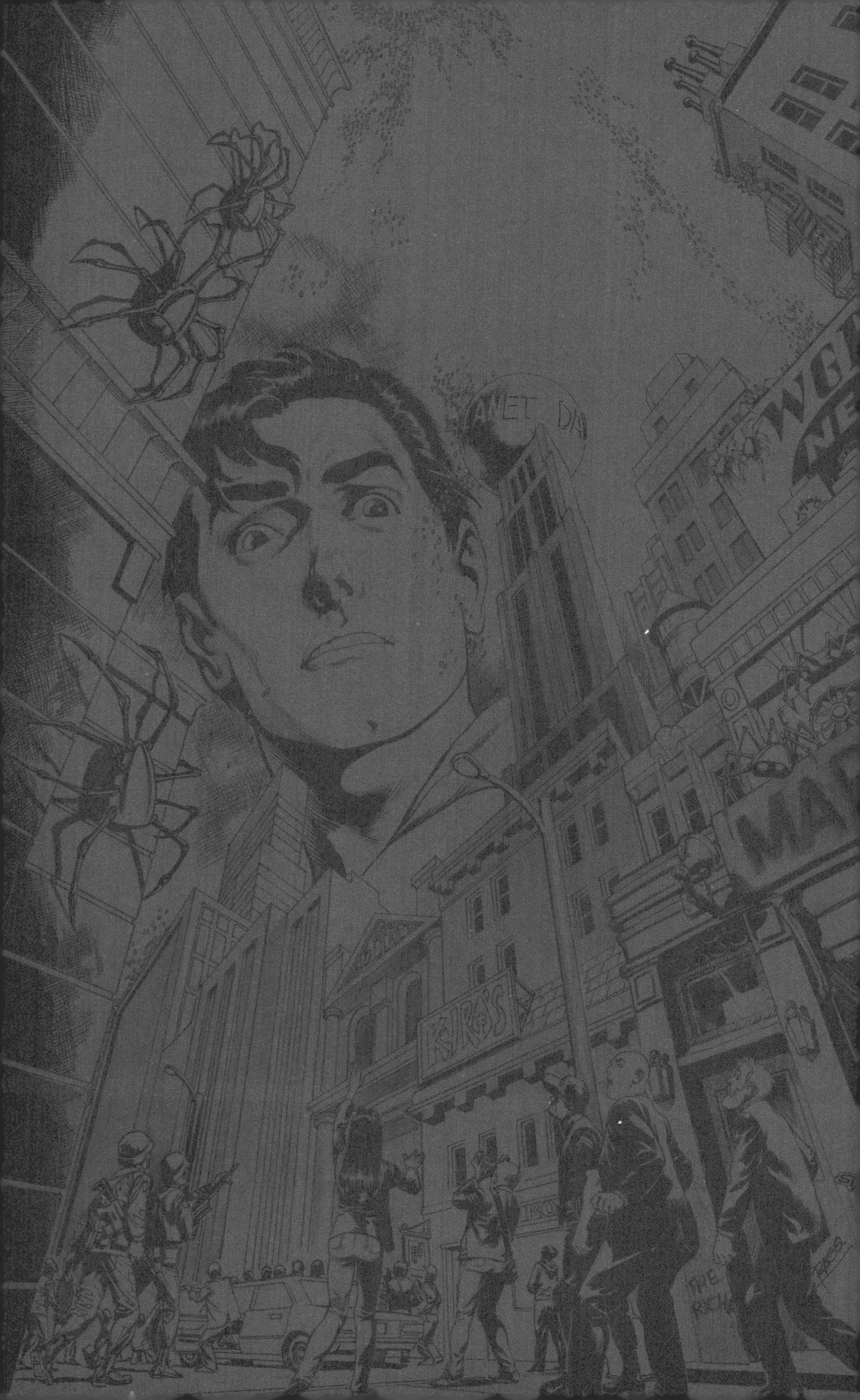

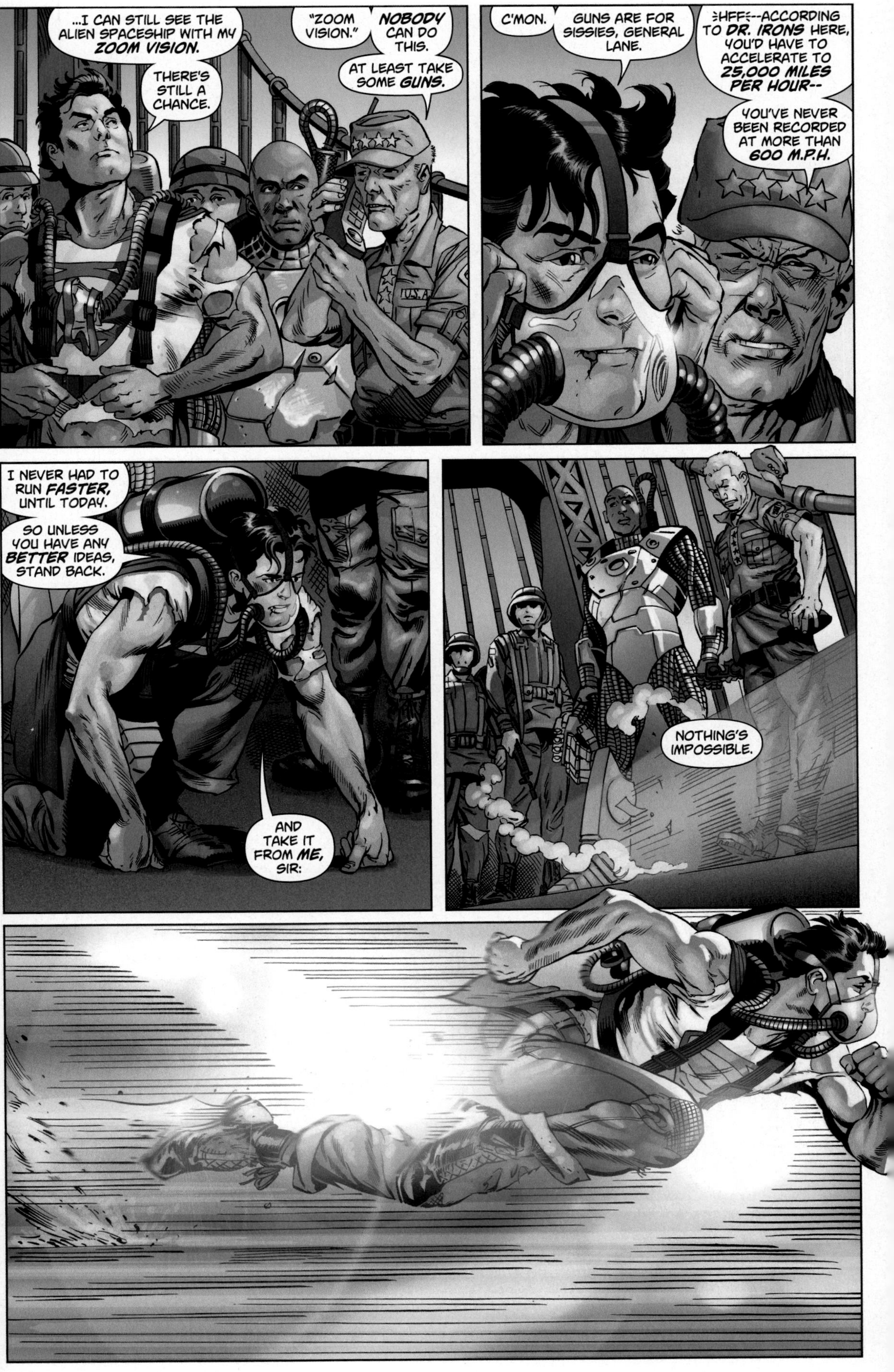

...I CAN STILL SEE THE ALIEN SPACESHIP WITH MY ZOOM VISION.
THERE'S STILL A CHANCE.
"ZOOM VISION."
NOBODY CAN DO THIS.
AT LEAST TAKE SOME GUNS.
C'MON.
GUNS ARE FOR SISSIES, GENERAL LANE.
HFF--ACCORDING TO DR. IRONS HERE, YOU'D HAVE TO ACCELERATE TO 25,000 MILES PER HOUR--
YOU'VE NEVER BEEN RECORDED AT MORE THAN 600 M.P.H.
I NEVER HAD TO RUN FASTER, UNTIL TODAY.
SO UNLESS YOU HAVE ANY BETTER IDEAS, STAND BACK.
AND TAKE IT FROM ME, SIR:
NOTHING'S IMPOSSIBLE.

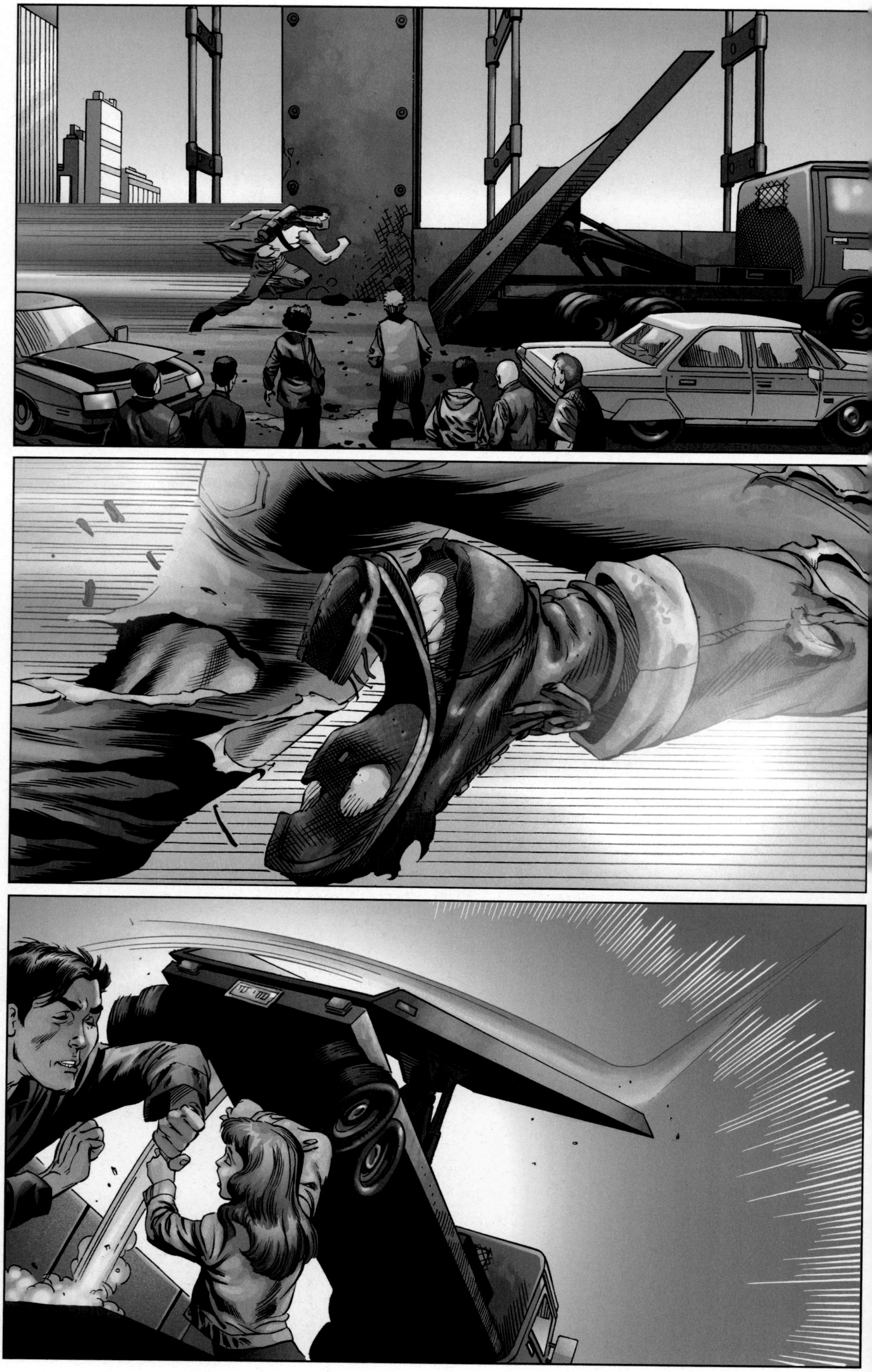

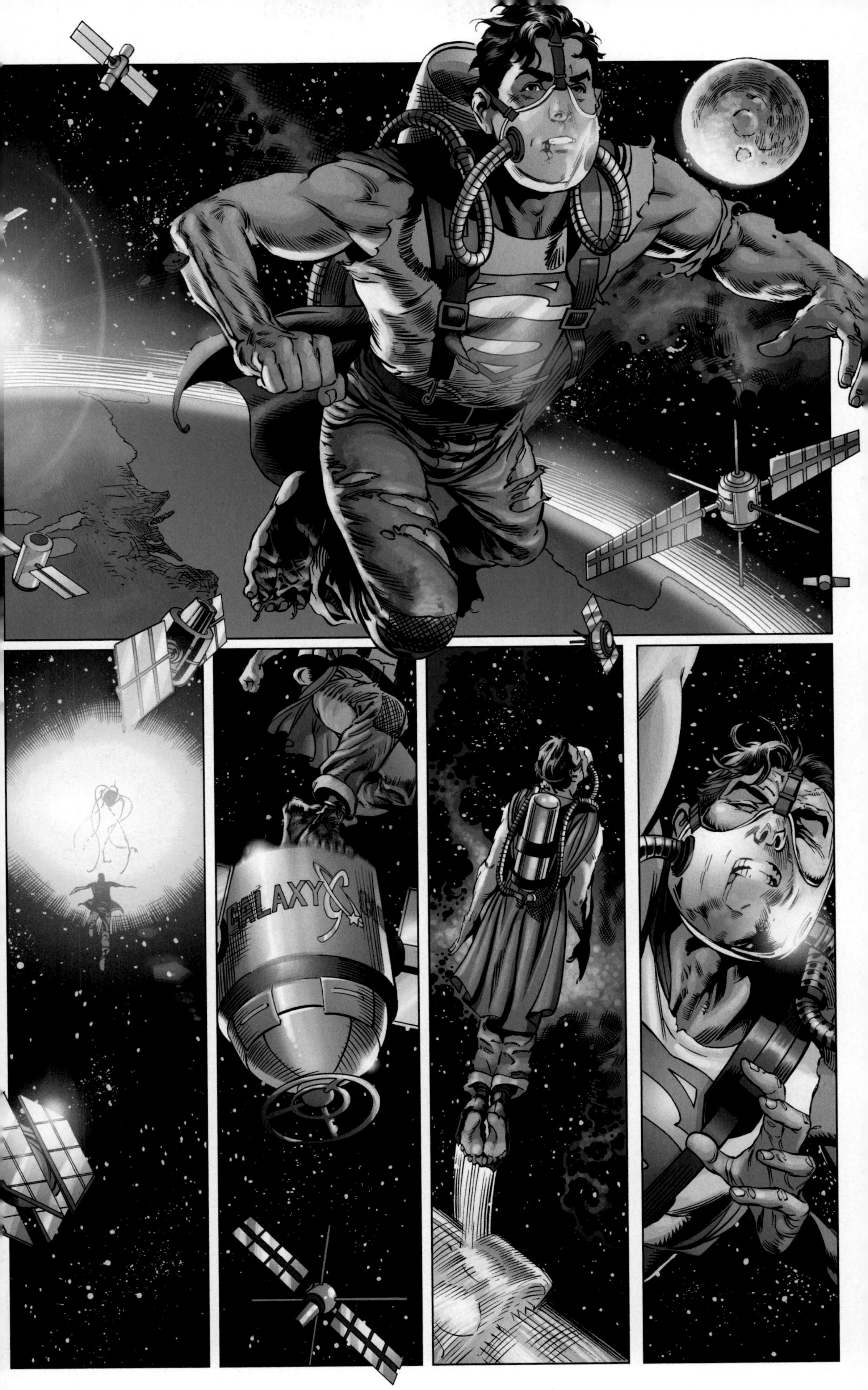
GALAXY

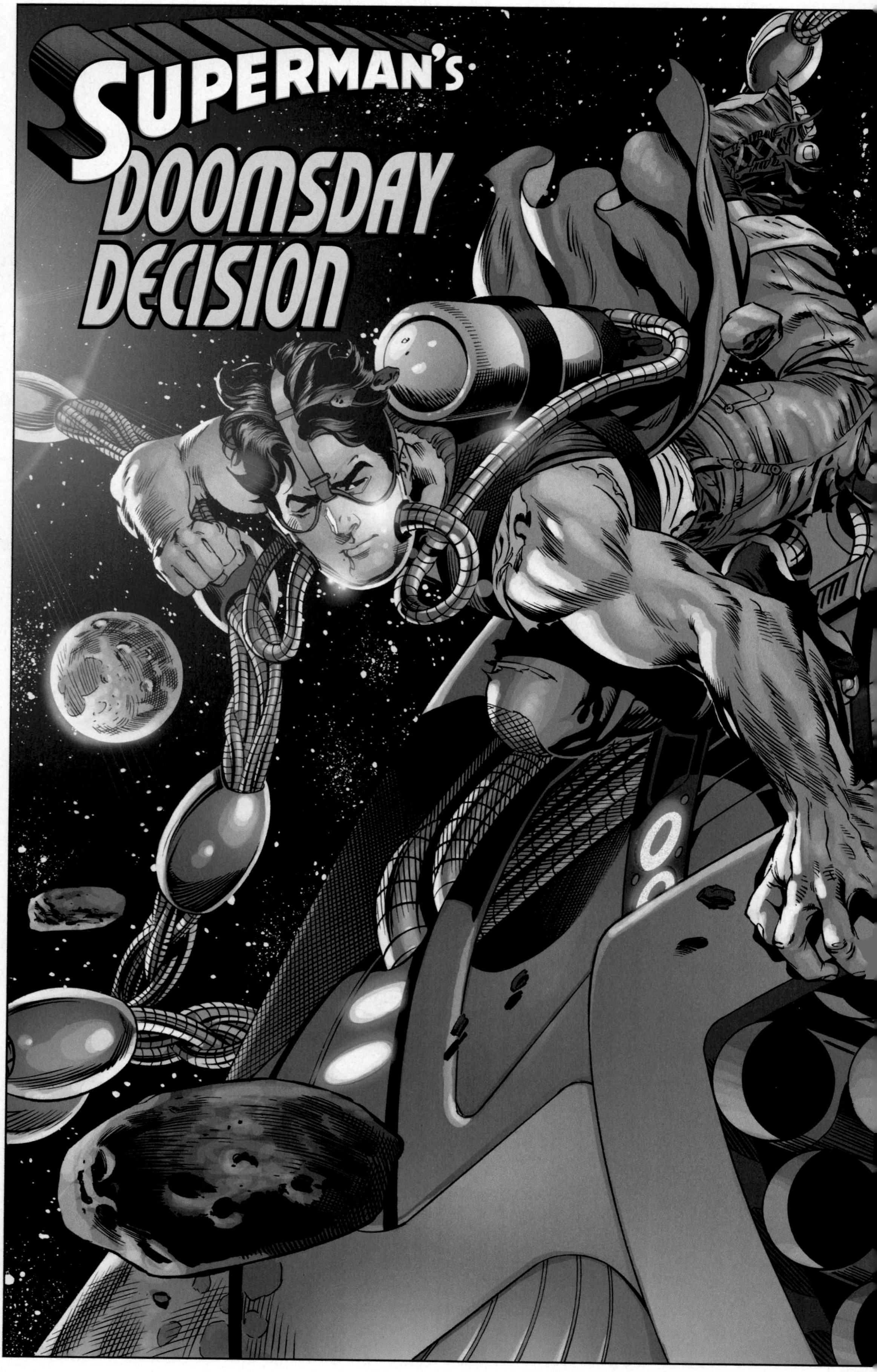
SUPERMAN'S
DOOMSDAY
DECISION

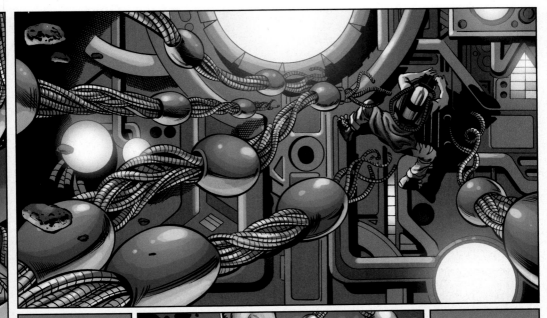

GRANT
MORRISON
WRITER
RAGS
MORALES
PENCILLER
RICK
BRYANT
INKER
BRAD
ANDERSON
COLORIST
PATRICK
BROSSEAU
LETTERER

RAGS
MORALES &
BRAD
ANDERSON
COVER
WIL
MOSS
ASSOC. EDITOR
MATT
IDELSON
EDITOR

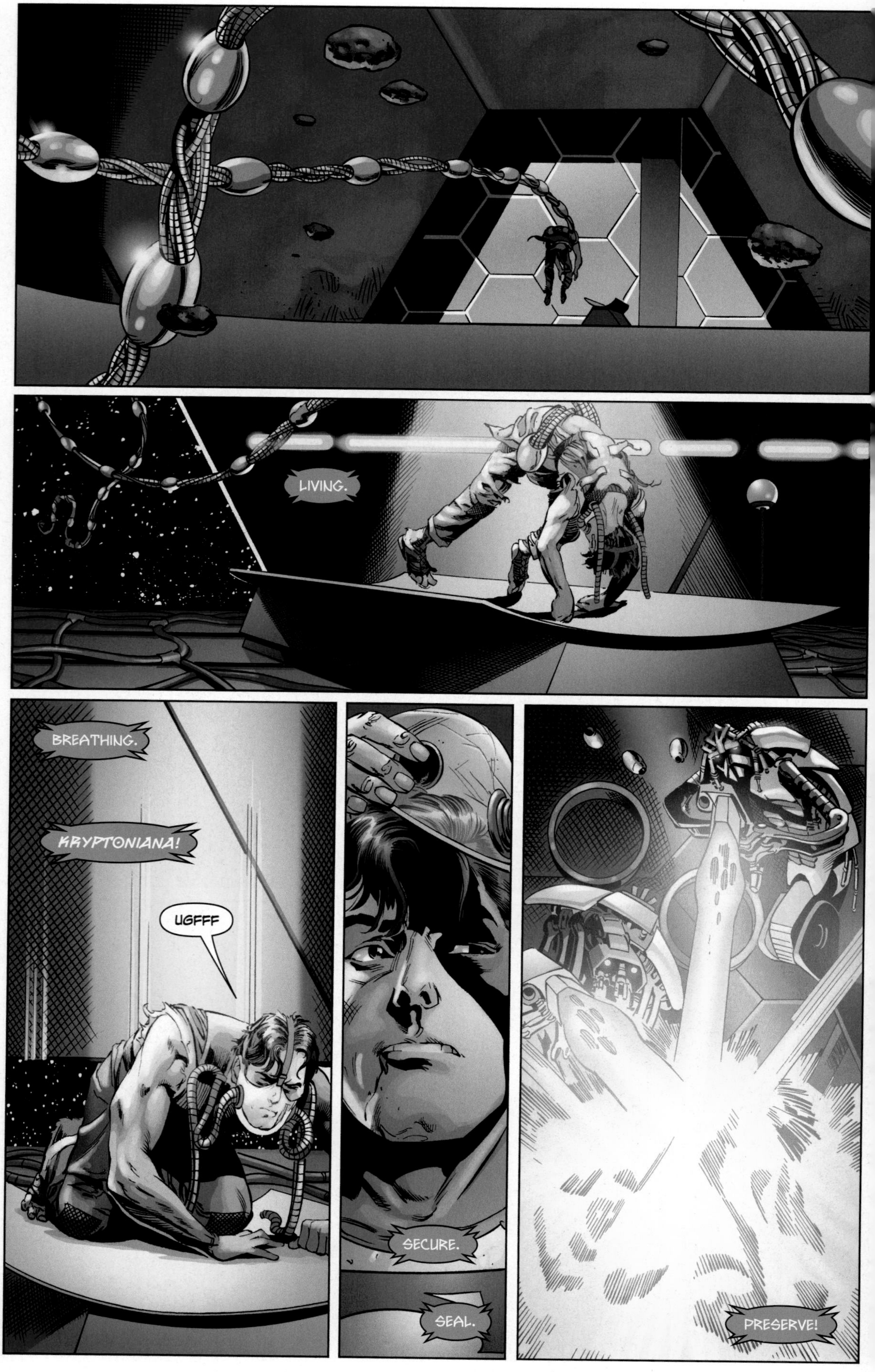
LIVING.
BREATHING.
KRYPTONIANA!
UGFFF
SECURE.
SEAL.
PRESERVE!

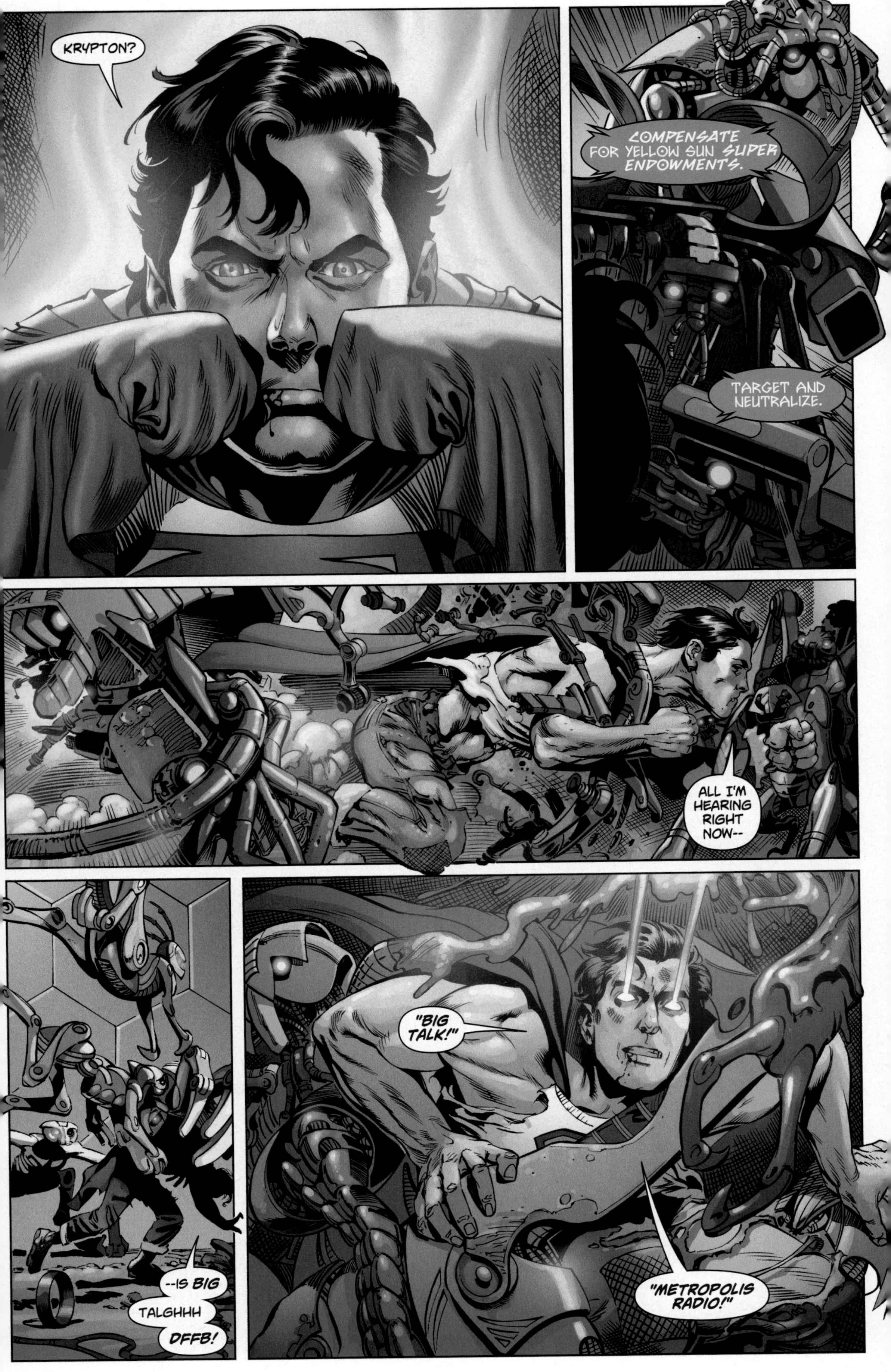
KRYPTON?
COMPENSATE FOR YELLOW SUN SUPER ENDOWMENTS.
TARGET AND NEUTRALIZE.
ALL I'M HEARING RIGHT NOW--
--IS BIG
TALGHHH
DFFB!
"BIG TALK!"
"METROPOLIS RADIO!"

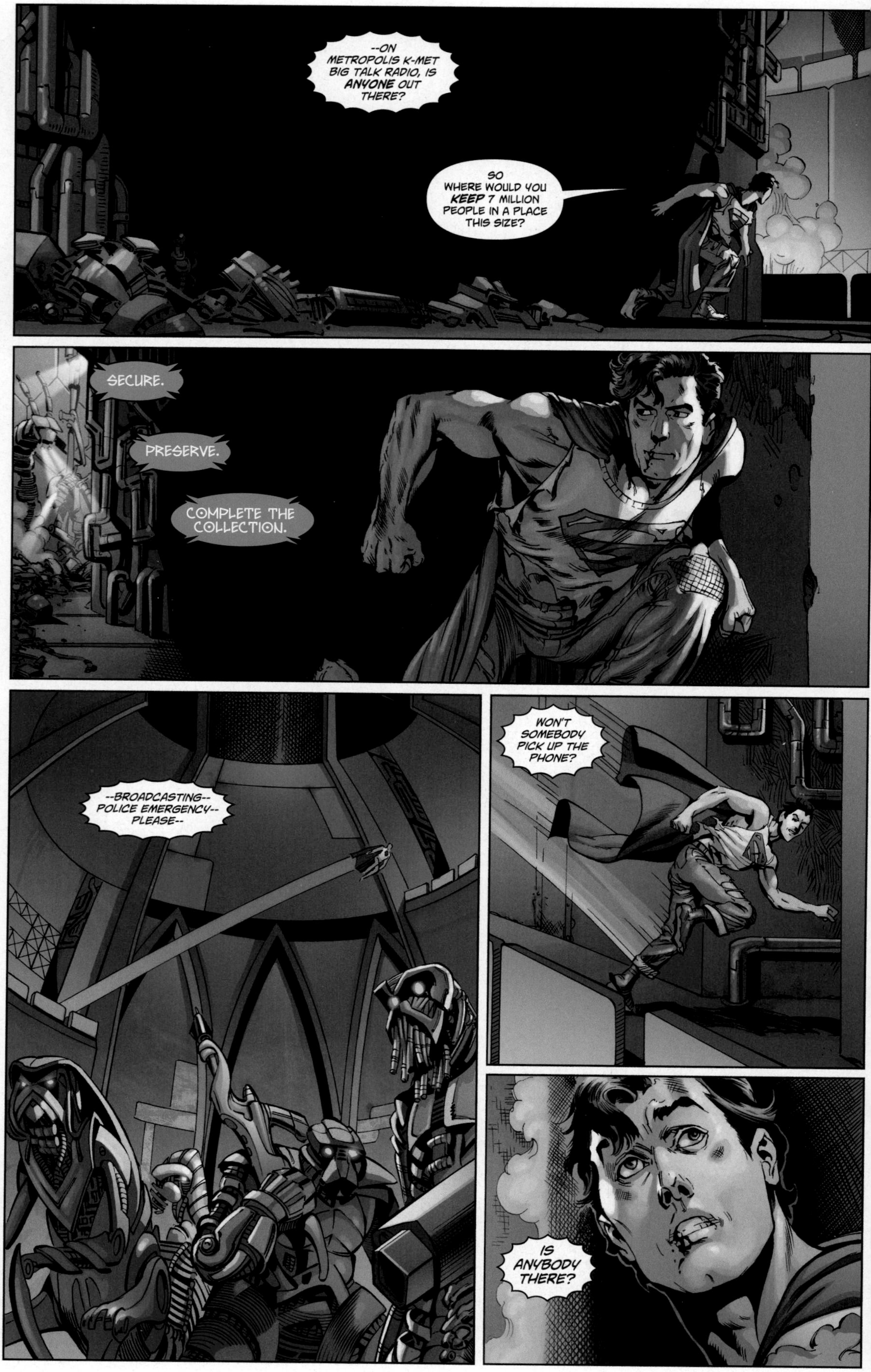
--ON METROPOLIS K-MET BIG TALK RADIO, IS ANYONE OUT THERE?
SO WHERE WOULD YOU KEEP 7 MILLION PEOPLE IN A PLACE THIS SIZE?
SECURE.
PRESERVE.
COMPLETE THE COLLECTION.
--BROADCASTING-- POLICE EMERGENCY-- PLEASE--
WON'T SOMEBODY PICK UP THE PHONE?
IS ANYBODY THERE?

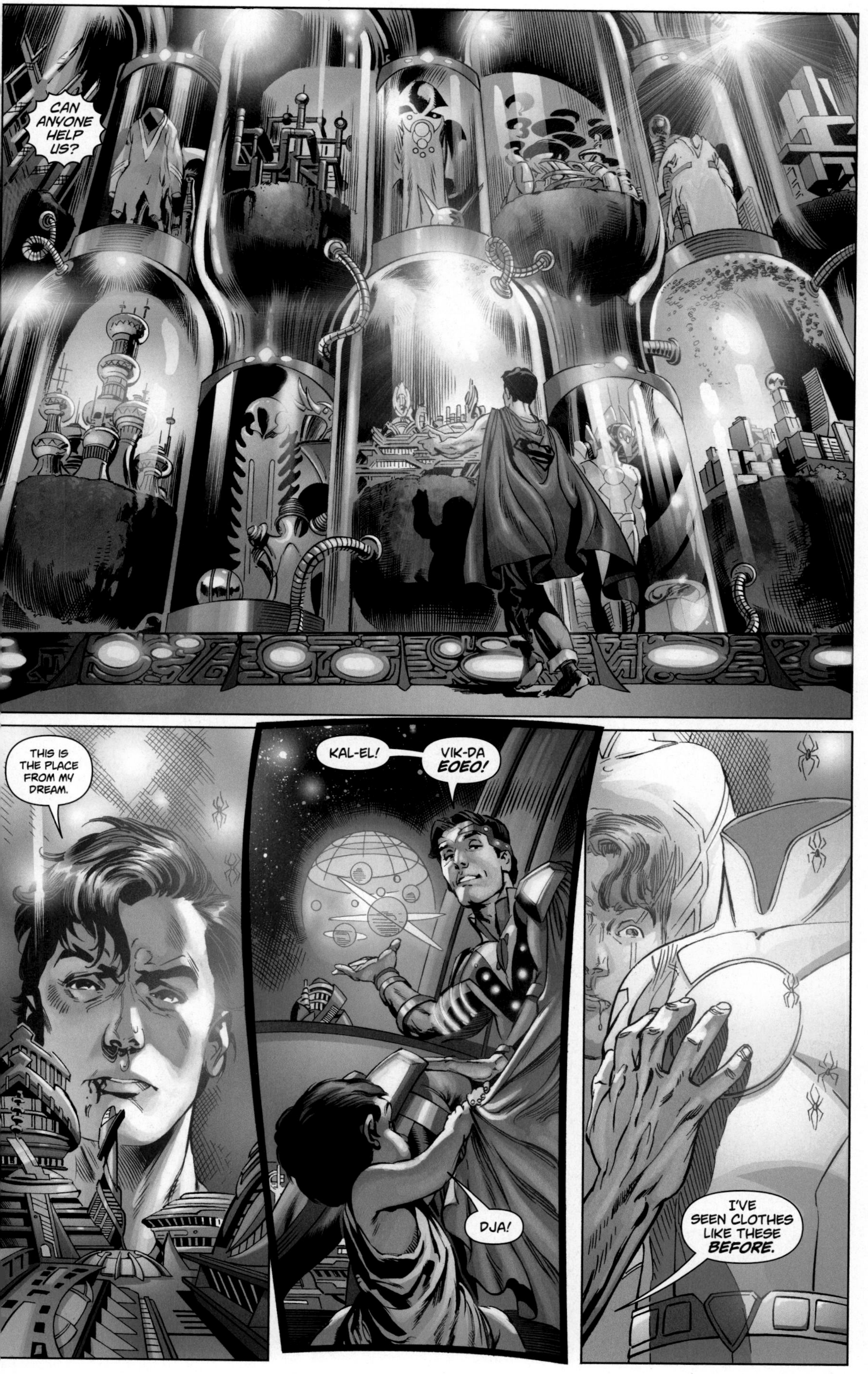
CAN ANYONE HELP US?
THIS IS THE PLACE FROM MY DREAM.
KAL-EL!
VIK-DA EOEO!
DJA!
I'VE SEEN CLOTHES LIKE THESE BEFORE.

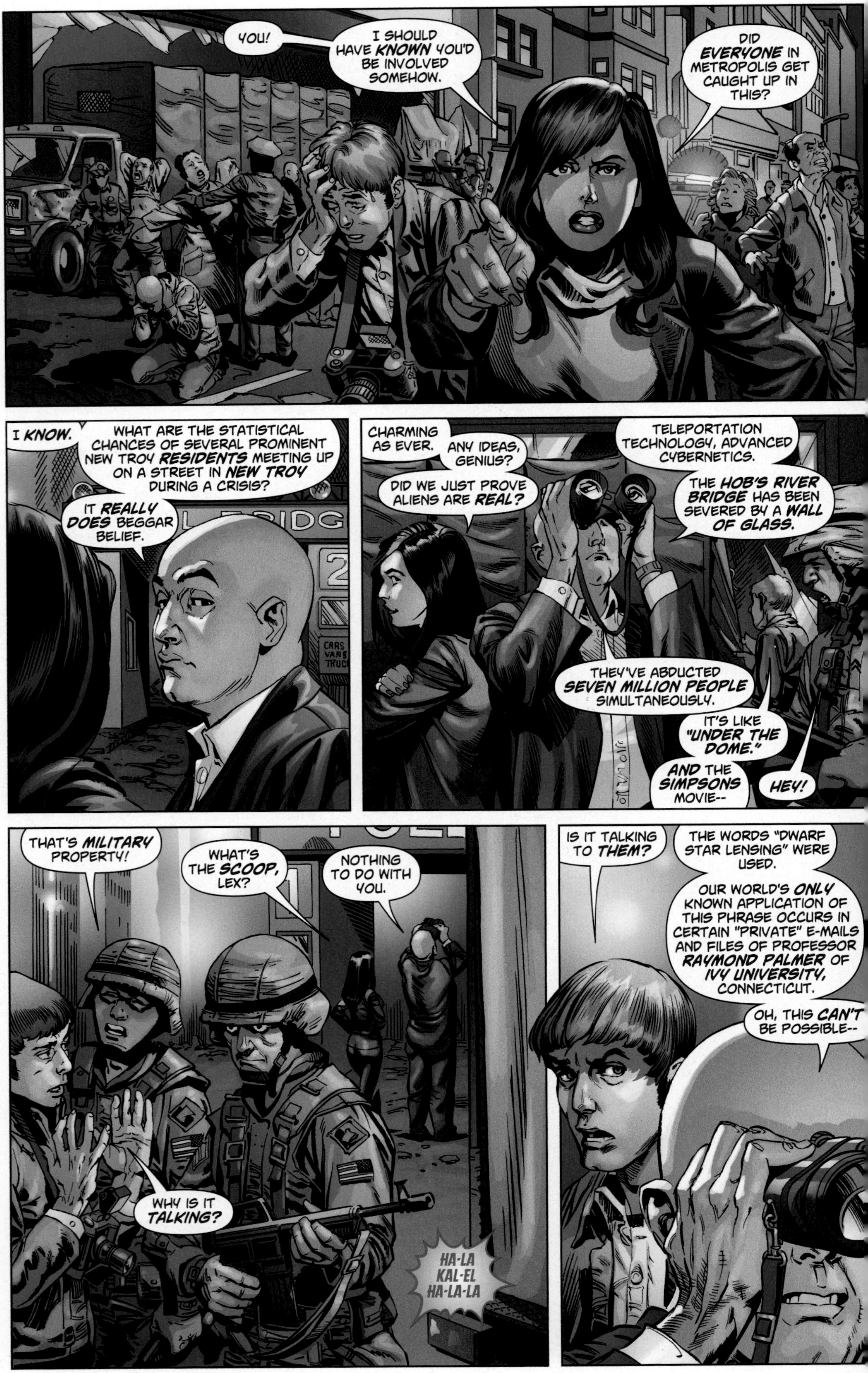
YOU!
I SHOULD HAVE KNOWN YOU'D BE INVOLVED SOMEHOW.
DID EVERYONE IN METROPOLIS GET CAUGHT UP IN THIS?
I KNOW.
WHAT ARE THE STATISTICAL CHANCES OF SEVERAL PROMINENT NEW TROY RESIDENTS MEETING UP ON A STREET IN NEW TROY DURING A CRISIS?
IT REALLY DOES BEGGAR BELIEF.
CHARMING AS EVER.
ANY IDEAS, GENIUS?
DID WE JUST PROVE ALIENS ARE REAL?
TELEPORTATION TECHNOLOGY, ADVANCED CYBERNETICS.
THE HOB'S RIVER BRIDGE HAS BEEN SEVERED BY A WALL OF GLASS.
THEY'VE ABDUCTED SEVEN MILLION PEOPLE SIMULTANEOUSLY.
IT'S LIKE "UNDER THE DOME."
AND THE SIMPSONS MOVIE--
HEY!
THAT'S MILITARY PROPERTY!
WHAT'S THE SCOOP, LEX?
NOTHING TO DO WITH YOU.
WHY IS IT TALKING?
HA-LA KAL-EL HA-LA-LA
IS IT TALKING TO THEM?
THE WORDS "DWARF STAR LENSING" WERE USED.
OUR WORLD'S ONLY KNOWN APPLICATION OF THIS PHRASE OCCURS IN CERTAIN "PRIVATE" E-MAILS AND FILES OF PROFESSOR RAYMOND PALMER OF IVY UNIVERSITY, CONNECTICUT.
OH, THIS CAN'T BE POSSIBLE--

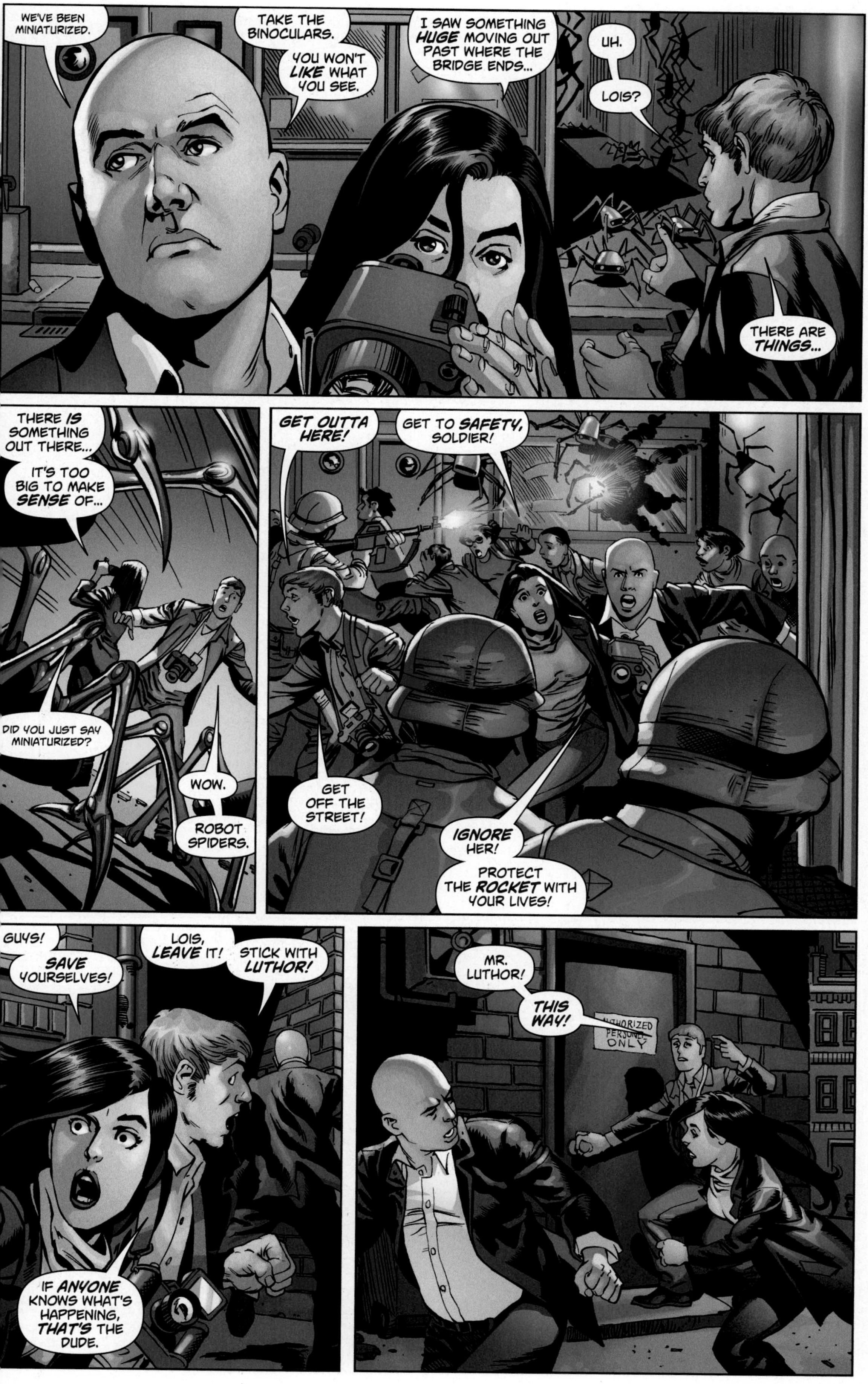
WE'VE BEEN MINIATURIZED.
TAKE THE BINOCULARS.
YOU WON'T LIKE WHAT YOU SEE.
I SAW SOMETHING HUGE MOVING OUT PAST WHERE THE BRIDGE ENDS...
UH.
LOIS?
THERE ARE THINGS...
THERE IS SOMETHING OUT THERE...
IT'S TOO BIG TO MAKE SENSE OF...
DID YOU JUST SAY MINIATURIZED?
WOW.
ROBOT SPIDERS.
GET OUTTA HERE!
GET TO SAFETY, SOLDIER!
GET OFF THE STREET!
IGNORE HER!
PROTECT THE ROCKET WITH YOUR LIVES!
GUYS!
SAVE YOURSELVES!
LOIS, LEAVE IT!
STICK WITH LUTHOR!
IF ANYONE KNOWS WHAT'S HAPPENING, THAT'S THE DUDE.
MR. LUTHOR!
THIS WAY!
ONLY

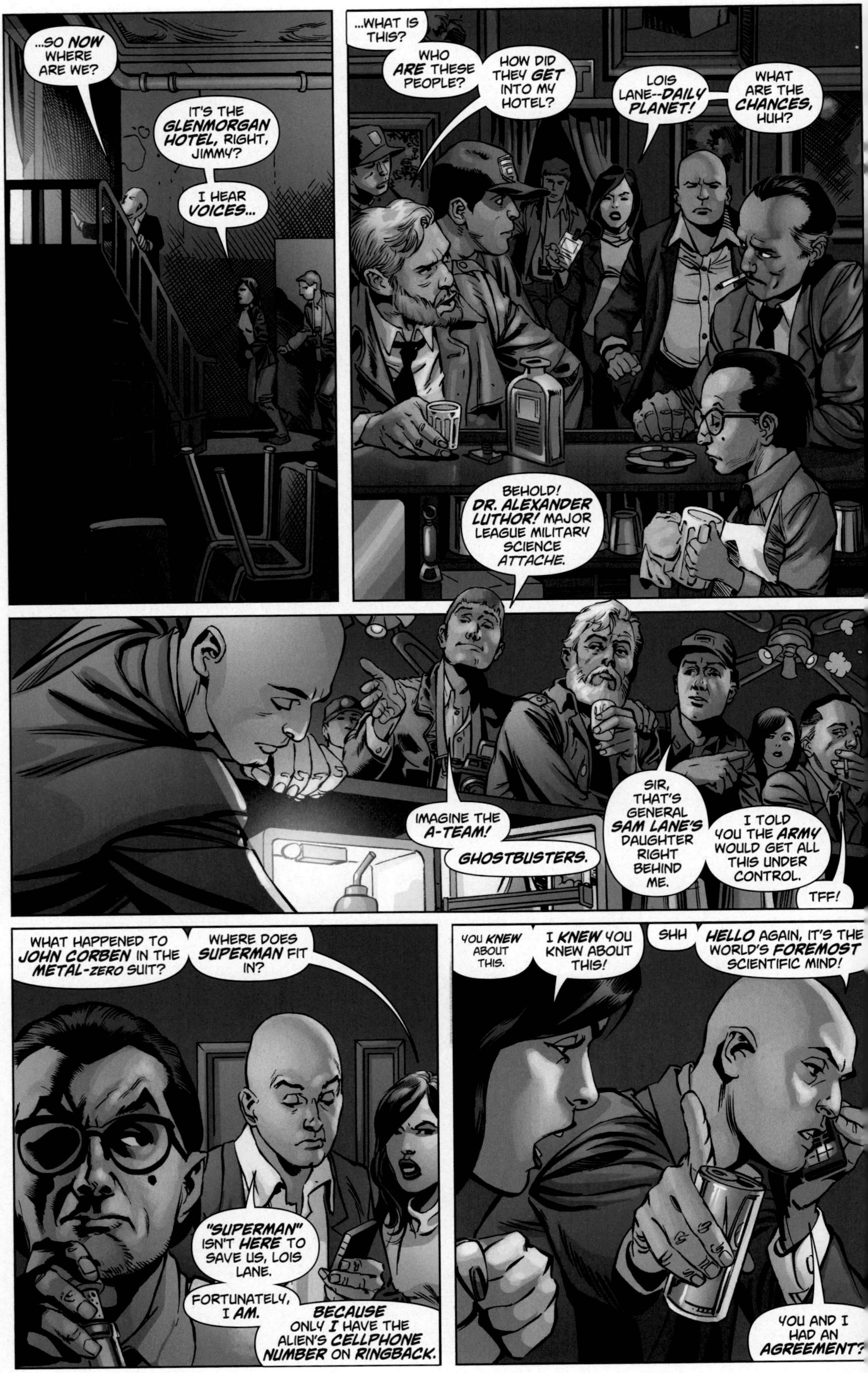
...SO NOW WHERE ARE WE?
IT'S THE GLENMORGAN HOTEL, RIGHT, JIMMY?
I HEAR VOICES...
...WHAT IS THIS?
WHO ARE THESE PEOPLE?
HOW DID THEY GET INTO MY HOTEL?
LOIS LANE--DAILY PLANET!
WHAT ARE THE CHANCES, HUH?
BEHOLD! DR. ALEXANDER LUTHOR! MAJOR LEAGUE MILITARY SCIENCE ATTACHE.
IMAGINE THE A-TEAM!
GHOSTBUSTERS.
SIR, THAT'S GENERAL SAM LANE'S DAUGHTER RIGHT BEHIND ME.
I TOLD YOU THE ARMY WOULD GET ALL THIS UNDER CONTROL.
TFF!
WHAT HAPPENED TO JOHN CORBEN IN THE METAL-ZERO SUIT?
WHERE DOES SUPERMAN FIT IN?
"SUPERMAN" ISN'T HERE TO SAVE US, LOIS LANE.
FORTUNATELY, I AM.
BECAUSE ONLY I HAVE THE ALIEN'S CELLPHONE NUMBER ON RINGBACK.
YOU KNEW ABOUT THIS.
I KNEW YOU KNEW ABOUT THIS!
SHH
HELLO AGAIN, IT'S THE WORLD'S FOREMOST SCIENTIFIC MIND!
YOU AND I HAD AN AGREEMENT?

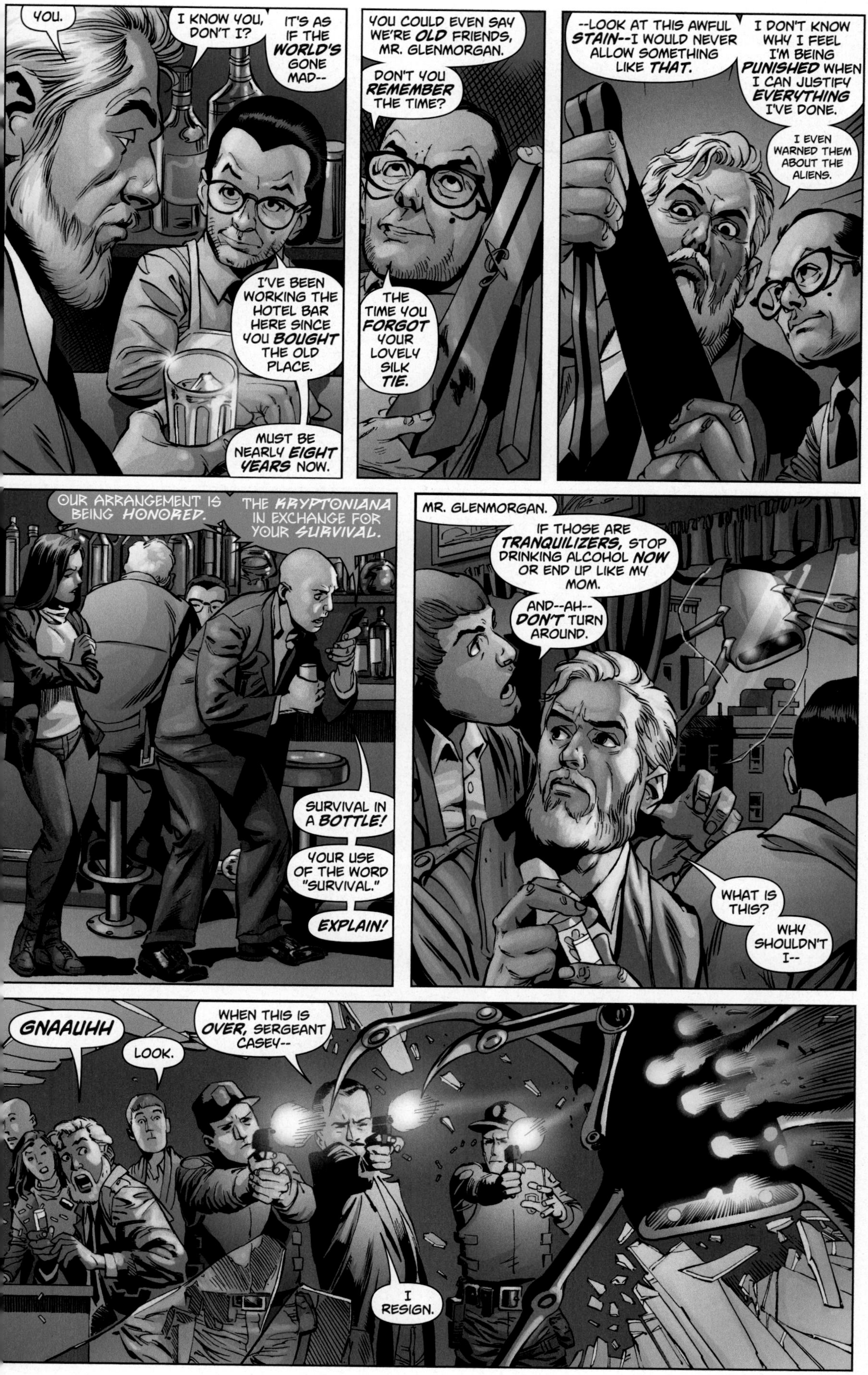
YOU.
I KNOW YOU, DON'T I?
IT'S AS IF THE WORLD'S GONE MAD--
I'VE BEEN WORKING THE HOTEL BAR HERE SINCE YOU BOUGHT THE OLD PLACE.
MUST BE NEARLY EIGHT YEARS NOW.
YOU COULD EVEN SAY WE'RE OLD FRIENDS, MR. GLENMORGAN.
DON'T YOU REMEMBER THE TIME?
THE TIME YOU FORGOT YOUR LOVELY SILK TIE.
--LOOK AT THIS AWFUL STAIN--I WOULD NEVER ALLOW SOMETHING LIKE THAT.
I DON'T KNOW WHY I FEEL I'M BEING PUNISHED WHEN I CAN JUSTIFY EVERYTHING I'VE DONE.
I EVEN WARNED THEM ABOUT THE ALIENS.
OUR ARRANGEMENT IS BEING HONORED.
THE KRYPTONIANA IN EXCHANGE FOR YOUR SURVIVAL.
SURVIVAL IN A BOTTLE!
YOUR USE OF THE WORD "SURVIVAL."
EXPLAIN!
MR. GLENMORGAN.
IF THOSE ARE TRANQUILIZERS, STOP DRINKING ALCOHOL NOW OR END UP LIKE MY MOM.
AND--AH--DON'T TURN AROUND.
WHAT IS THIS?
WHY SHOULDN'T I--
GNAAUHH
LOOK.
WHEN THIS IS OVER, SERGEANT CASEY--
I RESIGN.

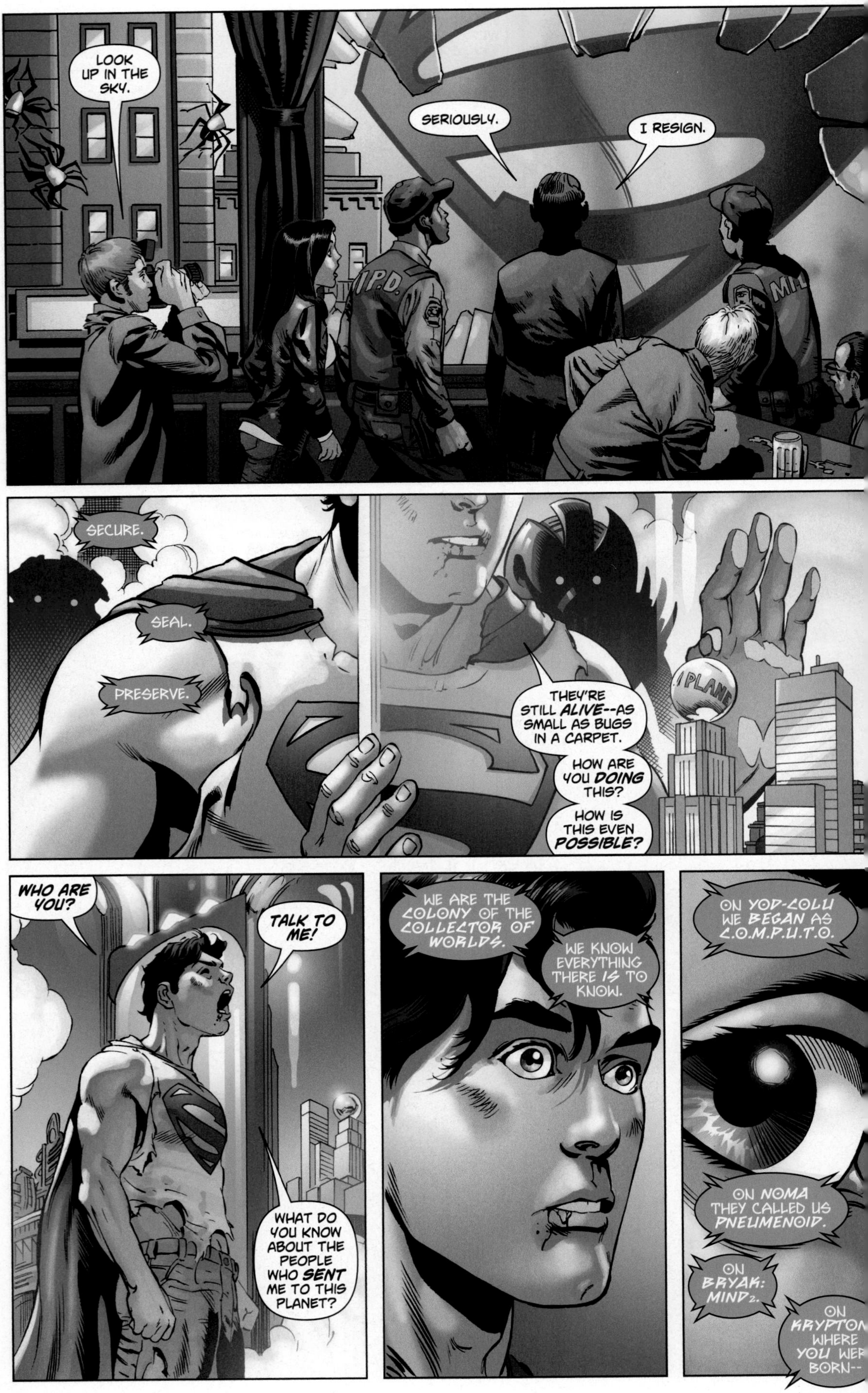
LOOK UP IN THE SKY.
SERIOUSLY.
I RESIGN.
SECURE.
SEAL.
PRESERVE.
THEY'RE STILL ALIVE--AS SMALL AS BUGS IN A CARPET.
HOW ARE YOU DOING THIS?
HOW IS THIS EVEN POSSIBLE?
WHO ARE YOU?
TALK TO ME!
WHAT DO YOU KNOW ABOUT THE PEOPLE WHO SENT ME TO THIS PLANET?
WE ARE THE COLONY OF THE COLLECTOR OF WORLDS.
WE KNOW EVERYTHING THERE IS TO KNOW.
ON YOD-COLU WE BEGAN AS C.O.M.P.U.T.O.
ON NOMA THEY CALLED US PNEUMENOID.
ON BRYAK: MIND2.
ON KRYPTON WHERE YOU WERE BORN--

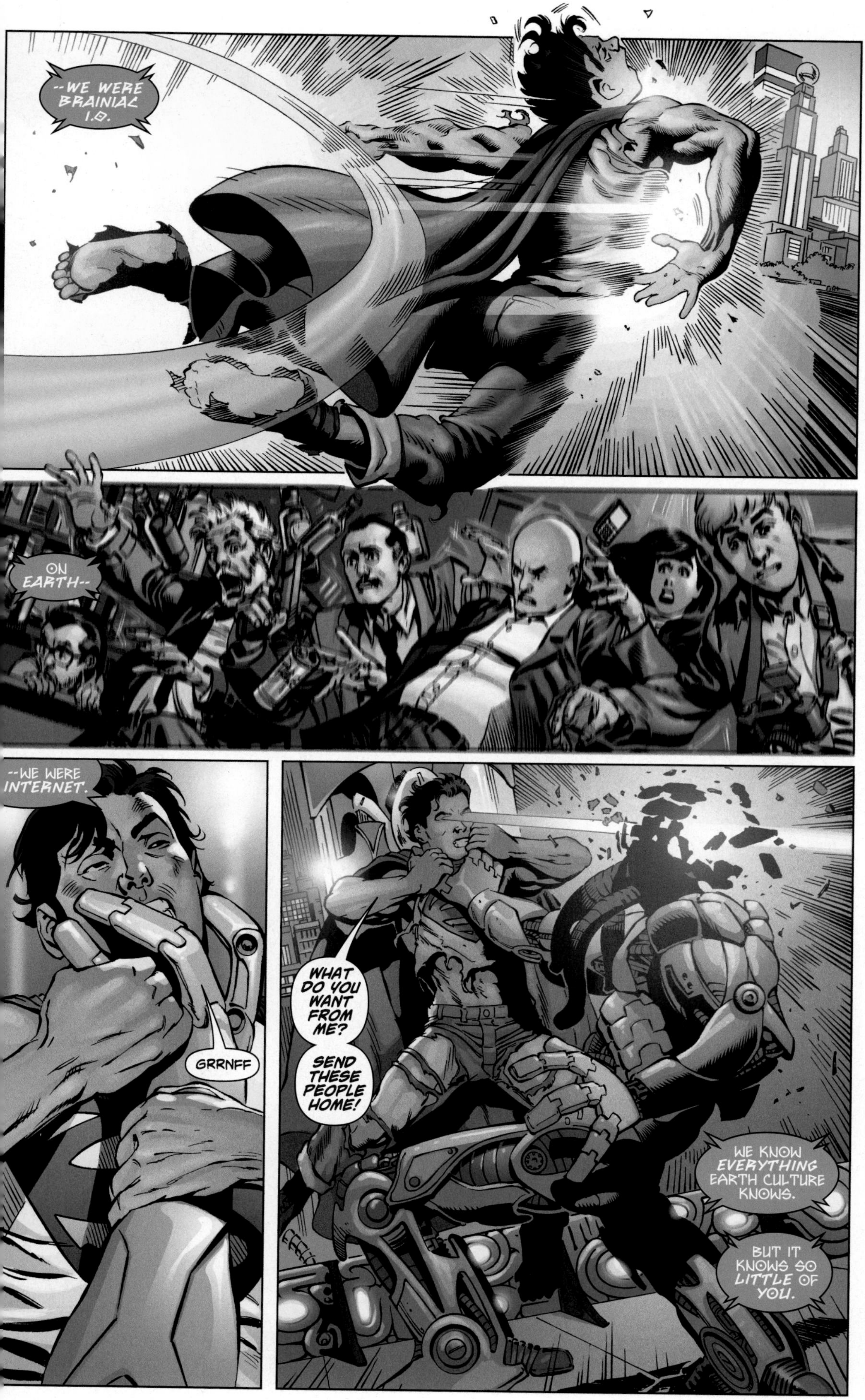
--WE WERE BRAINIAC 1.0.
ON EARTH--
--WE WERE INTERNET.
GRRNFF
WHAT DO YOU WANT FROM ME?
SEND THESE PEOPLE HOME!
WE KNOW EVERYTHING EARTH CULTURE KNOWS.
BUT IT KNOWS SO LITTLE OF YOU.

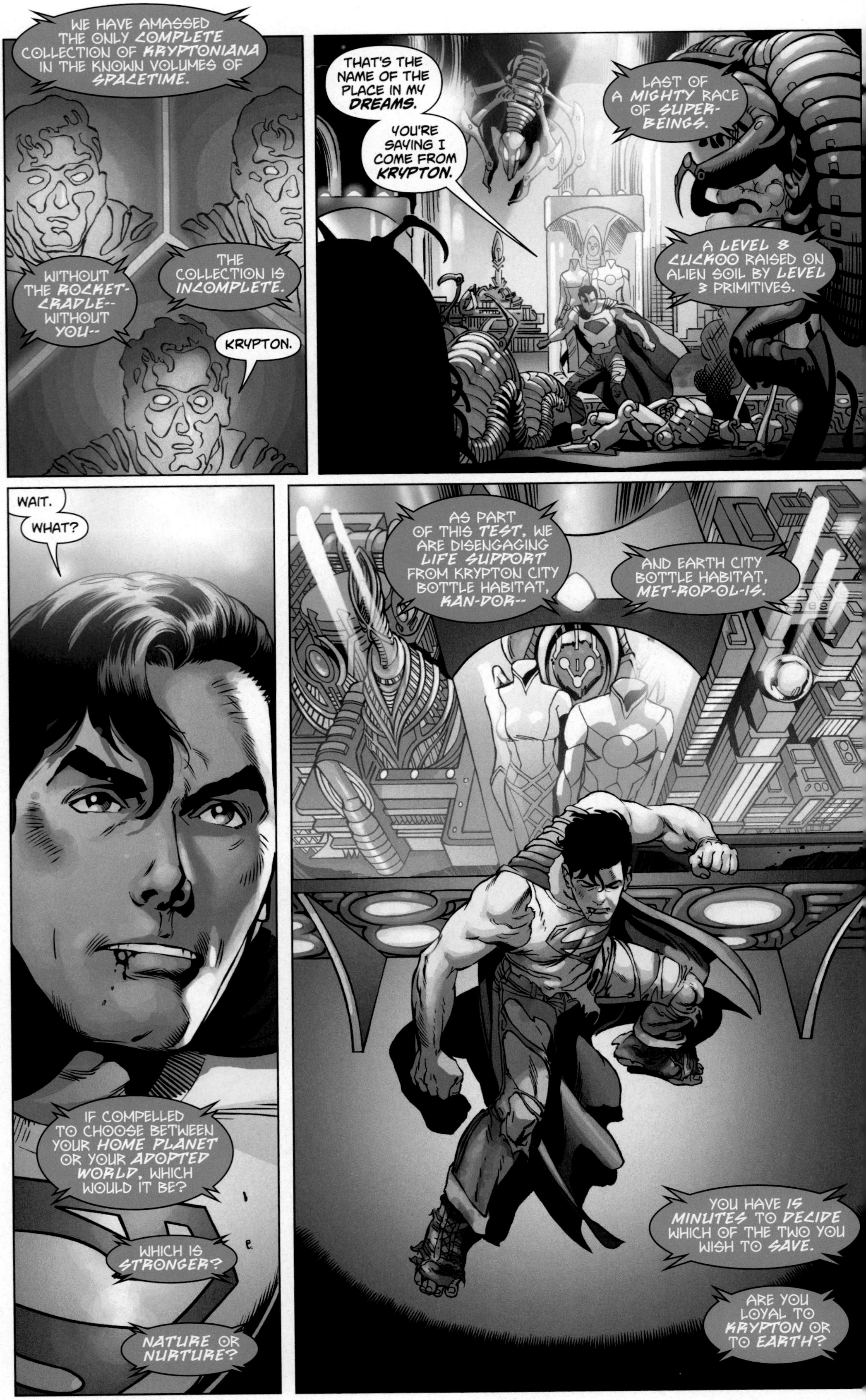
WE HAVE AMASSED THE ONLY COMPLETE COLLECTION OF KRYPTONIANA IN THE KNOWN VOLUMES OF SPACETIME.
WITHOUT THE ROCKET-CRADLE-- WITHOUT YOU--
THE COLLECTION IS INCOMPLETE.
KRYPTON.
THAT'S THE NAME OF THE PLACE IN MY DREAMS.
YOU'RE SAYING I COME FROM KRYPTON.
LAST OF A MIGHTY RACE OF SUPER-BEINGS.
A LEVEL 8 CUCKOO RAISED ON ALIEN SOIL BY LEVEL 3 PRIMITIVES.
WAIT.
WHAT?
IF COMPELLED TO CHOOSE BETWEEN YOUR HOME PLANET OR YOUR ADOPTED WORLD, WHICH WOULD IT BE?
WHICH IS STRONGER?
NATURE OR NURTURE?
AS PART OF THIS TEST, WE ARE DISENGAGING LIFE SUPPORT FROM KRYPTON CITY BOTTLE HABITAT, KAN-DOR--
AND EARTH CITY BOTTLE HABITAT, MET-ROP-OL-IS.
YOU HAVE 15 MINUTES TO DECIDE WHICH OF THE TWO YOU WISH TO SAVE.
ARE YOU LOYAL TO KRYPTON OR TO EARTH?

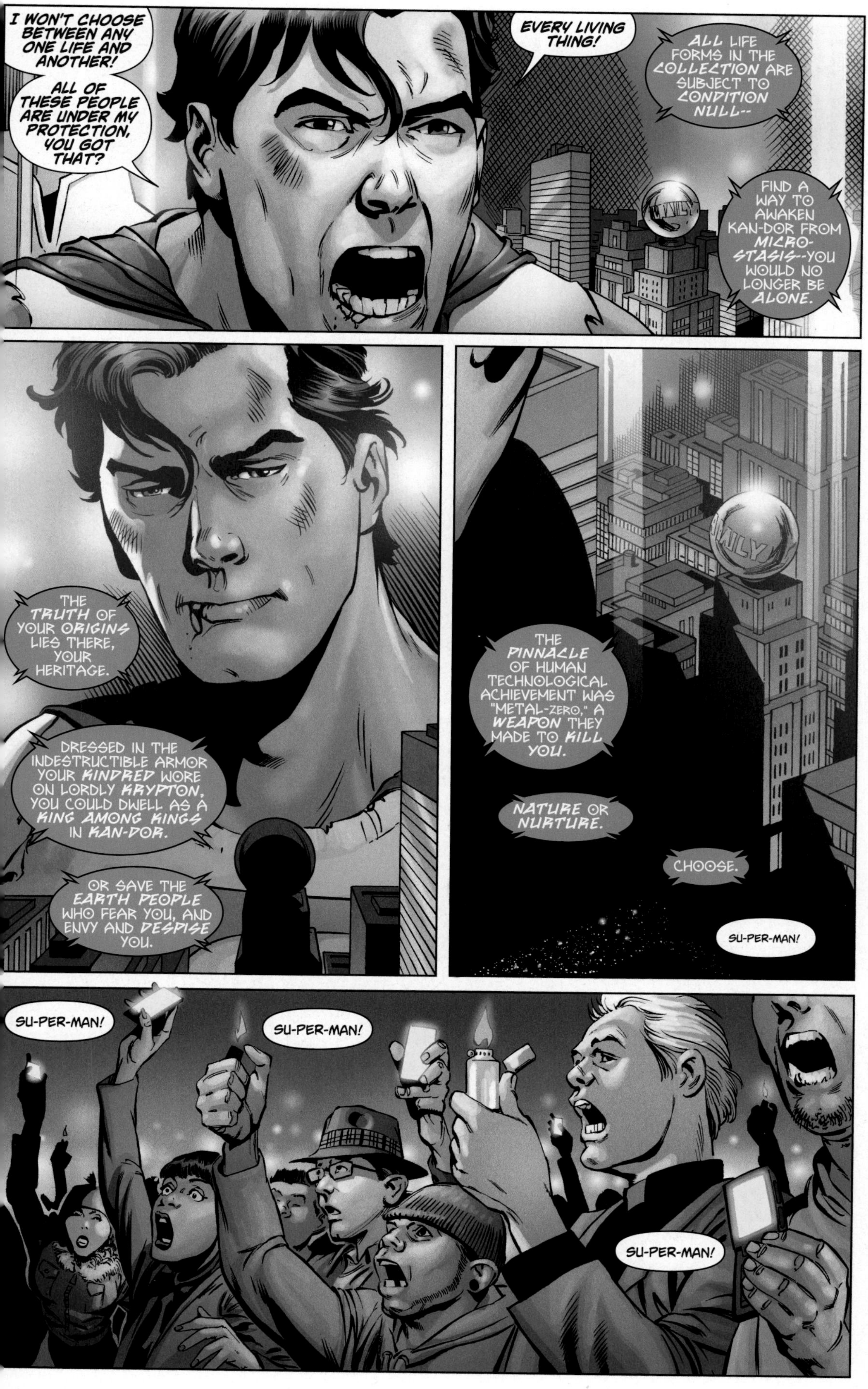

I WON'T CHOOSE BETWEEN ANY ONE LIFE AND ANOTHER!
ALL OF THESE PEOPLE ARE UNDER MY PROTECTION, YOU GOT THAT?
EVERY LIVING THING!
ALL LIFE FORMS IN THE COLLECTION ARE SUBJECT TO CONDITION NULL--
FIND A WAY TO AWAKEN KAN-DOR FROM MICRO-STASIS--YOU WOULD NO LONGER BE ALONE.
THE TRUTH OF YOUR ORIGINS LIES THERE, YOUR HERITAGE.
DRESSED IN THE INDESTRUCTIBLE ARMOR YOUR KINDRED WORE ON LORDLY KRYPTON, YOU COULD DWELL AS A KING AMONG KINGS IN KAN-DOR.
OR SAVE THE EARTH PEOPLE WHO FEAR YOU, AND ENVY AND DESPISE YOU.
THE PINNACLE OF HUMAN TECHNOLOGICAL ACHIEVEMENT WAS "METAL-ZERO," A WEAPON THEY MADE TO KILL YOU.
NATURE OR NURTURE.
CHOOSE.
SU-PER-MAN!
SU-PER-MAN!
SU-PER-MAN!
SU-PER-MAN!

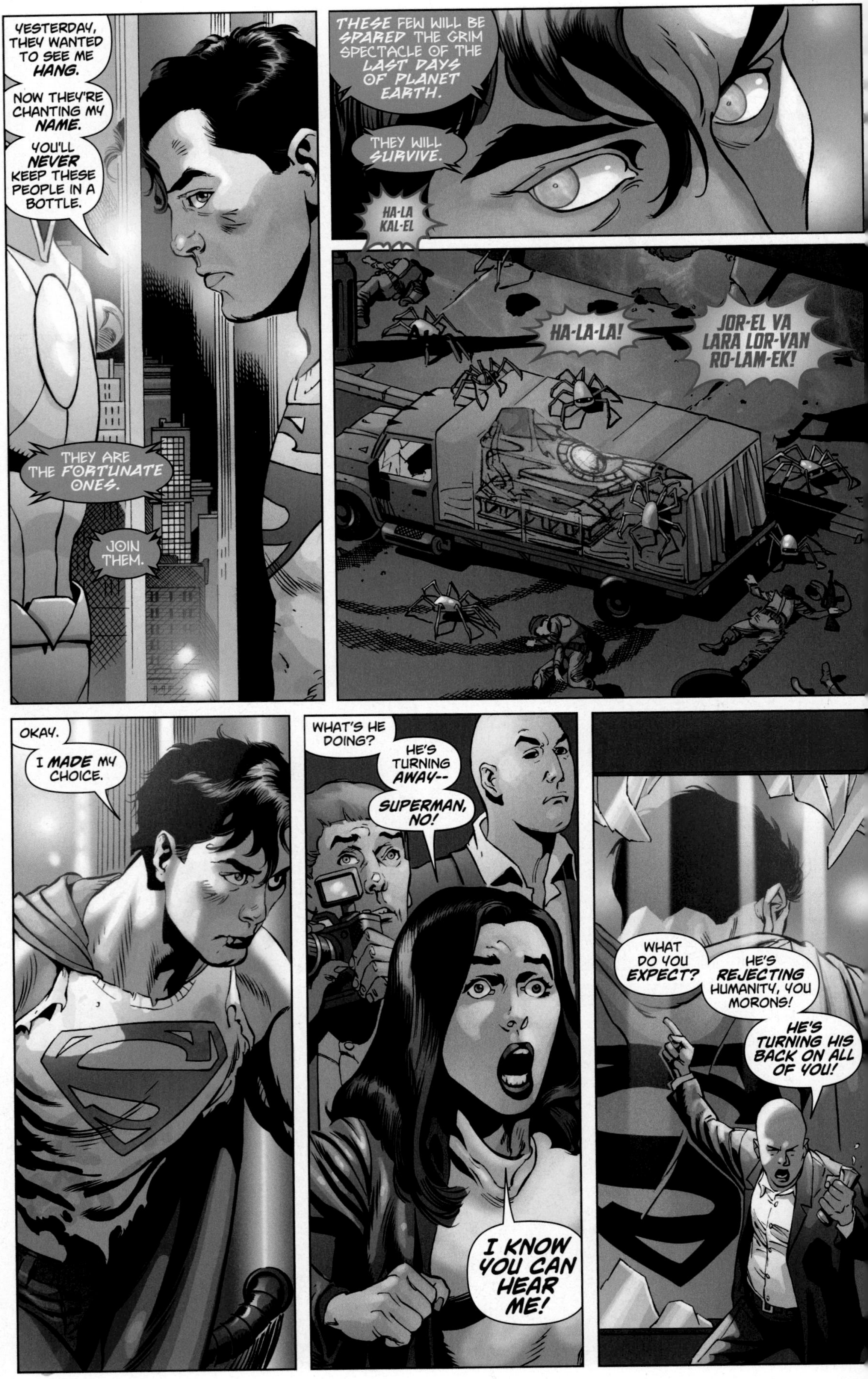

YESTERDAY, THEY WANTED TO SEE ME HANG.
NOW THEY'RE CHANTING MY NAME.
YOU'LL NEVER KEEP THESE PEOPLE IN A BOTTLE.
THEY ARE THE FORTUNATE ONES.
JOIN THEM.
THESE FEW WILL BE SPARED THE GRIM SPECTACLE OF THE LAST DAYS OF PLANET EARTH.
THEY WILL SURVIVE.
HA-LA KAL-EL
HA-LA-LA!
JOR-EL VA LARA LOR-VAN RO-LAM-EK!
OKAY.
I MADE MY CHOICE.
WHAT'S HE DOING?
HE'S TURNING AWAY--
SUPERMAN, NO!
I KNOW YOU CAN HEAR ME!
WHAT DO YOU EXPECT?
HE'S REJECTING HUMANITY, YOU MORONS!
HE'S TURNING HIS BACK ON ALL OF YOU!

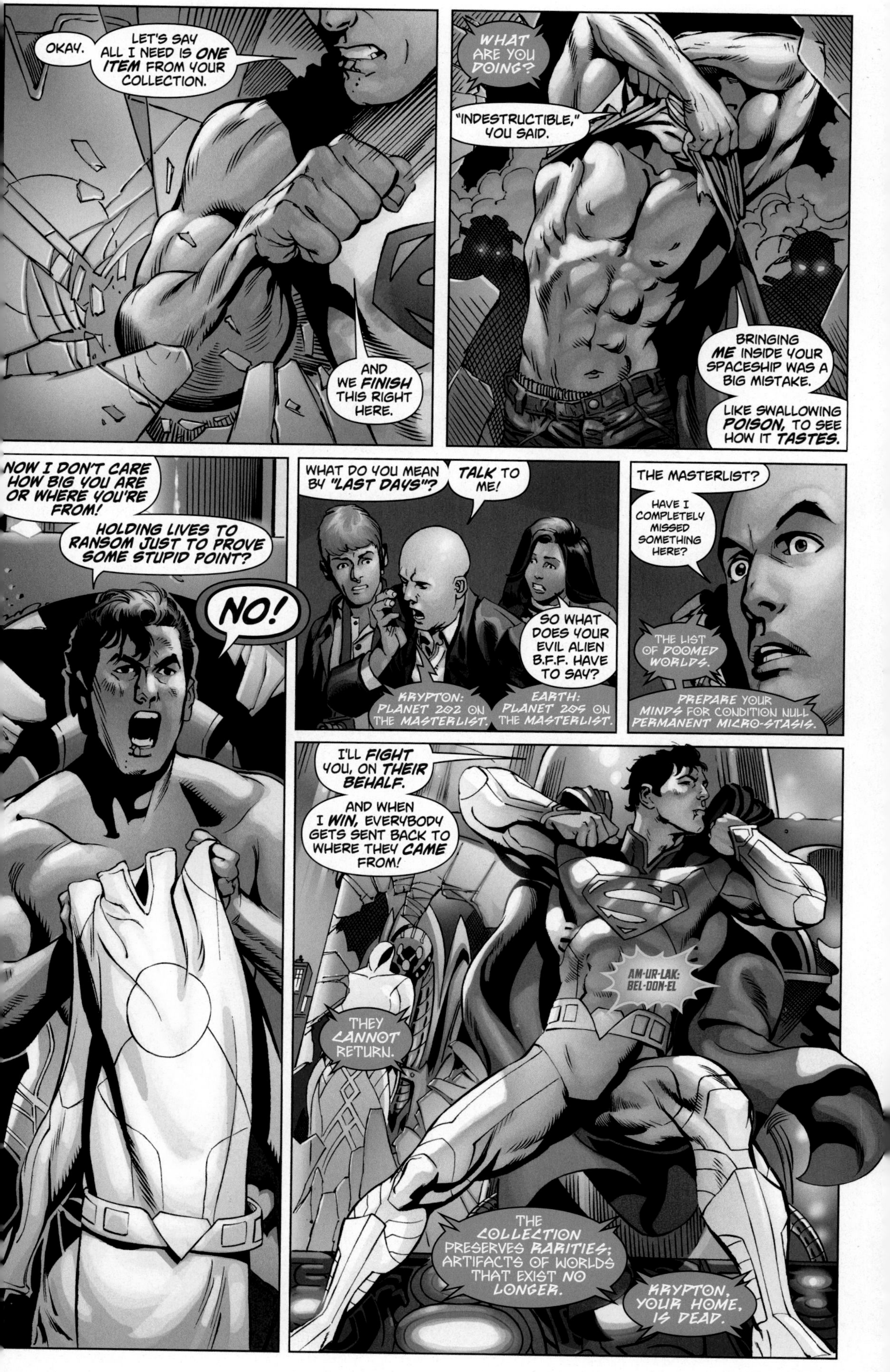
OKAY.
LET'S SAY ALL I NEED IS ONE ITEM FROM YOUR COLLECTION.
AND WE FINISH THIS RIGHT HERE.
WHAT ARE YOU DOING?
"INDESTRUCTIBLE," YOU SAID.
BRINGING ME INSIDE YOUR SPACESHIP WAS A BIG MISTAKE.
LIKE SWALLOWING POISON, TO SEE HOW IT TASTES.
NOW I DON'T CARE HOW BIG YOU ARE OR WHERE YOU'RE FROM!
HOLDING LIVES TO RANSOM JUST TO PROVE SOME STUPID POINT?
NO!
WHAT DO YOU MEAN BY "LAST DAYS"?
TALK TO ME!
SO WHAT DOES YOUR EVIL ALIEN B.F.F. HAVE TO SAY?
KRYPTON: PLANET 202 ON THE MASTERLIST.
EARTH: PLANET 205 ON THE MASTERLIST.
THE MASTERLIST?
HAVE I COMPLETELY MISSED SOMETHING HERE?
THE LIST OF DOOMED WORLDS.
PREPARE YOUR MINDS FOR CONDITION NULL PERMANENT MICRO-STASIS.
I'LL FIGHT YOU, ON THEIR BEHALF.
AND WHEN I WIN, EVERYBODY GETS SENT BACK TO WHERE THEY CAME FROM!
AM-UR-LAK: BEL-DON-EL
THEY CANNOT RETURN.
THE COLLECTION PRESERVES RARITIES: ARTIFACTS OF WORLDS THAT EXIST NO LONGER.
KRYPTON, YOUR HOME, IS DEAD.

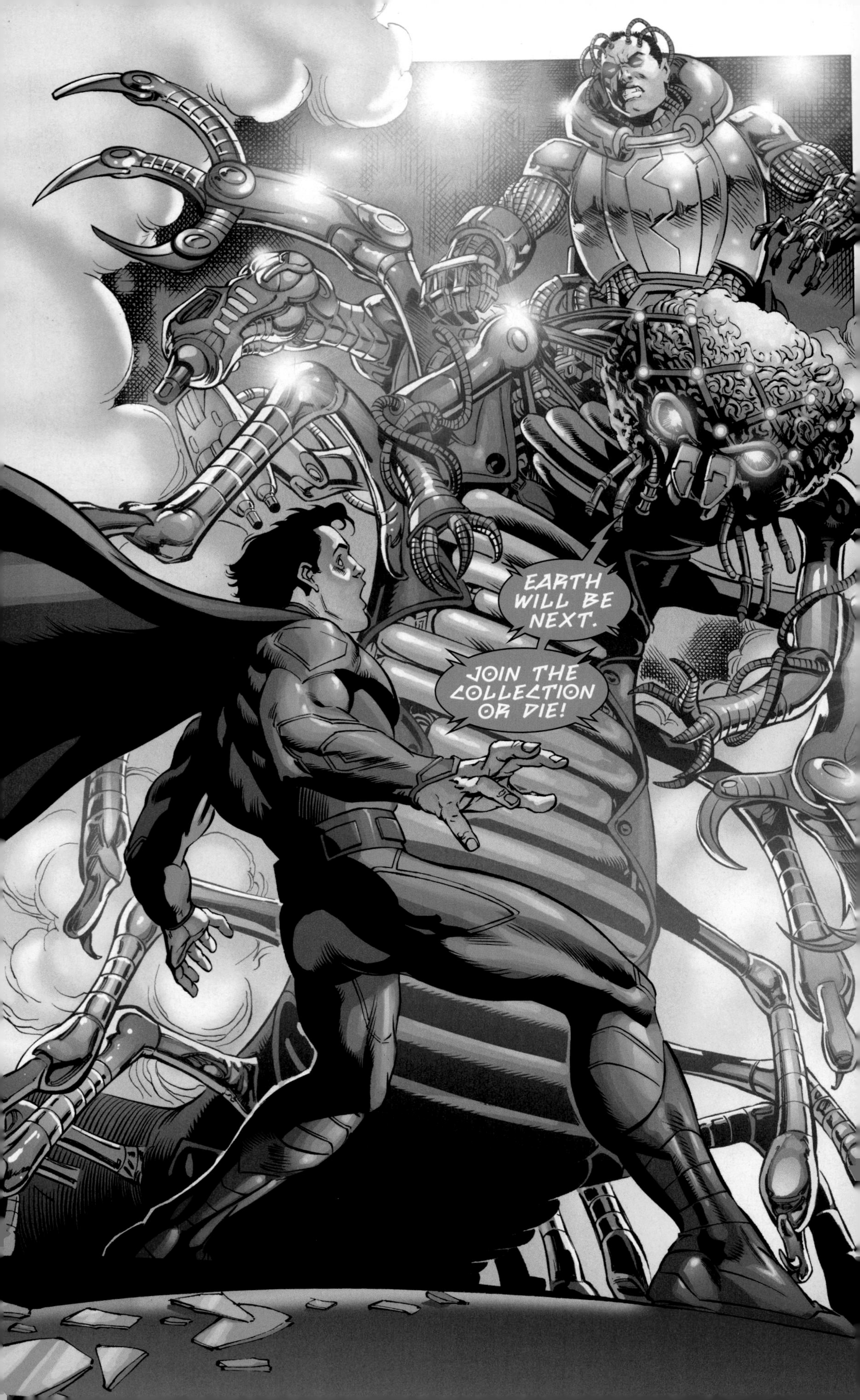
EARTH WILL BE NEXT.
JOIN THE COLLECTION OR DIE!

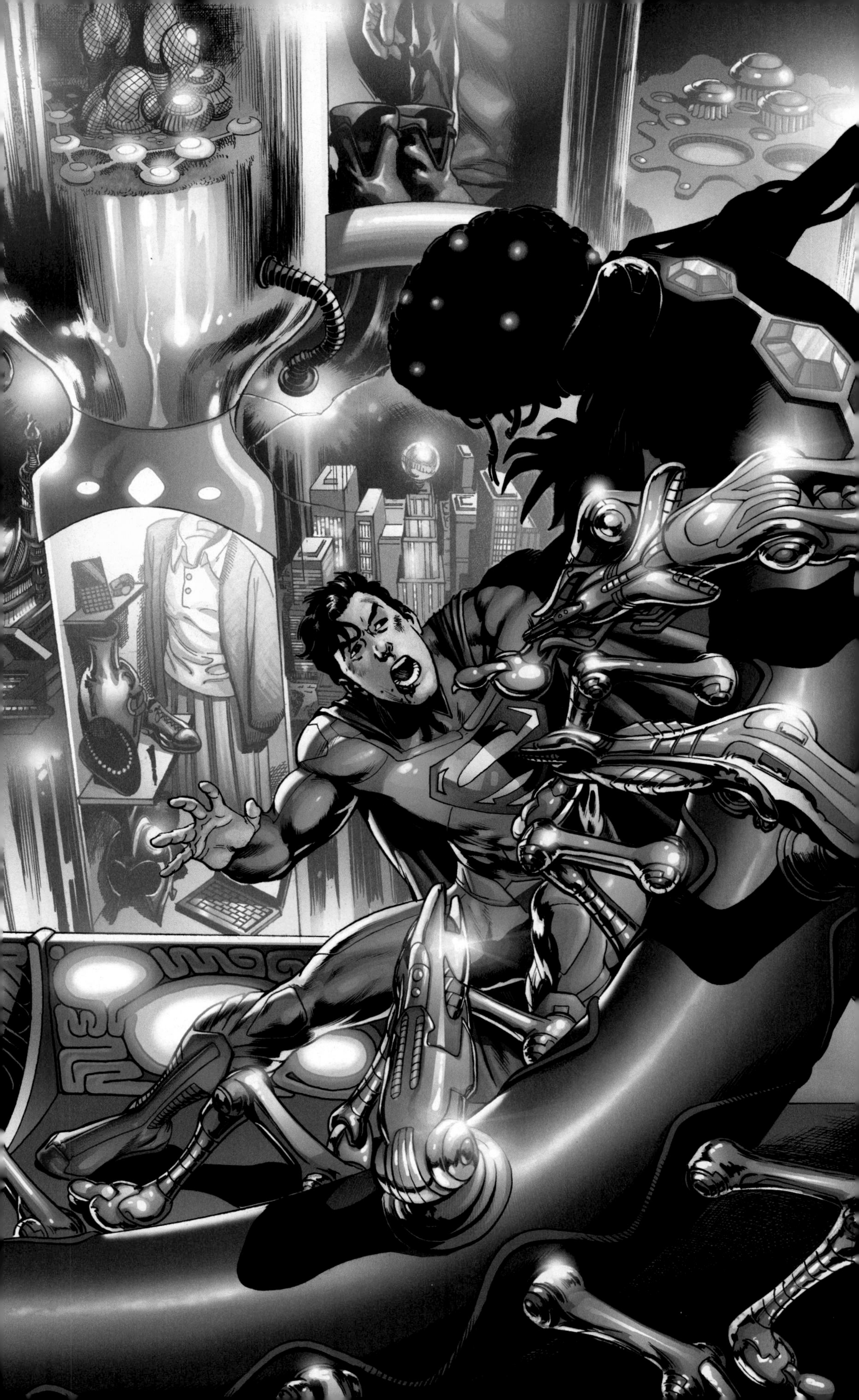

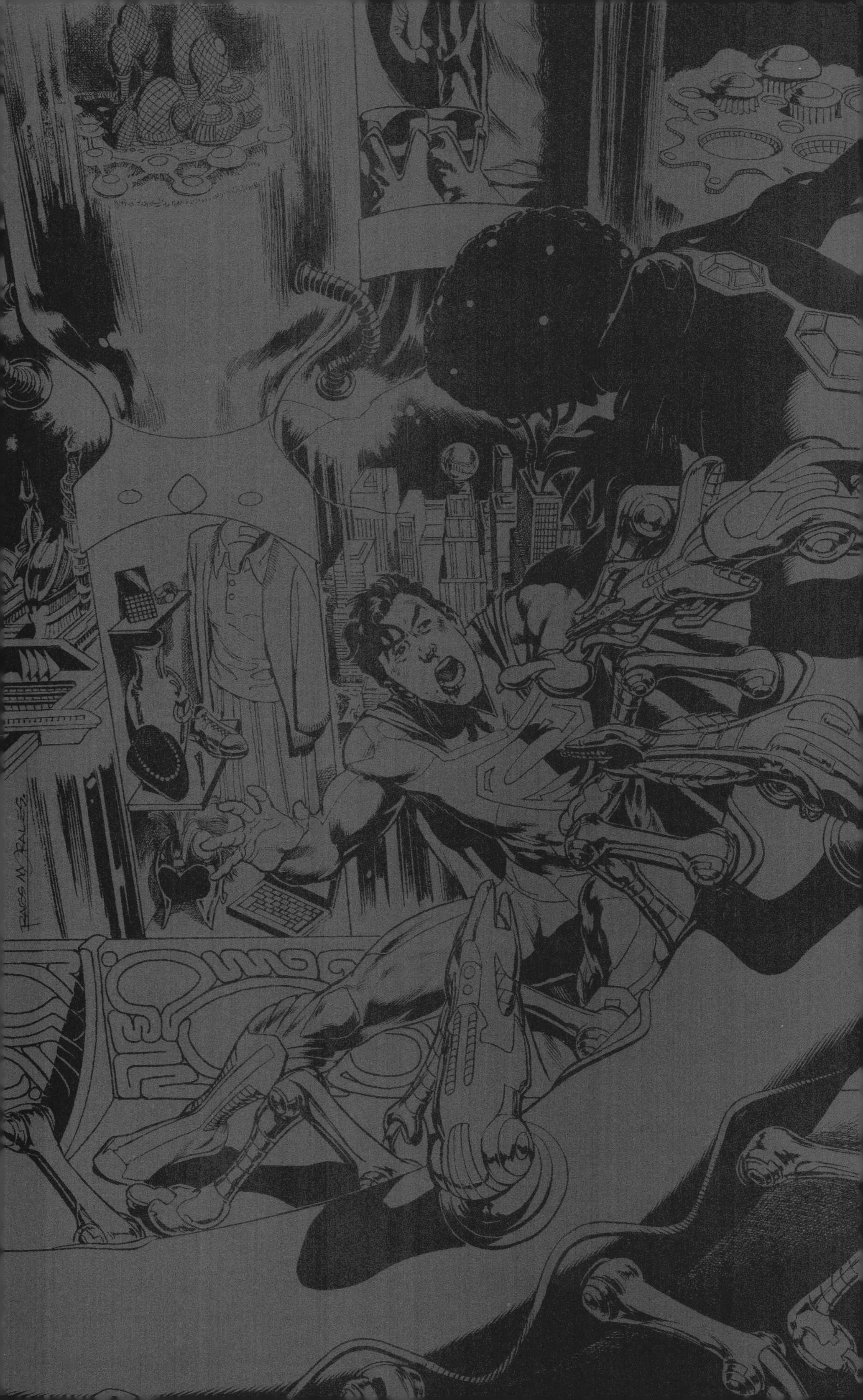

WHAT?

NO.
I SAID.
NO.

ABSOLUTELY
NO.

I EMPHATICALLY *DO NOT* WISH TO BE *RESCUED* BY "SUPERMAN."

WORST IDEA EVER.

TRUST ME, MISS LANE.

IT'S LIKE ONE OF *THOSE FILMS* WHERE--THOSE HORRIBLE *FILMS*--

THEY'RE TRAPPED IN *HELL* AND THE BARTENDER IS THE *DEVIL*...

THERE'S NO BARTENDER HERE, SIR.

PICTURE TWO WARRING ALIEN EMPIRES--ONE SYNTHETIC, MECHANIZED, *ANTISEPTIC;* THE OTHER SWEATING, BIOLOGICAL, *GERM-LADEN.*

PLANET EARTH *CAUGHT IN THE CROSSFIRE!*

WHEN IT *CONTACTED* ME, I DID MY BEST TO *DECEIVE* IT ON BEHALF OF ALL HUMANITY!

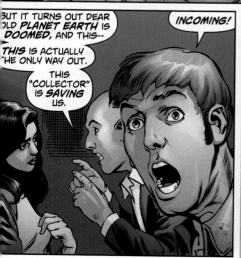

BUT IT TURNS OUT DEAR OLD *PLANET EARTH* IS *DOOMED,* AND THIS--

THIS IS ACTUALLY THE ONLY WAY OUT.

THIS "COLLECTOR" IS *SAVING* US.

INCOMING!

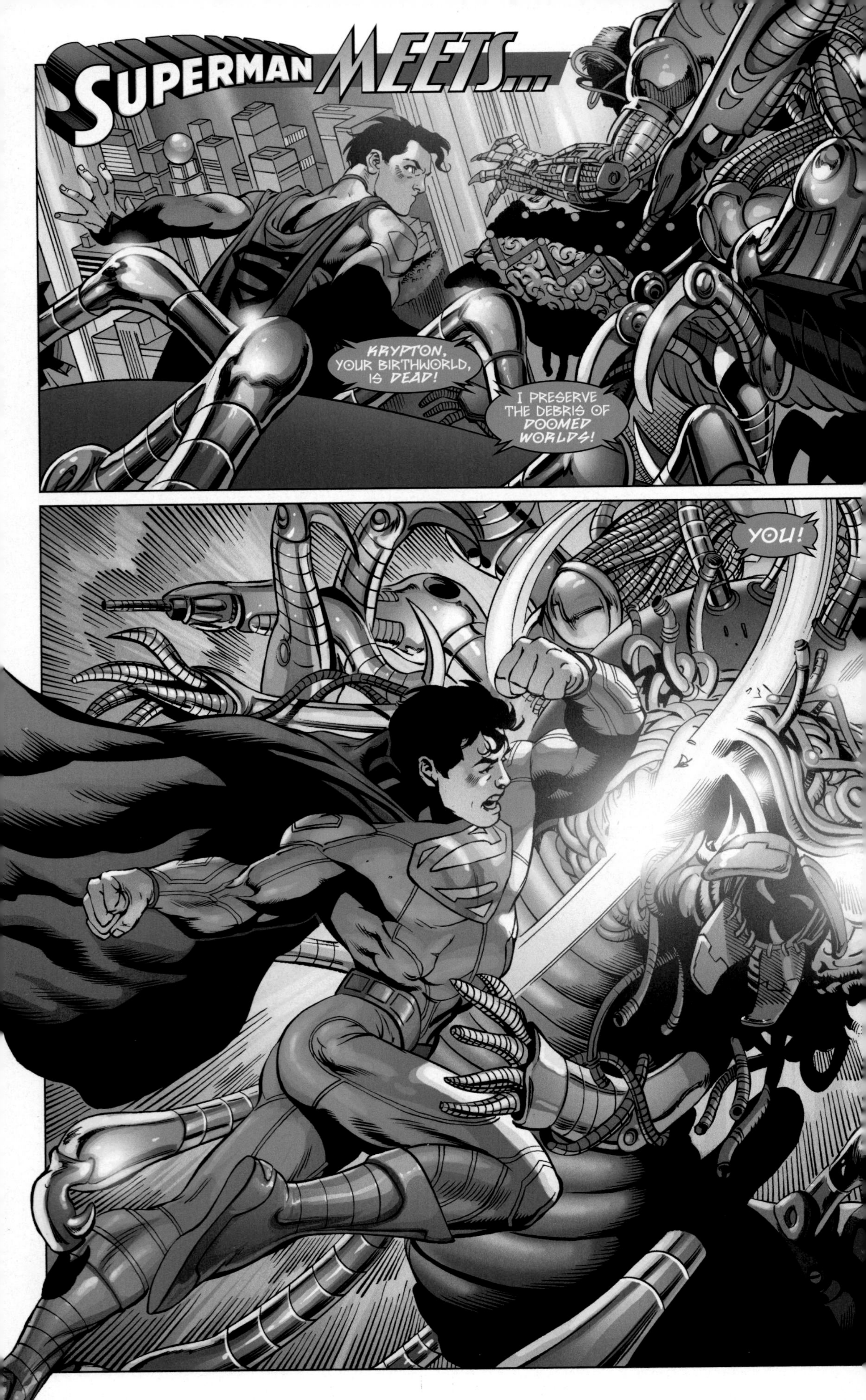
SUPERMAN MEETS...
KRYPTON, YOUR BIRTHWORLD, IS DEAD!
I PRESERVE THE DEBRIS OF DOOMED WORLDS!
YOU!

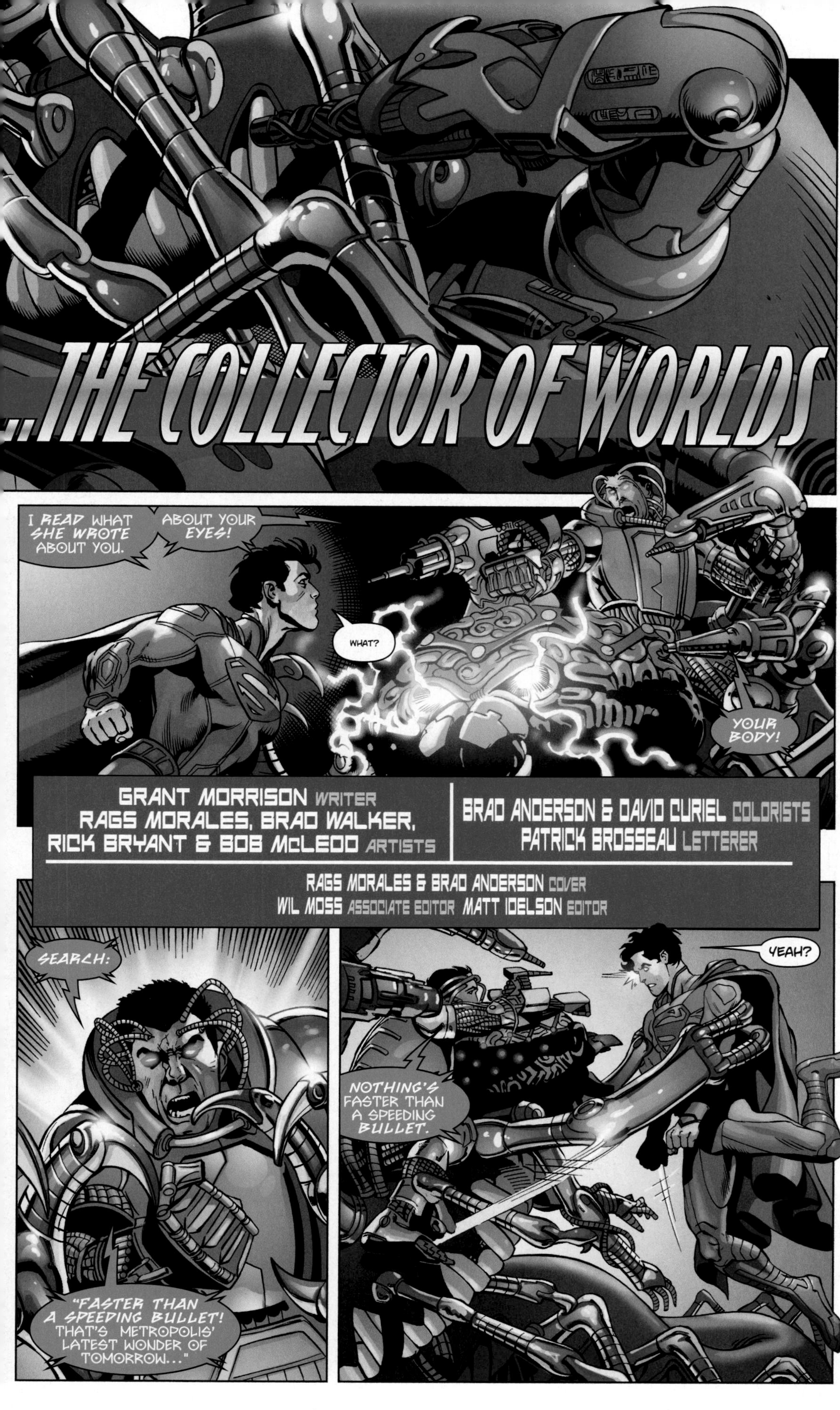
...THE COLLECTOR OF WORLDS
I READ WHAT SHE WROTE ABOUT YOU.
ABOUT YOUR EYES!
WHAT?
YOUR BODY!
GRANT MORRISON WRITER
RAGS MORALES, BRAD WALKER, RICK BRYANT & BOB McLEOD ARTISTS
BRAD ANDERSON & DAVID CURIEL COLORISTS
PATRICK BROSSEAU LETTERER
RAGS MORALES & BRAD ANDERSON COVER
WIL MOSS ASSOCIATE EDITOR MATT IDELSON EDITOR
SEARCH:
"FASTER THAN A SPEEDING BULLET! THAT'S METROPOLIS' LATEST WONDER OF TOMORROW..."
YEAH?
NOTHING'S FASTER THAN A SPEEDING BULLET.

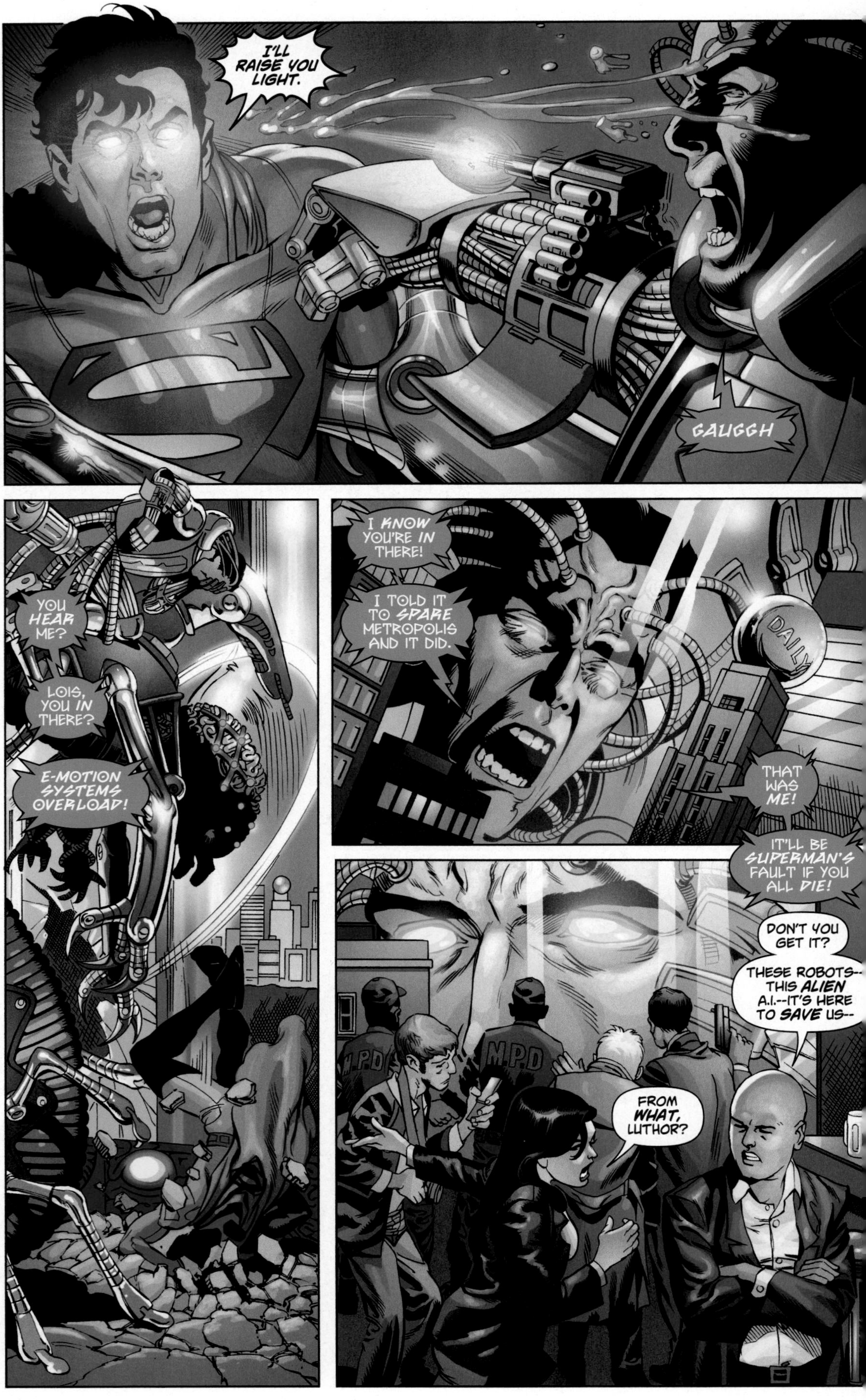
I'LL RAISE YOU LIGHT.
GAUGGH
YOU HEAR ME?
LOIS, YOU IN THERE?
E-MOTION SYSTEMS OVERLOAD!
I KNOW YOU'RE IN THERE!
I TOLD IT TO SPARE METROPOLIS AND IT DID.
DAILY
THAT WAS ME!
IT'LL BE SUPERMAN'S FAULT IF YOU ALL DIE!
DON'T YOU GET IT?
THESE ROBOTS--THIS ALIEN A.I.--IT'S HERE TO SAVE US--
M.P.D
M.P.D
FROM WHAT, LUTHOR?

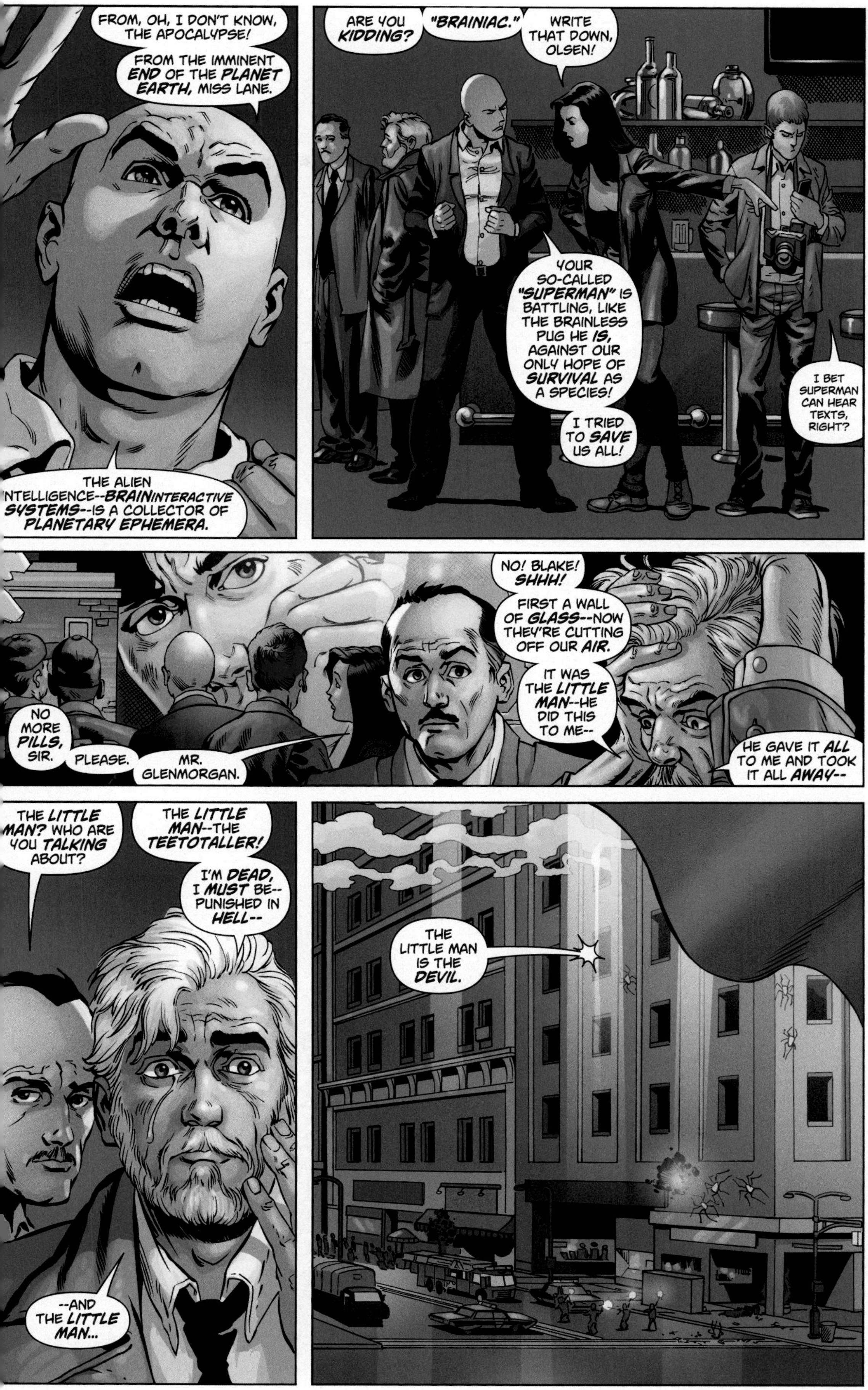
FROM, OH, I DON'T KNOW, THE APOCALYPSE!
FROM THE IMMINENT END OF THE PLANET EARTH, MISS LANE.
THE ALIEN INTELLIGENCE--BRAININTERACTIVE SYSTEMS--IS A COLLECTOR OF PLANETARY EPHEMERA.
ARE YOU KIDDING?
"BRAINIAC."
WRITE THAT DOWN, OLSEN!
YOUR SO-CALLED "SUPERMAN" IS BATTLING, LIKE THE BRAINLESS PUG HE IS, AGAINST OUR ONLY HOPE OF SURVIVAL AS A SPECIES!
I TRIED TO SAVE US ALL!
I BET SUPERMAN CAN HEAR TEXTS, RIGHT?
NO MORE PILLS, SIR.
PLEASE.
MR. GLENMORGAN.
NO! BLAKE! SHHH!
FIRST A WALL OF GLASS--NOW THEY'RE CUTTING OFF OUR AIR.
IT WAS THE LITTLE MAN--HE DID THIS TO ME--
HE GAVE IT ALL TO ME AND TOOK IT ALL AWAY--
THE LITTLE MAN? WHO ARE YOU TALKING ABOUT?
THE LITTLE MAN--THE TEETOTALLER!
I'M DEAD, I MUST BE--PUNISHED IN HELL--
--AND THE LITTLE MAN...
THE LITTLE MAN IS THE DEVIL.

KRYPTON
SPECIMEN.

PRESERVE.

WAIT!

HE
STILL HASN'T
MADE HIS
DECISION.

KANDOR OR
METROPOLIS?

NATURE!

UNNGGH!

OR
NURTURE?

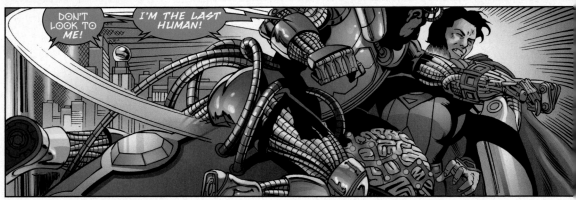

DON'T
LOOK TO
ME!

I'M THE LAST
HUMAN!

FIRST OF A
POST-HUMAN
MAN/MACHINE
RACE.

HUMANITY
IS DONE!

THAT'S
IT?

THAT'S ALL
YOU GOT,
SOLDIER?

I'M WEARING
INDESTRUCTIBLE
ARMOR.

SOME
SUPERMAN.

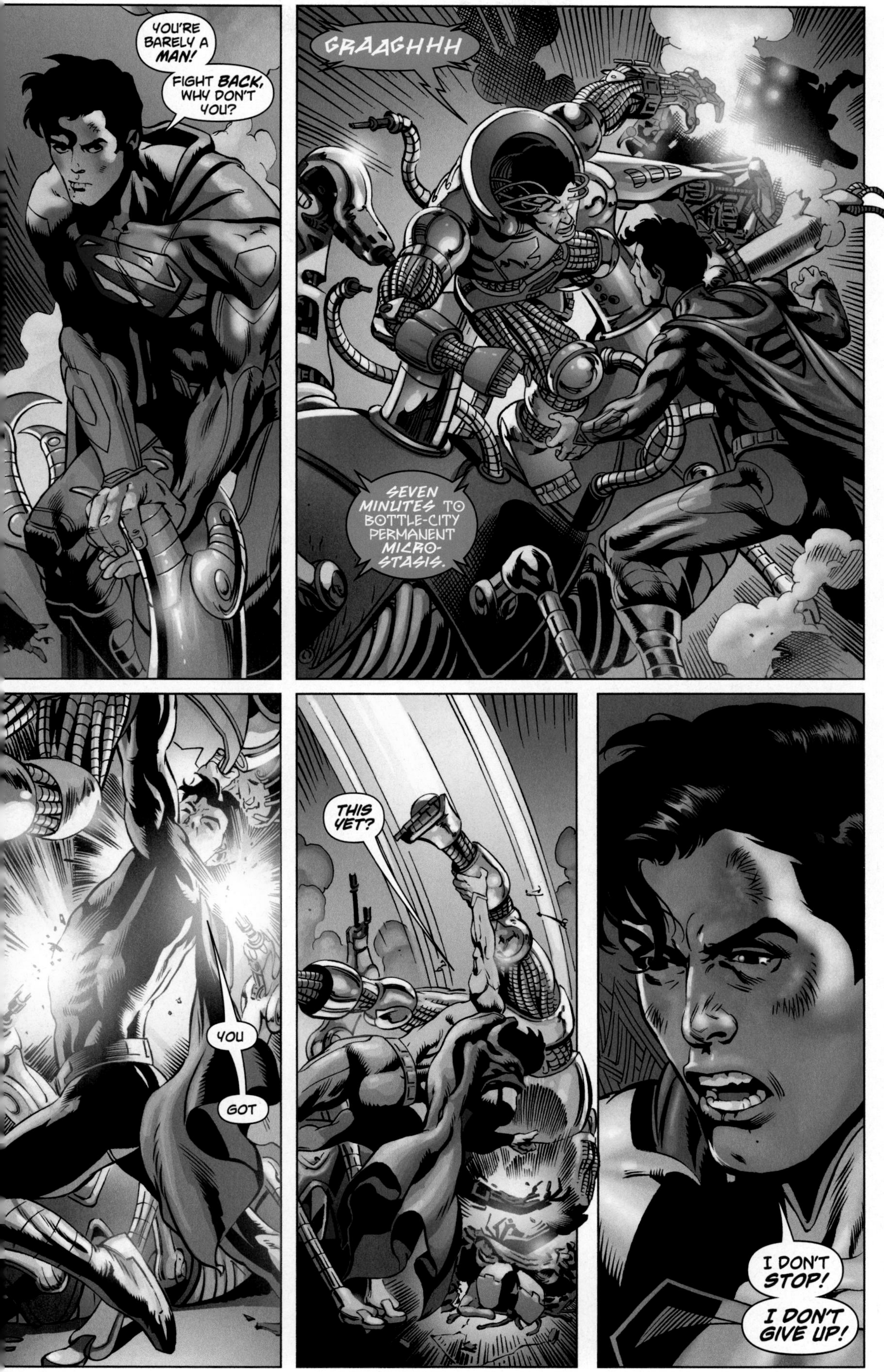
YOU'RE BARELY A MAN!
FIGHT BACK, WHY DON'T YOU?
GRAAGHHH
SEVEN MINUTES TO BOTTLE-CITY PERMANENT MICRO-STASIS.
YOU
GOT
THIS YET?
I DON'T STOP!
I DON'T GIVE UP!

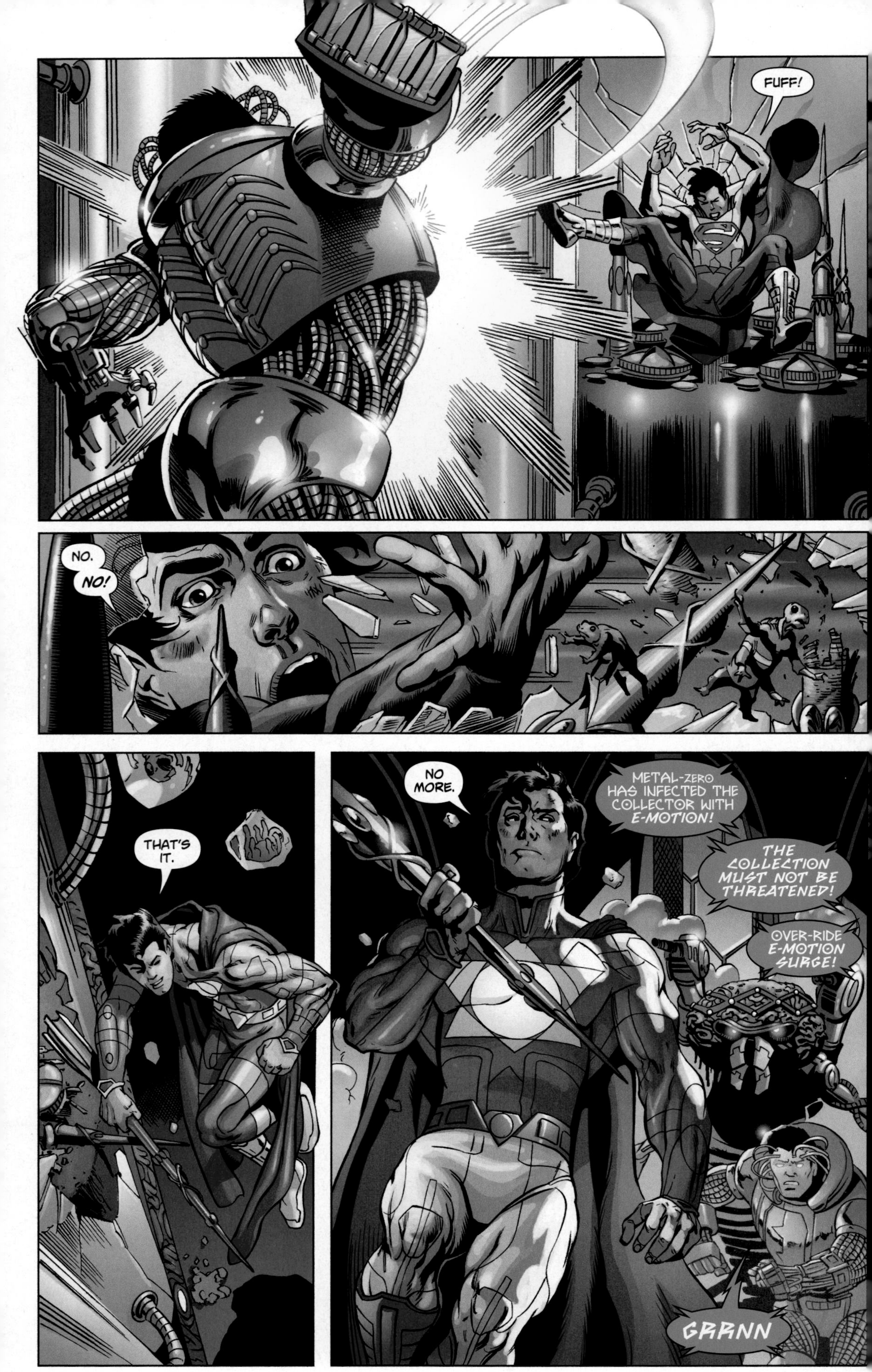
FUFF!
NO.
NO!
THAT'S IT.
NO MORE.
METAL-ZERO HAS INFECTED THE COLLECTOR WITH E-MOTION!
THE COLLECTION MUST NOT BE THREATENED!
OVER-RIDE E-MOTION SURGE!
GRRNN

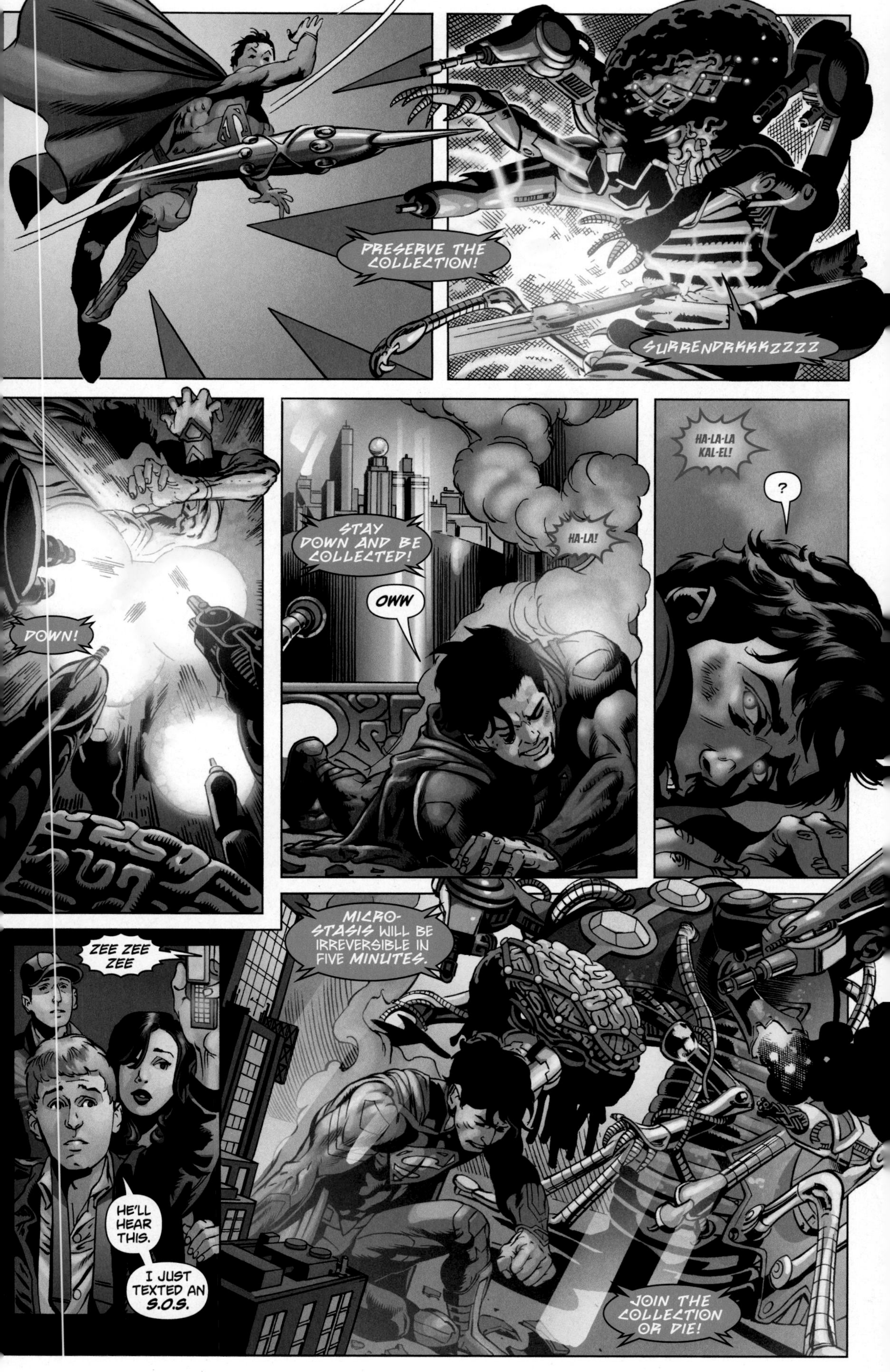
PRESERVE THE COLLECTION!
SURRENDRKKKZZZZ
DOWN!
STAY DOWN AND BE COLLECTED!
OWW
HA-LA!
HA-LA-LA KAL-EL!
?
ZEE ZEE ZEE
HE'LL HEAR THIS.
I JUST TEXTED AN S.O.S.
MICRO-STASIS WILL BE IRREVERSIBLE IN FIVE MINUTES.
JOIN THE COLLECTION OR DIE!

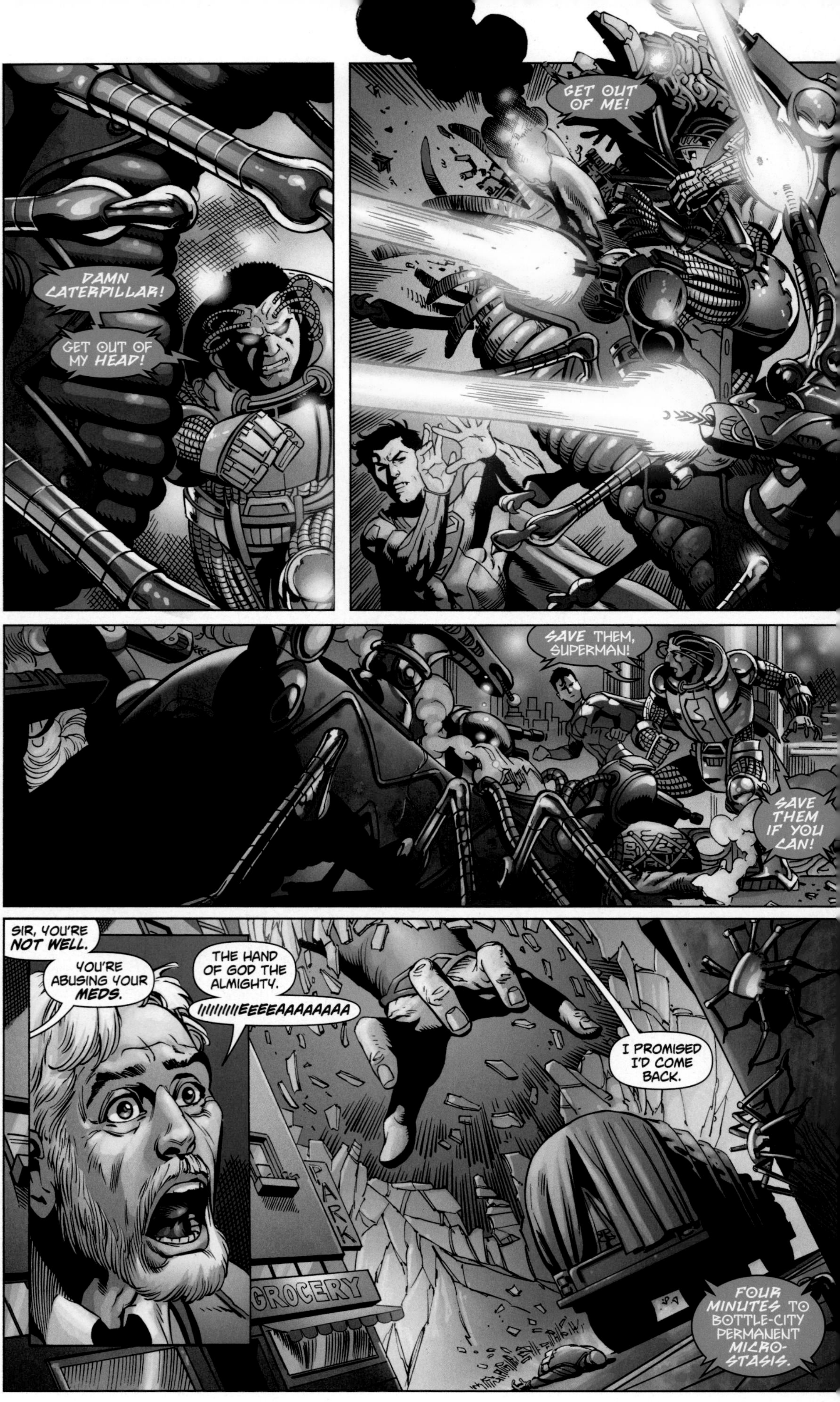
DAMN CATERPILLAR!
GET OUT OF MY HEAD!
GET OUT OF ME!
SAVE THEM, SUPERMAN!
SAVE THEM IF YOU CAN!
SIR, YOU'RE NOT WELL.
YOU'RE ABUSING YOUR MEDS.
THE HAND OF GOD THE ALMIGHTY.
IIIIIIIIEEEEAAAAAAAA
I PROMISED I'D COME BACK.
PARK
GROCERY
FOUR MINUTES TO BOTTLE-CITY PERMANENT MICRO-STASIS.

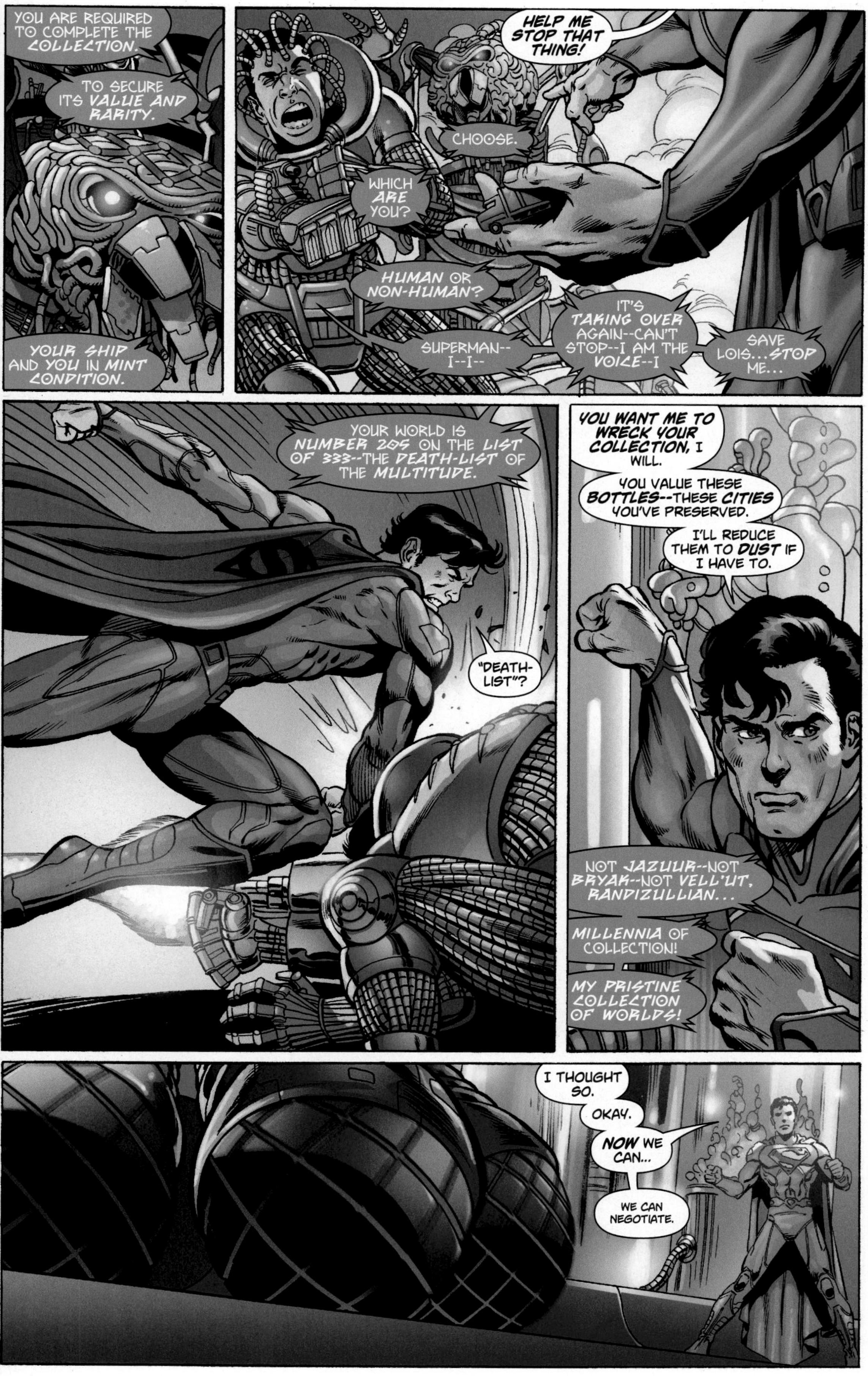

YOU ARE REQUIRED TO COMPLETE THE COLLECTION.
TO SECURE ITS VALUE AND RARITY.
YOUR SHIP AND YOU IN MINT CONDITION.
HELP ME STOP THAT THING!
CHOOSE.
WHICH ARE YOU?
HUMAN OR NON-HUMAN?
SUPERMAN-- I--I--
IT'S TAKING OVER AGAIN--CAN'T STOP--I AM THE VOICE--I
SAVE LOIS...STOP ME...
YOUR WORLD IS NUMBER 205 ON THE LIST OF 333--THE DEATH-LIST OF THE MULTITUDE.
"DEATH-LIST"?
YOU WANT ME TO WRECK YOUR COLLECTION, I WILL.
YOU VALUE THESE BOTTLES--THESE CITIES YOU'VE PRESERVED.
I'LL REDUCE THEM TO DUST IF I HAVE TO.
NOT JAZUUR--NOT BRYAK--NOT VELL'UT, RANDIZULLIAN...
MILLENNIA OF COLLECTION!
MY PRISTINE COLLECTION OF WORLDS!
I THOUGHT SO.
OKAY.
NOW WE CAN...
WE CAN NEGOTIATE.

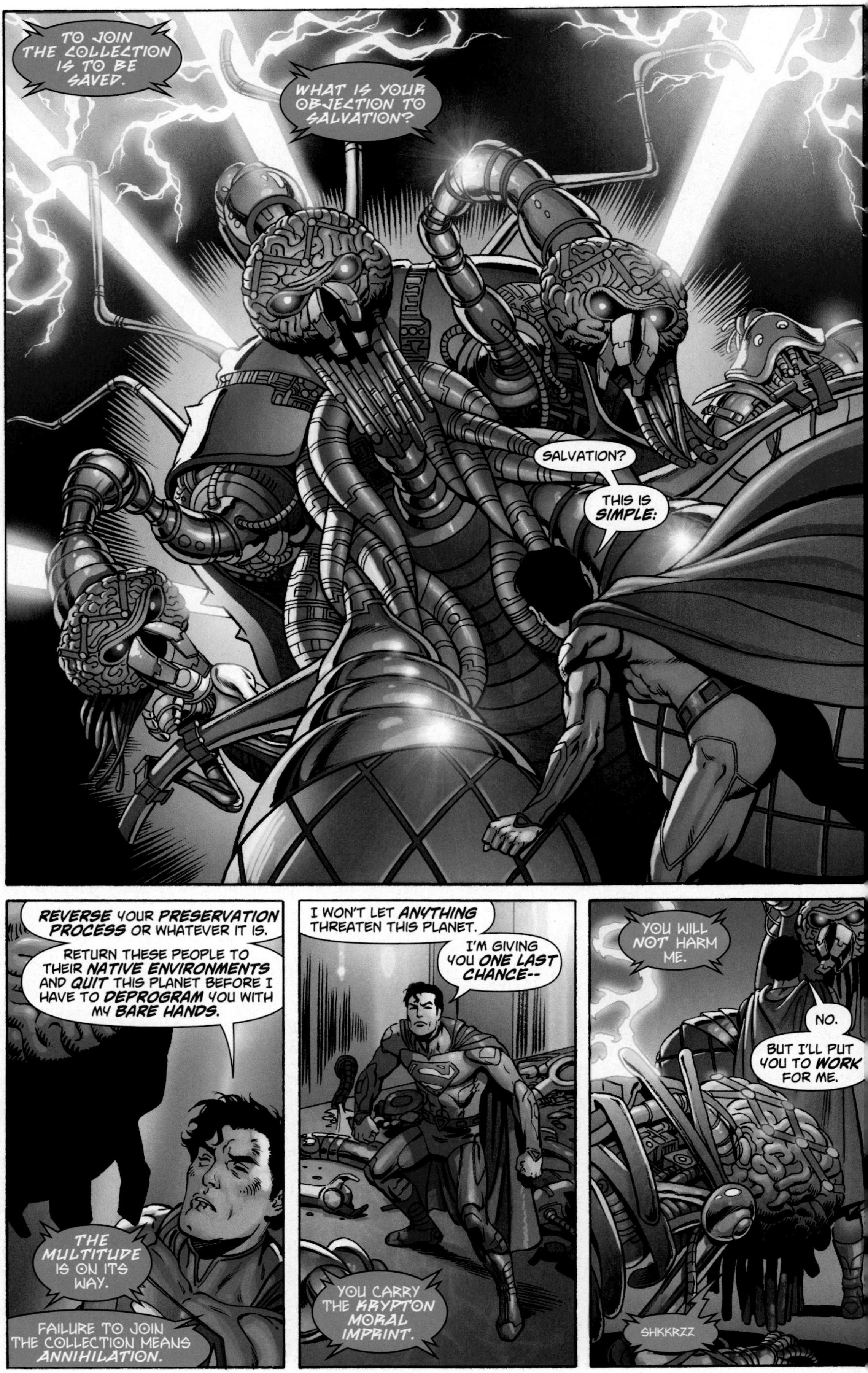
TO JOIN THE COLLECTION IS TO BE SAVED.
WHAT IS YOUR OBJECTION TO SALVATION?
SALVATION?
THIS IS SIMPLE:
REVERSE YOUR PRESERVATION PROCESS OR WHATEVER IT IS.
RETURN THESE PEOPLE TO THEIR NATIVE ENVIRONMENTS AND QUIT THIS PLANET BEFORE I HAVE TO DEPROGRAM YOU WITH MY BARE HANDS.
THE MULTITUDE IS ON ITS WAY.
FAILURE TO JOIN THE COLLECTION MEANS ANNIHILATION.
I WON'T LET ANYTHING THREATEN THIS PLANET.
I'M GIVING YOU ONE LAST CHANCE--
YOU CARRY THE KRYPTON MORAL IMPRINT.
YOU WILL NOT HARM ME.
NO.
BUT I'LL PUT YOU TO WORK FOR ME.
SHKKRZZ

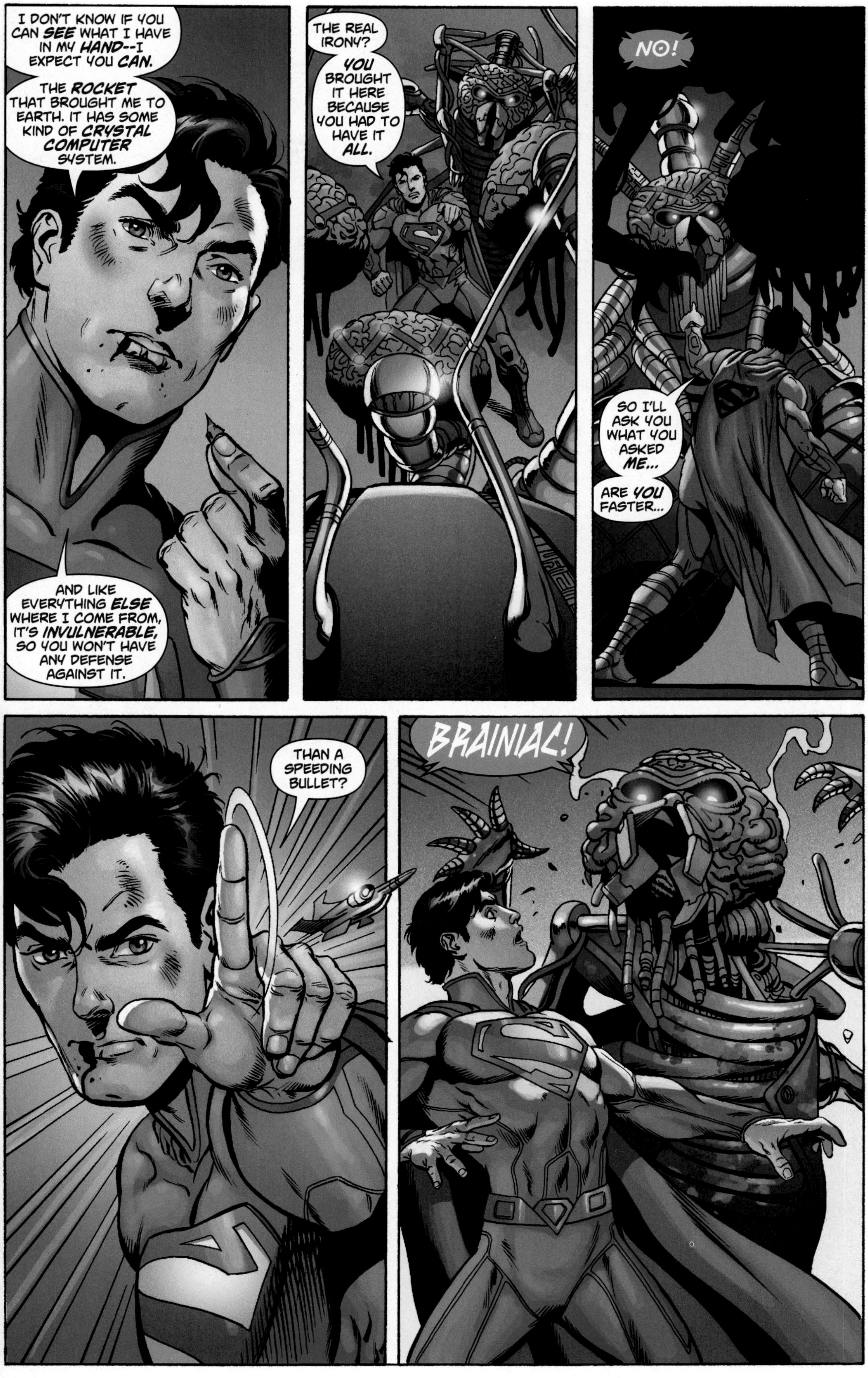
I DON'T KNOW IF YOU CAN SEE WHAT I HAVE IN MY HAND--I EXPECT YOU CAN.
THE ROCKET THAT BROUGHT ME TO EARTH. IT HAS SOME KIND OF CRYSTAL COMPUTER SYSTEM.
AND LIKE EVERYTHING ELSE WHERE I COME FROM, IT'S INVULNERABLE, SO YOU WON'T HAVE ANY DEFENSE AGAINST IT.
THE REAL IRONY?
YOU BROUGHT IT HERE BECAUSE YOU HAD TO HAVE IT ALL.
NO!
SO I'LL ASK YOU WHAT YOU ASKED ME...
ARE YOU FASTER...
THAN A SPEEDING BULLET?
BRAINIAC!

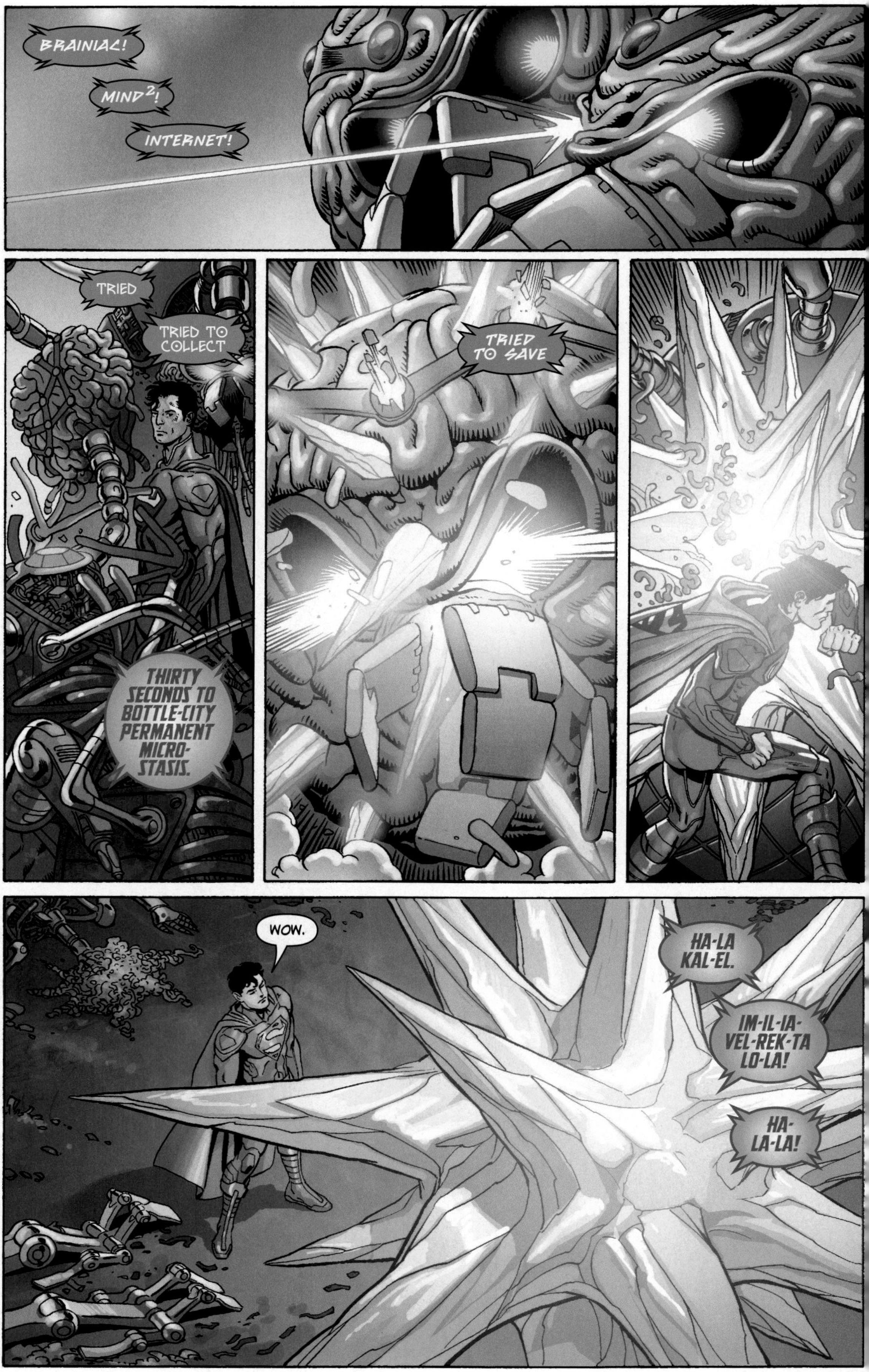
BRAINIAC!
MIND²!
INTERNET!
TRIED
TRIED TO COLLECT
THIRTY SECONDS TO BOTTLE-CITY PERMANENT MICRO-STASIS.
TRIED TO SAVE
WOW.
HA-LA KAL-EL.
IM-IL-IA-VEL-REK-TA LO-LA!
HA-LA-LA!

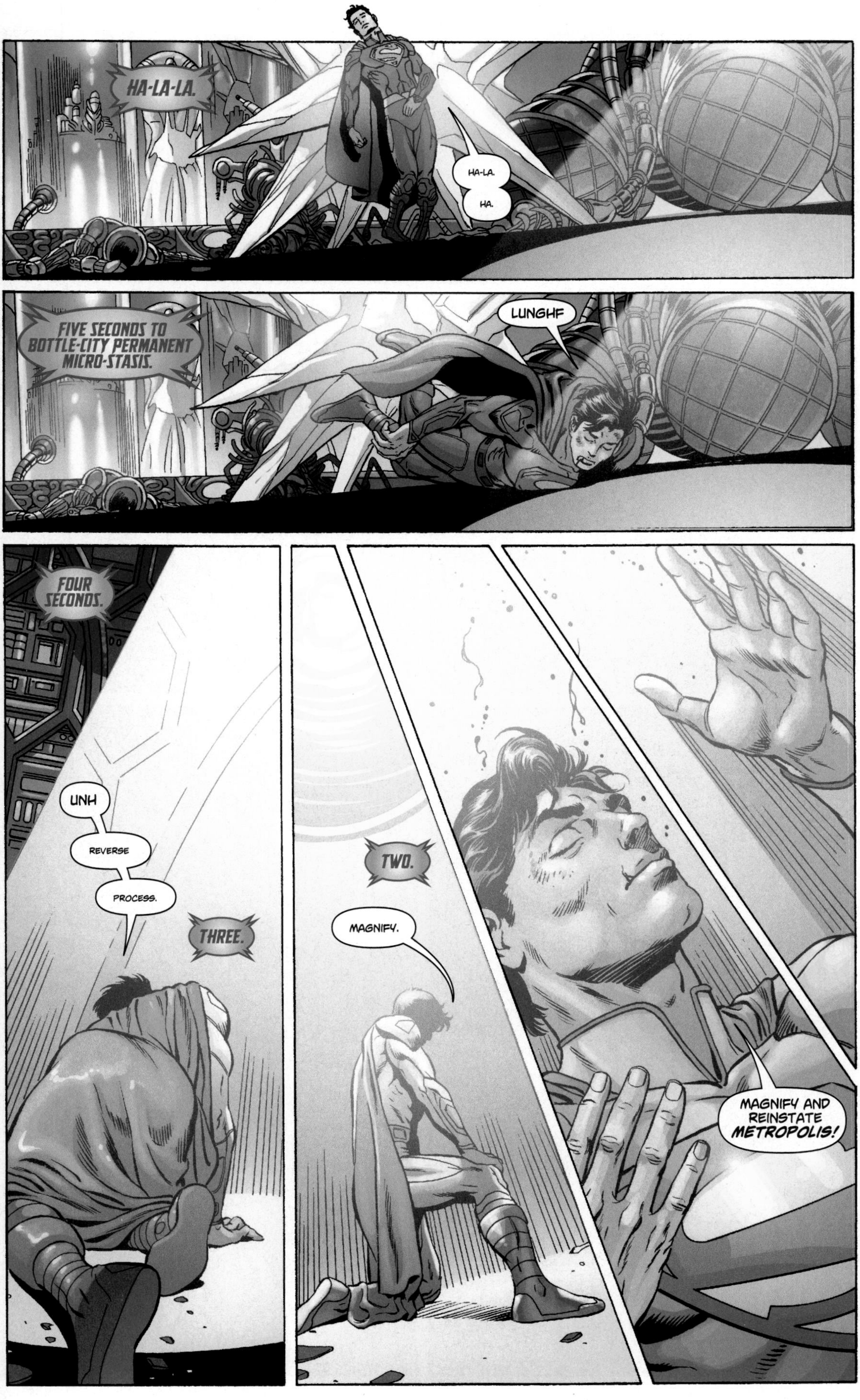
HA-LA-LA.
HA-LA.
HA.
FIVE SECONDS TO BOTTLE-CITY PERMANENT MICRO-STASIS.
LUNGHF
FOUR SECONDS.
UNH
REVERSE
PROCESS.
THREE.
TWO.
MAGNIFY.
MAGNIFY AND REINSTATE METROPOLIS!

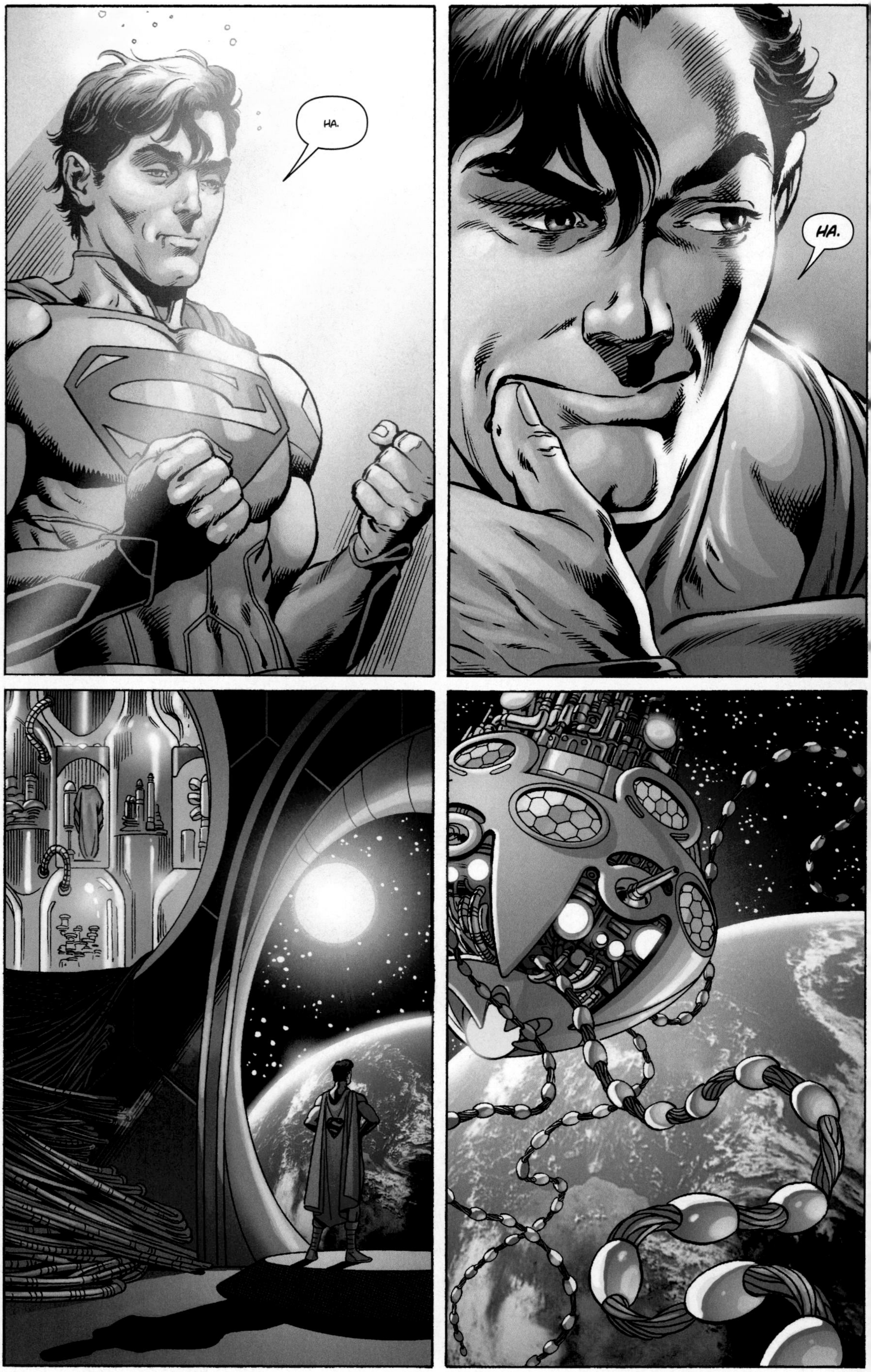
HA.
HA.

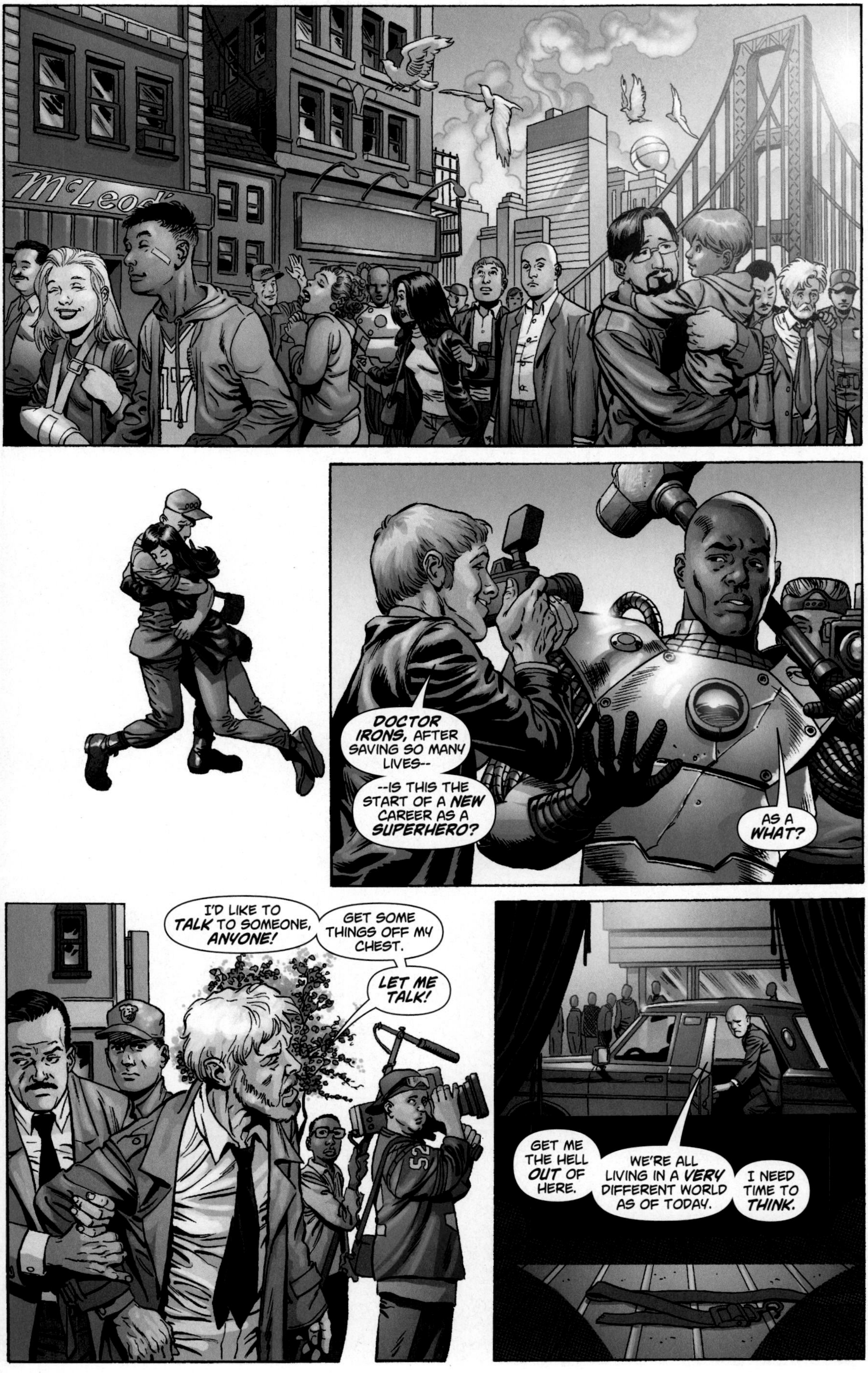
DOCTOR IRONS, AFTER SAVING SO MANY LIVES--
--IS THIS THE START OF A NEW CAREER AS A SUPERHERO?
AS A WHAT?
I'D LIKE TO TALK TO SOMEONE, ANYONE!
GET SOME THINGS OFF MY CHEST.
LET ME TALK!
GET ME THE HELL OUT OF HERE.
WE'RE ALL LIVING IN A VERY DIFFERENT WORLD AS OF TODAY.
I NEED TIME TO THINK.

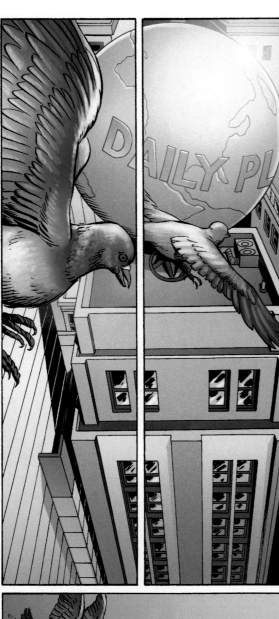

--I MET YOUR *MOM AND DAD* WHEN I WORKED ON THE *SMALLVILLE SENTINEL.*

THAT WAS DURING THE SO-CALLED "FARMER'S REBELLION."

EVERYBODY ELSE WAS SUSPICIOUS OF A SNOOPY REPORTER, BUT THEY TOOK ME IN.

YOUR FATHER AND I SHARED A--WELL, WE CAN CALL IT AN *ECCENTRIC* SENSE OF HUMOR AND A LOVE OF SURREAL *PRACTICAL JOKES.*

THEY'D BE *PROUD* OF YOU, CLARK.

EVEN *I'M* PROUD OF YOU, SON, HOW *ABOUT* THAT?

YOU *KEPT UP* YOUR CAMPAIGN, YOU MAINTAINED THE *PRESSURE.*

GLEN GLENMORGAN WAS A BAD, BAD MAN, BUT NONE OF US COULD EVER GET *NEAR* HIM.

DAILY ☆ ST

WARLORDS
WAR DIMS HOPE
FOR PEAC

IT TOOK SOMEONE LIKE YOU, WITH PRINCIPLES, PATIENCE, AND NOTHING TO *LOSE.*

AND A GENIUS FOR FACT-CHECKING.

IF YOU SAY SO, *MR. TAYLOR.*

I'M JUST SORRY "MR. METROPOLIS" LOST HIS MIND, THAT'S ALL.

WHATEVER IT WAS HE SAW IN THE *BOTTLE,* I GUESS HE COULDN'T *HANDLE* IT.

WOULDN'T BE THE FIRST MAN WHO FOUND GOD IN A *BOTTLE.*

WHAT IS IT, CLARK?

YOU'RE UNCOMFORTABLE.

I'VE BEEN AFTER GLENMORGAN AND ALL HIS CRONIES SINCE I *ARRIVED* IN METROPOLIS.

NOW HE'S *GONE--*

WHO FILLS THE *VACUUM?*

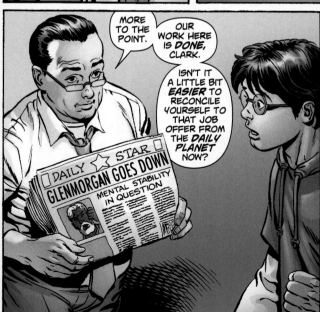

MORE TO THE POINT.

OUR WORK HERE IS *DONE,* CLARK.

ISN'T IT A LITTLE BIT *EASIER* TO RECONCILE YOURSELF TO THAT JOB OFFER FROM THE *DAILY PLANET* NOW?

DAILY ☆ STAR
GLENMORGAN GOES DOWN
MENTAL STABILITY IN QUESTION

--CAN WE TALK?

ALWAYS.

GIVE ME *FIVE* MINUTES, MRS. N.

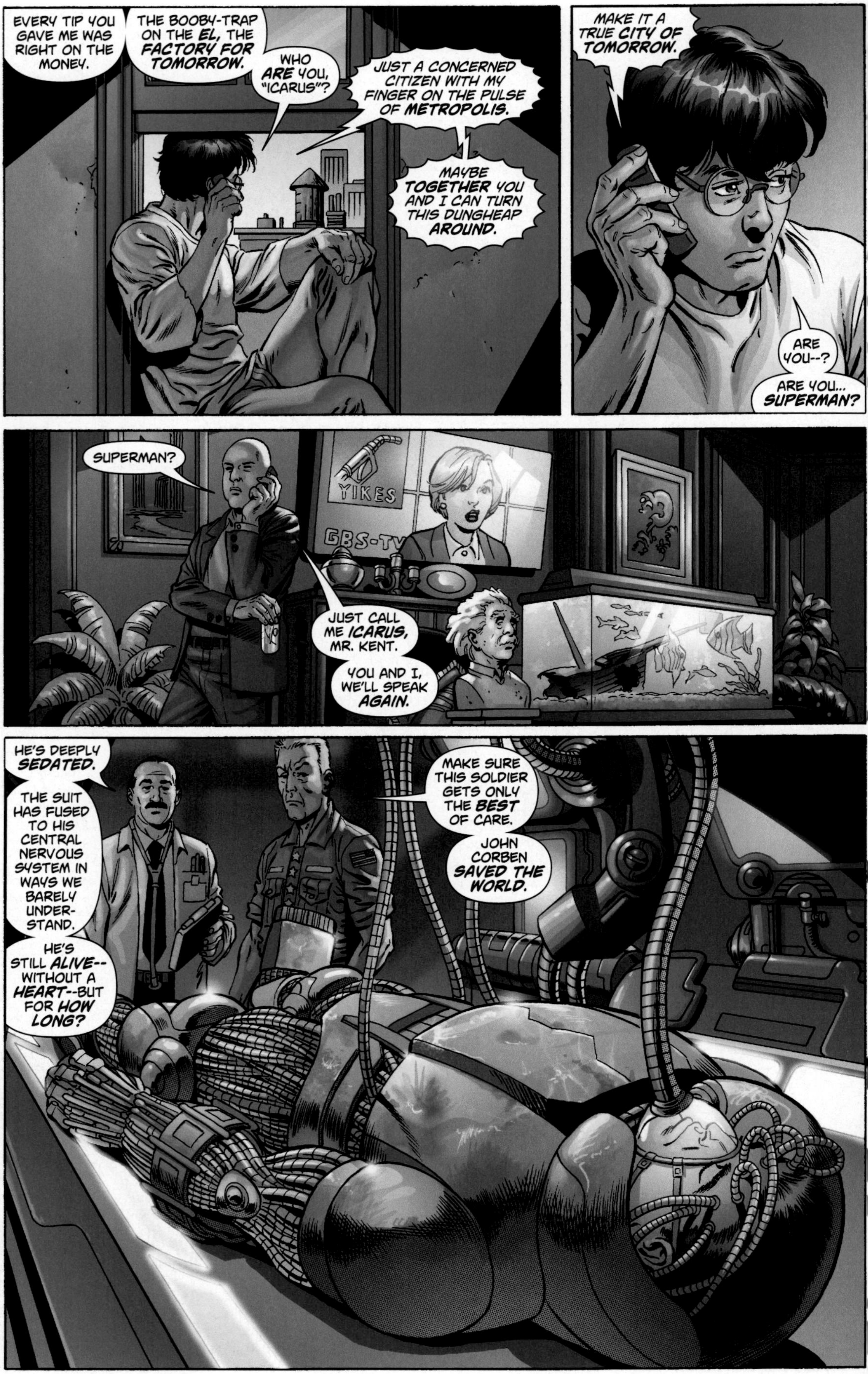
EVERY TIP YOU GAVE ME WAS RIGHT ON THE MONEY.
THE BOOBY-TRAP ON THE EL, THE FACTORY FOR TOMORROW.
WHO ARE YOU, "ICARUS"?
JUST A CONCERNED CITIZEN WITH MY FINGER ON THE PULSE OF METROPOLIS.
MAYBE TOGETHER YOU AND I CAN TURN THIS DUNGHEAP AROUND.
MAKE IT A TRUE CITY OF TOMORROW.
ARE YOU--?
ARE YOU... SUPERMAN?
SUPERMAN?
YIKES
GBS-TV
JUST CALL ME ICARUS, MR. KENT.
YOU AND I, WE'LL SPEAK AGAIN.
HE'S DEEPLY SEDATED.
THE SUIT HAS FUSED TO HIS CENTRAL NERVOUS SYSTEM IN WAYS WE BARELY UNDER-STAND.
HE'S STILL ALIVE--WITHOUT A HEART--BUT FOR HOW LONG?
MAKE SURE THIS SOLDIER GETS ONLY THE BEST OF CARE.
JOHN CORBEN SAVED THE WORLD.

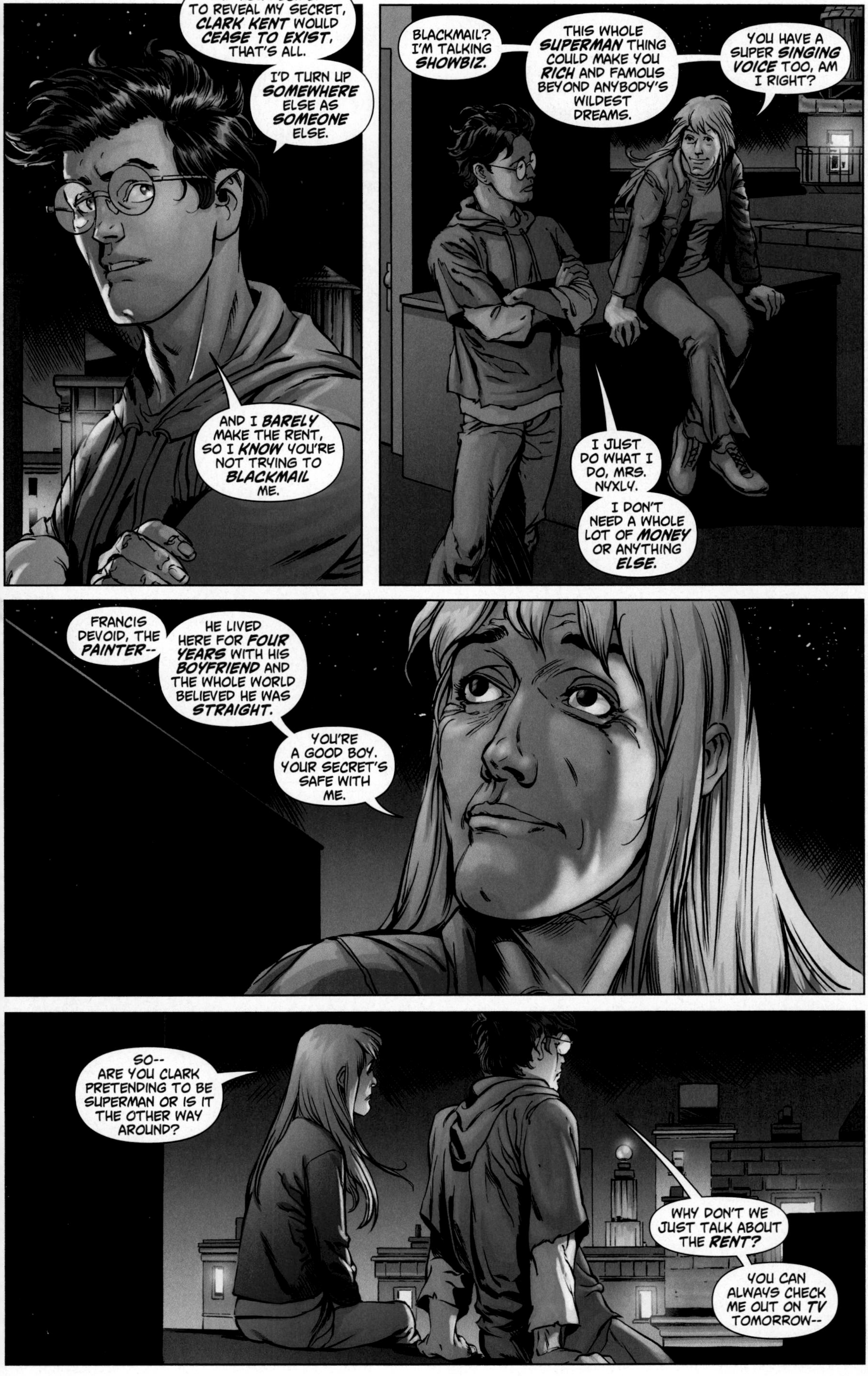
...IF YOU DECIDED TO REVEAL MY SECRET, CLARK KENT WOULD CEASE TO EXIST, THAT'S ALL.
I'D TURN UP SOMEWHERE ELSE AS SOMEONE ELSE.
AND I BARELY MAKE THE RENT, SO I KNOW YOU'RE NOT TRYING TO BLACKMAIL ME.
BLACKMAIL? I'M TALKING SHOWBIZ.
THIS WHOLE SUPERMAN THING COULD MAKE YOU RICH AND FAMOUS BEYOND ANYBODY'S WILDEST DREAMS.
YOU HAVE A SUPER SINGING VOICE TOO, AM I RIGHT?
I JUST DO WHAT I DO, MRS. NYXLY.
I DON'T NEED A WHOLE LOT OF MONEY OR ANYTHING ELSE.
FRANCIS DEVOID, THE PAINTER--
HE LIVED HERE FOR FOUR YEARS WITH HIS BOYFRIEND AND THE WHOLE WORLD BELIEVED HE WAS STRAIGHT.
YOU'RE A GOOD BOY. YOUR SECRET'S SAFE WITH ME.
SO-- ARE YOU CLARK PRETENDING TO BE SUPERMAN OR IS IT THE OTHER WAY AROUND?
WHY DON'T WE JUST TALK ABOUT THE RENT?
YOU CAN ALWAYS CHECK ME OUT ON TV TOMORROW--

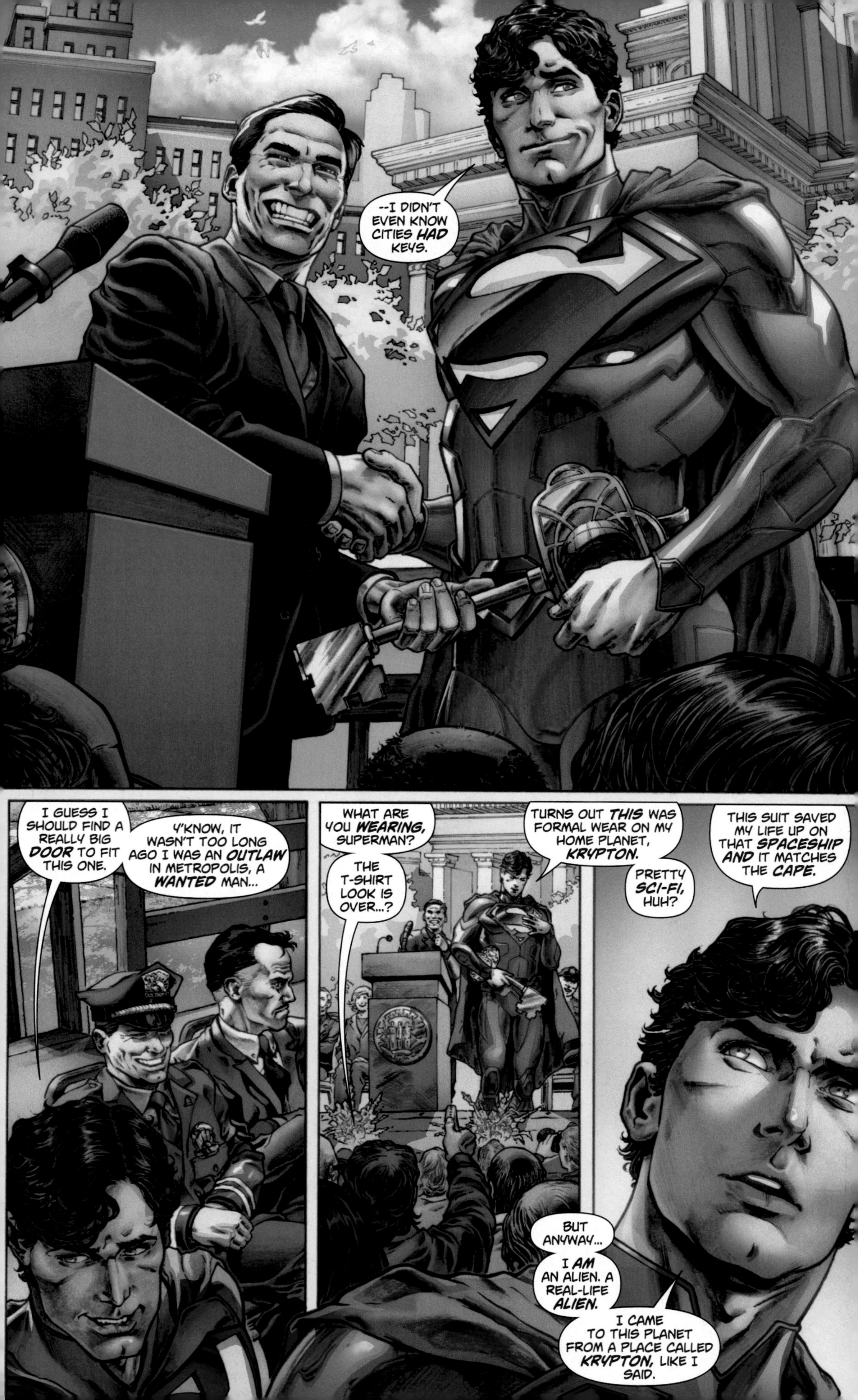
--I DIDN'T EVEN KNOW CITIES HAD KEYS.
I GUESS I SHOULD FIND A REALLY BIG DOOR TO FIT THIS ONE.
Y'KNOW, IT WASN'T TOO LONG AGO I WAS AN OUTLAW IN METROPOLIS, A WANTED MAN...
WHAT ARE YOU WEARING, SUPERMAN?
THE T-SHIRT LOOK IS OVER...?
TURNS OUT THIS WAS FORMAL WEAR ON MY HOME PLANET, KRYPTON.
PRETTY SCI-FI, HUH?
THIS SUIT SAVED MY LIFE UP ON THAT SPACESHIP AND IT MATCHES THE CAPE.
BUT ANYWAY...
I AM AN ALIEN. A REAL-LIFE ALIEN.
I CAME TO THIS PLANET FROM A PLACE CALLED KRYPTON, LIKE I SAID.

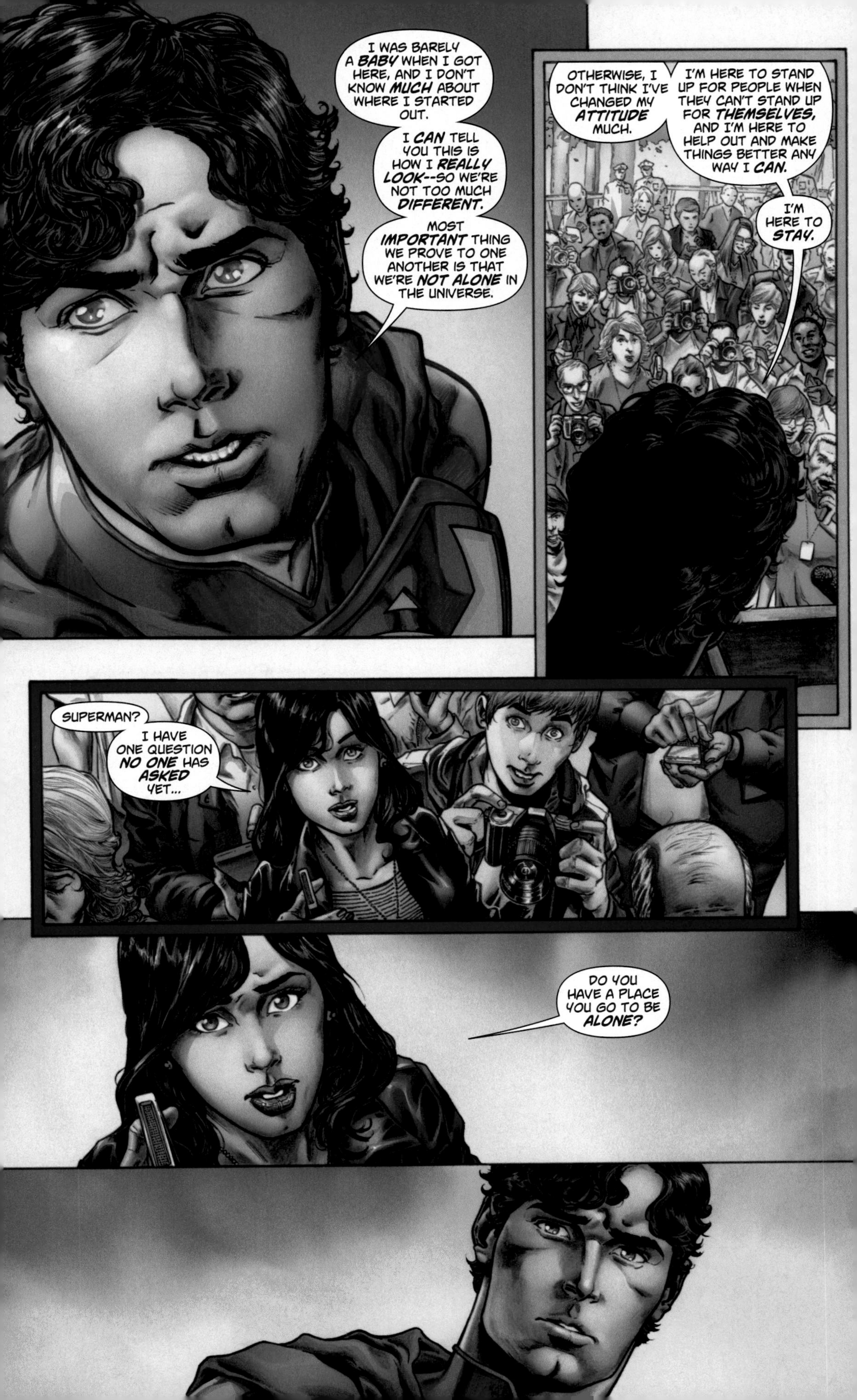
I WAS BARELY A BABY WHEN I GOT HERE, AND I DON'T KNOW MUCH ABOUT WHERE I STARTED OUT.
I CAN TELL YOU THIS IS HOW I REALLY LOOK--SO WE'RE NOT TOO MUCH DIFFERENT.
MOST IMPORTANT THING WE PROVE TO ONE ANOTHER IS THAT WE'RE NOT ALONE IN THE UNIVERSE.
OTHERWISE, I DON'T THINK I'VE CHANGED MY ATTITUDE MUCH.
I'M HERE TO STAND UP FOR PEOPLE WHEN THEY CAN'T STAND UP FOR THEMSELVES, AND I'M HERE TO HELP OUT AND MAKE THINGS BETTER ANY WAY I CAN.
I'M HERE TO STAY.
SUPERMAN?
I HAVE ONE QUESTION NO ONE HAS ASKED YET...
DO YOU HAVE A PLACE YOU GO TO BE ALONE?

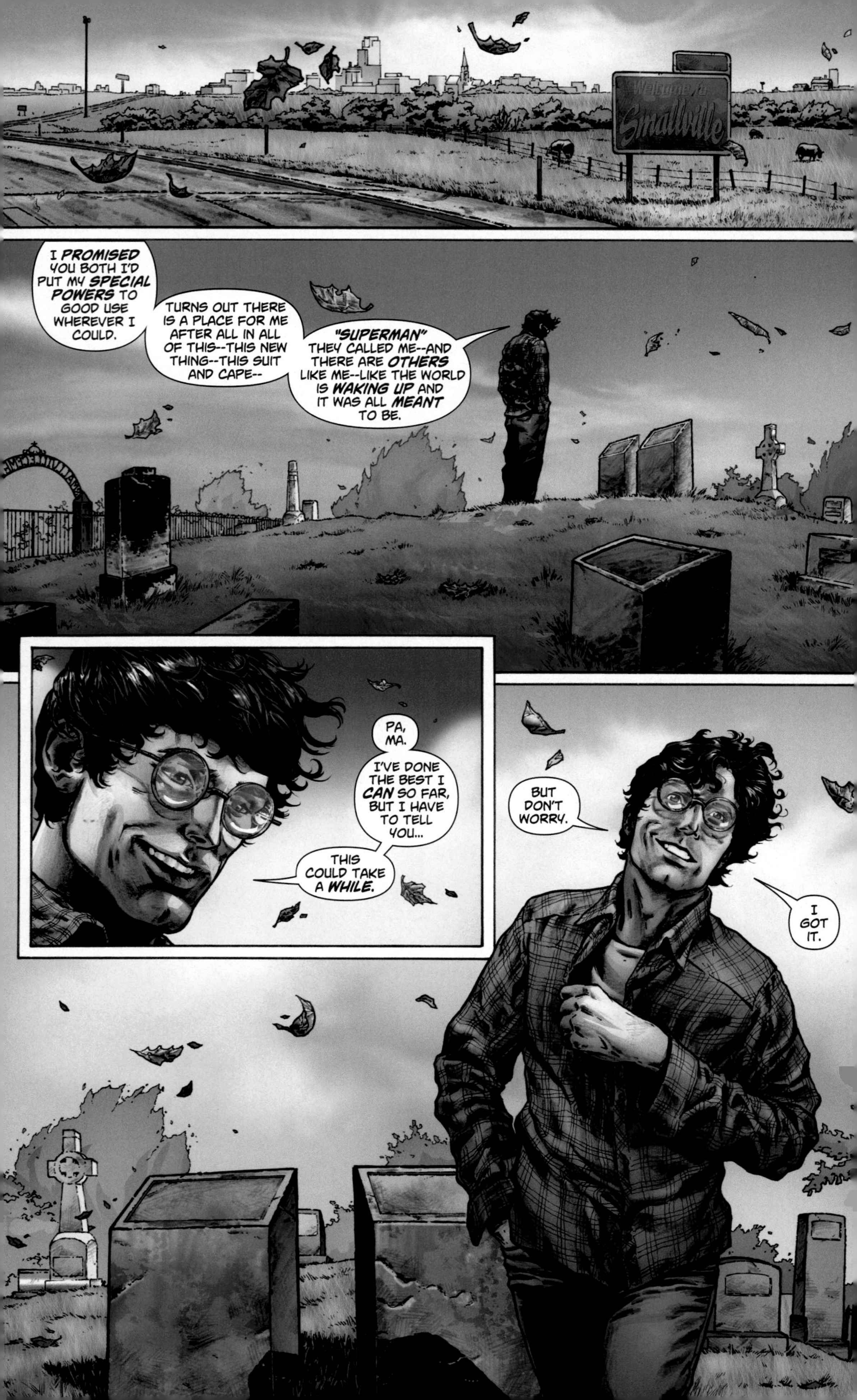
Welcome to Smallville
I PROMISED YOU BOTH I'D PUT MY SPECIAL POWERS TO GOOD USE WHEREVER I COULD.
TURNS OUT THERE IS A PLACE FOR ME AFTER ALL IN ALL OF THIS--THIS NEW THING--THIS SUIT AND CAPE--
"SUPERMAN" THEY CALLED ME--AND THERE ARE OTHERS LIKE ME--LIKE THE WORLD IS WAKING UP AND IT WAS ALL MEANT TO BE.
PA, MA.
I'VE DONE THE BEST I CAN SO FAR, BUT I HAVE TO TELL YOU...
THIS COULD TAKE A WHILE.
BUT DON'T WORRY.
I GOT IT.

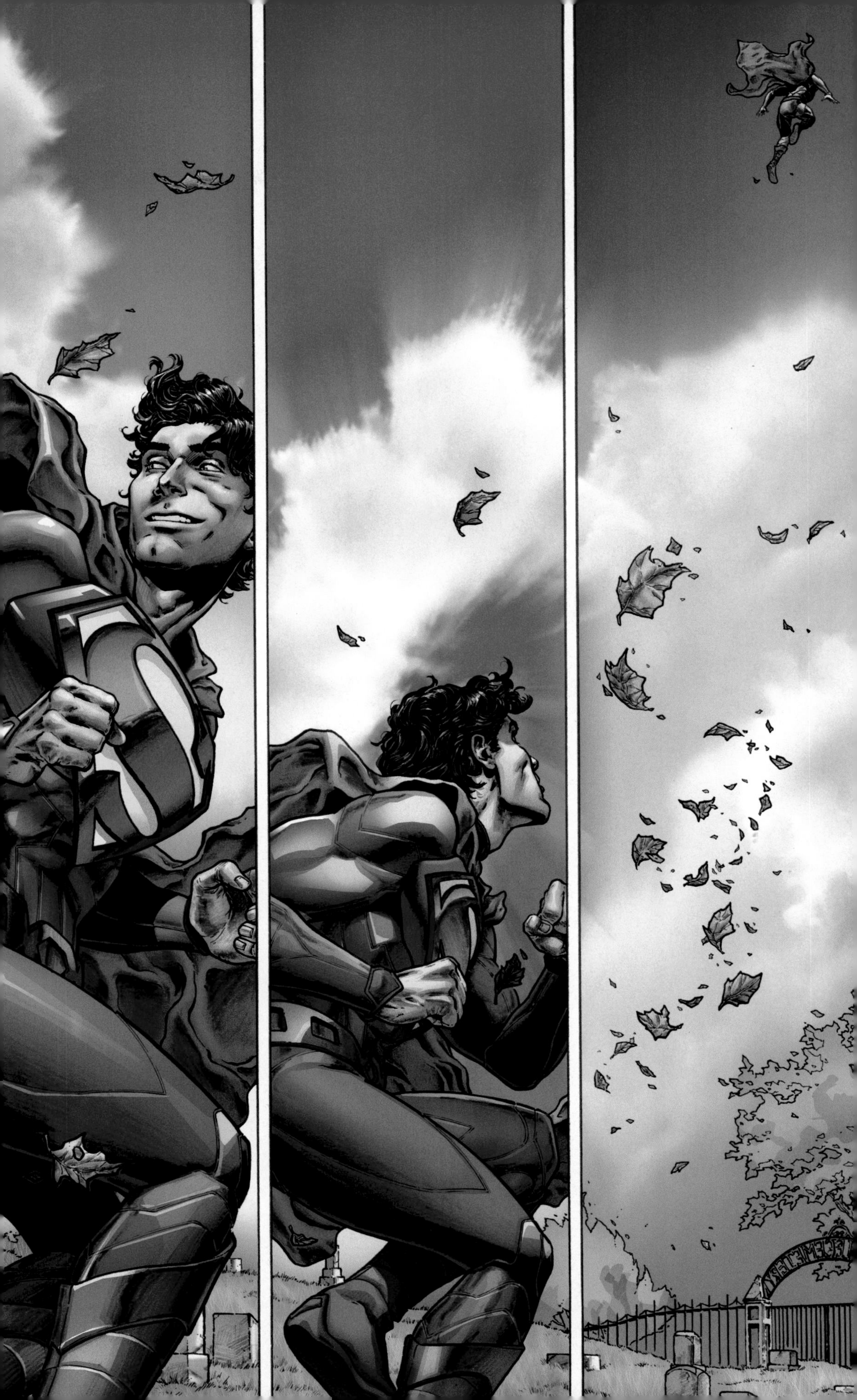

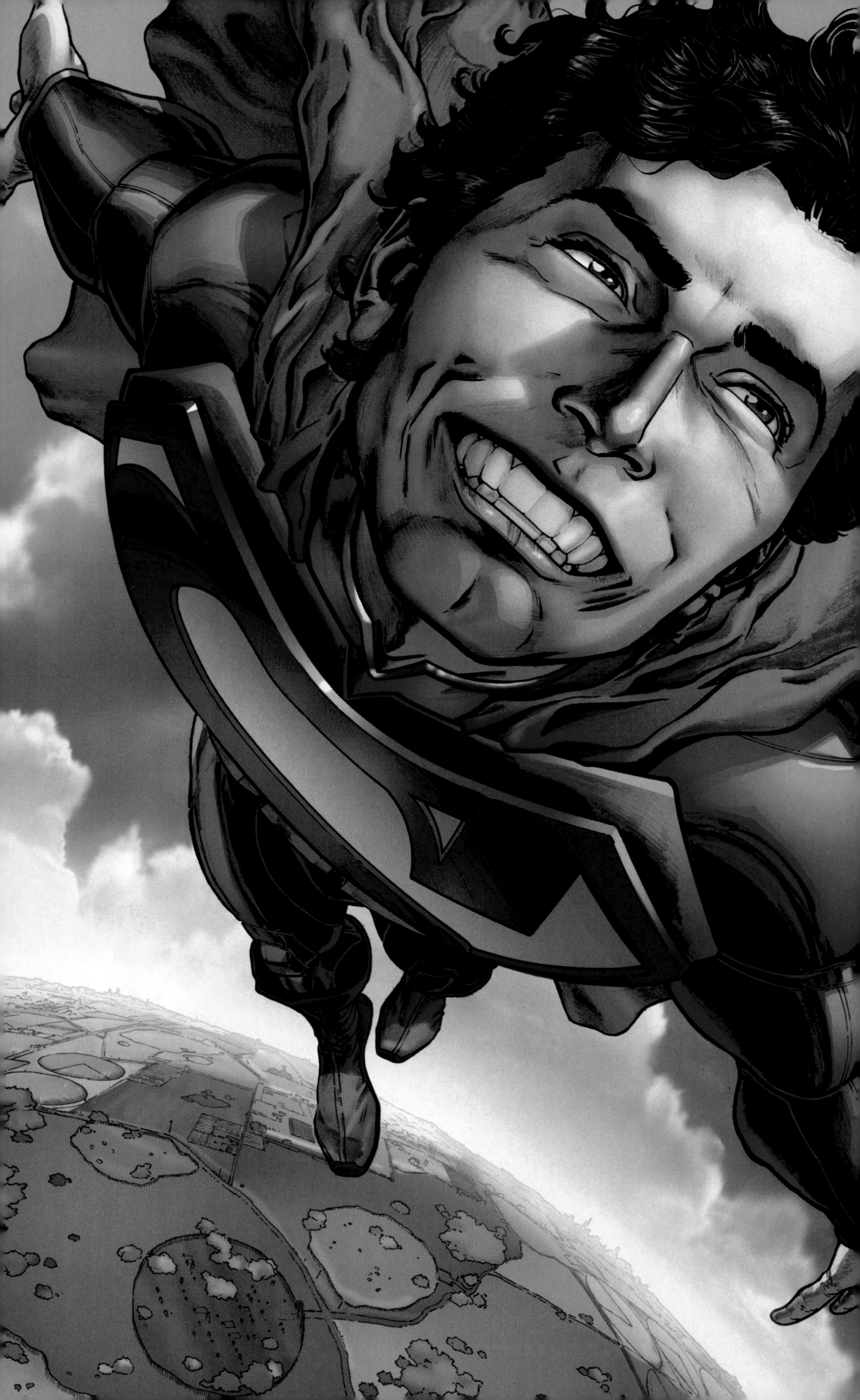

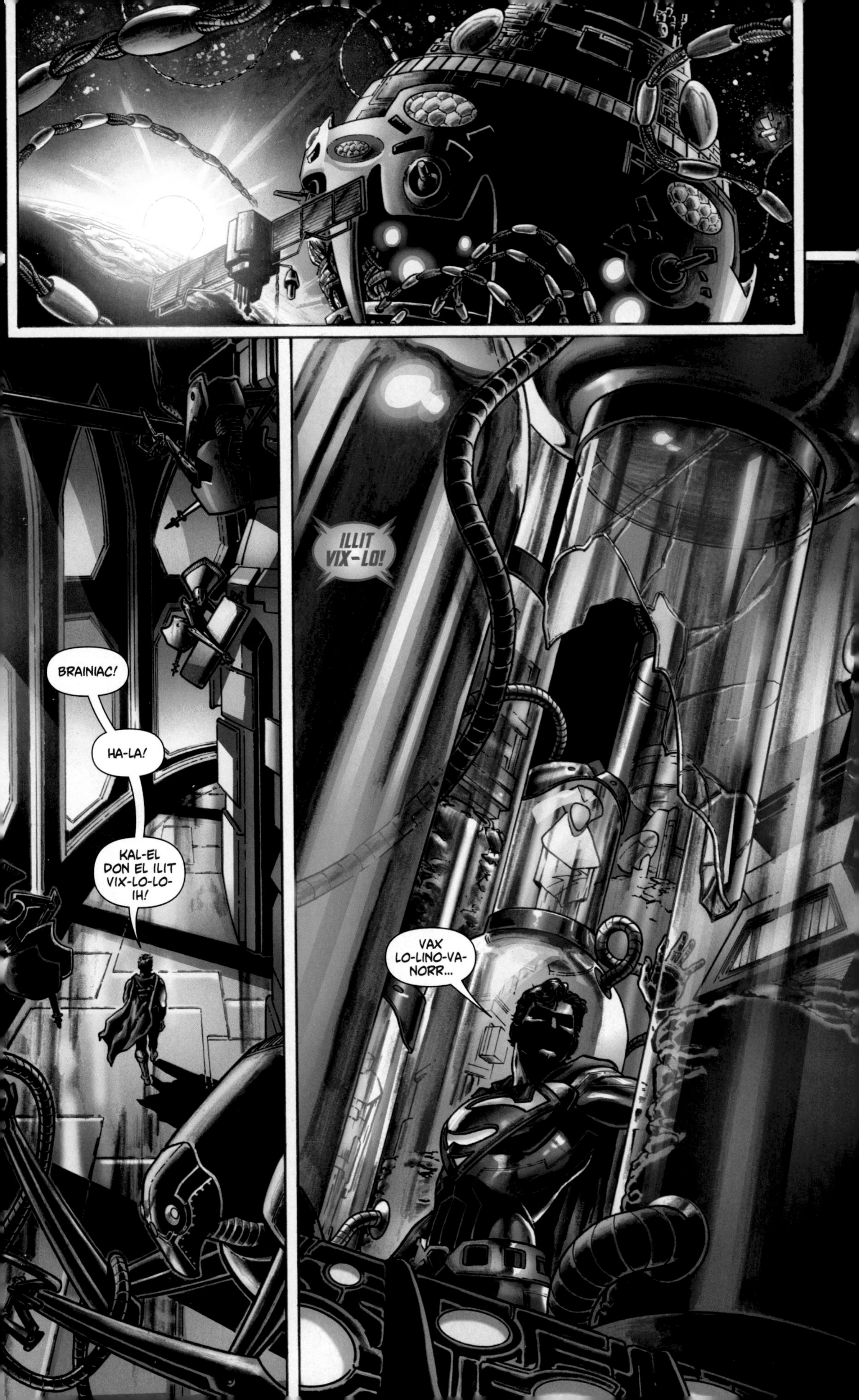
BRAINIAC!
HA-LA!
KAL-EL DON EL ILIT VIX-LO-LO-IH!
ILLIT VIX-LO!
VAX LO-LINO-VA-NORR...

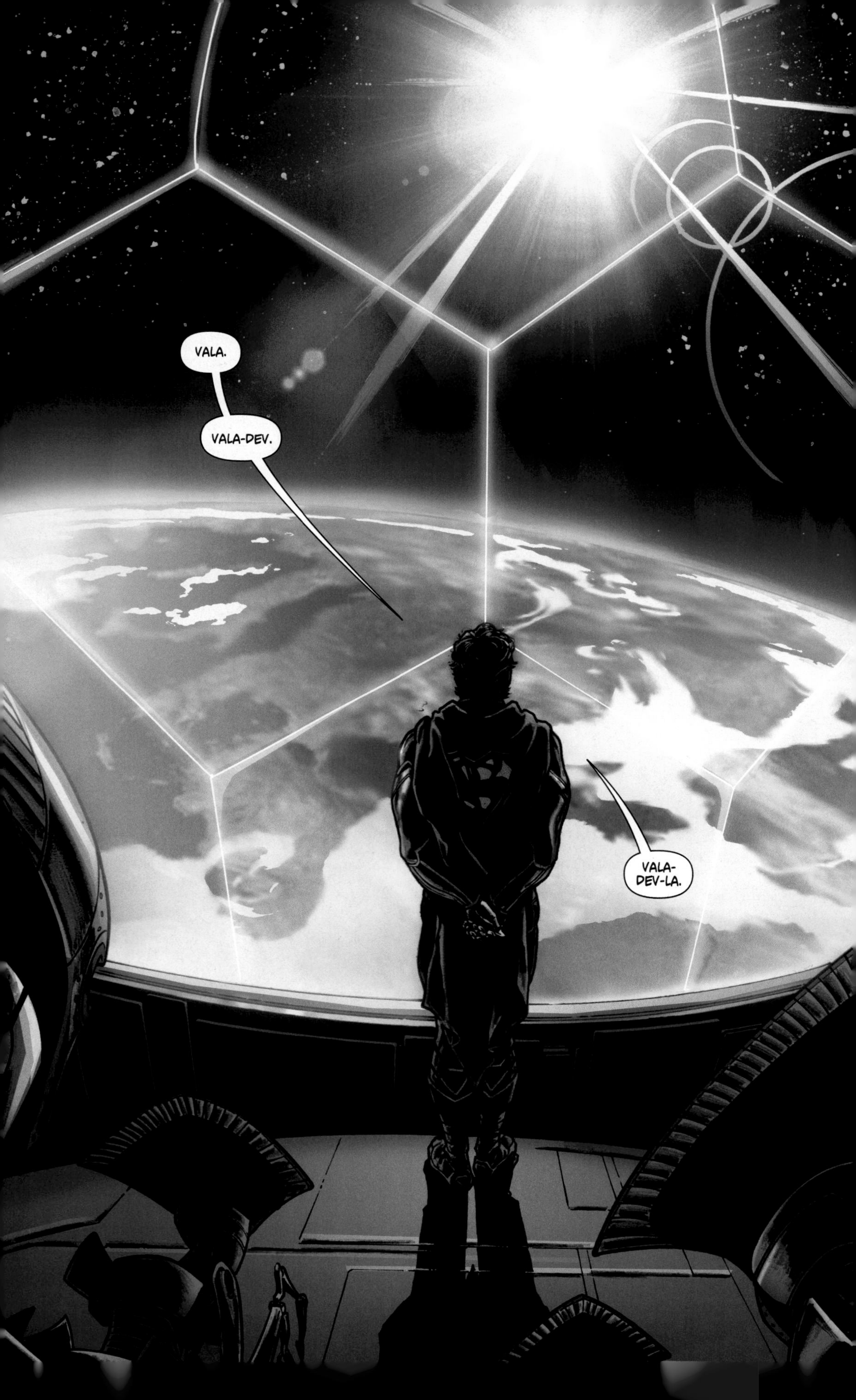
VALA.
VALA-DEV.
VALA-DEV-LA.

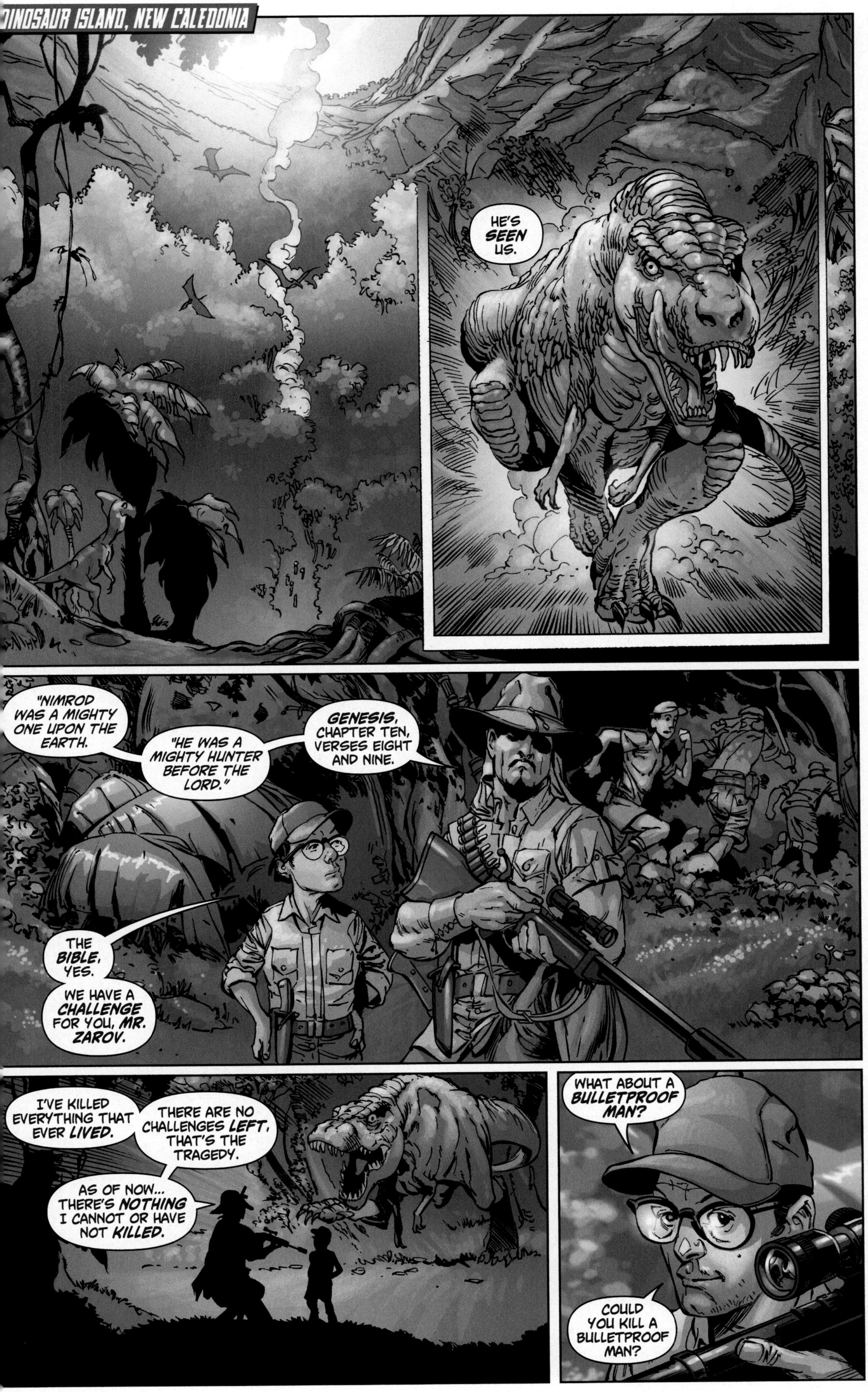
DINOSAUR ISLAND, NEW CALEDONIA
HE'S SEEN US.
"NIMROD WAS A MIGHTY ONE UPON THE EARTH.
"HE WAS A MIGHTY HUNTER BEFORE THE LORD."
GENESIS, CHAPTER TEN, VERSES EIGHT AND NINE.
THE BIBLE, YES.
WE HAVE A CHALLENGE FOR YOU, MR. ZAROV.
I'VE KILLED EVERYTHING THAT EVER LIVED.
THERE ARE NO CHALLENGES LEFT, THAT'S THE TRAGEDY.
AS OF NOW... THERE'S NOTHING I CANNOT OR HAVE NOT KILLED.
WHAT ABOUT A BULLETPROOF MAN?
COULD YOU KILL A BULLETPROOF MAN?

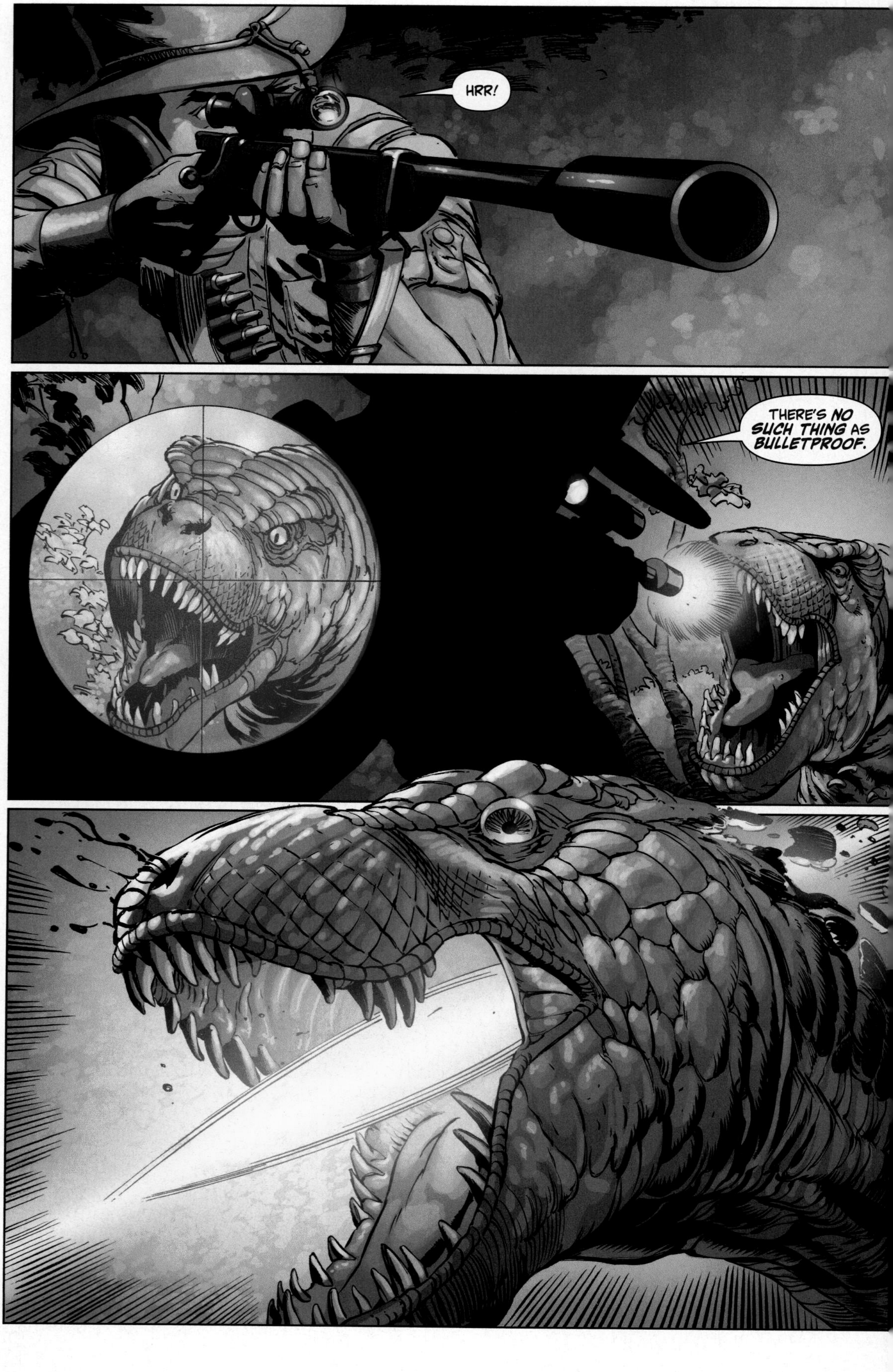
HRR!
THERE'S NO SUCH THING AS BULLETPROOF.

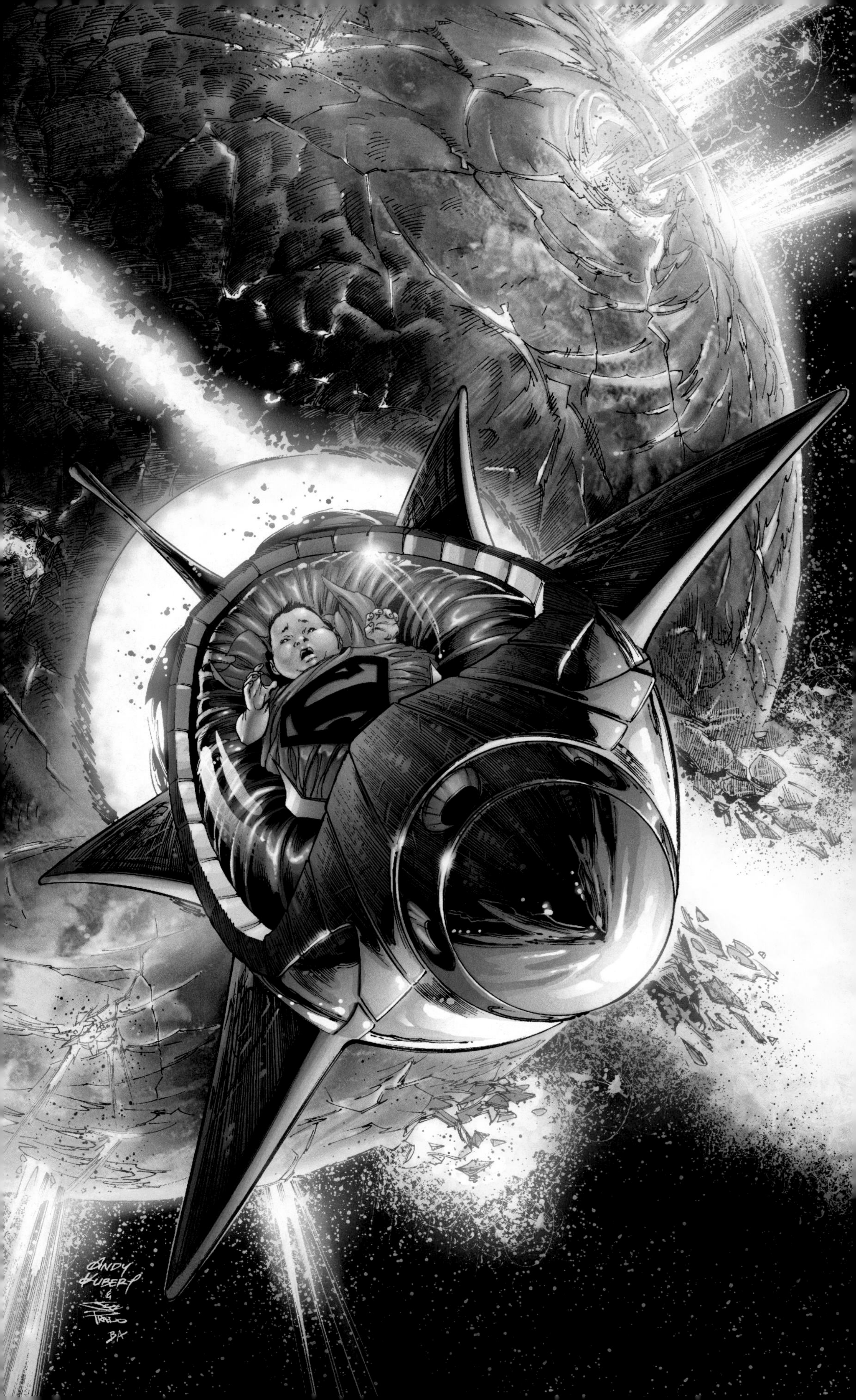
ANDY KUBERT
&

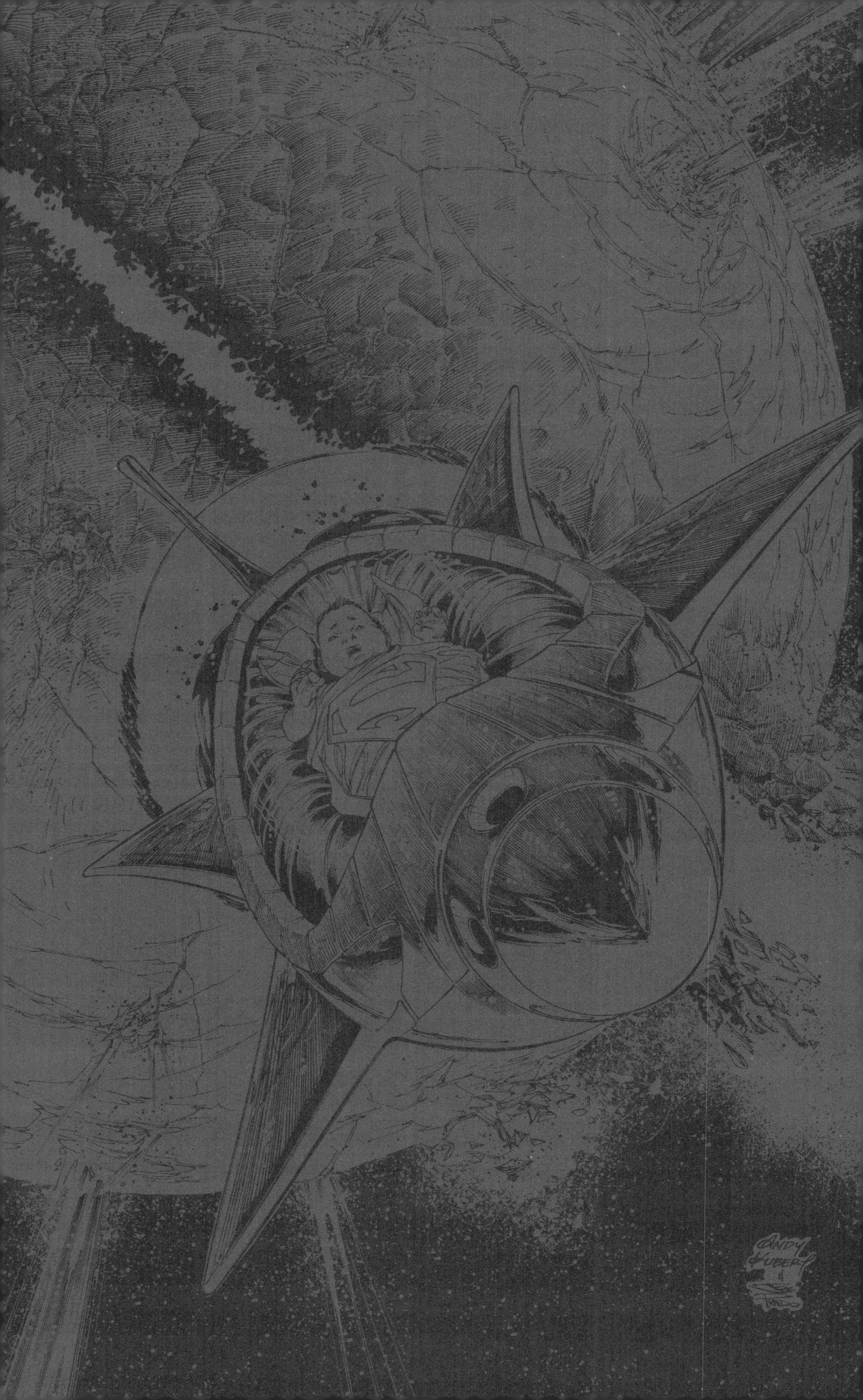

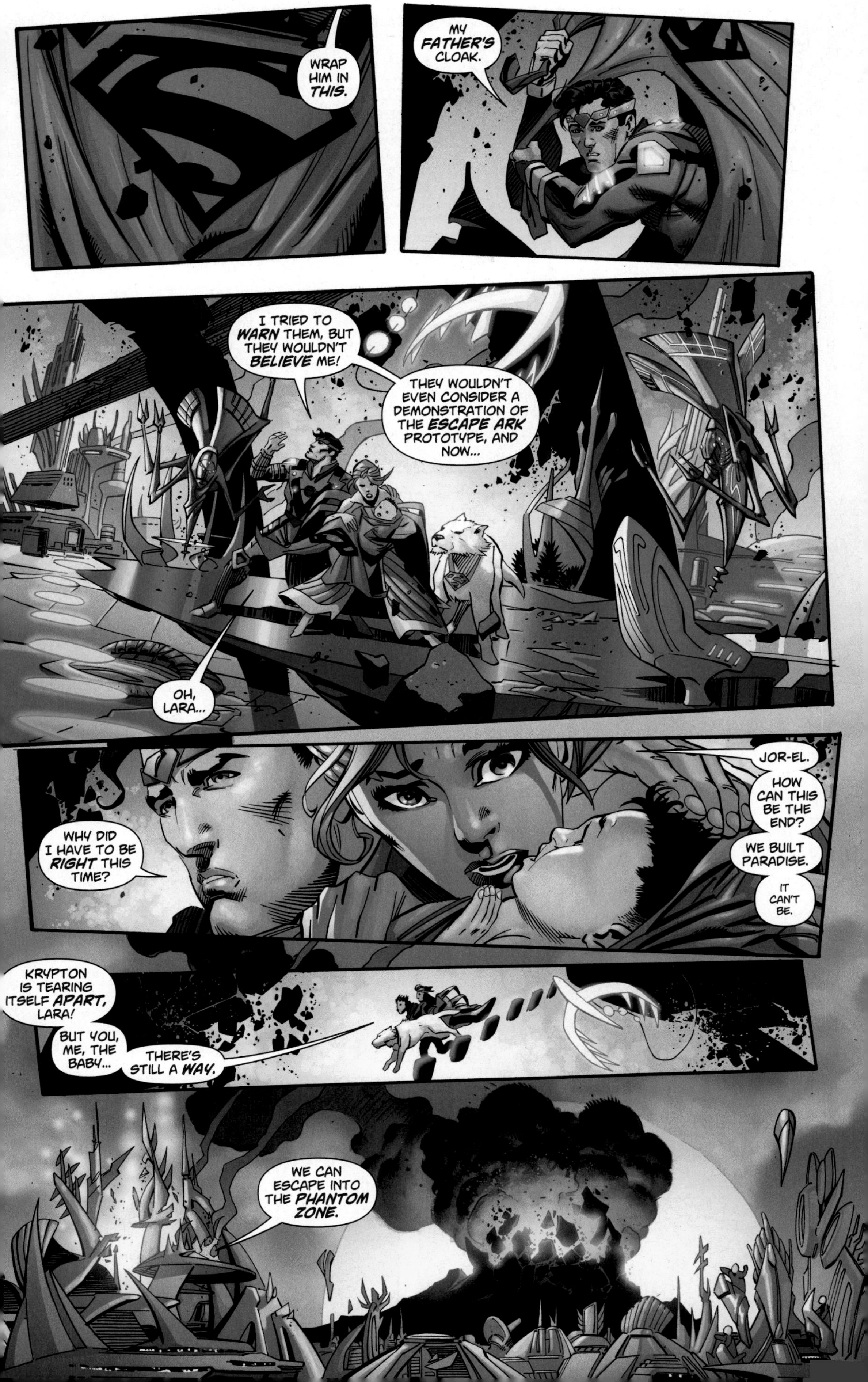
WRAP HIM IN *THIS.*
MY *FATHER'S* CLOAK.
I TRIED TO *WARN* THEM, BUT THEY WOULDN'T *BELIEVE* ME!
THEY WOULDN'T EVEN CONSIDER A DEMONSTRATION OF THE *ESCAPE ARK* PROTOTYPE, AND NOW...
OH, LARA...
JOR-EL.
HOW CAN THIS BE THE END?
WE BUILT PARADISE.
IT CAN'T BE.
WHY DID I HAVE TO BE *RIGHT* THIS TIME?
KRYPTON IS TEARING ITSELF *APART,* LARA!
BUT YOU, ME, THE BABY...
THERE'S STILL A *WAY.*
WE CAN ESCAPE INTO THE *PHANTOM ZONE.*

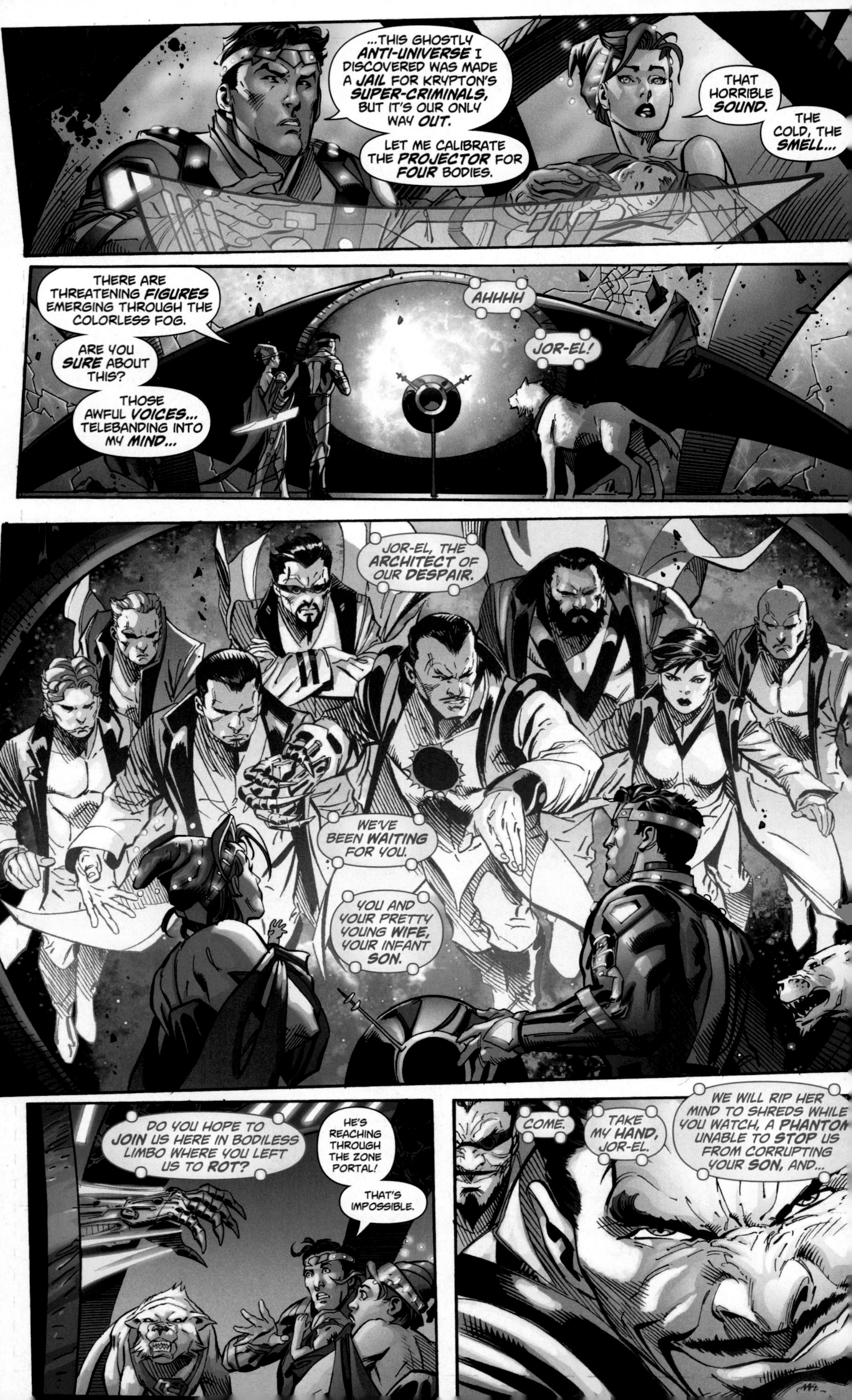
...THIS GHOSTLY ANTI-UNIVERSE I DISCOVERED WAS MADE A JAIL FOR KRYPTON'S SUPER-CRIMINALS, BUT IT'S OUR ONLY WAY OUT.
LET ME CALIBRATE THE PROJECTOR FOR FOUR BODIES.
THAT HORRIBLE SOUND.
THE COLD, THE SMELL...
THERE ARE THREATENING FIGURES EMERGING THROUGH THE COLORLESS FOG.
ARE YOU SURE ABOUT THIS?
THOSE AWFUL VOICES... TELEBANDING INTO MY MIND...
AHHHH
JOR-EL!
JOR-EL, THE ARCHITECT OF OUR DESPAIR.
WE'VE BEEN WAITING FOR YOU.
YOU AND YOUR PRETTY YOUNG WIFE, YOUR INFANT SON.
DO YOU HOPE TO JOIN US HERE IN BODILESS LIMBO WHERE YOU LEFT US TO ROT?
HE'S REACHING THROUGH THE ZONE PORTAL!
THAT'S IMPOSSIBLE.
COME.
TAKE MY HAND, JOR-EL.
WE WILL RIP HER MIND TO SHREDS WHILE YOU WATCH, A PHANTOM UNABLE TO STOP US FROM CORRUPTING YOUR SON, AND...

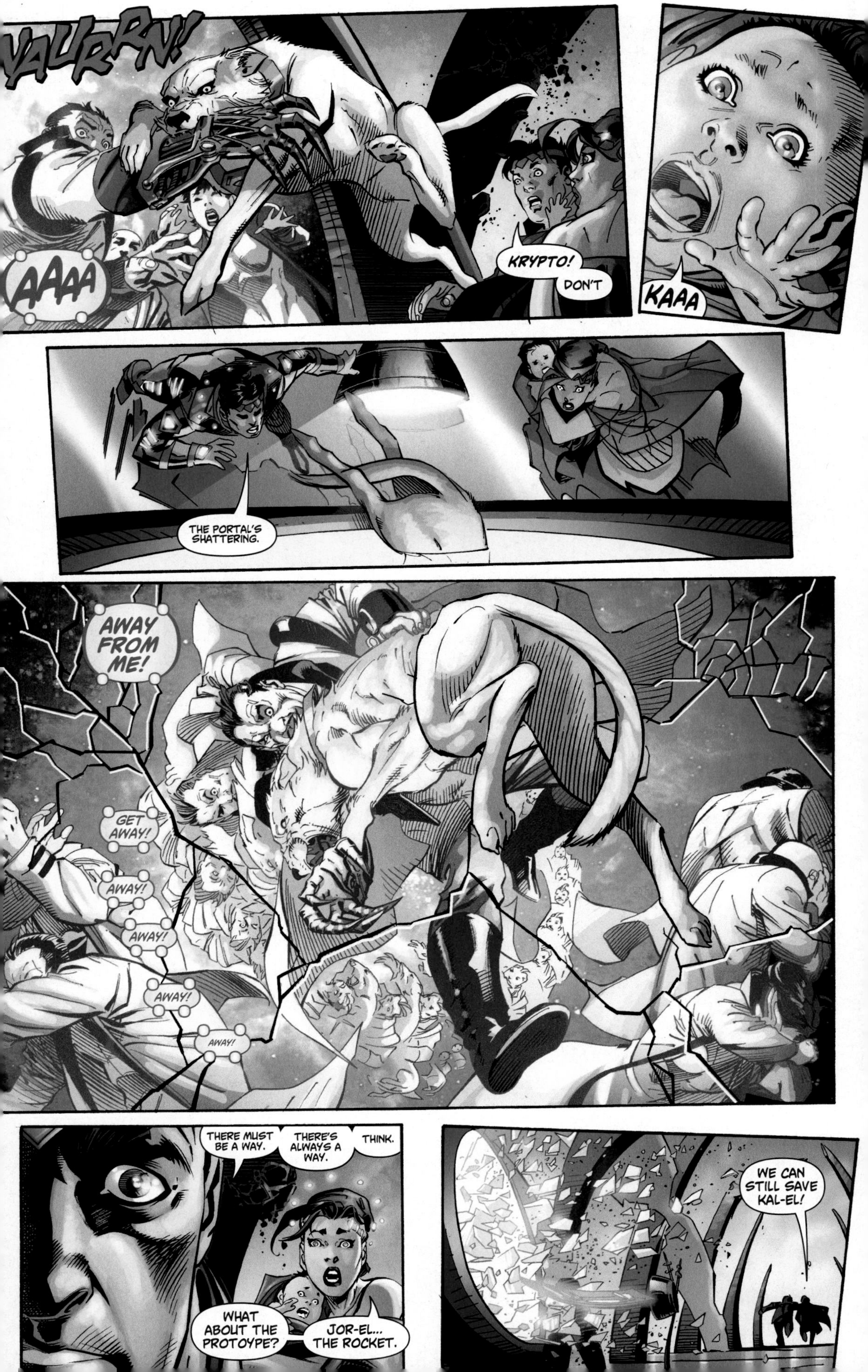

VAURRN!
AAAA
KRYPTO!
DON'T
KAAA
THE PORTAL'S SHATTERING.
AWAY FROM ME!
GET AWAY!
AWAY!
AWAY!
AWAY!
AWAY!
THERE MUST BE A WAY.
THERE'S ALWAYS A WAY.
THINK.
WHAT ABOUT THE PROTOYPE?
JOR-EL... THE ROCKET.
WE CAN STILL SAVE KAL-EL!

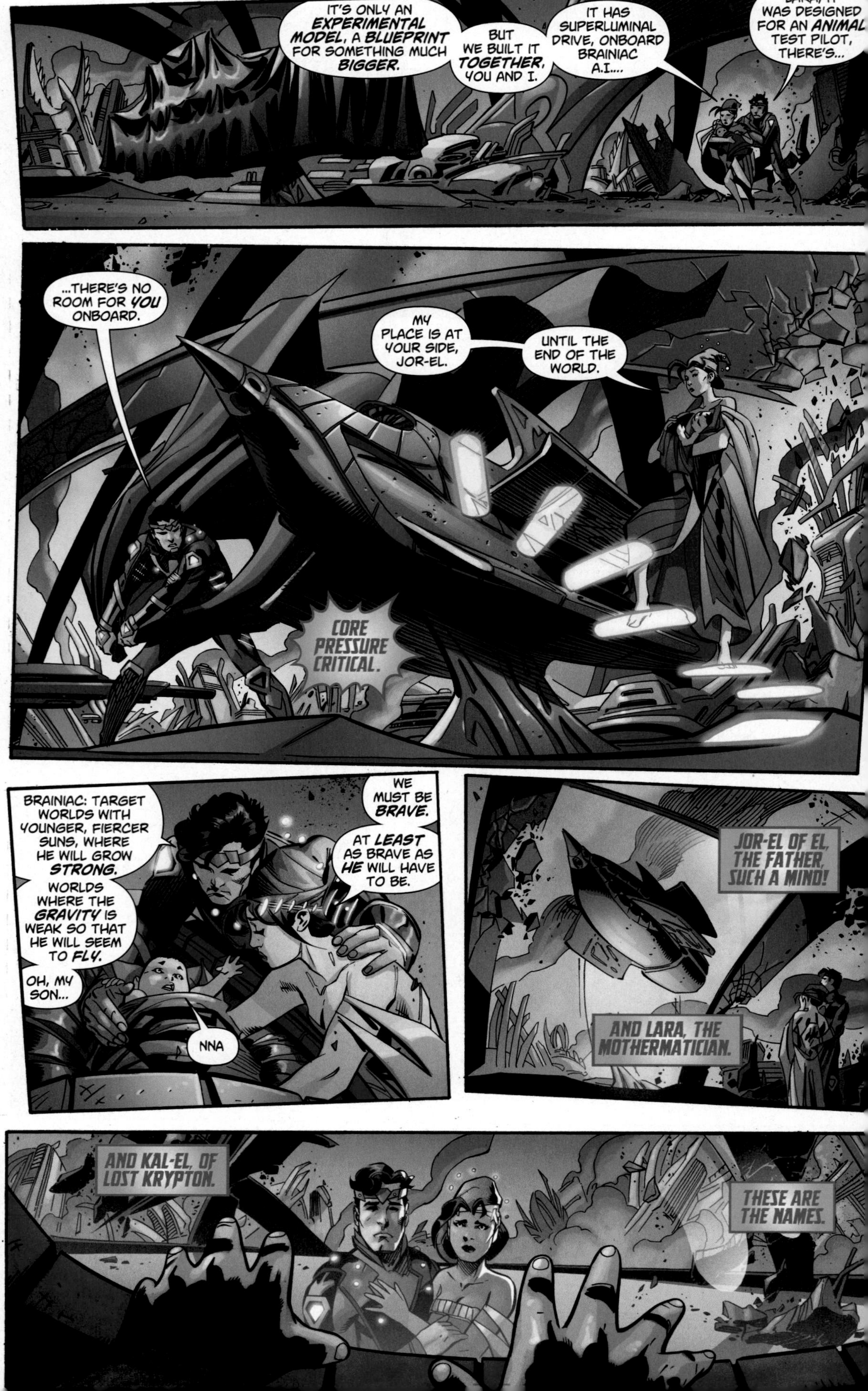

IT'S ONLY AN EXPERIMENTAL MODEL, A BLUEPRINT FOR SOMETHING MUCH BIGGER.
BUT WE BUILT IT TOGETHER, YOU AND I.
IT HAS SUPERLUMINAL DRIVE, ONBOARD BRAINIAC A.I....
LARA, IT WAS DESIGNED FOR AN ANIMAL TEST PILOT, THERE'S...
...THERE'S NO ROOM FOR YOU ONBOARD.
MY PLACE IS AT YOUR SIDE, JOR-EL.
UNTIL THE END OF THE WORLD.
CORE PRESSURE CRITICAL.
BRAINIAC: TARGET WORLDS WITH YOUNGER, FIERCER SUNS, WHERE HE WILL GROW STRONG.
WORLDS WHERE THE GRAVITY IS WEAK SO THAT HE WILL SEEM TO FLY.
WE MUST BE BRAVE.
AT LEAST AS BRAVE AS HE WILL HAVE TO BE.
OH, MY SON...
NNA
JOR-EL OF EL, THE FATHER, SUCH A MIND!
AND LARA, THE MOTHERMATICIAN.
AND KAL-EL, OF LOST KRYPTON.
THESE ARE THE NAMES.

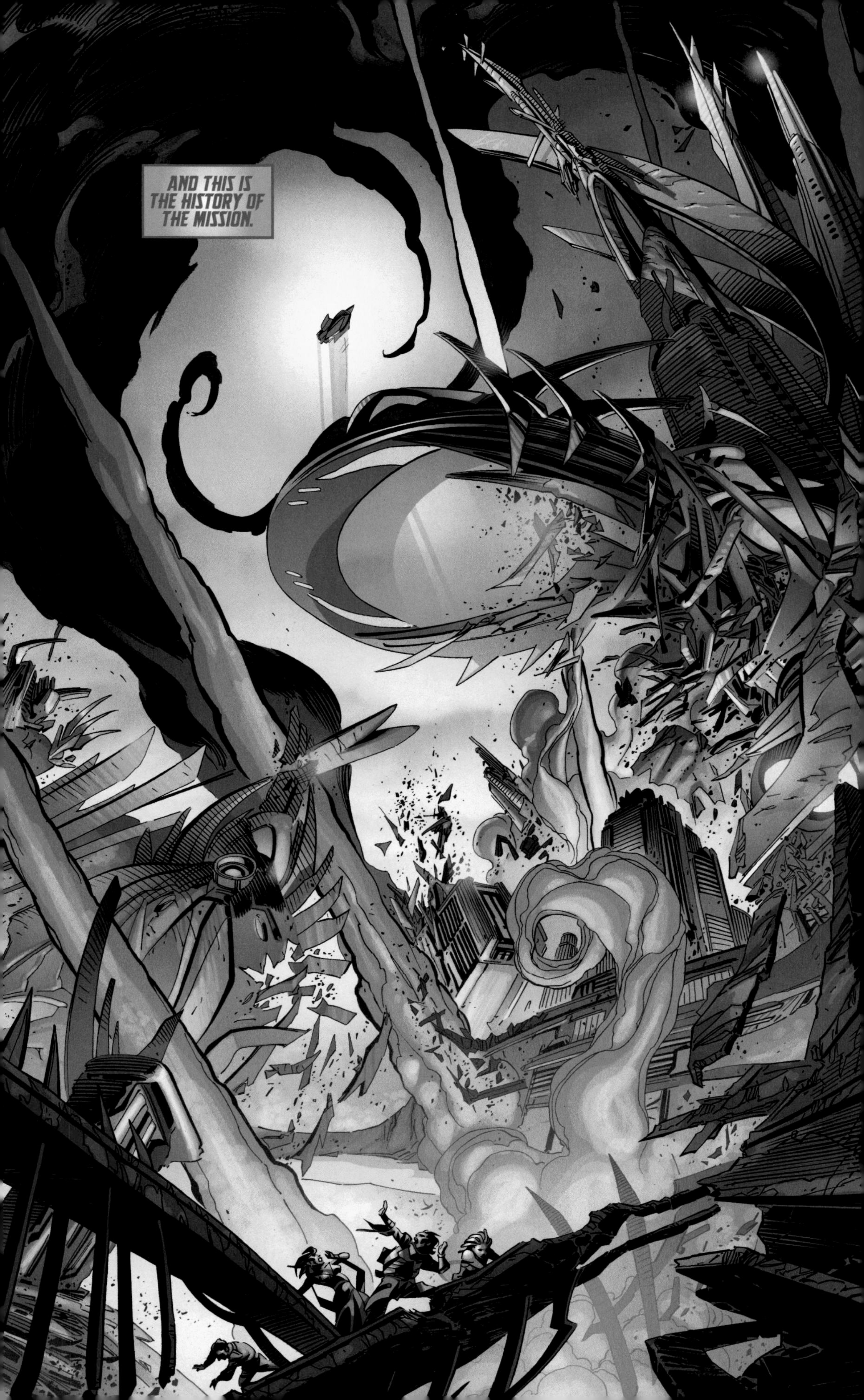
AND THIS IS THE HISTORY OF THE MISSION.

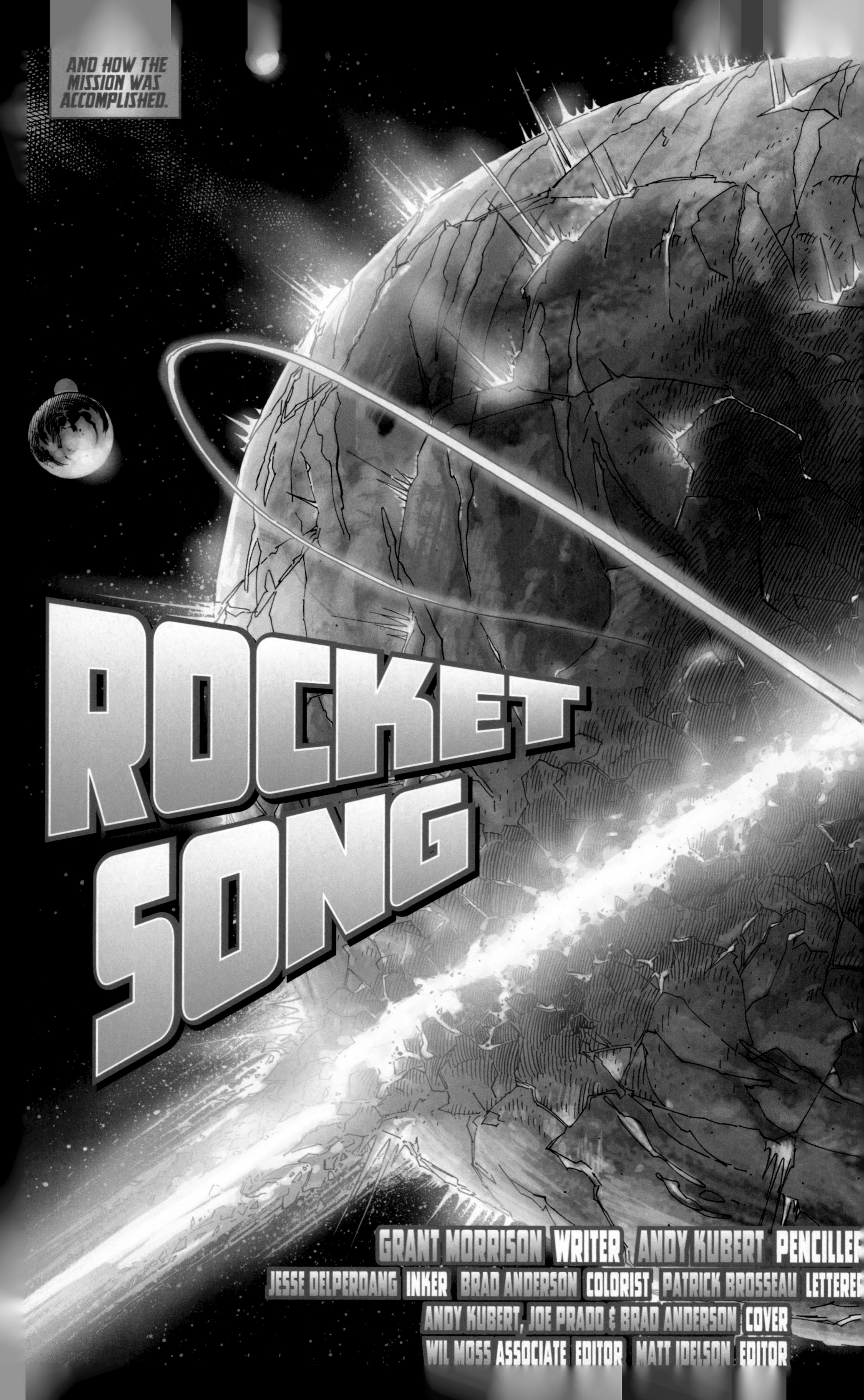
AND HOW THE MISSION WAS ACCOMPLISHED.
ROCKET SONG
GRANT MORRISON WRITER ANDY KUBERT PENCILLER
JESSE DELPERDANG INKER BRAD ANDERSON COLORIST PATRICK BROSSEAU LETTERER
ANDY KUBERT, JOE PRADO & BRAD ANDERSON COVER
WIL MOSS ASSOCIATE EDITOR MATT IDELSON EDITOR

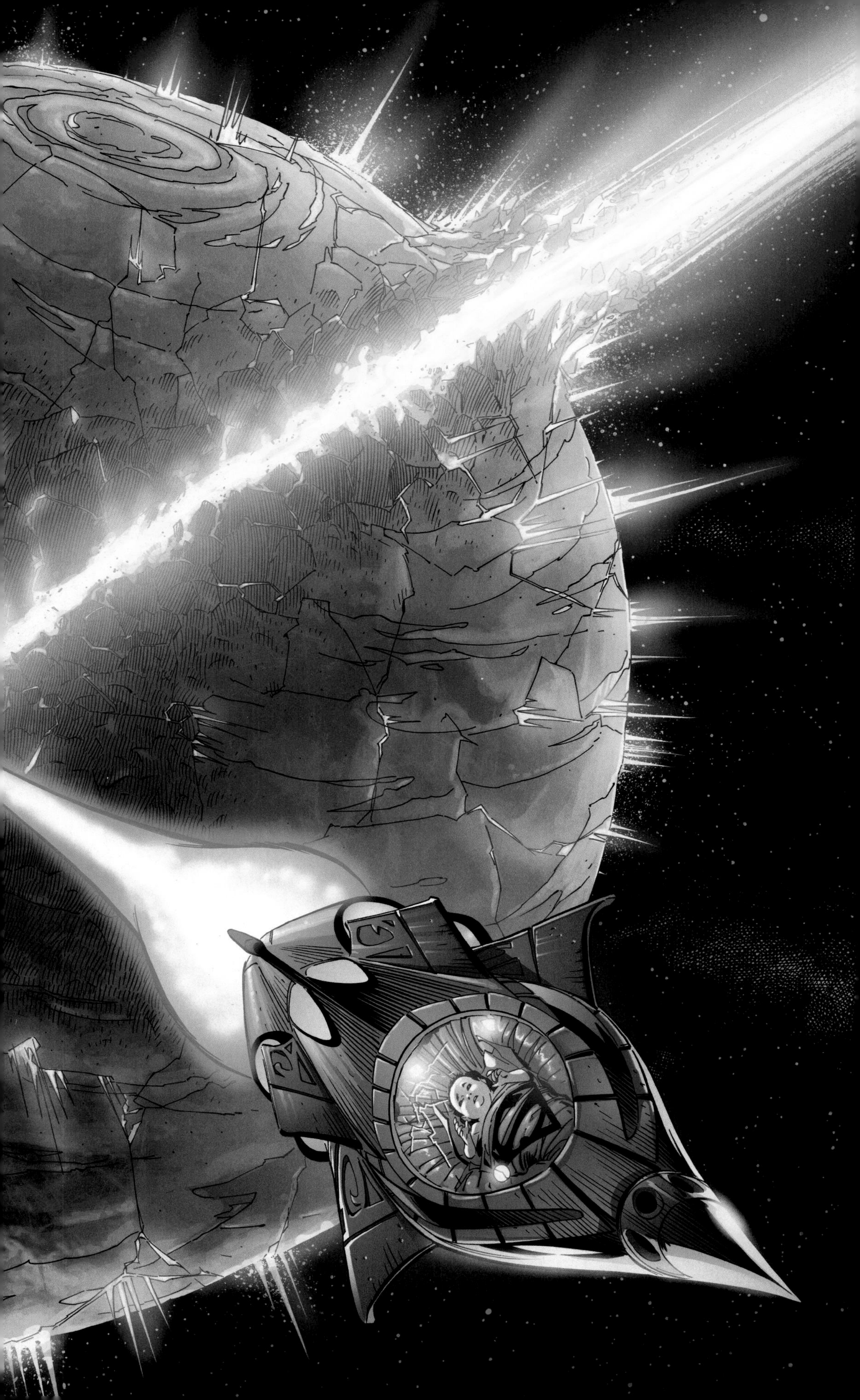

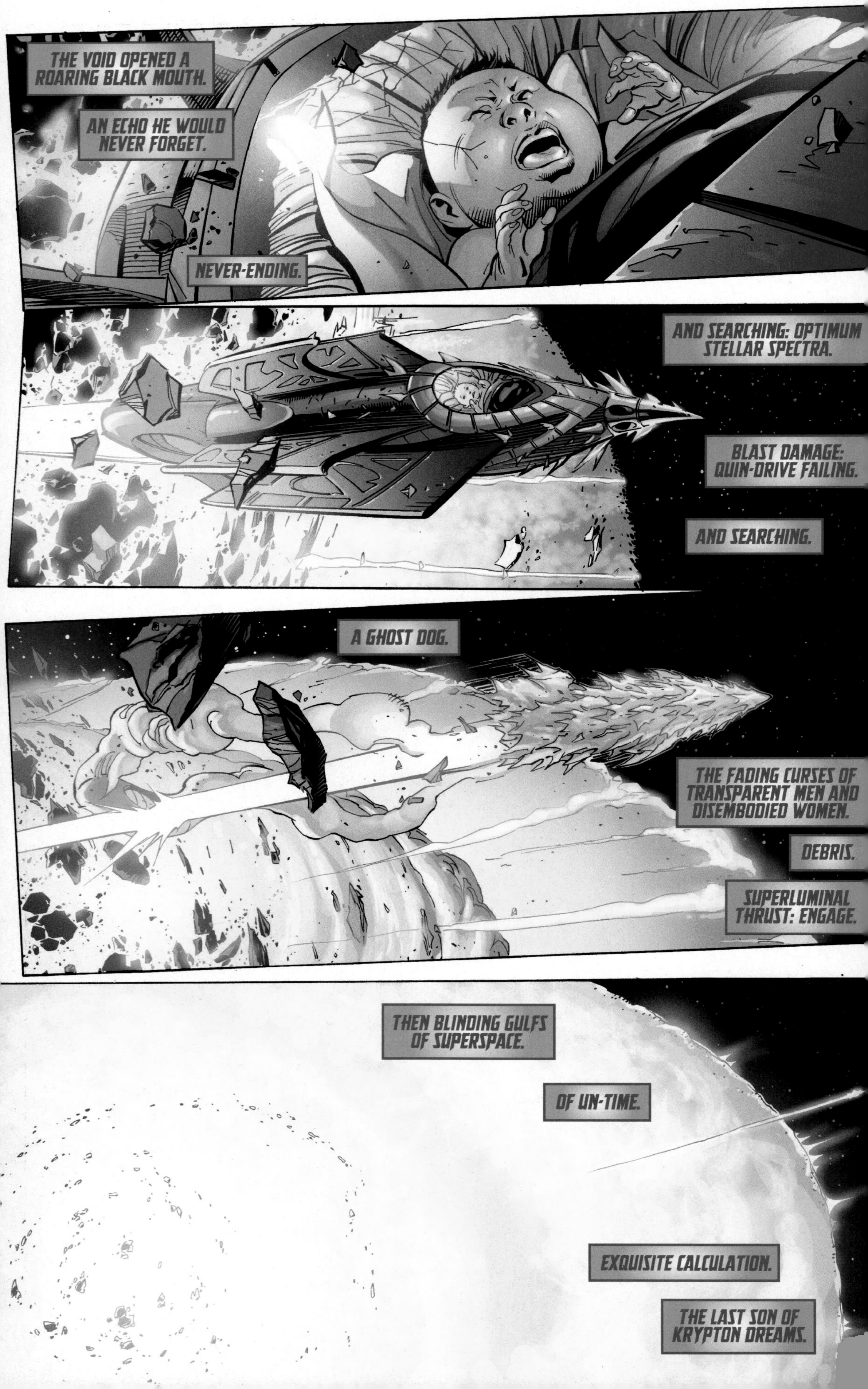
THE VOID OPENED A ROARING BLACK MOUTH.
AN ECHO HE WOULD NEVER FORGET.
NEVER-ENDING.
AND SEARCHING: OPTIMUM STELLAR SPECTRA.
BLAST DAMAGE: QUIN-DRIVE FAILING.
AND SEARCHING.
A GHOST DOG.
THE FADING CURSES OF TRANSPARENT MEN AND DISEMBODIED WOMEN.
DEBRIS.
SUPERLUMINAL THRUST: ENGAGE.
THEN BLINDING GULFS OF SUPERSPACE.
OF UN-TIME.
EXQUISITE CALCULATION.
THE LAST SON OF KRYPTON DREAMS.

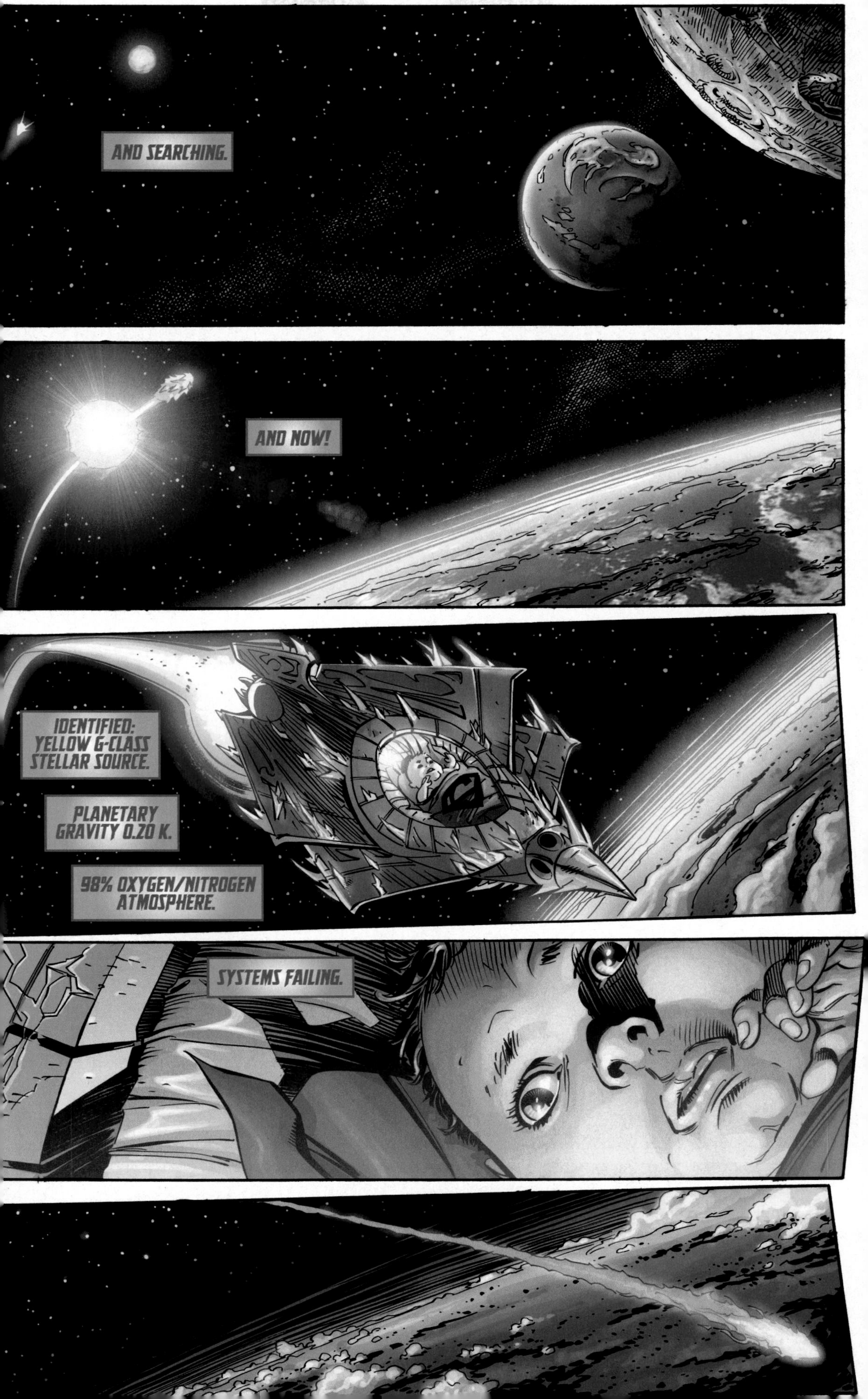
AND SEARCHING.
AND NOW!
IDENTIFIED: YELLOW G-CLASS STELLAR SOURCE.
PLANETARY GRAVITY 0.20 K.
98% OXYGEN/NITROGEN ATMOSPHERE.
SYSTEMS FAILING.

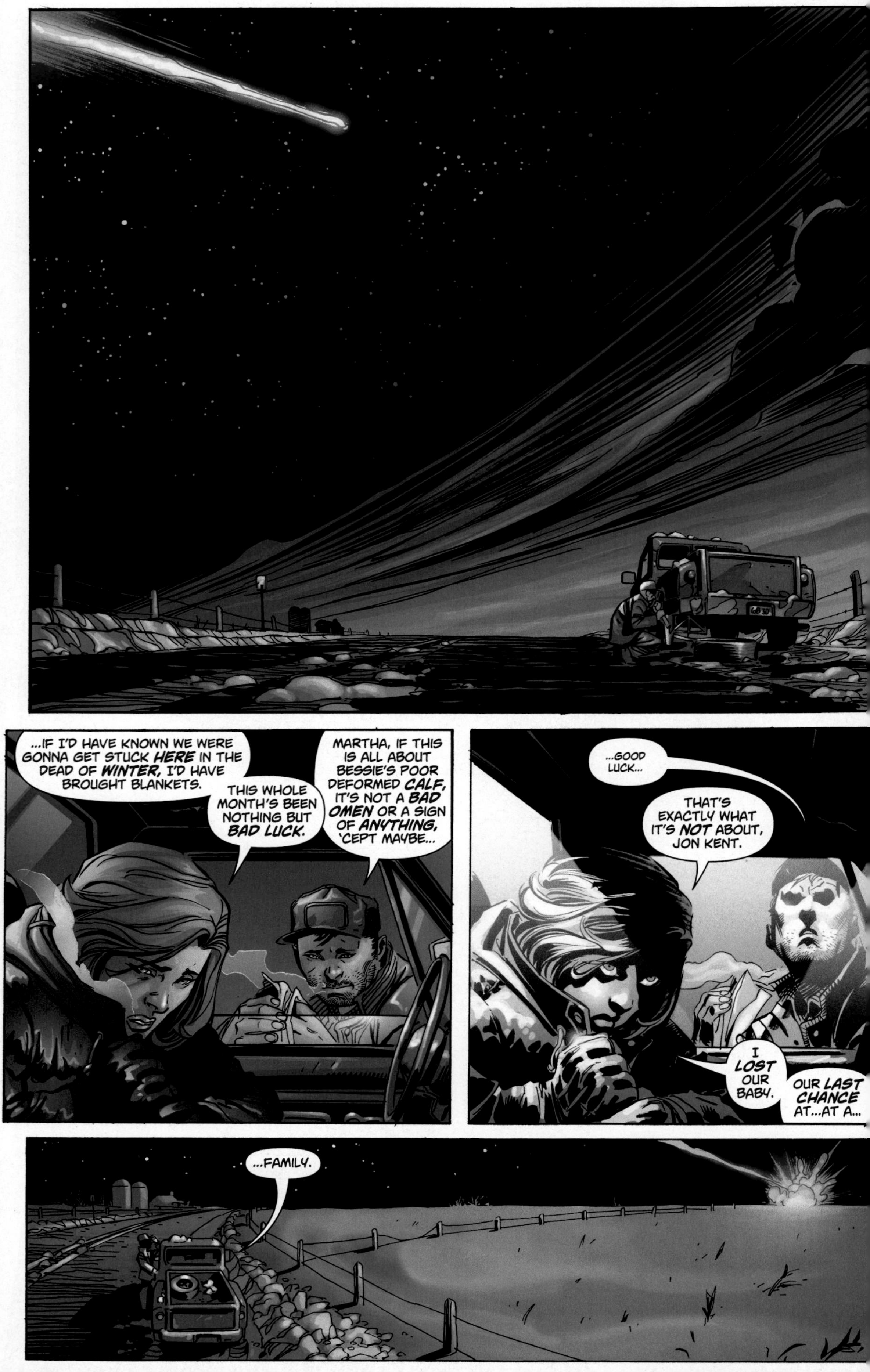

...IF I'D HAVE KNOWN WE WERE GONNA GET STUCK HERE IN THE DEAD OF WINTER, I'D HAVE BROUGHT BLANKETS.
THIS WHOLE MONTH'S BEEN NOTHING BUT BAD LUCK.
MARTHA, IF THIS IS ALL ABOUT BESSIE'S POOR DEFORMED CALF, IT'S NOT A BAD OMEN OR A SIGN OF ANYTHING, 'CEPT MAYBE...
...GOOD LUCK...
THAT'S EXACTLY WHAT IT'S NOT ABOUT, JON KENT.
I LOST OUR BABY.
OUR LAST CHANCE AT...AT A...
...FAMILY.

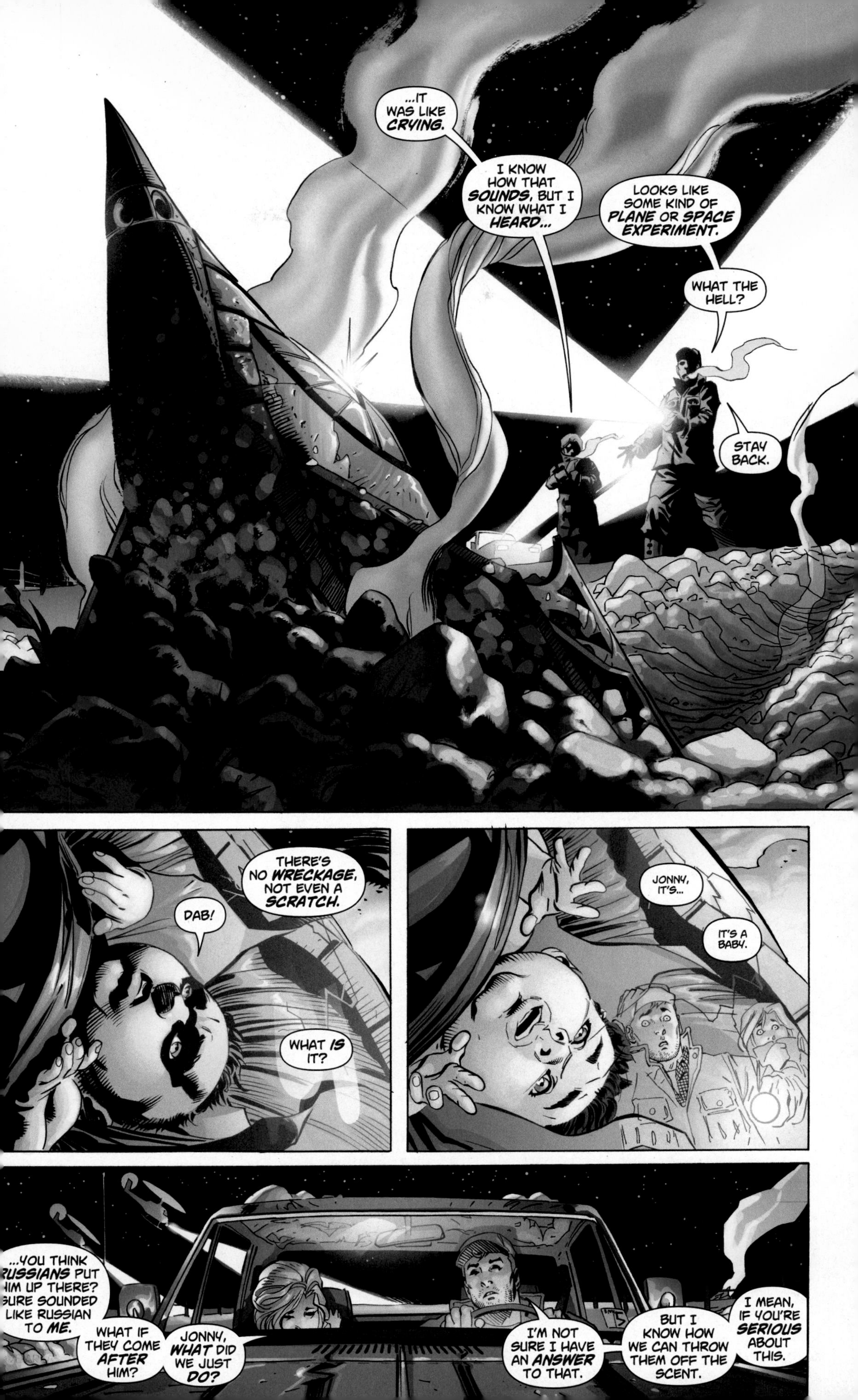
...IT WAS LIKE *CRYING*.
I KNOW HOW THAT *SOUNDS*, BUT I KNOW WHAT I *HEARD*...
LOOKS LIKE SOME KIND OF *PLANE* OR *SPACE EXPERIMENT*.
WHAT THE HELL?
STAY BACK.
THERE'S NO *WRECKAGE*, NOT EVEN A *SCRATCH*.
DAB!
WHAT *IS* IT?
JONNY, IT'S...
IT'S A BABY.
...YOU THINK *RUSSIANS* PUT HIM UP THERE? SURE SOUNDED LIKE RUSSIAN TO *ME*.
WHAT IF THEY COME *AFTER* HIM?
JONNY, *WHAT* DID WE JUST *DO?*
I'M NOT SURE I HAVE AN *ANSWER* TO THAT.
BUT I KNOW HOW WE CAN THROW THEM OFF THE SCENT.
I MEAN, IF YOU'RE *SERIOUS* ABOUT THIS.

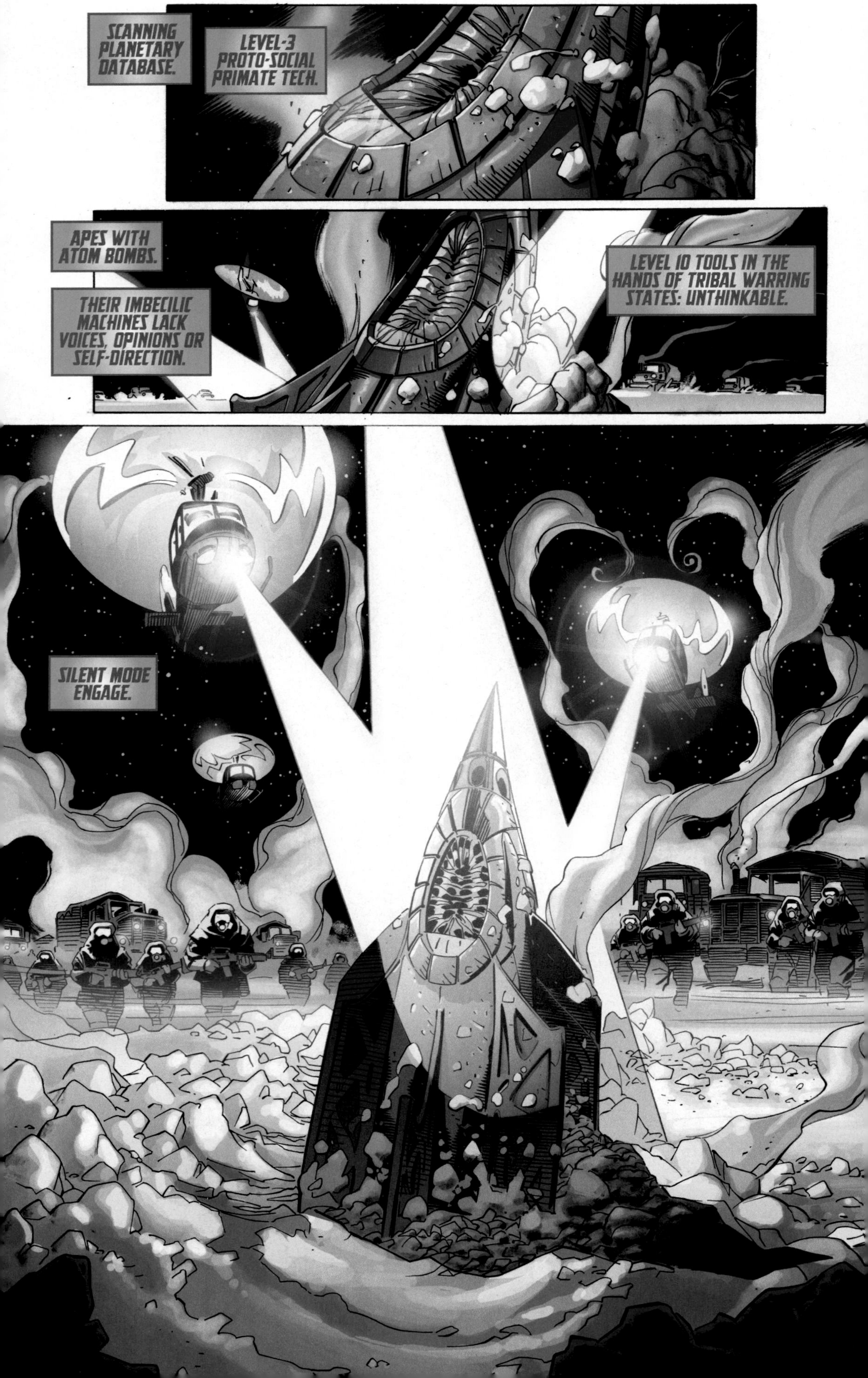
SCANNING PLANETARY DATABASE.
LEVEL-3 PROTO-SOCIAL PRIMATE TECH.
APES WITH ATOM BOMBS.
THEIR IMBECILIC MACHINES LACK VOICES, OPINIONS OR SELF-DIRECTION.
LEVEL 10 TOOLS IN THE HANDS OF TRIBAL WARRING STATES: UNTHINKABLE.
SILENT MODE ENGAGE.

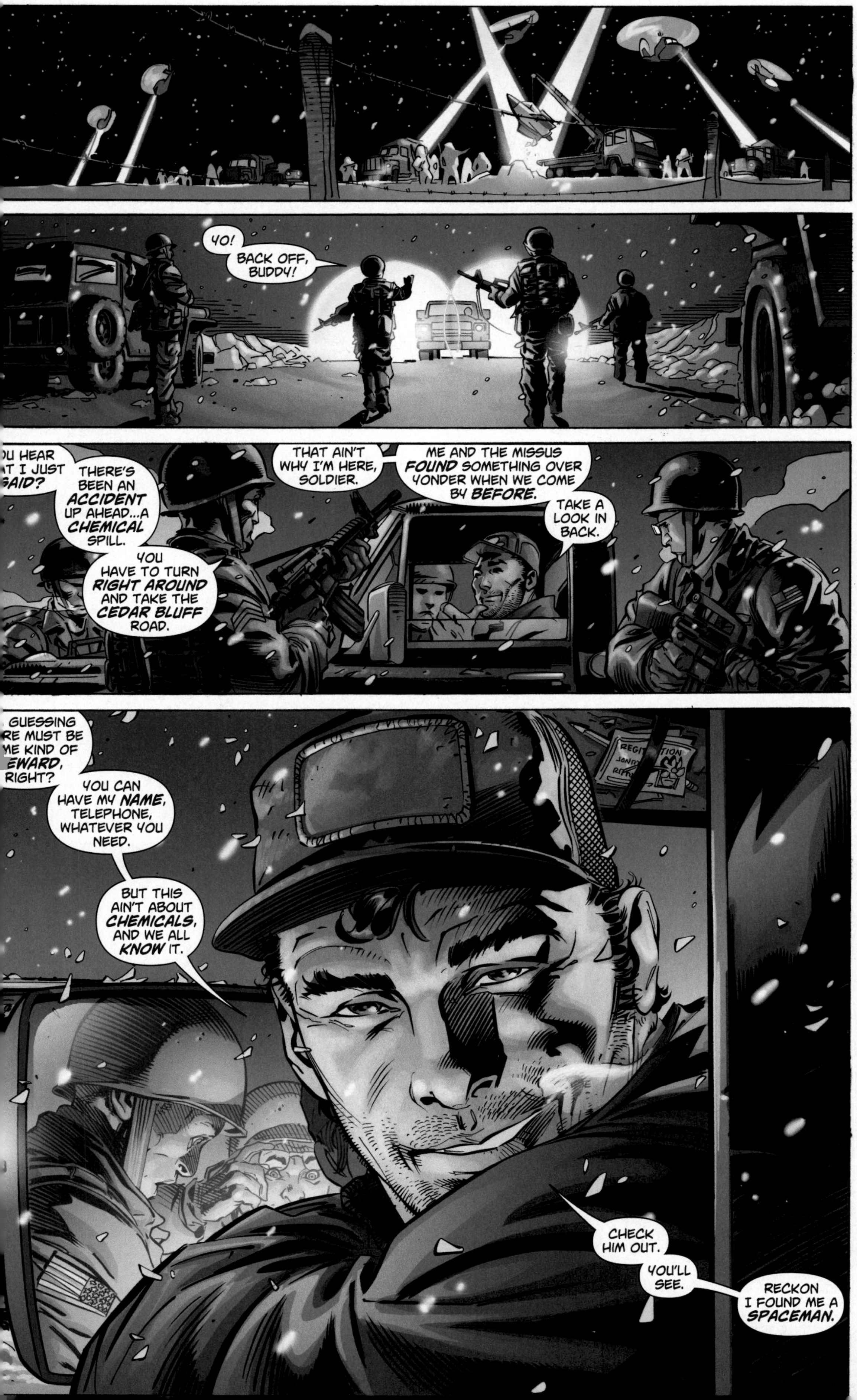

YO!
BACK OFF, BUDDY!
U HEAR T I JUST SAID?
THERE'S BEEN AN ACCIDENT UP AHEAD...A CHEMICAL SPILL.
YOU HAVE TO TURN RIGHT AROUND AND TAKE THE CEDAR BLUFF ROAD.
THAT AIN'T WHY I'M HERE, SOLDIER.
ME AND THE MISSUS FOUND SOMETHING OVER YONDER WHEN WE COME BY BEFORE.
TAKE A LOOK IN BACK.
GUESSING RE MUST BE ME KIND OF EWARD, RIGHT?
YOU CAN HAVE MY NAME, TELEPHONE, WHATEVER YOU NEED.
BUT THIS AIN'T ABOUT CHEMICALS, AND WE ALL KNOW IT.
CHECK HIM OUT.
YOU'LL SEE.
RECKON I FOUND ME A SPACEMAN.

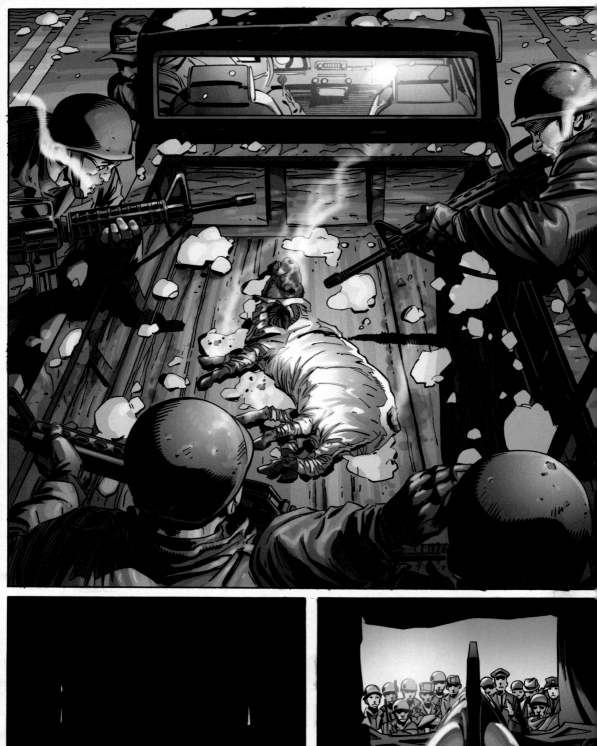

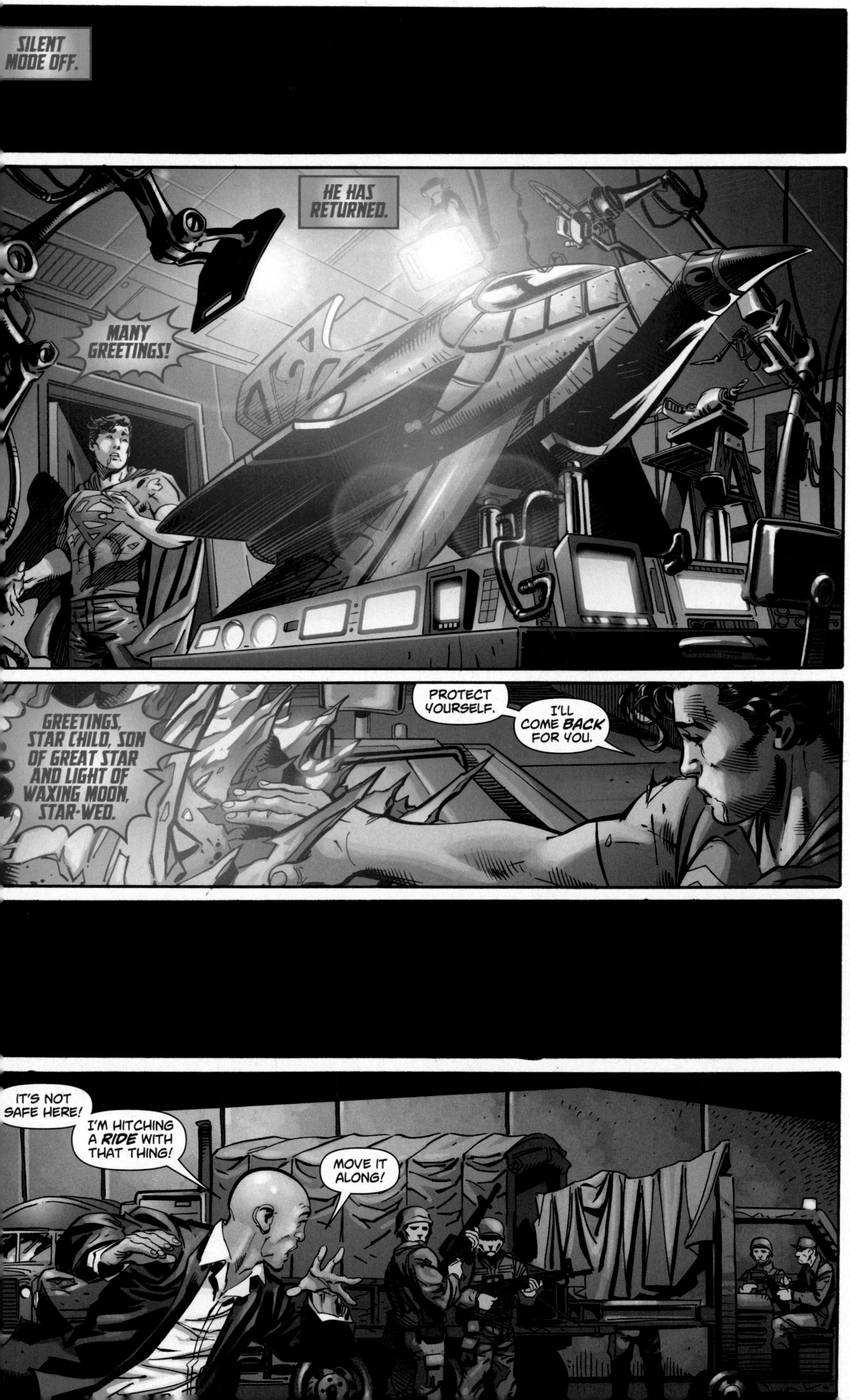
SILENT MODE OFF.
HE HAS RETURNED.
MANY GREETINGS!
GREETINGS, STAR CHILD, SON OF GREAT STAR AND LIGHT OF WAXING MOON, STAR-WED.
PROTECT YOURSELF.
I'LL COME BACK FOR YOU.
IT'S NOT SAFE HERE!
I'M HITCHING A RIDE WITH THAT THING!
MOVE IT ALONG!

THEN, AS ONCE IT CAME TO KRYPTON, THE COLLECTOR OF WORLDS REACHED LANDING SITE: "EARTH."

AND WHEN THE COLLECTOR WAS DON[E] EVERYTHING CHANGED FOREVER.

A DOOMED LEVEL 3 WORLD ACHIEVED LEVEL 4 DEVELOPMENTAL POTENTIAL.

WHAT HAD BEEN YIELDED T[O] WHAT WAS TO COME, AS TH[E] SEED OF KRYPTON GREW AND BLOOMED.

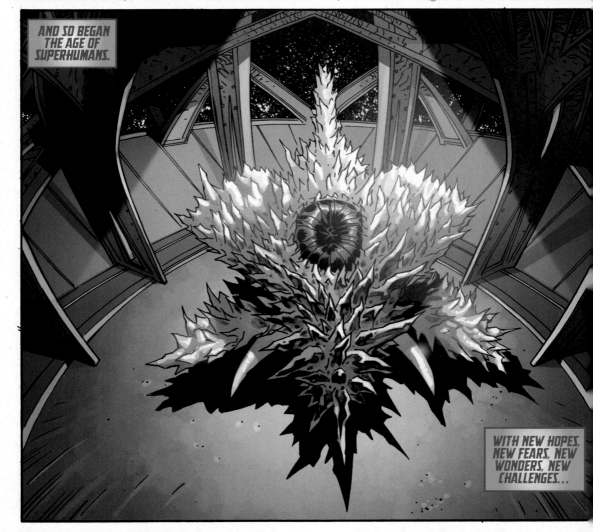

AND SO BEGAN THE AGE OF SUPERHUMANS.

WITH NEW HOPES, NEW FEARS, NEW WONDERS, NEW CHALLENGES...

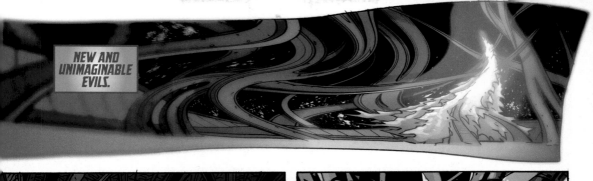

NEW AND UNIMAGINABLE EVILS.

IT SEEMS IMPOSSIBLE.

BUT WE'RE HERE AT A TIME *BEFORE* SUPERMAN'S *FORTRESS OF SOLITUDE* WAS ABLE TO PROTECT ITSELF AGAINST *TIME TRAVELERS.*

ngeniUS

ONLY *ONE* OF US HAS THE POWER TO SHATTER KRYPTONIAN *SUNSTONE.*

AND I HAVE WAITED SUCH A LONG TIME FOR REVENGE ON THE *HOUSE OF EL.*

SEE?

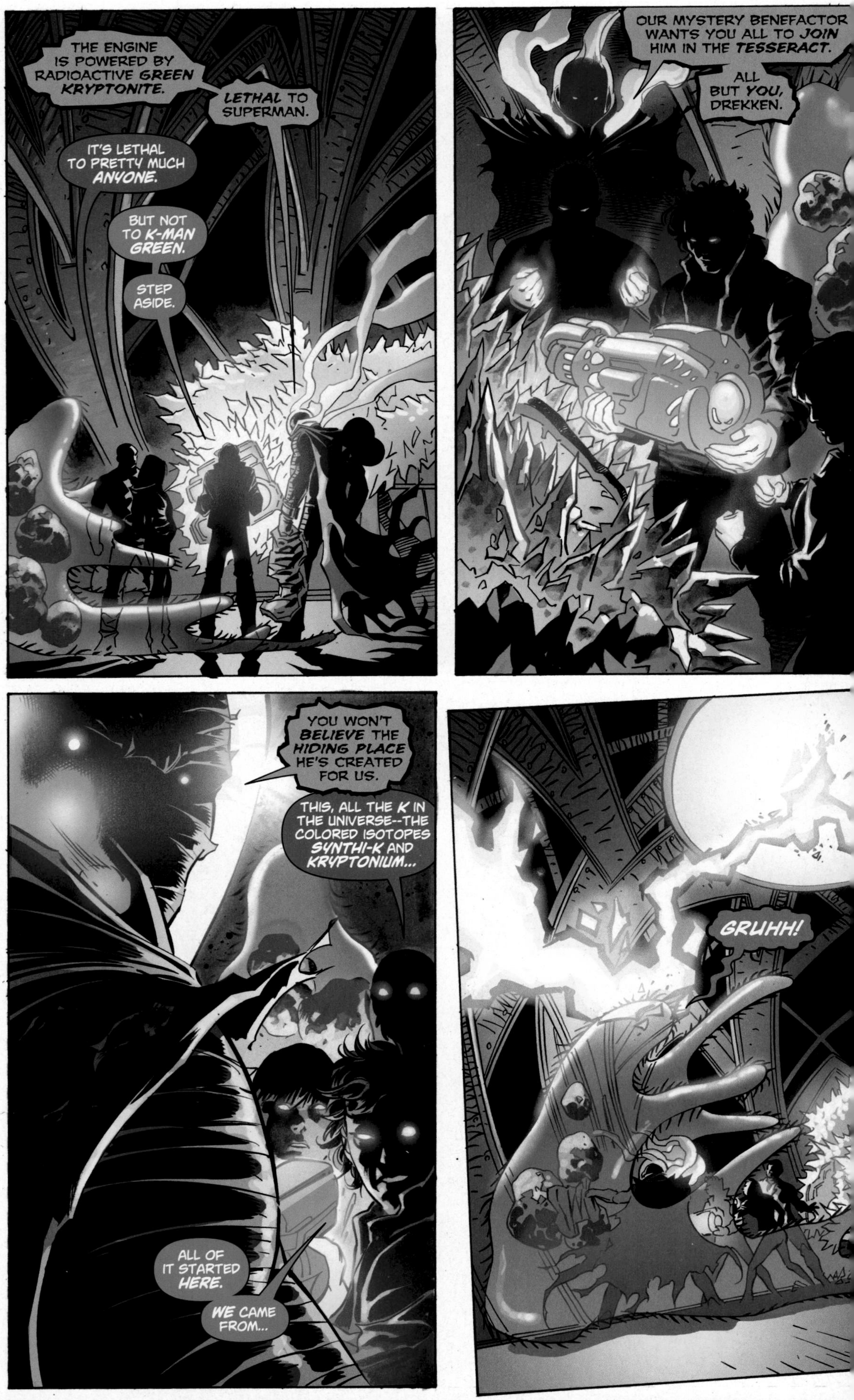
THE ENGINE IS POWERED BY RADIOACTIVE GREEN KRYPTONITE.
LETHAL TO SUPERMAN.
IT'S LETHAL TO PRETTY MUCH ANYONE.
BUT NOT TO K-MAN GREEN.
STEP ASIDE.
OUR MYSTERY BENEFACTOR WANTS YOU ALL TO JOIN HIM IN THE TESSERACT.
ALL BUT YOU, DREKKEN.
YOU WON'T BELIEVE THE HIDING PLACE HE'S CREATED FOR US.
THIS, ALL THE K IN THE UNIVERSE--THE COLORED ISOTOPES SYNTHI-K AND KRYPTONIUM...
ALL OF IT STARTED HERE.
WE CAME FROM...
GRUHH!

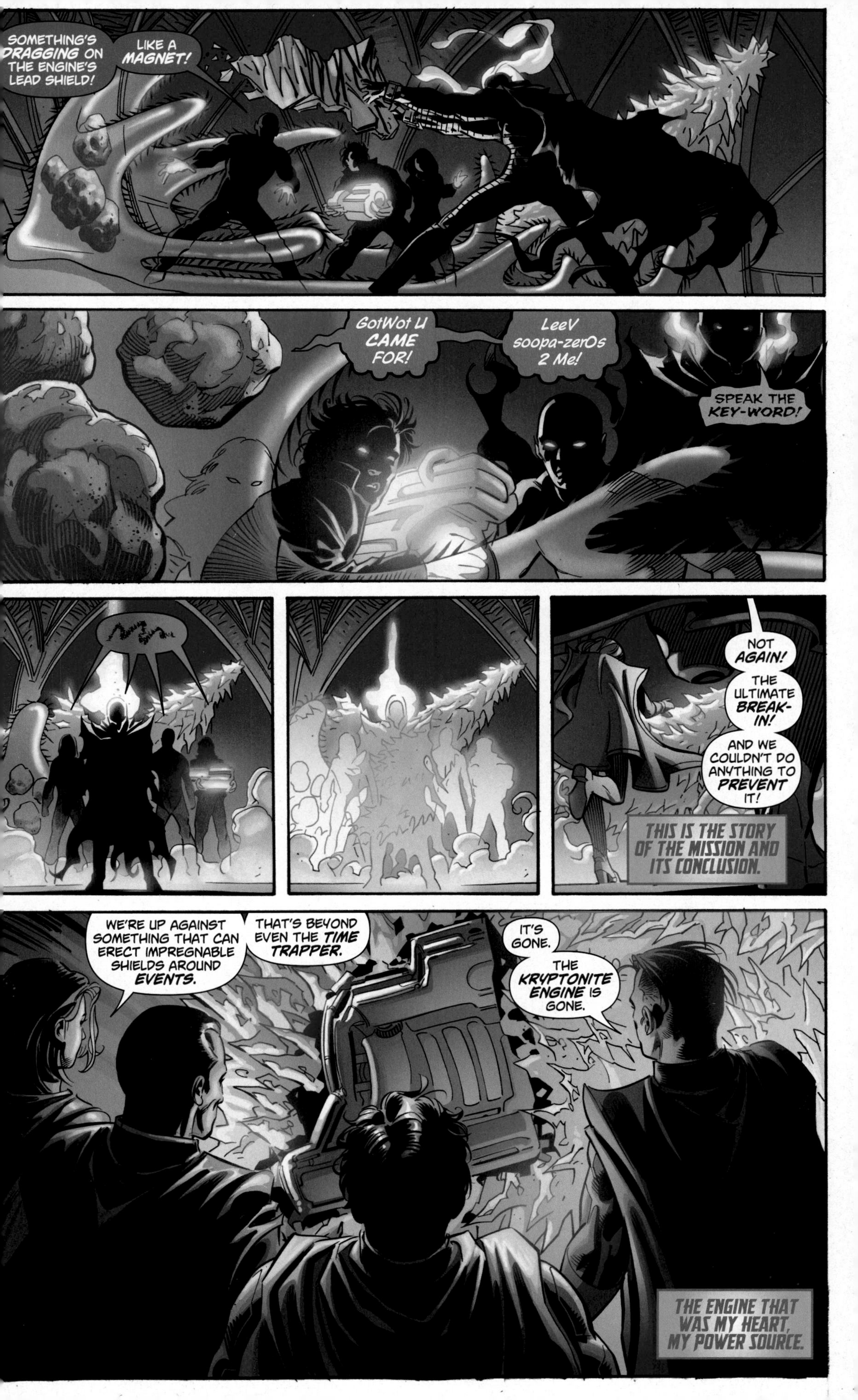
SOMETHING'S DRAGGING ON THE ENGINE'S LEAD SHIELD!
LIKE A MAGNET!
GotWot U CAME FOR!
LeeV soopa-zerOs 2 Me!
SPEAK THE KEY-WORD!
NOT AGAIN!
THE ULTIMATE BREAK-IN!
AND WE COULDN'T DO ANYTHING TO PREVENT IT!
THIS IS THE STORY OF THE MISSION AND ITS CONCLUSION.
WE'RE UP AGAINST SOMETHING THAT CAN ERECT IMPREGNABLE SHIELDS AROUND EVENTS.
THAT'S BEYOND EVEN THE TIME TRAPPER.
IT'S GONE.
THE KRYPTONITE ENGINE IS GONE.
THE ENGINE THAT WAS MY HEART, MY POWER SOURCE.

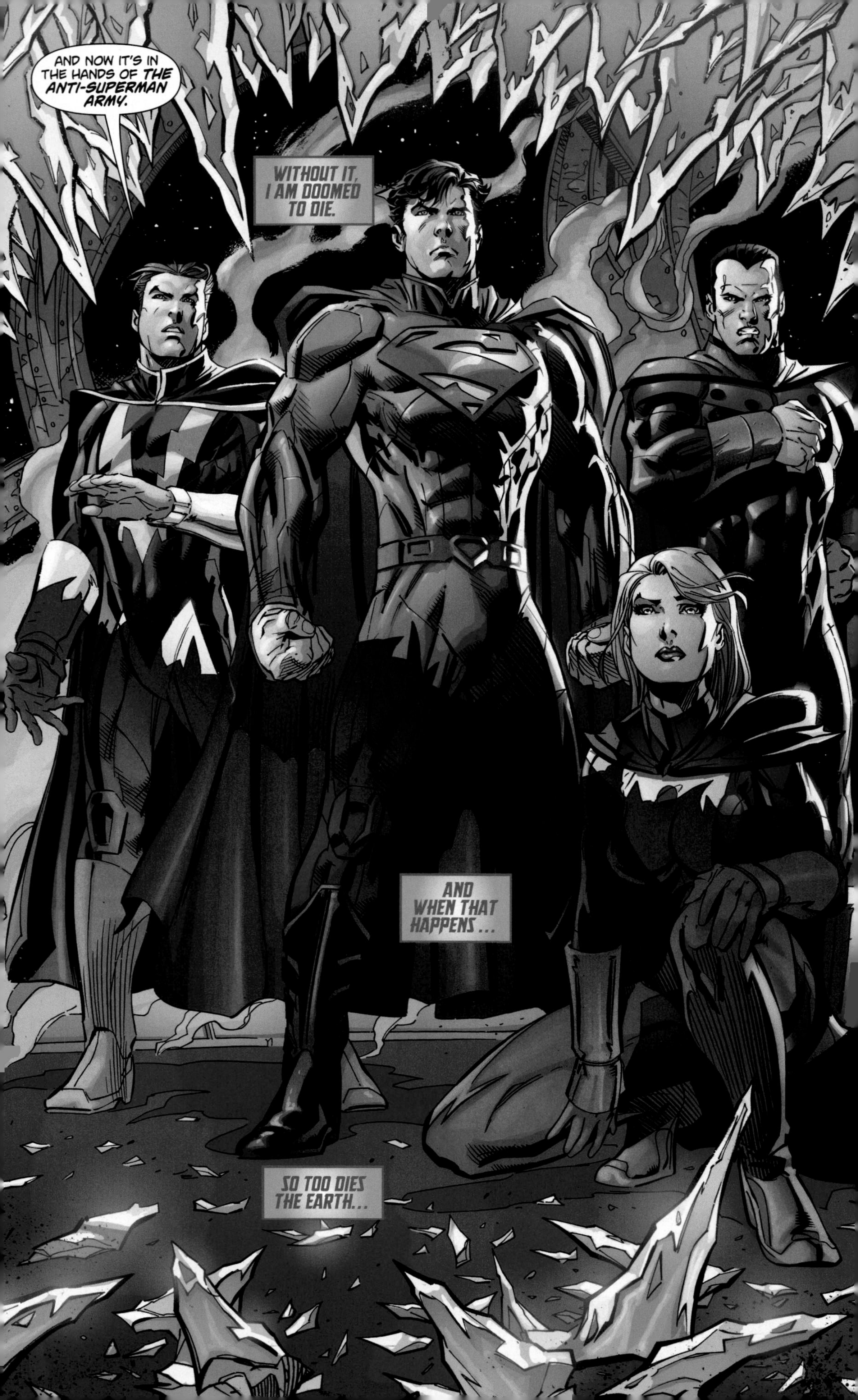
AND NOW IT'S IN THE HANDS OF THE ANTI-SUPERMAN ARMY.
WITHOUT IT, I AM DOOMED TO DIE.
AND WHEN THAT HAPPENS...
SO TOO DIES THE EARTH...

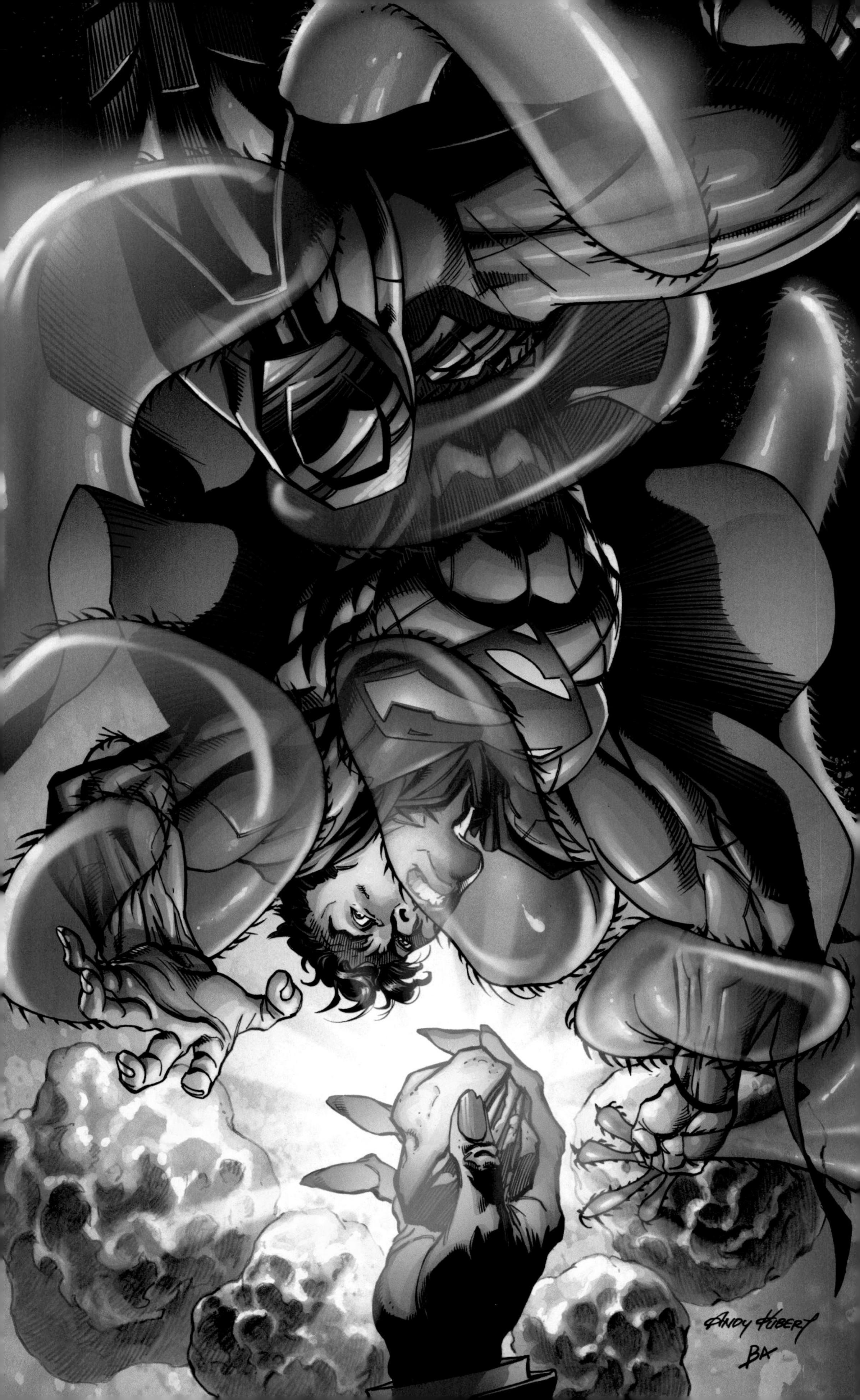
ANDY KUBERT
BA

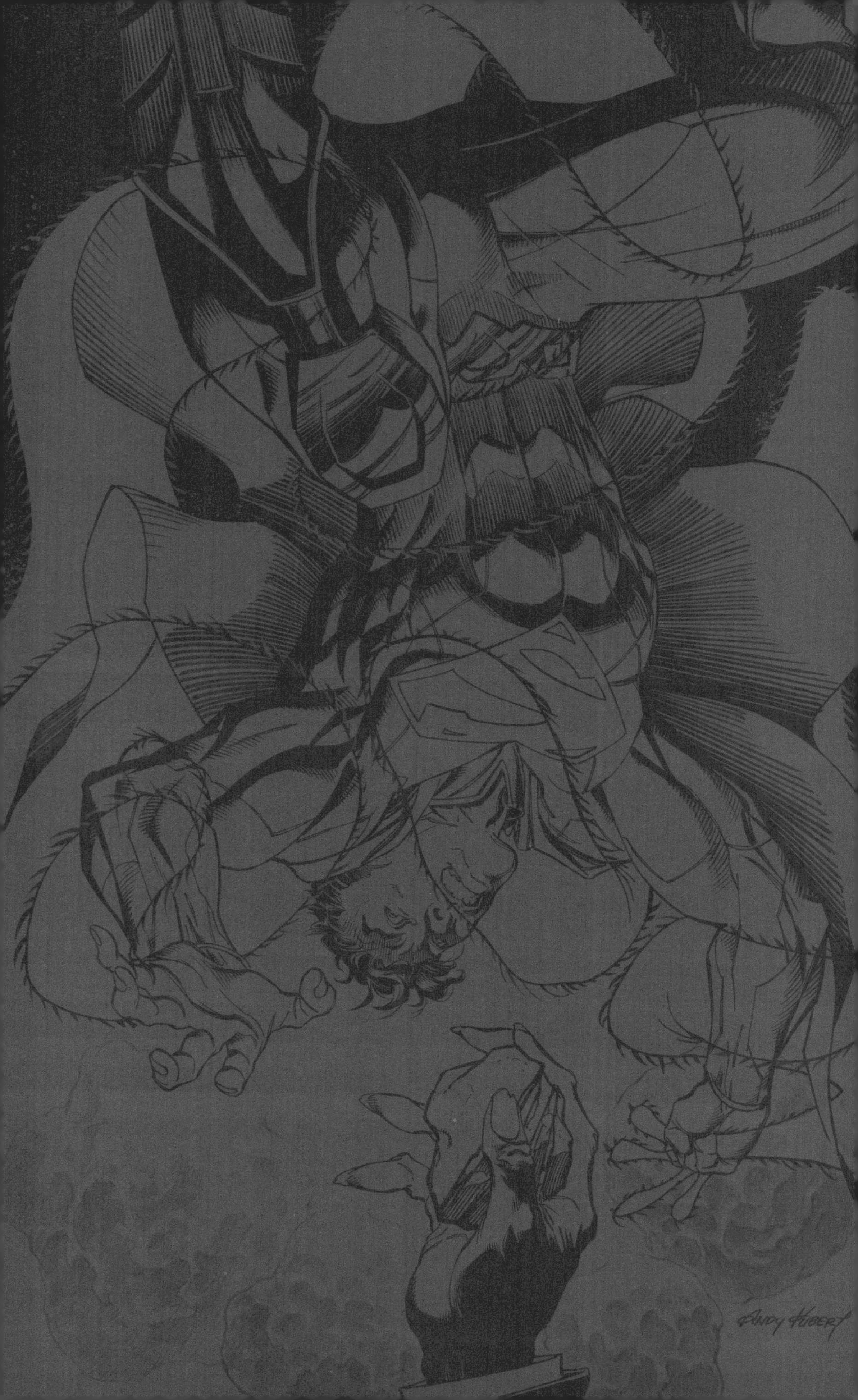
ANDY KUBERT

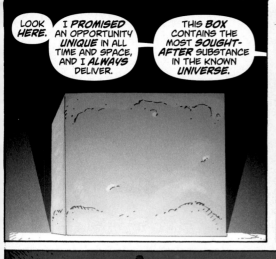

LOOK HERE. I PROMISED AN OPPORTUNITY UNIQUE IN ALL TIME AND SPACE, AND I ALWAYS DELIVER.

THIS BOX CONTAINS THE MOST SOUGHT-AFTER SUBSTANCE IN THE KNOWN UNIVERSE.

BECAUSE THIS, MY FRIENDS, IS THE ONLY MATERIAL GUARANTEED TO KILL SUPERMAN.

OR CHANGE HIM FOREVER.

UNSHIELDED, UNREFINED, THE UNLIMITED POWER SOURCE OF THE LOST PLANET KRYPTON IN THE FORM OF A ROCKET ENGINE CORE.

FROM THIS ORIGINAL DERIVE ALL THE UNSTABLE, EXOTIC ISOTOPES SUCH AS RED-K AND SILVER-K AND BLACK.

THESE DEADLY VARIANTS, INCLUDING BLUE, THE MOST TERRIBLE OF ALL, CAN AND WILL BE GROWN FROM THIS ONE PRIMARY CRYSTAL.

IF MY LOVELY ASSISTANT FROM THE PLANET TROM WILL CHANGE THE LEAD SHIELDING TO GLASS FOR A FEW MOMENTS ONLY...

I GIVE YOU KRYPTONITE.

SOLDIERS IN THE ANTI-SUPERMAN ARMY!

WHAT WILL YOU GIVE ME?

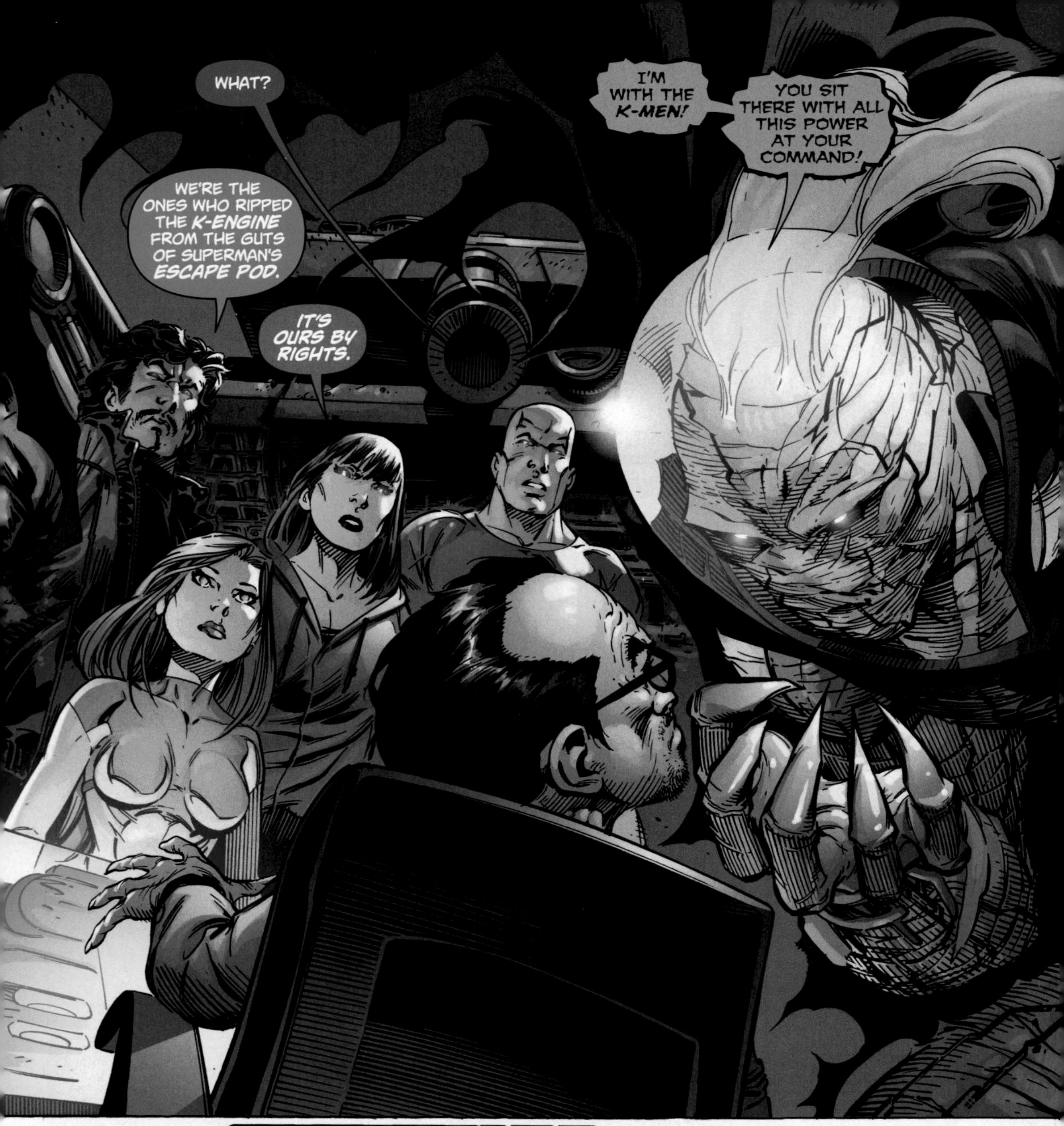
WHAT?
WE'RE THE ONES WHO RIPPED THE K-ENGINE FROM THE GUTS OF SUPERMAN'S ESCAPE POD.
IT'S OURS BY RIGHTS.
I'M WITH THE K-MEN!
YOU SIT THERE WITH ALL THIS POWER AT YOUR COMMAND!

WHEN SUPERMAN LEARNED TO FLY

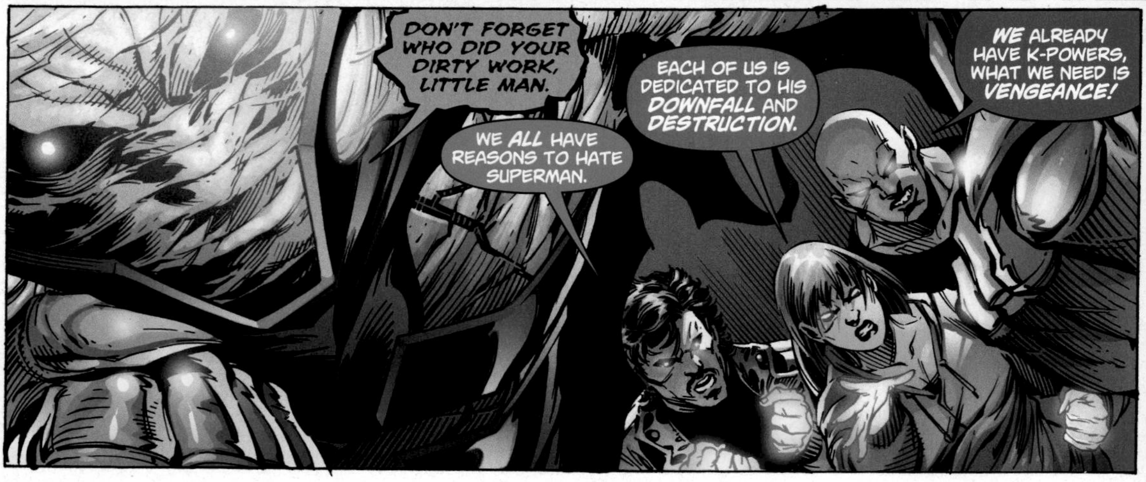
DON'T FORGET WHO DID YOUR DIRTY WORK, LITTLE MAN.
WE ALL HAVE REASONS TO HATE SUPERMAN.
EACH OF US IS DEDICATED TO HIS DOWNFALL AND DESTRUCTION.
WE ALREADY HAVE K-POWERS, WHAT WE NEED IS VENGEANCE!

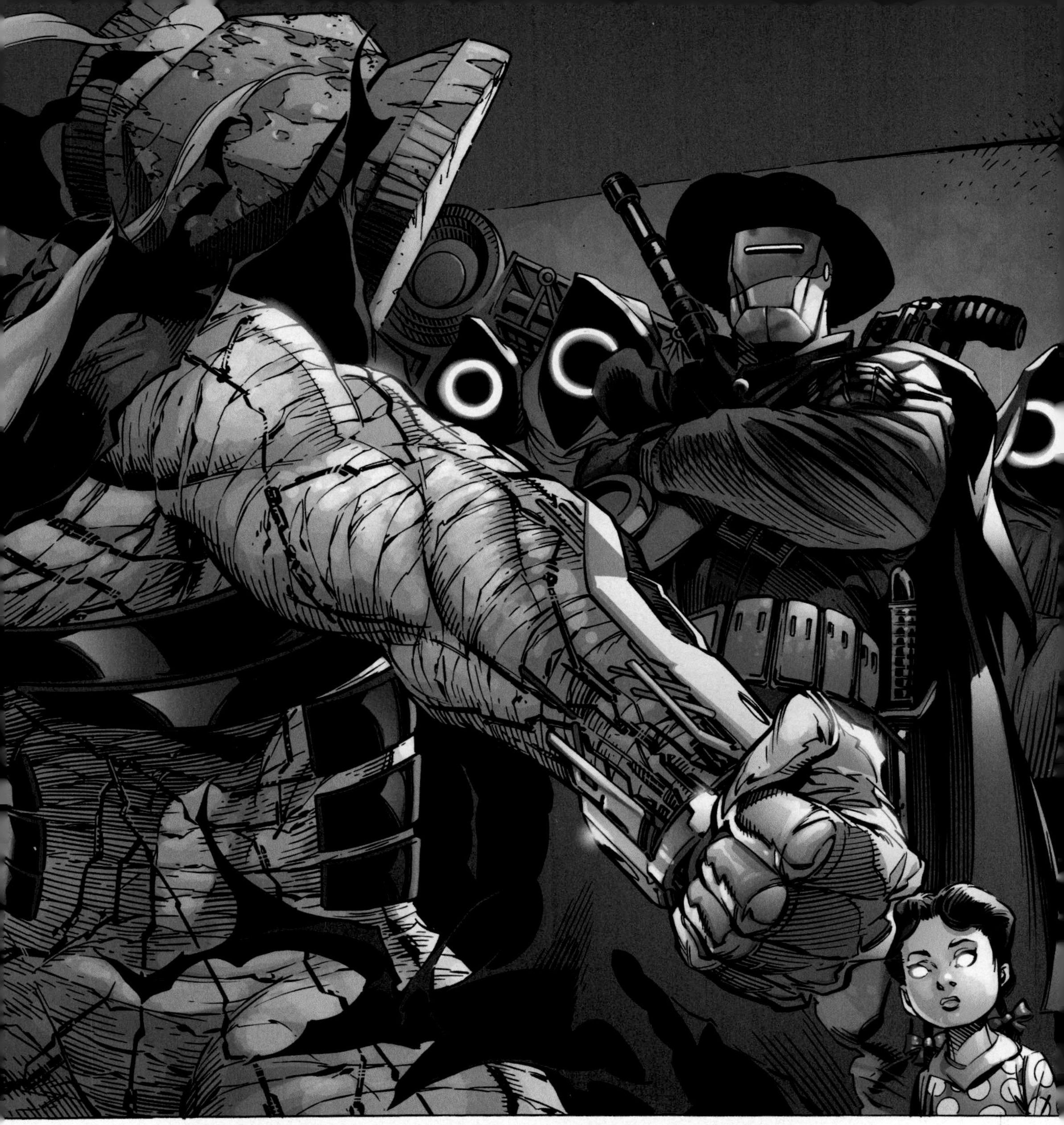

GRANT MORRISON WRITER ANDY KUBERT PENCILLER JOHN DELL INKER
BRAD ANDERSON COLORIST PATRICK BROSSEAU LETTERER ANDY KUBERT & BRAD ANDERSON COVER
WIL MOSS ASSOCIATE EDITOR MATT IDELSON EDITOR

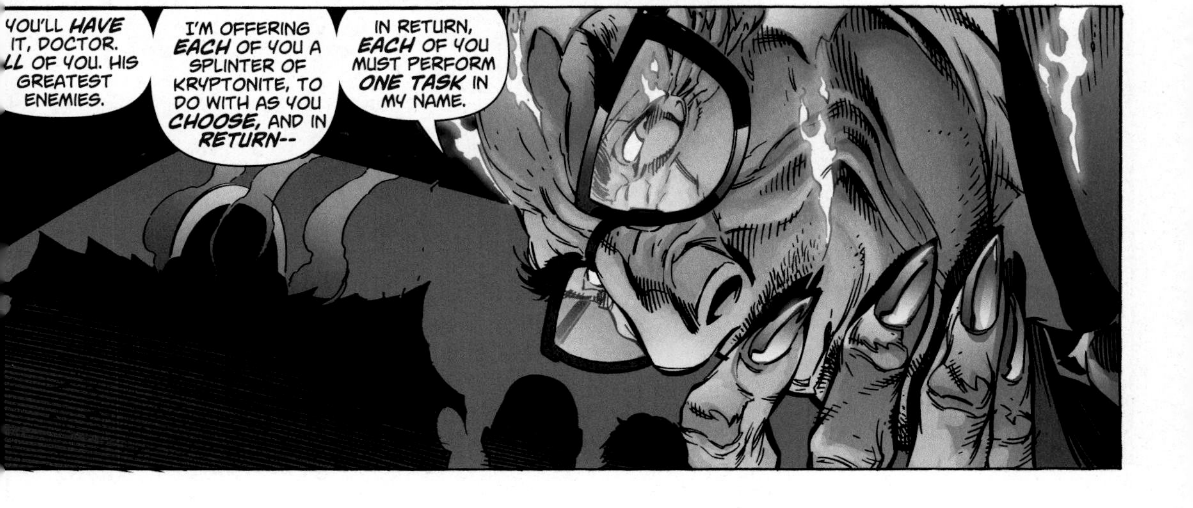
YOU'LL *HAVE* IT, DOCTOR. LL OF YOU. HIS GREATEST ENEMIES.
I'M OFFERING *EACH* OF YOU A SPLINTER OF KRYPTONITE, TO DO WITH AS YOU *CHOOSE,* AND IN *RETURN--*
IN RETURN, *EACH* OF YOU MUST PERFORM *ONE TASK* IN MY NAME.

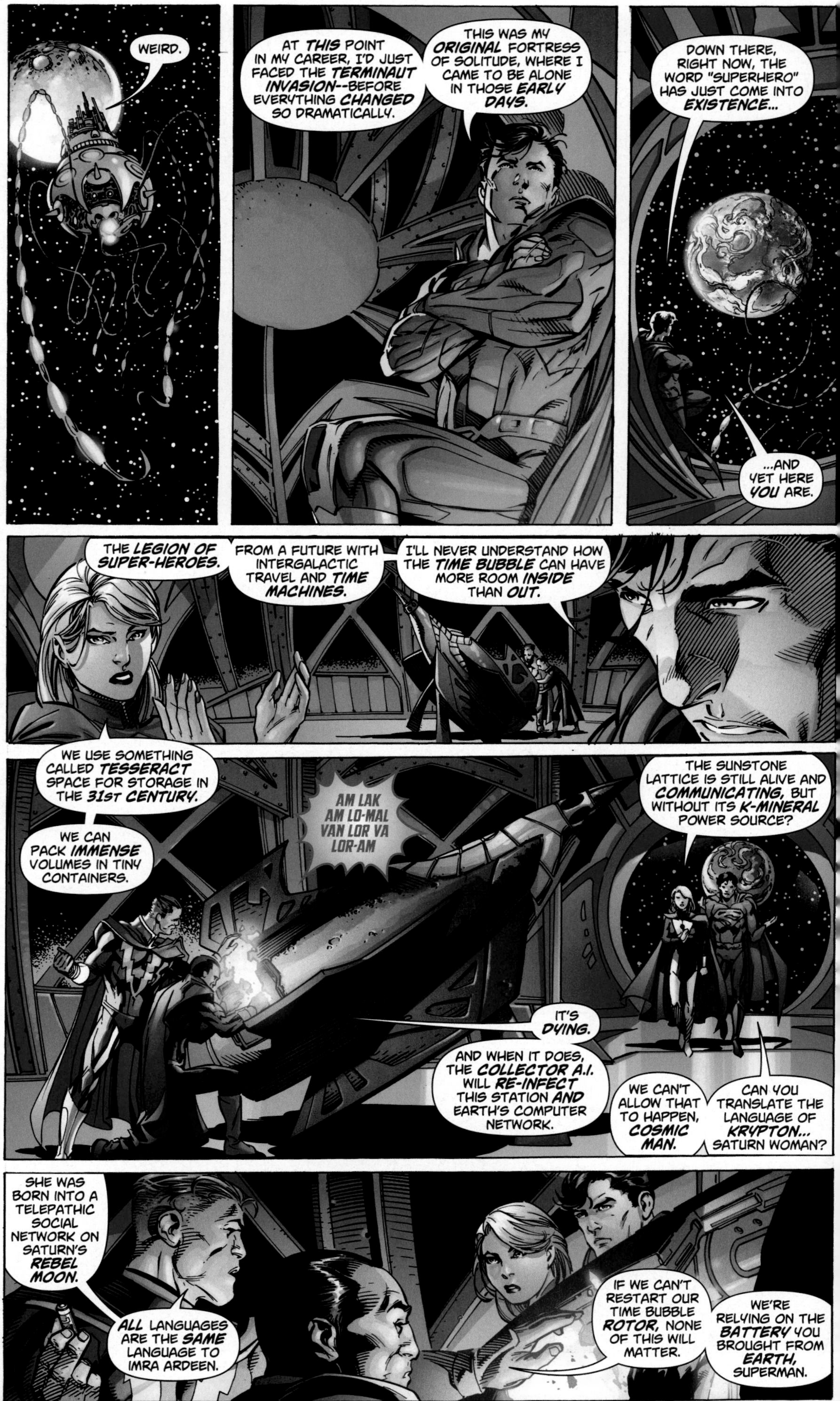
WEIRD.
AT THIS POINT IN MY CAREER, I'D JUST FACED THE TERMINAUT INVASION--BEFORE EVERYTHING CHANGED SO DRAMATICALLY.
THIS WAS MY ORIGINAL FORTRESS OF SOLITUDE, WHERE I CAME TO BE ALONE IN THOSE EARLY DAYS.
DOWN THERE, RIGHT NOW, THE WORD "SUPERHERO" HAS JUST COME INTO EXISTENCE...
...AND YET HERE YOU ARE.
THE LEGION OF SUPER-HEROES.
FROM A FUTURE WITH INTERGALACTIC TRAVEL AND TIME MACHINES.
I'LL NEVER UNDERSTAND HOW THE TIME BUBBLE CAN HAVE MORE ROOM INSIDE THAN OUT.
WE USE SOMETHING CALLED TESSERACT SPACE FOR STORAGE IN THE 31ST CENTURY.
WE CAN PACK IMMENSE VOLUMES IN TINY CONTAINERS.
AM LAK AM LO-MAL VAN LOR VA LOR-AM
THE SUNSTONE LATTICE IS STILL ALIVE AND COMMUNICATING, BUT WITHOUT ITS K-MINERAL POWER SOURCE?
IT'S DYING.
AND WHEN IT DOES, THE COLLECTOR A.I. WILL RE-INFECT THIS STATION AND EARTH'S COMPUTER NETWORK.
WE CAN'T ALLOW THAT TO HAPPEN, COSMIC MAN.
CAN YOU TRANSLATE THE LANGUAGE OF KRYPTON... SATURN WOMAN?
SHE WAS BORN INTO A TELEPATHIC SOCIAL NETWORK ON SATURN'S REBEL MOON.
ALL LANGUAGES ARE THE SAME LANGUAGE TO IMRA ARDEEN.
IF WE CAN'T RESTART OUR TIME BUBBLE ROTOR, NONE OF THIS WILL MATTER.
WE'RE RELYING ON THE BATTERY YOU BROUGHT FROM EARTH, SUPERMAN.

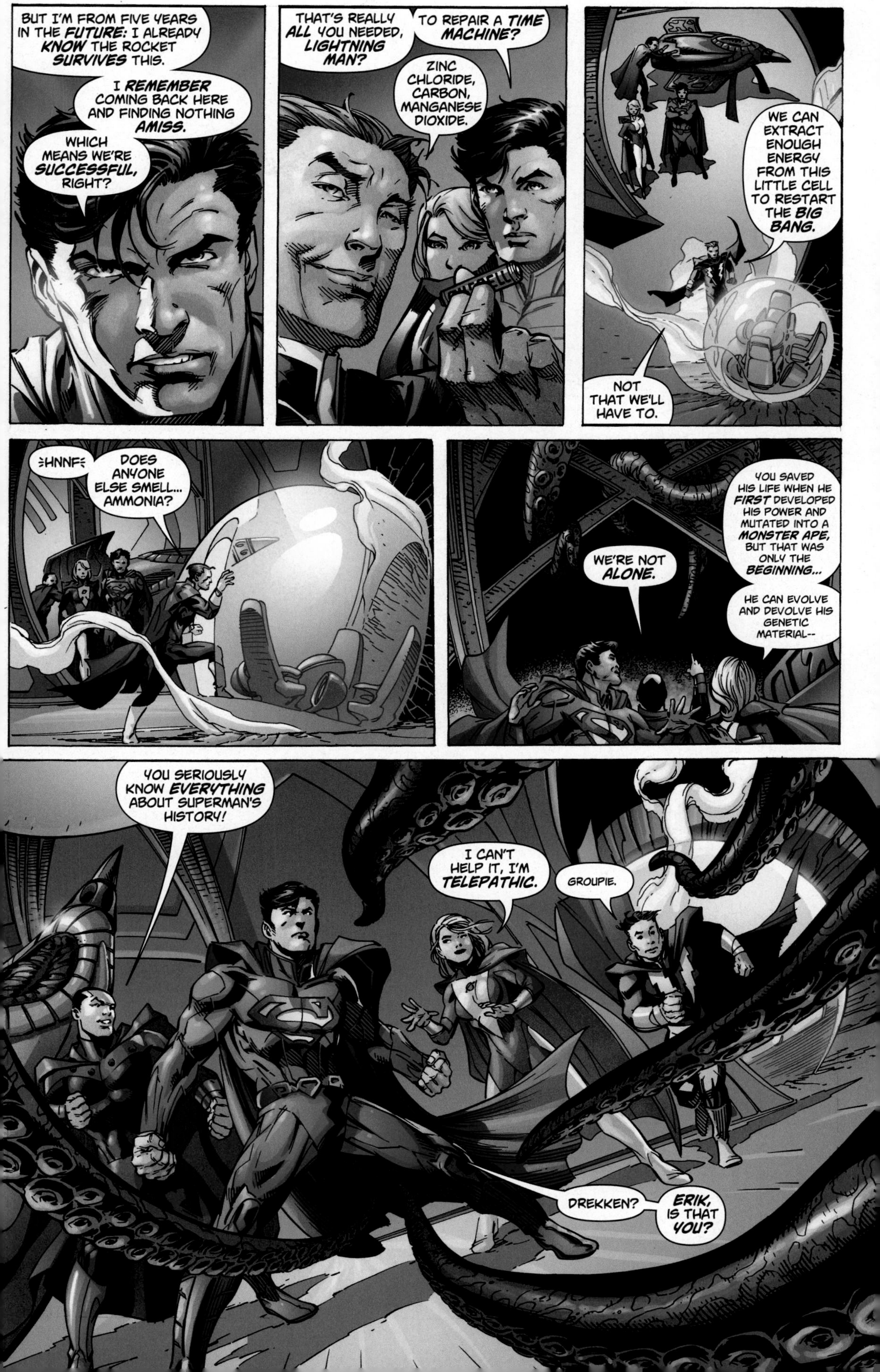
BUT I'M FROM FIVE YEARS IN THE FUTURE: I ALREADY KNOW THE ROCKET SURVIVES THIS.
I REMEMBER COMING BACK HERE AND FINDING NOTHING AMISS.
WHICH MEANS WE'RE SUCCESSFUL, RIGHT?
THAT'S REALLY ALL YOU NEEDED, LIGHTNING MAN?
TO REPAIR A TIME MACHINE?
ZINC CHLORIDE, CARBON, MANGANESE DIOXIDE.
WE CAN EXTRACT ENOUGH ENERGY FROM THIS LITTLE CELL TO RESTART THE BIG BANG.
NOT THAT WE'LL HAVE TO.
HNNF
DOES ANYONE ELSE SMELL... AMMONIA?
WE'RE NOT ALONE.
YOU SAVED HIS LIFE WHEN HE FIRST DEVELOPED HIS POWER AND MUTATED INTO A MONSTER APE, BUT THAT WAS ONLY THE BEGINNING...
HE CAN EVOLVE AND DEVOLVE HIS GENETIC MATERIAL--
YOU SERIOUSLY KNOW EVERYTHING ABOUT SUPERMAN'S HISTORY!
I CAN'T HELP IT, I'M TELEPATHIC.
GROUPIE.
DREKKEN?
ERIK, IS THAT YOU?

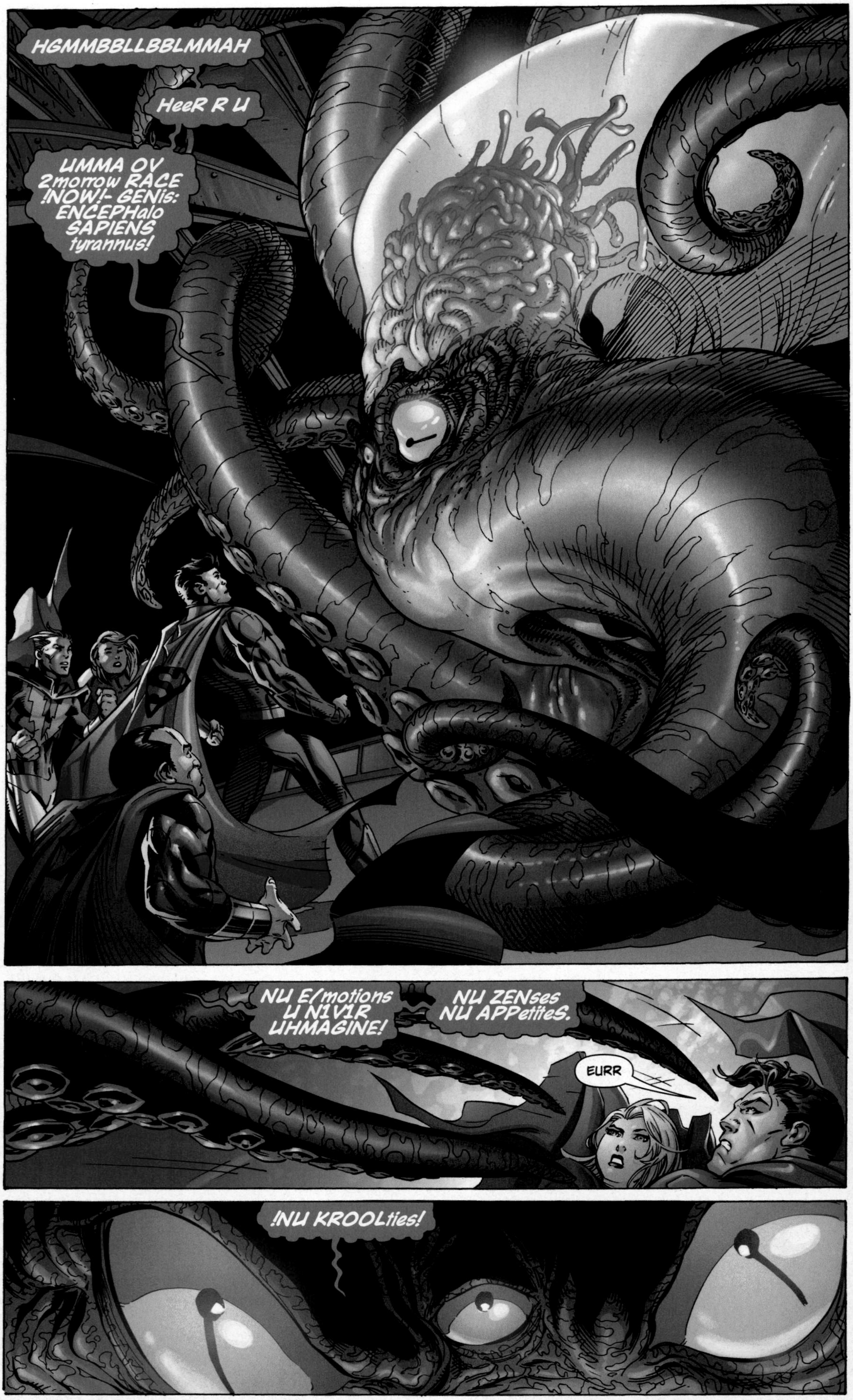
HGMMBBLLBBLMMAH
HeeR R U
UMMA OV 2morrow RACE !NOW!- GENis: ENCEPHalo SAPIENS tyrannus!
NU E/motions U N1V1R UHMAGINE!
NU ZENses NU APPetiteS.
EURR
!NU KROOLties!

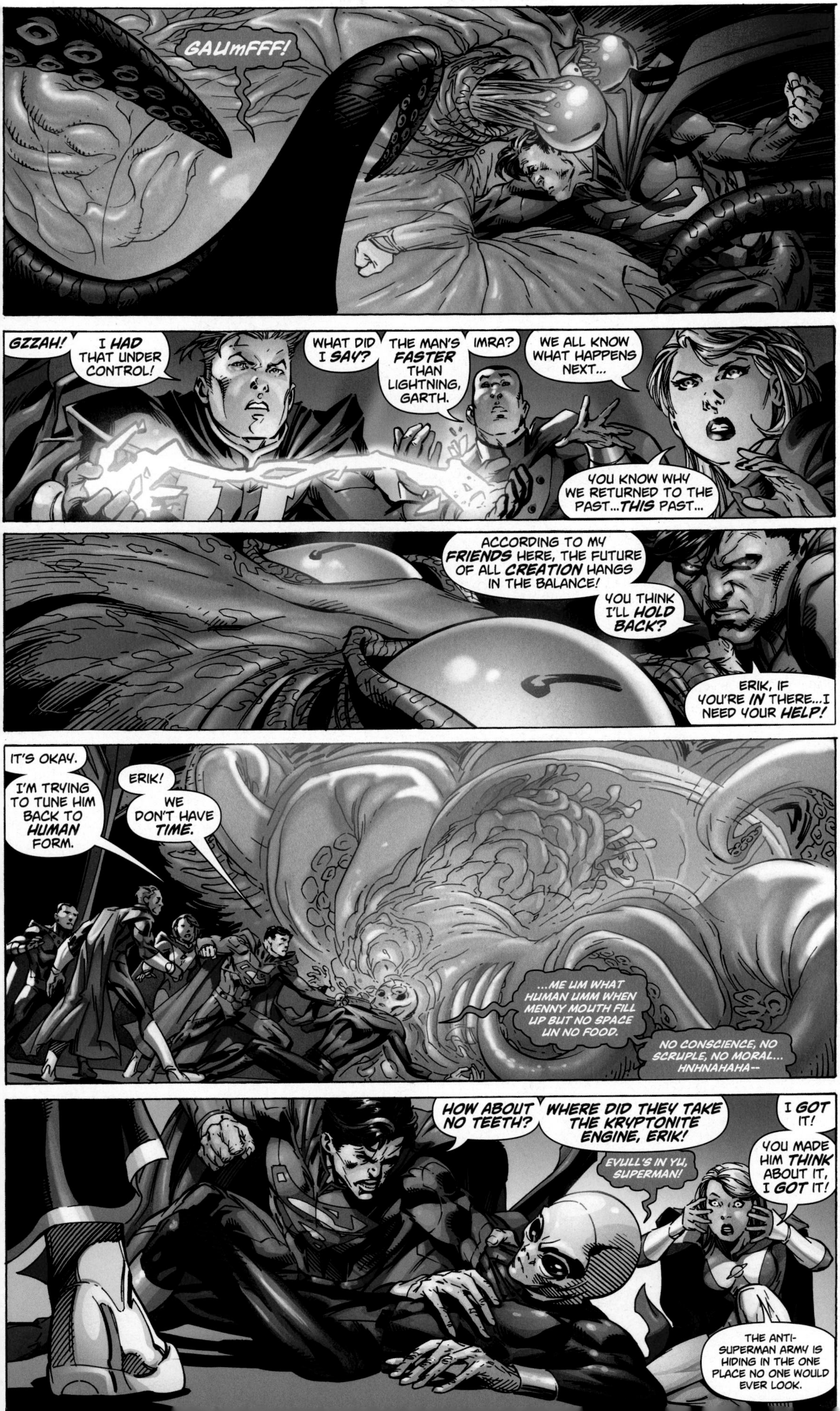
GAUmFFF!
GZZAH!
I HAD THAT UNDER CONTROL!
WHAT DID I SAY?
THE MAN'S FASTER THAN LIGHTNING, GARTH.
IMRA?
WE ALL KNOW WHAT HAPPENS NEXT...
YOU KNOW WHY WE RETURNED TO THE PAST...THIS PAST...
ACCORDING TO MY FRIENDS HERE, THE FUTURE OF ALL CREATION HANGS IN THE BALANCE!
YOU THINK I'LL HOLD BACK?
ERIK, IF YOU'RE IN THERE...I NEED YOUR HELP!
IT'S OKAY.
I'M TRYING TO TUNE HIM BACK TO HUMAN FORM.
ERIK!
WE DON'T HAVE TIME.
...ME UM WHAT HUMAN UMM WHEN MENNY MOUTH FILL UP BUT NO SPACE UN NO FOOD.
NO CONSCIENCE, NO SCRUPLE, NO MORAL... HNHNAHAHA--
HOW ABOUT NO TEETH?
WHERE DID THEY TAKE THE KRYPTONITE ENGINE, ERIK!
EVULL'S IN YU, SUPERMAN!
I GOT IT!
YOU MADE HIM THINK ABOUT IT, I GOT IT!
THE ANTI-SUPERMAN ARMY IS HIDING IN THE ONE PLACE NO ONE WOULD EVER LOOK.

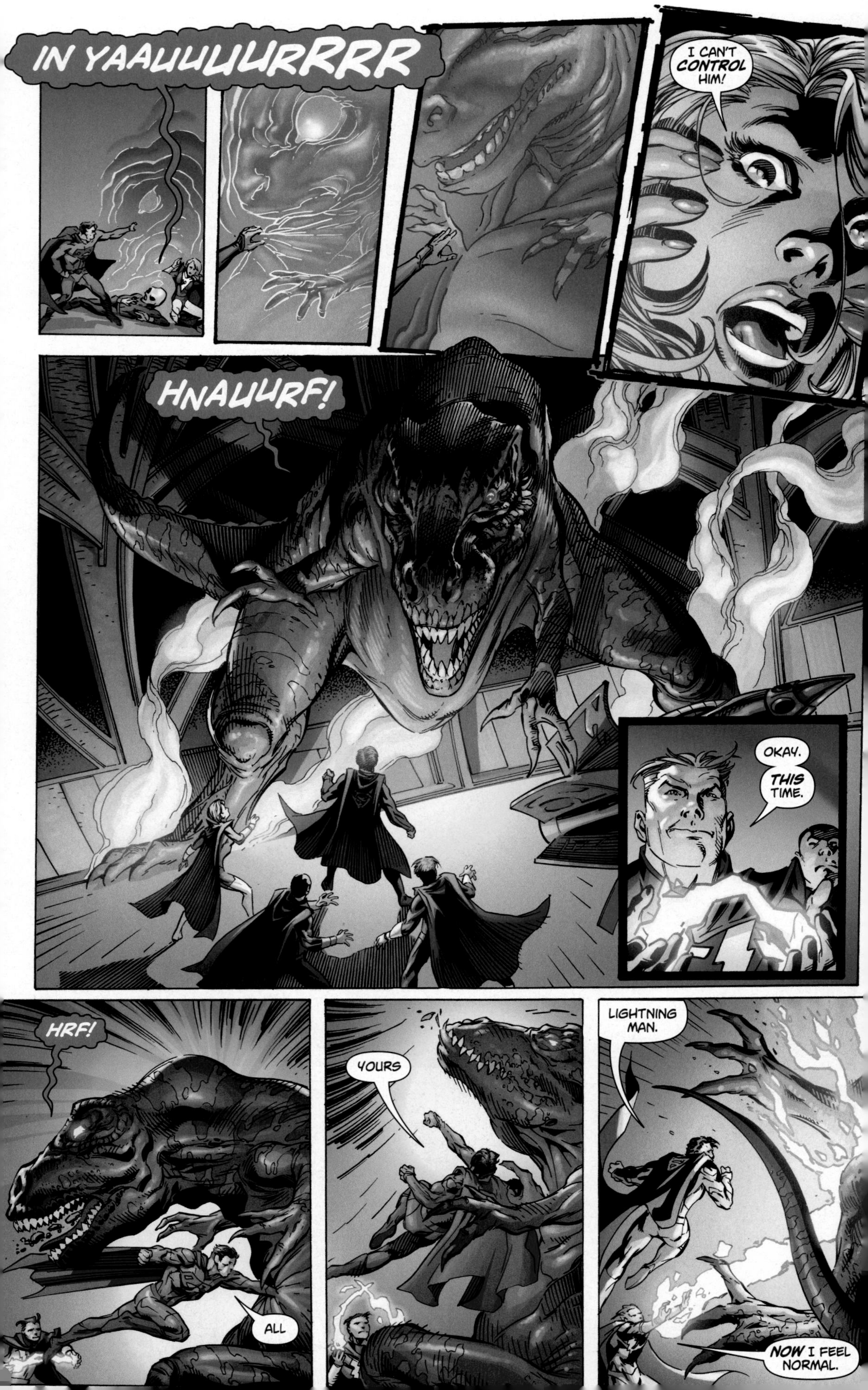
IN YAAUUUURRRR
I CAN'T CONTROL HIM!
HNAUURF!
OKAY. THIS TIME.
HRF!
ALL
YOURS
LIGHTNING MAN.
NOW I FEEL NORMAL.

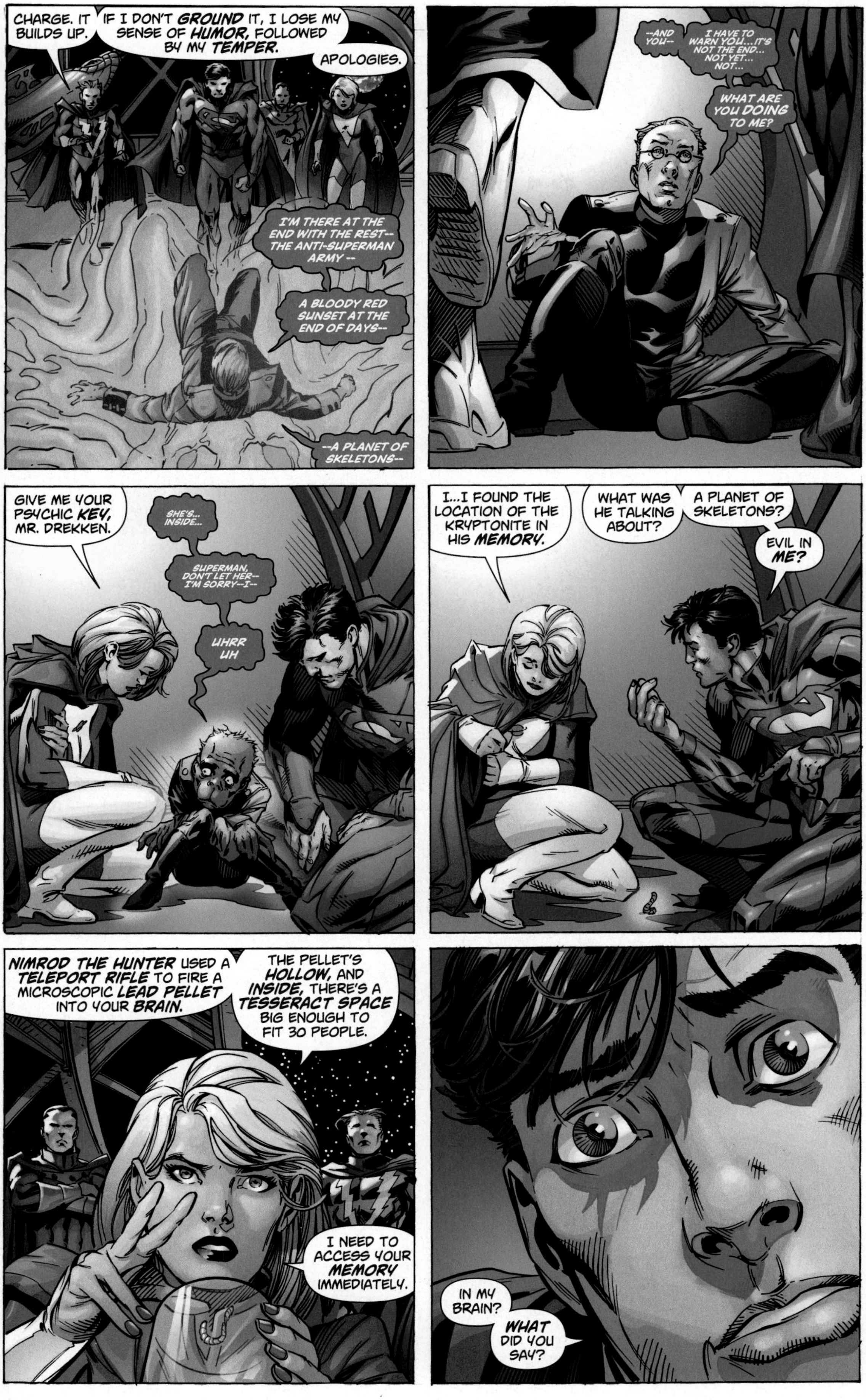
CHARGE. IT BUILDS UP.
IF I DON'T GROUND IT, I LOSE MY SENSE OF HUMOR, FOLLOWED BY MY TEMPER.
APOLOGIES.
I'M THERE AT THE END WITH THE REST-- THE ANTI-SUPERMAN ARMY --
A BLOODY RED SUNSET AT THE END OF DAYS--
--A PLANET OF SKELETONS--
--AND YOU--
I HAVE TO WARN YOU...IT'S NOT THE END... NOT YET... NOT...
WHAT ARE YOU DOING TO ME?
GIVE ME YOUR PSYCHIC KEY, MR. DREKKEN.
SHE'S... INSIDE...
SUPERMAN, DON'T LET HER-- I'M SORRY--I--
UHRR UH
I...I FOUND THE LOCATION OF THE KRYPTONITE IN HIS MEMORY.
WHAT WAS HE TALKING ABOUT?
A PLANET OF SKELETONS?
EVIL IN ME?
NIMROD THE HUNTER USED A TELEPORT RIFLE TO FIRE A MICROSCOPIC LEAD PELLET INTO YOUR BRAIN.
THE PELLET'S HOLLOW, AND INSIDE, THERE'S A TESSERACT SPACE BIG ENOUGH TO FIT 30 PEOPLE.
I NEED TO ACCESS YOUR MEMORY IMMEDIATELY.
IN MY BRAIN? WHAT DID YOU SAY?

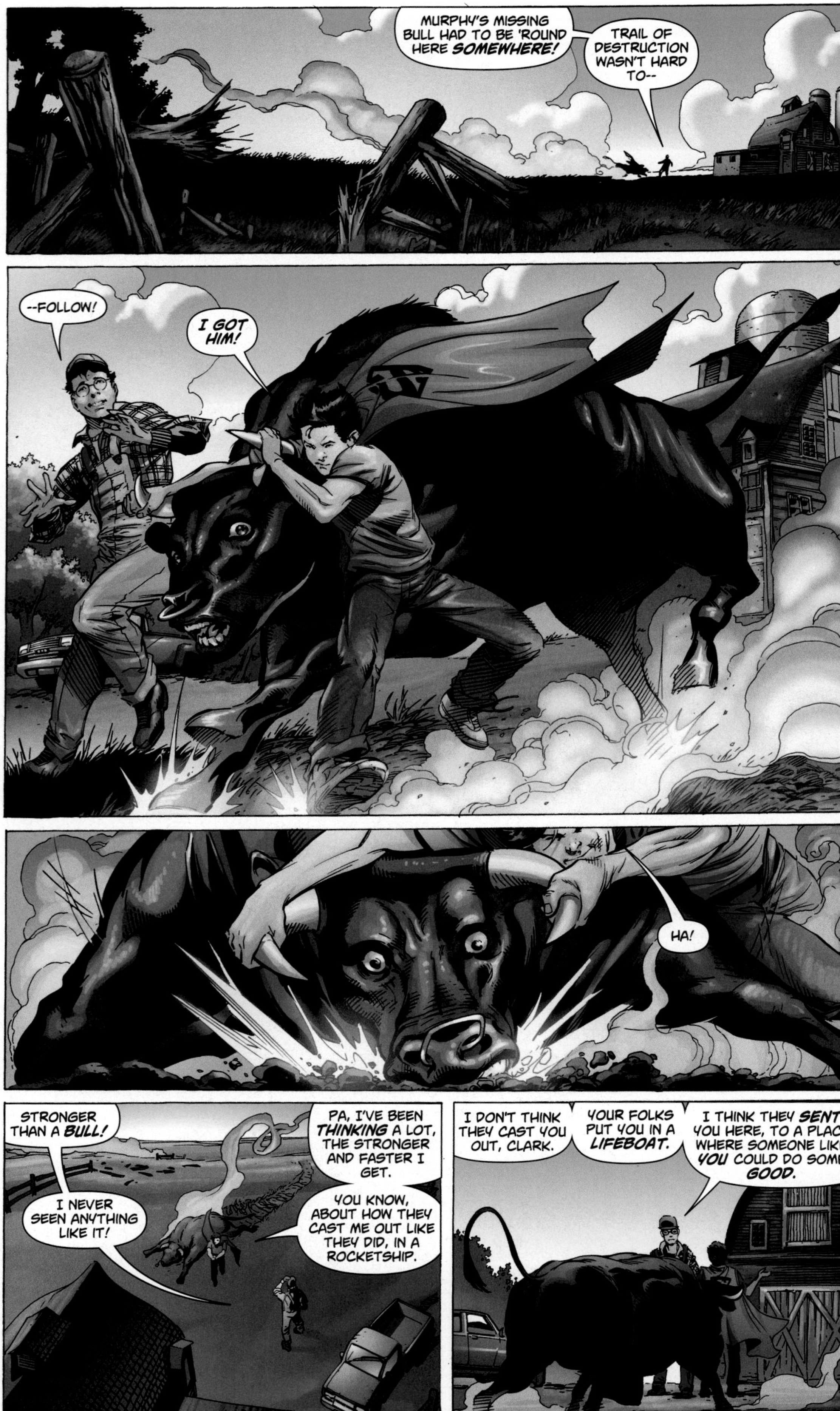
MURPHY'S MISSING BULL HAD TO BE 'ROUND HERE SOMEWHERE!
TRAIL OF DESTRUCTION WASN'T HARD TO--
--FOLLOW!
I GOT HIM!
HA!
STRONGER THAN A BULL!
I NEVER SEEN ANYTHING LIKE IT!
PA, I'VE BEEN THINKING A LOT, THE STRONGER AND FASTER I GET.
YOU KNOW, ABOUT HOW THEY CAST ME OUT LIKE THEY DID, IN A ROCKETSHIP.
I DON'T THINK THEY CAST YOU OUT, CLARK.
YOUR FOLKS PUT YOU IN A LIFEBOAT.
I THINK THEY SENT YOU HERE, TO A PLACE WHERE SOMEONE LIKE YOU COULD DO SOME GOOD.

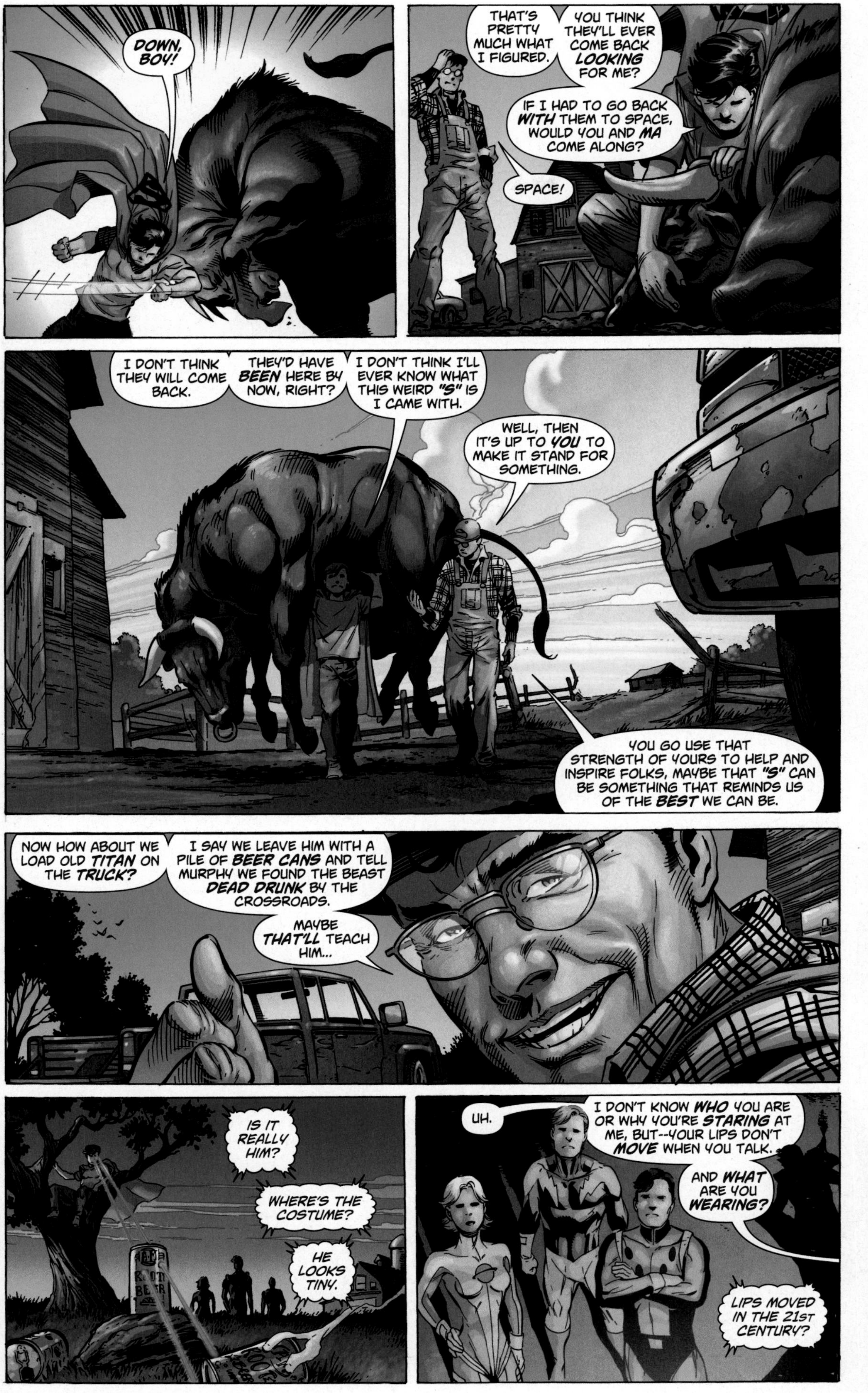
DOWN, BOY!
THAT'S PRETTY MUCH WHAT I FIGURED.
YOU THINK THEY'LL EVER COME BACK LOOKING FOR ME?
IF I HAD TO GO BACK WITH THEM TO SPACE, WOULD YOU AND MA COME ALONG?
SPACE!
I DON'T THINK THEY WILL COME BACK.
THEY'D HAVE BEEN HERE BY NOW, RIGHT?
I DON'T THINK I'LL EVER KNOW WHAT THIS WEIRD "S" IS I CAME WITH.
WELL, THEN IT'S UP TO YOU TO MAKE IT STAND FOR SOMETHING.
YOU GO USE THAT STRENGTH OF YOURS TO HELP AND INSPIRE FOLKS, MAYBE THAT "S" CAN BE SOMETHING THAT REMINDS US OF THE BEST WE CAN BE.
NOW HOW ABOUT WE LOAD OLD TITAN ON THE TRUCK?
I SAY WE LEAVE HIM WITH A PILE OF BEER CANS AND TELL MURPHY WE FOUND THE BEAST DEAD DRUNK BY THE CROSSROADS.
MAYBE THAT'LL TEACH HIM...
IS IT REALLY HIM?
WHERE'S THE COSTUME?
HE LOOKS TINY.
UH.
I DON'T KNOW WHO YOU ARE OR WHY YOU'RE STARING AT ME, BUT--YOUR LIPS DON'T MOVE WHEN YOU TALK.
AND WHAT ARE YOU WEARING?
LIPS MOVED IN THE 21ST CENTURY?

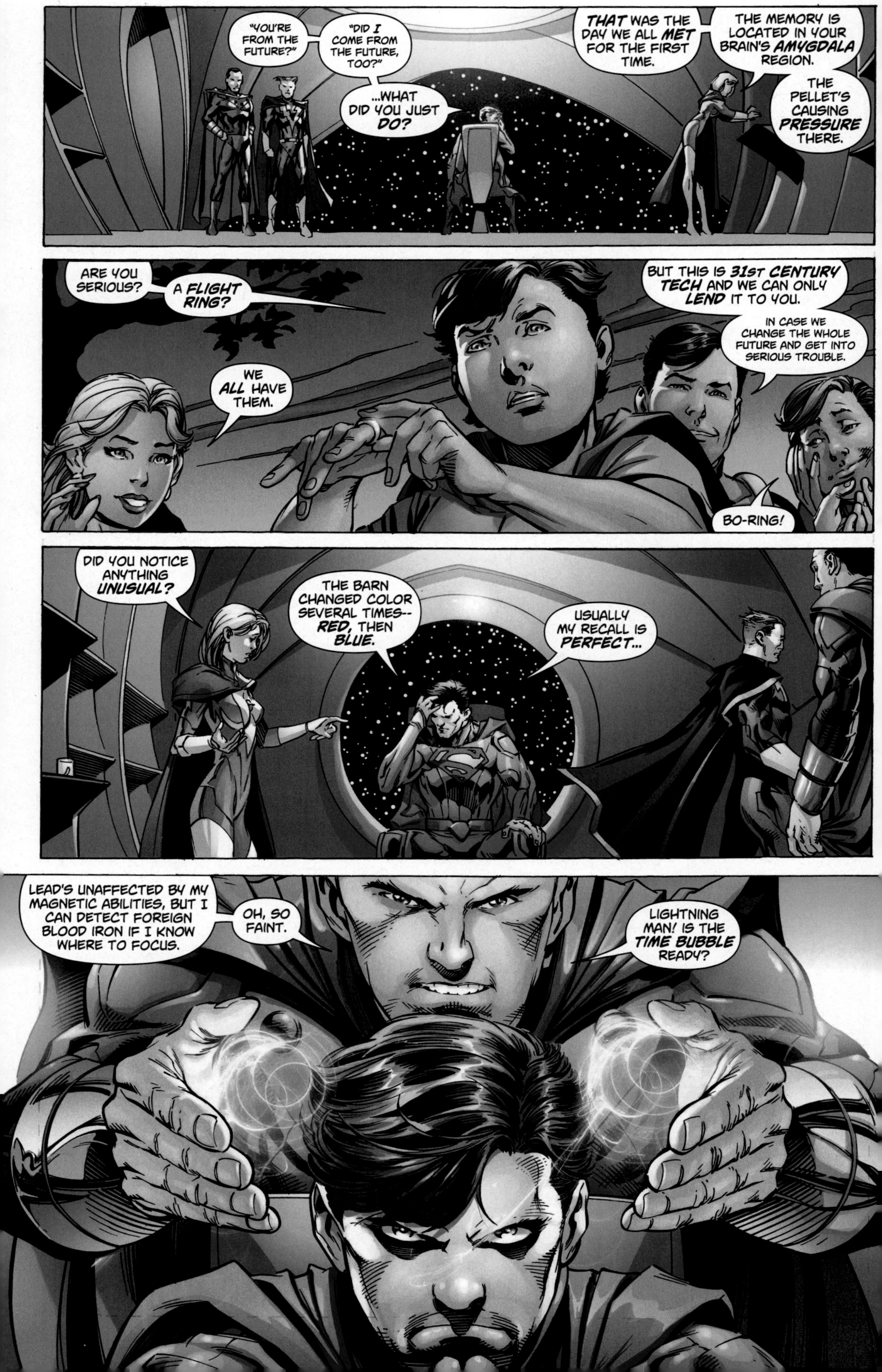
"YOU'RE FROM THE FUTURE?"
"DID I COME FROM THE FUTURE, TOO?"
...WHAT DID YOU JUST DO?
THAT WAS THE DAY WE ALL MET FOR THE FIRST TIME.
THE MEMORY IS LOCATED IN YOUR BRAIN'S AMYGDALA REGION.
THE PELLET'S CAUSING PRESSURE THERE.
ARE YOU SERIOUS?
A FLIGHT RING?
WE ALL HAVE THEM.
BUT THIS IS 31ST CENTURY TECH AND WE CAN ONLY LEND IT TO YOU.
IN CASE WE CHANGE THE WHOLE FUTURE AND GET INTO SERIOUS TROUBLE.
BO-RING!
DID YOU NOTICE ANYTHING UNUSUAL?
THE BARN CHANGED COLOR SEVERAL TIMES-- RED, THEN BLUE.
USUALLY MY RECALL IS PERFECT...
LEAD'S UNAFFECTED BY MY MAGNETIC ABILITIES, BUT I CAN DETECT FOREIGN BLOOD IRON IF I KNOW WHERE TO FOCUS.
OH, SO FAINT.
LIGHTNING MAN! IS THE TIME BUBBLE READY?

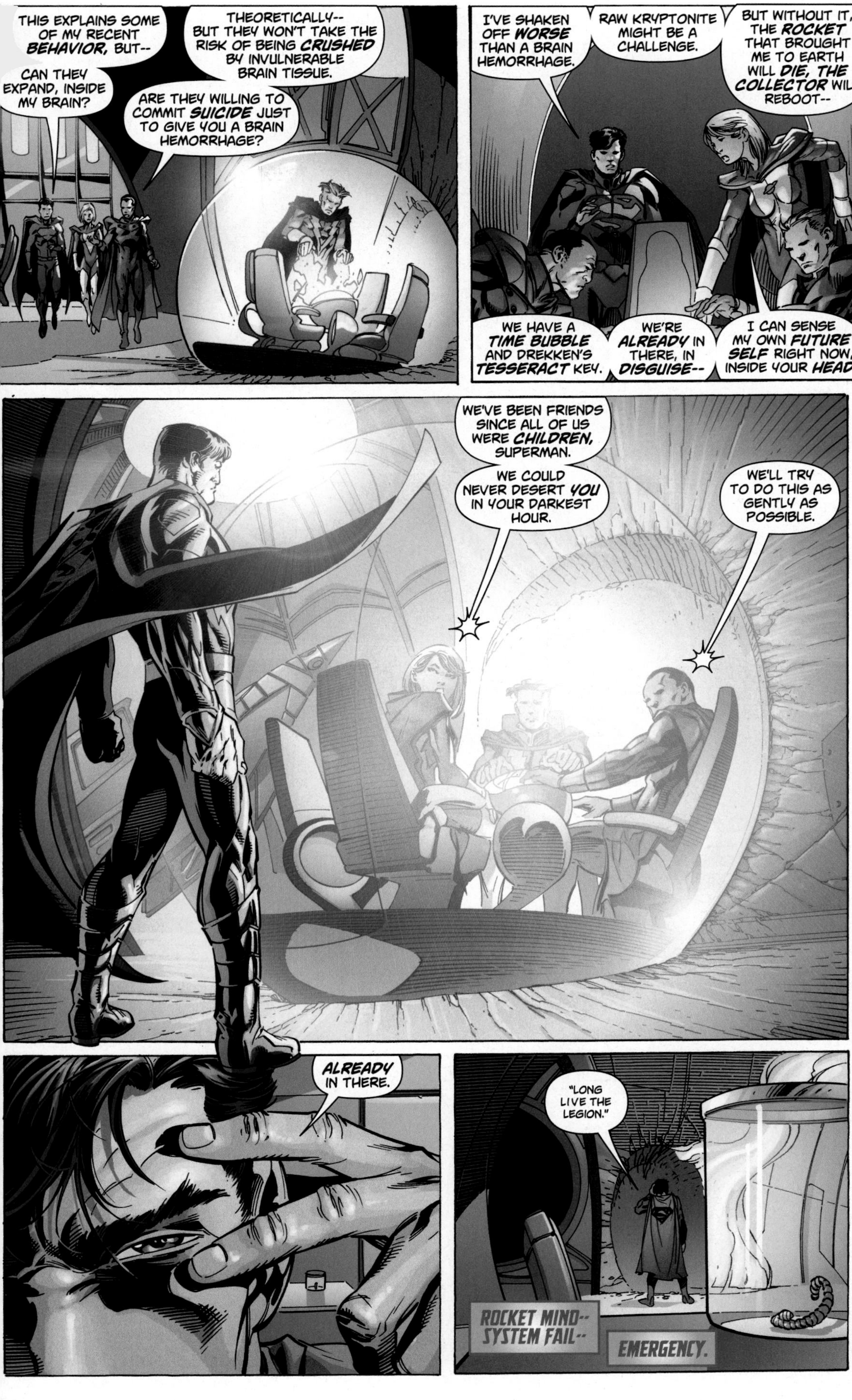
THIS EXPLAINS SOME OF MY RECENT BEHAVIOR, BUT--
CAN THEY EXPAND, INSIDE MY BRAIN?
THEORETICALLY-- BUT THEY WON'T TAKE THE RISK OF BEING CRUSHED BY INVULNERABLE BRAIN TISSUE.
ARE THEY WILLING TO COMMIT SUICIDE JUST TO GIVE YOU A BRAIN HEMORRHAGE?
I'VE SHAKEN OFF WORSE THAN A BRAIN HEMORRHAGE.
RAW KRYPTONITE MIGHT BE A CHALLENGE.
BUT WITHOUT IT, THE ROCKET THAT BROUGHT ME TO EARTH WILL DIE, THE COLLECTOR WILL REBOOT--
WE HAVE A TIME BUBBLE AND DREKKEN'S TESSERACT KEY.
WE'RE ALREADY IN THERE, IN DISGUISE--
I CAN SENSE MY OWN FUTURE SELF RIGHT NOW, INSIDE YOUR HEAD.
WE'VE BEEN FRIENDS SINCE ALL OF US WERE CHILDREN, SUPERMAN.
WE COULD NEVER DESERT YOU IN YOUR DARKEST HOUR.
WE'LL TRY TO DO THIS AS GENTLY AS POSSIBLE.
ALREADY IN THERE.
"LONG LIVE THE LEGION."
ROCKET MIND-- SYSTEM FAIL--
EMERGENCY.

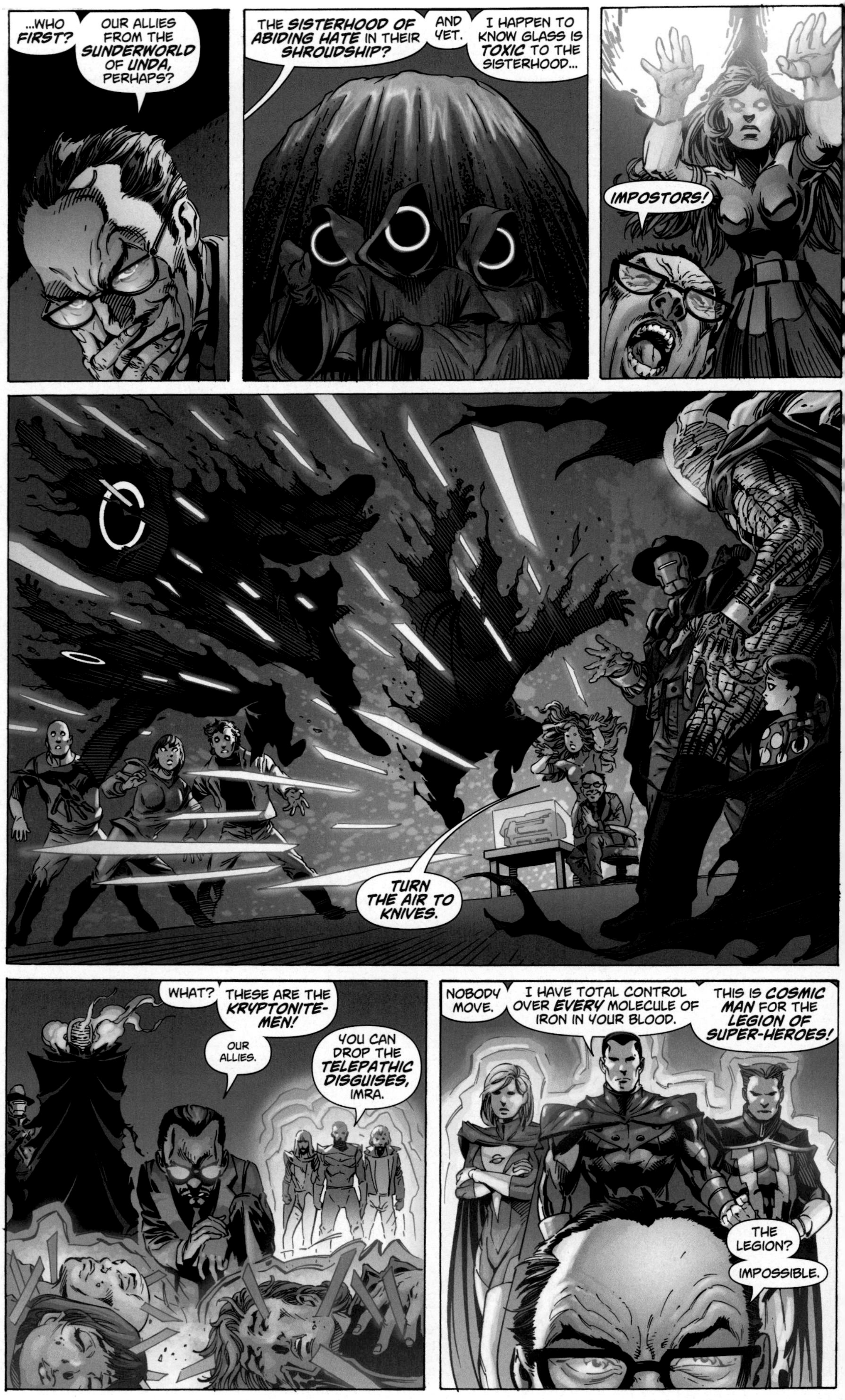
...WHO FIRST?
OUR ALLIES FROM THE SUNDERWORLD OF UNDA, PERHAPS?
THE SISTERHOOD OF ABIDING HATE IN THEIR SHROUDSHIP?
AND YET.
I HAPPEN TO KNOW GLASS IS TOXIC TO THE SISTERHOOD...
IMPOSTORS!
TURN THE AIR TO KNIVES.
WHAT?
THESE ARE THE KRYPTONITE-MEN!
OUR ALLIES.
YOU CAN DROP THE TELEPATHIC DISGUISES, IMRA.
NOBODY MOVE.
I HAVE TOTAL CONTROL OVER EVERY MOLECULE OF IRON IN YOUR BLOOD.
THIS IS COSMIC MAN FOR THE LEGION OF SUPER-HEROES!
THE LEGION?
IMPOSSIBLE.

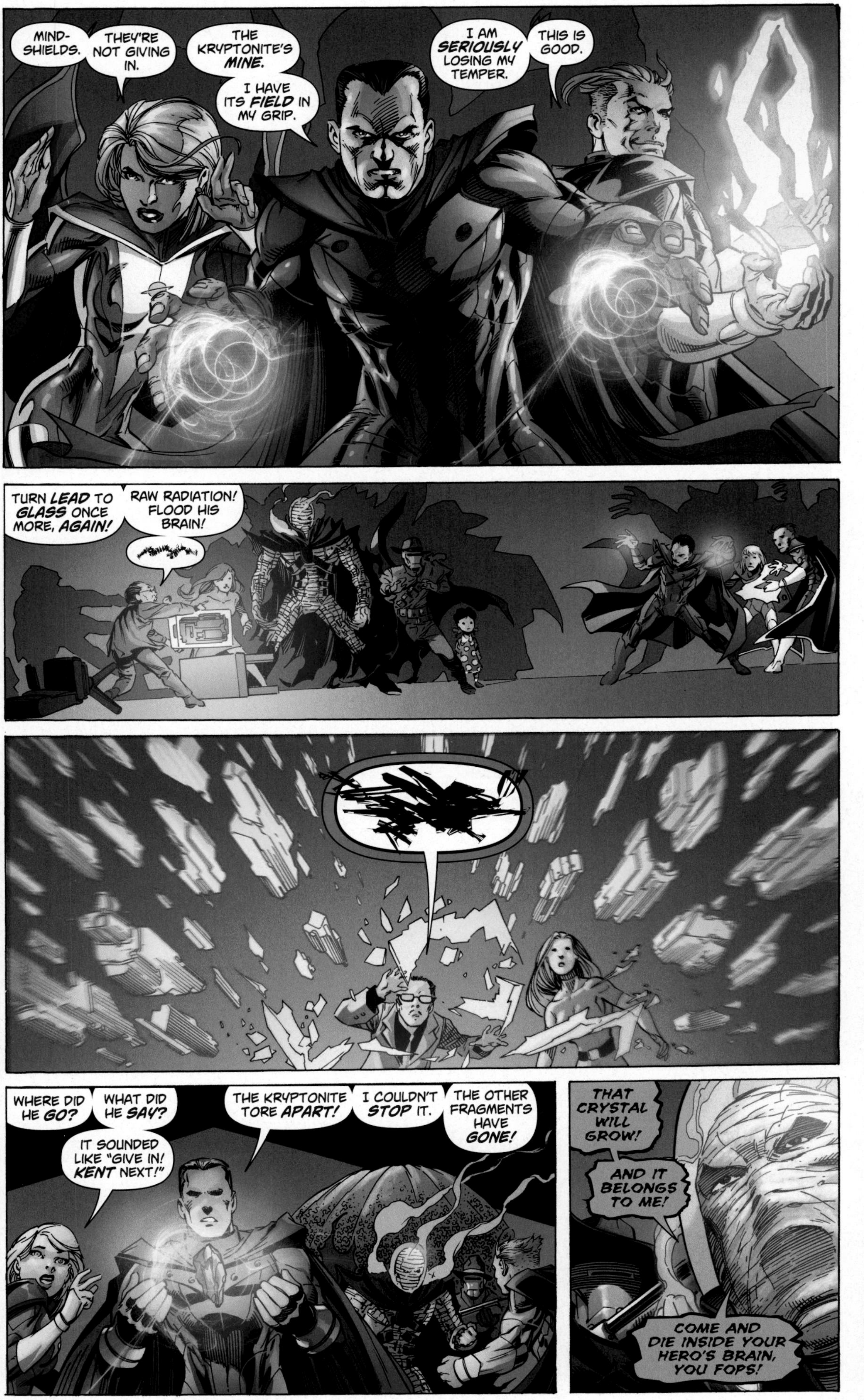
MIND-SHIELDS.
THEY'RE NOT GIVING IN.
THE KRYPTONITE'S MINE.
I HAVE ITS FIELD IN MY GRIP.
I AM SERIOUSLY LOSING MY TEMPER.
THIS IS GOOD.
TURN LEAD TO GLASS ONCE MORE, AGAIN!
RAW RADIATION! FLOOD HIS BRAIN!
WHERE DID HE GO?
WHAT DID HE SAY?
IT SOUNDED LIKE "GIVE IN! KENT NEXT!"
THE KRYPTONITE TORE APART!
I COULDN'T STOP IT.
THE OTHER FRAGMENTS HAVE GONE!
THAT CRYSTAL WILL GROW!
AND IT BELONGS TO ME!
COME AND DIE INSIDE YOUR HERO'S BRAIN, YOU FOPS!

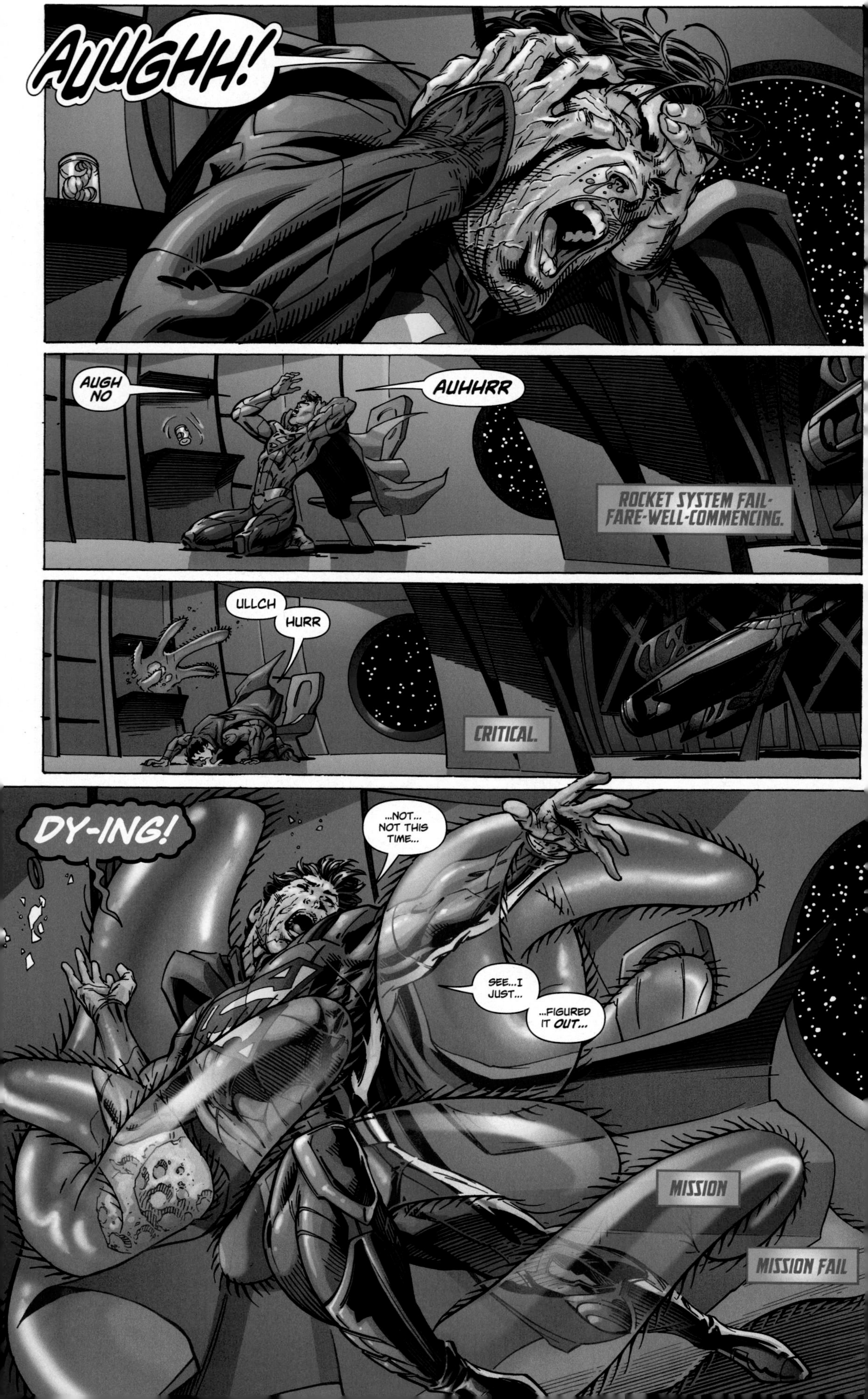
AUUGHH!
AUGH NO
AUHHRR
ROCKET SYSTEM FAIL-
FARE-WELL-COMMENCING.
ULLCH
HURR
CRITICAL.
DY-ING!
...NOT... NOT THIS TIME...
SEE...I JUST...
...FIGURED IT OUT...
MISSION
MISSION FAIL

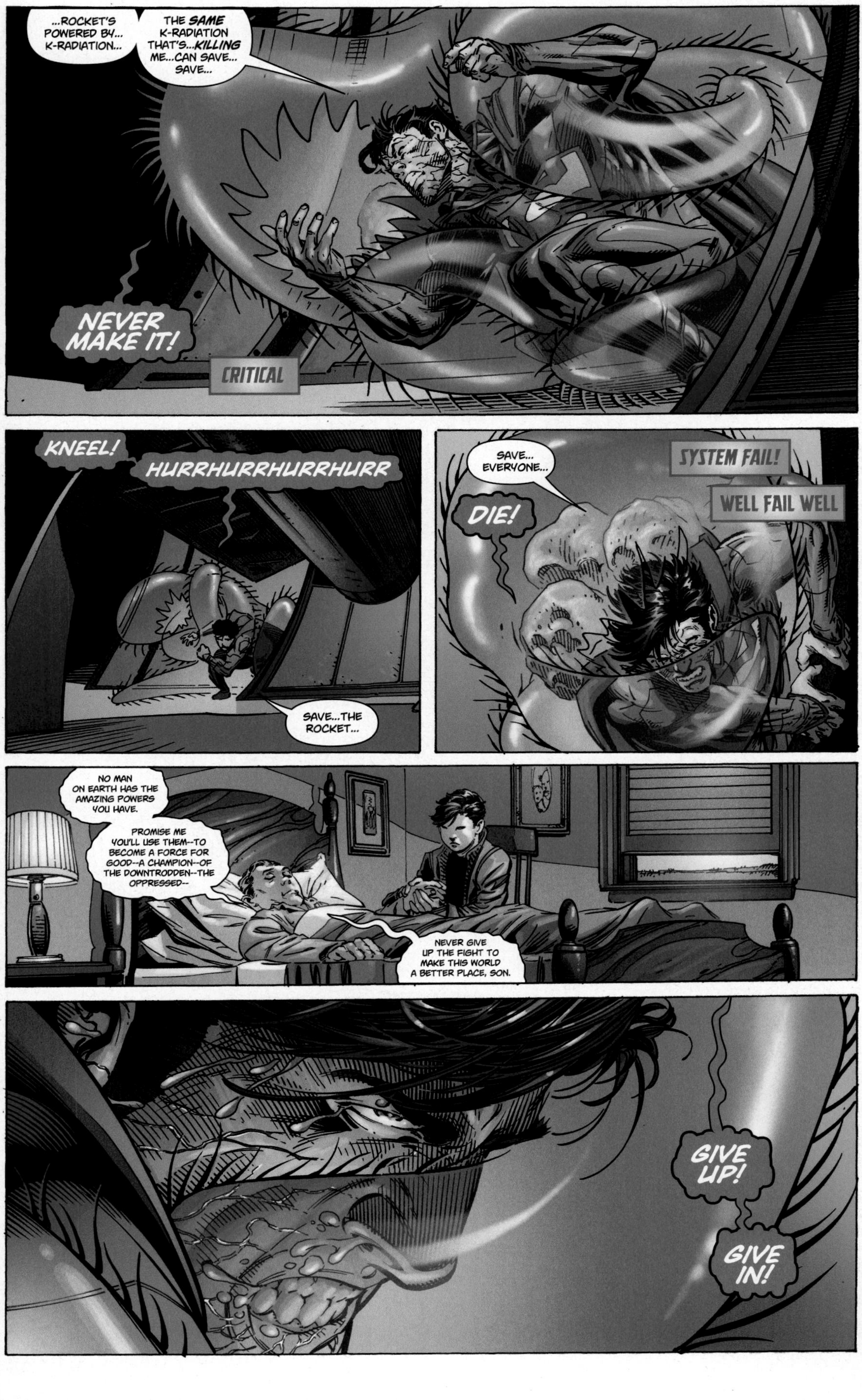
...ROCKET'S POWERED BY... K-RADIATION...
THE SAME K-RADIATION THAT'S...KILLING ME...CAN SAVE... SAVE...
NEVER MAKE IT!
CRITICAL
KNEEL!
HURRHURRHURRHURR
SAVE...THE ROCKET...
SAVE... EVERYONE...
SYSTEM FAIL!
WELL FAIL WELL
DIE!
NO MAN ON EARTH HAS THE AMAZING POWERS YOU HAVE.
PROMISE ME YOU'LL USE THEM--TO BECOME A FORCE FOR GOOD--A CHAMPION--OF THE DOWNTRODDEN--THE OPPRESSED--
NEVER GIVE UP THE FIGHT TO MAKE THIS WORLD A BETTER PLACE, SON.
GIVE UP!
GIVE IN!

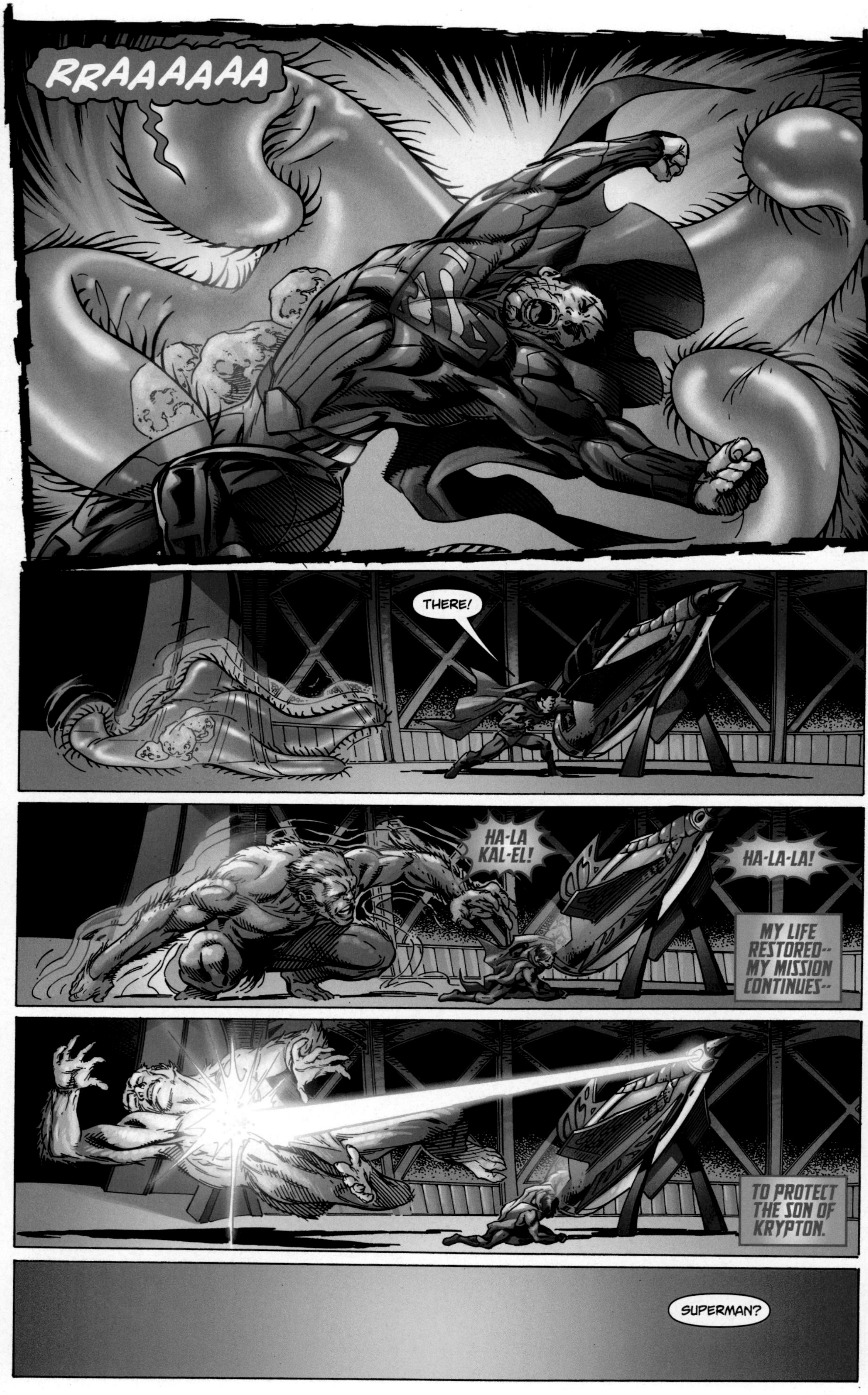
RRAAAAAA
THERE!
HA-LA KAL-EL!
HA-LA-LA!
MY LIFE RESTORED-- MY MISSION CONTINUES--
TO PROTECT THE SON OF KRYPTON.
SUPERMAN?

I HAD THAT.
SUPERMAN, WE BEAT THEM.
WE HAVE THE ENGINE. THE POWER SOURCE IS SAFE.
YOU CAN LET GO NOW.
URRRR
YOU DID IT.
YOU KEPT THE ROCKET ALIVE AND SAVED THE PAST, WHICH WE KNEW YOU'D DO, INCIDENTALLY.
AND NOW WE HAVE TO GET OUT OF HERE.
HELP
APPRECIATED
THE YOUNG SUPERMAN GETS BACK ANY SECOND.
HE'LL SOON HAVE ENOUGH TROUBLE ON HIS HANDS WITH SUSIE AND EARTH'S FIRST SUPERMAN WITHOUT HAVING TO DEAL WITH US.
NOW WHO'S THE GROUPIE, ROKK?
THIS SUPERMAN NEEDS SUNLIGHT AND REST AND TIME TO HEAL.
HIS GREATEST BATTLE'S STILL TO COME--AND OURS, TOO.
WHEN I LOOKED IN HIS MEMORIES, I FELT SO ASHAMED.
REMEMBER WE WERE SO DISAPPOINTED IN HIM THAT FIRST TIME?
WE'D BUILT HIM UP AS THIS IDOL IN OUR MINDS, THIS MYTH, AND HE WAS JUST A GAWKY CAVEMAN KID.
BUT FOR HIM...
MEETING US, THAT WAS WHEN HE KNEW THE UNIVERSE WAS BIGGER THAN HE EVER HOPED.
WE WERE THE PROOF THAT PLANET EARTH HAD A FUTURE WORTH FIGHTING FOR.
MEETING US WAS THE GREATEST DAY IN HIS LIFE.

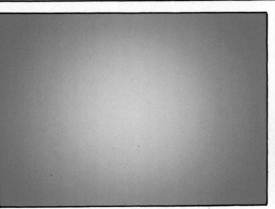

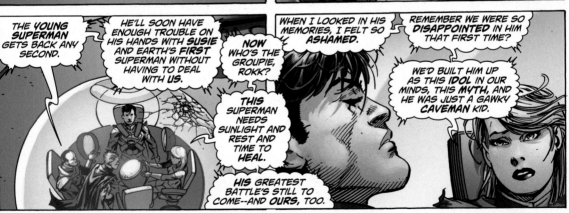

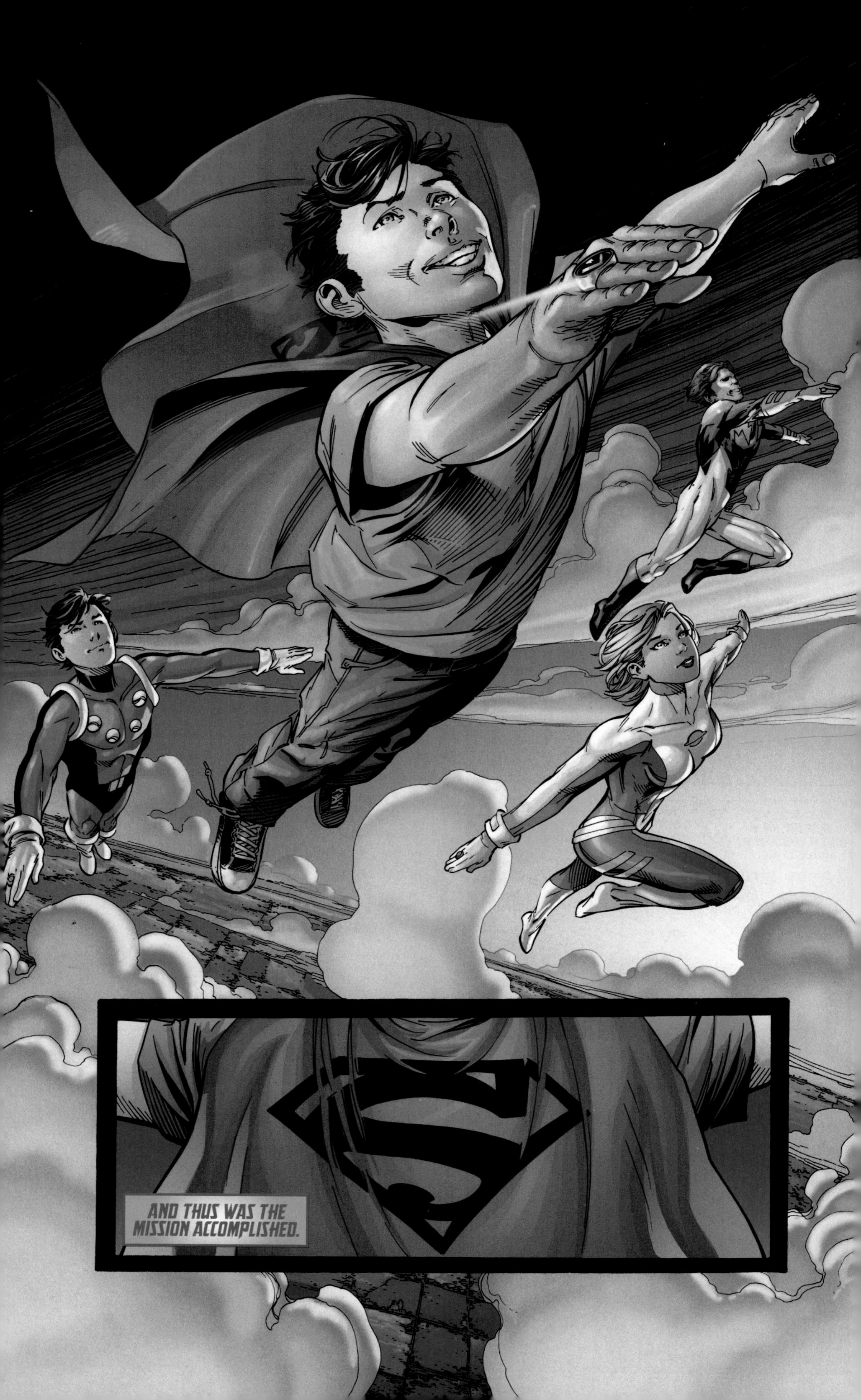
AND THUS WAS THE MISSION ACCOMPLISHED.

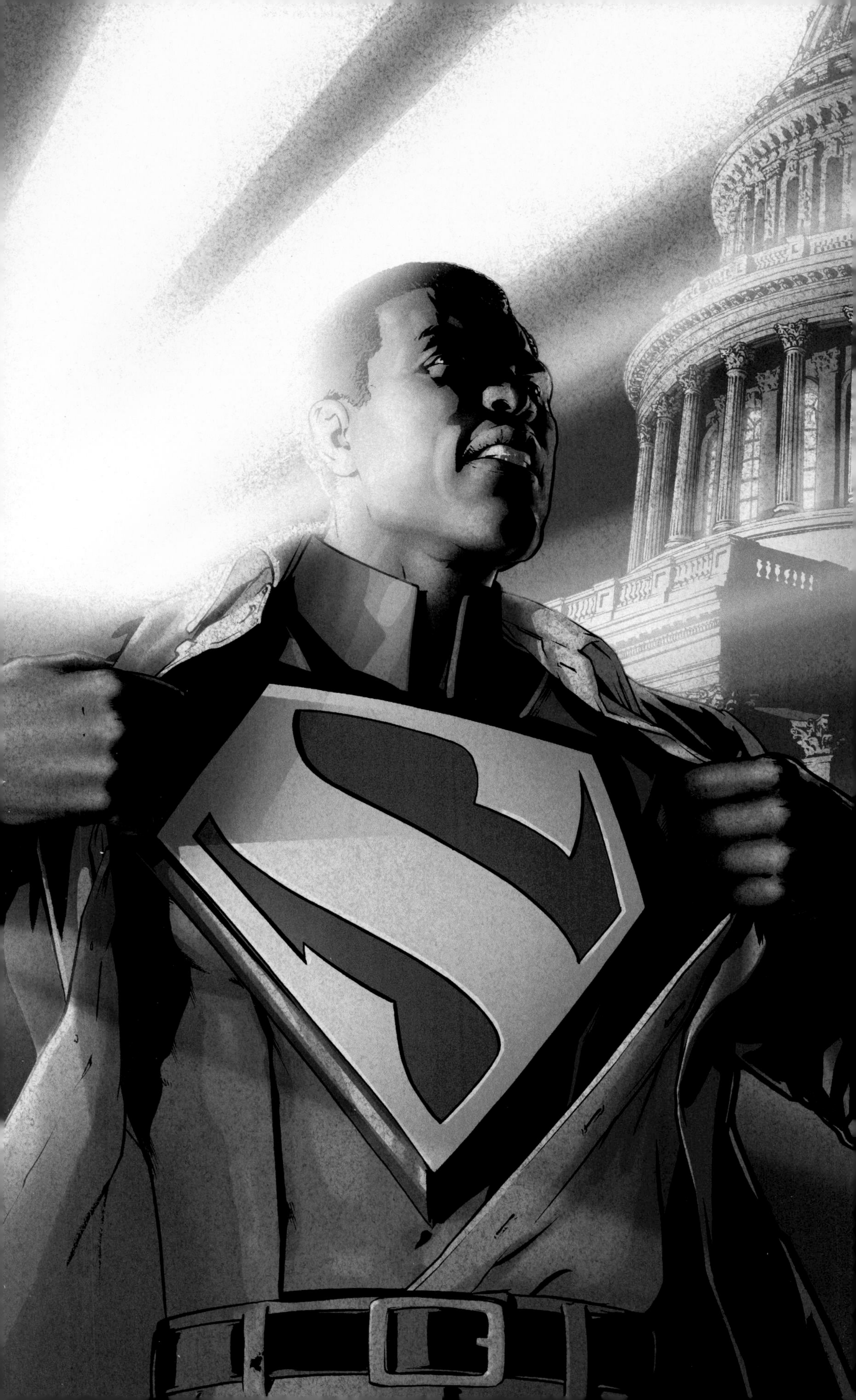

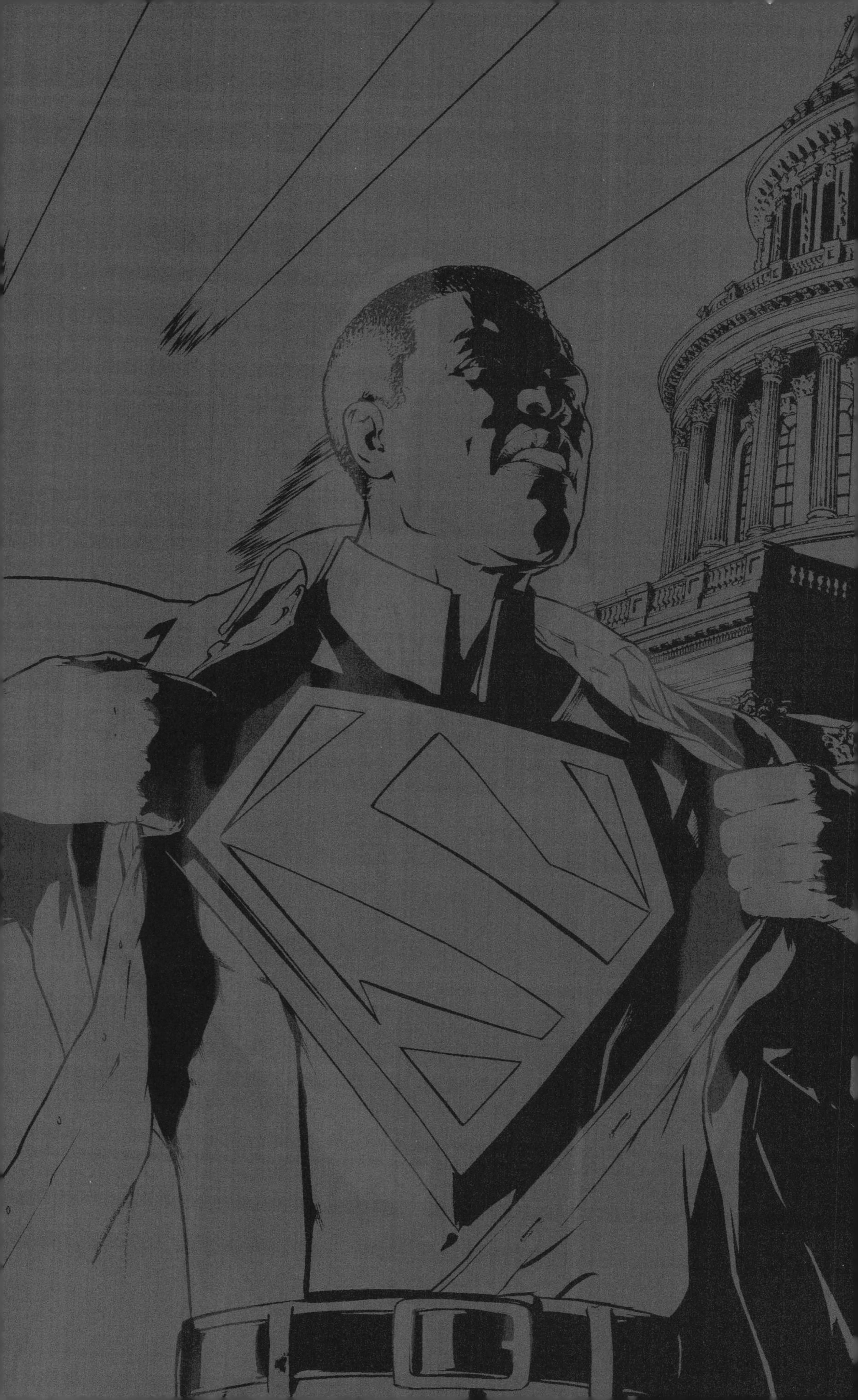

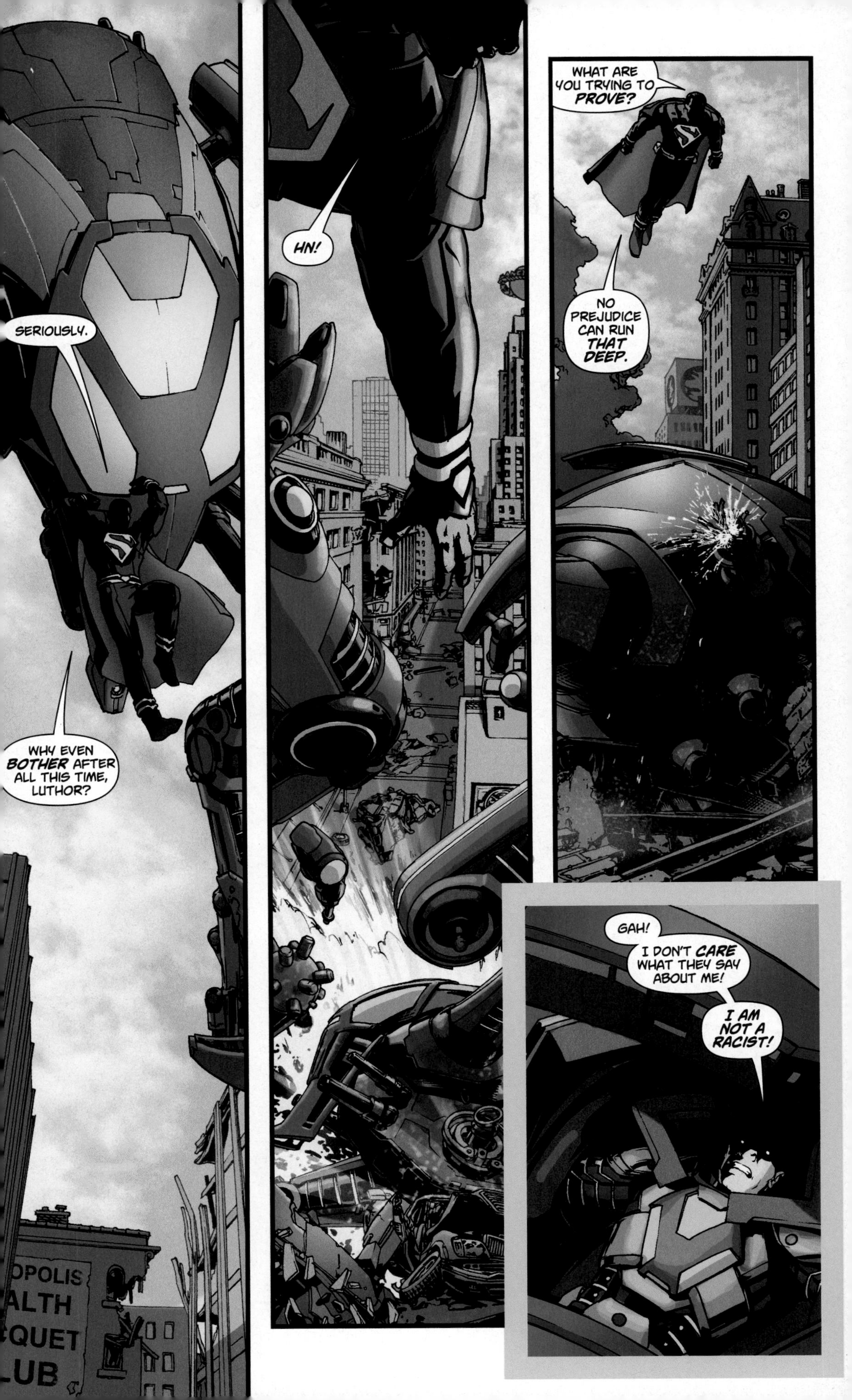
SERIOUSLY.
WHY EVEN BOTHER AFTER ALL THIS TIME, LUTHOR?
OPOLIS
ALTH
CQUET
LUB
HN!
WHAT ARE YOU TRYING TO PROVE?
NO PREJUDICE CAN RUN THAT DEEP.
GAH!
I DON'T CARE WHAT THEY SAY ABOUT ME!
I AM NOT A RACIST!

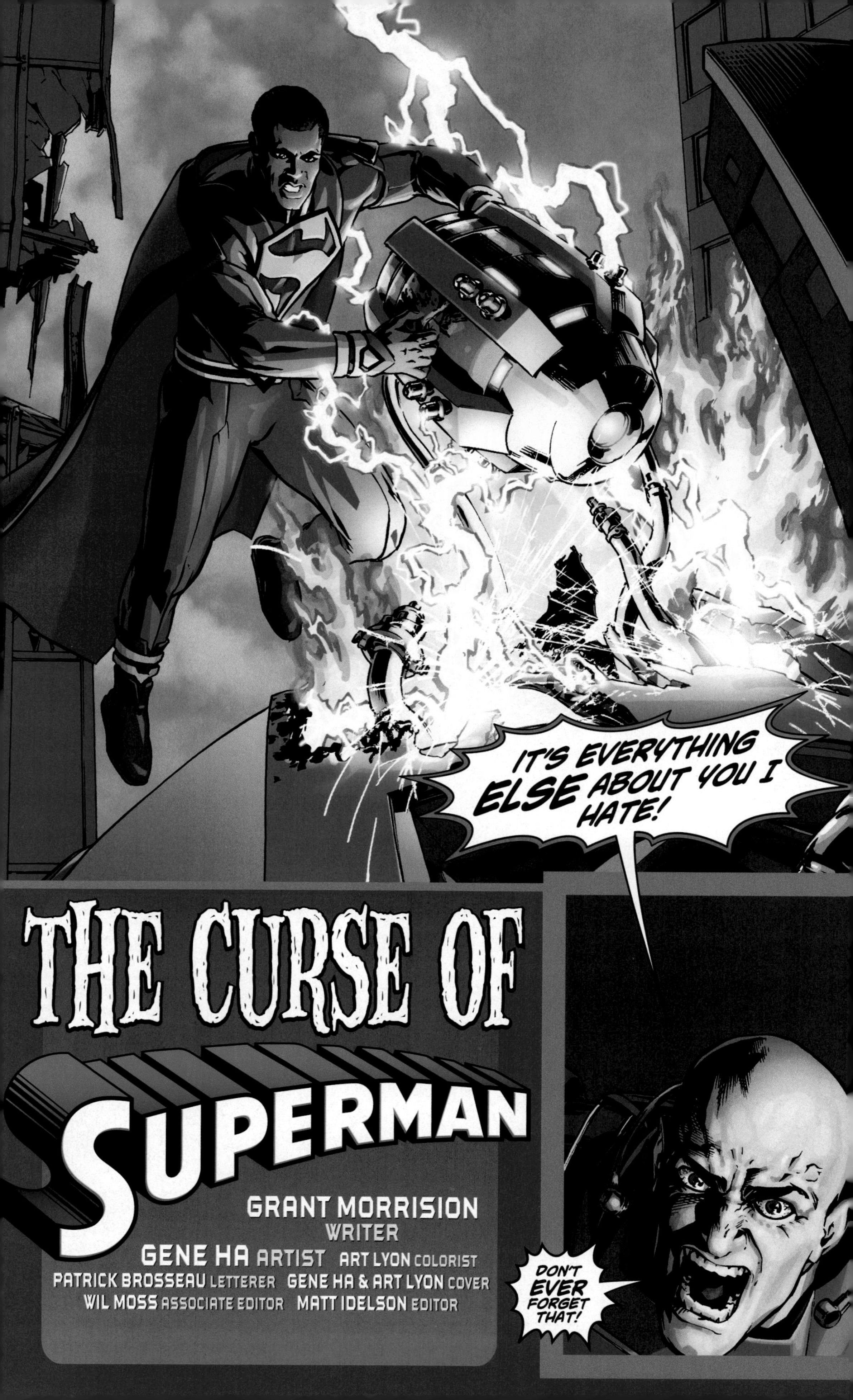
IT'S EVERYTHING ELSE ABOUT YOU I HATE!
THE CURSE OF SUPERMAN
GRANT MORRISION WRITER
GENE HA ARTIST ART LYON COLORIST
PATRICK BROSSEAU LETTERER GENE HA & ART LYON COVER
WIL MOSS ASSOCIATE EDITOR MATT IDELSON EDITOR
DON'T EVER FORGET THAT!

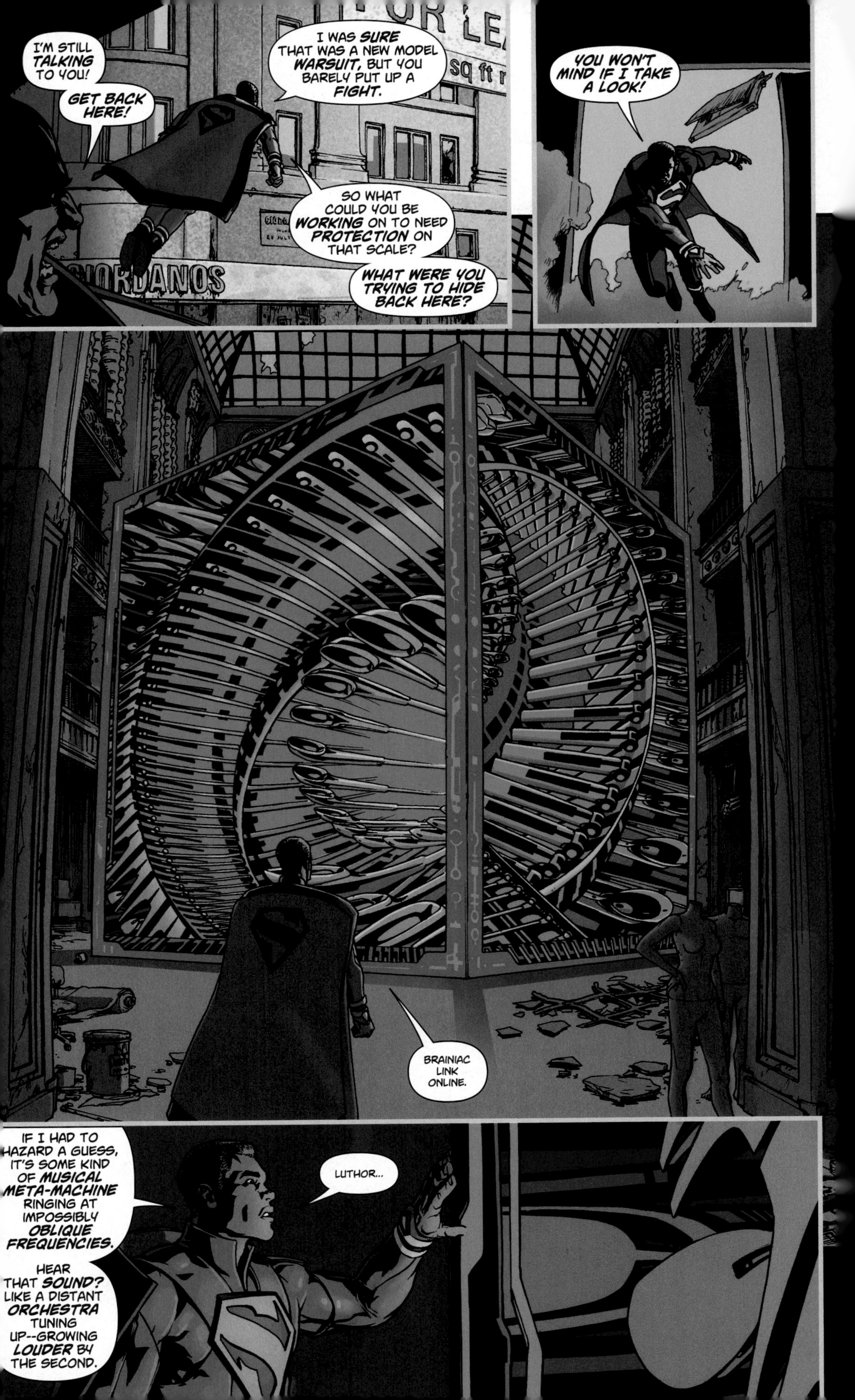
I'M STILL TALKING TO YOU!
GET BACK HERE!
I WAS SURE THAT WAS A NEW MODEL WARSUIT, BUT YOU BARELY PUT UP A FIGHT.
SO WHAT COULD YOU BE WORKING ON TO NEED PROTECTION ON THAT SCALE?
WHAT WERE YOU TRYING TO HIDE BACK HERE?
YOU WON'T MIND IF I TAKE A LOOK!
BRAINIAC LINK ONLINE.
IF I HAD TO HAZARD A GUESS, IT'S SOME KIND OF MUSICAL META-MACHINE RINGING AT IMPOSSIBLY OBLIQUE FREQUENCIES.
HEAR THAT SOUND? LIKE A DISTANT ORCHESTRA TUNING UP--GROWING LOUDER BY THE SECOND.
LUTHOR...

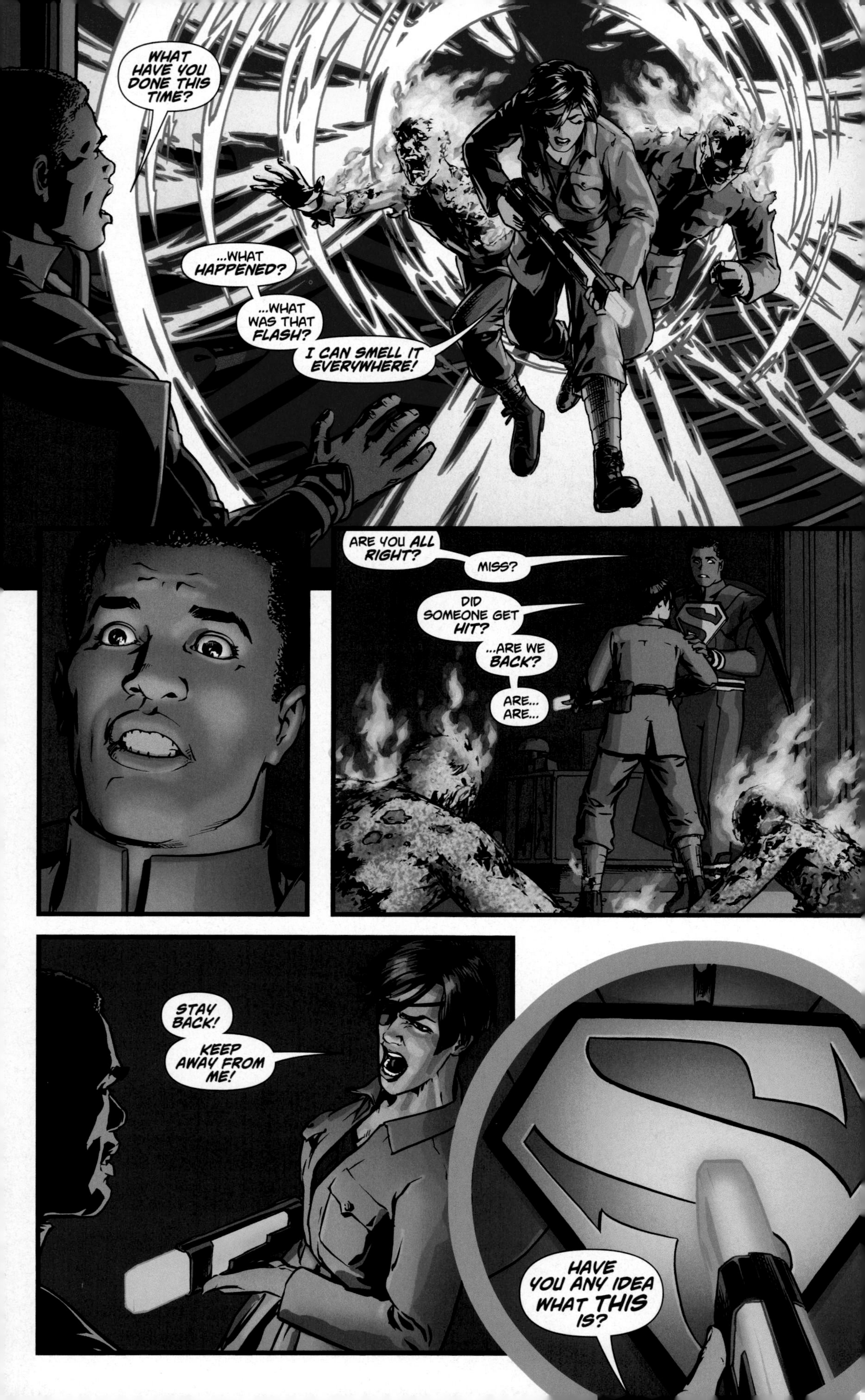
WHAT HAVE YOU DONE THIS TIME?
...WHAT HAPPENED?
...WHAT WAS THAT FLASH?
I CAN SMELL IT EVERYWHERE!
ARE YOU ALL RIGHT?
MISS?
DID SOMEONE GET HIT?
...ARE WE BACK?
ARE... ARE...
STAY BACK!
KEEP AWAY FROM ME!
HAVE YOU ANY IDEA WHAT THIS IS?

BACK!

...I...

YOU'RE IMMUNE TO K-LASER.

K-LASER?

IT'S--IT'S A HATE-POWERED WEAPON FROM THAT--THAT OTHER PLACE, WITH OPTIMAN--

CLARK WAS RIGHT-- CLARK...?

NNNN

LLLLUHH-LUH

CLARK!

OH, JIMMY!

OH NO, NO, NO!

JIMMY'S DEAD.

THEY DIDN'T DESERVE THIS.

THIS WASN'T SUPPOSED TO HAPPEN.

I HAVE NO IDEA WHAT'S GOING ON HERE.

I DON'T KNOW WHY YOU TRIED TO SHOOT ME.

I DON'T KNOW WHO YOU ARE--

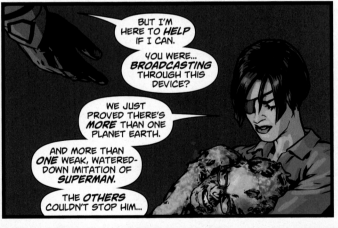

BUT I'M HERE TO HELP IF I CAN.

YOU WERE... BROADCASTING THROUGH THIS DEVICE?

WE JUST PROVED THERE'S MORE THAN ONE PLANET EARTH.

AND MORE THAN ONE WEAK, WATERED-DOWN IMITATION OF SUPERMAN.

THE OTHERS COULDN'T STOP HIM...

WHAT MAKES YOU SO DIFFERENT?

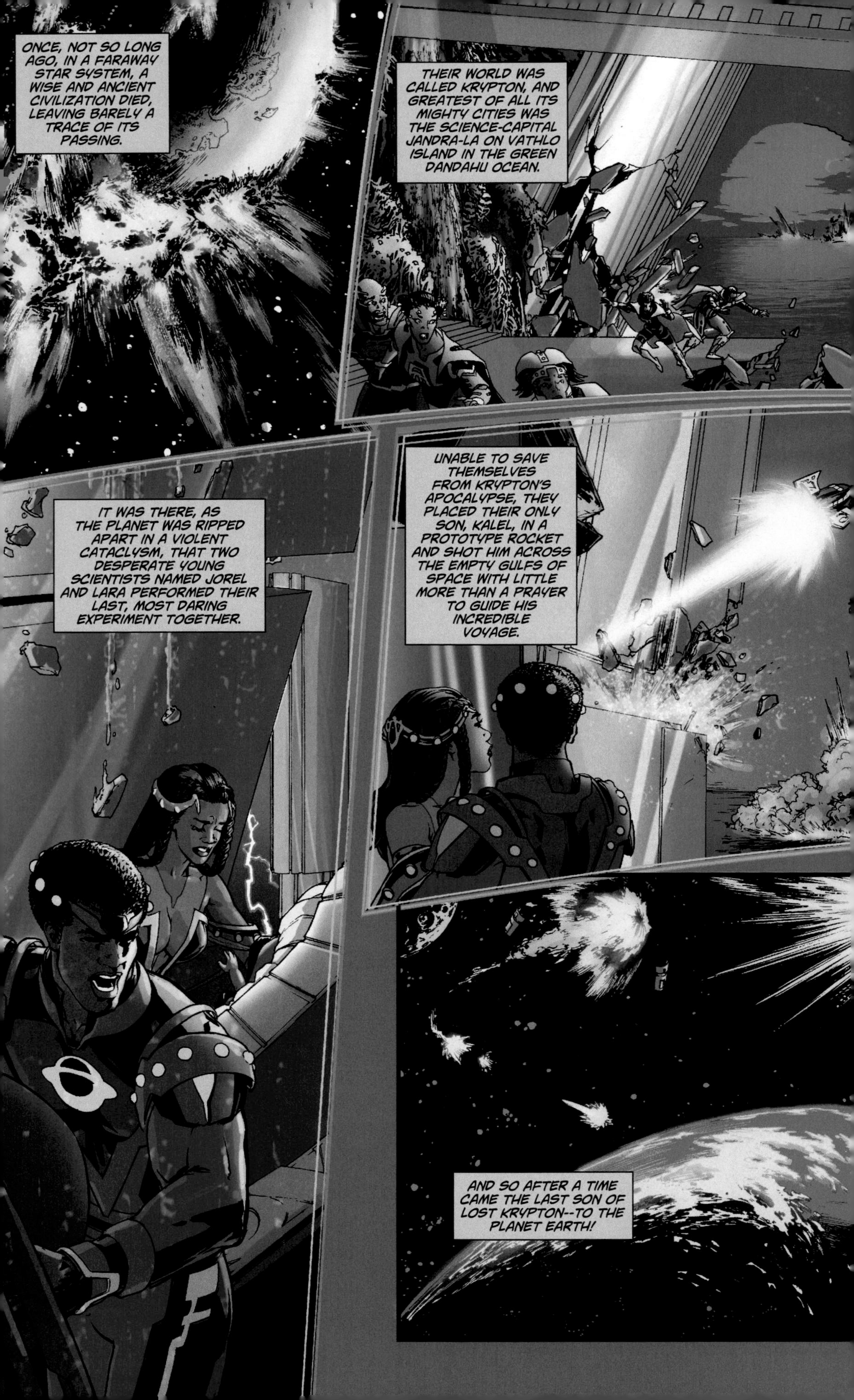
ONCE, NOT SO LONG AGO, IN A FARAWAY STAR SYSTEM, A WISE AND ANCIENT CIVILIZATION DIED, LEAVING BARELY A TRACE OF ITS PASSING.
THEIR WORLD WAS CALLED KRYPTON, AND GREATEST OF ALL ITS MIGHTY CITIES WAS THE SCIENCE-CAPITAL JANDRA-LA ON VATHLO ISLAND IN THE GREEN DANDAHU OCEAN.
IT WAS THERE, AS THE PLANET WAS RIPPED APART IN A VIOLENT CATACLYSM, THAT TWO DESPERATE YOUNG SCIENTISTS NAMED JOREL AND LARA PERFORMED THEIR LAST, MOST DARING EXPERIMENT TOGETHER.
UNABLE TO SAVE THEMSELVES FROM KRYPTON'S APOCALYPSE, THEY PLACED THEIR ONLY SON, KALEL, IN A PROTOTYPE ROCKET AND SHOT HIM ACROSS THE EMPTY GULFS OF SPACE WITH LITTLE MORE THAN A PRAYER TO GUIDE HIS INCREDIBLE VOYAGE.
AND SO AFTER A TIME CAME THE LAST SON OF LOST KRYPTON--TO THE PLANET EARTH!

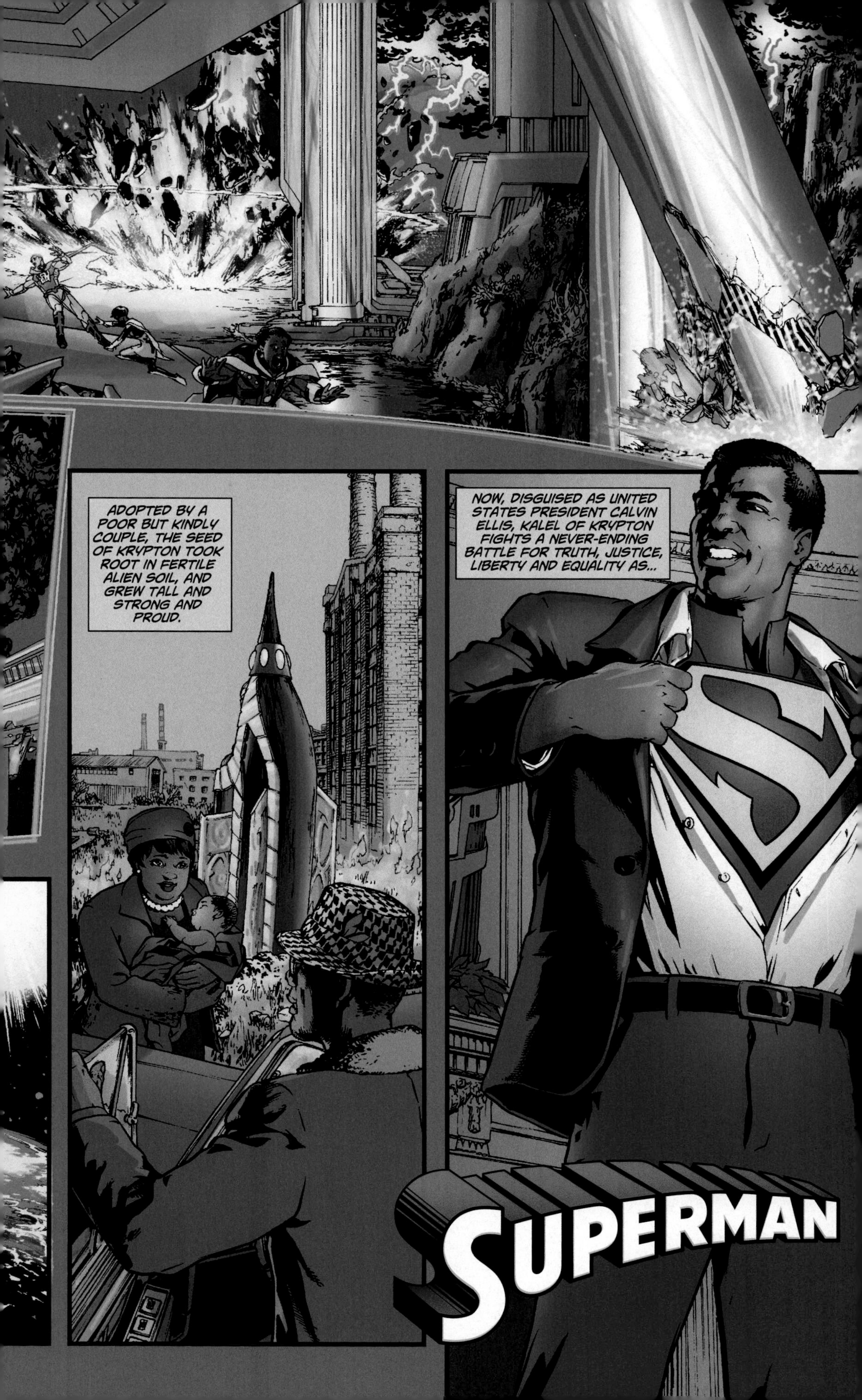
ADOPTED BY A POOR BUT KINDLY COUPLE, THE SEED OF KRYPTON TOOK ROOT IN FERTILE ALIEN SOIL, AND GREW TALL AND STRONG AND PROUD.
NOW, DISGUISED AS UNITED STATES PRESIDENT CALVIN ELLIS, KALEL OF KRYPTON FIGHTS A NEVER-ENDING BATTLE FOR TRUTH, JUSTICE, LIBERTY AND EQUALITY AS...
SUPERMAN

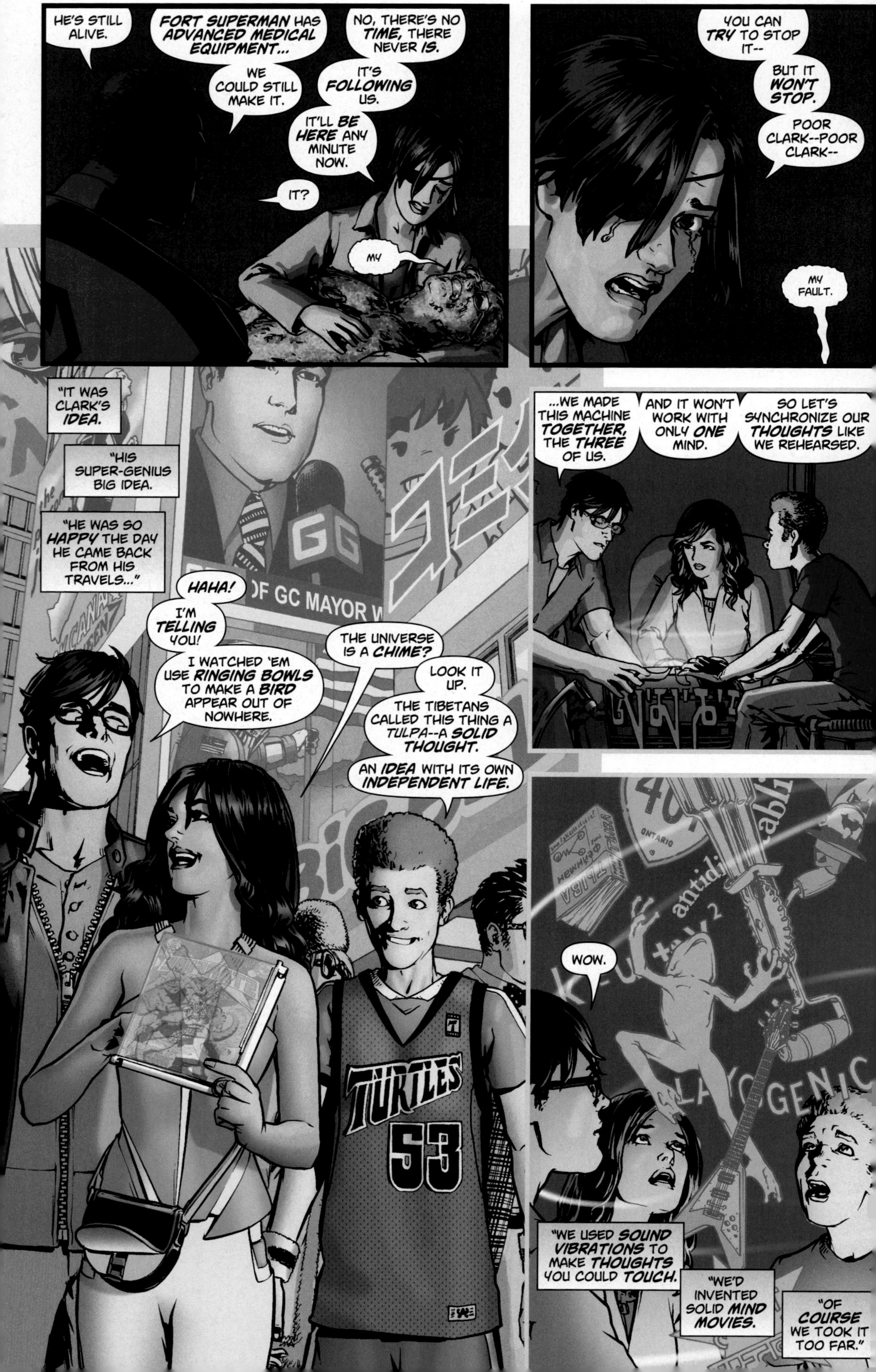

HE'S STILL ALIVE.
FORT SUPERMAN HAS ADVANCED MEDICAL EQUIPMENT...
WE COULD STILL MAKE IT.
NO, THERE'S NO TIME, THERE NEVER IS.
IT'S FOLLOWING US.
IT'LL BE HERE ANY MINUTE NOW.
IT?
MY
YOU CAN TRY TO STOP IT--
BUT IT WON'T STOP.
POOR CLARK--POOR CLARK--
MY FAULT.
"IT WAS CLARK'S IDEA.
"HIS SUPER-GENIUS BIG IDEA.
"HE WAS SO HAPPY THE DAY HE CAME BACK FROM HIS TRAVELS..."
HAHA!
I'M TELLING YOU!
I WATCHED 'EM USE RINGING BOWLS TO MAKE A BIRD APPEAR OUT OF NOWHERE.
THE UNIVERSE IS A CHIME?
LOOK IT UP.
THE TIBETANS CALLED THIS THING A TULPA--A SOLID THOUGHT.
AN IDEA WITH ITS OWN INDEPENDENT LIFE.
TURTLES
53
...WE MADE THIS MACHINE TOGETHER, THE THREE OF US.
AND IT WON'T WORK WITH ONLY ONE MIND.
SO LET'S SYNCHRONIZE OUR THOUGHTS LIKE WE REHEARSED.
WOW.
"WE USED SOUND VIBRATIONS TO MAKE THOUGHTS YOU COULD TOUCH.
"WE'D INVENTED SOLID MIND MOVIES.
"OF COURSE WE TOOK IT TOO FAR."

THESE PAINKILLERS SHOULD HELP FOR NOW.

I'M SORRY.

GO ON.

FIRST WE TRIED TO IMAGINE A *CHAMPION,* A THOUGHT-POWERED *REDEEMER* CAPABLE OF *SAVING THE WORLD.*

A MADE-UP *MESSIAH.* I CALLED OUR CREATION *SUPERMAN,* AFTER *NIETZSCHE* AND *GEORGE BERNARD SHAW.*

"OUR *FIRST* ATTEMPT LIVED FOR *TWENTY-FIVE GLORIOUS MINUTES.*

"NOT A *SINGLE SECOND* OF HIS BRIEF LIFE WAS WASTED, AS HE USED IT TO ARTICULATE A CODE OF *ETHICS* SO PURE AND SIMPLE AND GOOD WE ALL *WEPT.*

"TEN MINUTES LATER, NOT ONE OF US COULD RECALL A *SINGLE WORD* HE'D SAID.

"WE'D REACHED OUR *LIMITS.*

"TO GO FURTHER, WE NEEDED *MONEY,* FUNDING, MORE *BRAINPOWER.*"

UM.

WHAT'S IMPORTANT TO *ME* IS THE OPPORTUNITY TO CHANGE LIVES AND *INSPIRE* PEOPLE.

WE KNOW WE'RE ON TO SOMETHING *BIGGER* AND MORE ENDURING THAN *ACTORS* OR *ROCK STARS.*

WE KNOW WE'RE ON TO SOMETHING *BIG.*

WE WANT TO RETAIN DEVELOPMENT RIGHTS TO THE *SUPERMAN BRAND* IDEA.

IT'S IMPORTANT THAT WE WORK TOGETHER TO CREATE AN *INSPIRATIONAL* FIGURE.

INTERESTING.

HAVE YOU *THOUGHT* ABOUT WHAT THIS CURIOUS INVENTION OF YOURS MIGHT BE *WORTH?*

RIGHTS?

BUT *WE'D* BE TAKING *ALL* THE RISKS.

BUT THAT'S WHY WE HAVE *LAWYERS,* ISN'T IT?

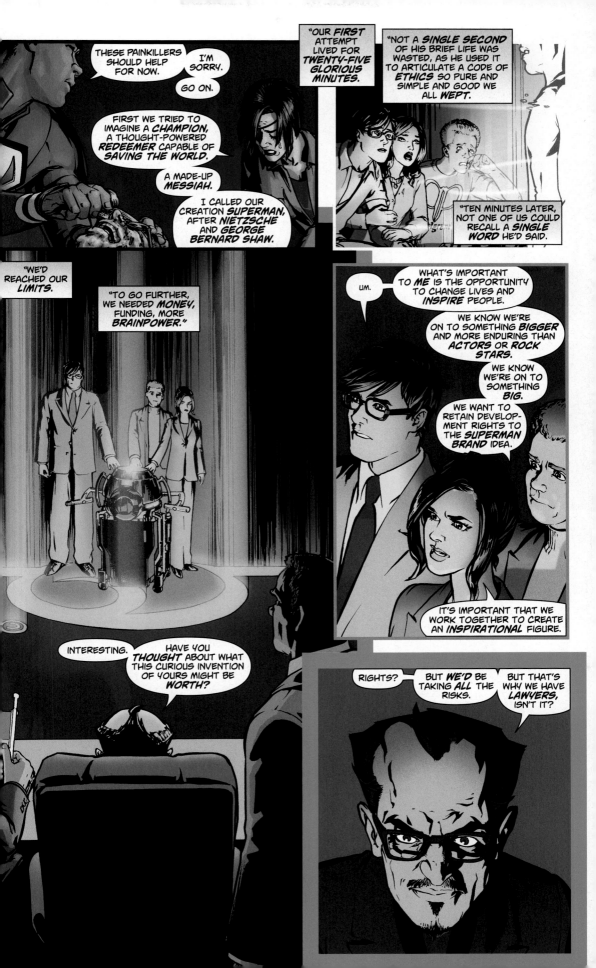

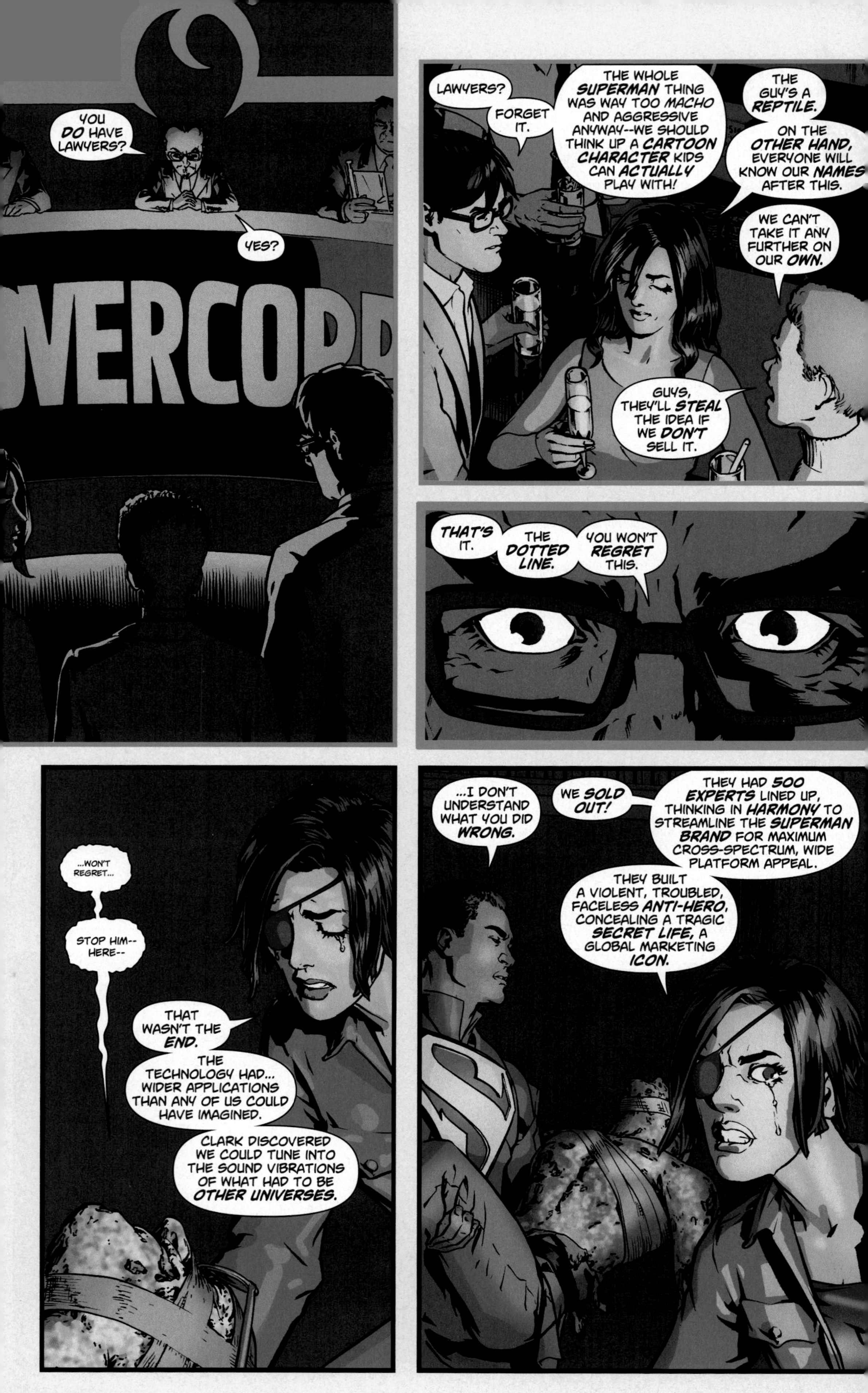
YOU DO HAVE LAWYERS?
YES?
LAWYERS?
FORGET IT.
THE WHOLE SUPERMAN THING WAS WAY TOO MACHO AND AGGRESSIVE ANYWAY--WE SHOULD THINK UP A CARTOON CHARACTER KIDS CAN ACTUALLY PLAY WITH!
THE GUY'S A REPTILE.
ON THE OTHER HAND, EVERYONE WILL KNOW OUR NAMES AFTER THIS.
WE CAN'T TAKE IT ANY FURTHER ON OUR OWN.
GUYS, THEY'LL STEAL THE IDEA IF WE DON'T SELL IT.
THAT'S IT.
THE DOTTED LINE.
YOU WON'T REGRET THIS.
...WON'T REGRET...
STOP HIM-- HERE--
THAT WASN'T THE END.
THE TECHNOLOGY HAD... WIDER APPLICATIONS THAN ANY OF US COULD HAVE IMAGINED.
CLARK DISCOVERED WE COULD TUNE INTO THE SOUND VIBRATIONS OF WHAT HAD TO BE OTHER UNIVERSES.
...I DON'T UNDERSTAND WHAT YOU DID WRONG.
WE SOLD OUT!
THEY HAD 500 EXPERTS LINED UP, THINKING IN HARMONY TO STREAMLINE THE SUPERMAN BRAND FOR MAXIMUM CROSS-SPECTRUM, WIDE PLATFORM APPEAL.
THEY BUILT A VIOLENT, TROUBLED, FACELESS ANTI-HERO, CONCEALING A TRAGIC SECRET LIFE, A GLOBAL MARKETING ICON.

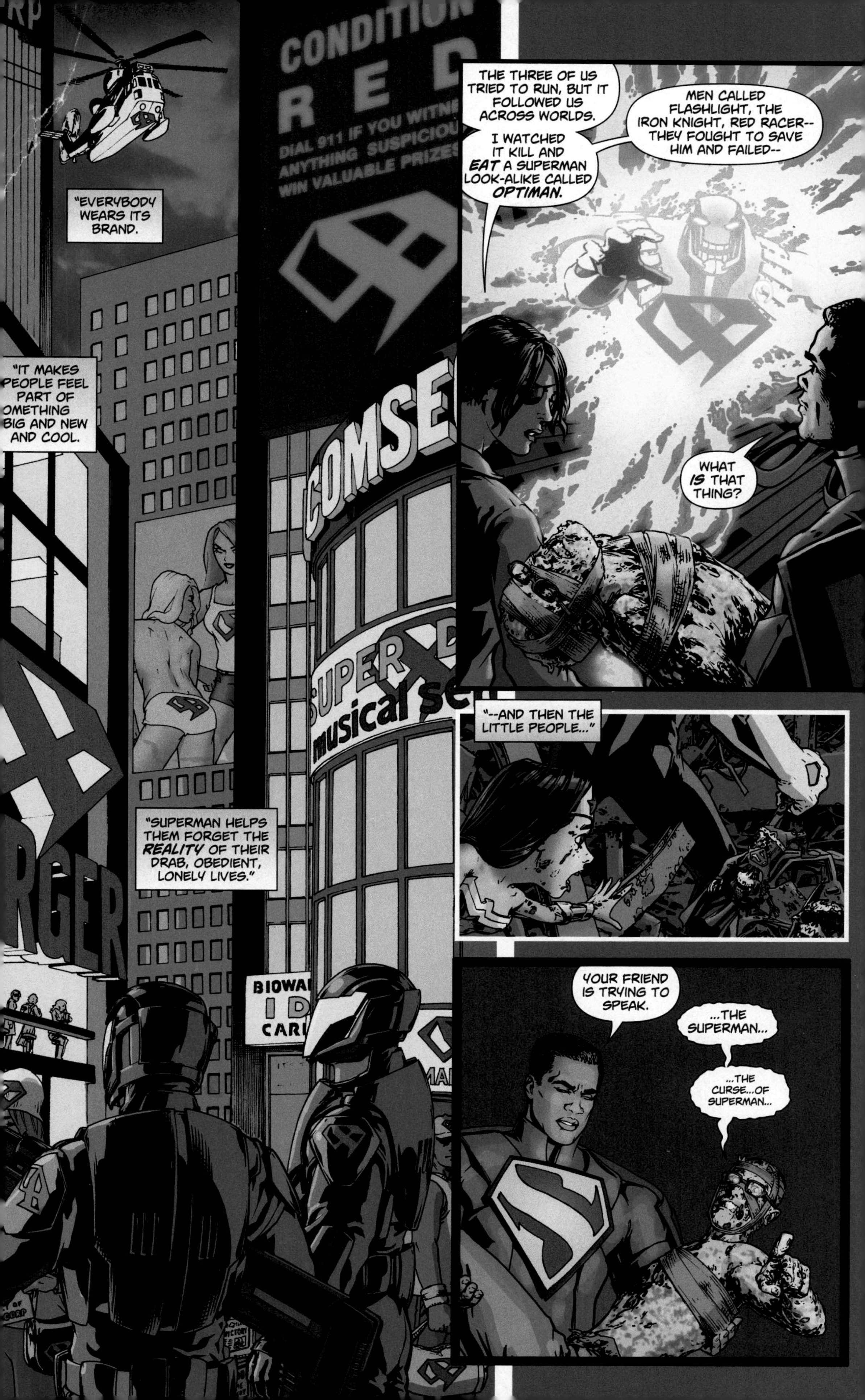
CONDITION
R E D
DIAL 911 IF YOU WITNE
ANYTHING SUSPICIOU
WIN VALUABLE PRIZES
"EVERYBODY WEARS ITS BRAND.
"IT MAKES PEOPLE FEEL PART OF OMETHING BIG AND NEW AND COOL.
COMSE
SUPER
musical se
"SUPERMAN HELPS THEM FORGET THE REALITY OF THEIR DRAB, OBEDIENT, LONELY LIVES."
RGER
BIOWA
CAR
THE THREE OF US TRIED TO RUN, BUT IT FOLLOWED US ACROSS WORLDS.
I WATCHED IT KILL AND EAT A SUPERMAN LOOK-ALIKE CALLED OPTIMAN.
MEN CALLED FLASHLIGHT, THE IRON KNIGHT, RED RACER-- THEY FOUGHT TO SAVE HIM AND FAILED--
WHAT IS THAT THING?
"--AND THEN THE LITTLE PEOPLE..."
YOUR FRIEND IS TRYING TO SPEAK.
...THE SUPERMAN...
...THE CURSE...OF SUPERMAN...

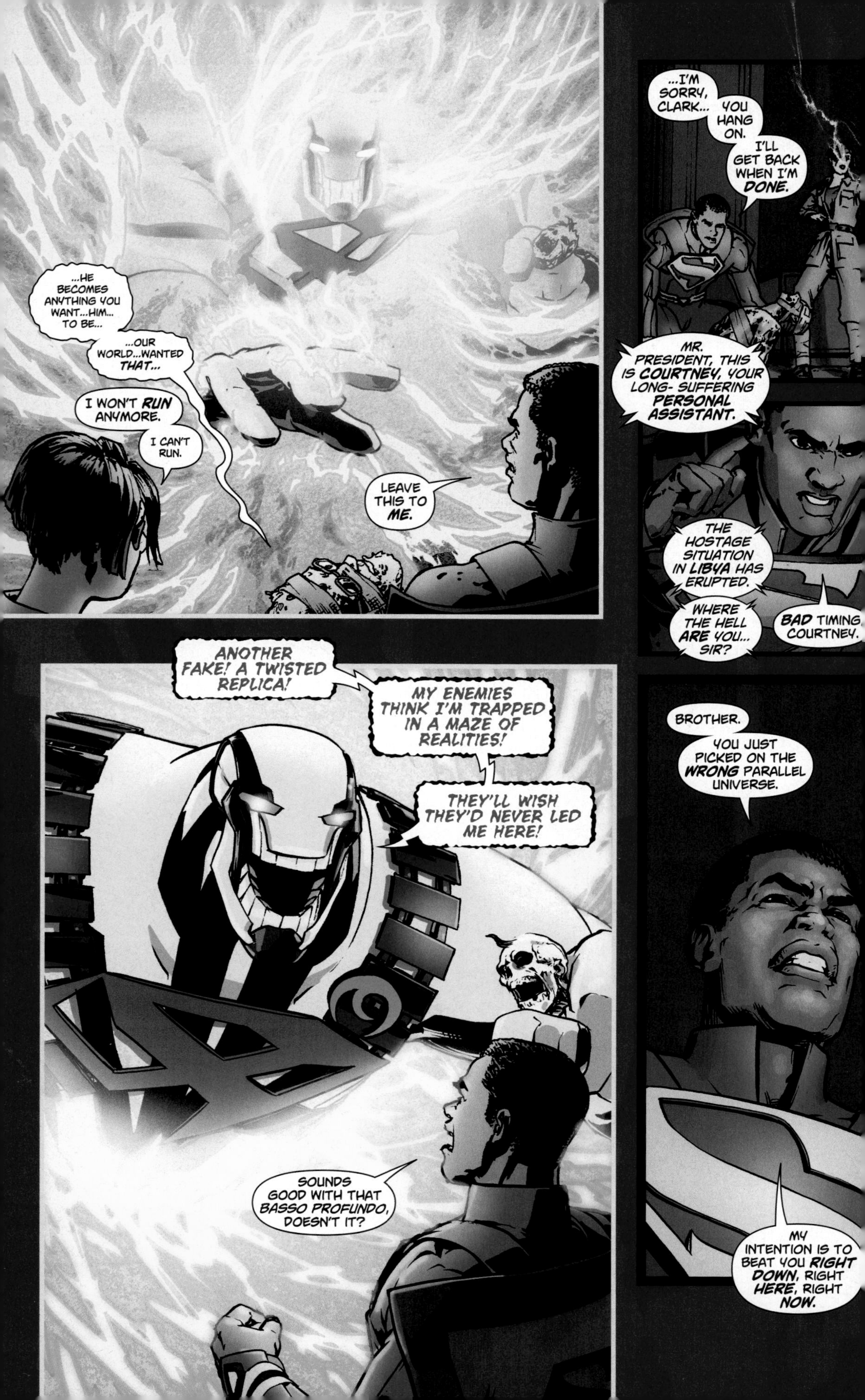
...HE BECOMES ANYTHING YOU WANT...HIM... TO BE...
...OUR WORLD...WANTED THAT...
I WON'T RUN ANYMORE.
I CAN'T RUN.
LEAVE THIS TO ME.
...I'M SORRY, CLARK...
YOU HANG ON.
I'LL GET BACK WHEN I'M DONE.
MR. PRESIDENT, THIS IS COURTNEY, YOUR LONG- SUFFERING PERSONAL ASSISTANT.
THE HOSTAGE SITUATION IN LIBYA HAS ERUPTED.
WHERE THE HELL ARE YOU... SIR?
BAD TIMING COURTNEY.
ANOTHER FAKE! A TWISTED REPLICA!
MY ENEMIES THINK I'M TRAPPED IN A MAZE OF REALITIES!
THEY'LL WISH THEY'D NEVER LED ME HERE!
SOUNDS GOOD WITH THAT BASSO PROFUNDO, DOESN'T IT?
BROTHER.
YOU JUST PICKED ON THE WRONG PARALLEL UNIVERSE.
MY INTENTION IS TO BEAT YOU RIGHT DOWN, RIGHT HERE, RIGHT NOW.

BRAINIAC!

WHILE I'M *BUSY,* YOU'RE IN *CHARGE.*

LIBYA.

BRAINIAC: RESPONDING.

ANALYZING DISTURBANCE IN GLOBAL HUMAN RELATIONS.

APPLYING BEHAVIORAL ALGORITHM TWO SEVEN.

MOBILE UNIT: ROBOT 3 ENGAGE.

RESPONDING.

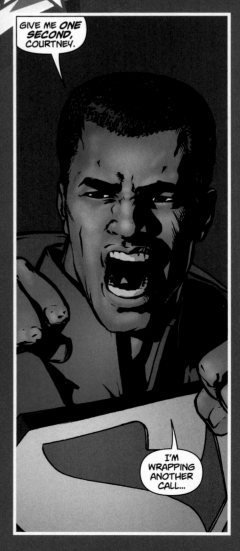

GIVE ME *ONE SECOND,* COURTNEY.

I'M WRAPPING ANOTHER CALL...

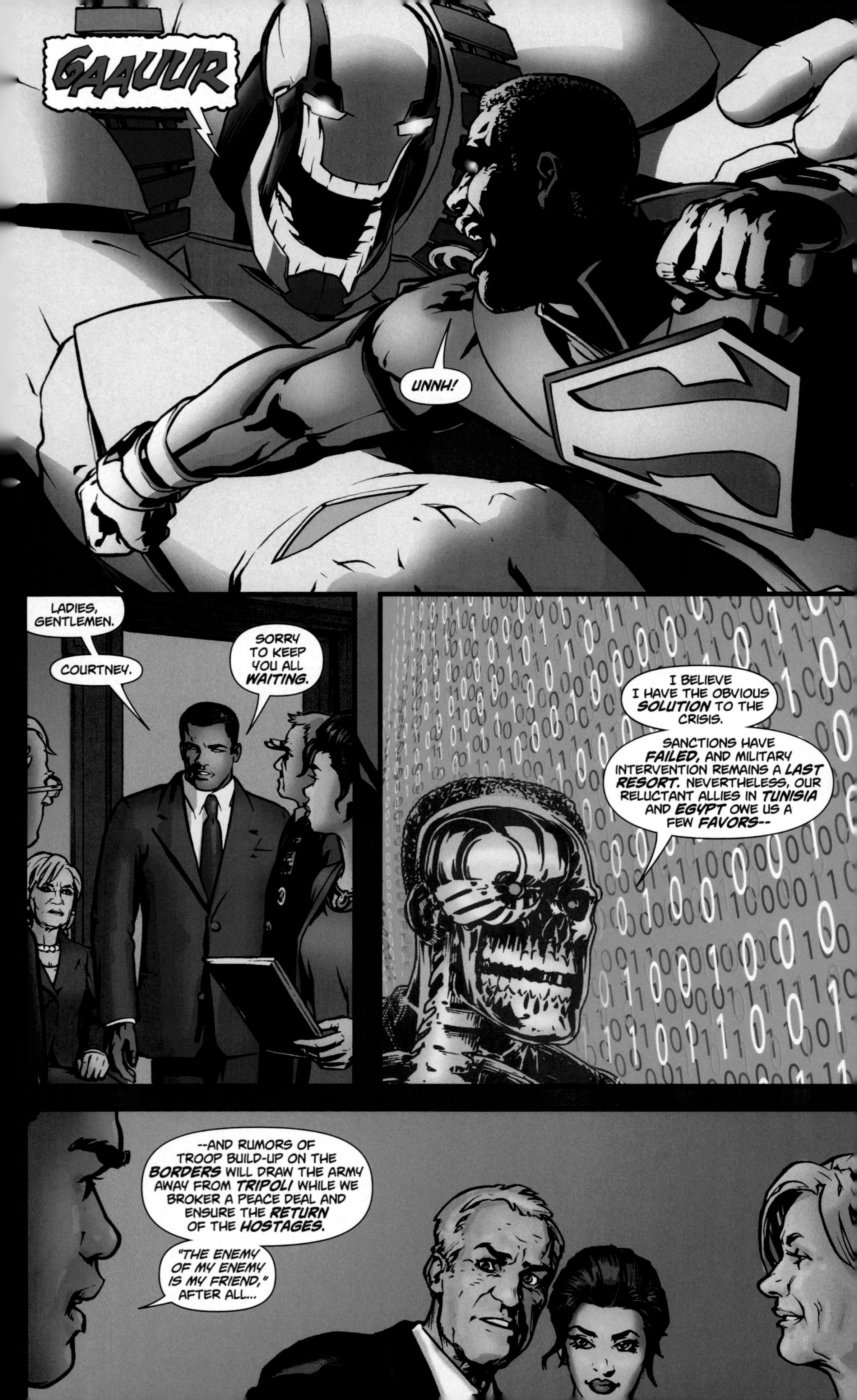

GAAUUR
UNNH!
LADIES, GENTLEMEN.
COURTNEY.
SORRY TO KEEP YOU ALL WAITING.
I BELIEVE I HAVE THE OBVIOUS SOLUTION TO THE CRISIS.
SANCTIONS HAVE FAILED, AND MILITARY INTERVENTION REMAINS A LAST RESORT. NEVERTHELESS, OUR RELUCTANT ALLIES IN TUNISIA AND EGYPT OWE US A FEW FAVORS--
--AND RUMORS OF TROOP BUILD-UP ON THE BORDERS WILL DRAW THE ARMY AWAY FROM TRIPOLI WHILE WE BROKER A PEACE DEAL AND ENSURE THE RETURN OF THE HOSTAGES.
"THE ENEMY OF MY ENEMY IS MY FRIEND," AFTER ALL...

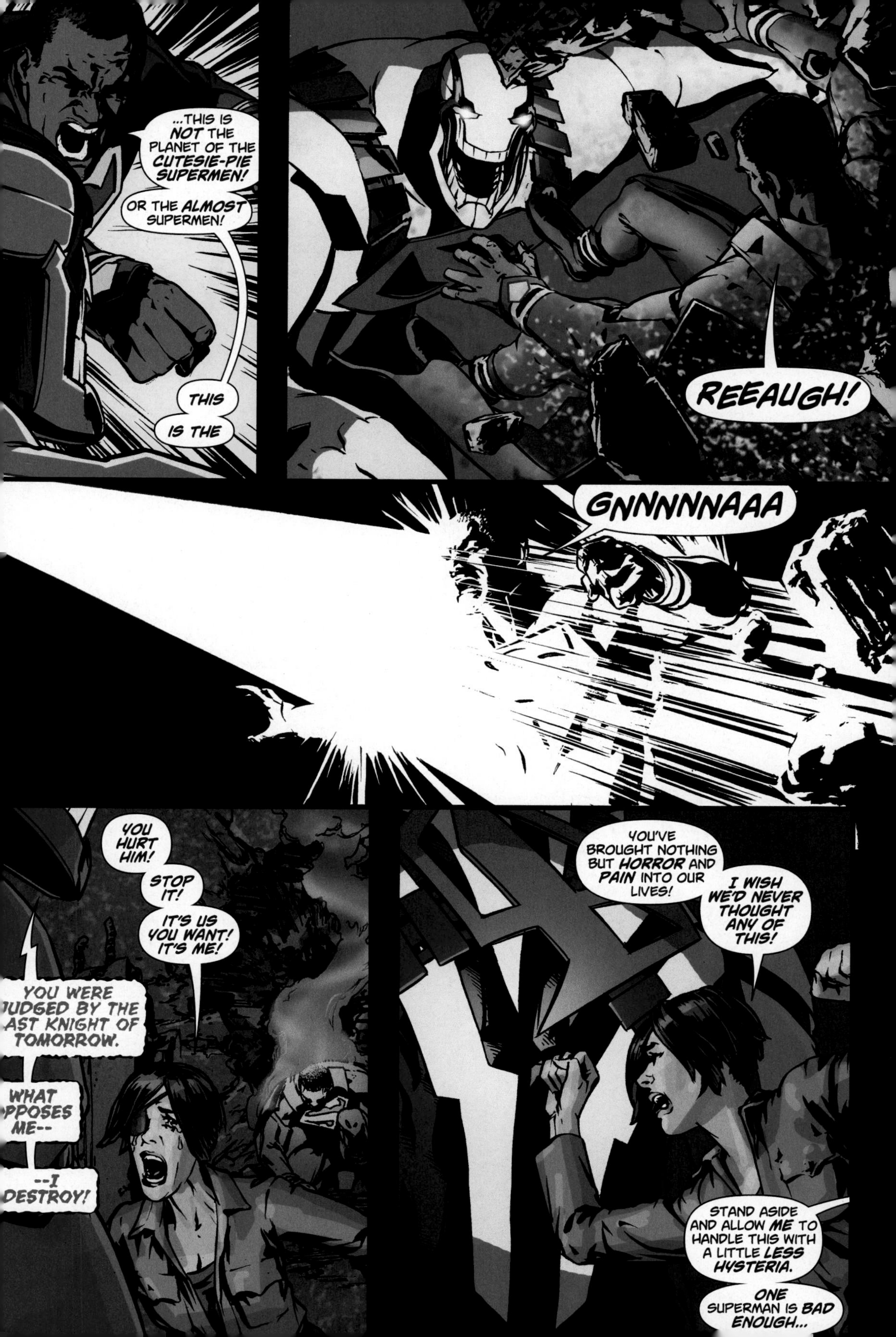
...THIS IS NOT THE PLANET OF THE CUTESIE-PIE SUPERMEN!
OR THE ALMOST SUPERMEN!
THIS
IS THE
REEAUGH!
GNNNNNAAA
YOU HURT HIM!
STOP IT!
IT'S US YOU WANT! IT'S ME!
YOU WERE JUDGED BY THE LAST KNIGHT OF TOMORROW.
WHAT OPPOSES ME--
--I DESTROY!
YOU'VE BROUGHT NOTHING BUT HORROR AND PAIN INTO OUR LIVES!
I WISH WE'D NEVER THOUGHT ANY OF THIS!
STAND ASIDE AND ALLOW ME TO HANDLE THIS WITH A LITTLE LESS HYSTERIA.
ONE SUPERMAN IS BAD ENOUGH...

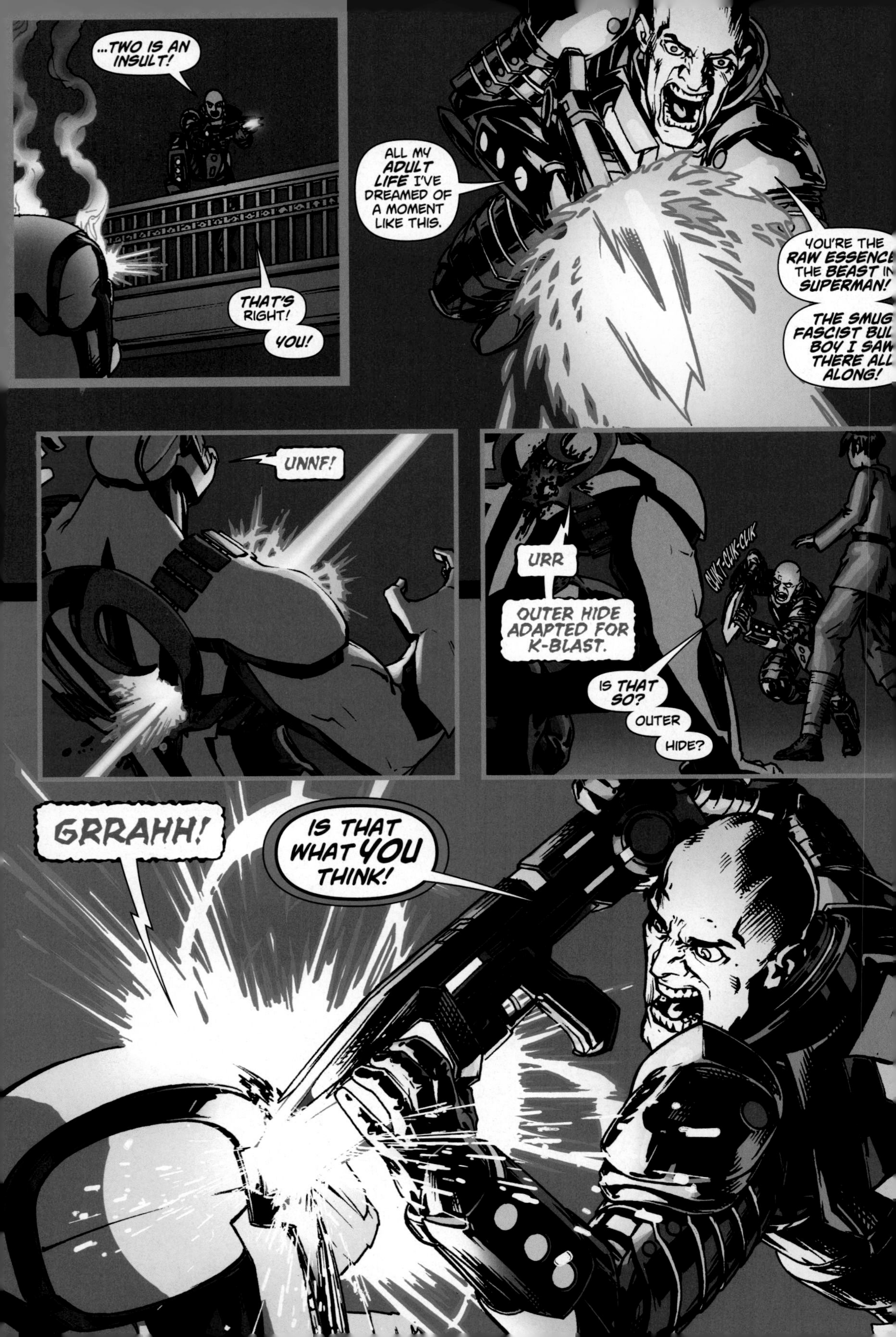
...TWO IS AN INSULT!
THAT'S RIGHT!
YOU!
ALL MY ADULT LIFE I'VE DREAMED OF A MOMENT LIKE THIS.
YOU'RE THE RAW ESSENCE THE BEAST IN SUPERMAN!
THE SMUG FASCIST BUL BOY I SAW THERE ALL ALONG!
UNNF!
URR
OUTER HIDE ADAPTED FOR K-BLAST.
CLIK-CLIK-CLIK
IS THAT SO?
OUTER
HIDE?
GRRAHH!
IS THAT WHAT YOU THINK!

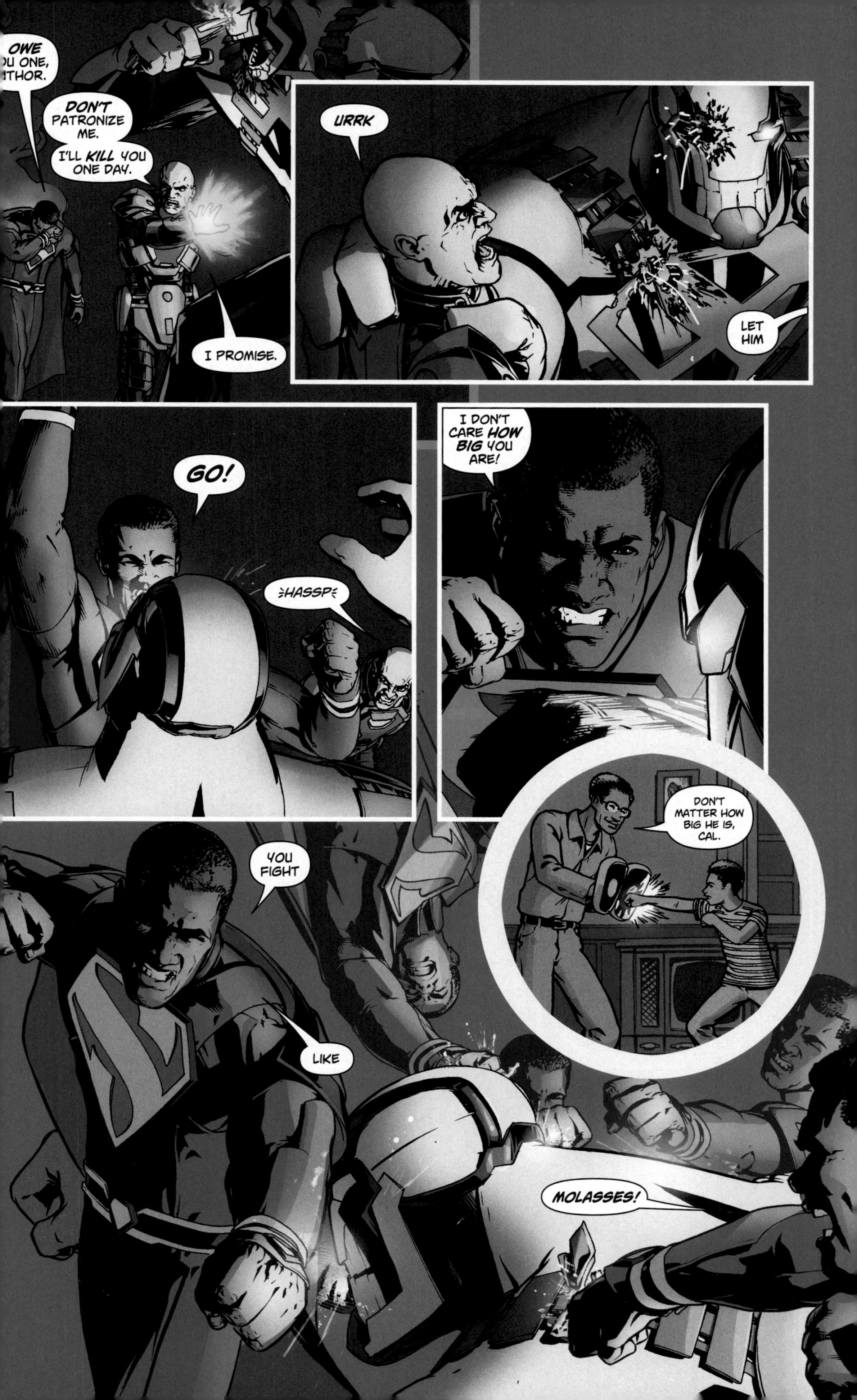
OWE
OU ONE,
UTHOR.
DON'T PATRONIZE ME.
I'LL KILL YOU ONE DAY.
I PROMISE.
URRK
LET HIM
GO!
HASSP
I DON'T CARE HOW BIG YOU ARE!
DON'T MATTER HOW BIG HE IS, CAL.
YOU FIGHT
LIKE
MOLASSES!

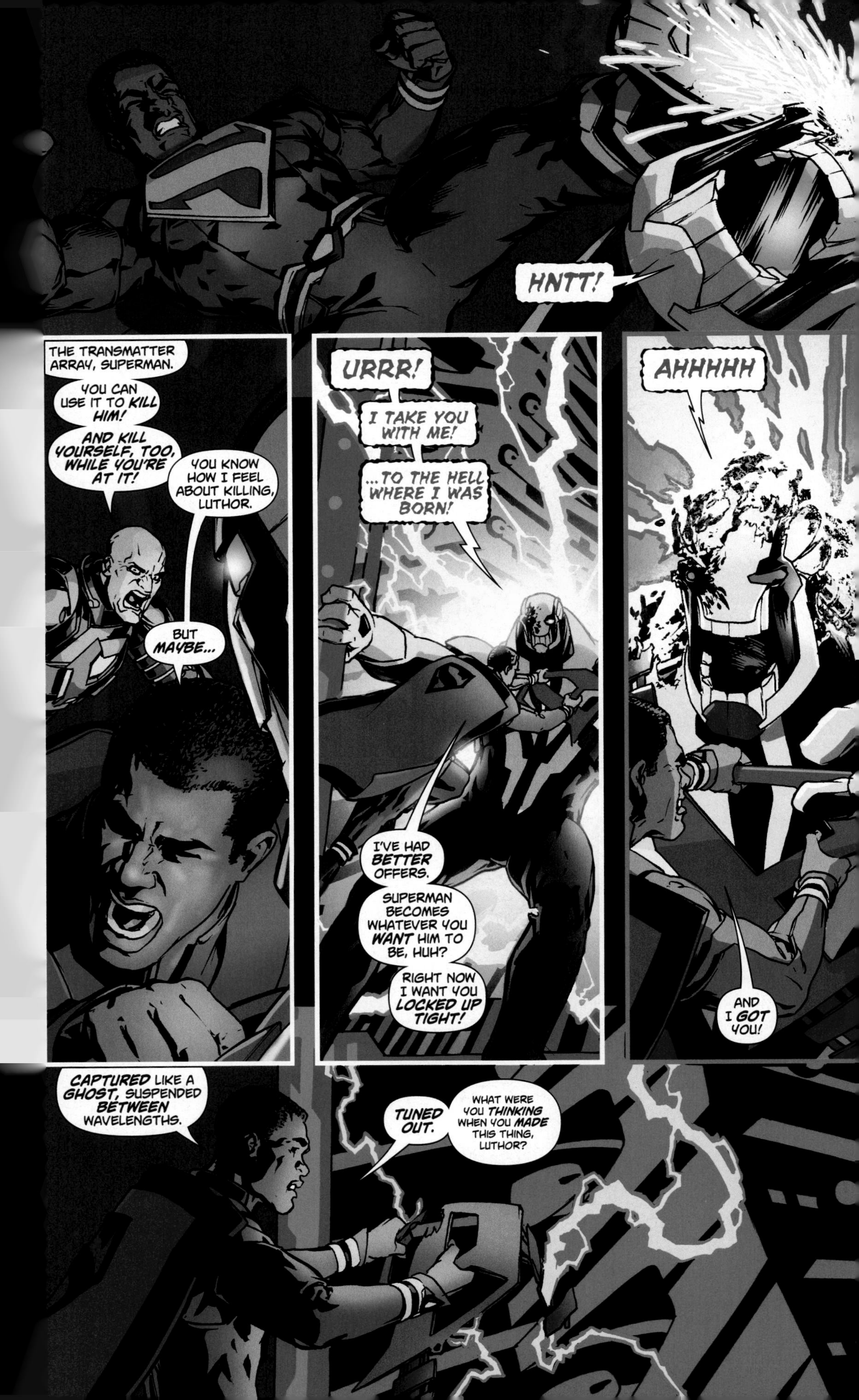
HNTT!
THE TRANSMATTER ARRAY, SUPERMAN.
YOU CAN USE IT TO KILL HIM!
AND KILL YOURSELF, TOO, WHILE YOU'RE AT IT!
YOU KNOW HOW I FEEL ABOUT KILLING, LUTHOR.
BUT MAYBE...
URRR!
I TAKE YOU WITH ME!
...TO THE HELL WHERE I WAS BORN!
I'VE HAD BETTER OFFERS.
SUPERMAN BECOMES WHATEVER YOU WANT HIM TO BE, HUH?
RIGHT NOW I WANT YOU LOCKED UP TIGHT!
AHHHHH
AND I GOT YOU!
CAPTURED LIKE A GHOST, SUSPENDED BETWEEN WAVELENGTHS.
TUNED OUT.
WHAT WERE YOU THINKING WHEN YOU MADE THIS THING, LUTHOR?

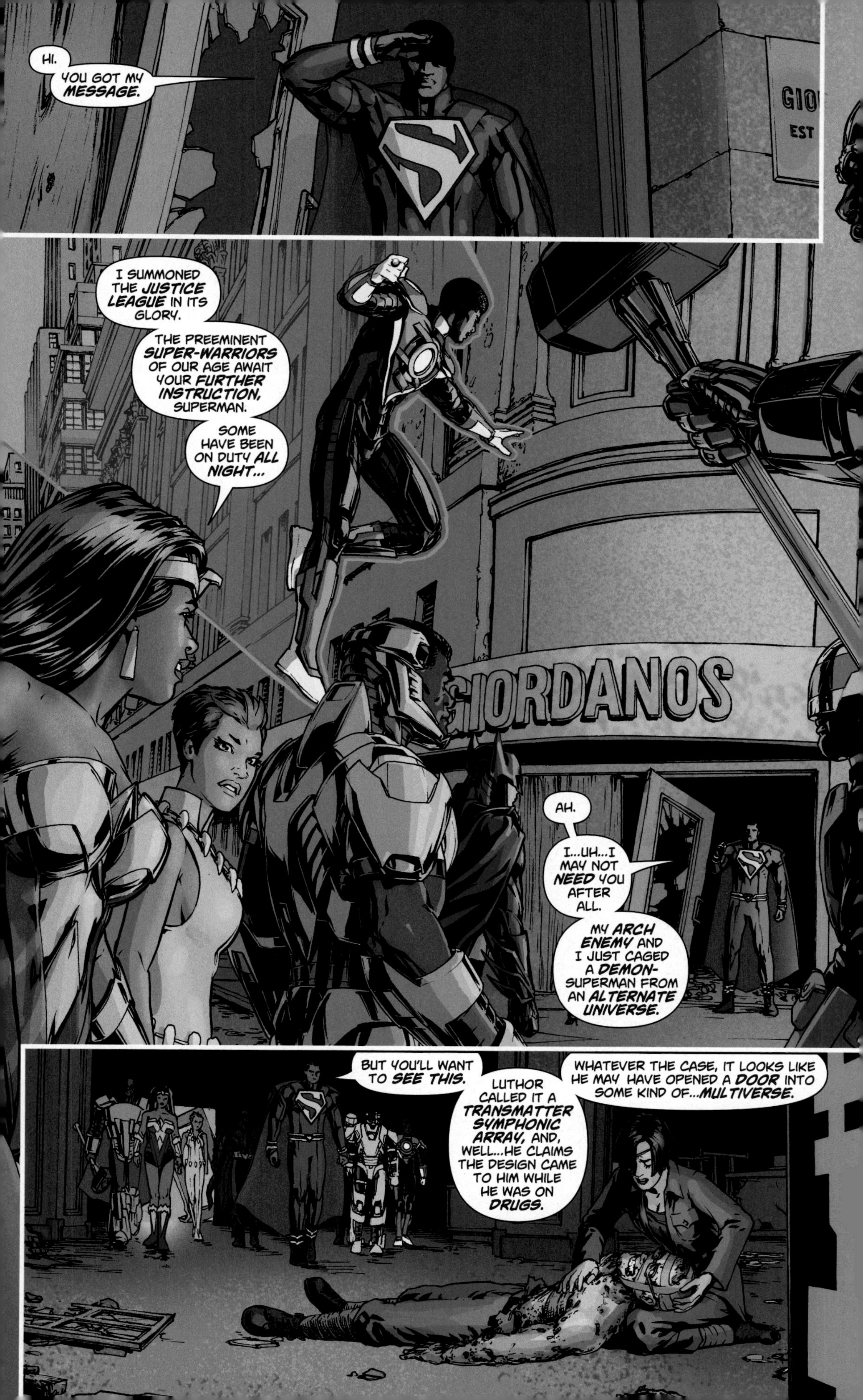
HI.
YOU GOT MY MESSAGE.
GIO
EST
I SUMMONED THE JUSTICE LEAGUE IN ITS GLORY.
THE PREEMINENT SUPER-WARRIORS OF OUR AGE AWAIT YOUR FURTHER INSTRUCTION, SUPERMAN.
SOME HAVE BEEN ON DUTY ALL NIGHT...
GIORDANOS
AH.
I...UH...I MAY NOT NEED YOU AFTER ALL.
MY ARCH ENEMY AND I JUST CAGED A DEMON-SUPERMAN FROM AN ALTERNATE UNIVERSE.
BUT YOU'LL WANT TO SEE THIS.
LUTHOR CALLED IT A TRANSMATTER SYMPHONIC ARRAY, AND, WELL...HE CLAIMS THE DESIGN CAME TO HIM WHILE HE WAS ON DRUGS.
WHATEVER THE CASE, IT LOOKS LIKE HE MAY HAVE OPENED A DOOR INTO SOME KIND OF...MULTIVERSE.

...I COULDN'T SAVE HIM.

BUT THERE'S A STILL THE CHANCE OF A SUCCESSFUL *LAZARUS REVIVAL* IN MY LAB.

IN THE MEANTIME--

YOU'RE WELCOME TO *STAY HERE* AS LONG AS YOU LIKE.

WHAT *CHOICE* DO I HAVE?

WHAT'S LEFT?

I'M IN *SHOCK.*

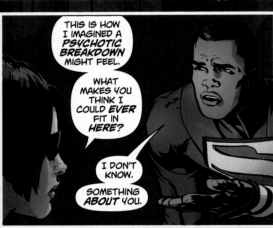

THIS IS HOW I IMAGINED A *PSYCHOTIC BREAKDOWN* MIGHT FEEL.

WHAT MAKES YOU THINK I COULD *EVER* FIT IN *HERE*?

I DON'T KNOW.

SOMETHING *ABOUT YOU.*

MAYBE THE FACT THAT YOU'RE A *SURVIVOR,* LIKE *ME.*

THAT'S *ALREADY* SOMETHING WE HAVE IN *COMMON.*

YOU DIDN'T TELL ME YOUR *NAME.*

ME?

I'M *LOIS.*

MY NAME'S *LOIS LANE.*

I GUESS YOU MUST BE *SUPERMAN* DONE RIGHT.

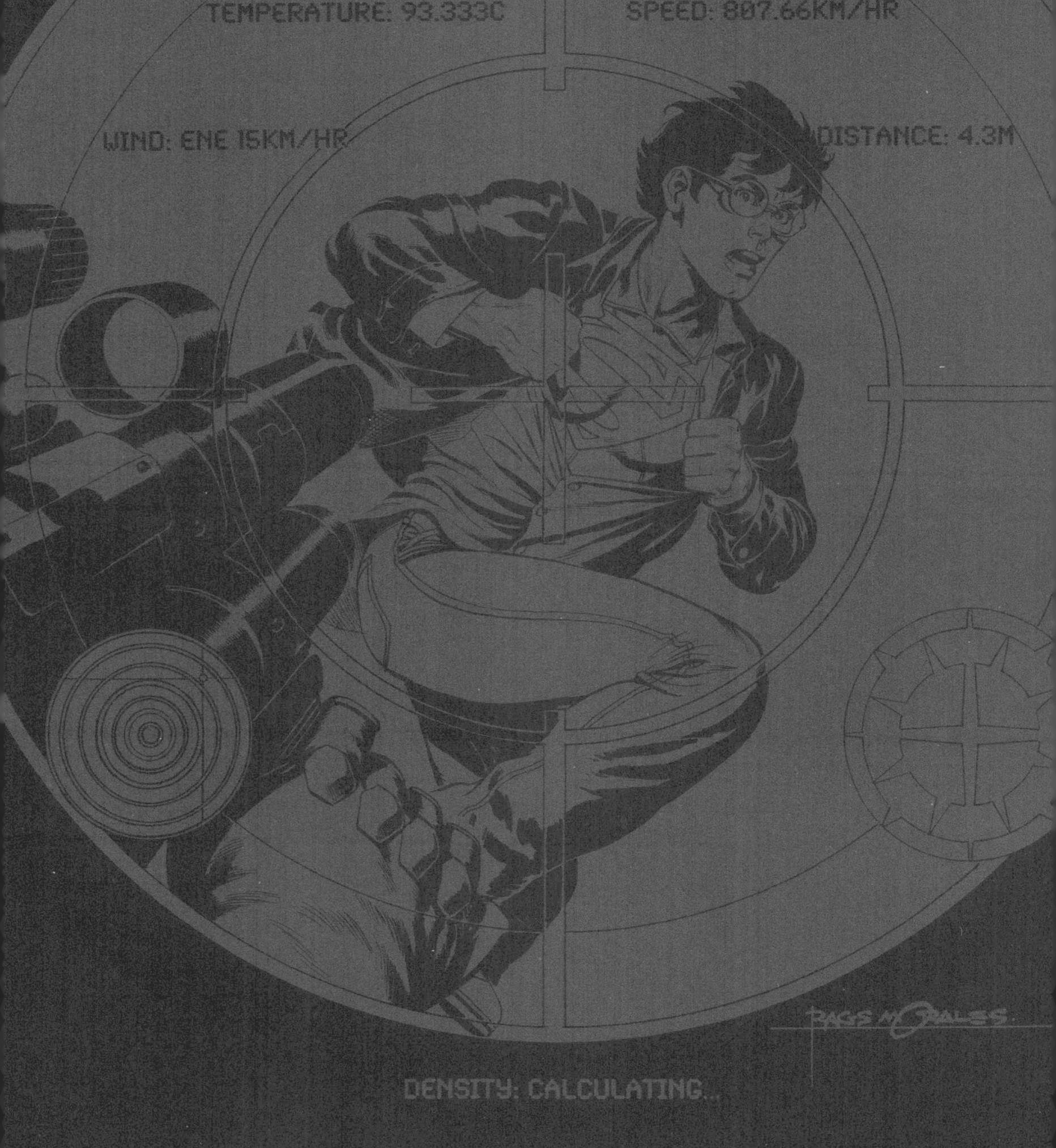
TEMPERATURE: 93.333C
SPEED: 807.66KM/HR
WIND: ENE 15KM/HR
DISTANCE: 4.3M
RAGS MORALES
DENSITY: CALCULATING...

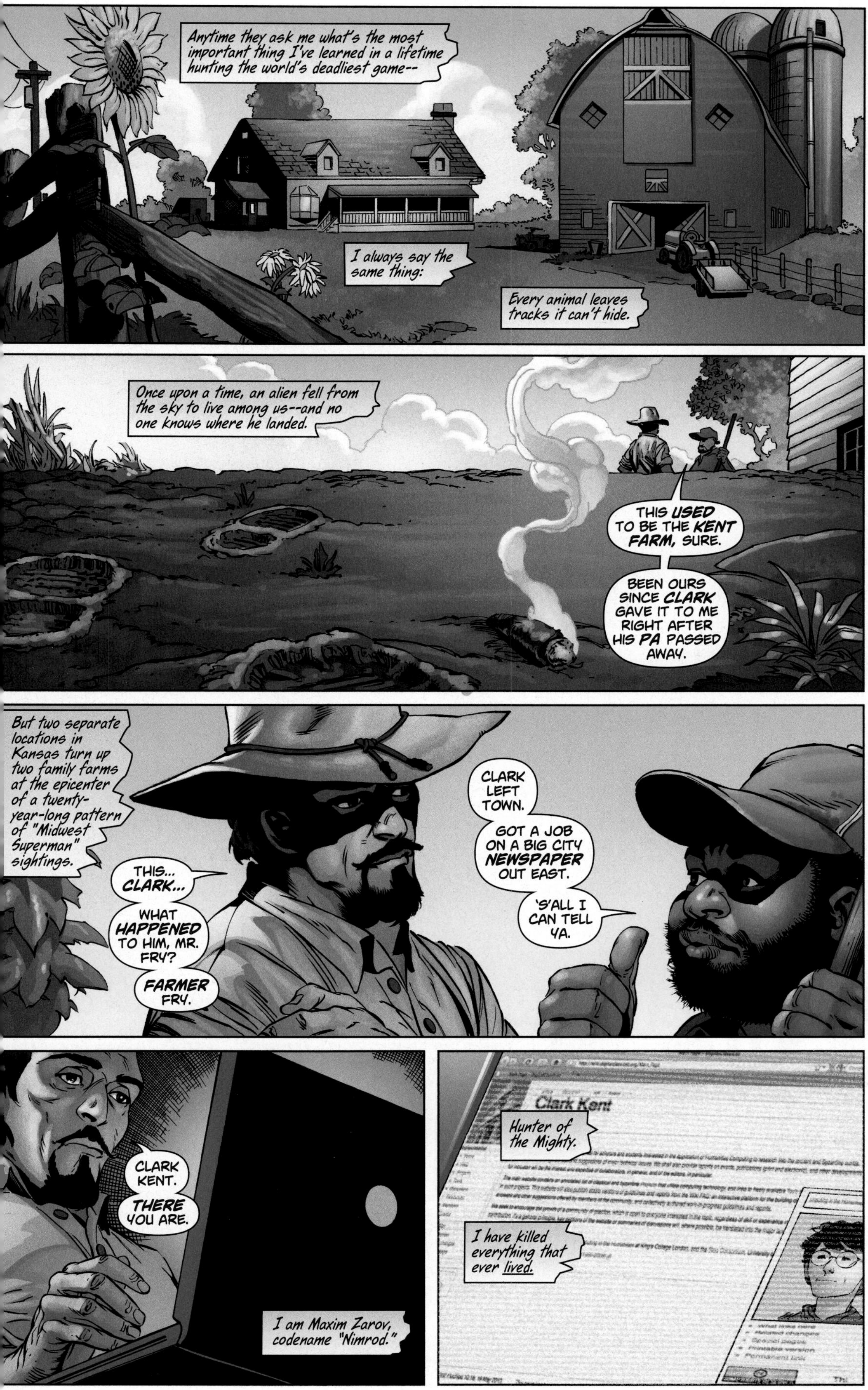

Anytime they ask me what's the most important thing I've learned in a lifetime hunting the world's deadliest game--
I always say the same thing:
Every animal leaves tracks it can't hide.
Once upon a time, an alien fell from the sky to live among us--and no one knows where he landed.
THIS USED TO BE THE KENT FARM, SURE.
BEEN OURS SINCE CLARK GAVE IT TO ME RIGHT AFTER HIS PA PASSED AWAY.
But two separate locations in Kansas turn up two family farms at the epicenter of a twenty-year-long pattern of "Midwest Superman" sightings.
THIS... CLARK...
WHAT HAPPENED TO HIM, MR. FRY?
FARMER FRY.
CLARK LEFT TOWN.
GOT A JOB ON A BIG CITY NEWSPAPER OUT EAST.
'S'ALL I CAN TELL YA.
CLARK KENT.
THERE YOU ARE.
I am Maxim Zarov, codename "Nimrod."
Clark Kent
Hunter of the Mighty.
I have killed everything that ever lived.

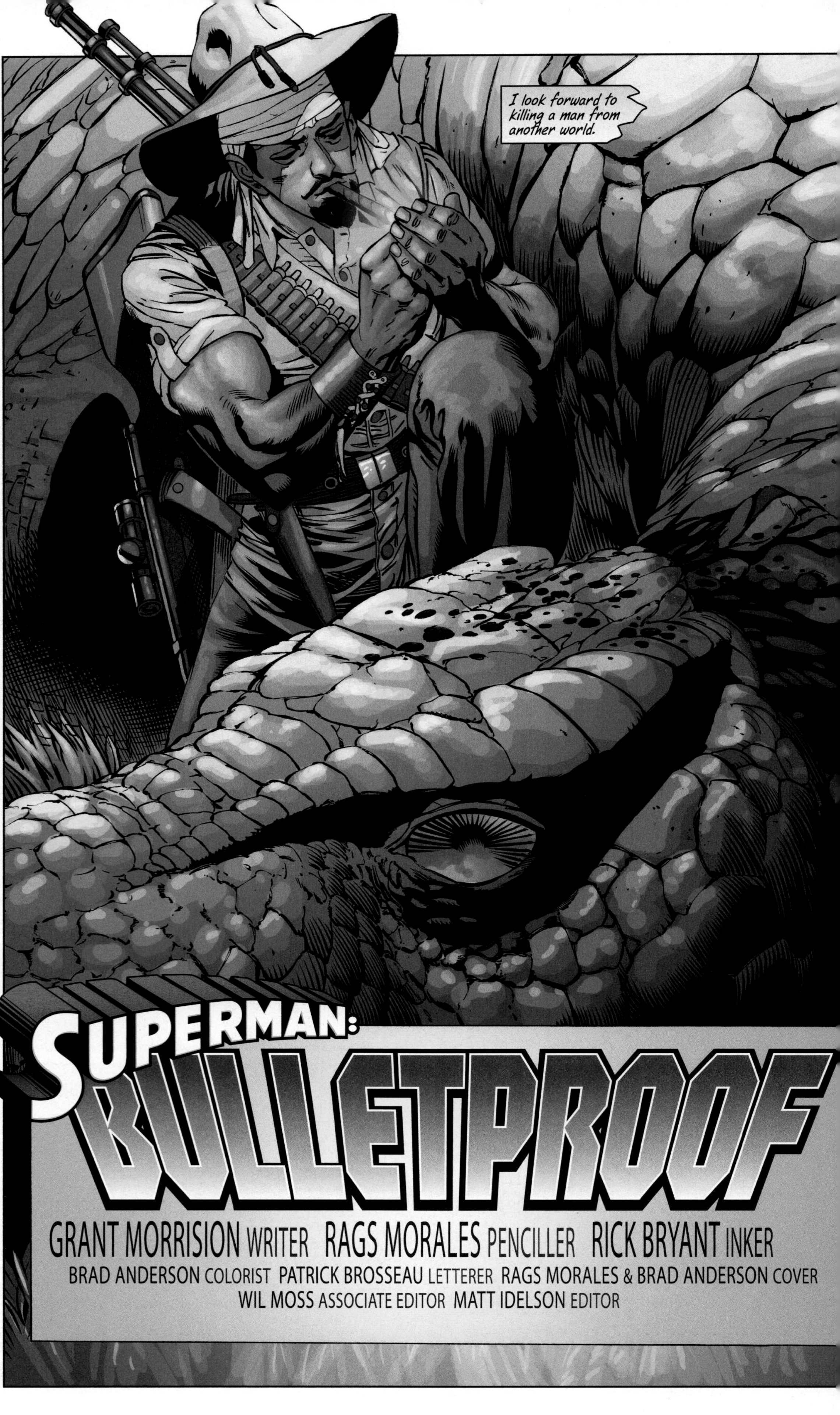
I look forward to killing a man from another world.
SUPERMAN:
BULLETPROOF
GRANT MORRISION WRITER RAGS MORALES PENCILLER RICK BRYANT INKER
BRAD ANDERSON COLORIST PATRICK BROSSEAU LETTERER RAGS MORALES & BRAD ANDERSON COVER
WIL MOSS ASSOCIATE EDITOR MATT IDELSON EDITOR

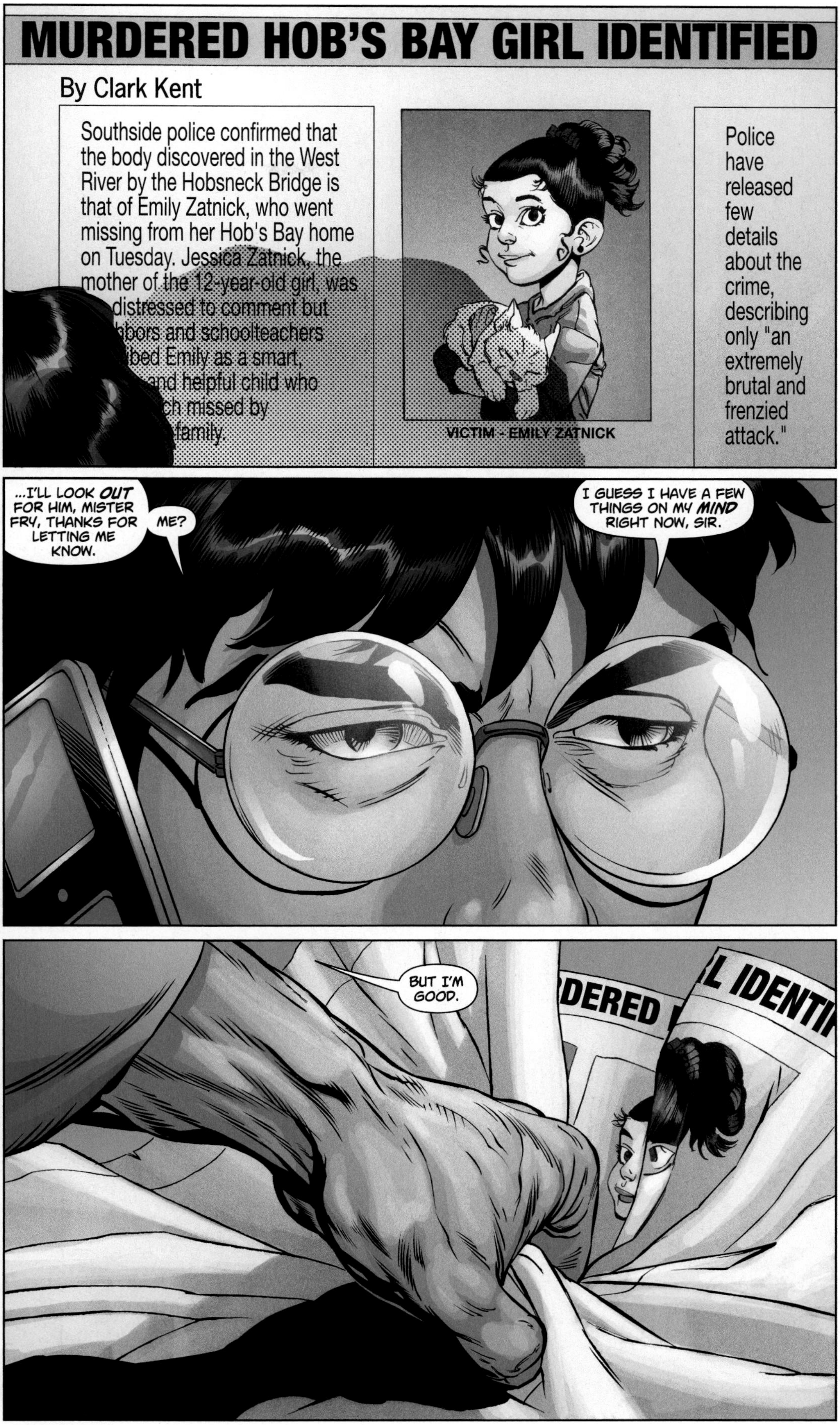
MURDERED HOB'S BAY GIRL IDENTIFIED
By Clark Kent
Southside police confirmed that the body discovered in the West River by the Hobsneck Bridge is that of Emily Zatnick, who went missing from her Hob's Bay home on Tuesday. Jessica Zatnick, the mother of the 12-year-old girl, was distressed to comment but bors and schoolteachers ibed Emily as a smart, and helpful child who ch missed by family.
VICTIM - EMILY ZATNICK
Police have released few details about the crime, describing only "an extremely brutal and frenzied attack."
...I'LL LOOK OUT FOR HIM, MISTER FRY, THANKS FOR LETTING ME KNOW.
ME?
I GUESS I HAVE A FEW THINGS ON MY MIND RIGHT NOW, SIR.
BUT I'M GOOD.
DERED
L IDENTI

CLARK?

37

38

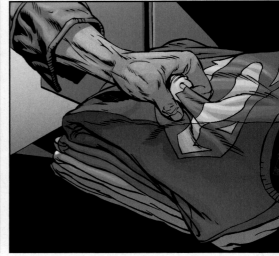

GOTHAM GATE 9
PHILADELPHIA GATE 9
WASHINGTON GATE 2
COAST CITY GATE 5

KEYSTO
FAWCET
CHICAG
NEW YO

3 TRAINS →

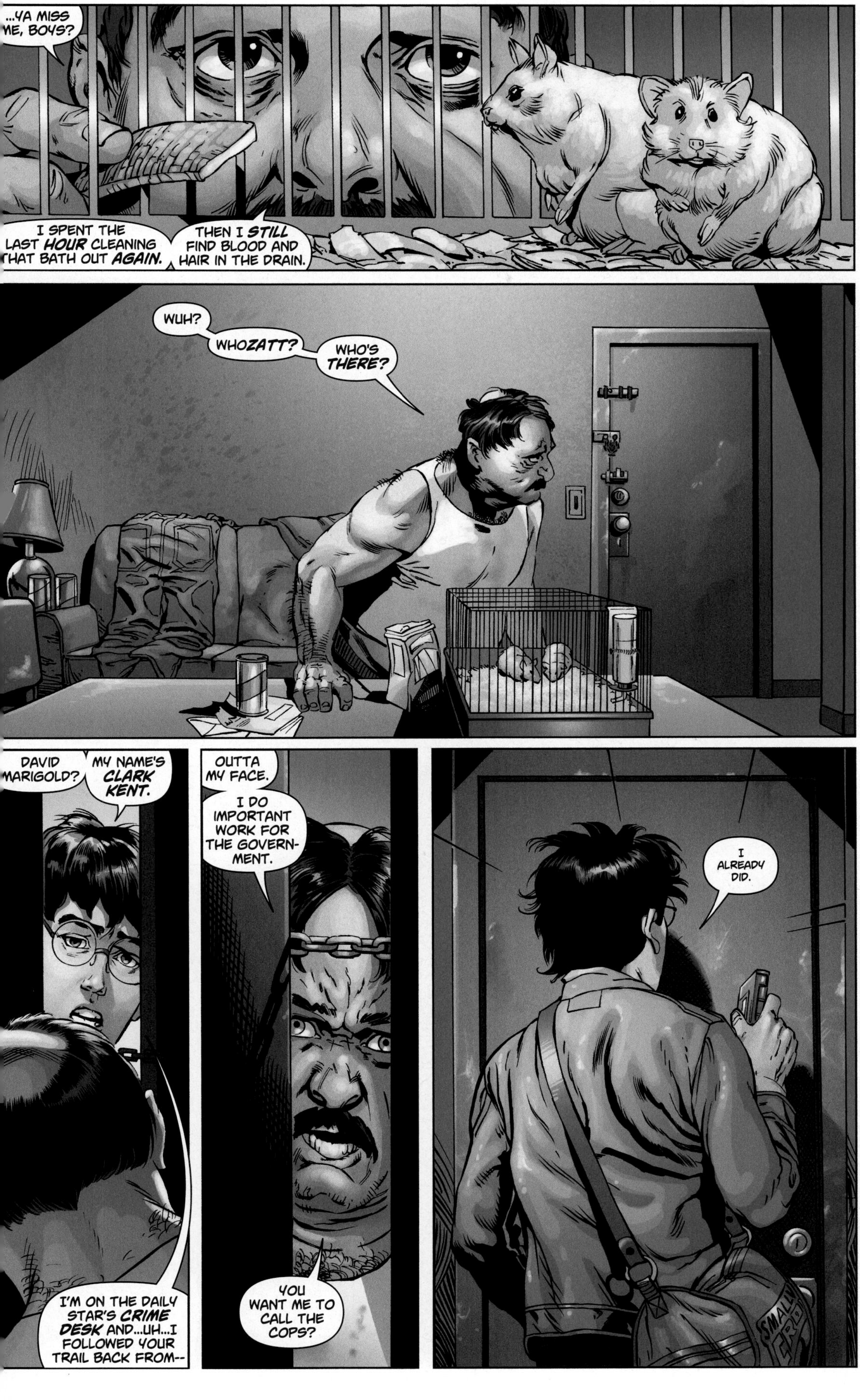
...YA MISS ME, BOYS?
I SPENT THE LAST HOUR CLEANING THAT BATH OUT AGAIN.
THEN I STILL FIND BLOOD AND HAIR IN THE DRAIN.
WUH?
WHOZATT?
WHO'S THERE?
DAVID MARIGOLD?
MY NAME'S CLARK KENT.
I'M ON THE DAILY STAR'S CRIME DESK AND...UH...I FOLLOWED YOUR TRAIL BACK FROM--
OUTTA MY FACE.
I DO IMPORTANT WORK FOR THE GOVERNMENT.
YOU WANT ME TO CALL THE COPS?
I ALREADY DID.

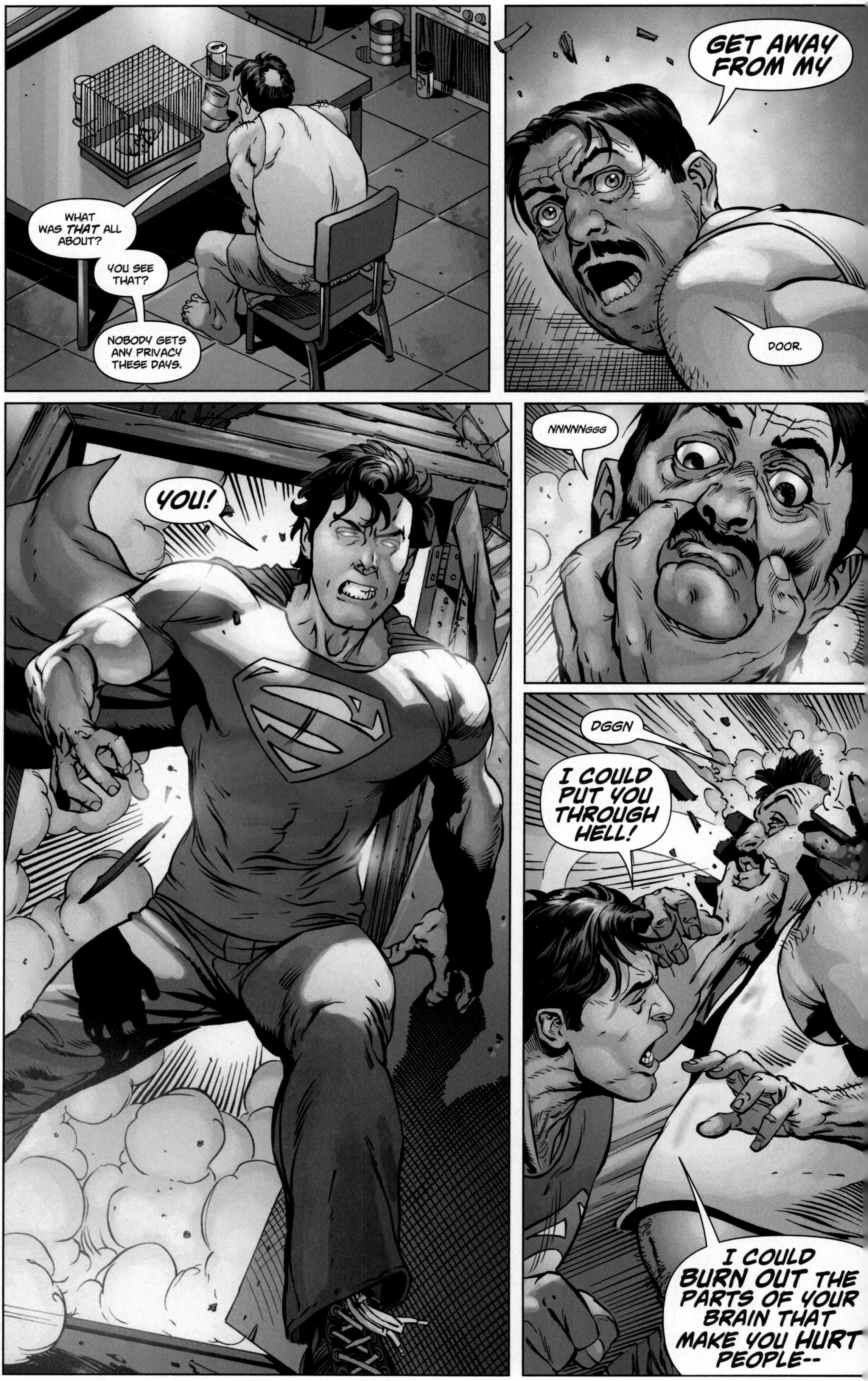
WHAT WAS THAT ALL ABOUT?
YOU SEE THAT?
NOBODY GETS ANY PRIVACY THESE DAYS.
GET AWAY FROM MY
DOOR.
YOU!
NNNNNGGG
DGGN
I COULD PUT YOU THROUGH HELL!
I COULD BURN OUT THE PARTS OF YOUR BRAIN THAT MAKE YOU HURT PEOPLE--

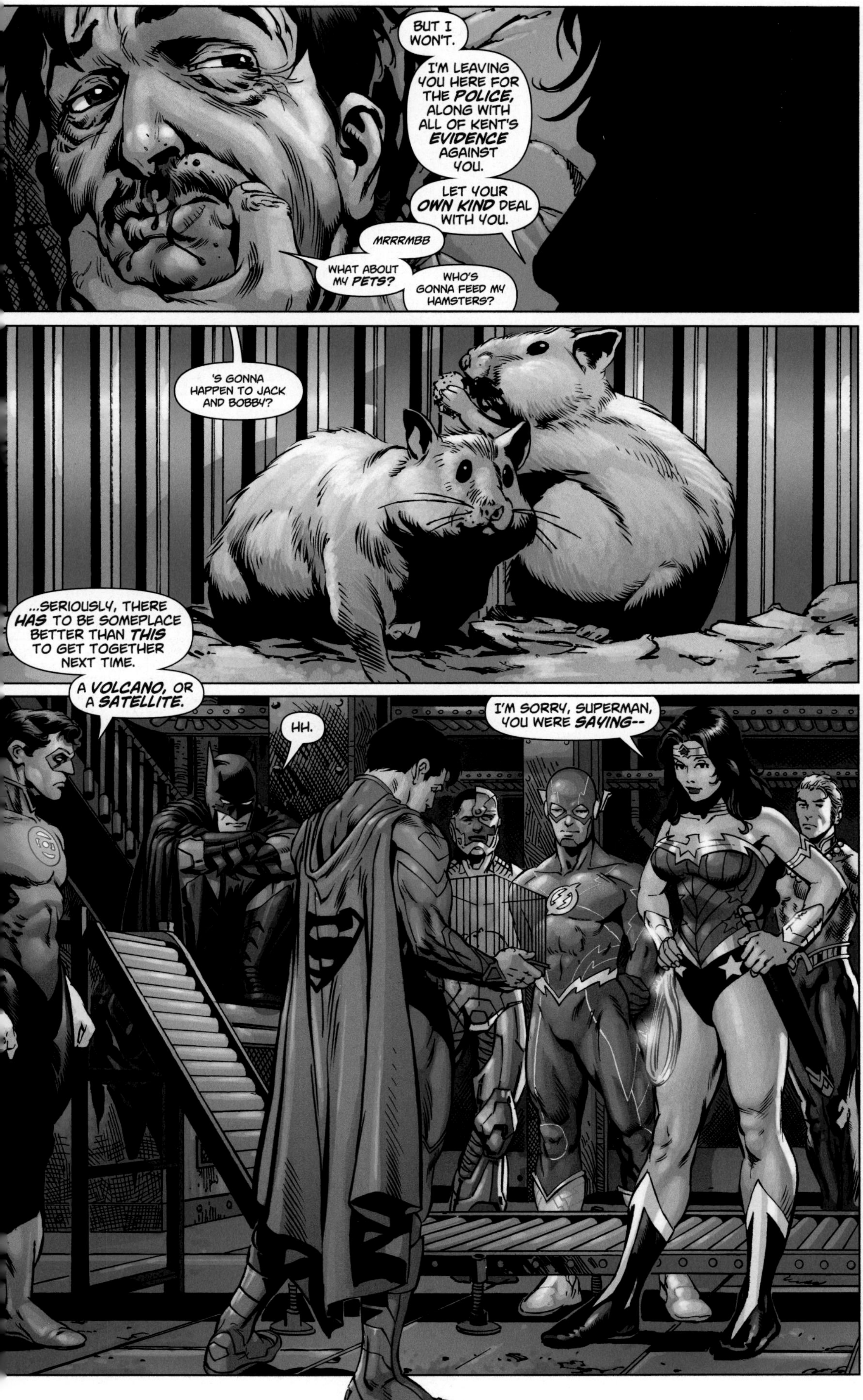
BUT I WON'T.
I'M LEAVING YOU HERE FOR THE POLICE, ALONG WITH ALL OF KENT'S EVIDENCE AGAINST YOU.
LET YOUR OWN KIND DEAL WITH YOU.
MRRRMBB
WHAT ABOUT MY PETS?
WHO'S GONNA FEED MY HAMSTERS?
'S GONNA HAPPEN TO JACK AND BOBBY?
...SERIOUSLY, THERE HAS TO BE SOMEPLACE BETTER THAN THIS TO GET TOGETHER NEXT TIME.
A VOLCANO, OR A SATELLITE.
HH.
I'M SORRY, SUPERMAN, YOU WERE SAYING--

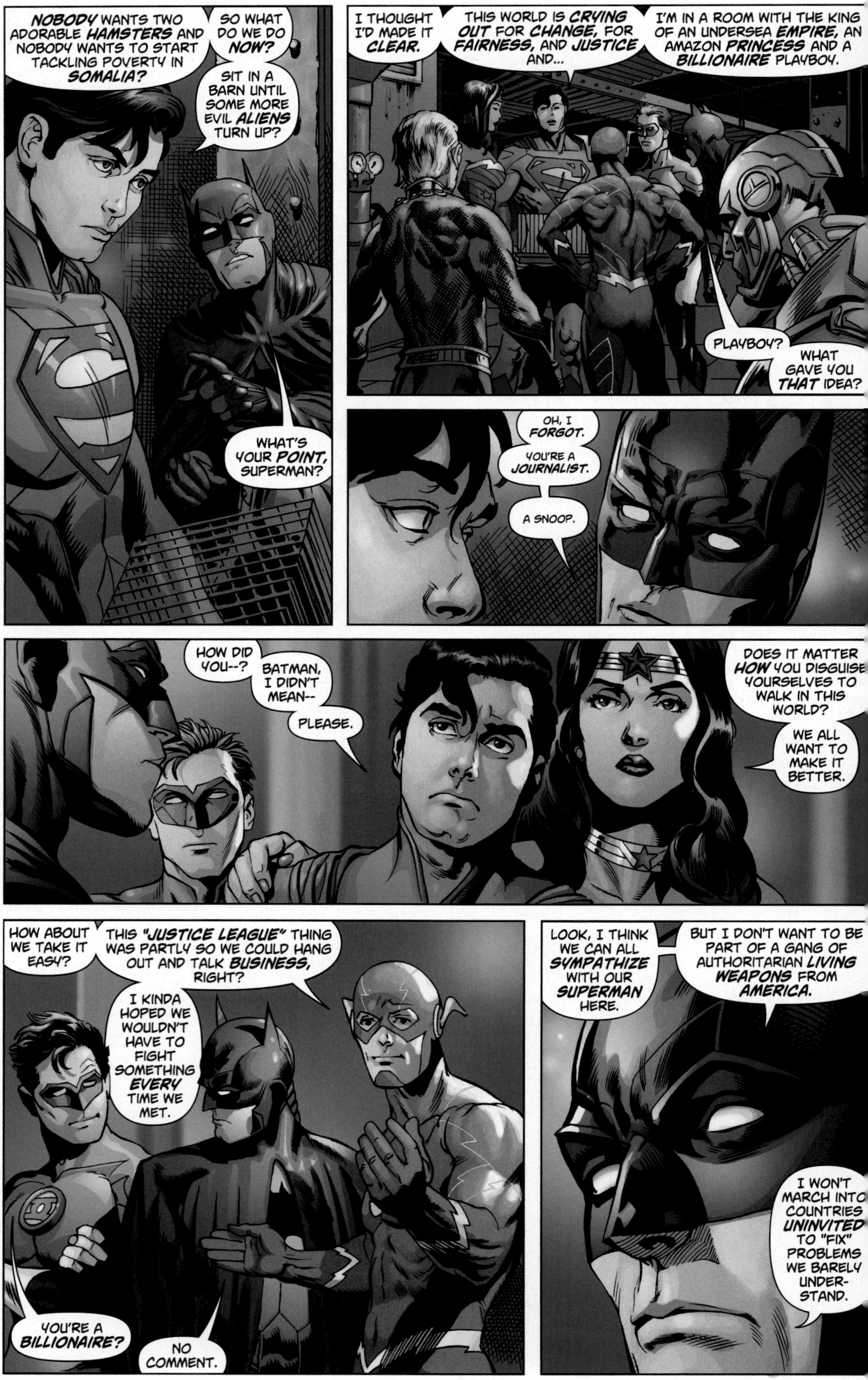

NOBODY WANTS TWO ADORABLE HAMSTERS AND NOBODY WANTS TO START TACKLING POVERTY IN SOMALIA?
SO WHAT DO WE DO NOW?
SIT IN A BARN UNTIL SOME MORE EVIL ALIENS TURN UP?
WHAT'S YOUR POINT, SUPERMAN?
I THOUGHT I'D MADE IT CLEAR.
THIS WORLD IS CRYING OUT FOR CHANGE, FOR FAIRNESS, AND JUSTICE AND...
I'M IN A ROOM WITH THE KING OF AN UNDERSEA EMPIRE, AN AMAZON PRINCESS AND A BILLIONAIRE PLAYBOY.
PLAYBOY?
WHAT GAVE YOU THAT IDEA?
OH, I FORGOT.
YOU'RE A JOURNALIST.
A SNOOP.
HOW DID YOU--?
BATMAN, I DIDN'T MEAN--
PLEASE.
DOES IT MATTER HOW YOU DISGUISE YOURSELVES TO WALK IN THIS WORLD?
WE ALL WANT TO MAKE IT BETTER.
HOW ABOUT WE TAKE IT EASY?
THIS "JUSTICE LEAGUE" THING WAS PARTLY SO WE COULD HANG OUT AND TALK BUSINESS, RIGHT?
I KINDA HOPED WE WOULDN'T HAVE TO FIGHT SOMETHING EVERY TIME WE MET.
YOU'RE A BILLIONAIRE?
NO COMMENT.
LOOK, I THINK WE CAN ALL SYMPATHIZE WITH OUR SUPERMAN HERE.
BUT I DON'T WANT TO BE PART OF A GANG OF AUTHORITARIAN LIVING WEAPONS FROM AMERICA.
I WON'T MARCH INTO COUNTRIES UNINVITED TO "FIX" PROBLEMS WE BARELY UNDER-STAND.

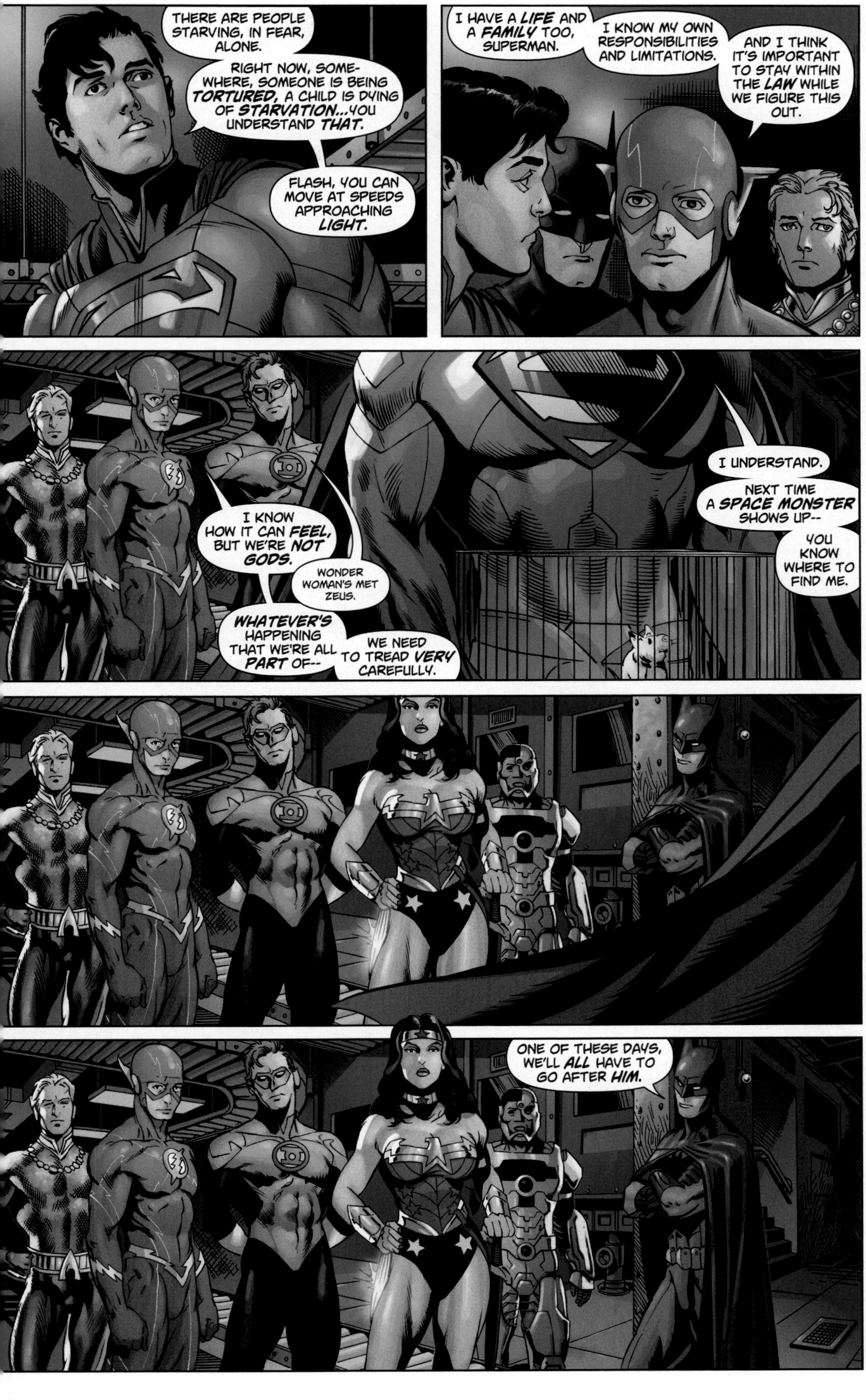
THERE ARE PEOPLE STARVING, IN FEAR, ALONE.
RIGHT NOW, SOMEWHERE, SOMEONE IS BEING *TORTURED*, A CHILD IS DYING OF *STARVATION*...YOU UNDERSTAND *THAT*.
FLASH, YOU CAN MOVE AT SPEEDS APPROACHING *LIGHT*.
I HAVE A *LIFE* AND A *FAMILY* TOO, SUPERMAN.
I KNOW MY OWN RESPONSIBILITIES AND LIMITATIONS.
AND I THINK IT'S IMPORTANT TO STAY WITHIN THE *LAW* WHILE WE FIGURE THIS OUT.
I KNOW HOW IT CAN *FEEL*, BUT WE'RE *NOT GODS*.
WONDER WOMAN'S MET ZEUS.
WHATEVER'S HAPPENING THAT WE'RE ALL *PART* OF--
WE NEED TO TREAD *VERY* CAREFULLY.
I UNDERSTAND.
NEXT TIME A *SPACE MONSTER* SHOWS UP--
YOU KNOW WHERE TO FIND ME.
ONE OF THESE DAYS, WE'LL *ALL* HAVE TO GO AFTER *HIM*.

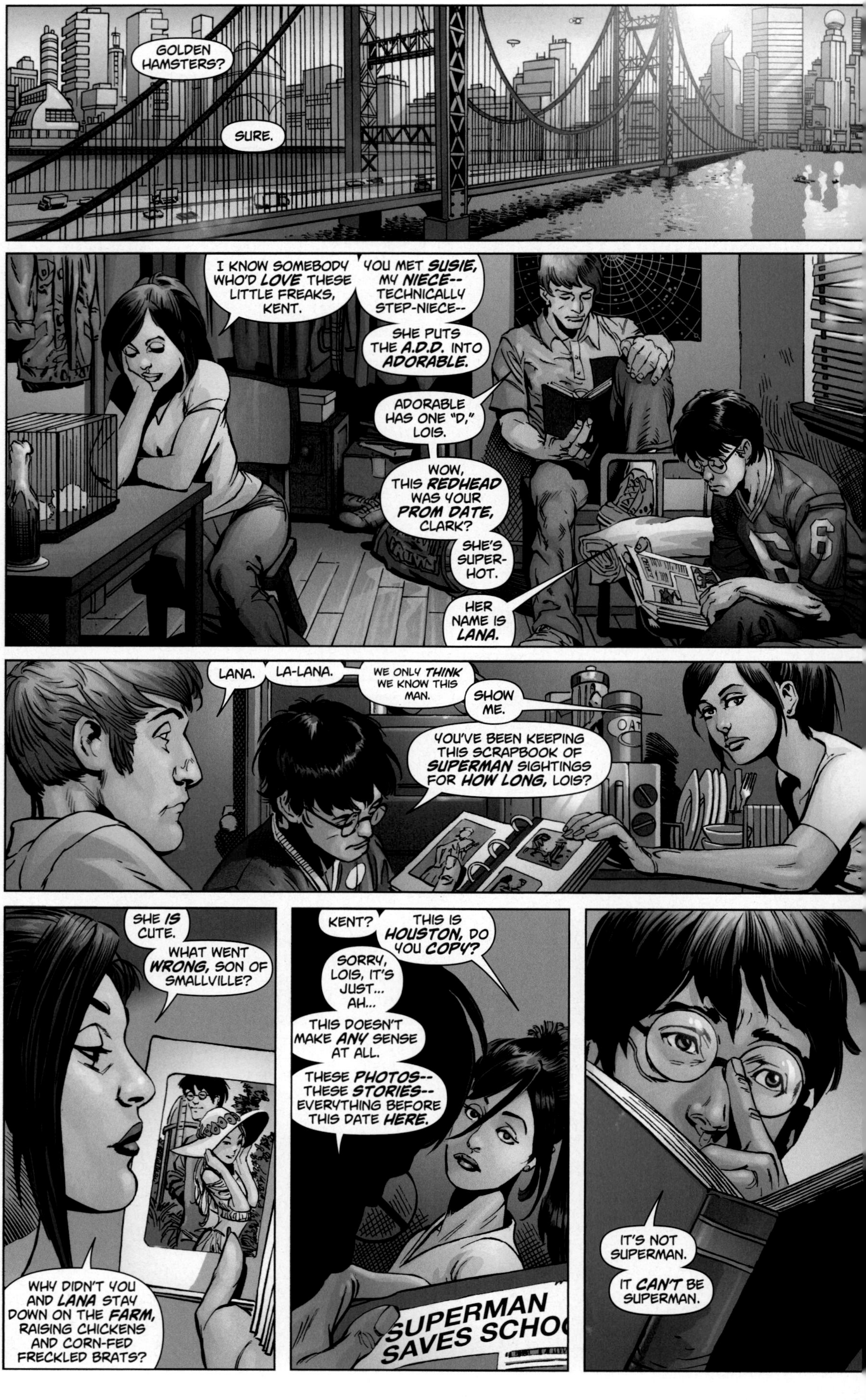
GOLDEN HAMSTERS?
SURE.
I KNOW SOMEBODY WHO'D LOVE THESE LITTLE FREAKS, KENT.
YOU MET SUSIE, MY NIECE-- TECHNICALLY STEP-NIECE--
SHE PUTS THE A.D.D. INTO ADORABLE.
ADORABLE HAS ONE "D," LOIS.
WOW, THIS REDHEAD WAS YOUR PROM DATE, CLARK?
SHE'S SUPER-HOT.
HER NAME IS LANA.
LANA.
LA-LANA.
WE ONLY THINK WE KNOW THIS MAN.
SHOW ME.
YOU'VE BEEN KEEPING THIS SCRAPBOOK OF SUPERMAN SIGHTINGS FOR HOW LONG, LOIS?
SHE IS CUTE.
WHAT WENT WRONG, SON OF SMALLVILLE?
WHY DIDN'T YOU AND LANA STAY DOWN ON THE FARM, RAISING CHICKENS AND CORN-FED FRECKLED BRATS?
KENT?
THIS IS HOUSTON, DO YOU COPY?
SORRY, LOIS, IT'S JUST... AH...
THIS DOESN'T MAKE ANY SENSE AT ALL.
THESE PHOTOS-- THESE STORIES-- EVERYTHING BEFORE THIS DATE HERE.
SUPERMAN SAVES SCHO
IT'S NOT SUPERMAN.
IT CAN'T BE SUPERMAN.

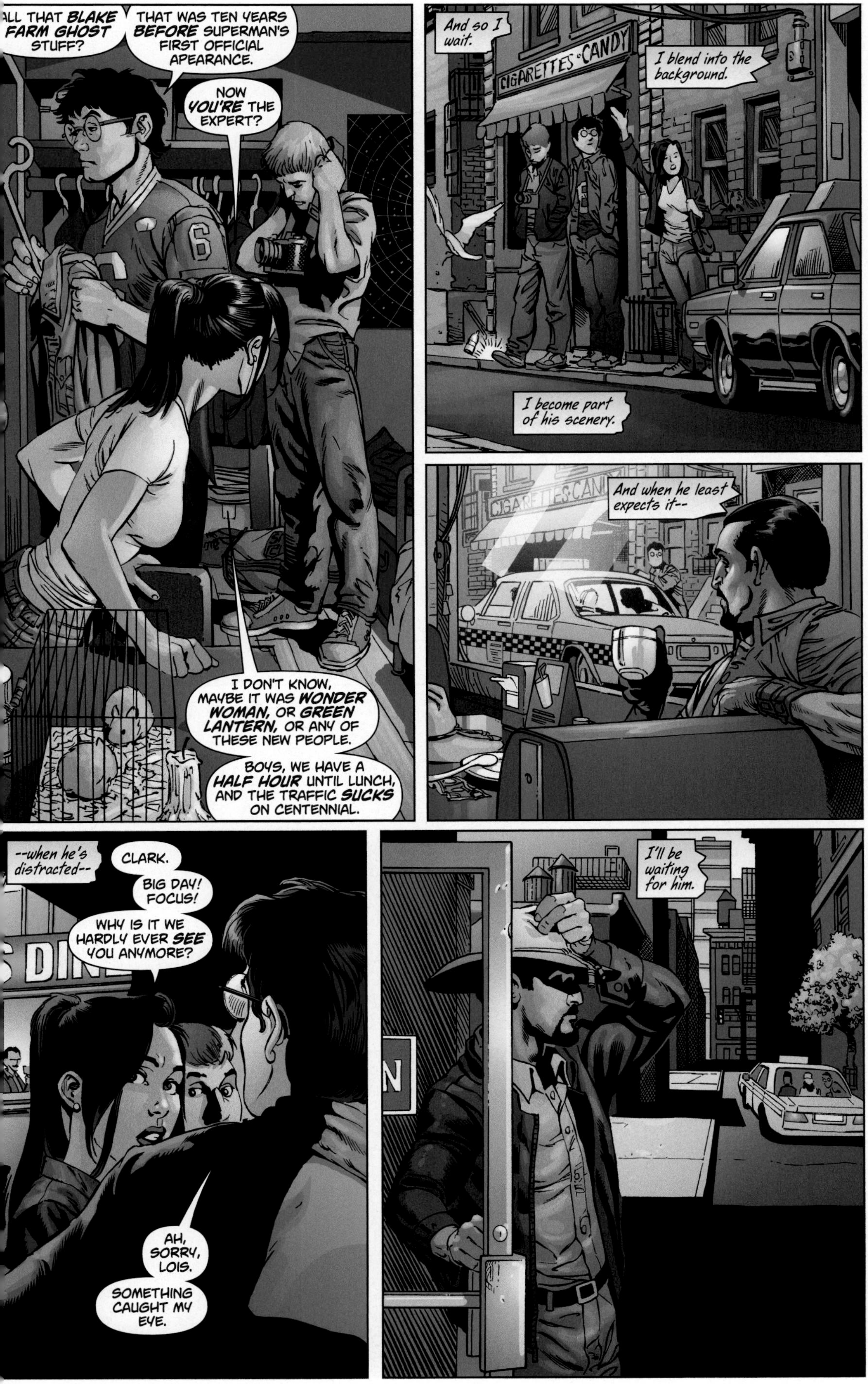
ALL THAT BLAKE FARM GHOST STUFF?
THAT WAS TEN YEARS BEFORE SUPERMAN'S FIRST OFFICIAL APEARANCE.
NOW YOU'RE THE EXPERT?
I DON'T KNOW, MAYBE IT WAS WONDER WOMAN, OR GREEN LANTERN, OR ANY OF THESE NEW PEOPLE.
BOYS, WE HAVE A HALF HOUR UNTIL LUNCH, AND THE TRAFFIC SUCKS ON CENTENNIAL.
And so I wait.
CIGARETTES CANDY
I blend into the background.
I become part of his scenery.
CIGARETTES CANDY
And when he least expects it--
--when he's distracted--
CLARK.
BIG DAY! FOCUS!
WHY IS IT WE HARDLY EVER SEE YOU ANYMORE?
AH, SORRY, LOIS.
SOMETHING CAUGHT MY EYE.
I'll be waiting for him.

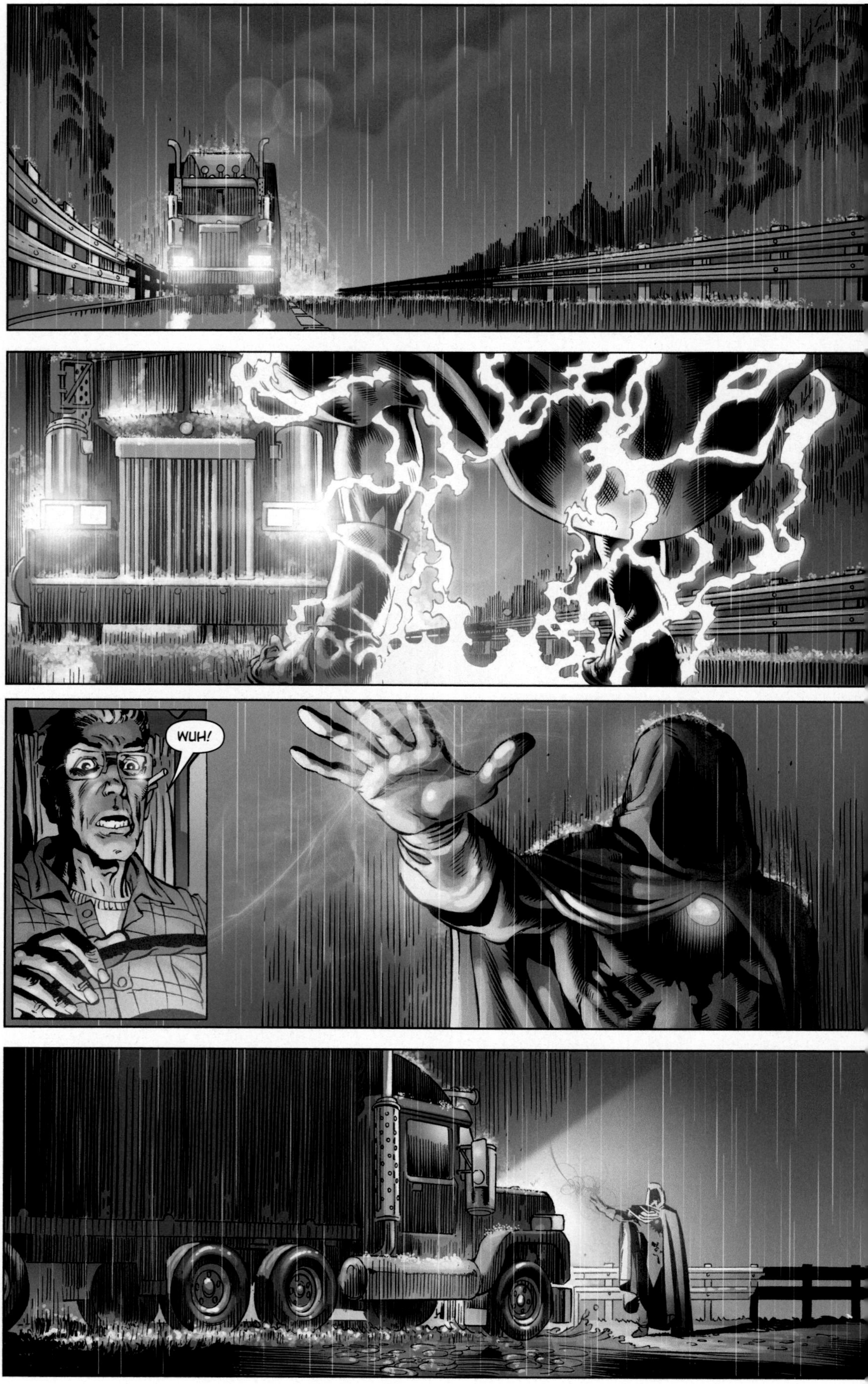
WUH!

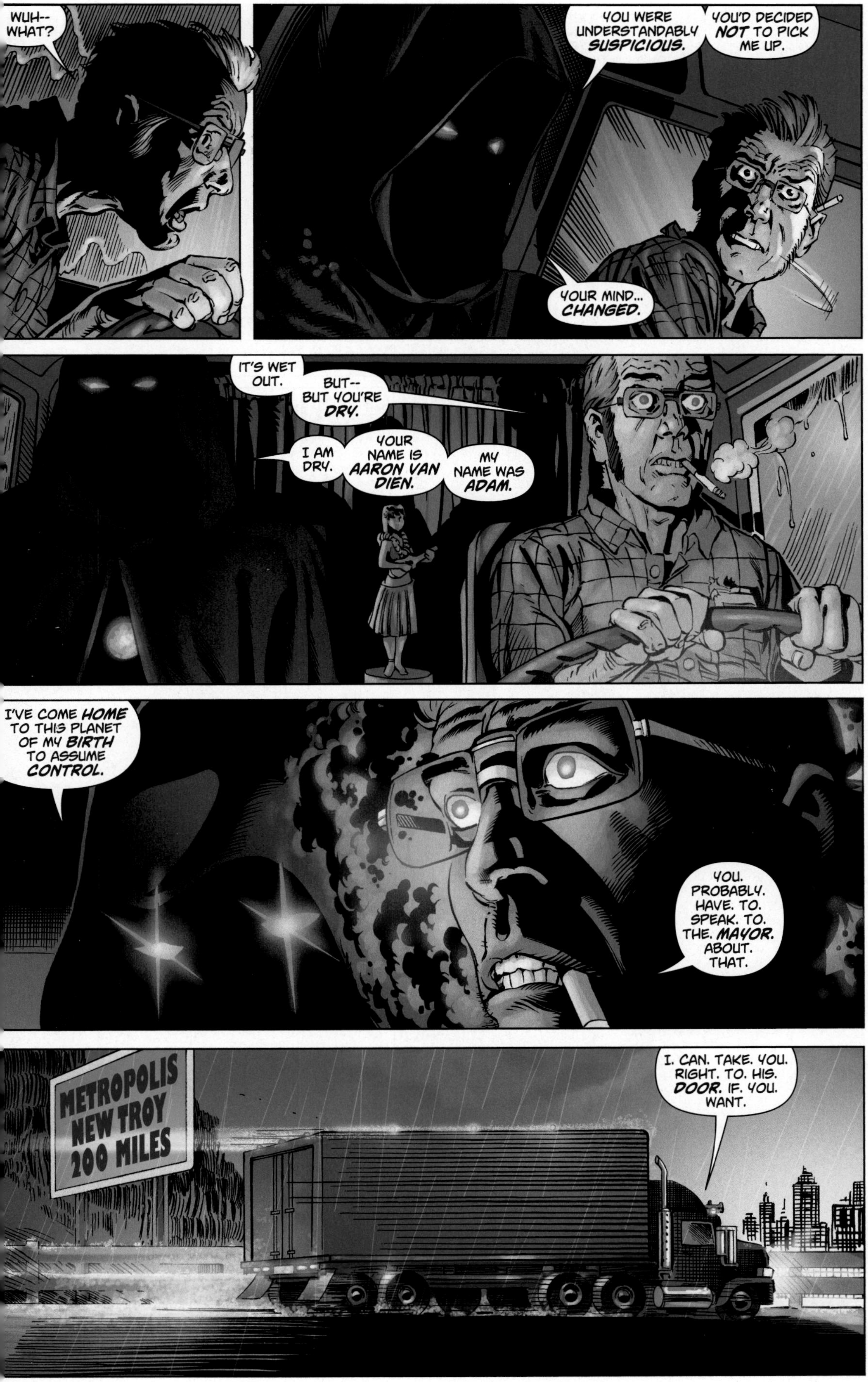

WUH-- WHAT?
YOU WERE UNDERSTANDABLY SUSPICIOUS.
YOU'D DECIDED NOT TO PICK ME UP.
YOUR MIND... CHANGED.
IT'S WET OUT.
BUT-- BUT YOU'RE DRY.
I AM DRY.
YOUR NAME IS AARON VAN DIEN.
MY NAME WAS ADAM.
I'VE COME HOME TO THIS PLANET OF MY BIRTH TO ASSUME CONTROL.
YOU. PROBABLY. HAVE. TO. SPEAK. TO. THE. MAYOR. ABOUT. THAT.
METROPOLIS NEW TROY 200 MILES
I. CAN. TAKE. YOU. RIGHT. TO. HIS. DOOR. IF. YOU. WANT.

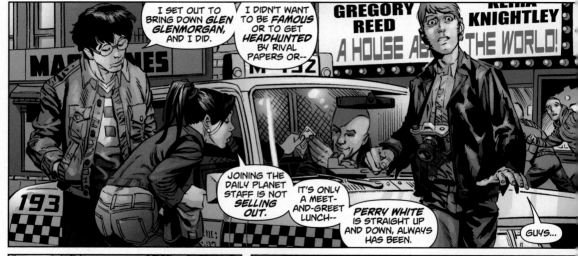

I SET OUT TO BRING DOWN *GLEN GLENMORGAN,* AND I DID.

I DIDN'T WANT TO BE *FAMOUS* OR TO GET *HEADHUNTED* BY RIVAL PAPERS OR--

GREGORY REED

KEIRA KNIGHTLEY

A HOUSE ABOVE THE WORLD!

JOINING THE DAILY PLANET STAFF IS NOT *SELLING OUT.*

IT'S ONLY A MEET-AND-GREET LUNCH--

PERRY WHITE IS STRAIGHT UP AND DOWN, ALWAYS HAS BEEN.

GUYS...

SOMETHING'S UP! THAT'S THE *DAILY STAR* BUILDING.

CLARK?

DAILY ★ STAR

YOUR CUE TO *RUN,* KENT!

WHERE'S *SUPERMAN?*

THIS IS THE SORT OF THING SUPERMAN DOES *REALLY WELL.*

WE DON'T *NEED* SUPERMAN.

STAY RIGHT THERE!

KENT!

I DIDN'T MEAN RUN *TOWARD* IT!

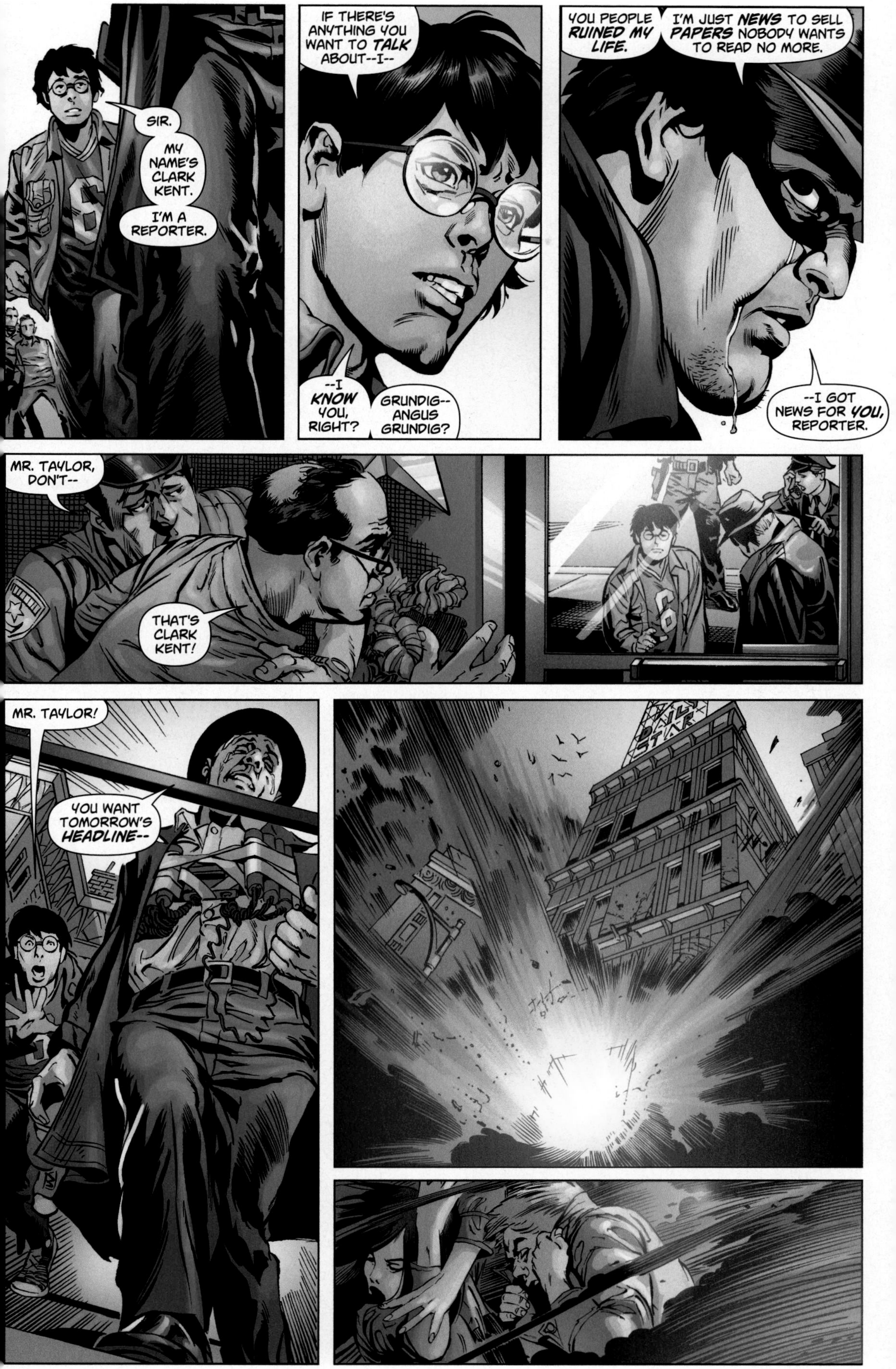
SIR.
MY NAME'S CLARK KENT.
I'M A REPORTER.
IF THERE'S ANYTHING YOU WANT TO TALK ABOUT--I--
--I KNOW YOU, RIGHT?
GRUNDIG-- ANGUS GRUNDIG?
YOU PEOPLE RUINED MY LIFE.
I'M JUST NEWS TO SELL PAPERS NOBODY WANTS TO READ NO MORE.
--I GOT NEWS FOR YOU, REPORTER.
MR. TAYLOR, DON'T--
THAT'S CLARK KENT!
MR. TAYLOR!
YOU WANT TOMORROW'S HEADLINE--

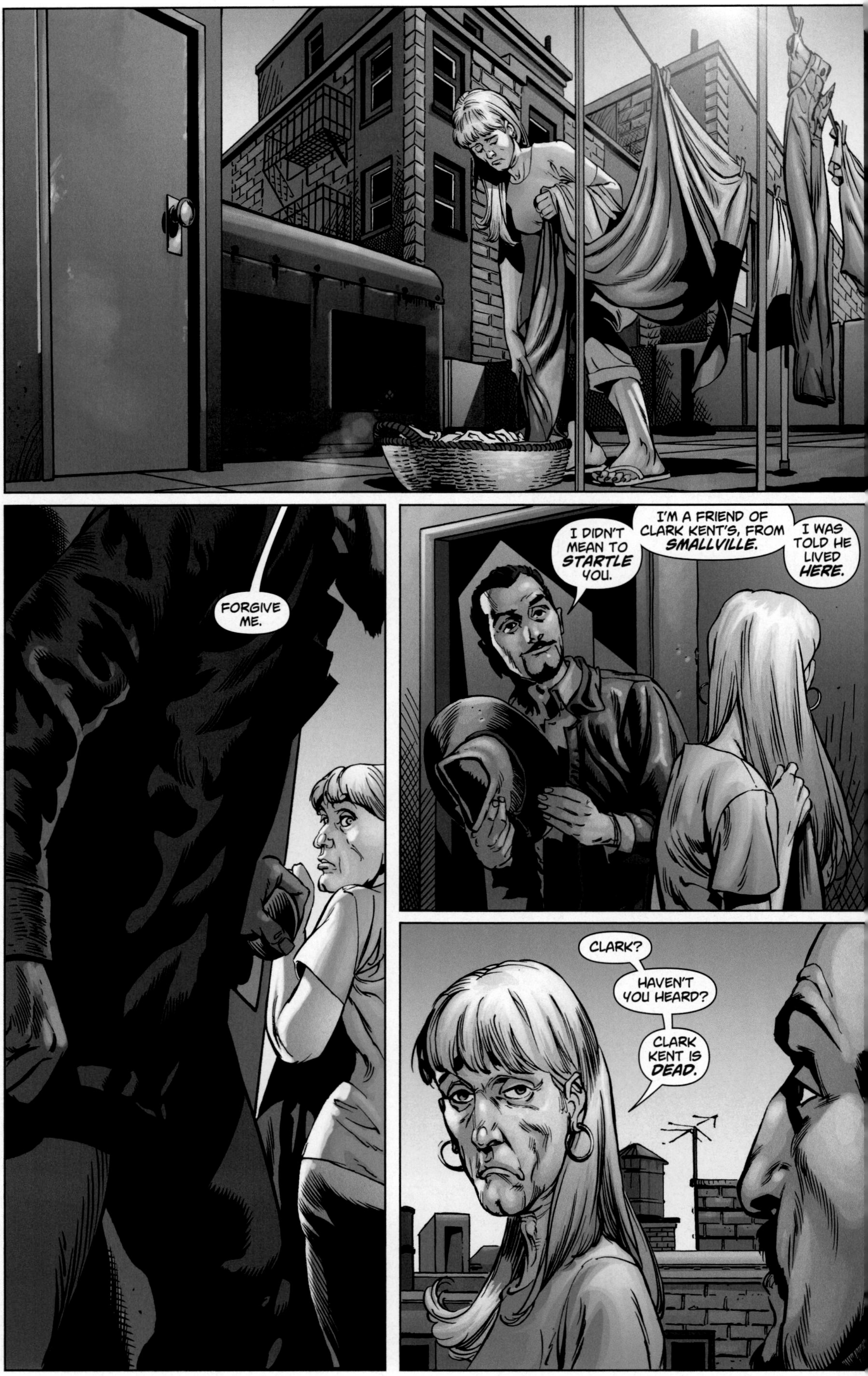
FORGIVE ME.
I DIDN'T MEAN TO STARTLE YOU.
I'M A FRIEND OF CLARK KENT'S, FROM SMALLVILLE.
I WAS TOLD HE LIVED HERE.
CLARK?
HAVEN'T YOU HEARD?
CLARK KENT IS DEAD.

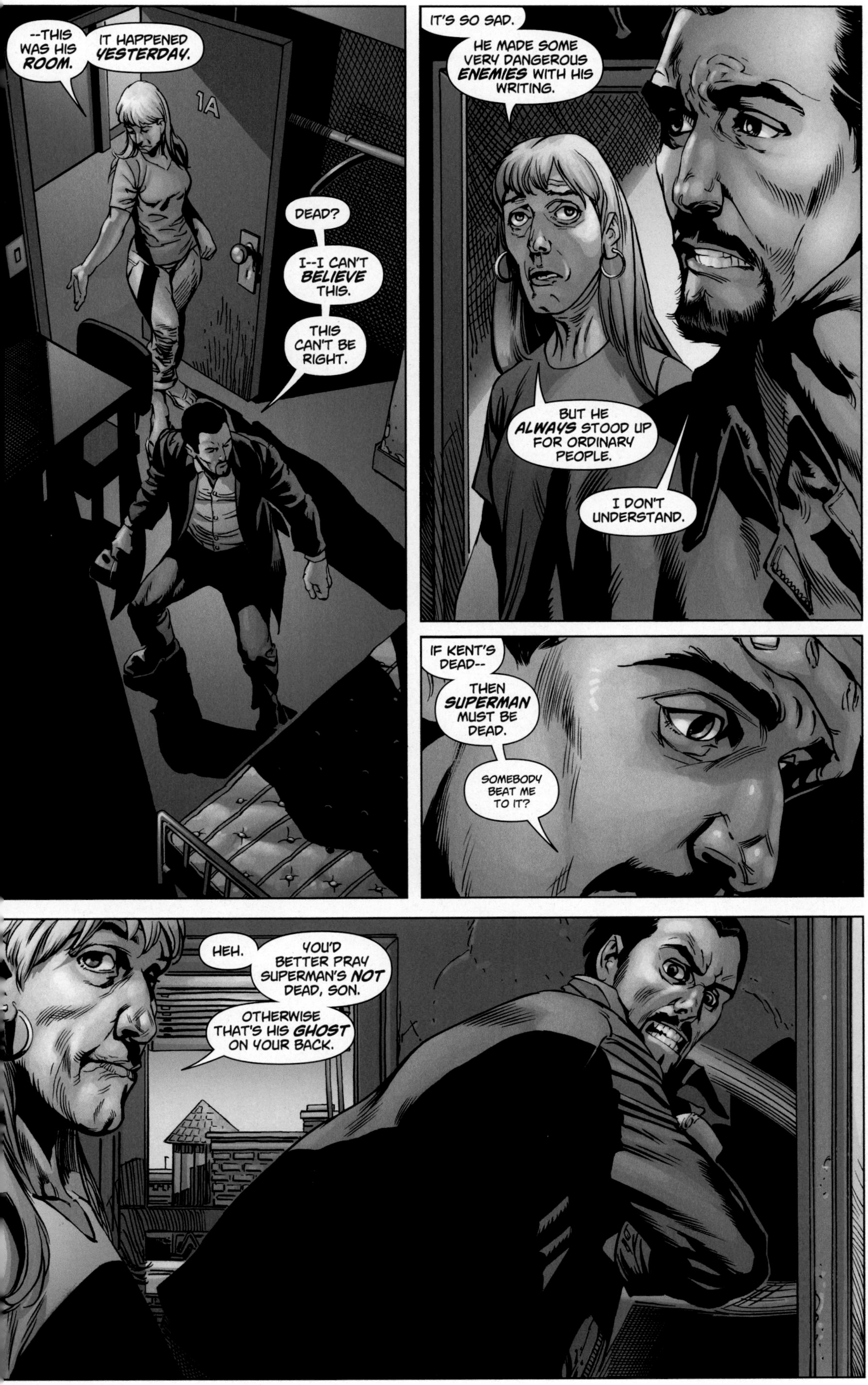
--THIS WAS HIS ROOM.
IT HAPPENED YESTERDAY.
DEAD?
I--I CAN'T BELIEVE THIS.
THIS CAN'T BE RIGHT.
IT'S SO SAD.
HE MADE SOME VERY DANGEROUS ENEMIES WITH HIS WRITING.
BUT HE ALWAYS STOOD UP FOR ORDINARY PEOPLE.
I DON'T UNDERSTAND.
IF KENT'S DEAD--
THEN SUPERMAN MUST BE DEAD.
SOMEBODY BEAT ME TO IT?
HEH.
YOU'D BETTER PRAY SUPERMAN'S NOT DEAD, SON.
OTHERWISE THAT'S HIS GHOST ON YOUR BACK.

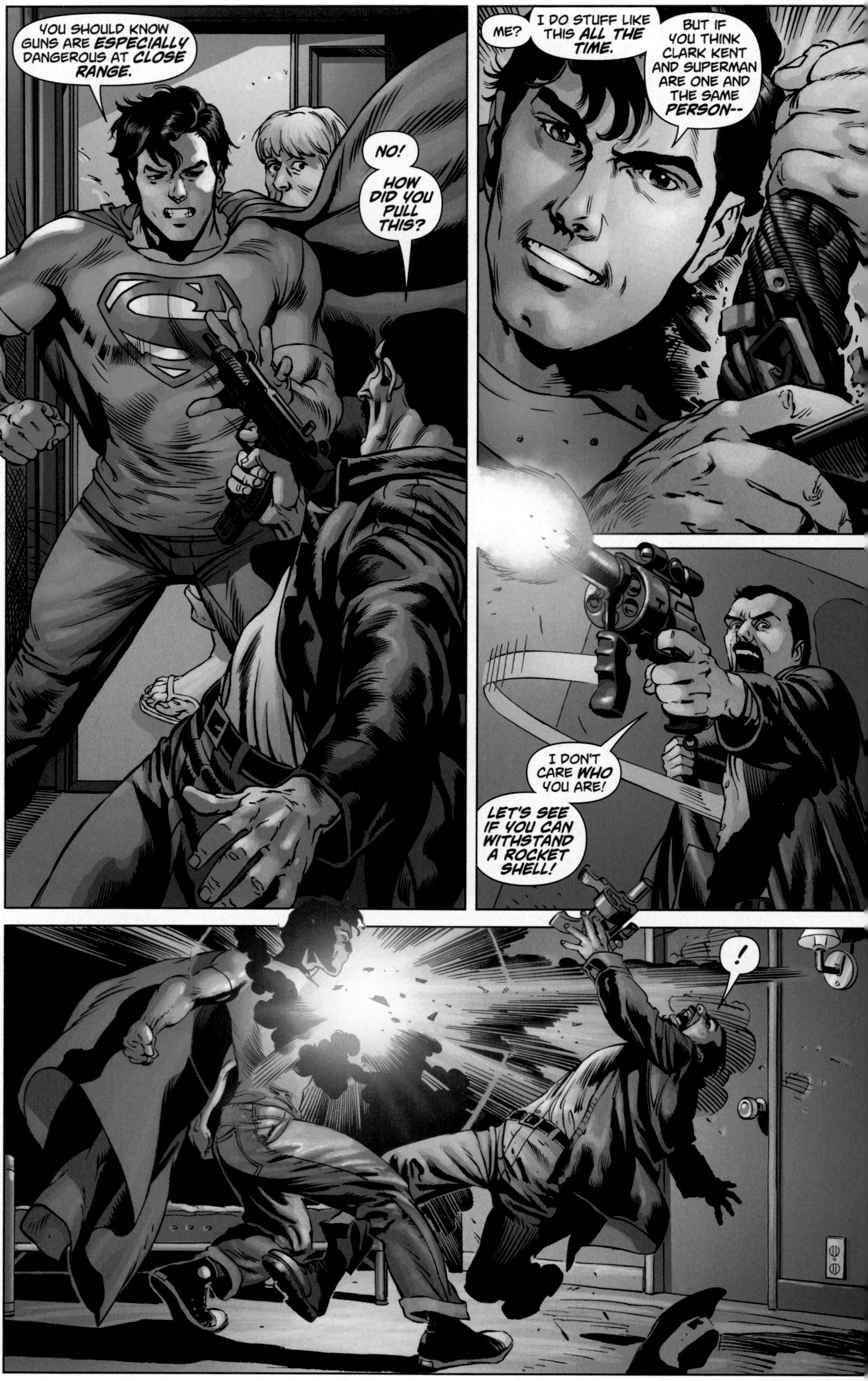
YOU SHOULD KNOW GUNS ARE ESPECIALLY DANGEROUS AT CLOSE RANGE.
NO!
HOW DID YOU PULL THIS?
ME?
I DO STUFF LIKE THIS ALL THE TIME.
BUT IF YOU THINK CLARK KENT AND SUPERMAN ARE ONE AND THE SAME PERSON--
I DON'T CARE WHO YOU ARE!
LET'S SEE IF YOU CAN WITHSTAND A ROCKET SHELL!
!

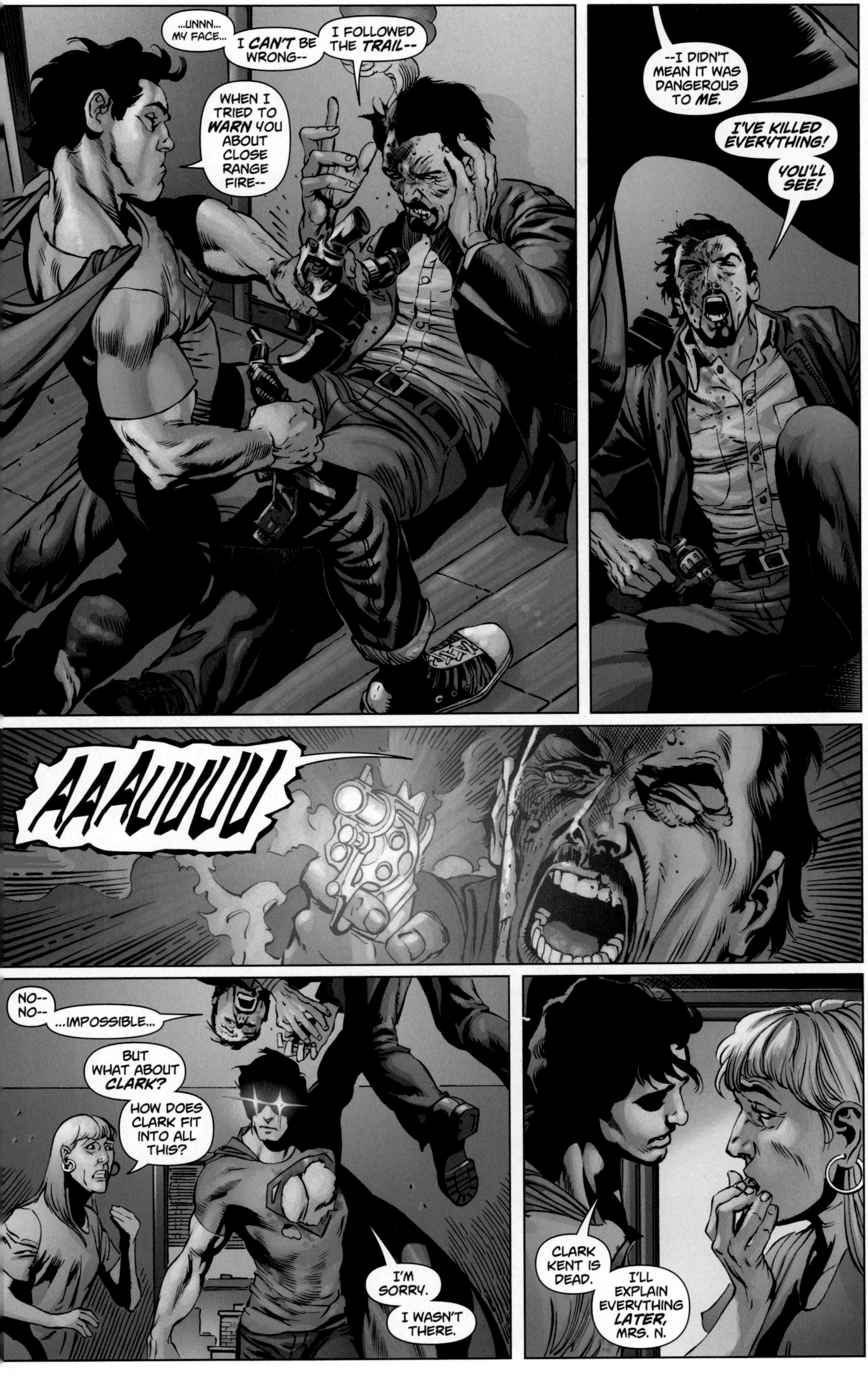
...UNNN... MY FACE...
I CAN'T BE WRONG--
I FOLLOWED THE TRAIL--
WHEN I TRIED TO WARN YOU ABOUT CLOSE RANGE FIRE--
--I DIDN'T MEAN IT WAS DANGEROUS TO ME.
I'VE KILLED EVERYTHING!
YOU'LL SEE!
AAAUUUUU
NO-- NO--
...IMPOSSIBLE...
BUT WHAT ABOUT CLARK?
HOW DOES CLARK FIT INTO ALL THIS?
I'M SORRY.
I WASN'T THERE.
CLARK KENT IS DEAD.
I'LL EXPLAIN EVERYTHING LATER, MRS. N.

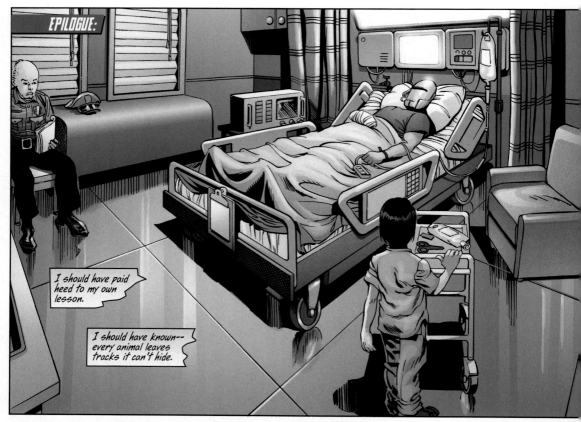

EPILOGUE:

I should have paid heed to my own lesson.

I should have known-- every animal leaves tracks it can't hide.

Even me.

...I *KNOW* WHAT YOU WANT, MR. ZAROV.

I'M HERE TO TELL YOU IT *CAN* BE DONE, BUT NOT WITH LITTLE *TOY GUNS.*

UHH?

I CAN PROVIDE YOU WITH WEAPONS--*STRONGER* WEAPONS FROM *OTHER* WORLDS.

ME?

I CAN MAKE YOU PART OF AN *ARMY* AGAINST SUPERMAN.

IT'S *SIMPLE.*

ALL YOU HAVE TO DO IS MAKE A *DEAL.*

BONUS SECTION

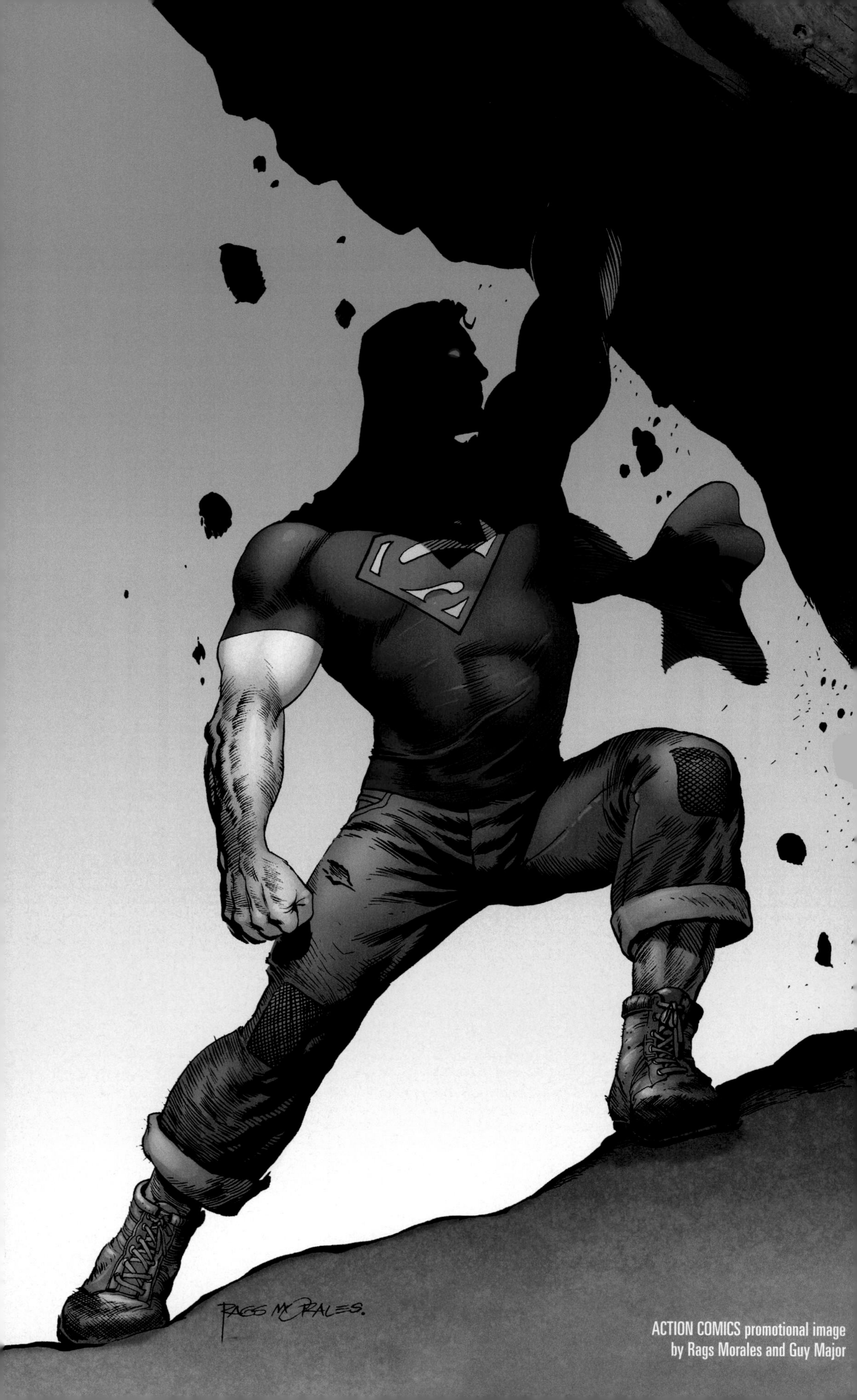
RAGS MORALES.

ACTION COMICS promotional image
by Rags Morales and Guy Major

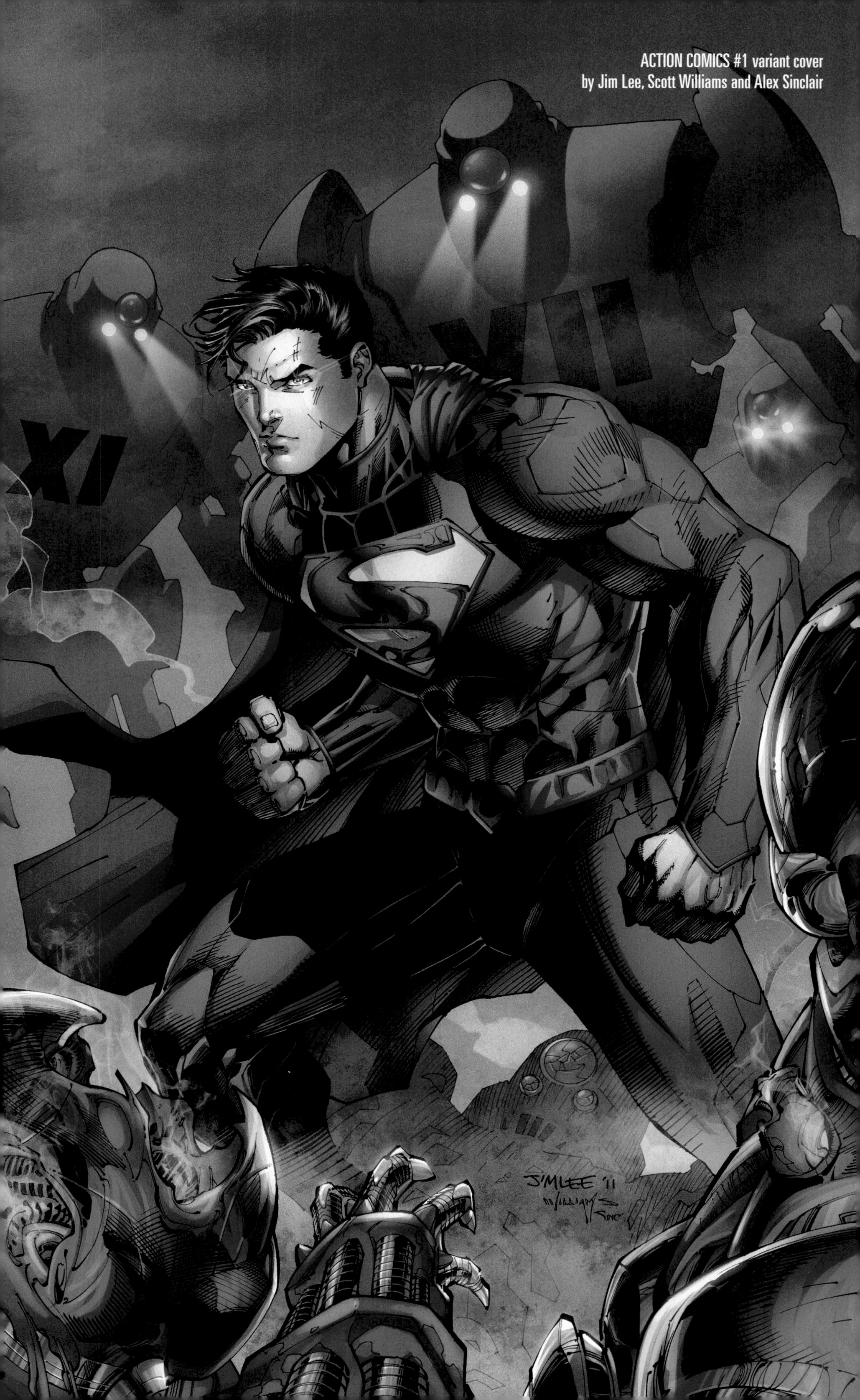
XI
VII

ACTION COMICS #1 variant cover
by Jim Lee, Scott Williams and Alex Sinclair

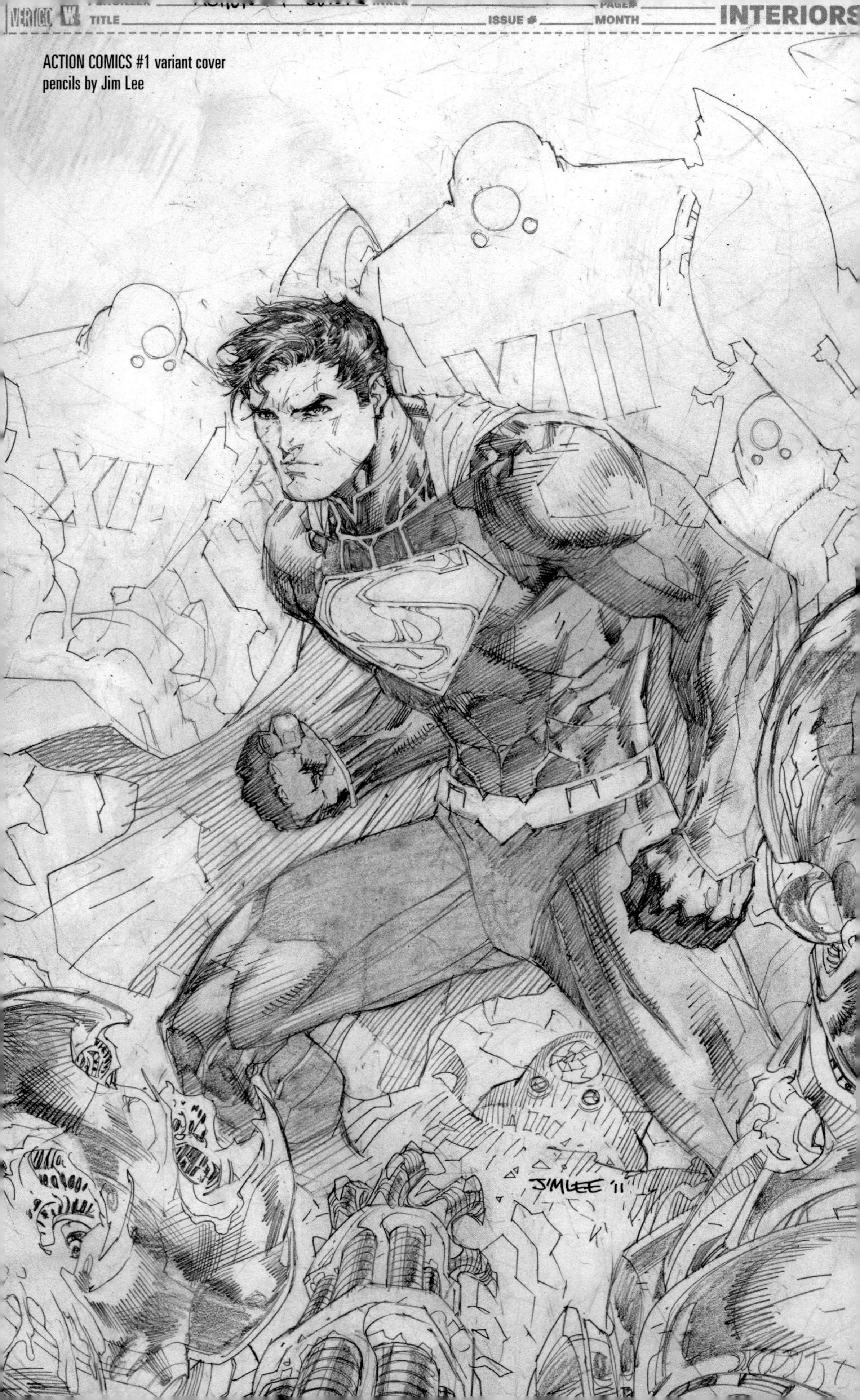
TITLE
ISSUE #
MONTH
PAGE#
INTERIORS
JIMLEE '11

ACTION COMICS #1 variant cover
pencils by Jim Lee

ACTION COMICS #2 variant cover
by Ethan Van Sciver

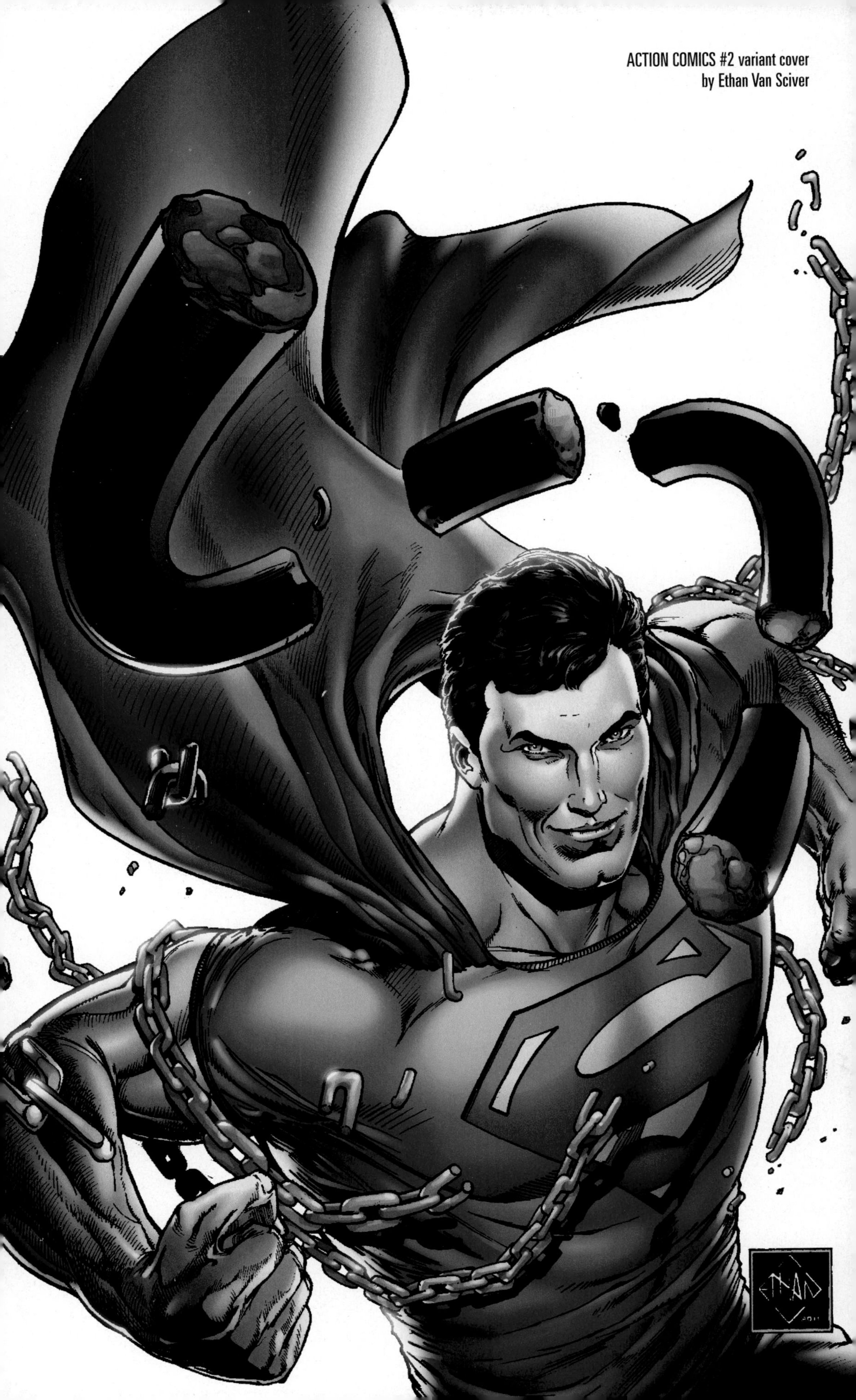

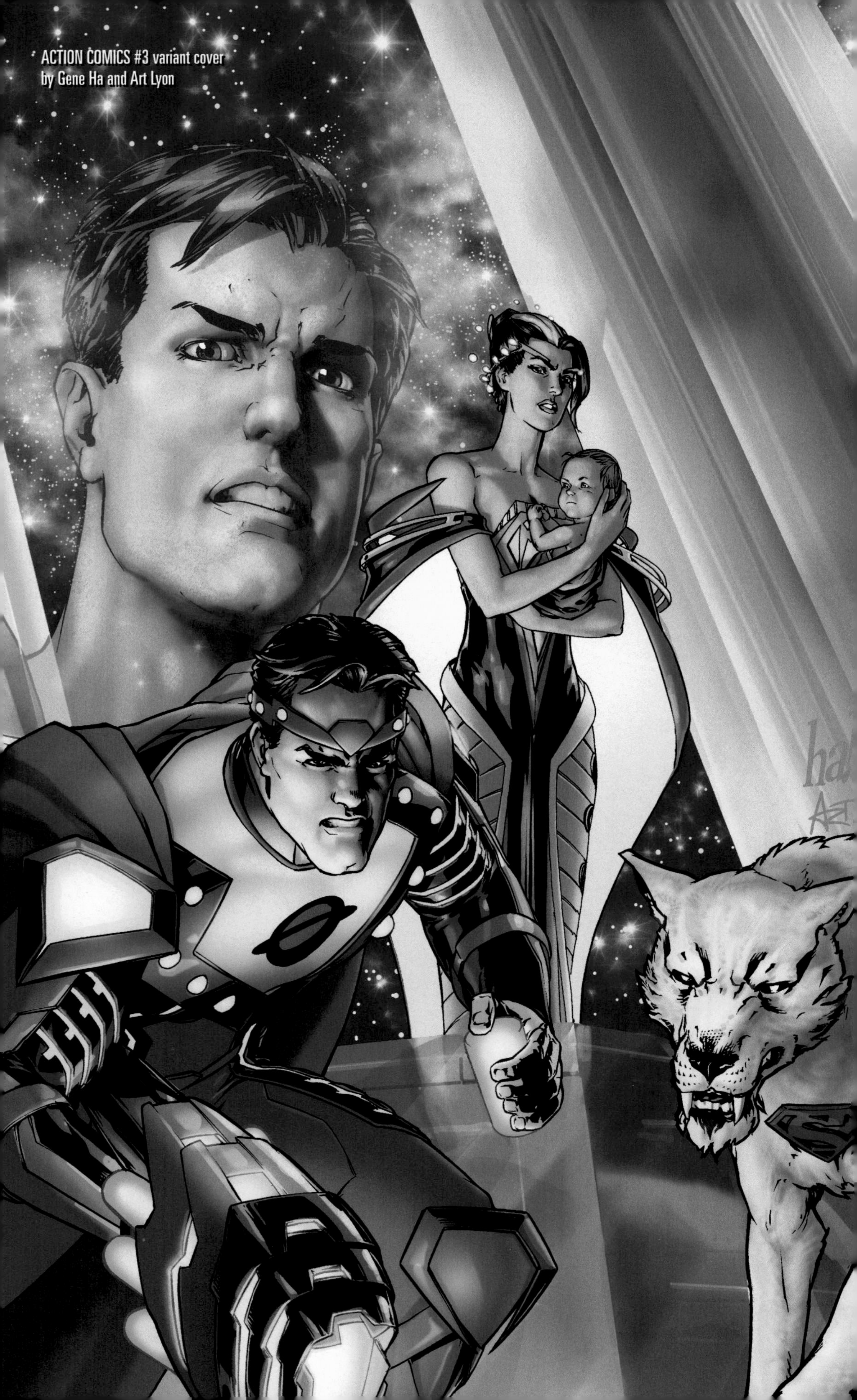
ACTION COMICS #3 variant cover
by Gene Ha and Art Lyon

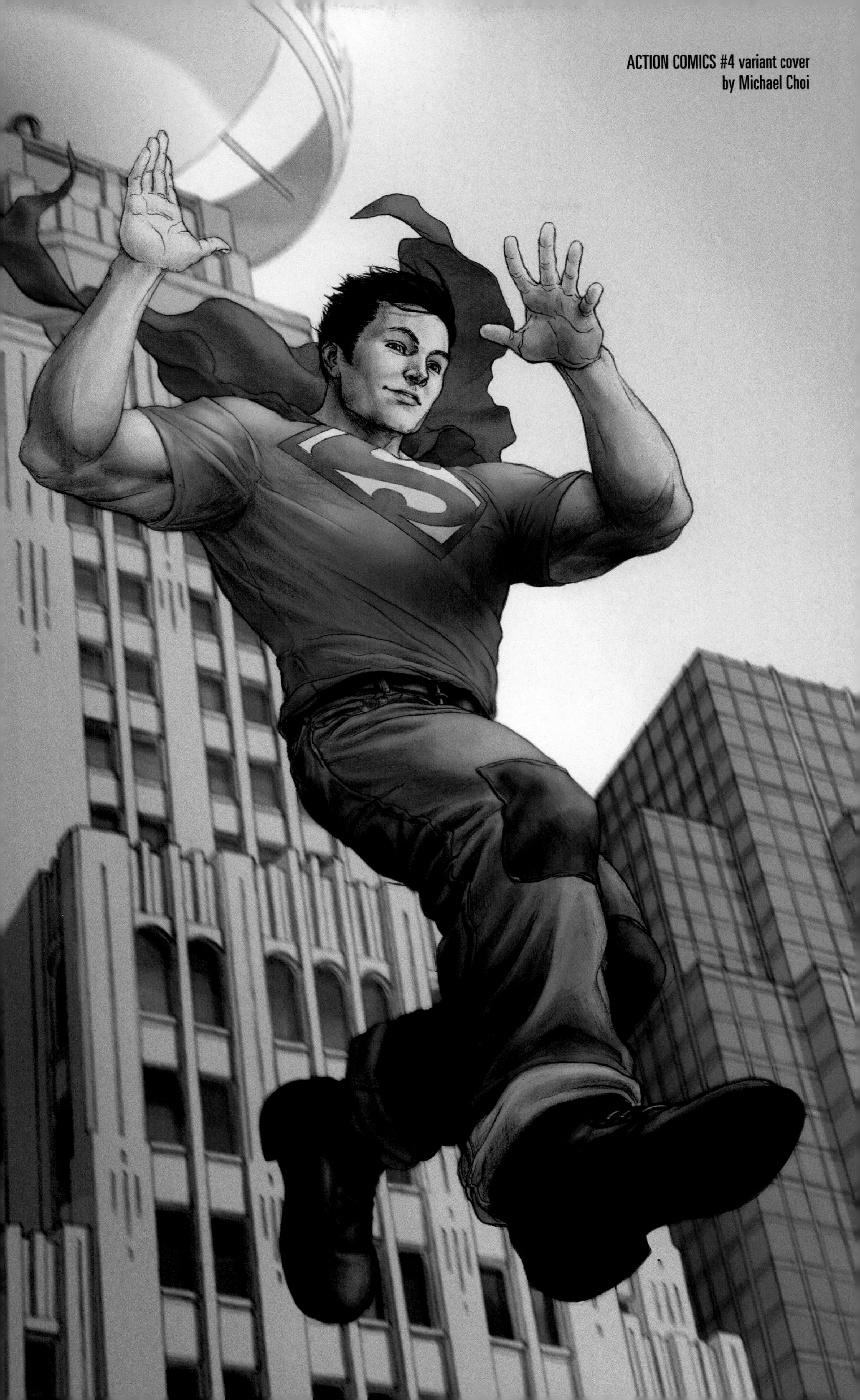

ACTION COMICS #4 variant cover
by Michael Choi

ACTION COMICS #5 variant cover
by Rags Morales and Brad Anderson

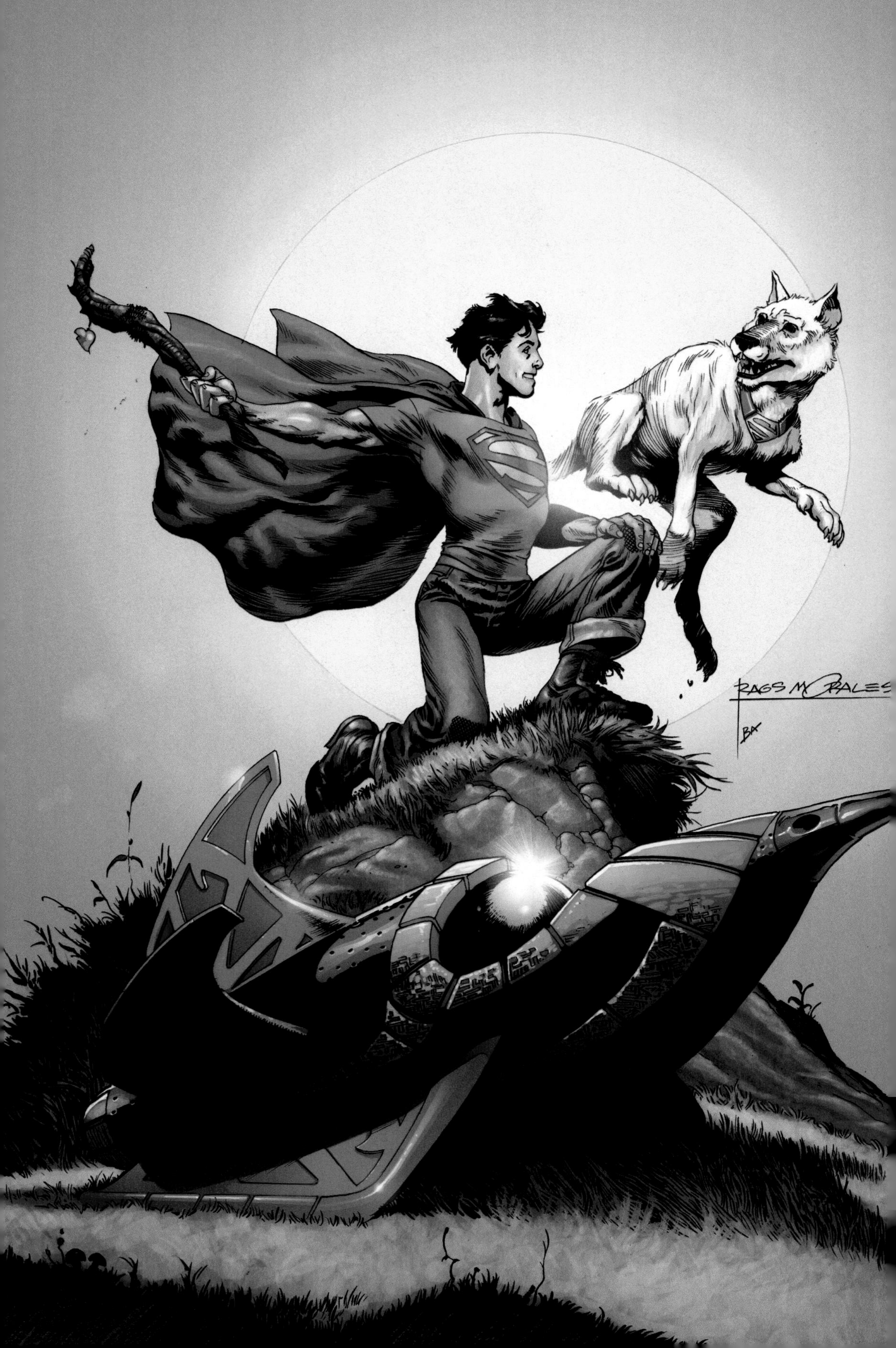
RAGS MORALES
BA

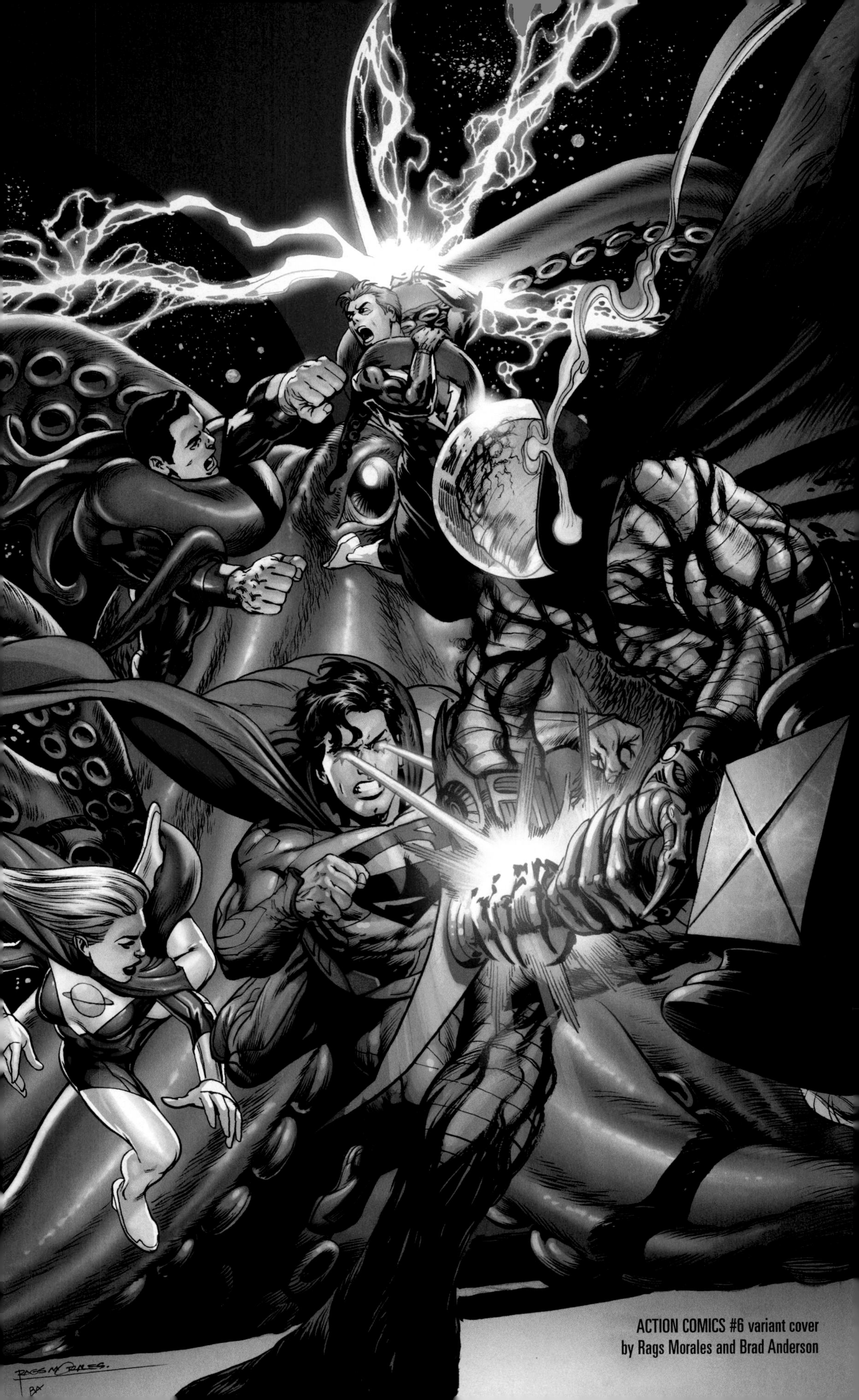

ACTION COMICS #6 variant cover
by Rags Morales and Brad Anderson

ACTION COMICS #7 variant cover
by Chris Burnham and Nathan Fairbairn

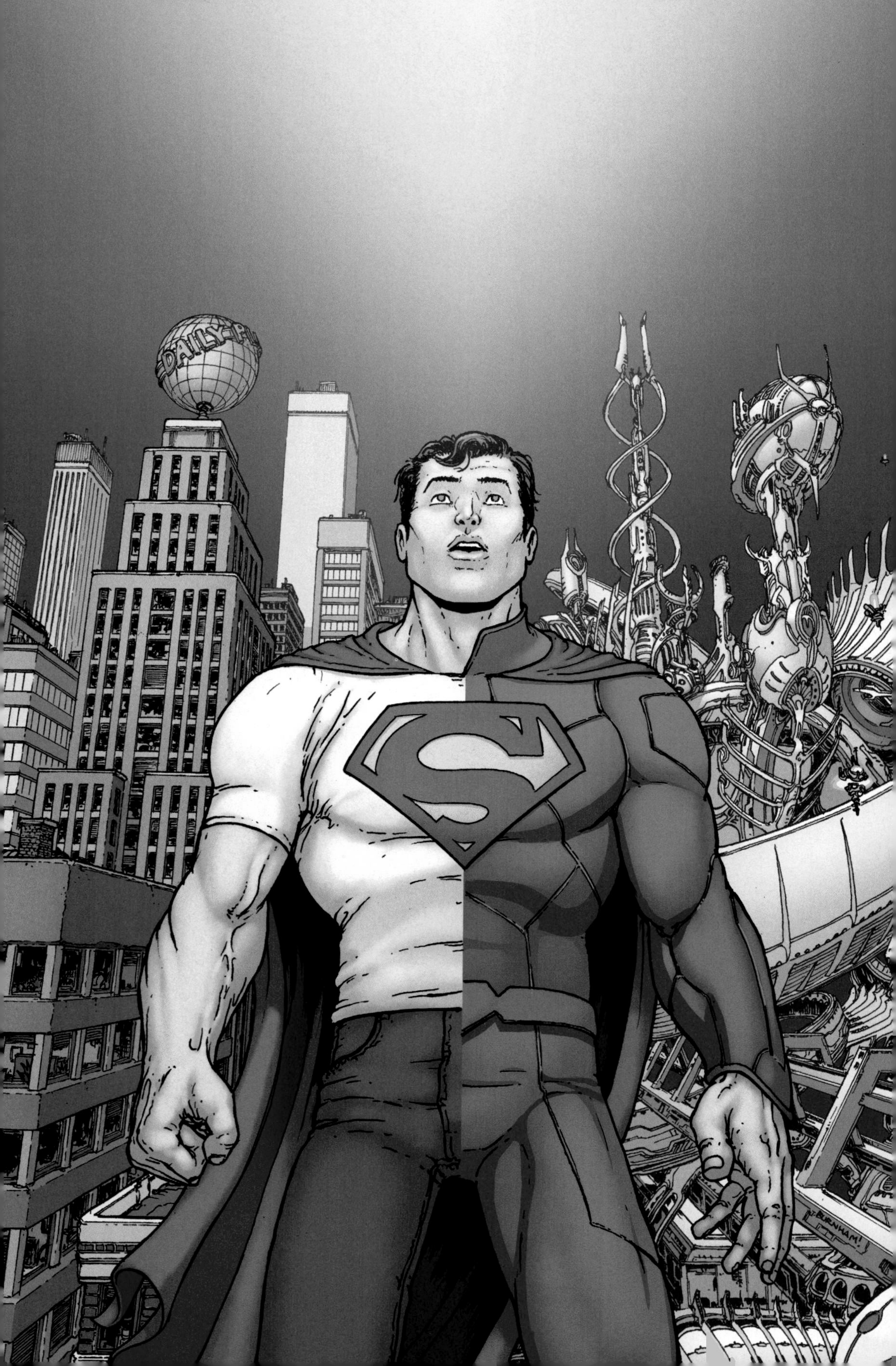
BURNHAM!

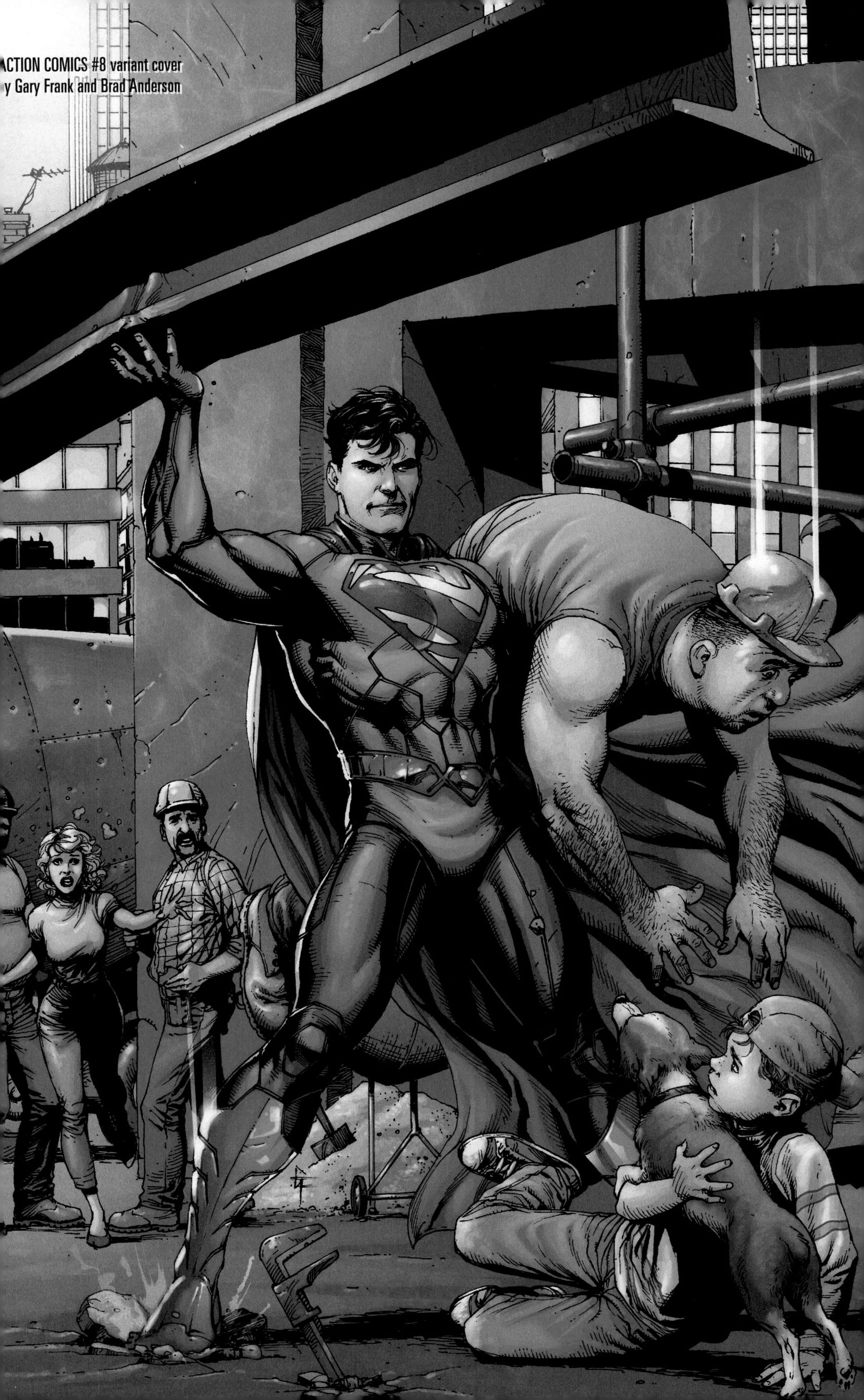
ACTION COMICS #8 variant cover
y Gary Frank and Brad Anderson

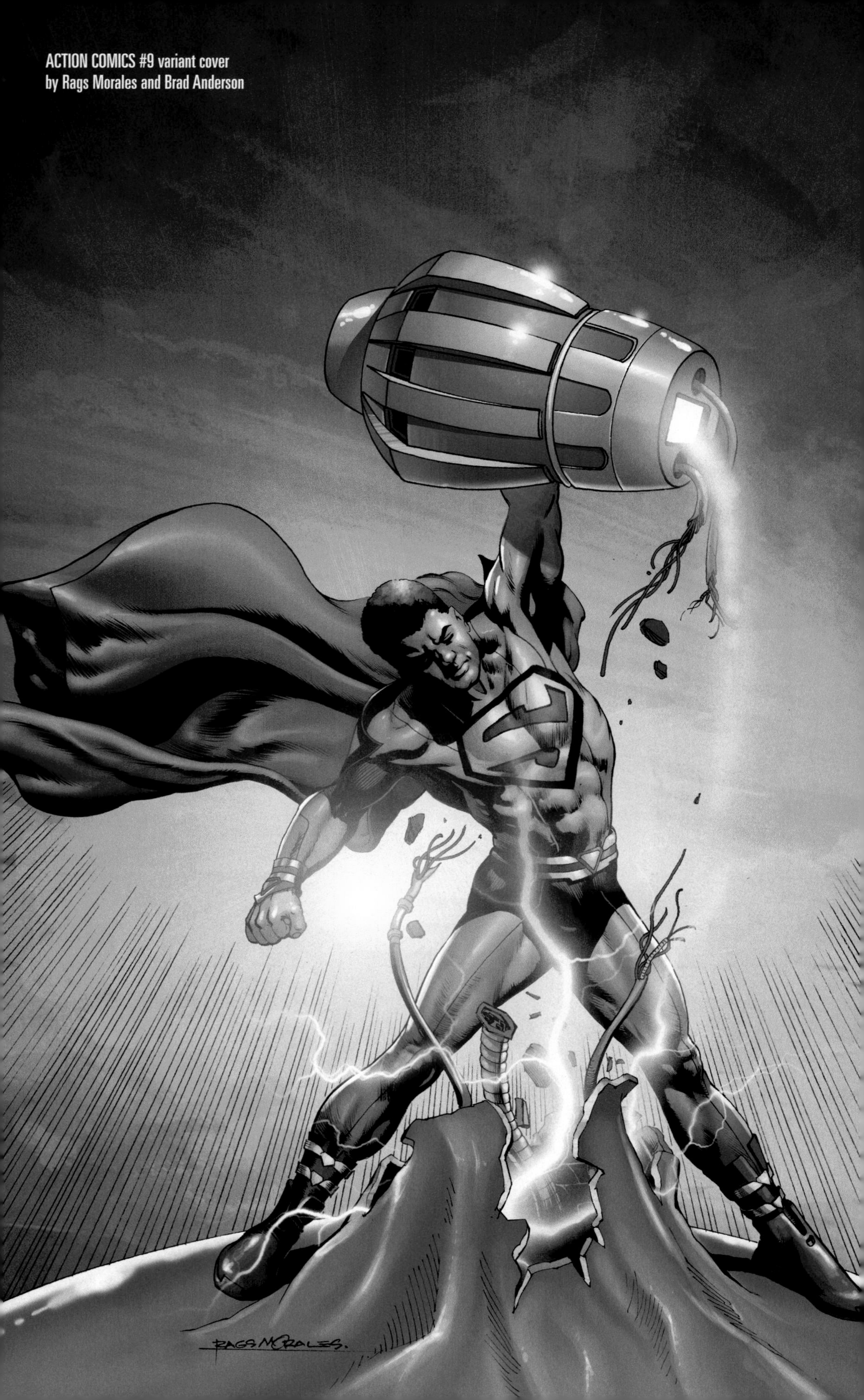
RAGS MORALES.

ACTION COMICS #9 variant cover
by Rags Morales and Brad Anderson

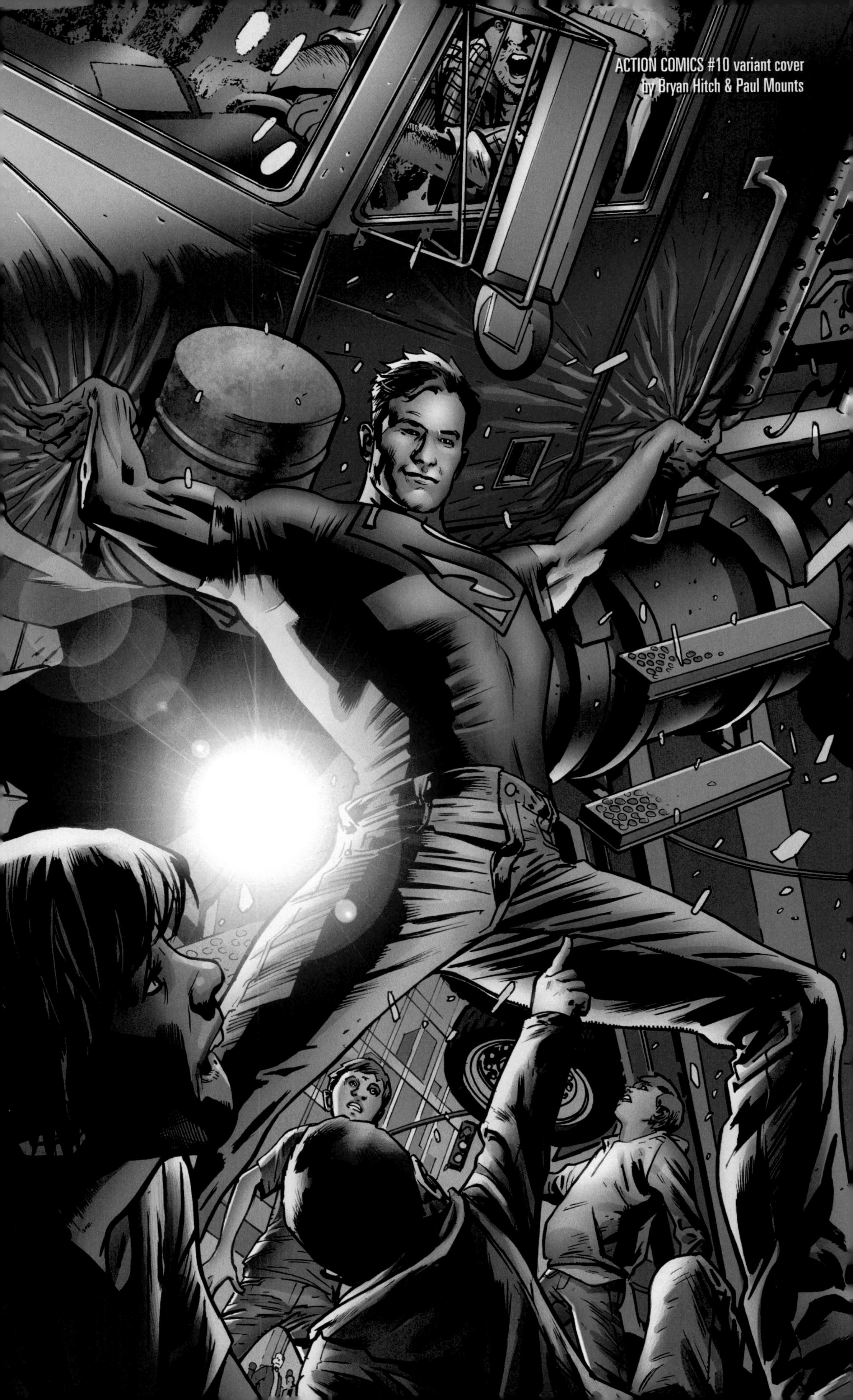

ACTION COMICS #10 variant cover
by Bryan Hitch & Paul Mounts

ACTION COMICS SKETCHBOOK

FEATURING COMMENTARY FROM WRITER **GRANT MORRISON** AND ARTIST **RAGS MORALES**

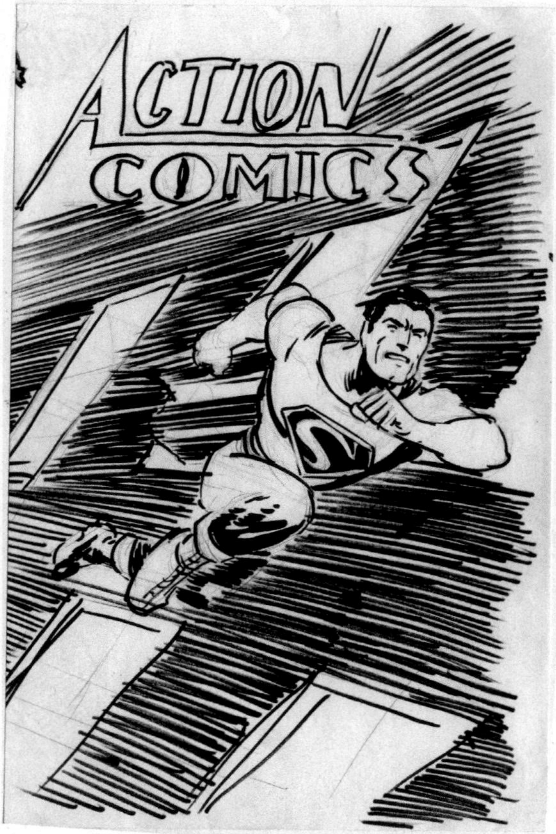
ACTION
COMICS

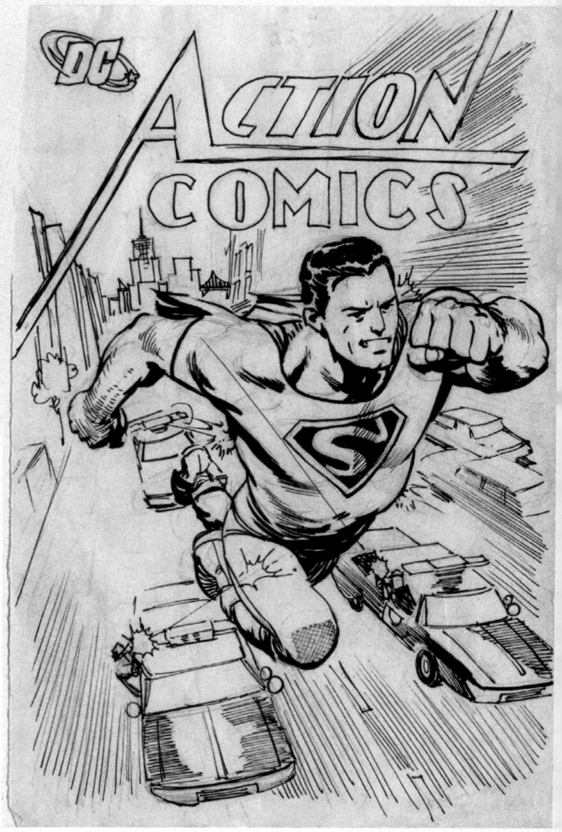
DC
ACTION
COMICS

Rags Morales' cover sketches for ACTION COMICS #1

ACTION!

GRANT MORRISON: The physical things Superman does came from the first year of ACTION COMICS, where they were doing this nonstop, kinetic, muscular action. I wanted to get that into the actual form and structure of this whole run, that feeling of motion and action. It's called ACTION COMICS—let's do that!

RAGS MORALES: For the first 20 years, flying with that pose I gave him on the first cover—the one bent leg and the one straight leg, and counterbalancing with the arms—was the Superman trademark, and it made him look like he was running. Here I am trying to do an homage to it. It brought it back to the essence of that character.

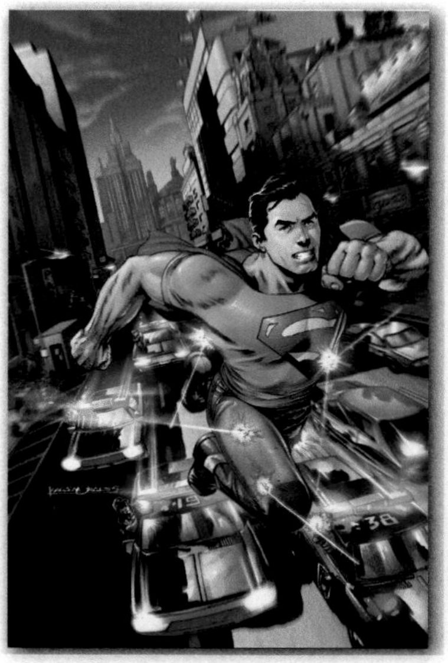

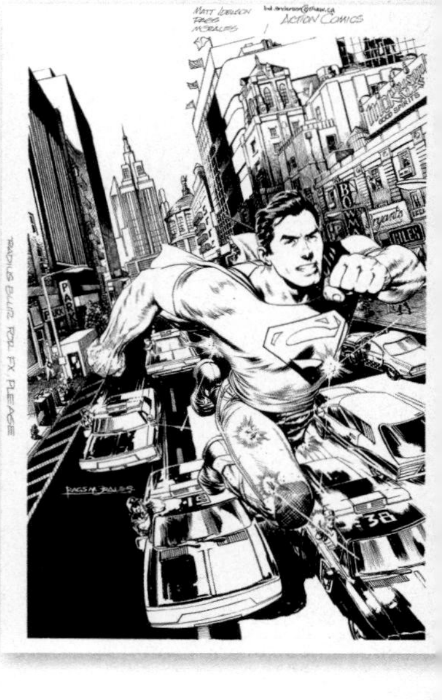
ACTION COMICS
RADIUS BLUR FOR FX, PLEASE

THE LITTLE MAN

MORRISON: I was thinking of the dwarf from *Twin Peaks*—a gnomelike figure, a creepy little elf.

MORALES: I relied more on the Robert Blake character from *Lost Highway*. Somehow he ended up looking a little bit like Elvis Costello, too... [Laughs]

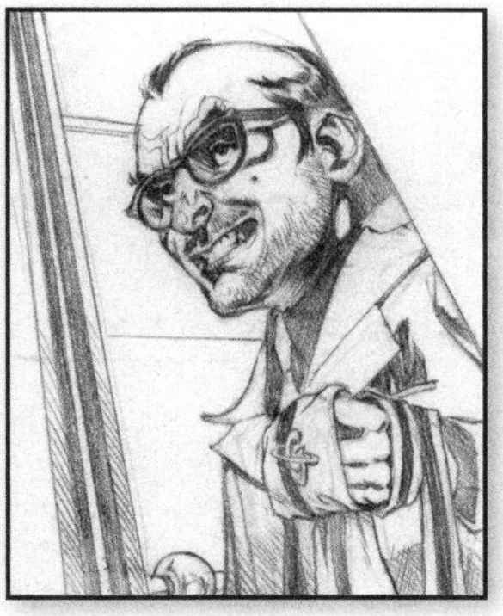

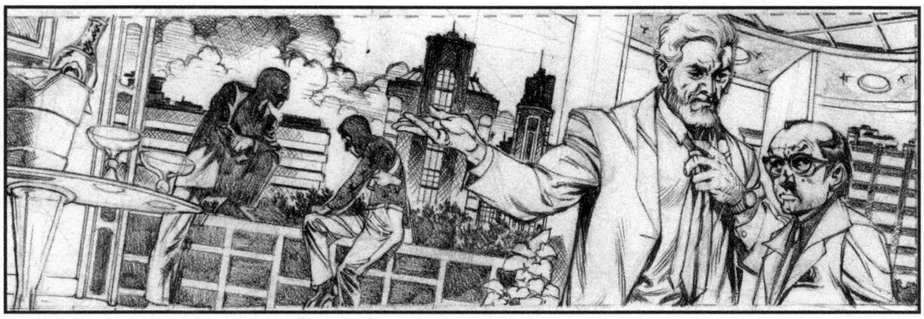

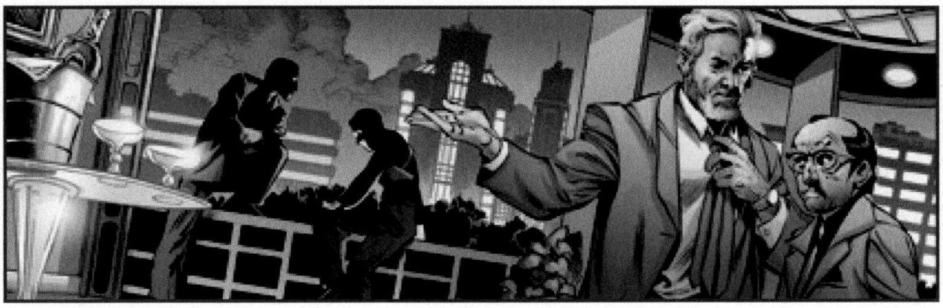

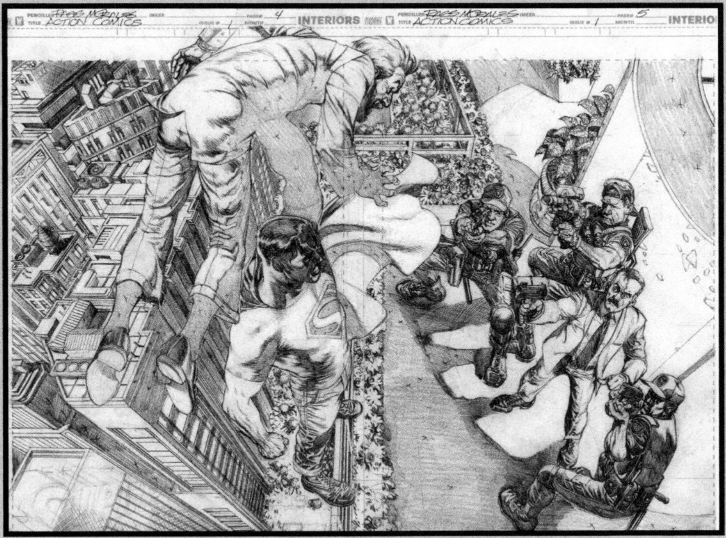
ACTION COMICS
INTERIORS
ACTION COMICS
INTERIO

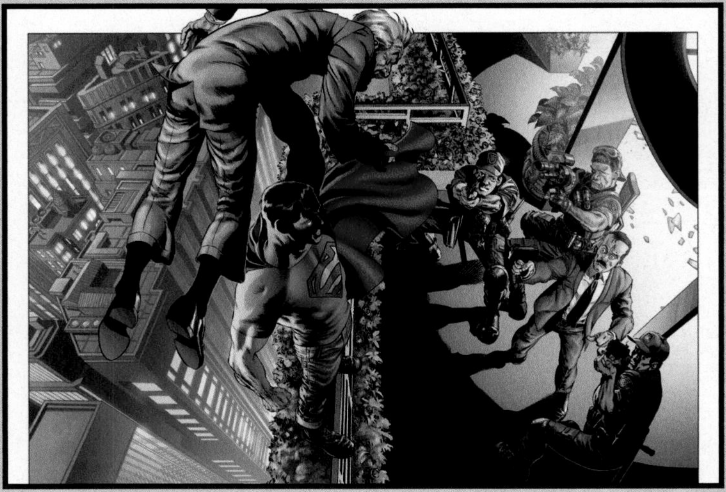

A WHOLE NEW SUPERMAN

MORRISON: Like a guitarist in a band of 17-year-olds, experience doesn't even come into it—he just does it. He's a superhero—he doesn't have to think. He's a kid who's been set free from Ma and Pa Kent. Both of them are dead, and suddenly he thinks, "I'm the most powerful thing on the planet. It's time to start cleaning up!" [Laughs] It seemed like you could get a really good story out of a young man who's not considering what he's doing—he's just doing it because it feels right.

MORALES: Honestly, I could never really get into Superman before. I even had a hard time drawing him, because he'd been done so many times by so many people. I'm glad we're going back to the beginning with him. It's a chance to do it all over again, knowing what we know now.

SUPER-SWAGGER

MORALES: I thought, "What are the two iconic things that Superman would be to me?" He'd be part Steve Reeves and part Elvis. [Laughs] When he's catching the bullet, he's got that Elvis light in the corner of his eye.

MORRISON: That swagger is part of what the rest of the world believes about America. "They're all John Wayne!" [Laughs] I wanted to put that back into Superman, that attitude of "I know what I'm doing, I'm the biggest guy on the block...but lucky for you, I'm a good guy!"

THE LABORS OF SUPERMAN

MORRISON: I constantly put Superman up against very physical objects: a wrecking ball, a tank, a train, solid stone. It was designed for the motion of that muscular, 1938 Superman—to really tie him into physical things, to big, heavy objects.

MORALES: I love that he's powered down. Love it, love it, love it, love it. I love that he's Herculean again. He's about doing the tasks. Superman back in the '40s was more relevant than Superman of recent years, because things hurt him. There was a danger to that.

CLARK KENT

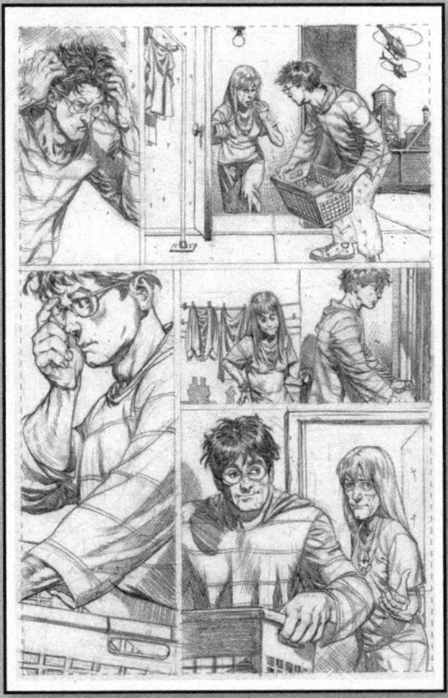

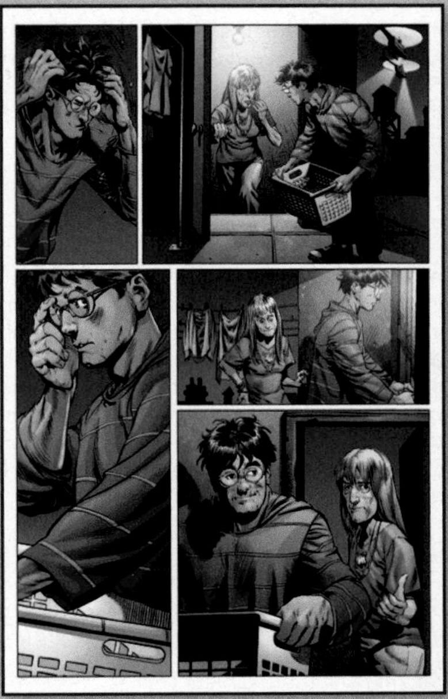

MORALES: I put him in baggy clothing to hide his muscles. Maybe stoop his posture a little bit, make him a little slack-jawed at certain moments so he doesn't look at all like a hero—more like a 22-year-old nerd, which is what he's trying to do. He's a very good actor, which is a superpower I don't think many other superheroes have. And I realized that there's a certain amount of thickness to the lenses of his glasses that can help distort the size of his eyes and make them seem larger.

MORRISON: I love Rags' Clark Kent. I think it's great, this Harry Potter Clark Kent. His face is so young and pliable! His eyes get bigger, so he looks more like a kid. That's why Rags is so good to work with—he really thinks about this stuff, and it makes such a big difference to the finished product. When I saw that Clark Kent, it changed the way I wrote the character. He suddenly seemed very young, and he could be a little bit brattish. Clark's obviously this little hardcore farmer's boy who's not taking any crap from anyone.

MORE POWERFUL THAN A LOCOMOTIVE?

MORRISON: When he's hit by a train, he's not the Superman we've seen for the last 25-30 years. This is someone who can be hurt. I wanted to show he has limits. But it's also this up-front connection to the Superman legend—he's actually punched in the chest by the "speeding bullet."

MORALES: Originally, when Superman took off, he was exerting effort. To stop a train was painful. To get electrocuted was painful. He survived it much better than we could, but we forget how impossible these things are to do. I love that he's been brought back down to Earth. That's the way it should be.

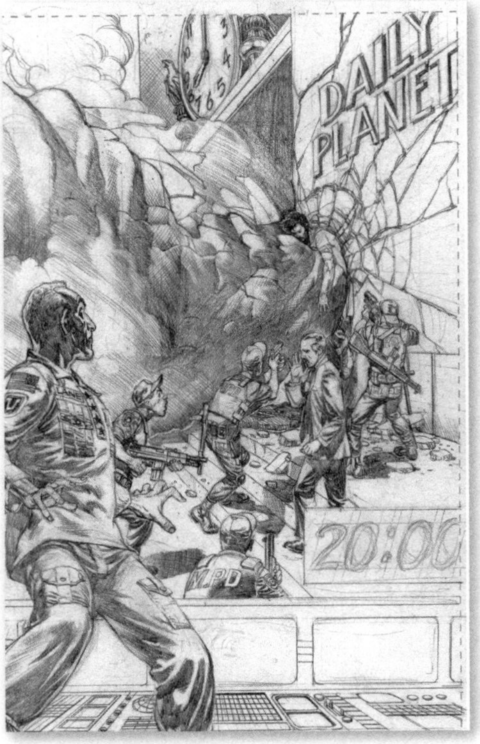
DAILY PLANET
20:00
MPD

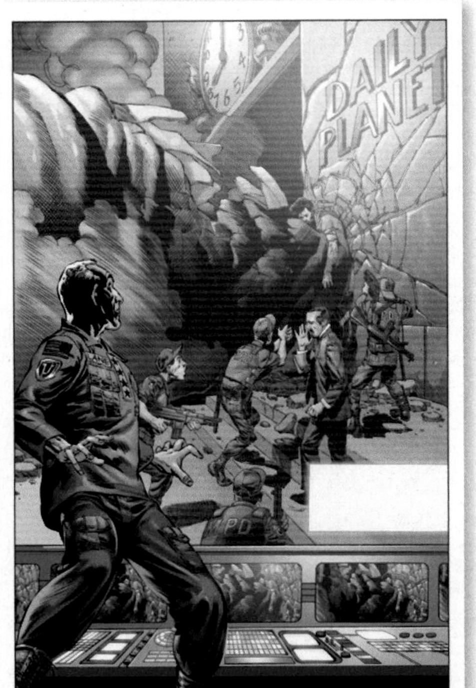
DAILY PLANET
MPD

MEET LEX LUTHOR

MORRISON: Superman is us at our best, and Lex is us at our worst...but they're both us. He's selfish, he's inwardly directed, he's greedy, he's egotistical, he pretends to hate Superman but really he wants to look like Superman, he's constantly chugging energy drinks, he talks crap...[Laughs] I wanted to make him an embodiment of all of our worst traits. They're what make us human, so that's what makes Lex human and relatable. That's why Lex Luthor's such a great villain: We all recognize those traits.

MORALES: Lex's weight is one of those little subliminal things. It adds a layer of jealousy and feeling insignificant and insecure about yourself. He's this out-of-shape, snide, condescending jerk who we're too mature now to stuff into a locker when we see him, but we still do it every time in our heads. [Laughs] Luthor's that guy from the electronics store who condescends to you when you ask about the difference between a megabyte and a gigabyte.

The following is a panel description from the script for ACTION COMICS #1:
Big pic. Now we cut to a military command center somewhere outside Metropolis. Nerve center atmosphere with military personnel hunched over computers. Big wall screen like they have at NASA. All yours, Rags. The picture is dominated by a big screen on which we see a GRAPHIC OF METROPOLIS with a pulsing circle in lower midtown east where Superman was last seen.
Silhouetted against the screen are two of our principal players—Lois Lane's dad GENERAL SAM LANE and Superman's arch-villain LEX LUTHOR. Lane is the archetypal tough American dad. Luthor, like Superman, is a little younger, perhaps a little heavier and sturdier. I like the idea that he was a little fat until his jealousy of Superman drove him to the gym to become the trim, muscular Luthor of the Silver Age and more recent stories. So he's not obese but he's veering a little more in the visual direction of Luthor's heavier build as it appeared in stories from 1941 to 1959.

LOIS LANE, REPORTER

MORRISON: Lois is an army girl, but she's become a crusading journalist to annoy her parents. She's like Clark Kent: she's crusading, she wants to do good, she's a hero in her own right. It changes the whole Superman dynamic, because Lois isn't tied to any guy. She's a party girl, she's smart, she's clever—she's Lady Gaga! She's the smartest girl on the planet.

MORALES: I think she has a poster of Woodward and Bernstein on the wall—that's what's important to her. I see her as constantly thinking. She may be saying one thing, but in her eyes you can tell she's thinking 15 steps ahead of you.

JIMMY OLSEN, ~~SUPERMAN'S~~ CLARK KENT'S PAL

MORRISON: Jimmy's playing the role of Clark's friend rather than Superman's friend. He's the guy that Clark connected with when he first turned up in Metropolis. The two of them are geeks together, talking about movies and sci-fi. Jimmy's a young kid who's getting into this whole photography thing and is really smart. These are characters who you can imagine all have blogs, and Jimmy has his photographs up on Flickr. They're modern kids.

MORALES: He's Clark's best friend. They're buds. They're on the same level. Initially, he was all, "Well, golly gee, Mr. Kent!" But now he's just kind of like, "Hey, Clark, man—dude." If you want to make Jimmy Olsen cool, stop making him such an obsequious sycophant. You bring Clark down to him—which is perfect for Clark, too. It puts them on equal terms and instantly makes Jimmy cooler.

"THAT BEAT-UP-LOOKING KID"

MORRISON: You can tell he's in danger simply because he's no longer in motion!

MORALES: All art comes from the center. All you have to do is remember all the scraps you got into as a kid...

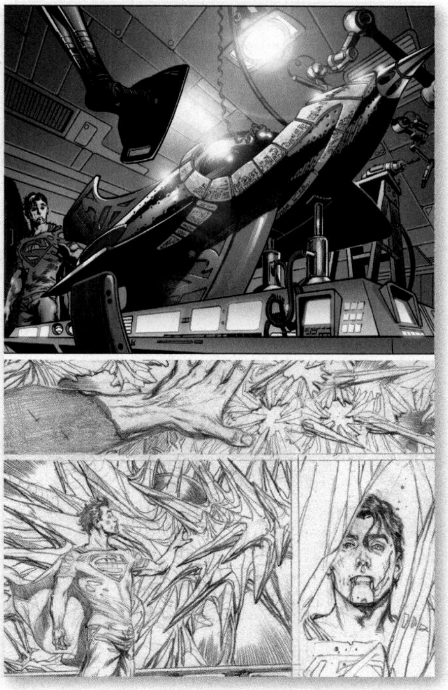

KAL-EL'S ROCKET

MORRISON: The rocket is Moses' basket, the basket that the Hindi hero Karna was placed in—the idea of people putting a child into the river of destiny. The cape, the rocket, the costume, the ship we see at the end of #2—everything is part of the story and has character arcs of its own. Every little bit of the Superman legend is turned into something meaningful in its own right.

MORALES: Those little squiggles are designed to be hieroglyphs. If you're Kryptonian, you can read them. But it's funny: As I was drawing it, I started seeing things that reminded me of Moses' basket. Then I'm thinking, "Kal-EL—'El' is a Hebrew word for God. The world's being destroyed, so he's being put into the basket and sent down the Nile." So I made it a little more basket-y.

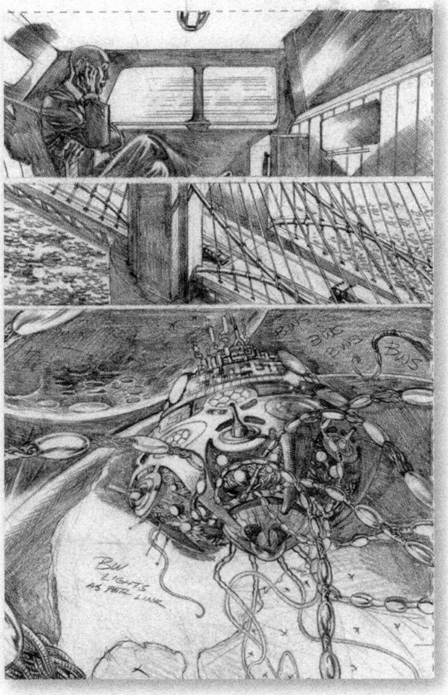

"IT CAME FROM OUTER SPACE"

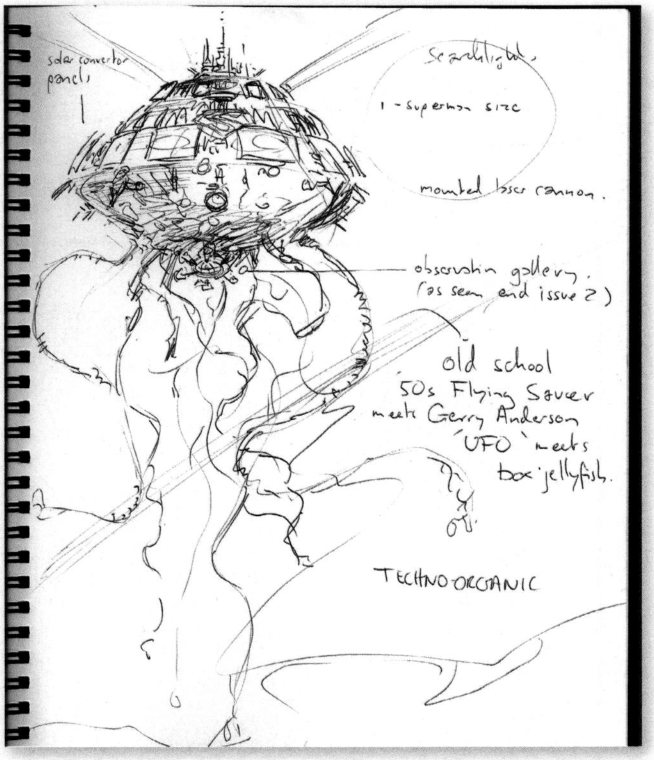
solar convertor panels
Searchlight
1 - superman size
mounted laser cannon.
observation gallery. (as seen end issue 2)
old school 50s Flying Saucer meets Gerry Anderson 'UFO' meets box jellyfish.
TECHNO ORGANIC

Grant Morrison's design of the spaceship from the last page of ACTION COMICS #2.

MORALES: When I first drew it, I had a mothership surrounded by little runabout ships straight out of *The Jetsons*. It was completely wrong. I sent it back and forth with the editor. Then Grant went ahead and did this jellyfish kind of design...

MORRISON: I think it's creepy that Lex is talking to something that doesn't reply, and then you see that image. That's the first hint of a bigger, overarching story to come. And tentacles are the creepiest things! [Laughs]

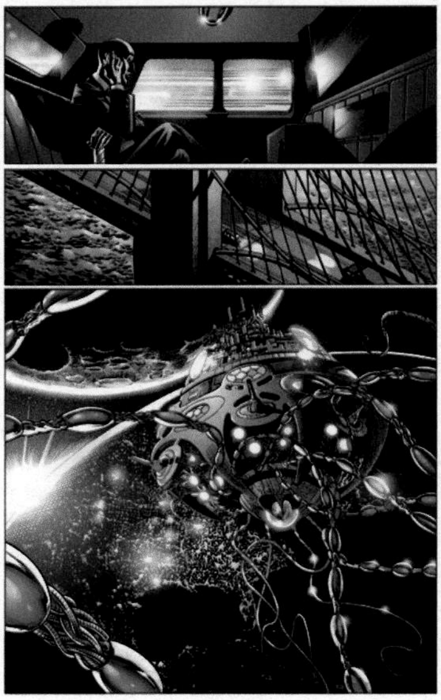

KRYPTON DESIGNS BY GENE HA!

MORRISON: It's the planet of your dreams. A scientific utopia. I wanted to explore Krypton as the world of super-people. What would happen if they worked it all out, if they lived for 500 years with amazing technology?

GENE HA: I'm going to vary Kryptonians by standard facial features and hair texture and placement, mixed with very unusual color of hair and skin. A cocktail party of supermodels attacked by a god-child with god-crayons. I see Kryptonian identity as being very tied to their bodies. They always want their bodies to be more perfect, though their concept of perfection can drift into surprising directions.

LIKE SON, LIKE FATHER

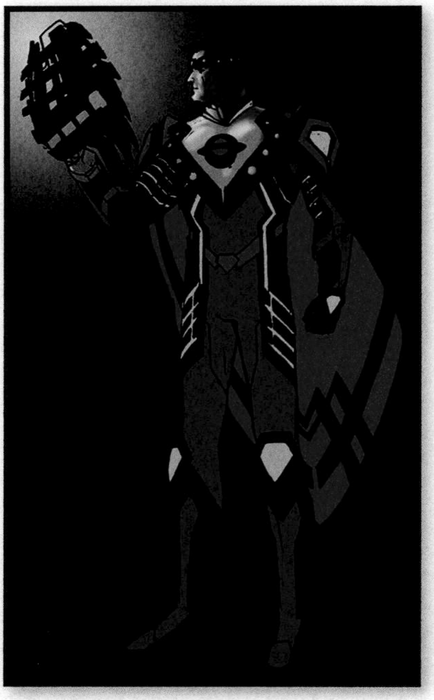

MORRISON: Jor-El looks just like the father of Superman should look. He's wearing an outfit that closely resembles the Jim Lee Superman suit, except in Jor-El's trademark green and red. He has the science guild symbol on his chest—a ringed planet.

MORE THAN JUST A LAMP

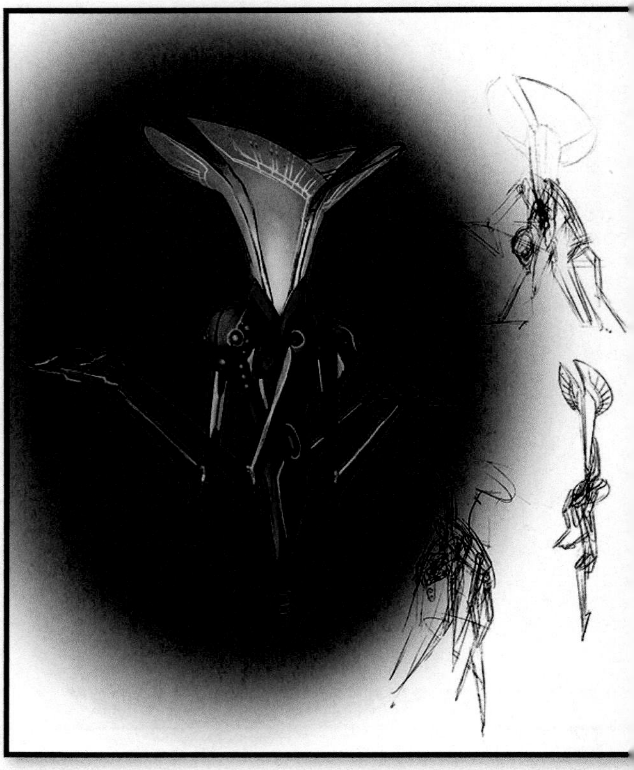

HA: The serving bots are both servants and decorative lamps with figura columns. The lily/insect wing/lampshade is their hover device. The robot are supposed to hint both at mantis arms, and also skeletons—lilies an skeletons being metaphors for the briefness of life and the permanenc of death.

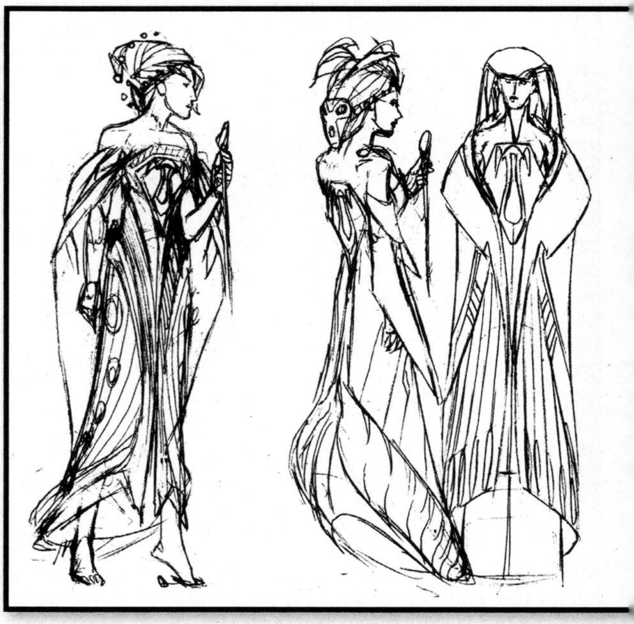

THE NEW FALL (OF KANDOR) COLLECTION

HA: At the basic level, Kryptonians could have body-defying technology and clothes. I imagine Lara's snarky sister Zara wearing a golden face mask on the back of her head, which lets her speak to and se people behind her back. She pretty much only uses her real mouth to emote and eat and drink Instead of drinking cocktails, they're sniffing from glass tubes. This plays with ideas like sniffin flowers, and sticking your nose into a wine glass before taking a sip. No idea what they get fro sniffing: aromatherapy, mild intoxication or even nutrition.

ANCING ON 'HE CEILING

A: The party platform akes heavy use of anti-ravity and other hover chnology. Each floor as normal Kryptonian ravity on each side, nd people are walking n each side. It has no airs, but instead the sun ystal columns also have eir own gravity for any-ne touching its surface.

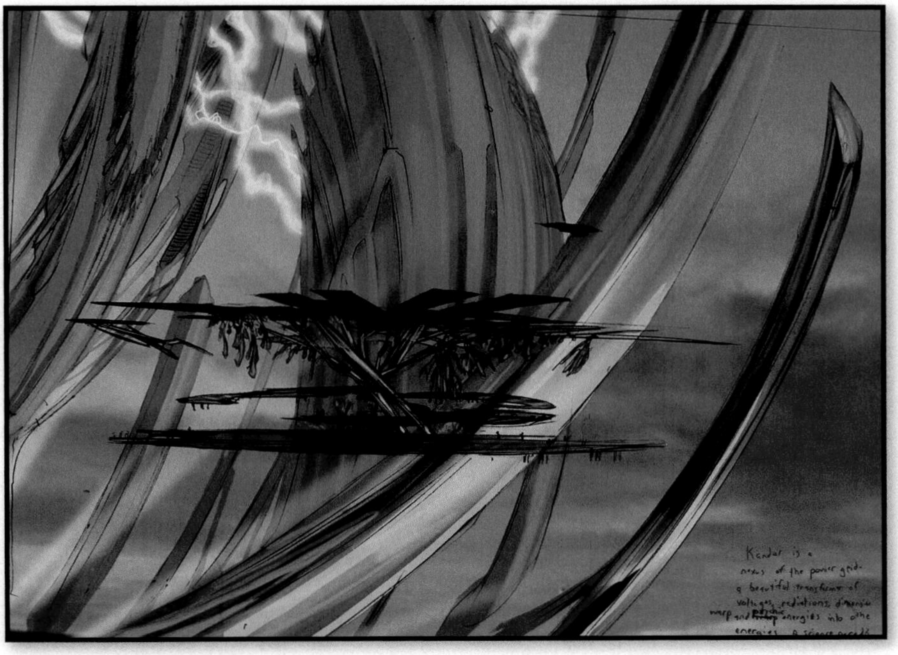

Kandar is a
nexus of the power grid-
a beautiful transformer of
voltages, radiations, dimension
warp and psychic energies into othe

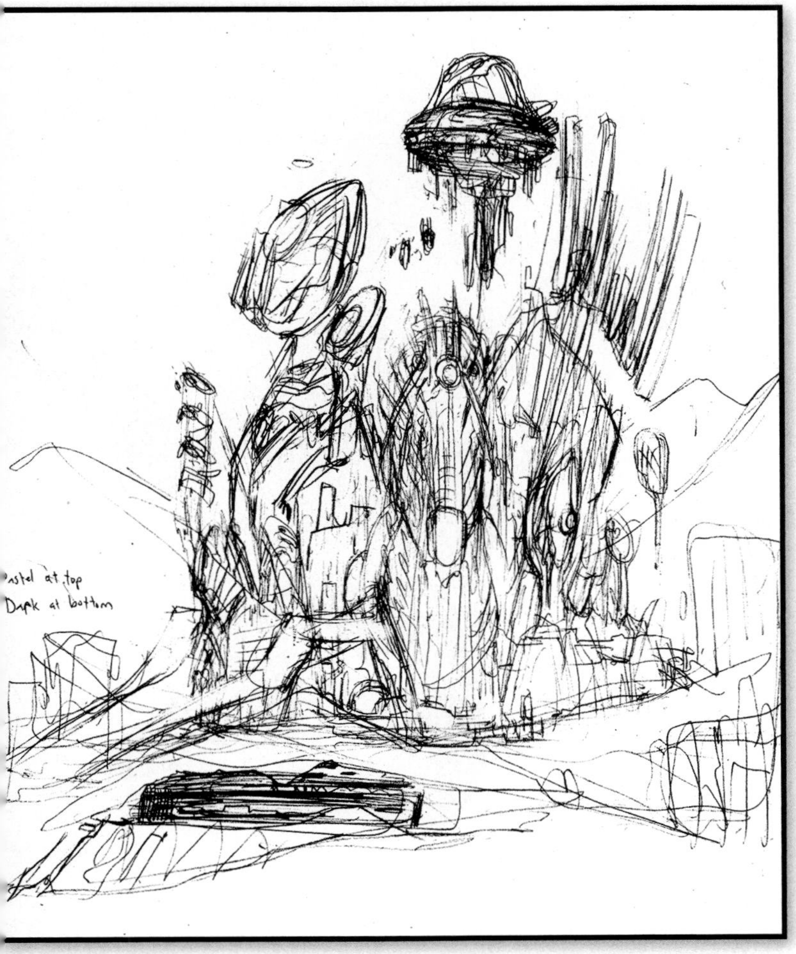

astel at top
Dark at bottom

CITY AS SCIENCE COLONY

HA: I'm imagining Kandor as a giant science colony. It's a mountain-sized power grid transformer, transforming and storing voltages, radiation, dimensional warps and perhaps even information and telepathic memories. The main administration is in the floating dome at the top of the city, but various other facilities have occupant space, too.

Interviews by Sean T. Collins

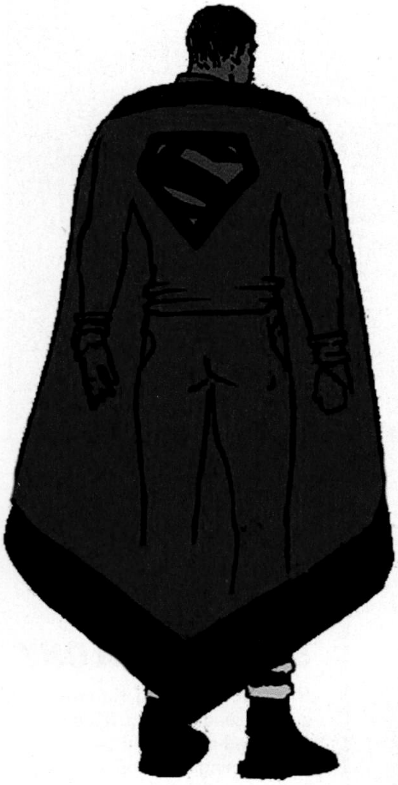

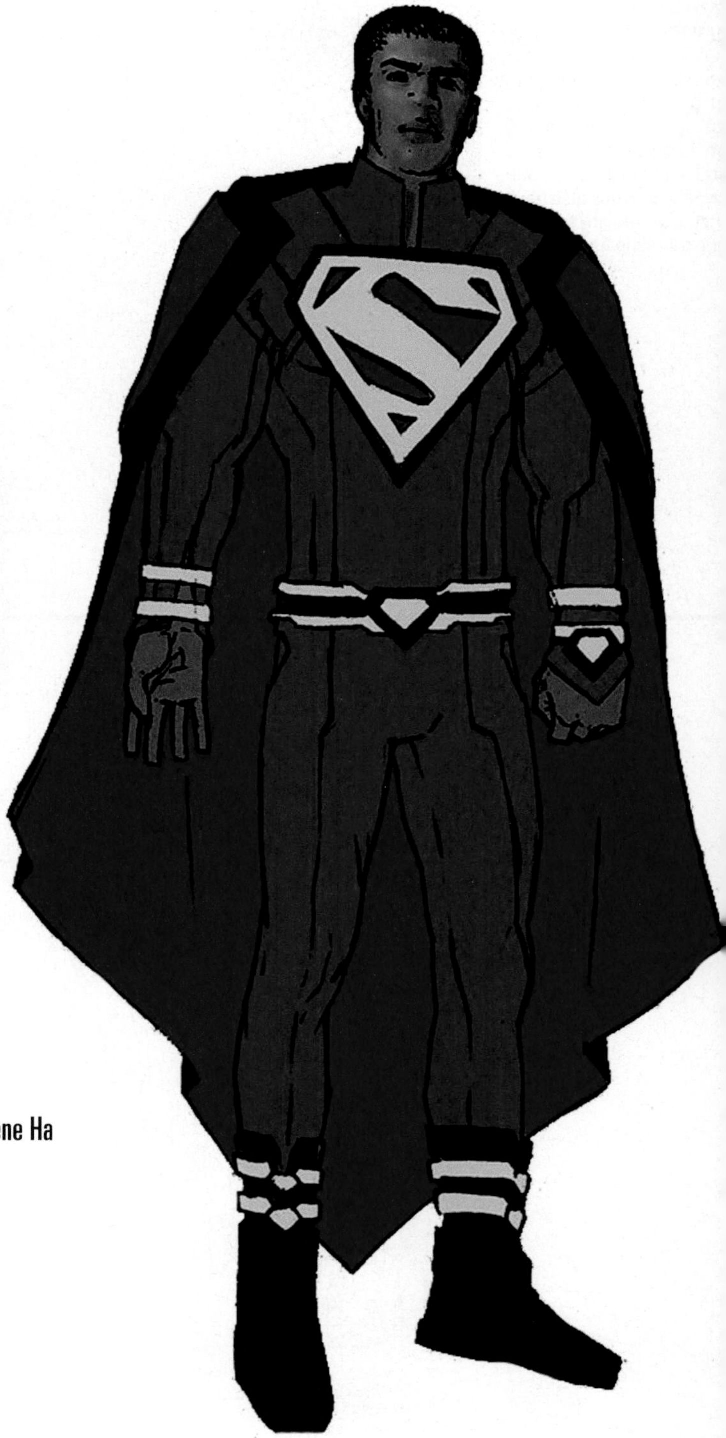

Designs for Superman of Earth-23 by Gene Ha

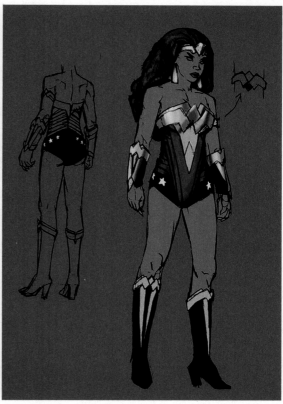

Designs for Wonder Woman of Earth-23 and Superdoom by Gene Ha

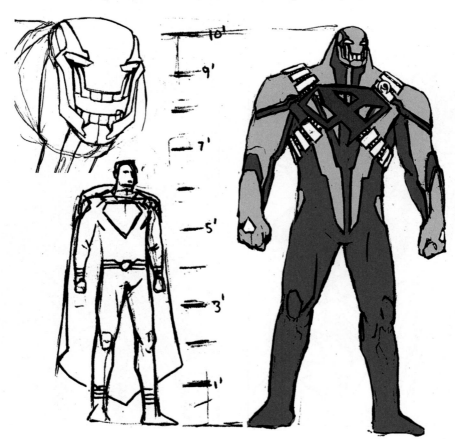

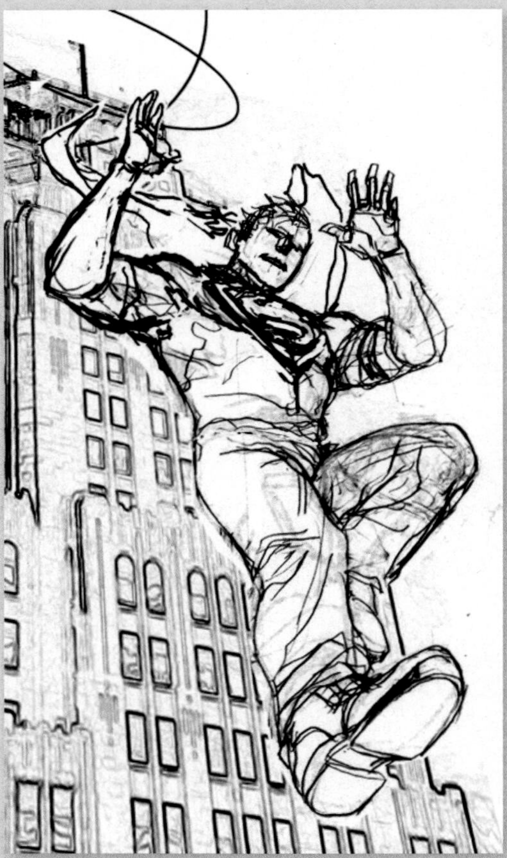

Cover sketches and pencils by Michael Choi

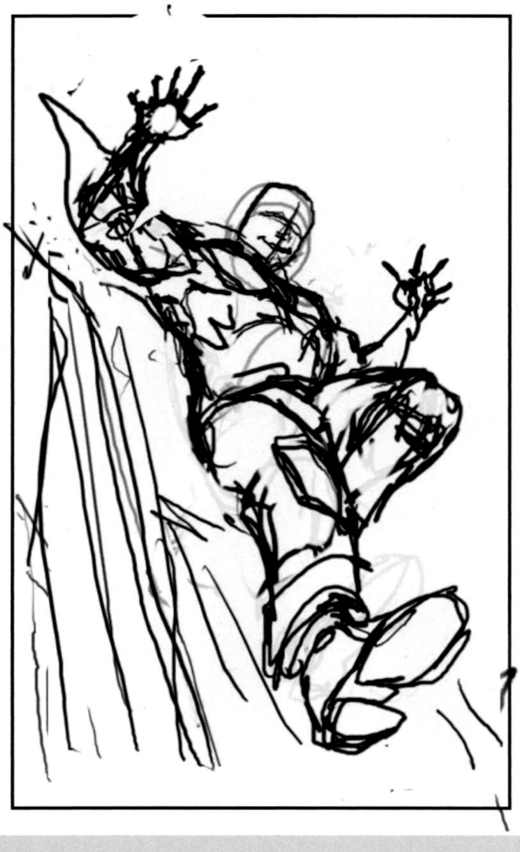

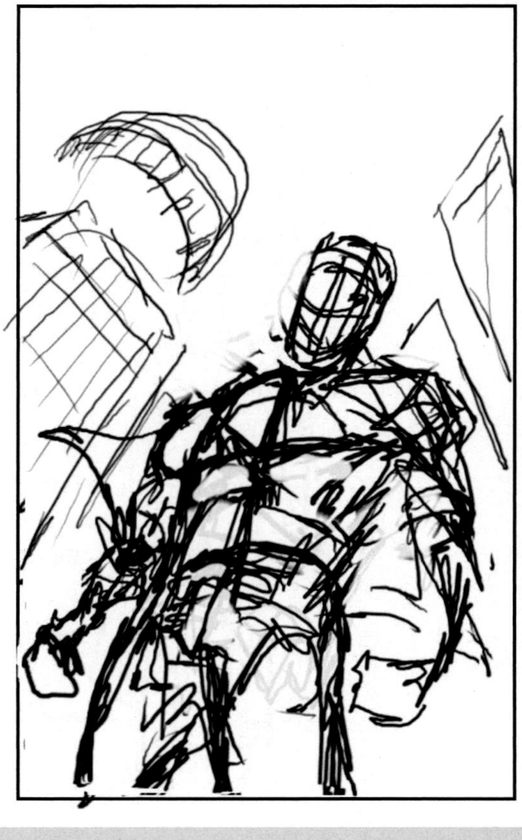

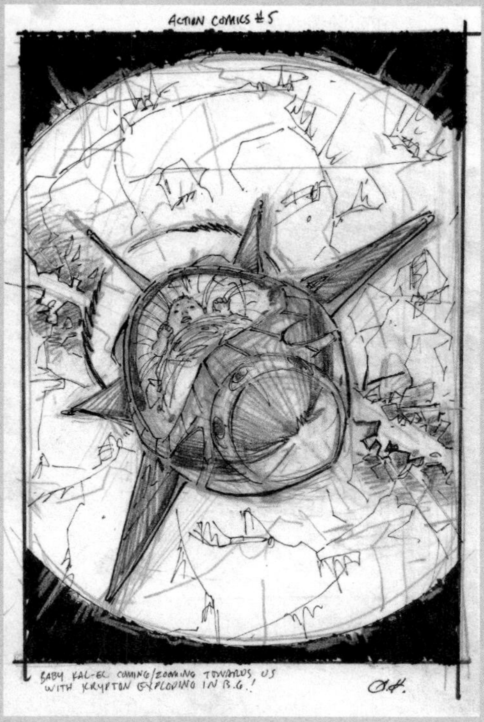
ACTION COMICS #5
BABY KAL-EL COMING/ZOOMING TOWARDS US WITH KRYPTON EXPLODING IN B.G.!

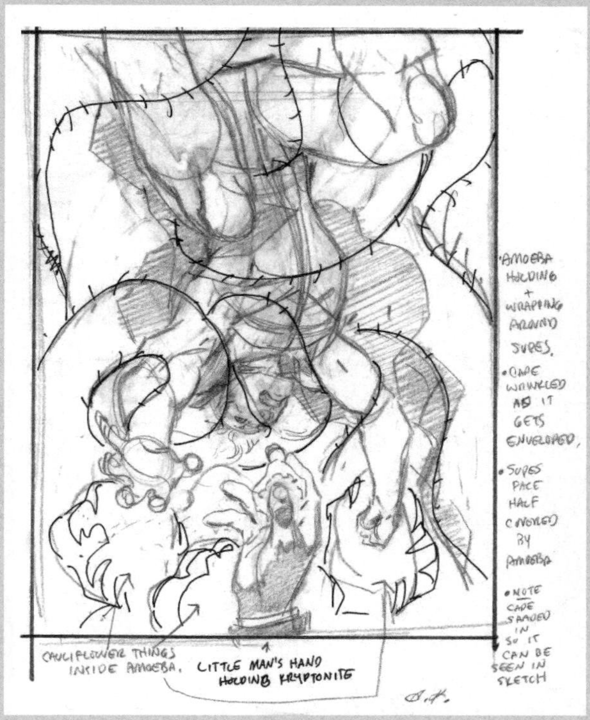
•AMOEBA HOLDING + WRAPPING AROUND SUPES.
•CAPE WRINKLED AS IT GETS ENVELOPED,
•SUPES FACE HALF COVERED BY AMOEBA
•NOTE CAPE SHADED IN SO IT CAN BE SEEN IN SKETCH
CAULIFLOWER THINGS INSIDE AMOEBA.
LITTLE MAN'S HAND HOLDING KRYPTONITE

Cover sketches by Andy Kubert

Cover sketches and pencils by Chris Burnham

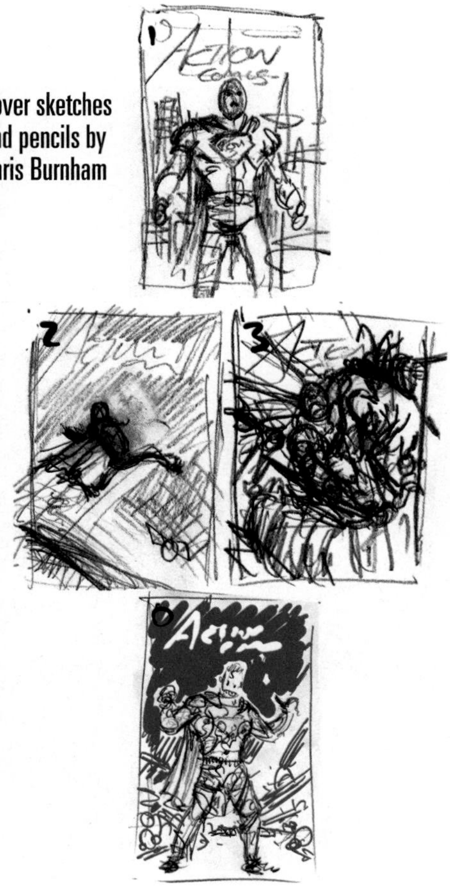

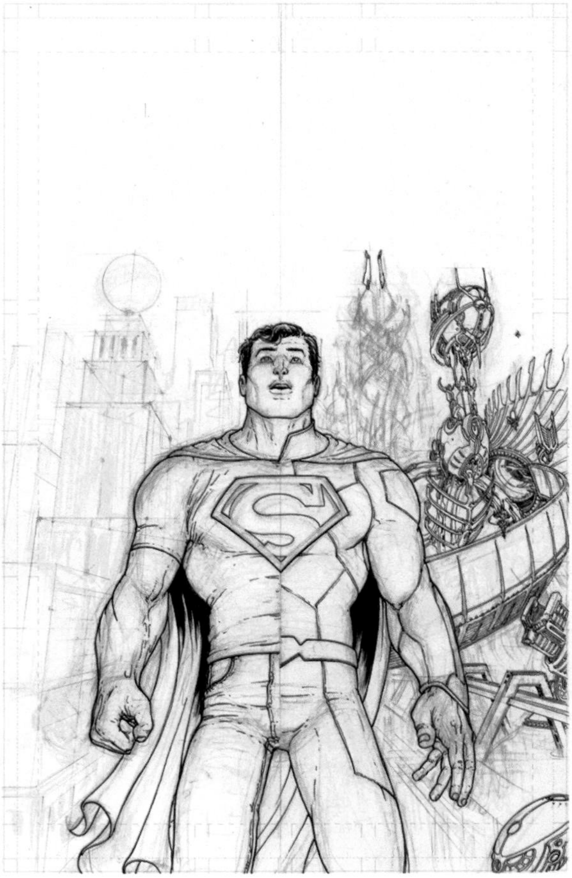

Cover sketches and pencils by Gene Ha

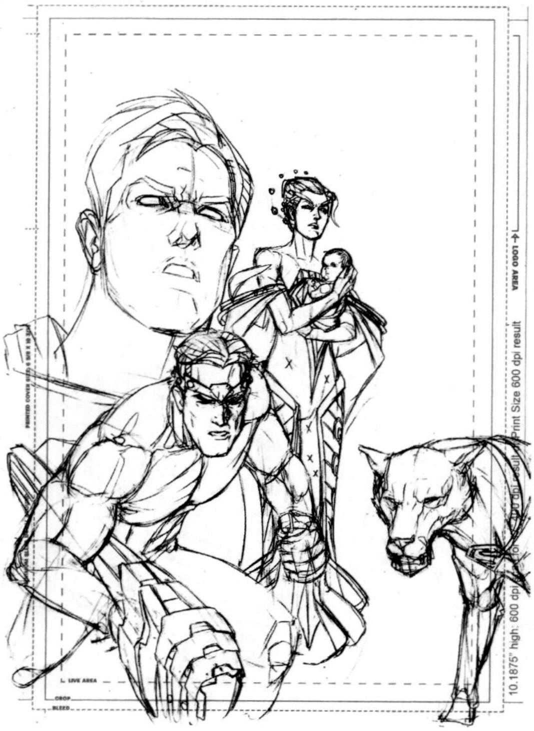
LOGO AREA
Print Size 600 dpi result
LIVE AREA
CROP
BLEED

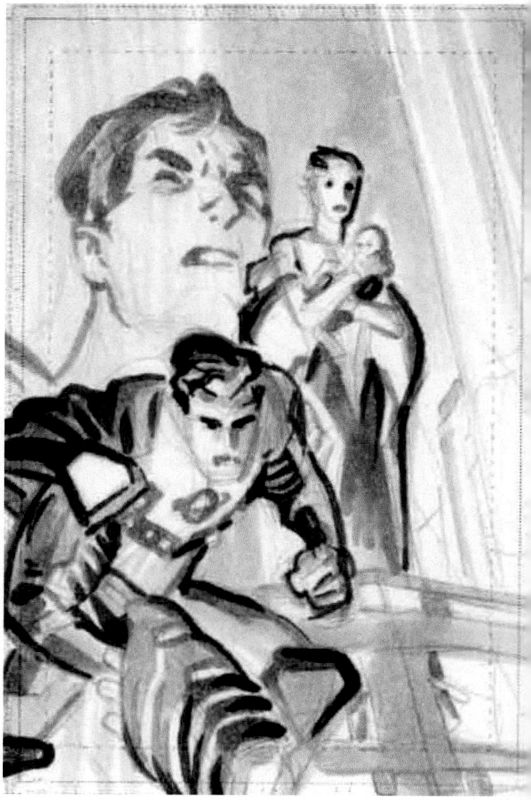

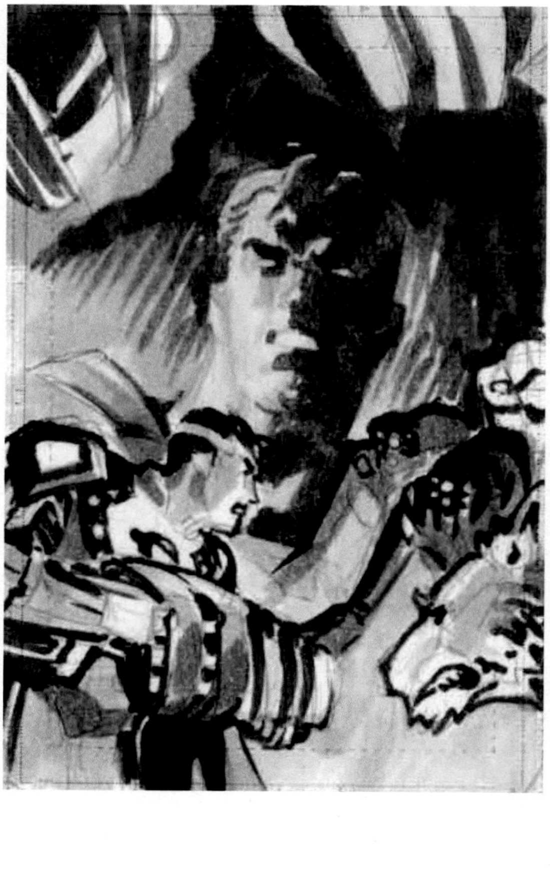

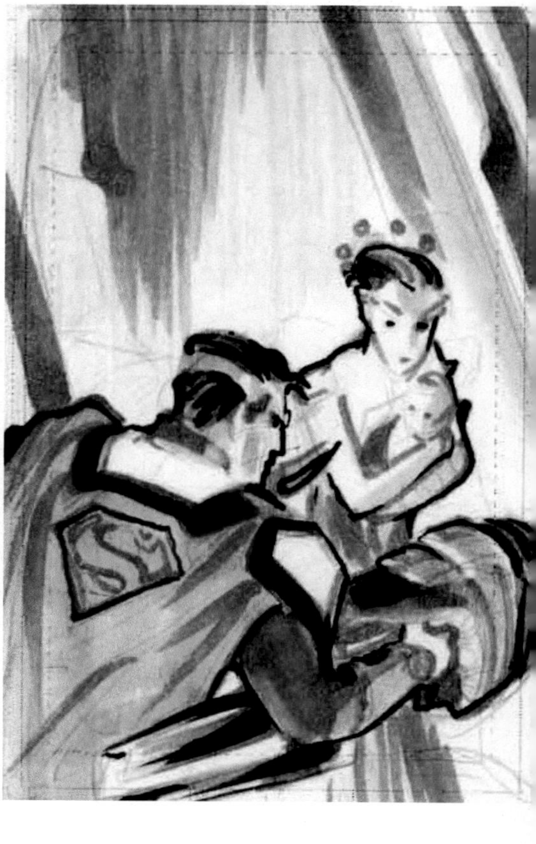

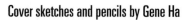

ACTION COMICS #9
cover sketches by Gene Ha

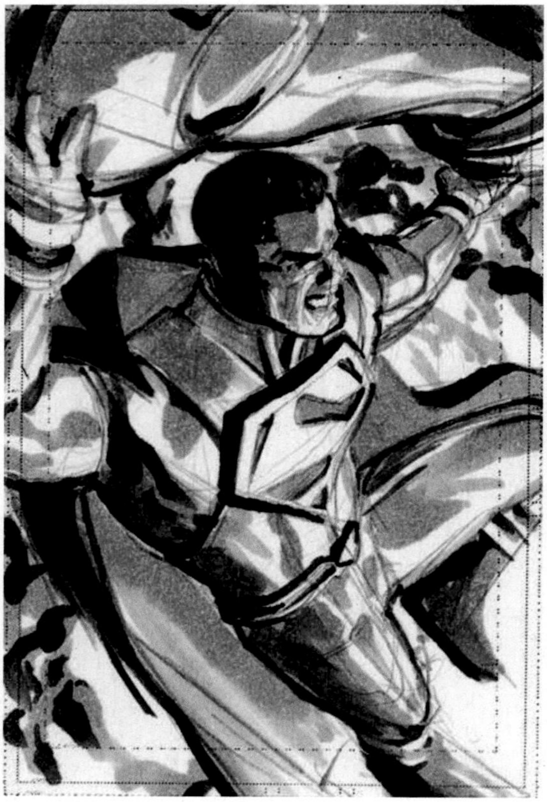

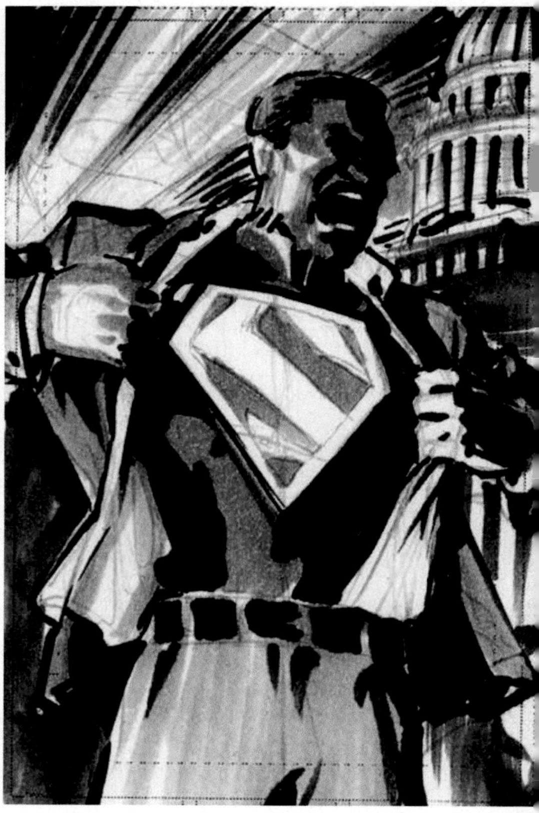

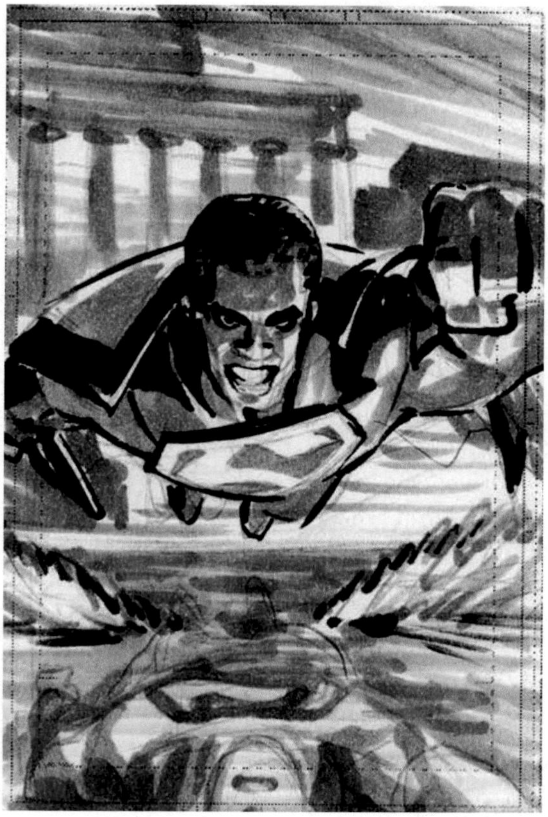